SIPRI Yearbook 1988

World Armaments and Disarmament

sipri

Stockholm International Peace Research Institute

OXFORD UNIVERSITY PRESS
1988

Oxford University Press, Walton Street, Oxford OX2 6DP
Oxford New York Toronto
Delhi Bombay Calcutta Madras Karachi
Petaling Jaya Singapore Hong Kong Tokyo
Nairobi Dar es Salaam Cape Town
Melbourne Auckland
and associated companies in
Berlin Ibadan

Oxford is a trade mark of Oxford University Press

Published in the United States
by Oxford University Press, New York

© SIPRI 1988

Yearbooks before 1987 published under title
'World Armaments and Disarmament:
SIPRI Yearbook [year of publication]'

All rights reserved. No part of this publication may be reproduced, stored
in a retrieval system, or transmitted, in any form or by any means,
electronic, mechanical, photocopying, recording, or otherwise, without the
prior permission of Oxford University Press

British Library Cataloguing in Publication Data
SIPRI yearbook of world armaments and
disarmament.—1988 –
1. Arms control & disarmament – Serials
2. military equipment: Weapons. Serials
I. Stockholm International Peace Research
Institute   II. World armaments and
disarmament, ISSN 0953–0282
623.4'05
ISBN 0–19–829126–4

Library of Congress Cataloguing in Publication Data
Data available

Set by Wyvern Typesetting, Bristol
Printed and bound in Great Britain by
Biddles Ltd., Guildford and King's Lynn

SIPRI Yearbook 1988
World Armaments and Disarmament

sipri

Stockholm International Peace Research Institute

SIPRI is an independent international institute for research into problems of peace and conflict, especially those of arms control and disarmament. It was established in 1966 to commemorate Sweden's 150 years of unbroken peace.

The Institute is financed mainly by the Swedish Parliament. The staff, the Governing Board and the Scientific Council are international.

The Governing Board and Scientific Council are not responsible for the views expressed in the publications of the Institute.

Governing Board

Ambassador Dr Inga Thorsson, Chairman (Sweden)
Egon Bahr (Federal Republic of Germany)
Professor Francesco Calogero (Italy)
Dr Max Jakobson (Finland)
Professor Dr Karlheinz Lohs (German Democratic Republic)
Professor Emma Rothschild (United Kingdom)
Sir Brian Urquhart (United Kingdom)
The Director

Director

Dr Walther Stützle (Federal Republic of Germany)

sipri

Stockholm International Peace Research Institute
Pipers väg 28, S-171 73 Solna, Sweden
Cable: PEACERESEARCH STOCKHOLM
Telephone: 46 8/55 97 00

Contents

Preface xiii

Glossary and conventions xv

Introduction

Chapter 1. 1987—the turning-point?
Walther Stützle

    I. Introduction   1
    II. The INF Treaty   3
    III. Conventional arms control in Europe   8
        CDE–the search for a new mandate in the old framework—Gorbachev challenges the West–from deterrence to co-operative defence?—NATO: dealing with a partner-like opponent
    IV. Conclusion   15
Notes and references   15

Part I. Weapons and technology

Chapter 2. Nuclear weapons   23
William M. Arkin, Andrew S. Burrows, Thomas B. Cochran, Richard W. Fieldhouse, Jozef Goldblat and Robert S. Norris

    I. Introduction   23
    II. US nuclear weapon programmes   24
        ICBMs—Strategic submarine programmes—Strategic bomber programmes—Theatre nuclear forces and the INF Treaty—NATO nuclear war planning—Naval nuclear weapons—Congressional initiatives
    III. Soviet nuclear weapon programmes   33
        ICBMs—Strategic submarine programmes—Strategic bomber programmes—Strategic defence developments—Soviet non-strategic nuclear forces—Naval nuclear forces
    IV. British nuclear weapon programmes   45
        British–French nuclear co-operation—Polaris/Chevaline—Trident submarine and warhead
    V. French nuclear weapon programmes   48
        Hadès missile—Air Force programmes—Force Océanique Stratégique—Strategic communications—Future nuclear programmes
    VI. Chinese nuclear weapon programmes   52
        Land-based missile programmes and technology—Other programmes
    VII. Developments in nuclear proliferation   54
        Israel—Pakistan and India—South Africa—Brazil and Argentina—Other countries

vi   SIPRI YEARBOOK 1988

Notes and references   59

Table 2.1.   US strategic nuclear forces, 1988   36
Table 2.2.   US theatre nuclear forces, 1988   37
Table 2.3.   US nuclear warheads in Europe, 1965–92   38
Table 2.4.   Soviet strategic nuclear forces, 1988   39
Table 2.5.   Soviet theatre nuclear forces, 1988   40
Table 2.6.   British nuclear forces, 1988   42
Table 2.7.   French nuclear forces, 1988   43
Table 2.8.   Chinese nuclear forces, 1988   44

Chapter 3. Nuclear explosions   65
Ragnhild Ferm

    I. Introduction   65
    II. Information on nuclear explosions   65
        US and Soviet tests—The United Kingdom—France—China
    III. Violations and verification   68
    IV. Talks and negotiations   70
Notes and references   70

Appendix 3A. Nuclear explosions, 1945–87   72

Table 3A.1. Observed nuclear explosions in 1987   72
Table 3A.2. Estimated number of nuclear explosions 16 July 1945–5 August 1963   73
Table 3A.3. Estimated number of nuclear explosions 6 August 1963–31 December 1987   74
Table 3A.4. Estimated number of nuclear explosions 16 July 1945–31 December 1987   74

Chapter 4. Military use of outer space   75
Bhupendra Jasani

    I. Introduction   75
    II. Military satellites   75
        US military satellites—Soviet military satellites—Military satellites of other nations
    III. Space weapons   81
        Sensor technology—Some advances in computer technology—Interceptor technology
    IV. Conclusions   89
Notes and references   90

Appendix 4A. Tables of satellites launched in 1987   93

Table 4A.1. Photographic reconnaissance satellites launched in 1987   93
Table 4A.2. Electronic reconnaissance satellites launched in 1987   95

Table 4A.3.	Ocean surveillance satellites launched in 1987	96
Table 4A.4.	Early-warning satellites launched in 1987	96
Table 4A.5.	Meteorological satellites launched in 1987	97
Table 4A.6.	Communications satellites launched in 1987	97
Table 4A.7.	Navigation satellites launched in 1987	98
Table 4A.8.	Possible geodetic satellites launched in 1987	98
Table 4A.9.	Manned space flights in 1987	99

Chapter 5. Chemical and biological warfare: developments in 1987 101
S. J. Lundin, J. P. Perry Robinson and Ralf Trapp

    I. Chemical weapons 101
        Proliferation aspects—Developments in chemical-warfare armament—Visits to destruction sites
    II. Developments related to the Biological Weapons Convention 112
    III. Allegations of non-compliance with the CBW treaties 113
    IV. Chemical weapon-free zones 115
    V. Developments influencing the CWC negotiations 116
    VI. Conclusions 120
Notes and references 121

Table 5.1.	States known to have been past possessors or repositories of chemical weapons	103
Table 5.2.	The chemicals on the Australian Group lists	105
Table 5.3.	Allegations of CBW arms control violations during 1987	106
Table 5.4.	US production of binary munitions: start-up schedule as of May 1987	109
Table 5.5.	US CBW expenditure as of March 1987: programme for FYs 1987–89	110
Table 5.6.	Soviet chemical weapons as displayed during the visit to the Shikhany testing facility	111

Part II. Military expenditure, the arms trade and armed conflicts

Chapter 6. SIPRI military expenditure data 129
Rita Tullberg and Gerd Hagmeyer-Gaverus

    I. Introduction 129
    II. NATO 130
    III. The WTO 133
        Soviet military expenditure—Intelligence agency approaches—Other approaches—The rest of the WTO
    IV. Other Europe 138
    V. The Middle East 139
    VI. Africa 140
    VII. South Asia 142
    VIII. The Far East 143
    IX. Oceania 146

viii SIPRI YEARBOOK 1988

X.	Central America	147
XI.	South America	149
XII.	Economic data used by SIPRI	152
Notes and references		154

Table 6.1. The British defence budget: domestic and NATO definitions 132
Table 6.2. Estimates of Soviet military expenditure 136

Appendix 6A. Tables of world military expenditure, 1978–87 158

Table 6A.1. World military expenditure, in current price figures 158
Table 6A.2. World military expenditure, in constant price figures 163
Table 6A.3. World military expenditure as a percentage of gross domestic product 168

Chapter 7. The trade in major conventional weapons 175
Aaron Karp

I.	Introduction	175
II.	The trade in major weapons	175
	The USSR—The United States—France—The UK—China—Other suppliers	
III.	The rising importance of smaller arms deals	188
IV.	The rise of the grey and black markets	190
V.	International implications	192
VI.	Will Third World arms sales return?	195
VII.	Conclusion	197
Notes and references		198

Table 7.1. The leading exporters of major weapons, 1983–87 176
Table 7.2. The leading importers of major weapons, 1983–87 178
Table 7.3. Some recently disclosed grey and black market arms deals 191

Appendix 7A. Aggregate tables of the value of the trade in major weapons with the Third World, 1968–87 202

Table 7A.1. Values of imports of major weapons by the Third World: by region, 1968–87 202
Table 7A.2. Values of exports of major weapons to regions listed in table 7A.1: by supplier, 1968–87 204

Appendix 7B. Register of the trade in major conventional weapons with industrialized and Third World countries, 1987 206

Appendix 7C. Register of licensed production of major conventional weapons in industrialized and Third World countries, 1987 248

Appendix 7D. Sources and methods 256

Chapter 8. The naval arms trade and implications of changes in maritime law   265
Ian Anthony

    I. Introduction   265
    II. Implications of Part V of the LOS Convention   266
    III. The need for sea surveillance   269
    IV. The LOS Convention and other maritime law   276
    V. Prospects for regional co-operation in maritime surveillance and patrol   278
    VI. A co-operative programme in action   280
    VII. Conclusions   281

Notes and references   282

Table 8.1.   An inventory of maritime patrol aircraft and their surveillance capabilities   270

Chapter 9. Major armed conflicts in 1987   285
G. Kenneth Wilson and Peter Wallensteen

    I. Introduction   285
    II. Conflict characteristics   286
    III. Armed conflicts and the international community   287

Notes and references   288

Table 9.1.   Major armed conflicts in the world, 1987   288

Part III. Developments in arms control

Chapter 10. US–Soviet nuclear arms control   301
Christoph Bertram

    I. Introduction   301
    II. START: narrowing the gap   301
        Defining and counting the arsenals—Mobile ICBMs—Air-launched cruise missiles—Sea-launched cruise missiles—Structuring for deterrence: the problem of sub-limits—Verifying START
    III. Strategic defence: a bridge over troubled waters?   308
    IV. A step towards stability?   311

Notes and references   312

Table 10.1.   Soviet and US strategic forces under START   302

Chapter 11. Conventional arms control in Europe: problems and prospects   315
Jane Sharp

    I. The negotiation forums   315
    II. Recurrent problems   316
        Geographic asymmetries—Economic asymmetries—Political asymmetries
    III. WTO arms control goals   319
    IV. NATO arms control goals   321

V. MBFR	322
Prospects for an MBFR agreement—Virtues of an MBFR agreement	
VI. The CSCE–CDE	324
The Stockholm CSBMs—Prospects for the stability talks	
VII. WTO goals at the stability talks	327
Proposals to defuse the offensive aspects of military doctrines—The Jaruzelski proposal	
VIII. NATO goals at the stability talks	330
IX. Conclusion	333
Potential for unilateral initiatives	
Notes and references	335
Table 11.1. European negotiation forums	316
Table 11.2. NATO–WTO differences on the mandate for the stability talks	326
Figure 11.1. European negotiation forums	317

Appendix 11A. Calendar of planned notifiable military activities in 1988 and forecast for 1989, as required by the Stockholm Document   338

Chapter 12. Multilateral arms control efforts   347
Jozef Goldblat

I. Introduction	347
II. Chemical disarmament	347
Areas of agreement—Areas of major disagreement—Other outstanding issues—Conclusion	
III. Nuclear non-proliferation	358
Strengthening the non-proliferation regime—Non-explosive uses of nuclear energy—Conclusion	
IV. Nuclear test ban	365
Arms control impact of a test ban—New proposals—Verification—Partial limitation of tests—Possible transitional measures	
Notes and references	369

Part IV. Special features

Chapter 13. The INF Treaty negotiations   375
Jonathan Dean

I. Introduction	375
II. Genesis of the INF issue	376
III. NATO's two-track decision	378
IV. A slow beginning for the INF talks	379
V. Rapid movement at the new negotiations	383
VI. Terms of the Treaty	385
VII. Verification	387
VIII. What the INF Treaty does not do	388
IX. Significance of the agreement	389
Notes and references	393

Appendix 13A. Treaty between the United States of America and the Union of Soviet Socialist Republics on the elimination of their intermediate-range and shorter-range missiles   395

Appendix 13B. Memorandum of Understanding regarding the establishment of the data base for the Treaty   407

Appendix 13C. Protocol on procedures governing the elimination of the missile systems subject to the Treaty   463

Appendix 13D. Protocol regarding inspections relating to the Treaty   472

Appendix 13E. Agreement between the United States of America and the Union of Soviet Socialist Republics on the establishment of nuclear risk reduction centers   486

Chapter 14. The ABM Treaty and the strategic relationship: an uncertain future   491
Regina Cowen

    I. Introduction   491
    II. Ballistic missile defence and the Treaty reinterpretation issue   492
    III. Treaty reinterpretation, grey areas and loopholes   494
    IV. The Soviet position   497
    V. The Treaty's uncertain future   500
Notes and references   503

Chapter 15. The United Nations and the Iraq–Iran War   507
Co-ordinated by Brian Urquhart

    I. Introduction   507
    II. The mandate of the Security Council   507
    III. UN peace initiatives in the Iraq–Iran War   508
    IV. Iraqi and Iranian relations with the United Nations   512
    V. Prospects for an arms embargo   514
    VI. Conclusions   515
Notes and references   516

Chapter 16. The United Nations International Conference on the Relationship between Disarmament and Development   517
Saadet Deger

    I. Introduction   517
    II. Basic definitions   518
    III. The Conference   521
        Background—The US absence—The Final Document
    IV. The analytical framework   528
        The linkages for the Third World—US defence spending and the international economy—The economic effects of military spending—The North–South dimensions—Summary
    V. Conclusion   536
Notes and references   536
Table 16.1. Comparative economic and military data for industrial market economies and the Third World, 1985   519

Table 16.2. A comparison of import shares for industrial market economies and the Third World, 1985   519

Table 16.3. Disarmament and development in the Third World: the potential linkages   528

Table 16.4. External debt of the Third World, 1987   531

Chapter 17. The SIPRI 1987 Olof Palme Memorial Lecture—'Security and disarmament: change and vision'   539
Willy Brandt

Annexes

Annexe A. Major multilateral arms control agreements   549

    I. Summaries of the agreements   549
    II. Status of the implementation of the major multilateral arms control agreements, as of 1 January 1988   552
    III. UN member states and year of membership   578

Annexe B. Chronology   579

Errata   590

Index   591

Preface

SIPRI's Yearbook 1988 is presented in the same format as its predecessor in 1987. It offers four standard parts: I. Weapons and Technology, II. Arms Trade, Military Expenditure and Armed Conflicts, III. Developments in Arms Control, IV. Special Features.

Since the INF Treaty, concluded in December 1987 in Washington, D.C. between the United States of America and the Soviet Union, certainly represents an extremely important event, this Yearbook devotes quite some space to the analysis and the documentation of it, although this endeavour is partly in conflict with our objective to limit the Yearbook to a handy size. For reasons which are obvious, under 'Special Features' we have also included the greatly worrying Iraq–Iran War, the UN Conference on 'Disarmament and Development' and the discussion about the interpretation of the ABM Treaty.

We are proud to have again secured the co-operation of several distinguished international researchers and experts outside the SIPRI staff: Dr Christoph Bertram, Dr Jonathan Dean, Dr Bhupendra Jasani, Sir Brian Urquhart and Professor Dr Peter Wallensteen. And we are grateful to those who, in response to my appeal, cared to provide us with valuable suggestions as to how to improve the Yearbook work to the benefit of a globally dispersed readership.

A dedicated staff produced the Yearbook, including, under Connie Wall's experienced leadership, the institute's editors and secretaries. Special thanks are due to Bella Kjellgren, Barbara Adams, Gabrielle Bartholomew, Billie Bielckus, Jetta Gilligan Borg, Cynthia Loo, Marianne Lyons, Gillian Stanbridge, Miyoko Suzuki and Gun Winqvist.

Dr Walther Stützle
Director, SIPRI
31 March 1988

GLOSSARY AND CONVENTIONS

Acronyms

AAM	Air-to-air missile	EDI	European Defence Initiative
ABM	Anti-ballistic missile	EMP	Electromagnetic pulse
ACE	Allied Command Europe (NATO)	Enmod	Environmental modification
ACM	Advanced cruise missile	ERW	Enhanced radiation (neutron) weapon
ADM	Atomic demolition munition	Eureka	European Research Co-ordination Agency
ALCM	Air-launched cruise missile	FOFA	Follow-on forces attack
ASAT	Anti-satellite	GLCM	Ground-launched cruise missile
ASM	Air-to-surface missile	HLTF	High Level Task Force
ASUW	Anti-surface warfare	IAEA	International Atomic Energy Agency
ASW	Anti-submarine warfare	ICBM	Intercontinental ballistic missile
ATBM	Anti-tactical ballistic missile	INF	Intermediate-range nuclear forces
ATM	Anti-tank missile	IOC	Initial operating capability
AWACS	Airborne warning and control system	IRBM	Intermediate-range ballistic missile
BMD	Ballistic missile defence	JVE	Joint verification experiment
BWC	Biological Weapons Convention	KEW	Kinetic-energy weapon
CBM	Confidence-building measure	Laser	Light amplification by simulated emission of radiation
CBW	Chemical and biological warfare	MAD	Mutual assured destruction
CD	Conference on Disarmament (Geneva)	MARV	Manoeuvrable re-entry vehicle
CDE	Conference on Disarmament in Europe (Stockholm)	MBFR	Mutual and Balanced Force Reduction talks
CEP	Circular error probable	MIRV	Multiple independently targetable re-entry vehicle
CMEA	Council for Mutual Economic Assistance	MRV	Multiple (but not independently targetable) re-entry vehicle
CORRTEX	Continuous reflectometry for radius versus time experiments	MOU	Memorandum of Understanding
CSBM	Confidence- and security-building measure	MURFAAMCE	Mutual Reductions of Forces and Armaments and Associated Measures in Central Europe
CSCE	Conference on Security and Co-operation in Europe (Helsinki, Belgrade, Madrid, Vienna)	NATO	North Atlantic Treaty Organization
CTB	Comprehensive test ban	NNA	Neutral and non-aligned countries
CWC	Chemical Weapons Convention	NPT	Non-Proliferation Treaty
CWFZ	Chemical weapon-free zone		
DC	Disarmament Commission		
DEW	Directed-energy weapon		

xvi   SIPRI YEARBOOK 1988

NST	Nuclear and Space Talks (Geneva)	SLBM	Submarine-launched ballistic missile
OECD	Organization for Economic Co-operation and Development	SLCM	Sea-launched cruise missile
		SRAM	Short-range attack missile
PNE(T)	Peaceful Nuclear Explosions (Treaty)	SRBM	Short-range ballistic missile
PTB(T)	Partial Test Ban (Treaty)	SSBN	Nuclear-powered, ballistic-missile submarine
PWR	Pressurized water reactor	SSN	Nuclear-powered attack submarine
R&D	Research and development		
RPV	Remotely piloted vehicle	START	Strategic Arms Reduction Talks
RV	Re-entry vehicle	SWS	Strategic weapon system
SALT	Strategic Arms Limitation Talks	TEL	Transporter-erector-launcher
SAM	Surface-to-air missile	TNF	Theatre nuclear forces
SCC	Standing Consultative Commission	TTB(T)	Threshold Test Ban (Treaty)
		VLTTB	Very-low-threshold test ban
SDI	Strategic Defense Initiative	WTO	Warsaw Treaty Organization (Warsaw Pact)
SICBM	Small ICBM		

Glossary

Anti-ballistic missile (ABM) system	Weapon system for intercepting and destroying ballistic missiles in flight.
Binary chemical weapon	A shell or other device filled with two chemicals of relatively low toxicity which mix and react while the device is being delivered to the target, the reaction product being a supertoxic chemical warfare agent, such as nerve gas.
Biological weapon (BW)	Living organisms or infective material derived from them, which are intended for use in warfare to cause disease or death in man, animals or plants, and the means of their delivery.
Chemical weapon (CW)	Chemical substances—whether gaseous, liquid or solid—which might be employed as weapons in combat because of their direct toxic effects on man, animals or plants, and the means of their delivery.
Circular error probable (CEP)	A measure of missile accuracy: the radius of a circle, centred on the target, within which 50 per cent of the weapons aimed at the target are expected to fall.
Conference on Disarmament (CD)	Multilateral arms control negotiating body, based in Geneva, which is composed of 40 states, including all the nuclear weapon powers.
Conference on Disarmament in Europe (CDE)	Unofficial name for the Conference on Confidence- and Security-Building Measures and Disarmament in Europe, held in Stockholm, Sweden, 1984–86. The Stockholm Document was signed on 19 September 1986. Part of the CSCE process. *See also*: Conference on Security and Co-operation in Europe.
Conference on Security and Co-operation in Europe (CSCE)	Conference of 33 European NATO, WTO and neutral and non-aligned states plus the USA and Canada, which began in 1972 and in 1975 adopted a Final Act (also called the Helsinki Declaration) containing, among others, a Document on confidence-building measures and disarmament. Follow-up meetings were held in Belgrade (1977–78), Madrid (1980–83) and Vienna (1986–).

GLOSSARY xvii

Conventional weapon	Weapon not having mass destruction effects. *See also*: Weapon of mass destruction.
Cruise missile	Unmanned, self-propelled, guided weapon-delivery vehicle which sustains flight through aerodynamic lift, generally flying at very low altitudes to avoid radar detection, sometimes following the contours of the terrain. It can be air-, ground- or sea-launched and deliver a conventional or nuclear warhead.
Disarmament Commission (DC)	A subsidiary, deliberative organ of the UN General Assembly for disarmament matters, composed of all UN members.
First-strike capability	Theoretical capability to launch a pre-emptive nuclear attack which would destroy all of an adversary's retaliatory nuclear forces.
Flexible response	The NATO doctrine for reaction to an attack with a full range of military options, including the use of nuclear weapons.
Helsinki Declaration	*See*: Conference on Security and Co-operation in Europe.
Initial operating capability (IOC)	Date by which a weapon system is first operationally deployed, ready for use in the field.
Intercontinental ballistic missile (ICBM)	Ground-launched ballistic missile with a range in excess of 5500 km. Speed: 20 000–25 000 km per hour.
Intermediate-range nuclear forces (INF)	Theatre nuclear forces with a range of from 1000 up to and including 5500 km. *See also*: Theatre nuclear forces.
Kiloton (kt)	Measure of the explosive yield of a nuclear weapon equivalent to 1000 tons of trinitrotoluene (TNT) high explosive. (The bomb detonated at Hiroshima in World War II had a yield of some 12–15 kilotons.)
Launcher	Equipment which launches a missile. For example, ICBM launchers are land-based launchers which can be either fixed or mobile. SLBM launchers are missile tubes on submarines.
Launch-weight	Weight of a fully loaded ballistic missile at the time of launch.
Megaton (Mt)	Measure of the explosive yield of a nuclear weapon equivalent to one million tons of trinitrotoluene (TNT) high explosive.
Multiple independently targetable re-entry vehicle (MIRV)	Re-entry vehicle, carried by a missile, which can be directed to separate targets along separate trajectories (as distinct from MRVs).
Mutual assured destruction (MAD)	Concept of reciprocal deterrence which rests on the ability of the nuclear weapon powers to inflict intolerable damage on one another after receiving a nuclear attack. *See also*: Second-strike capability.
Mutual reduction of forces and armaments and associated measures in Central Europe (MURFAAMCE)	Subject of negotiations between NATO and the Warsaw Treaty Organization, which began in Vienna in 1973. Often referred to as the Mutual and Balanced Force Reduction (MBFR) talks.
Nuclear and Space Talks (NST)	Negotiations between the USA and the USSR on strategic and intermediate-range nuclear weapons and on space weapon issues, held in Geneva from March 1985. Include the INF and START negotiations.
Peaceful nuclear explosion (PNE)	Application of a nuclear explosion for non-military purposes such as digging canals or harbours or creating underground cavities.
Re-entry vehicle (RV)	That part of a ballistic missile designed to carry a nuclear warhead or penetration aids and to re-enter the earth's atmosphere in the terminal phase of the missile's trajectory.
Second-strike capability	Ability to survive a nuclear attack and launch a retaliatory blow large enough to inflict intolerable damage on the opponent. *See also*: Mutual assured destruction.

Standing Consultative Commission (SCC)	US–Soviet consultative body established in accordance with the SALT agreements, to promote the objectives and implementation of the agreements.
Strategic Arms Limitation Talks (SALT)	Negotiations between the Soviet Union and the United States, held from 1969 to 1979, which sought to limit the strategic nuclear forces, both offensive and defensive, of both sides. Two agreements were reached, SALT I (1972) and SALT II (1979).
Strategic Arms Reduction Talks (START)	Negotiations between the Soviet Union and the United States, initiated in 1982, which seek to reduce the strategic nuclear forces of both sides. Suspended in December 1983 but resumed under the Nuclear and Space Talks that opened in Geneva in March 1985. *See also*: Nuclear and Space Talks.
Strategic nuclear weapons	ICBMs, SLBMs and bomber aircraft carrying nuclear weapons of intercontinental range (over 5500 km).
Terminal guidance	Guidance provided in the final, near-target phase of the flight of a missile.
Theatre nuclear forces (TNF)	Nuclear weapons with ranges of up to and including 5500 km, more recently called non-strategic nuclear forces. In the 1987 INF Treaty, land-based missiles with ranges of 500–5500 km are subdivided into intermediate-range (1000–5500 km) and shorter-range (500–1000 km). Nuclear weapons with ranges below 500 km are often termed short-range, tactical or battlefield nuclear weapons.
Throw-weight	The sum of the weight of a ballistic missile's re-entry vehicle(s), dispensing mechanisms, penetration aids, and targeting and separation devices.
Toxins	Poisonous substances which are products of organisms but are inanimate and incapable of reproducing themselves. Some toxins may also be produced by chemical synthesis.
Warhead	That part of a weapon which contains the explosive or other material intended to inflict damage.
Weapon of mass destruction	Nuclear weapon and any other weapon which may produce comparable effects, such as chemical and biological weapons.
Yield	Released nuclear explosive energy expressed as the equivalent of the energy produced by a given number of tons of trinitrotoluene (TNT) high explosive. *See also*: Kiloton and Megaton.

Conventions

. .	Data not available or not applicable
—	Nil or a negligible figure
( )	Uncertain data
[ ]	Estimate with a high degree of uncertainty
m.	Million
b.	Billion (thousand million)
$	US $, unless otherwise indicated

Introduction

Chapter 1. 1987—the turning-point?

1. 1987—the turning-point?

WALTHER STÜTZLE

I. Introduction

While East–West relations appeared to dominate international relations in 1987 and early 1988, world politics of course had many other crucial subjects on its agenda. With the view broadened beyond the boundaries of the established East–West framework, the sad balance is that mankind has again failed to apply the noble principles of the United Nations Charter to the policies of states. Unfortunately, it is true that, once again, mankind has not given new credibility to its alleged desire for unarmed peace, social justice and respect for human rights: the number of political prisoners is still frighteningly high— Nelson Mandela, for example, is still held in a South African prison. The war between Iran and Iraq, now in its eighth year, has escalated further, and Soviet troops have still not completely withdrawn from Afghanistan. However, since the principle decision to withdraw has been taken and an agreement between Pakistan and Afghanistan has been signed on 14 April 1988 to that effect, to which the USA and the USSR both serve as guarantor powers, hope now exists that this stumbling-block on the road to a better international climate can be removed.[1]

With the development in 1987–88 of the Iraq–Iran War, it has become very questionable whether the UN still has the ability to live up at least to the duty to prevent small- and medium-size powers from becoming a threat to world peace.

On the one hand, while the five permanent members of the UN Security Council, for the first time, agreed to call on the two countries to end the war immediately and to withdraw their troops behind the internationally accepted borders (Resolution 598),[2] on the other hand, the United Nations proved to be completely incapable of turning its words into actions. In fact, as time went by, the situation became worse. In February 1988 Baghdad and Tehran engaged in a missile war, wherein ground-launched ballistic missiles with a range of more than 500 kilometres were used; considerable damage was inflicted on the civilian populations of both cities, and the war was 'lifted' to the quality of capitals fighting each other directly.[3] Iran and Iraq also continued throughout 1987 and the beginning of 1988 to defy international law demonstratively by attacking international ship traffic in the Persian Gulf.[4]

Turning to the other Middle East powder-keg, the Israeli–Palestinian conflict, the situation is hardly more encouraging. In December 1987 civil war erupted in the Gaza Strip between Israel, which has occupied this territory since 1948, and its Arab population. Out of the 689 000 Arab inhabitants of Israel, 633 000 are concentrated in the Gaza Strip, half of them being refugees who are spread out among eight refugee camps. More than 60 per cent of these refugees are in their youth, younger than 18 years of age—'a revolutionary force as typical as one can possibly imagine'.[5]

SIPRI Yearbook 1988: World Armaments and Disarmament

This civil war has given a new political dimension to the old problem. The war, and the brutality with which it is fought, signal that the peace process named after Camp David, where former US President Jimmy Carter forged the Israeli–Egyptian Peace Treaty of 26 March 1979,[6] has finally failed. Today Camp David must be considered as a lost opportunity.

What started in December 1987 in the Gaza Strip has rendered the centre-piece of the peace settlement totally insufficient, that is, to grant autonomy to the Palestinian people in the Gaza Strip and on the West Bank.[7] One day it may come to be looked upon as the beginning of a conflict that holds the potential to set fire to the entire region, with the added danger of involving countries from outside the region, such as the United States and the Soviet Union. And the picture does not become brighter when complemented by the fact that Israel is a nuclear threshhold country, which would certainly be capable of using the weapon of last resort if the alternative were losing a safe home for the Jewish people. After all, it has to be understood that Israel's definition of security and safety for its people is the definition of those who survived the holocaust.[8]

However, in spite of the fact that the international community could easily be aware of all of the risks involved in the conflict and the fact that there is no shortage of resolutions of all kinds, today no international organization is strong enough to enforce compliance with the basic principles of international law: the guarantee of Israel's right to exist within secure borders, and effective respect for the right to self-determination of the Palestinian people.

In South and southern Africa—another troubled area—the international community has continued to fail in bringing down the apartheid regime and in preparing the ground for a fundamental reorientation of political power, that is, from white to black. By the year 2000, the number of black students who will have graduated from high school will be three times more than the number of whites.[9] This fact alone may illustrate the mounting pressure for change, violent change if a peaceful one is not engineered in time. Unlike Latin America, Eastern Europe or the Middle East, southern Africa is not a zone of vital interest to either superpower. But also because of the fact that South Africa has to be regarded as a nuclear threshhold country and that its nuclear potential is at the disposal of the white class, whose clock is ticking away, it should be in the interest of all nations not to allow the opportunity to exist for a minority to cause substantial damage not only to South Africa itself but also potentially to the entire region. It is clear that the two superpowers should recognize their special responsibility in this context.[10]

Finally, in Central America, another major conflict threatens a region of the world. However, in this case the states in the region have taken a peace initiative, the so-called Arias Plan.[11] Despite the difficulties to put the plan into effect, the process it has set in motion seems to suggest that regional powers have an important role to play in solving the region's problems and do not entirely depend on actions by the two superpowers or either one of them.

Of course, in an era of global interdependence, there is more to security than the type that is provided for and threatened by military means. The ticking debt bomb is the perfect case in point. Although heavily indebted, Chile and Mexico have been allowed to use new instruments to cut some of their debts by restructuring their liabilities (debt/equity conversion); however, the overall debt problem remains unsolved. The debt bomb has not been defused. At the end of 1986, the total foreign debt of all developing countries amounted to US $1095 billion. This sum equals 167.5 per cent of the total value of exports (goods and services) of these countries. It is now common knowledge that only the concerted effort of the involved debtor and creditor countries could deal with this problem appropriately.[12] Still, this effort is not in sight.

Thus, 1987 and the beginning of 1988 represent no exception to the rule that, in most cases, mankind finds it extremely difficult to find solutions to some of its main problems.

And yet, it is justified not to be overly pessimistic as one looks at these events. After all, with Gorbachev in firm command of Soviet policy, during 1987 (more than in any other year since he assumed power in 1985) the General Secretary demonstrated his leadership in correcting some of the major mistakes of his predecessors. Nevertheless, it is equally true that his concept of how to go from there has yet to emerge. The INF Treaty between Washington and Moscow is the most salient case in point: it corrects a major mistake of the past, and it also offers some important details (such as the verification regime) which any broader arms control arrangements in the future have to embrace, although it does not point to the architecture such an arrangement might shape into. With their signatures, the two superpowers—as the principal players in world affairs—have managed to cross over the threshold to a new era of arms control efforts. And, although this breakthrough is first and foremost an East–West event, it may have wider implications. The Washington summit meeting held in December 1987 again confirmed the longstanding East–West experience, namely, that the solution of regional conflicts may be an easier task if the Washington–Moscow relationship is buttressed by a favourable arms control atmosphere, but it is equally true that arms control can easily be damaged by major events in the overall political environment.[13]

II. The INF Treaty

1987 marks a breakthrough in the long history of arms control efforts. A key move was that, for the first time in history, an entire class of already deployed weapons (plus the non-deployed ones) was eliminated from the arms arsenals. The signing of the Treaty between the United States of America and the Union of Soviet Socialist Republics on the Elimination of Their Intermediate-Range and Shorter-Range Missiles (INF Treaty), signed in Washington on 8 December 1987, marked a politically important but militarily rather modest event in the East–West relationship. The INF Treaty requires the United States and the Soviet Union to throw into history's waste-bin 2695 intermediate-range ground-launched missiles with ranges between 1000 and 5500 kilometres and ground-launched shorter-range missiles with ranges between 500 and 1000 kilometres. The USSR will have to scrap 1836 missiles, and the USA will have to destroy 867 missiles.[14]

Although the Treaty does not require the elimination of any warhead *per se*, a result of the Treaty will nevertheless be the removal of some 2200 warheads from deployed missiles, including 100 US warheads on the 72 West German Pershing 1a missiles.[15] These warheads will be returned to stockpiles or recycled in the United States or the Soviet Union. The Treaty rules out the right 'to produce, flight-test or launch any intermediate-range missiles', 'any shorter-range missiles' or 'any stages of such missiles' (Article VI). But it prohibits neither research nor development; thus on this point the INF Treaty is not comprehensive and radical.

The real value of the Treaty does not lie in its military significance. In fact, only a small percentage of delivery vehicles with nuclear charges, deployed in Europe by either side, will be removed. Even with the INF Treaty put into effect, Europe will be far from being denuclearized. As Christoph Bertram has said: 'In comparison with other regions, Europe remains, even after the removal of INF missiles, positively stuffed with nuclear weapons.'[16]

It is the Treaty's political value that matters most. And this is true for both its positive and negative aspects. Consequently, there are good reasons not to exaggerate the value of the INF Treaty. Yet, some of the positive developments it represents clearly outweigh its shortcomings:

1. The Treaty represents a fundamental change in Soviet foreign policy towards the Atlantic Alliance in general and its West European component in particular. Brezhnev and Gromyko somehow completely failed to understand the *psychological damage* caused by their policy that sought *parity with the United States* on the nuclear strategic level, while simultaneously striving for *superiority over Western Europe* in long-range theatre nuclear forces that could only strike at Western Europe (the policy for which the SS-20 missile was the major symbol). Even with hindsight, the question is not whether the concern in Western Europe was justified or not, for instance, when looked at through the eyes of a superpower. Rather, what matters is that General Secretary Gorbachev considered the situation in need of redress and acted accordingly. In so doing he not only corrected a profound mistake of his predecessors, but he also exploited the situation for breaking new ground in arms control.

2. Gorbachev accepted the fact that the Soviet Union had more to reduce than the United States, thereby acknowledging that it is capabilities that count rather than numbers. Although this results logically from the fact that the party that has more has to sacrifice more, it was new for a Soviet leader to subscribe to this rule, which has possible consequences for negotiations about conventional forces and armaments in Europe.

3. The acceptance of the most comprehensive verification regime, at the centre of which lie very intrusive and discriminative on-site inspection arrangements and the exchange of all available data, marks a genuine breakthrough in arms control. Hence the INF Treaty proves that Gorbachev's readiness, under the Stockholm Document of September 1986 which deals with confidence- and security-building measures,[17] to open, for the first time, Soviet territory to obligatory on-site inspections was meant to be more than only a one-time concession. In the light of the INF Treaty, the Stockholm Document was the beginning of a much bolder Soviet verification policy that does not stop

short of abandoning some of the treasured traditions in Soviet security policy.

Gorbachev has broken with the traditional, deeply rooted Soviet preference for secrecy. Accepting permanent on-site inspection at the Soviet missile production facility, the Votkinsk Machine Building Plant, west of the Urals (where both the SS-20s covered by the Treaty and the SS-25s not covered by the Treaty are assembled) amounts to no less than making the Soviet public (and military) aware that close and constant observation by one's arch-rival helps to maintain peace. This is not an easy proposition in a society that is educated to entrust the country's security to the professional military only, though under the leadership of the Party, and in a country where the government system is based on the key notion that, besides the military, only the Party leadership is entitled to know detailed military data.

4. In an almost dramatic way, the INF Treaty testifies to Gorbachev's and the Party's leadership over the military. Making the Chief of the General Staff of the Soviet Union act, visibly to the public, as the principal arms control adviser to the General Secretary at crucial international events, such as the summit meetings with President Reagan, indicates basically three things: (*a*) it demonstrates that the military have to play according to the rules established by the Party; (*b*) it secures the support of the armed forces by giving their top representative a prominent and influential role in the negotiations; and (*c*) it commits the military to the results of such negotiations. With Marshal Sergei Akhromeyev serving in that function, Gorbachev's intentions become even more tangible, since Akhromeyev is not known to be supportive of a bold arms control approach.[18]

5. Gorbachev's approach to the INF problem suggests (and the same is true for his policy on the total ban of chemical weapons)[19] that the time is over when Western politicians could take refuge in far-reaching arms control proposals knowing that there would be no risk that the leadership in the Kremlin would ever accept them. It may be called an irony of history that it was exactly this firm belief that made President Reagan and his then key arms control advisers—Defense Secretary Caspar Weinberger and Assistant Secretary of Defense for International Security Affairs Richard Perle—give way to pressure from US allies to propose the INF zero solution to the Soviet leadership, although without including the shorter-range systems. This action, of course, made it possible for the new Soviet leader to call the President's bluff and take him up on his proposal.

6. With the INF Treaty, Gorbachev has added substance to what he had already announced as a new policy during his first visit abroad (Paris in 1986) as General Secretary of the Soviet Communist Party. He abandoned, at least for the time being, the longstanding Soviet effort of his predecessors to get a handle on French and British nuclear weapons through negotiations with Washington. He has also given further credibility to his skill to satisfy Western expectations from public policy, as long as there is no substantial risk involved for Soviet interest.[20]

7. With the INF Treaty Gorbachev has presumably strengthened his position *vis-à-vis* critics of his new course in that he can claim to have turned the originally anti-Soviet and anti-arms control policy of President Reagan and the

US–Soviet arms control impasse into a productive co-operative arms control approach.[21]

In agreeing to the INF Treaty, Gorbachev can claim to have turned a major mistake of his predecessors into a maximum political advantage at minimal cost.

Without sacrificing anything of crucial importance for Soviet security and defence, the INF Treaty stands as a significant example of Soviet responsiveness to Western security and arms control concerns. The Treaty, in general, and its verification regime, in particular, have laid the foundation for a new political atmosphere in Washington and in other Western capitals. At least the way may be paved for addressing fundamental US–Soviet issues in such a way that the 1972 Anti-Ballistic Missile (ABM) Treaty will be explicitly adhered to in its original meaning, the Strategic Defense Initiative (SDI) will finally stop far from what it was originally meant to be (thus preventing a costly competition in space weapons), and consequently a substantial cut in offensive nuclear strategic weaponry will become possible.

Even before he arrived in Washington for the 1987 summit meeting, Gorbachev had scored on two of the three major points: ABM and SDI. The powerful Chairman of the Armed Services Committee, Senator Sam Nunn, had made it crystal-clear to the Reagan Administration that a violation of the original meaning of the ABM Treaty was not acceptable to Congress.[22] And, at the beginning of December 1987, on the budget side congressional leaders had agreed on language that 'expresses support for SDI, but only as a research program'.[23]

Gorbachev's ambitious goal—to produce substantially better economic performance for the benefit of his people and to the advantage of the Soviet Union's international competitiveness—determines the means of his policy vis-à-vis the United States. His goal requires obviating a new and costly arms competition with the United States, as such a competition would absorb the know-how and the investment capital needed for the civil sector of the Soviet economy. Since more efficient economic performance is also in the interest of the military, provided it is not achieved at the expense of central security interests, Gorbachev could also hope for support on this point.[24]

In fact, there exists every reason to suggest that the INF Treaty is an important part of Gorbachev's political strategy, announced at the 27th Party Congress of February 1986. There the General Secretary unequivocally stated that 'the fundamental tasks of the country's economic and social development also determine the CPSU'S [Communist Party of the Soviet Union] international strategy'.[25]

The Washington summit meeting, in December 1987, has ratified Gorbachev's strategy: it secured a breather on SDI and ABM in that both sides settled for an agreement to disagree[26] while leaving the door open for a brighter arms control future through a Strategic Arms Reduction Talks (START) treaty to be signed either with the Reagan Administration or his successor's.[27]

Other than just after the Reykjavik meeting of 1986,[28] Gorbachev expressed no alarm about the Washington summit meeting nor was he shy about displaying self-confidence at his meeting with Reagan, although his confidence was not always in line with reality.[29] In short, the Washington summit meeting demonstrated strikingly that it is the political resolve to control technology which produces arms control results rather than the hope that the prevention of new technological developments could lead to arms control agreements. Still, the major arms control result produced at the Washington summit is in the non-strategic area (INF); but the meeting failed to produce substantial progress on the subjects of strategic importance (ABM and SDI).

The INF success, important as it is, must not, however, blur two facts: (*a*) the Treaty as such has major shortcomings; and (*b*) there are still vastly more arms control questions to be solved than are already settled. This will become particularly obvious when examining the prospects for conventional arms control in Europe, a problem which the INF success has served as a catalyst for bringing its prospects into sharper focus:

1. It tends to be forgotten that it took almost 10 years to reach the INF Treaty: on 28 October 1977 Helmut Schmidt, then Chancellor of the Federal Republic of Germany, presented publicly what was referred to as the 'grey area' problem.[30]

2. Schmidt's speech already embraced what two years later became official North Atlantic Treaty Organization (NATO) policy, embodied in the two-track decision of 12 December 1979, that is, the desirability and possibility of a zero solution for the systems with ranges between 1000 and 5500 km.[31] The elimination of shorter-range systems was not included until Gorbachev, in an interview on 22 July 1987, offered a global zero solution also for this weapon category.[32]

3. The INF Treaty is a bilateral agreement between only two of the five nuclear powers, four of which hold direct responsibility for nuclear armaments deployed in Europe. The Treaty does not prohibit any other country from developing, deploying and even using, as currently done in the Iraq–Iran War, delivery vehicles with ranges between 500 and 5500 km and from equipping them with nuclear warheads where the country has not forgone the nuclear option by having ratified the Treaty for the Non-Proliferation of Nuclear Weapons (NPT). The missile war between Iraq and Iran, started in February 1988, and the deployment of Chinese-made ground-launched ballistic missiles with a range of 2000 miles (320 km) in Saudi Arabia, commented on in unambiguous terms by Israel, indicate to what degree the INF Treaty marks progress in the European region only.[33] Neither does it manage to draw France and the United Kingdom into the process of reducing their nuclear arsenals. In fact, in the light of political reactions to the INF Treaty in both of these countries, it can be argued that the Treaty has already visibly hardened the traditional French and British opposition to non-strategic nuclear arms control, although for different reasons.[34] In view of the fact that there remain only fewer than eight years until the 1968 NPT (in force since March 1970) might expire,[35] this situation is not an encouraging sign for the preservation of this important treaty. After all, why should any of the threshhold countries give way to pressure from nuclear countries to join the NPT regime if the three nuclear powers which sponsored the Treaty, namely, the USA, the USSR and the UK,

within 18 years of the Treaty's 25 years of initial duration, did not manage to live up to their pledge 'to pursue negotiations in good faith on effective measures relating to cessation of the nuclear arms race *at an early date* and to nuclear disarmament'.[36]

4. Although security in Europe is at the centre of the problem that INF represents, Western Europe played no visible role, aside from being regularly consulted, in bringing about the result of the discussions. Clearly, it was not represented at the negotiating table. Nor has there been a West European effort to offer collective West European advice to the United States, for example, as a result of political co-operation within the European Political Co-operation, an essential consultation body of the European Community. Not even the host countries for the Pershing II and the ground-launched cruise missiles (GLCMs)—Belgium, the Federal Republic of Germany, Italy, the Netherlands and the United Kingdom—launched a visible effort to play a more decisive role. Thus, it was not without logic that President Reagan, on the level of public diplomacy, reciprocated by not even calling for a special meeting of the NATO allies at the level of Foreign Ministers, neither before nor even after having put his signature to the Treaty.

The time span needed to reach the agreement and the great number of political obstacles to be overcome confirm that arms control is a very vulnerable political creature and is almost entirely dependent on the political climate produced by non-arms control matters. If there is a relationship between the political environment and arms control, it is this: in order to survive or to rebuild it, both need to be protected from damaging influences.

III. Conventional arms control in Europe

There are four features that mainly characterize the situation:

1. The Conference on Security and Co-operation in Europe (CSCE) Follow-up Meeting, which commenced its work on 4 November 1986 in Vienna, has not produced to date (March 1988) a negotiating mandate under which to continue—according to the Madrid mandate of 6 September 1983—the efforts of the 35 states 'to make progress in strengthening confidence and security and in achieving disarmament'.[37]

2. Throughout 1987 and during the first part of 1988, the Soviet Union remained on the arms control offensive, initiated with the Budapest appeal of the Warsaw Treaty Organization (WTO) on 11 June 1986, although more on the level of political rhetoric than substance.

3. As a collective body, the Atlantic Alliance had to content itself with a low arms control profile because of substantial differences among its major partners.

4. The East–West forum (which has by far the longest experience with conventional arms control in Europe)—the Mutual and Balanced Force Reductions (MBFR) negotiations in Vienna, now in their fourteenth year—has not produced an agreement and is not likely to do so.

CDE—the search for a new mandate in the old framework

Since the successful completion of the Conference on Confidence- and Security-Building Measures and Disarmament in Europe (commonly referred to as CDE, the Conference on Disarmament in Europe) in Stockholm on 19 September 1986, three positive developments can be recorded:

1. In the light of the Stockholm experience, the CDE countries, under the Madrid mandate, could have opted to devote also the next CDE round to confidence- and security-building measures only. It was a major step forward that this possibility was not seriously considered. The success of the CDE in Stockholm seems to have generated sufficient courage to broaden the endeavours and hence to put arms reductions on the agenda of the next stage of negotiations.

2. It is especially noteworthy that France is part of this new approach; thus the country's co-operation is secured. France had always resisted participation in the MBFR negotiations. Without its active participation in a positive way, however, arms control negotiations for Europe from 'the Atlantic to the Urals' (leaving aside 'disarmament') would be bound to fail.

3. Agreement has also been established among the 35 CDE states that 'the core problem of the conventional forces' in Europe, that is, 'weapons with an offensive capability',[39] will be dealt with by those who possess them: the 23 member states of the two alliances.

But, in the first place, arms control is not about soldiers and weapons. Guided by the fundamental principle that national defence must not be impaired, arms control represents a diplomatic effort to allay the political suspicion of either side that armed forces could be used offensively by political leaders for the promotion of offensive political goals. For negotiations, a number of consequences flow from here.

The main consequence is the need to identify carefully one's political goal in negotiations before turning to the details. If the goal of either side is to seek a substantial reduction of troops and armaments, the consequences for any negotiating concept to be pursued in the European context will be inherently more complex than one that aims 'only' at the advancement of political confidence between the two alliances.

NATO and the WTO exist and function under very different strategic conditions. Consequently, they will approach the arms control subject from very different angles (thus making it extremely difficult to reach a balanced reduction of troops and armaments).

Three member countries of the Atlantic Alliance are nuclear weapon states with specific views about the role of nuclear weapons within the deterrence framework and also during a war. Despite the perennial demand from the Soviet Union and its allies, NATO refuses to include nuclear weapons in the CDE. The French position is probably the strongest one, basically saying: either 'France in' but no nuclear weapons on the agenda, or 'France out' and 'nuclear weapons in'. In fact, given the complex relationship between the three Western nuclear powers, it is very unlikely, perhaps not even desirable, that they would want to search for a joint position to be represented at an East–West negotiating table.

As indicated by its name, the Atlantic Alliance is built around an ocean and depends on unimpeded availability of sea lines of communication. Neither could industry continue to work without the raw materials imported via the high seas, nor could the USA carry out a joint defence plan with its European allies if the Atlantic Ocean was controlled by an unfriendly country. The same is not true for the WTO. In strategic raw materials, the Soviet Union is almost 100 per cent independent. In fact, in terms of raw material resources, the Soviet Union is not only a superpower: it is the greatest power of all. It also leads an alliance of land powers, with all the technical advantages associated with it. A threat to sea lines of communication would in no way impinge on the WTO's military security.[40]

But ever since the Madrid mandate when the CSCE countries included 'the whole of Europe as well as the adjoining sea area and air space', supplemented with a note saying that 'in this context, the notion of adjoining sea area is understood to refer also to ocean areas adjoining Europe', the content of this passage has been a stumbling-block between East and West. The WTO countries perceive it as in their interests to include in the control regime as many Western naval operations as possible plus the land- and and sea-based tactical air force, while the West, at most, was and is prepared to talk about such operations that were part of combined operations with land forces on the European continent and covered by the regime of prior notification.

Since the United States and the Soviet Union are global powers, they cannot be expected to tailor their armed forces exclusively to the needs of regional security in Europe.

As a consequence of World War II, the Soviet Union, the United States, the United Kindom and France enjoy a special responsibility for Germany as a whole and for Berlin.[41] It is unlikely that the Four Powers will allow restrictions that could hinder them from exercising their respective rights and duties (e.g., for the three Western powers to guarantee the security and freedom of West Berlin).

Soviet forces in Eastern Europe and in the German Democratic Republic serve a dual purpose: (*a*) they contribute to the military security of the Soviet Union proper and of its allies; and (*b*) they help to preserve political systems which none of the countries has adopted voluntarily. Nothing in Soviet foreign policy suggests that Moscow would tolerate, let alone actively seek, a loosening of the strategic cohesiveness of the WTO or that it would be prepared to risk the military infrastructure on which its dominant role over Eastern Europe and the GDR is based. This must not be confused with the question of whether, in the long run, Soviet policy can retain the degree of control exercised today. But the Soviet Union must not be expected to discuss this policy rationale and ensuing military consequences with its allies and/or with the NATO countries, neither off the record nor at an international negotiating table.[42]

The assured stability of the current political systems in adjoining East European countries is in fact a central element of national security as the Soviet Union defines it for itself. This characteristic feature, more than any other, contributes to the complex situation that the military balance in Europe is stable enough to prevent armed conflict but, at the same time, is too unbalanced to allow genuine confidence to develop. In short, the balance that exists today is anything but conducive to arms control.

While the United States does not need to worry about maintaining forces in Western Europe for the sake of protecting imposed political systems, Washington has to be concerned with maintaining the political cohesion of the Alliance. Among other things, this requires maintaining a balance, for example, between the West German and the French forces and the equal distribution of the benefits that result from the reductions aimed at. While the preservation of dominance over its allies represents Moscow's overriding concern, well reflected in its share of WTO troops,[43] Washington needs to concern itself about equality among its allies.

In fact, no Soviet leader can be expected to encourage the East European allies to form a political union of the kind with which the USA has constantly tried to tempt Western Europe ever since the visionary Philadelphia speech of John F. Kennedy on 4 July 1962.[44]

In the extreme, the United States would not feel its national security to be deadly threatened if it were to withdraw its military forces from Europe. The Soviet Union, however, would not be expected to have the same view in the event that it had to withdraw militarily from the GDR and Eastern Europe. The experience of the two world wars during this century does not permit the WTO political leaders even to entertain such an idea if they are interested in getting into or staying in power. Arms control in Europe is as much a problem within the two alliances as it is between them.

In essence, conventional arms control in Europe is about the political structure of the old continent and not only about manpower and equipment; it is about the qualitative change of the *status quo* without moving borders.

Apart from the political complexities, the purely technical difficulties involved render conventional arms control in Europe an extremely ambitious and complicated undertaking. To illustrate the point, a broad comparison with the INF Treaty may be helpful: 35 countries, not 2, deal with *all* conventional armed forces (soldiers and equipment), not only with one class of weapon, spread out over all of Europe from the Atlantic to the Urals.

This, of course, is not to suggest that arms control is impossible. But it would not be surprising if the Soviet Union initially opted for unilateral troop reductions of some less than substantial order rather than negotiated ones, since such a step would evade all the intricacies of a negotiated East–West settlement while perhaps offering the opportunity to put Western public opinion in the right frame of mind. What confidence building needs, however, is mutually agreed measures, not unilateral ones, since, in the sensitive area of security and defence, confidence will not come about except through visibly adhered to commitments to respect others' security concerns as much as one's own.

It is, however, equally logical to assume that mutually agreed, verifiable and militarily significant reductions of troops and armaments in Europe represent a very ambitious political goal, reachable only after overcoming enormous difficulties. Thus, it may just be adequate for the promotion of the Helsinki–Stockholm process not to look for the perfect negotiating concept, but rather to start the next stage of the process, hoping that at some point it will lead in the right direction, which is to bolster further the non-use of force principle. In fact, if a considerably higher degree of transparency of military activities in Europe through refined confidence-building measures and constraints takes place first, it may then be easier to agree on reductions.

Rather than trying to make the armed forces slowly disappear, the history- and psychology-loaded, sensitive political system in Europe may find it easier to guarantee the non-use of force through measures that make it visibly impossible for the political leadership to use armed forces for offensive political goals. After all, arms control is a continuing process, sensitive to concomitant positive political circumstances as much as to negative ones. Arms control is not a finished product.

Gorbachev challenges the West—from deterrence to co-operative defence?

While with respect to INF the General Secretary has not only applied bold language but has also initiated radical solutions in order to correct the major mistake of his predecessors, he has been remarkably less precise in addressing the future. Although it was he who more than two years ago, in his April 1986 Prague speech,[45] coined the notion 'our common house of Europe', thereby signalling that he had some new political structure in mind, and despite his frequently returning to the subject with new metaphors, Gorbachev has failed to produce new ideas about what the elements of this Europe should look like.

But this must not be misconstrued as a simple continuation of the rusty Soviet approach centred around the notion 'peaceful coexistence'. From his book *Perestroika*, as well as from numerous speeches and other public remarks, three noticeable changes that Gorbachev has introduced emerge:

1. To call the hitherto existing three CSCE stages, as symbolized by Helsinki, Stockholm and Vienna, almost complete designs for the construction of a 'common European house',[46] amounts to no less than accepting that a political process has been set in motion, the outcome of which is uncertain but open to influence.

2. It certainly marks a departure from previous days not only to admit that the military balance in Europe holds problems for neighbours of the WTO but also to offer to hold discussions with the West about the matter[47] (in particular if seen in conjunction with the WTO offer of May 1987 to 'consult' with NATO about doctrine).[48]

3. To talk about 'hitherto unknown norms of openness and transparency, to verify mutually scope and depth of accepted commitments' and to hold out a prospect of producing defence-budget figures within the next 'two to three years'[49] also represent an opening, which, if not followed fairly soon by respective substance, carries the risk of being identified as nothing but a propaganda ploy.

The discussion among Soviet military leaders and the civil experts on military matters who work for Gorbachev indicates that the military is far from keen on entering into a doctrinal discussion with the West.[50] However, this did not lead Gorbachev to soften his demand. On the contrary, in his September 1987 article in *Pravda* and *Izvestiya*, Gorbachev broadened considerably the WTO demand of May 1987 for 'consultations' in that he proposed an agreement about a 'strategy of defence' and about 'military sufficiency'—the latter being a notion for which he, as the highest political authority, offered a definition in order to end the dispute between military and civil experts. The definition claims that both a 'strategy of defence' and 'military sufficiency' 'require the armed forces of states to have a structure which is sufficient for defence against a potential aggression, but not sufficiently strong to launch offensive attacks'.[51]

Largely owing to NATO's failure to test Gorbachev's ideas, it remains unclear whether the Soviet leader means serious business. Does he, in fact, intend to use a discussion about crucial military subjects for the purpose of establishing solid ground for a genuine restructuring of the armed forces in all of Europe? Or has he in fact only designed a tactical game to exploit the discussion about 'non-provocative defence'? (This concept is of West German origin and, on the political-parliamentary levels, is almost exclusively promoted by the German Social Democratic Party; moreover, it has not yet attracted the support of any NATO government.)

It is also not clear in which forum Gorbachev would want to conduct the doctrinal 'consultations' and the search for an 'agreement', for example, within the CDE II framework currently being worked on in Vienna or in a special set-up, separate from or loosely linked to the CDE. Moreover, it is unclear whether Gorbachev holds enough power to enforce the publication of military data of the kind needed to do what the Soviet Defence Minister, General of the Army Dmitry Yazov, in an article in *Pravda*, termed 'an accomplishable task': 'to objectively assess the military balance of the forces of the Warsaw Treaty Organization and of the NATO bloc'.[52] And this uncertainty is not going to vanish until either NATO musters enough courage and unanimity to take Gorbachev at his word or the General Secretary, in another unilateral move, provides interesting data; or, in the worst case, until the entire effort collapses, for whatever reason.

NATO: dealing with a partner-like opponent

The North Atlantic Treaty Organization's lack of 'a positive political strategy for dealing with the Soviet Union',[53] as rightly diagnosed already in 1983 by the then soon-to-be NATO Secretary General Lord Carrington, has in no way been cured. In fact, it has become worse: with the old safety system gone, that is, that disagreements between alliance partners could be covered up with bold ideas since Moscow would reject them anyway, the search for acceptable, workable concepts has become imperative.[54] So far, this search has not borne any fruit.

The reason for failure is not new. Basically, it centres around the question: What role are nuclear weapons to play in maintaining deterrence in an era of accepted nuclear parity between the United States and the Soviet Union?[55] Or:

How much nuclear is enough? Without an answer to these questions, no concept about the reduction of nuclear weapons can realistically emerge. And as the Soviet Union was not, until recently, ready to negotiate arms reductions seriously, NATO did not feel hard pressed to produce such concepts.

With Gorbachev, however, the situation has changed. He has called NATO's bluff. Thus, the old rifts that separate two schools of thought have reappeared. On the one side, there are those who think that a further reduction of non-strategic nuclear weapons would be acceptable only after the WTO's edge on conventional forces has been cut by a negotiated settlement. And, on the other side, there are those who believe that, in the wake of the INF Treaty, a drastic cut in non-strategic nuclear weapons should be sought at once and that there is no need to effectuate the modernization of NATO's shorter-range nuclear weapons now, as agreed upon in 1983 in Montebello. The Montebello decision had not been taken in isolation anyway, but rather under circumstances when there was absolutely no hope that Moscow could agree to the reduction of nuclear weapons in Europe.

As a consequence of this, in June 1987 NATO designed the so-called Reykjavik formula, which served everybody's needs. It states that an arms control and disarmament concept would also serve the requirements of NATO's flexible response strategy if, among other objectives, it sought 'in conjunction with the establishment of a conventional balance and the global elimination of chemical weapons, tangible and verifiable reductions of American and Soviet land-based nuclear missile systems of shorter range, leading to equal ceilings'.[56]

Obviously, this formula offered something for everybody:

1. For Washington, it did not rule out the argument that there should be no further reduction of shorter-range nuclear weapons without preceding East–West agreements about the establishment of a conventional balance in Europe.[57]

2. For the Federal Republic of Germany, it covered Bonn's request first to work out an 'overall concept' for all three components—conventional, chemical and nuclear—before taking further decisions about what to solve through modernization and what to solve through negotiations.[58]

3. For France, it secured very visibly its policy of protecting the French nuclear forces against arms control effects while it also allayed obvious French nervousness about the future orientation of West German security policy (unjustified as it is, and which was recently highlighted by the French reactions to the INF Treaty). Centred around the fear that the arms control process could ultimately lead to a nuclear weapon-free Europe, INF quite nicely served French purposes in that it gave a denuclearization appetizer to the Federal Republic of Germany without basically affecting nuclear reality in Europe. The FRG's alleged anti-nuclear stance has now become so visible that Mitterrand even found it necessary to attend a NATO summit meeting, something which the French President has not done ever since de Gaulle left the military integration of NATO in 1966.[59]

Of course, the Brussels summit meeting of 3 March 1988 could not achieve more than to confirm the basic disagreement within the Western Alliance. Hence, it not only reaffirmed the Reykjavik formula[60] but also made it clear that the NATO allies clearly denied President Reagan a mandate to go beyond this unworkable formula when he goes to Moscow in May 1988 for his fourth and final summit meeting with General Secretary Gorbachev. At the 11–12 October 1986 preparatory meeting in Reykjavik, both Gorbachev and Reagan turned the explicitly dubbed non-summit meeting into a negotiating forum and basically agreed on the evil nature of nuclear weapons and the need to eliminate all of them.[61] The NATO allies' concern that the US President should not repeat what he did with Gorbachev in Reykjavik was shrouded in the formula behind the conspicuous non-reference to the Reykjavik meeting and the demonstrative mention of the Washington summit meeting of 7–8 December 1987.[62]

IV. Conclusion

1987 and the beginning of 1988 are not unlike a holding operation. Both superpowers have travelled a long way and in so doing have managed to overcome some of the main obstacles to reaching more profound agreements. The INF Treaty is the most salient case in point although not the only one. However, with no new negotiating mandate for conventional arms control in Europe agreed upon, no START agreement signed, and agreement on the substance of the future of the ABM Treaty pending, it is still uncertain whether the holding operation will result in a safe landing, meaning a beginning of a substantially new era in arms control, marked by agreements that cut into the muscles rather than only reduce the redundancy. With the presidential elections in France (May 1988) and in the United States (November 1988) and with the global situation being far from satisfactory (e.g., Iraq–Iran, Afghanistan, the debt crisis, South Africa, Central America, etc.), it is uncertain when, how and in what direction the situation will change.

Notes and references

[1] In a statement published by TASS on 8 Feb. 1988, Gorbachev announced that 'the Government of the USSR and the Republic of Afghanistan agreed to set a specific date for beginning the withdrawal of Soviet troops, 15 May 1988, and to complete the withdrawal within 10 months'. See 'USA begrüssen Gorbatschows Abzugsplan', *Süddeutsche Zeitung*, 10 Feb. 1988, p. 9; for the text of the agreement, see *Süddeutsche Zeitung*, 15 Apr. 1988, p. 11.

[2] See 'The United Nations and the Iran–Iraq War', *A Ford Foundation Conference Report*, New York, Aug. 1987; here Sir Brian Urquhart and Gary Sick note: 'When the United Nations Charter was written in 1945, the world had suffered six years of devastating war. Governments were convinced of the need to devise an international system that could deal with international disputes or acts of aggression or whatever else threatened to disrupt the peace. . . . After forty years, much of the sense of urgency about dealing co-operatively with threats to or breaches of the peace has evaporated'. See also Urquhart, B., *SIPRI Yearbook 1988*, chapter 15.

[3] According to data compiled by Agnès Allebeck, SIPRI, from Agence France Press, *Defense and Foreign Affairs Weekly* and *Mednews*, by 23 Mar. 1988 the picture is as follows: Iraq claims to have fired 103 missiles (93 on Teheran, 8 on Quam, 2 on Isphahan); Iran claims to have fired 36 missiles on Baghdad, but Iraqi officials acknowledge only 28. According to Iranian sources, by 21 Mar. 1988 Iran suffered 600 civilian casualties and 1000 wounded. According to Pott, M., 'Diplomatie im Städtekrieg', *Die Zeit*, 11 Mar. 1988, p. 12. By 9 Mar. 1988, Tehran is reported to

16 INTRODUCTION

have suffered 270 civilian casualties; Iraq has released no figures on Iraqi casualties. Concerning the class of missiles fired, no confirmed news exists either. Iran claims to have the know-how to produce the missiles, perhaps copies of the Soviet Scud B with an extended range (original: 300 km; needed: above 500 km); Iraq claims the same, although observers believe that the missiles fired are either of Soviet origin (Scud Bs) or result from secret co-operation with other countries. Brazil has been named in this context.

  [4] According to the information collected by the Center for Defense Information in Washington, DC, 165 ships were attacked in the Persian Gulf during 1987 (1986: 111; 1985: 47); since the beginning of the Iraq–Iran War in 1980, 437 ships have been attacked by either party to the War (275 Iraqi attacks; 162 Iranian). Ninety merchant fleet seamen were reported to have lost their lives as a result of these attacks; see 'Amerikanische Bilanz des Tankerkrieges im Golf', *Neue Zürcher Zeitung*, 30 Dec. 1987, p. 3. Another 51 seamen were killed in an Iraqi attack on two Iranian tankers on 21 Mar. 1988. It was the worst incident since the tanker war began in earnest in 1984; see *Financial Times*, 22 Mar. 1988, p. 1.

  [5] See Strothmann, D., 'Messer am Hals. Ein Flüchtlingsland unter Blockade', *Die Zeit*, no. 5 (29 Jan. 1988), p. 9. A senior Israeli defence official is quoted to have said that 'what Israel was witnessing was no less than "the beginning of the Palestinians' war of independence"'; see 'West Bank violence claims six dead as protests sweep region', *Financial Times*, 8 Feb. 1988, p. 2.

  [6] For a well-documented analysis of the peace negotiations, see Hünseler, P., 'Die ägyptisch–israelischen Friedensverhandlungen', *Die Internationale Politik 1979–1980*, Jahrbuch des Forschungsinstituts der Deutschen Gesellschaft für Auswärtige Politik (R. Oldenbourg: München, Wien, 1983), pp. 126–51.

  [7] See Flottau, H., 'Camp David ist tot. Doch auch die arabischen Staaten haben Vorbehalte gegen einen palästinensischen Staat', *Süddeutsche Zeitung*, no. 48 (27–28 Feb. 1988), p. 11.

  [8] See interview with Israel's Defence Minister Jizchak Rabin, 'Sollen wir mit Blumen werfen?', *Der Spiegel*, no. 12 (21 Mar. 1988), pp. 176–81.

  [9] Hanf, Th., 'Konflikte im südlichen Afrika', in K. Kaiser and H. P. Schwarz, *Weltpolitik. Strukturen-Akteure-Perspektiven* (Klett-Cotta: Stuttgart, 1985), p. 661.

  [10] See Campbell, K. M., *Southern Africa in Soviet Foreign Policy*, Adelphi Papers no. 227 (winter 1987/88) (International Institute for Strategic Studies: London, 1988).

  [11] In February 1987 President Oscar Arias of Costa Rica proposed a peace plan, based on a cease-fire in the countries in Central America where armed struggle is under way and an end to US funding for the Nicaraguan Contras, and the institution of a process leading to amnesties, democratic rights and social justice. On 7 August 1987 the presidents of Honduras, Guatemala, Costa Rica, Nicaragua and El Salvador signed their own Regional Peace Plan Agreement, which called for a cease-fire within 90 days of the conflicts in Nicaragua, El Salvador and Guatemala, for the suspension of all assistance to insurgent groups in the region, as well as for the establishment of verifiable democracies; see the Documentation in *Survival*, vol. 30, no. 1 (1988), pp. 79–85.

  [12] For further details, in particular concerning Latin America—the most serious part of the debt problem—see Westphalen, J., 'Das internationale Schuldenmanagement vor neuen Aufgaben', *Europa Archiv*, vol. 24 (1987), pp. 701–8. See also the analysis of the President of the Inter-American Development Bank, Antonio Ortiz Mena, 'Zustand und Aussichten der Wirtschaft Lateinamerikas', *Europa Archiv*, no. 15 (1987), pp. 437–42. According to data from the UN Commission on Latin America, between 1982 and 1987 the debt of Latin American countries has risen by 24 per cent to US $409.8 billion in 1987; see 'Latin America: hopes and fears', *International Herald Tribune*, 11 Feb. 1988, p. 7 (1982/1987): Mexico 87.6/105.6; Uruguay 4.2/5.2; Brazil 91.3/116.9; Venezuela 35.1/32.2; Colombia 10.3/15.7. The IMF global debt figure for developing countries in 1987 is US $1184 billion (1980: 634), broken into regions: Latin America, 409 (231); Africa, 170 (97); Asia, 300 (138); Middle East, 159 (74); Europe, 146 (94); see 'Auslandsverschuldung der Entwicklungsländer', *Süddeutsche Zeitung*, 8/9 Aug. 1987, p. 21.

  [13] The Soviet invasion of Afghanistan in December 1979 is perhaps the most dramatic case in point, given the fact that it caused President Carter to withdraw the SALT Treaty (signed by him and Brezhnev in June 1979) from the Senate ratification table, even though it had taken seven years to negotiate the result.

  [14] For the text of the Treaty, see appendix 13A. The Memorandum of Understanding lists only 859 US missiles, but 8 defective Pershing 1a's were located and, according to Article IX of the Treaty, reported to the USSR, after its signature.

  [15] See *Arms Control Today*, vol. 18, no. 11 (1988), INF supplement, p. 1; here one also finds a good summary of the INF Treaty and the Protocols.

  [16] Bertram, C., 'Europe's security dilemmas', *Foreign Affairs*, summer 1987, p. 951. A good overview of the shorter-range nuclear-capable delivery systems in the European area is presented in 'Threat assessment', Document 1115 of Assembly of Western European Union, Report

1987—THE TURNING-POINT? 17

submitted on behalf of the Committee on Defense Questions and Armaments by Mr Stokes, Rapporteur, 2 Nov. 1987, p. 19; according to this authoritative account, NATO retains 1392 launchers and the WTO 1609, after elimination of intermediate-range nuclear forces according to the Washington Treaty of 8 Dec. 1987, not including the dual-capable artillery systems.

[17] See 'Document of the Stockholm Conference on Confidence- and Security-Building Measures and Disarmament in Europe', paras. 66–99, *SIPRI Yearbook 1987: World Armaments and Disarmament* (Oxford University Press: Oxford, 1987), pp. 364–7.

[18] See the excellent study by Herspring, D. R., 'Marshal Akhromeyev and the future of the Soviet armed forces', *Survival*, vol. 28, no. 6, pp. 524–35; Herspring refers *inter alia* to Akhromeyev's article in *Pravda* of 15 Oct. 1985 wherein he expresses concern over verification and argues that mutual forces reduction 'monitoring must not turn into intelligence activity' and also emphasizes the importance of French and British nuclear weapons for the arms control negotiations (Herspring, p. 530). Only nine days after the INF Treaty was signed, Akhromeyev reaffirmed his concern about the British and French nuclear forces, although he obviously chose to put it into a larger framework. In an interview with *Pravda* on 16 Dec. 1987, he stated his 'hope that Britain and France will join the process of nuclear arms reductions after the prospective 50 per cent reduction of strategic offensive armaments, that is to say after the sizeable reduction of the nuclear weapons of the USSR and the USA'; see also Reifenberg, J., 'Der Blick in die Küche ist möglich. Achromejews Ja ermöglicht den Durchbruch in Genf', *Frankfurter Allgemeine Zeitung*, 26 Nov. 1987, p. 2.

[19] See Lundin, S. J., Perry Robinson, J. P. and Trapp, R., in *SIPRI Yearbook 1988*, chapter 5.

[20] Among the most notable events to that effect is the following: the decision to contract the Liebherr company in the Federal Republic of Germany, the country whose political leadership was most concerned about the Soviet missiles, to convert some of the SS–20 transporter vehicles into chassis for civilian ambulances.

Before the Washington meeting Gorbachev had reached a better positive-to-negative poll rating among Americans than Ronald Reagan, 'something few would have thought possible even a year ago'; see *Wall Street Journal*, 4 Dec. 1987, p. 1. According to a *Wall Street Journal*/NBC poll, conducted with 1599 adults nationwide in the United States, the favourable/unfavourable relation for Reagan was 59 per cent to 35 per cent, for Gorbachev 53 per cent to 20 per cent.

[21] See Schmidt-Haeuser, Ch., 'Die neue Stufe. Der Gipfel stärkt Gorbatschow', *Die Zeit*, vol. 52 (18 Dec. 1987), p. 1.

[22] Nunn: 'I have concluded that the preponderance of evidence in the negotiating record supports the Senate's original understanding of the treaty—that is the traditional interpretation.... I believe the administration is wrong in its analysis of the negotiating record itself'; see 'Interpretation of the ABM Treaty, Senate', March 11, 1987, *Congressional Record*, Proceedings and Debates of the 100th Congress, First Session, vol. 133, no. 40, p. 2.

[23] See 'Reagan expects pact on strategic arms with Soviets in 1988', *Wall Street Journal*, 4 Dec. 1987, p. 6. The changing emphasis emerges also from the budget figures: for fiscal year 1989, running from 1 Oct. 1988 through 30 Sep. 1989, the budget request from the Defense Department amounts to US $4.6 billion, which is $1.7 billion below what was originally planned ($6.3 billion) and only $1.1 billion above the level provided for by Congress for 1988 ($3.5 billion); see 'Defense budget cut, essential strength maintain' (excerpts: national defense section of the Reagan budget), *Document Defense Policy*, 8 Feb. 1988, Stockholm, USIS, p. 5. Between US $13 billion and $14 billion have now been spent on the SDI programme, according to 'Congressional sources'; see 'SDI is better than political manoeuvring, says Teller', *Document Defense Policy*, 14 Mar. 1988, p. 16. See also 'Reagan legt den bescheidendsten Etatentwurf für das Pentagon vor', *Frankfurter Allgemeine Zeitung*, 20 Feb. 1988, p. 3.

[24] See Schroeder, H. H., 'Gorbatschow und die Generäle. Militärdoktrin, Rüstungspolitik und öffentliche Meinung in der "Perestrojka"', *Berichte des Bundesinstituts für ostwissenschaftliche und internationale Studien*, vol. 45 (1987), pp. 34–9.

[25] See Gorbachev's speech to the Twenty-Seventh Party Congress of the CPSU, 25 Feb. 1986, *Europa Archiv*, no. 8 (1986), p. D.215.

[26] See 'Gemeinsame Erklärung über die Gespräche zwischen dem Präsidenten der Vereinigten Staaten, Ronald Reagan und dem Generalsekretäri der KPdSU, Michail Gorbatschow, in Washington vom 7 bis zum 10 Dezember 1987', *Europa Archiv*, vol. 1 (1988), pp. D.32–8. Both sides instructed their negotiators in Geneva 'to work out an agreement that would commit the sides to observe the ABM Treaty as signed in 1972' (p. D.35).

[27] Already in Apr. 1987, Soviet Foreign Minister Shevardnadze stated publicly that an INF Treaty with the Reagan Administration seemed to be in the offing, but not START and SDI; see *Europa Archiv*, vol. 9 (1987), p. Z.84.

[28] See Gorbachev's Press Conference directly after the Reykjavik meeting, where the General

Secretary in an alarmist tone stated, e.g., that 'he could not allow himself for a minute to think that the next summit in Washington could result in a failure', and that his and the President's views on 'how to stop the arms race and prohibit nuclear weapons clashed' (translation from German), *Europa Archiv*, no. 24 (1986), pp. D.669–81.

[29] During the Washington summit meeting, Gorbachev is reported to have suggested to Reagan that the Soviet Union disposed of technology to verify reliably from some distance sea-launched cruise missiles deployed on ships and submarines; when hard pressed at the START negotiating table in Geneva, where verification of SLCMs is a major problem, the Soviet delegation, so far, seemed not to be able to substantiate this statement; in his press conference after the summit meeting, Gorbachev implicitly referred to this part of his conversation with Reagan, reporting that he had suggested to the President that Soviet scientists had made headway in solving the verification problem, while US scientists had not. Speaking about what national verification means could do for the SLCM problem, Gorbachev stated: 'We could share our achievements'; see Gorbachev, Press Conference on 10 Dec. 1987, Washington, DC, TASS, 1 Dec. 1987.

[30] Schmidt, H., 'Politische und wirtschaftliche Aspekte der westlichen Sicherheit. 1977 Alastair Buchan Memorial Lecture', *Bulletin der Bundesregierung*, no. 112 (1977), pp. 1013–20.

[31] Schmidt (note 30): 'Eine auf die Weltmächte USA und Sowjetunion begrenzte strategische Rüstungsbeschränkung muss das Sicherheitsbedürfnis der westeuropäischen Bündnispartner gegenüber der in Europa militärisch überlegenen Sowjetunion beeinträchtigen, wenn es nicht gelingt, die in Europa bestehenden Disparitäten parallel zu den SALT–Verhandlungen abzubauen', p. 1014/1015. A NATO Communiqué of 12 Dec. 1979, para. 11, reads: 'NATO's TNF requirements will be examined in the light of concrete results reached through negotiations'. Indirectly, the decision also referred to the goal of curbing the shorter-range system situation by saying 'the *immediate* objective of these (INF) negotiations should be the agreed limitations on US and Soviet land-based long-range theatre nuclear missile systems' (emphasis added); Special Meeting of Foreign and Defence Ministers, Brussels, 12 Dec. 1979, Text of Final Communiqués, vol. 2, 1975–1980, NATO Information Service, Brussels, pp. 121–3. It is noteworthy, however, that in the light of the prevailing conditions of the time, i.e., the conduct of Soviet foreign policy, NATO, in its decision documents, rightly judged the 'total elimination' as 'highly unlikely'.

[32] See excerpts of the interview with the Indonesian newspaper *Merdeka*, 22 July 1987, in *Europa Archiv*, no. 20 (1987), pp. D559–63; see also 'Gorbachev says Soviet is ready to eliminate missiles in Asia', *International Herald Tribune*, 23 July 1988, p. 1.

[33] See Karp, A., 'The frantic Third World quest for ballistic missiles', *Bulletin of the Atomic Scientists*, vol. 44, no. 5 (June 1988), pp. 14–21. The Chinese sale of missiles to Saudi Arabia reported in Mar. 1988 is the most recent case in point. According to the information reported, China has confirmed the sale of surface-to-surface missiles with non-nuclear warheads and with a range of 3600 km (CSS-2 Class) to Saudi Arabia; *International Herald Tribune*, 19–20 Mar. 1988, p. 1, and 22 Mar. 1988, pp. 1–2. The US State Department felt sufficiently alarmed to seek China's and Saudi Arabia's assurance that the missiles are not nuclear-tipped. Israeli Defence Minister Shamir demanded the immediate removal of the missiles, coupled with warnings from unnamed Israeli officials that the Saudi Arabian launch sites could be bombed; see 'Israelis warn Saudis on missiles', *Financial Times*, 21 Mar. 1988, p. 22.

[34] See de Weck, R., 'Angst im Abseits. Frankreichs Sorge vor dem Abrüstungssog', *Die Zeit*, vol. 51 (11 Dec. 1987), p. 4. French policy is still more concerned with preserving its status advantage over the Federal Republic, which would be endangered by any radical anti-nuclear weapon policy. In his interview with *Nouvel Observateur*, conducted after the signing of the INF Treaty, President Mitterrand, not for the first time, referred specifically to the 'special restrictions' imposed on the Federal Republic of Germany since World War II; see excerpts in *Europa Archiv*, no. 2 (1988), p. D49. The UK is more concerned with preserving some kind of assured nuclear deterrence *vis-à-vis* the Soviet Union; despite the special sort of relationship Margaret Thatcher enjoys with Gorbachev, she does not become tired of warning about the 'Russian bear'; see, e.g., Bertram, C., 'Margaret Thatcher lässt nicht locker. London will moderne Atomwaffen', *Die Zeit*, 11 Mar. 1988, p. 4.

[35] Article X, para. 2 of the NPT stipulates: 'Twenty-five years after the entry into force of the Treaty, a conference shall be convened to decide whether the Treaty shall continue in force indefinitely, or shall be extended for an additional fixed period or periods. This decision shall be taken by a majority of the Parties to the Treaty'; see Goldblat, J., SIPRI, *Agreements for Arms Control* (Taylor & Francis: London, 1982), pp. 172–4. It is logical that under this provision the decision could also be taken in favour of a 'zero' period.

[36] Article VI of the Treaty (emphasis added).

[37] Final Document of Madrid CSCE, 6 Sep. 1983, Extracts, in SIPRI, *World Armaments and Disarmament: SIPRI Yearbook 1984* (Taylor & Francis: London, 1984), p. 570.

[38] See note 17.

[39] Schenk, B., 'Die KVAE aus der Sicht der neutralen Schweiz', *Europa Archiv*, no. 3 (1987), p. 84. (The author was head of the Swiss delegation at the CDE in Stockholm and also heads his country's delegation at the CSCE Follow-up Meeting in Vienna.)

[40] See Stützle, W., *Politik und Kräfteverhältnis. Die Bundesrepublik im Wechselspiel der wirtschaftlichen, politischen und militärischen Kräfte von Ost und West* (E. S. Mittler & Sohn: Herford, 1983).

[41] It is not by chance that the Soviet Union, to this very day and despite many other changes in its policy, has not altered the official name of its contingent in the GDR (plus the permanent guard of honour at the Soviet War Memorial in Berlin (West) and also the three Soviet Military Liaison Missions to the US Forces (Frankfurt am Main), the British Army on the Rhine (Buente in Westfalen) and the French Forces in Germany (Baden Baden)): Group of Soviet Forces in Germany.

[42] The dual-purpose role of Soviet forces in Eastern Europe and in the GDR is not only secured through the integrated structure within the WTO but also by a close network of bilateral treaties with the individual WTO member states; see Hacker, J., *Der Ostblock. Entstehung, Entwicklung und Struktur 1939–1980* (Nomos: Baden Baden, 1983); Brzezinski, Z., *The Soviet Bloc Unity and Conflict*, revised enlarged edn (Harvard University Press, Cambridge, Mass., 1967).

[43] With the exception of land forces, where the USSR deployed some 60 per cent of all WTO forces, its share in WTO air and naval forces amounts to more than 80 per cent, and in WTO defence spending it is close to 90 per cent; the respective US figures are 29 per cent (land), 49 per cent (air), 61 per cent (naval) and 56 per cent (defence spending); for 1970 and 1980 figures, see Stützle (note 40), p. 49.

[44] It was in this speech that Kennedy argued for an Atlantic Alliance resting on two strong pillars: the USA and a politically united Europe. See Hacke, Ch., *Von Kennedy bis Reagan. Grundzüge der amerikanischen Aussenpolitik 1960–1984* (Klett Cotta: Stuttgart, 1984).

[45] For the text of the speech, see *Europa Archiv*, no. 10 (1987), pp. D.280–4: 'Im Lichte der neuen Denkweise brachten wir die Idee des "gesamteuropäischen Hauses" vor. Das ist keine schöne Phantasie, sondern das Ergebnis einer ernsthaften Analyse der Situation auf dem Kontinent. Der Begriff "gesamteuropäisches Haus" bedeutet vor allem die Anerkennung einer bestimmten Ganzheit, obwohl es um Staaten geht, die unterschiedlichen sozialen Systemen und entgegengesetzten militärpolitischen Blöcken angehören. Er verbindet in sich die herangereiften Probleme mit dem Vorhandensein realer Möglichkeiten für ihre Lösung' (p. D.283/84); see also the interesting account Gorbachev offers about the genesis of this very idea in his book *Perestroika. New Thinking for our Country and the World* (Collins: London, 1987), p. 194. It is also noteworthy that the German edition of the book has a different subtitle, that is, 'Die zweite russische Revolution. Eine neue Politik für Europa und die Welt', thus emphasizing Europe (German edn: Gorbatschow, M., *Perestroika. Die Zweite russische Revolution. Eine neue Politik für Europa und die Welt* [Droemer Knaur: München, 1987], pp. 252ff.).

[46] 'It has to its credit such a unique accomplishment in the history of international relations as the Helsinki process. Hopeful results were produced by the Stockholm Conference. Then the torch was taken up by Vienna where, we hope, a new step in the development of the Helsinki process will be made. So, the blueprints for the construction of a common European home are all but ready'; Gorbachev, *Perestroika* (note 45), p. 197.

[47] At its summit meeting in East Berlin on 28 and 29 May 1987, the WTO countries offered NATO 'consultations with the aim of comparing the military doctrines of both alliances, analysing their character and jointly studying the directions of their further evolution with a view to removing the mutual suspiciousness and mistrust that have accumulated for years'; see *Military Bulletin*, no. 11(17), Supplement, May 1987.

[48] For an excellent analysis, see Schroeder, H. H., 'Gorbatschow und die Generäle. Militärdoktrin, Rüstungspolitik und öffentliche Meinung in der "Perestrojka"', *Berichte des Bundesinstituts für ostwissenschaftliche und internationale Studien*, vol. 45 (1987); and Shenfield, S., *The Nuclear Predicament. Explorations in Soviet Ideology*, Chatham House Papers 37 (Routledge & Kegan Paul: London, New York, Andover, 1987), pp. 87–91.

[49] Gorbachev, M., 'Realities of and guarantees for secured peace', *Pravda* and *Izvestiya*, 17 Sep. 1987.

[50] Yazov, D., 'On military balance of forces and nuclear-missile parity', *Pravda*, 8 Feb. 1988; this article addresses in an amazingly encouraging tone some of the requirements for a promising data discussion that goes beyond bean-counting. However, Yazov does not answer the question: When is the Soviet Union going to live up to the self-imposed challenge? Hardly any other feature could indicate more strikingly the difference between rhetoric and reality than the fact that Yazov refers to Western data sources in order to make his point about the 'military balance'.

20   INTRODUCTION

⁵¹ Gorbachev (note 49).
⁵² Yazov (note 50).
⁵³ Lord Carrington, 'Alastair Buchan Memorial Lecture', 21 Apr. 1983, *Survival*, London (July/Aug. 1983), pp. 146–53.

⁵⁴ The politician in the West who has caught the situation better than any other is Walther Leisler Kiep, Member of the Presidium of the Christian Democratic Party (CDU) in the FRG, who, in an interview, remarked that 'Western policy towards the Soviet Union is guided too much by the past. That is to say, we still take comfort in the idea that Moscow is a reliable foe, whose "no" to Western proposals is a foregone conclusion. Today we possibly deal with a partner, although this assessment may be a slight exaggeration. We find it endlessly difficult to adjust to that situation' (translation from German added); Kiep, W. L., 'Die Allianz ist kein gepanzerter Konsumverein', *Neue Ruhr Zeitung*, 30 Nov. 1987, p. 6.

⁵⁵ The following facts may briefly illustrate NATO's problems: it took NATO seven years to accept the US decision to replace 'massive retaliation' with 'flexible response', adopted in 1967. It took another two years to agree on a small segment of the nuclear problem, i.e., the use of tactical nuclear weapons, laid down in the Provisional Political Guidelines of 1969. Seventeen more years were needed—until 1986—until NATO reached an agreement on General Political Guidelines 'covering all aspects of nuclear use'; see the informative and fine analysis of Kelleher, C. McArdle, 'Managing NATO's tactical nuclear operations', *Survival*, vol. 30, no. 1 (1988), pp. 59–78; see also Stützle, W., 'Abschreckung und Verteidigung. Für eine politische Strategie der Allianz', *Europa Archiv*, no. 5 (1983), pp. 139–48.

⁵⁶ See 'Erklärung der Ministertagung des Nordatlantikrats vom 12. Juni 1987', *Europa Archiv*, no. 14 (1987), pp. 382–4.

⁵⁷ See, e.g., 'Carlucci outlines U.S. Defense Strategy' (excerpts: Annual Report to Congress), 18 Feb. 1988, *Document Defense Policy*, USIS, Stockholm, 22 Feb. 1988, p. 4.

⁵⁸ See 'Erklärung der Bundesregierung über die Ergebnisse des Europäischen Rates in Brüssel und die Gespräche des Bundeskanzlers in Washington', Regierungserklärung von Bundeskanzler H. Kohl, 25 Februar 1988, *Bulletin der Bundesregierung*, no. 29, 26 February 1988, pp. 245–9; it is here where the Federal Chancellor stresses the need for an 'overall concept', embracing conventional and nuclear armament and arms reductions, and where he argues against a decision about the modernization of the shorter-range nuclear systems before such a concept is available. Volker Rühe, Foreign Policy spokesman of the Christian Democratic Union in the German Bundestag, explained in great detail the need to first work out 'an overall concept' in order then to determine 'the absolute minimal nuclear requirement'. The President of the Federal Republic, Richard von Weizsäcker, stated publicly: 'The INF agreement must not be seen in isolation; its real value depends on the next steps that it will lead to. Conventional forces in Europe pose the real test for security in Europe' (translation from German); Rede des Bundespräsidenten vor der Internationalen Aspen-Instituts-Konferenz, 27.Oktober 1987, *Der Tagesspiegel* (Berlin), 28 Oct. 1987.

⁵⁹ See, e.g., Heisbourg, F., 'An urgent agenda for the NATO summit', *International Herald Tribune*, 17 Feb. 1988, p. 6. The French Director of the IISS talks about a 'growing sense of alienation in West Germany'. See also Lellouche, P., 'All this talk of singularity weakens the alliance', *International Herald Tribune*, 17 Feb. 1988, p. 6; here the Deputy Director of the French Institute for International Affairs (IFRI) alleges that 'German nationalists are uniting against NATO's nuclear posture' and concludes: 'The last thing Europe needs today is a new wave of German *angst* in the form of anti-nuclear, neutralist nationalism'.

⁶⁰ For them, the comprehensive concept of arms control and disarmament includes: 'in conjunction with the establishment of a conventional balance and the global elimination of chemical weapons, tangible and verifiable reductions of American and Soviet land-based nuclear missile systems of shorter range, leading to equal ceilings'; see 'Declaration by NATO leaders, 3 March 1988', *Document Defense Policy*, USIS, 4 Mar. 1988, US Embassy, Stockholm.

⁶¹ For an assessment of the Reykjavik preparatory summit meeting, in particular, for the question of 'A world free of nuclear weapons?', see Stützle, W., '1986—a year of peace?', in SIPRI, *SIPRI Yearbook 1987: World Armaments and Disarmament* (Oxford University Press: Oxford, 1987), pp. xxix–xxxvi.

⁶² 'We hope that at their forthcoming summit in Moscow, President Reagan and General Secretary Gorbachev will be able to build upon the progress achieved at their Washington meeting last December'; Declaration by NATO leaders of 3 Mar. 1988.

Part I. Weapons and technology

Chapter 2. Nuclear weapons

Chapter 3. Nuclear explosions

Chapter 4. Military use of outer space

Chapter 5. Chemical and biological warfare: developments in 1987

2. Nuclear weapons

Prepared by the *Nuclear Weapons Databook* staff and SIPRI*

I. Introduction

The most significant event of 1987 was the signing of the Treaty on the Elimination of Intermediate-Range and Shorter-Range Missiles (the INF Treaty) by President Reagan and General Secretary Gorbachev (see also chapter 13). While the INF Treaty includes approximately 4 per cent of the world's total arsenal of some 55 000 nuclear weapons, the Strategic Arms Reduction Talks (START) cover some 24 000 nuclear warheads, or about 40 per cent of the total (see also chapter 10).

None the less, amidst great progress in arms control negotiations, nuclear weapon deployments continued during the year. The USA and the USSR deployed approximately 1250 new strategic weapons: almost 700 for the USA and over 550 for the USSR. For the USA, these include: the last 90 air-launched cruise missiles (ALCMs) which are now operational on B-52G/Hs at six Strategic Air Command (SAC) bases; 20 more MX missiles carrying 200 warheads at F. E. Warren Air Force Base (AFB), Wyoming; and approximately 400 new B83 gravity bombs for 50 B-1B bombers delivered during the year. The US ballistic-missile submarine force remained the same size. The USA removed approximately 20 Minuteman III missiles from silos to be able to deploy the new MX missiles. The most dramatic recent trend for the United States has been an increase in bomber weapons with the introduction of ALCMs for a portion of the B-52 force and new gravity bombs for the B-1B bomber.

The Soviet Union deployed new weapons in all three 'legs' of its triad. Approximately 50 SS-25 intercontinental ballistic missiles (ICBMs) were deployed, and the first few rail-mobile SS-24s were fielded. The fourth Typhoon and third Delta IV Class submarines became operational, and the next units of each model were launched. Bear bombers continued to be converted to the G model, and new H models were produced. Approximately 20 Bear-Hs with 160 new AS-15 long-range ALCMs were deployed during the year. The Soviet Union continued to retire SS-11s under the SALT (Strategic Arms Limitation Talks) agreements and began removing SS-17s and SS-19s as the SS-24 was fielded. The last 15 Bison bombers were removed from service during 1987. The MIRVing (equipping with multiple independently targetable re-entry vehicles) of the Soviet ballistic-missile submarine force continued, and expansion of the bomber force, both in quality and numbers of bomber weapons, continued.

During 1987, Britain and France moved towards a new level of defence co-operation that could include collaboration on developing a new air-

---

* Robert S. Norris, Thomas B. Cochran and Andrew S. Burrows, Natural Resources Defense Council, Inc., Washington, DC; William M. Arkin, Institute for Policy Studies, Washington, DC; and Jozef Goldblat (section VII) and Richard W. Fieldhouse, SIPRI.

24 WEAPONS AND TECHNOLOGY

launched, nuclear-armed missile. Joint development of such a missile would mark the first time Britain has collaborated with a country other than the United States on nuclear armaments and the first joint European nuclear weapon project.

China continued with its gradual nuclear force modernization programme in 1987 and pursued the development of a short-range ballistic missile using solid fuel. This missile could be the first step in an effort to use solid fuel for the rest of China's land-based nuclear missiles.

The tables showing the nuclear forces of all five nations (tables 2.1–2.8) appear in section III of this chapter.

II. US nuclear weapon programmes

The total US nuclear weapon stockpile contained 23 400 warheads at the beginning of 1987.[1] This figure, which was inadvertently revealed in congressional hearings, is about 3 per cent lower than when the Reagan Administration entered office. Ironically, one of the military goals of the Reagan Administration was to increase the size of the nuclear stockpile by some 13 per cent between 1983 and 1988.

US strategic nuclear forces have grown by over 5400 warheads since the signing of the SALT I Treaty (1972) and by almost 2400 warheads during the Reagan Administration (1981–88).[2] The Administration has almost completed the first wave of its strategic nuclear weapon modernization programme. A second wave, planned to begin in 1988, could be more expensive than the first.[3] These programmes include the small intercontinental ballistic missile (SICBM), 50 rail-based MX ICBMs, Trident II submarine-launched ballistic missiles (SLBMs), Advanced Technology Bombers (ATBs), Advanced Cruise Missiles (ACMs) and SRAM IIs. The broad-based modernization which has occurred during the Reagan Administration has not been without troubles, in terms of the capabilities of new weapons. During 1987 a number of nuclear weapon systems, notably the MX, B-1B bomber and ACM, were strongly criticized for technological problems and/or cost over-runs.

ICBMs

By the end of 1987, 30 MX missiles were deployed in underground silos, although some (reportedly 12) were unusable because of defective guidance systems. Throughout the year reports revealed problems with the inertial measurement unit (IMU), a key component of the guidance and control system. On 16 March 1987 the Air Force suspended payments to the prime contractor, Northrop Electronics Division in Hawthorne, California. In June a special panel of the House Armed Services Committee (HASC) conducted a review and criticized the systemic flaws in the acquisition process.[4]

On 19 December 1986 President Reagan announced that funds would be included in the FY 1988 defence budget to design an MX basing scheme, called rail-garrison, which would deploy the missiles on trains.[5] Current plans call for 50 MX missiles to be deployed on 25 trains at seven or more secure garrisons on existing Air Force bases. The main base would be at F. E. Warren AFB, Wyoming, the deployment site for silo-based MX missiles.[6] On 11 February 1987 the Air Force identified 10 more candidate installations for possible rail-garrison basing (all currently Strategic Air Command (SAC) bomber and/or missile bases).[7]

Each MX garrison would cover about 45–50 acres (about 0.2 km^2) of land. Each train would have seven cars: a locomotive, two missile cars, two security cars, a launch command and control car, and a maintenance car. The specially designed missile launch cars would weigh in excess of 227 273 kg and be 27 metres long and 5.1 metres high. Three or four trains at each site would be parked in shelters constructed of earthen berms and corrugated steel. During normal day-to-day operations, the trains would be on strategic alert in their garrisons. They would be guarded by 15–20 security personnel on a 24-hour-a-day basis similar to bomber security operations today. Upon 'strategic warning' the trains would be dispersed on to the US civil railway system. The Reagan Administration received $300 million (of a requested $593 million) in FY 1988 for development of this basing mode. It is scheduled to become operational in December 1991.

Development of the SICBM continued, but by the end of the year the programme was in serious trouble. The FY 1988 budget request was cut from $2.2 billion to $700 million. Under directives by Secretary of Defense Frank Carlucci to reduce the FY 1989 Department of Defense (DOD) budget by $31 billion the Air Force offered to cancel the missile. Some in the Air Force have reportedly never been very enthusiastic about the missile and have from the start preferred the multi-warhead MX instead. Their strategy was to feign enthusiasm for the SICBM in order to get funding for 50 more MX missiles from the US Congress, which has promoted the SICBM. In technical developments, two in a series of three SICBM canister-ejection tests were conducted at Vandenberg AFB, California. A static first-stage rocket motor test was also conducted. A SICBM warhead was also selected during the year; it will be a modified higher-yield (475-kt) version of the W87 used on the MX missile.

Strategic submarine programmes

The Trident II (or D-5) missile test programme began on 15 January 1987; the missile was fired from Launch Complex 46 at Cape Canaveral. During the year, a total of eight Trident II development test flights were made, with various numbers of re-entry vehicles (RVs).[8] There was controversy over the eighth test, which had been planned to carry 12 RVs.[9] Because of the implications for a START agreement and for the future size of the ballistic-missile submarine fleet, the test with 12 RVs was not conducted. At the US–Soviet summit meeting in Washington, it was decided that the warhead counting rule for the Trident II would be eight, thus limiting the USA (and indirectly the UK) to no more than eight warheads for each Trident II missile. It is unclear what impact this development will have on the Navy's plan to put two different kinds of RV on Trident II missiles.

The D-5 test programme will be the largest and most expensive in the history of US ballistic missiles; it will have four parts and will use a total of 386 missiles.[10] The research and development (R&D) flight-test programme will use 30 missiles, 20 of which will be ground launched, and 10 of which will be used in performance evaluation tests and be fired from operational submarines beginning in the summer of 1989. A launch in this series is scheduled to be made on an average of every 40 days.[11]

The Operational Test (OT) programme will constitute 40 flights during the first three years that the Trident II is deployed. The purpose is to establish reliability and accuracy parameters for use in the development of targeting guidance for the Single Integrated Operational Plan (SIOP), the US nuclear war plan.

The Follow-on Test (FOT) programme, currently planned for 260 flight-tests over 20 years (16 flights per year during 1993–97 and 12 per year thereafter until the year 2012),[12] is designed to update SIOP parameters, to detect developing problems and to test potential remedies. The size of the FOT programme exceeds the minimum necessary to comply with the Joint Chiefs of Staff (JCS) guidance for identifying deterioration in missile reliability. Meeting JCS guidance would require only six flights a year. The Navy claims that it needs a larger than usual FOT programme to improve the quality of the accuracy estimate. It further justifies a large FOT programme by noting that launching SLBMs presents special operating requirements that increase the demand for test data. Unlike ICBMs, SLBMs may be launched from a variety of ranges and must be able to conduct a ripple launch—the sequential firing of a group of missiles from a single submarine. Finally, the Navy claims that because the Trident II missiles could carry two different RVs—the low-yield Mark 4 (100 kt) and the higher-yield Mark 5 (475 kt)—extra tests are required.[13]

Finally, the Demonstration and Shakedown Operations (DASO) launches will use 53 missiles to help detect and remedy engineering problems and to demonstrate that a newly completed or overhauled submarine is fully capable. The Navy plans to test two missiles from each of the first four submarines that carry the Trident II (i.e., SSBNs 734–737). One missile will be tested from each of the eight subsequent SSBNs (SSBNs 738–745, assuming a fleet of 20) and the initial eight Trident SSBNs that will be backfitted during their first overhauls (SSBNs 726–733). Finally, each Trident SSBN receiving a major overhaul will test-launch one missile; 32 overhauls are planned.

Strategic bomber programmes

Developments in US bomber forces were numerous during the year, including continued deployment of the B-1B and two nuclear bombs (B61 and B83), continued development of the 'stealth' ATB, and continued development of the SRAM II and a stealth ACM.

The second B-1B base—Ellsworth AFB, South Dakota—received its allotted 35 aircraft during the year, and the third, Grand Forks AFB, North Dakota, began to receive the first of its 17 B-1Bs in October. By the end of

1987, approximately 75 B-1Bs had been delivered. On 20 January 1988 the 100th, and last, B-1B bomber was rolled out of the Rockwell factory in Palmdale, California. Delivery of the final aircraft to the Strategic Air Command is expected in April 1988. Currently most bombers are being used for training, with only two on 15-minute ground alert. About 30 bombers will eventually be on alert.[14]

Throughout 1987 certain problems that have plagued the aircraft came to light.[15] The General Accounting Office reported that the B-1B would cost $6 billion more to build than the Reagan Administration originally stated.[16] A B-1B crashed on 28 September in southern Colorado, killing three of the six-member crew. The crash was caused by the plane hitting a large (6.8-kg) bird which in turn started a fire that ignited hydraulic systems and led to loss of control of the aircraft. The SAC suspended low-level B-1 flight training, pending the results of an investigation of the incident, throughout the rest of the year.

During the year it became clear that the ATB, now officially designated the B-2, is behind schedule and over-cost. A variety of technical and management problems associated with the ATB resulted in the FY 1988/89 DOD Authorization Act mandating that the Secretary of Defense improve the programme.[17] Despite the problems, the Northrop Corporation received a $2 billion contract on 19 November to begin producing the bomber.[18]

During 1987 the Air Force revealed that the ACM (AGM-129) programme was having difficulties.[19] The missile had not, as of April, completed six successful tests, which was a milestone required for a full rate of production. On 4 November McDonnell Douglas was awarded a second source contract to produce the ACM along with General Dynamics, partly as a safeguard against poor workmanship and management by General Dynamics. The ACM will be deployed first at K. I. Sawyer AFB, Michigan.[20]

Boeing Aerospace was selected on 8 December 1986 to develop a second-generation SRAM II to augment and eventually replace the current SRAM missiles. The SRAM is a nuclear-armed air-to-surface missile that would be used largely to destroy Soviet air defence installations. Additional roles are conceived for the SRAM II. It will be two-thirds the size of the current SRAM and will have greater range, accuracy and performance. One of the major innovations for the new missile is rapid targeting, a capability which will be used to target Soviet mobile systems. Plans call for the production of 1633 SRAM IIs for initial deployment on B-1B and B-2 bombers.

A new nuclear warhead for the SRAM II is about to enter engineering development (Phase 3 of Department of Energy R&D). Engineering development is the phase of a warhead's life cycle where a final design is selected from either the Los Alamos National Laboratory or the Lawrence Livermore National Laboratory. Thirteen designs were considered for the SRAM II warhead, and the final selection was made in November 1986. The first warhead was planned to be produced in July 1991 when the missile was planned to be operational in March 1992; the SRAM II is now scheduled to be operational in April 1993. This 13-month delay was ordered by the Office of the Secretary of Defense because of concerns over rushing into production without adequate testing. The new warhead will have a lower explosive yield than that originally requested by the Air Force.

When contemplating the impending INF Treaty, the SAC proposed a $3 billion plan to modify 150 B-52G bombers to carry only conventional weapons for NATO non-nuclear missions.[21] However, this would pose considerable problems for a START agreement.

Theatre nuclear forces and the INF Treaty

The bilateral INF Treaty calls for the elimination of all US and Soviet ground-launched missiles with a range of 500-5500 km (300-3400 miles) over a three-year period. The impact of the Treaty on the nuclear force structures of the USA and the USSR will be significant:

1. The USA will destroy 120 deployed Pershing II missiles and 309 deployed ground-launched cruise missiles (GLCMs).[22]

2. The USSR will destroy 405 deployed SS-20 Saber missiles, 65 deployed SS-4 Sandal missiles, 220 deployed shorter-range SS-12 Scaleboard missiles, and 167 deployed SS-23 Spider missiles.

3. Approximately 520 US and 2150 Soviet nuclear warheads will be deactivated.

4. Future missile modernization (nuclear or conventional), including development, production and flight-testing, is banned.

Even without INF reductions, the number of US European nuclear warheads has steadily declined during the Reagan Administration. By the end of 1987 the USA had approximately 4300 warheads deployed in Europe—fewer nuclear warheads than at any time since the early 1960s (see table 2.3). By 1992, when the INF missiles have been withdrawn, about 3250 US nuclear warheads will remain on European soil.

The publication of the INF Treaty provided unprecedented official detail concerning the numbers and locations of US and Soviet missiles (for the text of the Treaty and the MOU, see appendices 14A and 14B). The Memorandum of Understanding (MOU) revealed that, as of 1 November, 309 GLCMs were in Europe, 45 more than was publicly known. Also of interest was the fact that 178 Pershing 1a missiles, many of which had been withdrawn from the Federal Republic of Germany in 1983-85, still existed at an Army depot in Colorado. All Soviet information was new, since the Soviet Government has never previously released information on its nuclear weapon deployments (see section III).

In light of the INF Treaty many, including NATO Ministers, have called for the modernization and re-equipping of NATO's nuclear arsenal. Pressure has mounted to proceed with new programmes to 'compensate' for the impending removal of Pershing IIs and GLCMs from Europe. Any modernization of NATO's nuclear forces will be controversial. There are four conceivable means to increase NATO's nuclear capabilites: a nuclear Lance missile replacement; a new nuclear-armed, aircraft-delivered, air-to-surface missile (called the TASM); an increase in the number of nuclear artillery shells; and increased pressure on European governments to agree to deploy the neutron warheads which are stored in the USA.

Perhaps the only real option open to NATO is to increase the number and capability of nuclear-armed fighter aircraft and to introduce a medium-range nuclear ASM for them. Nuclear-capable fighter aircraft are not as controversial as artillery or short-range missiles, and numerous modernization programmes (including the ongoing production of modern non-strategic nuclear bombs for aircraft) are under way to bolster the fighter force. Fighter aircraft, in addition, would provide the flexibility to execute both short- and long-range nuclear strikes, a feature attractive to nuclear war planners.

During 1987 the US Air Force moved forward with development of a new tactical fighter, the F-15E, which will become the primary nuclear bomber and deep-interdiction aircraft in Europe starting in 1988, augmenting and eventually replacing the F-111.[23] The F-15E will perform all-weather, day-or-night, long-range bombing missions while retaining an air-to-air combat capability as well. The first research model of the F-15E was flight-tested by McDonnell Douglas in St Louis, Missouri, on 11 December. Current plans call for delivery of 392 F-15Es to four wings at a rate of 42 a year until 1997. The first operational wing will be at Seymour Johnson AFB, North Carolina.

After 18 months of negotiation, on 10 December Spain told the USA to remove its 72 F-16 aircraft from Torrejon Air Base over a three and one-half-year period. Under the current arrangement, the aircraft have a wartime mission to fly to Italy and Turkey to load their nuclear bombs.[24] Although one alternative was to relocate the planes in Italy, the US DOD announced plans to deactivate the 401st Air Wing as part of its reduced FY 1989 budget plan.

NATO nuclear war planning

During 1987 details of changes in the political guidelines for the employment of nuclear weapons in Europe came to light.

At the NATO Ministers' meeting in Gleneagles, Scotland, on 20–21 October 1986 NATO adopted new political guidelines for the use of its nuclear forces. Although a process of re-evaluating NATO's nuclear capabilities had been going on for about eight years, the deployment of long-range nuclear forces and the withdrawal of major portions of NATO's European stockpile required a restatement of nuclear strategy as it related to the initiation of the use of nuclear weapons, follow-on nuclear strikes and strikes on Soviet territory.

These new General Political Guidelines (GPG) are the NATO equivalent of the Carter Administration Presidential Directive 59 (PD-59), the Nuclear Weapons Employment Policy for US strategic forces that was approved in July 1980. The GPG, like PD-59 (and the Reagan Administration affirmation in National Security Decision Directive 13 in October 1981), sought to articulate better a counterforce nuclear doctrine that had been evolving during the 1970s.

The new GPG were prepared by a NATO working group of the Defence Planning Committee[25] which resulted in four drafts (the last was in 1982) that were discussed and debated at Defence Planning Committee, Nuclear Planning Group and ministerial meetings. They update and replace the 1969 Provisional Political Guidelines (known as the PPG) on the initial (or first) use of nuclear weapons, and the 1970 General Release guidelines. These, together with two other NATO statements previously in effect on the use of nuclear weapons, constituted NATO's nuclear employment policy:[26]

1. *Provisional Political Guidelines for the Initial Defensive Tactical Use of Nuclear Weapons by NATO* (DPC/D(69)58 (Revised)) (November 1969);
2. *Concept for the Role of Theater Nuclear Strike Forces in ACE* [Allied Command Europe] (DPC/D(70)59 (Revised)) (October 1970);
3. Guidelines for consultation procedures on use of nuclear weapons (November 1969);[27] and
4. Political guidelines for use of atomic demolition munitions (October 1970).[28]

The new General Political Guidelines do the following:

1. Reaffirm NATO's 1967 flexible response strategy, which calls for NATO to defend itself against attack in three phases: 'direct defense', 'deliberate escalation' and 'general nuclear response'.[29]
2. Reaffirm the policy of initial (first) use of NATO nuclear weapons in response to a Soviet conventional attack and discuss in great detail the selective use of NATO nuclear weapons. The GPG put greater emphasis on 'follow-on' nuclear strikes, assuming a Warsaw Treaty Organization (WTO) nuclear response to 'initial' NATO use. Since the assumption is one of a series of selective strikes, the priority for the 'deliberate escalation' phase of the flexible response strategy is to strike beyond the battlefield (i.e., not on NATO territory). Initial attacks, under the GPG, would be made 'mainly on the territory of the aggressor, including the Soviet Union'.[30] Strikes on Soviet territory in previous NATO employment policy were highly restricted to specific circumstances such as warfare on the Soviet–Turkish border.
3. State that nuclear weapons will be developed and deployed, to implement the new long-range employment doctrine: 'TNF [Theater Nuclear Force] modernization in Europe has shifted the weight of regional nuclear armaments and target options away from the battlefield towards the adversary's side with a tendency of striking deep in WP [Warsaw Pact] territory'.[31]
4. Contain guidance for nuclear targeting, stating that priority be given to militarily significant ('counterforce') strikes as a means to convey political messages, rather than 'countervalue' strikes. This is in contrast to the 1969 guidelines which stated that the objective of the initial NATO use of nuclear weapons 'would be essentially political and that initial use would therefore be very selective'.[32]
5. Contain new guidance on NATO declaratory policy dealing with nuclear weapons.
6. Contain new guidance on communicating NATO intentions to the Soviet Union in a crisis, as well as after selective use of nuclear weapons (such as in the case of demonstration nuclear strikes).

7. Provide new guidelines for political consultation to ensure control over battlefield commanders and reaffirm the traditional 'Athens' guidelines that consultation would be subject to, 'time and circumstances permitting'.

8. Provide guidelines on the use of sea-based nuclear weapons for the first time. The 1969 guidelines considered only the initial use of land-based nuclear weapons in response to an attack.

Naval nuclear weapons

The US Navy has apparently decided to shift the emphasis of its Tomahawk sea-launched cruise missile programme away from steady production of nuclear-armed land-attack missiles towards conventionally armed variants. The current five-year plan (FY 1988–92) significantly reduces the number of nuclear missiles to be purchased during that period. The plan in 1986 called for buying the remaining 440 of 758 nuclear Tomahawks during FYs 1988–91. The 1987 plan calls for buying only 93 missiles during the same period (19 in FY 1988, 28 in FY 1989, 46 in FY 1990, and none in FY 1991 and FY 1992), shifting the last 327 nuclear missiles to be produced to FY 1993. The Navy is currently buying three conventionally armed Tomahawk variants: a precision land-attack missile, an anti-ship missile, and a combined-effects bomblet missile for airfield attack. Previous projections were to purchase 618 of these in FYs 1988 and 1989, but the 1987 budget asked for 937. In 1987 the Navy was planning to buy 262 nuclear-armed Tomahawks in FYs 1988 and 1989 but now plans to purchase only 47.

The longer-range Sea Lance anti-submarine standoff weapon (ASW/SOW) was originally planned to replace the SUBROC in 1992, initially carrying the non-nuclear lightweight Mk-50 torpedo. However, budget reductions and technical dificulties will delay this programme considerably. The Navy would like to develop a nuclear warhead for the Sea Lance but has been unable to convince Congress to fund it. The Navy has said that it will decide in December 1990 whether it will try to develop a nuclear version.

Congress is also not convinced about the need for a nuclear version of the Standard Missile-2 (SM-2(N)) as a replacement for the Terrier (RIM-2F) surface-to-air missile (SAM) now on 31 cruisers and destroyers. The US Congress deleted funds for the nuclear version in the FY 1987 budget, and the Navy did not request R&D funding in the FY 1988 or FY 1989 budgets. The future of the programme is uncertain, but it appears that the Navy has lost interest in a nuclear SAM.

On 23 December the Navy selected General Dynamics and the McDonnell Douglas Corporation to develop and build the Advanced Tactical Aircraft (ATA). The ATA will be the next generation of carrier-borne attack aircraft, intended to replace the A-6 and A-7 aircraft, and will have a nuclear attack role and use low-observable (or stealth) technologies.

Congressional initiatives

Immediately upon convening in January, the Democrat-controlled 100th Congress took up from where it left off in 1986 and began to introduce arms control legislation. The major initiatives had to do with protecting the traditional interpretation of the 1972 Anti-Ballistic Missile (ABM) Treaty (see also chapter 14), returning the USA to compliance with the SALT limits and mandating limitations on nuclear weapon testing.

In October 1985 the Reagan Administration began to promote an interpretation of the ABM Treaty that would allow the development and testing of many of its Strategic Defense Initiative (SDI) programmes.[33] This 'broad' or permissive interpretation is almost universally rejected by all but one member of the US delegation that negotiated the Treaty, by NATO allies, by the Soviet Union and by many members of Congress.

The Administration claimed that the true meaning of the ABM Treaty can be found only in the detailed negotiating record and not in the public statements or hearings. Senator Nunn asked for and eventually received access to the negotiating record. In three speeches to the Senate on 11, 12 and 13 March he presented his report, which upheld the traditional interpretation.[34]

Beyond legalistic points about the meaning of the Treaty was the constitutional issue of the Senate's role in approving a treaty. Senator Nunn challenged the Administration's claim to reinterpret unilaterally a treaty and to disregard past official congressional testimony. In a letter of 2 September to the President he threatened to complicate the Senate approval process of the INF Treaty unless the Administration changed its position with regard to ABM Treaty interpretation. In early February 1988 he made good his threat by proposing to delay a Senate vote until the issue of the authoritativeness of Administration testimony is resolved.[35]

Republican senators who support the SDI conducted a four-month filibuster (from May until 11 September) to block the DOD authorization bill because it included SDI testing limitations. Eventually Congress passed legislation that requires that any SDI tests would have to fall within the traditional interpretation of the ABM Treaty.

On 2 October the Senate voted 57 to 41, as part of its authorization bill, to compel the USA to abide by the SALT limitations.[36] With a veto threatened by the President, Congress resolved the issue by denying money to overhaul the *USS Andrew Jackson* (SSBN 619).[37]

The year also saw the superpowers create nuclear risk reduction centres in Washington and Moscow. On 15 September Soviet Foreign Minister Eduard Shevardnadze and Secretary of State George Shultz signed the US–Soviet Agreement on the Establishment of Nuclear Risk Reduction Centers (for the text, see appendix 13E).

The inspiration for this idea began with Senators Henry Jackson, Sam Nunn and John W. Warner who in 1980 suggested the concept of a 'crisis control center'.[38] A more refined concept was eventually contained in a 1984 Senate resolution, sponsored by Nunn and Warner, which later became part of the FY 1985 DOD authorization bill. On 26 August 1985 the Reagan Administration gave its endorsement to a scaled-down version, and Senators Nunn and Warner discussed the idea with General Secretary Gorbachev on 3 September 1985. At the Geneva summit meeting in November 1985, Reagan and Gorbachev agreed 'to study the question of establishing centres to reduce nuclear risk at the expert level'.[39] Formal discussions began in 1986. The original Senate recommendation envisioned jointly (US–Soviet) manned centres which would focus on incidents or threats of nuclear terrorism, on matters of nuclear proliferation and on potential miscalculations during international crises. The signed agreement instead provides for the transmission of notifications, through the centres, of ballistic-missile launches and other information as agreed by the two nations. The Reagan Administration stressed that the centres would have no crisis-management role. According to the DOD, 'their principal function will be to exchange information and notifications as required under certain existing and possible future arms control and confidence building agreements'.[40] The centres will thus be used to provide the notifications and data updates required by the INF Treaty.

III. Soviet nuclear weapon programmes

Soviet strategic offensive forces continued to grow and be modernized in 1987; a net increase of nine launchers and 343 warheads was added. At the end of 1987, Soviet strategic forces comprised 1392 ICBMs with 6846 warheads, 968 SLBMs with 3408 warheads, and 155 bombers with 1170 warheads. Soviet strategic forces have grown by 8600 warheads since the signing of the SALT I Treaty and by 3100 warheads during the period of the Reagan Administration.[41]

The US Defense Intelligence Agency has predicted that, excluding a START agreement, the Soviet Union will have 12 000 strategic nuclear weapons (missile warheads and bombs) by 1990 and 16 000 by the mid-1990s.[42] Growth in strategic nuclear forces will continue to reflect MIRVing of the submarine missile force as well as expansion of bomber capabilities. According to the JCS, 'The Soviets have more than 30 new strategic offensive systems in various stages of development'.[43]

ICBMs

Deployment of new Soviet ICBMs continues. During 1987, the USSR deployed approximately 50 new road-mobile, single-warhead SS-25 missiles and the first few rail-mobile SS-24s. By the end of the year, some 126 SS-25 Sickle and 15 SS-24 Scalpel missiles were believed to be operational.

The SS-24 Scalpel, which was first deployed in August, is a new MX-size, 10-warhead, solid-propellant ICBM.[44] On 7 August, Senator Jesse Helms stated that the USA had detected at least five SS-24 launchers, a number which he claimed put the Soviet Union over the SALT sublimit for MIRVed ICBMs. Helms's disclosure was confirmed by the White House on 9 August. On 11 August, Victor Karpov, head of the arms control and disarmament directorate of the Soviet Foreign Ministry, confirmed that the SS-24 missile was being deployed. Karpov stated that the USSR was abiding by the SALT missile and MIRVing limits, and that the SS-24 was the one new ICBM permitted under the SALT II Treaty.

The US Central Intelligence Agency estimates that the Soviet Union will deploy more than 200 SS-24 launchers (with 2000 warheads).[45] Speculation continues about possible SS-24 deployment in silos, although evidence thus far indicates only mobile basing. Throughout the year, SS-11s continued to be retired to keep within the SALT limits; SS-17s and SS-19s also began to be withdrawn as SS-24s were fielded.[46]

The deployment of the two new, accurate Soviet ICBMs may change assessments of Soviet hard-target-kill capability. Since 1985 the US intelligence community has been reassessing its estimate of Soviet ICBM accuracy. Initially the multiple-warhead ICBMs deployed in the 1970s (SS-17, SS-18 and SS-19) were considered capable of destroying hardened targets. The new assessment concludes that only the SS-18s, or perhaps also the new SS-25s, are capable of destroying hardened targets.[47]

According to a US Air Force report of early 1987, 'three new ICBMs are expected to enter flight testing in the next four years'.[48] One of these new ICBMs, reportedly labelled the TT-09 (and to be designated the SS-X-26), was successfully flight-tested for the first time in December 1986, after two previous flight-test failures.[49] The TT-09 has been described as a liquid-propellant follow-on to the SS-18, with increased accuracy and throw-weight. The other two missiles, according to the US DOD, are a follow-on to the SS-24, and a new, possibly MIRVed version of the SS-25.[50] The DOD has predicted that the ICBM force (including the SS-24 and SS-25) will be almost entirely replaced with new systems by the mid-1990s.[51] On 29 and 30 September the USSR test-fired two ICBMs to within 575 km north-west of Hawaii, which caused a strong US protest.[52]

Strategic submarine programmes

The fourth Typhoon and third Delta IV Class ballistic-missile submarines became operational during the year, while the next units of each model were also launched. Sea trials of a fourth Delta IV submarine began in 1987; the submarine is expected to become operational in early 1988. Sea trials of the fifth Typhoon submarine also began in mid-1987.[53] It is assumed that older Yankee I Class submarines continue to be retired under the SALT II limits, but the number of those retired during 1987 is not publicly known.

At the Washington summit meeting in December 1987, the USA and the USSR agreed on new START counting rules for warhead levels, *inter alia* for SLBMs deployed after the SALT II Treaty was signed. The SS-N-18 SLBM (on Delta III submarines), which was previously estimated to carry an average of 7 warheads, will be counted as carrying 6. The SS-N-20 Sturgeon (on Typhoon submarines), which was previously estimated to carry 6–9 warheads,[54] is now to be counted as carrying 10. The SS-N-23 Skiff SLBM (on Delta IV submarines), which was previously estimated to carry 10 warheads, is now to be counted as carrying only 4.[55]

The new counting rules significantly change the overall assessment of the SS-N-23 missiles deployed on Delta IV submarines. When the missile was in development, it was compared to the US Trident II missile regarding hard-target-kill capability and warhead load. After it was deployed, it was reported by DOD as having 10 warheads and accorded great importance in the growth of Soviet strategic submarine force capabilities. The Joint Chiefs of Staff and the US Navy now believe that the missile will be backfitted in the Delta III Class submarines, replacing the SS-N-18. This would result in a significant net decrease in MIRV warheads, important for the Soviet force structure under the START ceiling of 6000 warheads.[56]

According to DOD, 'The Soviets are developing replacements for the SS-N-20 and SS-N-23 SLBMs for their next round of modernization'.[57] A new class of nuclear-powered ballistic-missile submarine (SSBN) is also reported to be under development, for deployment in the early 1990s.[58]

Strategic bomber programmes

Overall modernization of the Soviet bomber forces continues and is taking on a more important role in the strategic force structure. Three types of bomber continue in production. The new variant of the Bear bomber, the Bear-H, continues to be deployed carrying the first Soviet long-range cruise missile, the 1600-nautical mile (3000-km) range AS-15 Kent. Approximately 20 Bear-Hs with 160 new AS-15s were deployed during the year. Bear-H bomber training has been repeatedly documented, and the bombers have reportedly been conducting 'regular combat patrols to various points off the North American coast'.[59]

A new long-range strategic bomber, the Blackjack-A, continues in flight-testing and could be deployed in 1988–89, although it experienced at least one crash during 1987.[60] The Blackjack will reportedly be capable of carrying the AS-15 Kent cruise missile as well. The Soviet Union continues to build about 30 Backfire medium bombers per year.

In addition to new production, older Bear bombers continue to be retrofitted. Older Bear-B/C models have been upgraded to the new Bear-G model, which permits the aircraft to carry two nuclear-capable AS-4 Kitchen air-to-surface missiles (ASMs) in place of the single nuclear AS-3 Kangaroo ASM. A new Soviet supersonic ASM, similar to the US SRAM and designated the AS-X-16, is also under development for deployment on the Blackjack-A and Bear-H bombers.[61] The Soviet Union also has a refuelling aircraft under development, the Il-76 Midas, which could be used to increase the range of strategic bombing missions. The last 15 Bison bombers were removed from service during 1987.

Strategic defence developments

Soviet strategic defensive capabilities continued to be a major focus of reporting and propaganda during 1987. Many of the contentious issues—the purpose of the Soviet radar under construction at Krasnoyarsk, Soviet laser and anti-satellite (ASAT) capabilities, and Soviet strategic defence research and capabilities—were directly tied to the fortunes of the US SDI programme.[62] General Secretary Gorbachev announced that the Soviet Union would cease construction of the controversial Krasnoyarsk radar for one year.[63]

36 WEAPONS AND TECHNOLOGY

Table 2.1. US strategic nuclear forces, 1988

Weapon system				Warheads		
Type	No. deployed	Year deployed	Range (km)	Warhead × yield	Type	No. deployed
ICBMs						
Minuteman II	450	1966	11 300	1 × 1.2 Mt	W56	450
Minuteman III (Mk 12)	220	1970	13 000	3 × 170 kt	W62	660
Minuteman III (Mk 12A)	300	1979	13 000	3 × 335 kt	W78	900
MX	30	1986	11 000	10 × 300 kt	W87	300
Total	**1 000**					**2 310**
SLBMs						
Poseidon	256	1971	4 600	10 × 40 kt	W68	2 560
Trident I	384	1979	7 400	8 × 100 kt	W76	3 072
Total	**640**					**5 632**
Bombers[a]						
B-1B	72	1986	9 800	ALCM	W80-1	1 614
B-52G/H	263	1958/61	16 000	SRAM	W69	1 140
FB-111A	61	1969	4 700	Bombs	[b]	2 316
Total	**396**					**5 070**
Refuelling aircraft						
KC-135	615	1957	. .	. .	. .	. .

[a] Bombers are loaded in a variety of ways, depending on mission. B-1Bs and B-52s can carry a mix of 8–24 weapons, and FB-111s can carry 6 weapons, excluding ALCMs and B53 and B28 bombs.

[b] Bomber weapons include six different nuclear bomb designs (B83, B61-0, -1, -7, B57, B53, B43, B28) with yields from sub-kt to 9 Mt, ALCMs with selectable yields from 5 to 150 kt, and SRAMs with a yield of 170 kt.

Sources: Cochran, T. B., Arkin, W. M. and Norris, R. S., *Nuclear Weapons Databook, Volume 1: US Forces and Capabilities*, 2nd edn (Ballinger: Cambridge, Mass., forthcoming); Joint Chiefs of Staff, *United States Military Posture for FY 1989*; authors' estimates.

The ABM system around Moscow has now been upgraded to a two-layer system that includes improved silo-based Galosh exo-atmospheric missiles and new silo-based Gazelle endo-atmospheric high-acceleration missiles, plus a modernized array of early-warning, acquisition and battle-management radars.

Soviet surface-to-air missile (SAM) forces also continued to be modernized. The SA-X-12B Giant mobile SAM continued to be developed. The missile is believed by DOD to have limited anti-cruise missile and anti-tactical ballistic missile capabilities.[64] Meanwhile, the SA-10 Grumble continued to be deployed, both around Moscow and in the Far East. The SA-10 is believed to have some capability against ballistic missiles, according to DOD.

On 28 May a West German teenager flew a single-engine Cessna aircraft across the Soviet Union to Moscow and into Red Square. This incident was used by General Secretary Gorbachev to consolidate his power within the military.[65]

Table 2.2. US theatre nuclear forces, 1988

Weapon system				Warheads		
Type	No. deployed	Year deployed	Range (km)	Warhead × yield	Type	No. in stockpile
Land-based systems:						
Aircraft[a]	2 250	..	1 060–2 400	1–3 × bombs	Bombs[a]	1 800
Missiles						
Pershing II	120	1983	1 790	1 × 0.3–80 kt	W85	125
GLCM	309	1983	2 500	1 × 0.2–150 kt	W84	325
Pershing 1a	72	1962	740	1 × 60–400 kt	W50	100
Lance	100	1972	125	1 × 1–100 kt	W70	1 282
Honest John	24	1954	38	1 × 1–20 kt	W31	132
Nike Hercules	27	1958	160	1 × 1–20 kt	W31	75
Other systems						
Artillery[b]	3 850	1956	30	1 × 0.1–12 kt	[b]	1 540
ADM (special)	150	1964	..	1 × 0.01–1 kt	W54	150
Naval systems:						
Carrier aircraft[c]	1 100	..	550–1 800	1–2 × bombs	Bombs[c]	1 450
Land-attack SLCMs						
Tomahawk	150	1984	2 500	1 × 5–150 kt	W80-0	150
ASW systems						
ASROC	..	1961	1–10	1 × 5–10 kt	W44	574
SUBROC	..	1965	60	1 × 5–10 kt	W55	285
ASW aircraft[d]	710	..	1 160–3 800	1 × <20 kt	B57	897
Naval SAMs						
Terrier	..	1956	35	1 × 1 kt	W45	290

[a] Aircraft include US Air Force F-4D/E, F-16A/B/C/D and F-111A/D/E/F. Bombs include four types (B28, B43, B57 and B61) with yields from sub-kt to 1.45 Mt.

[b] There are two types of nuclear artillery (155-mm and 203-mm) with four different warheads: a 0.1-kt W48, 155-mm shell; a 1- to 12-kt W33, 203-mm shell; a 0.8-kt W79-1, enhanced-radiation, 203-mm shell; and a variable-yield (up to 1.1 kt) W79-0 fission warhead. The enhanced-radiation warheads will be converted to standard fission weapons.

[c] Aircraft include Navy A-6E, A-7E, F/A-18A/B and Marine Corps A-4M, A-6E and AV-8B. Bombs include three types with yields from 20 kt to 1 Mt.

[d] Aircraft include US Navy P-3A/B/C, S-3A/B and SH-3D/H helicopters. Some US B57 nuclear depth bombs are allocated to British Nimrod, Italian Atlantic and Netherlands P-3 aircraft.

Sources: Cochran, T. B., Arkin, W. M. and Norris, R. S., *Nuclear Weapons Databook, Volume 1: US Forces and Capabilities*, 2nd edn (Ballinger: Cambridge, Mass., forthcoming); Joint Chiefs of Staff, *United States Military Posture for FY 1989*; authors' estimates.

Table 2.3. US nuclear warheads in Europe, 1965–92

Type	May 1965	Dec. 1981	Dec. 1987	After INF (1992)
Artillery				
8-inch	975	938	738	240
155-mm	0	732	732	732
Tactical SSMs				
Lance	0	692	692	692
Pershing I	200	293	100	0
Pershing II	0	0	108	0
Honest John	1 900	198	0	0
Sergeant	300	0	0	0
Nike Hercules SAMs	990	686	100	0
Bombs	1 240	1 729	1 400	1 400
B57 NDB	–	192	192	192
ADMs	340	372	0	0
GLCMs	0	0	256	0
Total	**5 945**	**5 832**	**4 318**	**3 256**

Source: Authors' estimates.

Soviet non-strategic nuclear forces

The INF Treaty, signed by the USA and the USSR in December 1987, will have a considerable impact on Soviet land-based non-strategic nuclear forces. The Treaty requires the elimination of six Soviet missile systems that were either part of their non-strategic nuclear forces or that had been tested for future deployment. These include the SS-20, the SS-4, the SS-12 and the SS-23 (all operational); the non-deployed SS-5 missile, undergoing retirement and in storage; and the SSC-X-4 ground-launched cruise missile under development (tested but not deployed).

The Treaty also bans all future ground-launched ballistic or cruise missile systems with ranges between 500 and 5500 km. This will terminate or prevent any development programmes for INF systems not specifically mentioned in the Treaty, such as a follow-on missile for the SS-20, or a GLCM—the SSC-X-5—believed by the USA to be in development.

Thus, one unheralded benefit of the Treaty is that it will cancel the Soviet GLCM development programme before any missiles are operationally deployed. At least one and possibly two Soviet long-range GLCMs were under development: the SSC-X-4, which the USA expected would be deployed in 1988, and possibly the SSC-X-5, a large supersonic GLCM (derived from the naval SS-NX-24), which the USA believed was in development. The SSC-X-4 had been flight-tested, and the INF Treaty Memorandum of Understanding (MOU) revealed that 6 SSC-X-4 launchers and 84 missiles were at Jelgava, near Riga in Latvia.[66]

The INF Treaty MOU revealed extraordinary, new, detailed information

Table 2.4. Soviet strategic nuclear forces, 1988

Weapon system					Warheads	
Type	NATO code-name	No. deployed	Year deployed	Range (km)	Warhead × yield	No. deployed
ICBMs						
SS-11 Mod. 2	Sego	184	1973	13 000	1 × .950–1.1 Mt	184
Mod. 3		210	1973	10 600	3 × 100–350 kt (MRV)	630[a]
SS-13 Mod. 2	Savage	60	1973	9 400	1 × 600–750 kt	60
SS-17 Mod. 2	Spanker	139	1979	10 000	4 × 750 kt (MIRV)	556
SS-18 Mod. 4	Satan	308	1979	11 000	10 × 550 kt (MIRV)	3 080
SS-19 Mod. 3	Stiletto	350	1979	10 000	6 × 550 kt (MIRV)	2 160
SS-24	Scalpel	5	1987	10 000	10 × 100 kt (MIRV)	50
SS-25	Sickle	126	1985	10 500	1 × 550 kt	126
Total		**1 382**				**6 846**
SLBMs						
SS-N-6 Mod. 3	Serb	256	1973	3 000	2 × .375–1 Mt (MRV)	512[a]
SS-N-8 Mod. 1/2	Sawfly	286	1973	7 800	1 × 1–1.5 Mt	286
SS-N-17	Snipe	12	1977	3 900	1 × .5–1 Mt	12
SS-N-18 Mod. 1/3	Stingray	224	1978	6 500	7 × 200–500 kt	1 568
Mod. 2			1978	8 000	1 × .45–1 Mt	
SS-N-20	Sturgeon	80	1983	8 300	10 × 100 kt	800
SS-N-23	Skiff	64	1986	7 240	4 × 100 kt	256
Total		**922**				**3 434**
Bombers						
Tu-95	Bear A	30	1956	8 300	4 bombs	120
Tu-95	Bear B/C	30	1962	8 300	5 bombs or 1 AS-3	150
Tu-95	Bear G	40	1984	8 300	4 bombs and 2 AS-4	240
Tu-95	Bear H	55	1984	8 300	8 AS-15 ALCMs and 4 bombs	660
Total		**155**				**1 170**
Refuelling aircraft	..	140–170	..	..	..	..
ABMs						
ABM-1B	Galosh Mod.	16	1986	320	1 × unknown	16
ABM-3	Gazelle	80	1985	70	1 × low yield	80
Total		**96**				**96**

[a] SS-11 and SS-N-6 MRV warheads are counted individually.

Sources: Authors' estimates derived from: Cochran, T. B., Arkin, W. M. and Sands, J. I., *Nuclear Weapons Databook, Volume IV, Soviet Nuclear Weapons* (Ballinger: Cambridge, Mass., forthcoming); Arkin, W. M. and Sands, J. I., 'The Soviet nuclear stockpile', *Arms Control Today*, June 1984, pp. 1–7; US Department of Defense, *Soviet Military Power*, 1st, 2nd, 3rd, 4th, 5th, 6th edns; NATO, *NATO–Warsaw Pact Force Comparisons*, 1st, 2nd edns; Berman, R. P. and Baker, J. C., *Soviet Strategic Forces: Requirements and Responses* (Brookings Institution: Washington, DC, 1982); US Defense Intelligence Agency, *Unclassified Communist Naval Orders of Battle*, DDB-1200-124-85, Dec. 1985; Congressional Budget Office, *Trident II Missiles: Capability, Costs, and Alternatives*, July 1986; Collins, J. M. and Victory B. C., *U.S./Soviet Military Balance*, Library of Congress/Congressional Research Service, Report No. 87-745-S, 1 Sep. 1987; Background briefing on *SMP, 1986*, 24 Mar. 1986; SASC/SAC, *Soviet Strategic Force Developments*, Senate Hearing 99–335, June 1985; Polmar, N., *Guide to the Soviet Navy*, 4th edn (US Naval Institute: Annapolis, Md., 1986); Joint Chiefs of Staff, *United States Military Posture for FY 1989*.

Table 2.5. Soviet theatre nuclear forces, 1988

Type	NATO code-name	No. deployed[a]	Year first deployed	Range[b] (km)	Warhead × yield	No. deployed
Land-based systems:						
Aircraft						
Tu-26	Backfire	160	1974	4 000	1–3 × bombs or ASMs	320
Tu-16	Badger A/G	272	1954	3 100	1–2 × bombs or ASMs	272
Tu-22	Blinder A/B	120	1962	2 900–3 300	1–2 × bombs or 1 ASM	120
Tactical aircraft[c]		2 700	. .	700–1 300	1–2 × bombs	2 700
Missiles						
SS-20	Saber	405	1977	5 000	3 × 250 kt	1 215
SS-4	Sandal	65	1959	2 000	1 × 1 Mt	65
SS-12	Scaleboard	135	1969/78	900	1 × 500 kt	405
SS-1c	Scud B	500	1965	280	1 × 1–10 kt	500
SS-23	Spider	102	1985	500	1 × 100 kt	167
. .	FROG 7	370	1965	70	1 × 1–25 kt	200
SS-21[d]	Scarab	130	1978	120	1 × 10–100 kt	1 100
SS-C-1b	Sepal	100	1962	450	1 × 50–200 kt	100
SAMs[e]	. .	. .	. .	40–300	1 × low kt	. .
Other systems						
Artillery[f]	. .	<7 700	1973–80	10–30	1 × low kt	. .
ADMs	. .	?	?	?	?	?
Naval systems:						
Ballistic missiles						
SS-N-5	Sark	39	1963	1 400	1 × 1 Mt	39
Aircraft						
Tu-26	Backfire	130	1974	4 000	1–3 × bombs or ASMs	260
Tu-16	Badger A/C/G	205	1955	3 100	1–2 × bombs or ASMs	205
Tu-22	Blinder	35	1962	2 900–3 300	1 × bombs	35
ASW aircraft[g]	. .	390	1966–82	. .	1 × depth bombs	390
Anti-ship cruise missiles[h]						
SS-N-3 b/a,c	Shaddock/Sepal	228	1960	450	1 × 350 kt	120
SS-N-7	Starbright	90	1968	65	1 × 200 kt	44
SS-N-9	Siren	208	1969	280	1 × 200 kt	78
SS-N-12	Sandbox	200	1976	550	1 × 350 kt	76
SS-N-19	Shipwreck	136	1980	550	1 × 500 kt	56
SS-N-22	Sunburn	80	1981	100	1 × 200 kt	24
Land-attack cruise missiles						
SS-N-21	Sampson	12	1987	3 000	1 × n.a.	12
SS-NX-24	?	0	1988?	<3 000	1 × n.a.	0
ASW missiles and torpedoes						
SS-N-15	Starfish	400	1973	37	1 × 10 kt	?
SS-N-16	Stallion		1979	120	1 × 10 kt	?
FRAS-1	. .	10	1967	30	1 × 5 kt	10
Torpedoes[i]	Type 65	?	1965	16	1 × low kt	?
	ET-80	?	1980	>16	1 × low kt	?

Table 2.5 *cont.*

Type	Weapon system NATO code-name	No. deployed[a]	Year first deployed	Range[b] (km)	Warheads Warhead × yield	No. deployed
Naval SAMs						
SA-N-1	Goa	65	1961	22	1 × 10 kt	65
SA-N-3	Goblet	43	1967	37	1 × 10 kt	43
SA-N-6	Grumble	33	1981	65	1 × 10 kt	33

[a] For missile systems, the number is for operational or deployed missiles on launchers (see the Memorandum of Understanding of the INF Treaty).
[b] Range for aircraft indicates combat radius, without refuelling.
[c] Nuclear-capable tactical aircraft models include MiG-21 Fishbed L/N, MiG-27 Flogger D/J, Su-7 Fitter A, Su-17 Fitter C/D, and Su-24 Fencer A/B/C/D/E.
[d] Includes SS-21s in GDR and Czechoslovakian units.
[e] Nuclear-capable land-based surface-to-air missiles probably include SA-1 Guild, SA-2 Guideline, SA-5 Gammon, SA-10 Grumble and SA-12 Gladiator.
[f] Nuclear-capable artillery include systems of three calibres: 152-mm (M-1976, 2S3 and 2S5), 203-mm (2S7 and M-1980) and 240-mm (2S4 and M-240). Some older systems may also be nuclear-capable.
[g] Includes 95 Be-12 Mail, 50 Il-38 May and 55 Tu-142 Bear F patrol aircraft. Land- and sea-based helicopters include 140 Ka-25 Hormone and 50 Ka-27 Helix models.
[h] Based on an average of two nuclear-armed cruise missiles per nuclear-capable surface ship, except for 4 per Kiev and Kirov Classes, and 4 per nuclear-capable cruise missile submarine, except for 12 on the Oscar Class.
[i] The two types of torpedo are the older and newer models, respectively, with the ET-80 probably replacing the Type 65.

Sources: Cochran, T. B., Arkin, W. M. and Sands, J. I., *Nuclear Weapons Databook, Volume IV, Soviet Nuclear Weapons* (Ballinger: Cambridge, Mass., forthcoming); Arkin, W. M. and Sands, J. I., 'The Soviet nuclear stockpile', *Arms Control Today*, June 1984, pp. 1–7; Polmar, N., *Guide to the Soviet Navy*, 4th edn (US Naval Institute: Annapolis, Md., 1986); Department of Defense, *Soviet Military Power*, 1st, 2nd, 3rd, 4th, 5th, 6th edns; NATO, *NATO–Warsaw Pact Force Comparisons*, 1st, 2nd edns; Joint Chiefs of Staff, *United States Military Posture for FY 1989*; interviews with US DOD officials, Apr. and Oct. 1986; 'More self-propelled gun designations', *Jane's Defence Weekly*, 7 June 1986, p. 1003; Handler, J. and Arkin, W. M., *Nuclear Warships and Naval Nuclear Weapons: A Complete Inventory*, Neptune Paper no. 2 (Greenpeace/Institute for Policy Studies: Washington, DC, 1988).

---

about the location, support, production, storage and repair facilities for the SS-20, SS-4, SS-12 and SS-23 missiles. Virtually all previous public estimates of the size of Soviet INF forces were in error. As of 1 November 1987:

1. 405 SS-20 missiles were deployed with 405 launchers at 48 bases. The DOD continued to use the number 441, refusing to acknowledge that 36 launchers were removed. An additional 245 missiles and 122 launchers will have to be eliminated under the terms of the INF Treaty.

2. 65 SS-4 Sandal missiles were deployed at 13 bases, as opposed to 112 missiles commonly cited by DOD. Another 105 missiles and a total of 81 launchers will have to be destroyed.

3. 220 SS-12 Scaleboard missiles were deployed on 115 launchers at 6 bases in the Soviet Union, 4 bases in the German Democratic Republic and 1 base in Czechoslovakia. In addition there were 506 non-deployed missiles and 20 launchers.

4. 167 SS-23 Spider missiles were deployed with 82 launchers at 5 bases in the

Table 2.6. British nuclear forces, 1988[a]

Weapon system				Warheads		
Type	No. deployed	Year deployed	Range (km)[b]	Warhead × yield	Type	No. in stockpile[c]
Aircraft						
Buccaneer S2B	25[d]	1962	1 700	1 × 5–200 kt bomb	WE-177[e]	25
Tornado GR-1	220[f]	1982	1 300	1–2 × 5–200 kt bombs	WE-177	220
SLBMs						
Polaris A3-TK	64	1982[g]	4 700	2 × 40 kt	MRV	128
Carrier aircraft						
Sea Harrier FRS. 1	34	1980	450	1 × 5–200 kt bomb	WE-177	34
ASW helicopters						
Sea King HAS 5	56	1976	–	1 × depth bomb	?[h]	56
Lynx HAS 2/3	78	1976	–	1 × depth bomb	?	78

[a] British systems certified to use US nuclear weapons include 31 Nimrod ASW aircraft based in the UK, and 20 Lance launchers (1 regiment of 12 launchers, plus spares) and 135 artillery guns in 5 regiments (120 M109 and 15 M110 howitzers) based in FR Germany.

[b] Range for aircraft indicates combat radius, without refuelling.

[c] Some sources put the total number of nuclear warheads in the British stockpile as low as 185 warheads, comprised of: 80 WE-177 gravity bombs, 25 nuclear depth bombs and 80 Chevaline A3-TK warheads.

[d] Plus 18 in reserve and 9 undergoing conversion, probably the remainder from FR Germany.

[e] The WE-177 is thought to be a tactical 'lay-down' type bomb.

[f] Some Buccaneer and Jaguar aircraft, withdrawn from bases in FR Germany and replaced by Tornado GR-1, may still be assigned nuclear roles in the UK.

[g] The Polaris A3-TK (Chevaline) was first deployed in 1982 and has now completely replaced the original Polaris A-3 missile (which was first deployed in 1968).

[h] The RN nuclear depth bomb is believed to be a low-yield variation of the RAF tactical bomb.

Sources: UK Ministry of Defence, *Statement on the Defence Estimates*, 1980 through 1986 (Her Majesty's Stationery Office: London, annual); Rogers, P., *Guide to Nuclear Weapons 1984–85* (University of Bradford: Bradford, 1984); Campbell, D., 'Too few bombs to go round', *New Statesman*, 29 Nov. 1985, pp. 10–12; US Defense Intelligence Agency, *Ground Order of Battle: United Kingdom*, DDB-1100-UK-85 (secret, partially declassified), Oct. 1985; Nott, J., 'Decisions to modernise U.K.'s nuclear contribution to NATO strengthen deterrence', *NATO Review*, vol. 29, no. 2 (Apr. 1981); International Institute for Strategic Studies, *The Military Balance 1987–1988* (IISS: London, 1987); authors' estimates.

Soviet Union and 2 bases in the GDR. Before the Treaty was signed, a figure of 36 launchers was commonly cited by official Western sources.

The INF Treaty data confirmed the deployment of SS-12 *and* SS-23 missiles in Eastern Europe. Previously, it had been believed that only SS-12 missiles had been forward deployed.

Table 2.7. French nuclear forces, 1988

Weapon system				Warheads		
Type	No. deployed	Year deployed	Range (km)[a]	Warhead × yield	Type	No. in stockpile
Aircraft						
Mirage IVP/ASMP	18	1986	1 500[b]	1 × 300 kt	TN 80	20
Jaguar A	45	1974[e]	750	1 × 6–8/30 kt bomb	ANT-52[d]	50
Mirage IIIE	30	1972[e]	600	1 × 6–8/30 kt bomb	ANT-52[d]	35
Refuelling aircraft						
C-1325F/FR	11	1965	..	..	..	..
Land-based missiles						
S3D[e]	18	1980	3 500	1 × 1 Mt	TN-61	18
Pluton	44	1974	120	1 × 10/25 kt	ANT-51[f]	70
Submarine-based missiles						
M-20	64	1977	3 000	1 × 1 Mt	TN-61	64
M-4A	16	1985	4 000–5 000	6 × 150 kt (MIRV)	TN-70[g]	96
M-4 (modified)	16	1987	6 000	4–6 × 150 kt (MIRV)	TN-71	<96
Carrier aircraft						
Super Etendard	36	1978	650	1 × 6–8/30 kt bomb	ANT-52[d]	40

[a] Range for aircraft indicates combat radius, without refuelling.

[b] Range does not include the 80- to 250-km range of the ASMP air-to-surface missile.

[c] The Mirage IIIE and Jaguar A aircraft were first deployed in 1964 and 1973, respectively, although they did not carry nuclear weapons until 1972 and 1974, respectively.

[d] Gravity bombs for these aircraft include: the ANT-52 warhead (incorporating the same basic MR 50 charge as that used for the Pluton SSM), reported as being of 25- and 30-kt by CEA and DIA, respectively; and an alternate low-yield gravity bomb of 6-8 kt.

[e] S3D ('Durcie') is the designation for the hardened S3 missile. The original S3 missile was deployed in 1980.

[f] Warheads for the Pluton include the ANT-51 (incorporating the same basic MR 50 charge as the ANT-52) with a yield of 25 kt, and a specially designed alternate warhead of 10 kt.

[g] The *Inflexible* will be the only SSBN to receive the TN-70. All subsequent refits of the M-4 into Redoutable Class SSBNs will incorporate the improved TN-71 warhead. The M-4As of the *Inflexible* will eventually also be changed to hold the TN-71, dockyard space and budgets permitting.

Sources: Commissariat à l'Energie Atomique (CEA), 'Informations non classifiées sur l'armement nucléaire français', 26 June 1986; CEA, 'Regard sur l'avenir du CEA', *Notes d'Information*, Jan.–Feb. 1986, p. 7; CEA, *Rapport Annuel 1985*, pp. 77–79; US Defense Intelligence Agency (DIA), *A Guide to Foreign Tactical Nuclear Weapon Systems under the Control of Ground Force Commanders*, DST-1040S-541-83, 9 Sep. 1983, with CHG 1 and 2 (secret, partially declassified), 17 Aug. 1984 and 9 Aug. 1985; DIA, *Air Forces Intelligence Study (AFIS): France*, DDI-1300-FR-77 (secret, partially declassified), Apr. 1977; DIA, *Military Capability Study of NATO Countries*, DDB-2680-15-85 (secret, partially declassified), Sep. 1985 and Dec. 1977; Laird, R. F., 'French nuclear forces in the 1980s and the 1990s', *Comparative Strategy*, vol. 4, no. 4 (1984), pp. 387–412; International Institute for Strategic Studies, *The Military Balance 1987–1988* (IISS: London, 1987); authors' estimates.

44 WEAPONS AND TECHNOLOGY

Table 2.8. Chinese nuclear forces, 1988

Weapon system				Warheads	
Type	No. deployed	Year deployed	Range (km)	Warhead × yield	No. in stockpile
Aircraft[a]					
B-5 (Il-28 Beagle)	15–30	1974	1 850	1 × bomb[b]	15–30
B-6 (Tu-16 Badger)	100	1966	5 900	1–3 × bombs	100–130
Land-based missiles					
DF-2 (CSS-1)	40–60	1966	1 100	1 × 20 kt	40–60
DF-3 (CSS-2)	85–125	1972	2 600	1 × 1–3 Mt	85–125
DF-4 (CSS-3)	~10	1978	7 000	1 × 1–3 Mt	10
DF-5 (CSS-4)	~10	1980	12 000	1 × 4–5 Mt	10
Submarine-based missiles[c]					
CSS-N-3	24	1983	3 300	1 × 200 kt–1 Mt	26–38

[a] All figures for these bomber aircraft refer to nuclear-capable versions only. Hundreds of these aircraft are also deployed in non-nuclear versions.

[b] Yields of bombs are estimated to range from below 20 kt to 3 Mt.

[c] Two missiles are presumed to be available for rapid deployment on the Golf Class submarine (SSB). Additional missiles are being built for new Xia Class submarines.

Sources: Joint Chiefs of Staff, *Military Posture (annual report) FY 1978, 1982, 1983*; Department of Defense, *Annual Report for 1982*; Defense Intelligence Agency, *Handbook on the Chinese Armed Forces*, Apr. 1976; Defense Intelligence Agency, 'A guide to foreign tactical nuclear weapon systems under the control of ground force commanders', DST-1040S-541-83-CHG 1 (secret, partially declassified), 17 Aug. 1984; Godwin, P. H., *The Chinese Tactical Airforces and Strategic Weapons Program: Development, Doctrine, and Strategy* (Air University: Maxwell AFB, Ala., 1978); Washburn, T. D., *The People's Republic of China and Nuclear Weapons: Effects of China's Evolving Arsenal*, ADA 067350 (National Technical Information Service, US Department of Commerce: Washington, DC, 1979); US Congress, Joint Economic Committee, *Allocation of Resources in the Soviet Union and China* (annual hearing) 1976, 1981, 1982, 1983; Anderson, J., 'China shows confidence in its missiles', *Washington Post*, 19 Dec. 1984, p. F11.

Meanwhile, deployment of the new short-range SS-21 Scarab missile continued at a steady rate with Soviet ground forces. Virtually all of the 130 SS-21 transporter-erector-launchers (TELs) deployed until the end of the year have been assigned to the Western Theatre of Military Operations (*Teatr Voennykh Deistvii*, abbreviated TVD).[67] By the end of the year, all of the FROG missiles in Soviet divisions in the GDR had been equipped with the SS-21. Nuclear-capable self-propelled artillery also continued in production during the year. The US Defense Intelligence Agency estimates that, when fully deployed, the number of new nuclear-capable artillery guns and the older 152-mm howitzers will exceed 10 000.[68]

Naval nuclear forces

The Soviet Navy continued to increase its nuclear weapon capabilities during 1987, particularly with a long-range sea-launched cruise missile (SLCM). In contrast, the year witnessed the continued slow-down in shipbuilding, foretelling a shrinking but more capable Soviet Navy.

The first Soviet long-range nuclear SLCM, the SS-N-21 Sampson, was made operational in 1987.[69] The SS-N-21, a land-attack SLCM with a maximum range of approximately 3000 km, is small enough to be fired from a standard Soviet torpedo tube. Possible launch platforms include the Akula, Sierra, Victor II and converted Yankee Class attack submarines. Another Soviet SLCM, the supersonic SS-NX-24, continued to be tested during the year. This large SLCM, estimated to be more than 12-m long and to have a wingspan of more than 5 m,[70] will be flight-tested again from a converted Yankee Class submarine (SSGN). It is expected to be deployed during 1988–89.

In addition to its many models of nuclear-capable anti-ship cruise missiles, the Soviet Navy has a wide variety of naval nuclear weapons, including nuclear-armed torpedoes. The US JCS identified two of these nuclear torpedoes as the Type 65 and the ET-80.[71] In the Soviet Navy, according to the JCS, 'almost all major surface combatants (about 290), all submarines (about 340), as well as a few other combatants (some 31) are armed with at least one, or a mix of, nuclear weapon systems'.[72]

In the shipbuilding programme, the first aircraft-carrier of the 65 000-ton Kremlin Class, the *Leonid Brezhnev*, continued under construction. The US Navy told Congress early in the year that the *Brezhnev* should commence sea trials within two years, that a second aircraft-carrier is being built, and that two more will be built by the year 2000.[73] Significantly, the USA acknowledged for the first time that it will be a V/STOL (vertical/short take off and landing) carrier with a 'ski-jump', instead of the US large deck-type for operating advanced aircraft with catapults and arresting gear.[74] This means that the Soviet Navy will not, contrary to US predictions, be able to operate high-performance aircraft from carriers for many years.

Other naval deployments during 1987 included:

1. A fourth Kiev Class aircraft-carrier began sea trials.
2. A third Kirov Class nuclear cruiser was launched.
3. An eighth Sovremennyy Class guided-missile cruiser became operational.
4. A second Slava Class guided-missile cruiser became operational.
5. The first Sierra Class nuclear-powered attack submarine became operational.

All these vessels are nuclear-capable.

The Backfire-C bomber continued in production and was assigned to both Strategic Air Armies and Soviet Naval Aviation (SNA), replacing the Badger bomber in SNA. The nuclear-capable Su-24 Fencer also continued in production, for the Air Force and the Navy, and a strike/reconnaissance version of the aircraft, the Fencer-E, was introduced in SNA during the year.

IV. British nuclear weapon programmes

Britain moved forward in 1987 with the idea of developing a nuclear-armed air-launched cruise missile jointly with France. This would be the first such joint effort between the two nations and the first time Britain has worked on a joint nuclear weapon programme with a country other than the USA. All other British nuclear weapon programmes were continued during 1987, including possibly the last Chevaline-equipped SLBM modernization before the Trident submarines and missiles are introduced in the mid-1990s. The fourth and last British SSBN to be equipped with the Chevaline system began operations in 1987.

British–French nuclear co-operation

British Defence Secretary Younger and French Defence Minister Giraud met seven times in 1987 to discuss joint nuclear weapon development and procurement. Following their last meeting in December 1987 in London, the British and French defence staffs were ordered to study the feasibility of jointly developing a nuclear-armed, air-launched cruise missile as a 1990s successor to older nuclear weapons in their respective arsenals.[75]

The proposed jointly developed missile is currently envisioned as arming the British Tornado aircraft in the late 1990s and replacing the current French ASMP missile on French aircraft (see section V for details). The missile would have a range of more than 480 km, which is similar to that planned for a French missile under development, or about 180 km greater than that of the current French ASMP. Whether any future missile development work would be based on the ASMP or would start from a new design has not as yet been determined.[76]

The nuclear warheads for the joint missile would be developed by each country independently. As far as the British warhead is concerned, it was reported that the Atomic Weapons Research Establishment (AWRE) has considered fitting a modified Trident warhead to the cruise missile, which could give it a 150-kt warhead.[77]

In addition to the emerging British–French ALCM programme, the United Kingdom has expressed interest in joining the USA in developing a nuclear stand-off air-to-surface missile (ASM) for NATO.[78] (This nuclear ASM is one of the 'modernization' ideas which have been under consideration by NATO since before 1983.) The Royal Air Force (RAF) has previously expressed interest in a nuclear ASM for the late 1990s to replace their ageing WE-177 gravity bomb.[79] Such a missile would enable the Tornado aircraft to survive improved WTO air defences.

Polaris/Chevaline

It is estimated that Britain's strategic squadron number 10, comprising four Resolution Class SSBNs, has completed some 188 operational patrols since the maiden patrol of *HMS Resolution* in 1968.[80]

A mid-life refurbishment of the 'front end module' of the Chevaline A3-TK missile started in January 1988 and is expected to take a number of years.[81] This programme could be the last major contract on the Chevaline before the system is replaced by the Trident system in the mid-1990s. All four submarines equipped with Chevaline are now operational.

The US Navy Strategic Systems Project Office (SSPO) sells Polaris[82] and Trident II missiles (without the warheads), equipment and supporting services to the UK under the Polaris Sales Agreement, and certain services under the 1958 USA–UK Agreement for Cooperation on the Uses of Atomic Energy for Mutual Defense Purposes. Since the inception of the Polaris Sales Agreement on 6 April 1963, the UK has spent (through the SSPO) some $2.1 billion (through the end of FY 1987) in the USA on the Polaris, Chevaline and Trident weapon systems.[83] Expenditures in FY 1987 are estimated to have been $30.6 million for the Polaris and Chevaline.[84]

Trident submarine and warhead

Rear Admiral Slater, Chief, Strategic Systems Executive, announced after the re-election of Prime Minister Thatcher in early 1987 that the entire Trident programme is 'on time, on target for full deployment of four subs, each carrying 16 Tridents, by 1994–95'.[85] While all four SSBNs will probably be commissioned by 1994, full deployment may not be achieved until a few years later because of the time required for sea trials and for demonstration and shakedown operations. The first submarine, *HMS Vanguard*, is scheduled to put to sea in 1991.

The British Government stated in 1987 that each British Vanguard Class SSBN 'will carry no more than a maximum of 128 warheads'.[86] This would be 8 MIRV warheads per missile, although individual missiles might be loaded with fewer than 8 warheads. Following the December 1987 US–Soviet counting rule agreement (see sections II and III) that would prevent the USA from testing Trident II SLBMs with more than eight RVs, the British Trident SLBMs could have no more than eight RVs, as the British SLBMs are tested by the USA at the Eastern Test Range in Florida.

Although shrouded in heavy secrecy, the issue of warhead production for the Trident programme was raised again in 1987. After newspaper investigations, Defence Ministry sources acknowledged in January 1988 that the planned production facility A90 at Aldermaston is several years behind schedule.[87] As a result, it will not be able to produce components for Trident warheads until at least 1992, thus raising the prospect of a shortage of warheads for the Trident programme. There was no open public or parliamentary debate on the issue since such details are considered secrets.

The introduction of the Trident II D-5 SLBM aboard the new Vanguard Class SSBNs will result in a great increase in the numbers, accuracy and destructiveness of the British sea-based nuclear force. Britain will no longer have a 'minimum deterrent'. The deployment of Trident will result in a fourfold increase in total warheads over the present Resolution Class SSBNs armed with Polaris A3-TK missiles (Chevaline), each with two MRV warheads and decoys.[88]

The introduction of a MIRVed missile allows for greater target coverage. Basically the two Chevaline front-ends on each Polaris missile have only one target, whereas the eight warheads possible on each Trident II missile could have up to eight separate targets. However, even with this extra capability, the British Ministry of Defence (MOD) has stated that 'the essential capability for us is to be able to continue to hold at risk key aspects of Soviet state power, not to threaten the maximum possible number of individual targets'.[89] Thus the main target area will continue to be Moscow, although the fact of having hundreds of additional warheads may force changes in targeting policy.[90]

As of 31 March 1987, total expenditure for the Trident programme was approximately £1000 million, with a further £2000 million committed.[91] Expenditures through the SSPO in FY 1987 were US $33.1 million for Trident,[92] most of which is accounted for by the Trident Strategic Weapons System (SWS) (missiles, related support equipment, etc.). Ninety-five per cent of the costs for the Trident SWS are incurred in the USA,[93] and most fall under the provisions of the Polaris Sales Agreement which has been extended to cover the sale of Trident II.

A report issued by the British National Audit Office on 14 July 1987 disclosed some puzzling statistics about the work on the British Trident warhead.[94] Of the three major areas of expenditure (development, production and fissile material), the document stated that 'most of the expenditure on development and production is incurred in the US'.[95] This revelation runs contrary to official British statements that the British Trident warhead will be of 'British design and manufacture'.[96]

There are two possible explanations: first, as concerns 'production', the National Audit Office (NAO) may be confused as to what constitutes a warhead. It is possible that the NAO was referring to the re-entry vehicles instead of actual nuclear warheads, which may explain the NAO statement that 'most of the development and production expenditure is incurred in the US', and the USA will supply 'certain warhead-related components and services'. Second, there may be confusion concerning 'development' and 'production', which were included in the same category. Some development will take place in the USA, such as costs incurred at the Nevada Test Site, while production will not.[97]

The document also disclosed that the largest element of British expenditure on the Trident nuclear warhead was on fissile materials. The current estimate for procurement has gone down 16 per cent in real terms since 1981.

V. French nuclear weapon programmes

There were a number of important developments in French nuclear forces during 1987, including the delivery of the first Mirage 2000N nuclear aircraft and the operational deployment of the modernized strategic submarine *Le Tonnant*, that will have a considerable effect on the character and composition of these forces through the end of the century. These developments are described below (see table 2.7).

Hadès missile

The Hadès tactical nuclear missile programme remains on schedule, to be deployed in 1992, presumably with a neutron warhead. In April 1987 Prime Minister Jacques Chirac announced that the French Government will decide 'in the near future' whether to produce and deploy neutron warheads. However, a decision is needed soon if the neutron warheads are to be mounted on the Hadès missile in 1992.[98] A 22 October 1987 dispatch from the German Press Agency quotes President Mitterrand as saying that France will soon have the neutron bomb in its arsenal but hopes they will never be used.[99]

The enhanced-radiation weapons will cost France about 6 million francs ($1.03 million) each, while development of the warhead is costing 1 billion francs ($171 million), according to a report published by the Finance and Economic Affairs Committee of the French National Assembly.[100]

The first development flight of France's Hadès tactical nuclear missile is planned in 1988 from the French Centre d'Essais des Landes (CEL). Hadès will be launched from mobile tractor/trailers and will have a range of more than 480 km, a fourfold increase from the 120-km range of the Pluton tactical missile it will replace.[101] The development costs of the Hadès missile (excluding the warhead) are likely to reach 4.5 billion francs. The total cost, taking into account the manufacture of about 100 transporters, is about 15 billion francs.[102]

In October 1987 President Mitterrand conducted a high-profile visit to FR Germany during which he sought to calm the longstanding fears in the FRG over whether France would ever fire its short-range Pluton nuclear missiles at a WTO invasion force after it entered the FRG. German officials welcomed Mitterrand's carefully worded suggestions that France should not use its Pluton missiles against West German territory, even though the weapons' 120-km range makes them unsuitable for any other purpose. The Hadès, which would have a range of 480 km, would be able to reach the GDR (as well as eastern Czechoslovakia). However, Bonn takes little comfort at this statistic and believes that France should not use nuclear weapons over German territory, east *or* west.[103]

According to a document released by the US Army War College in 1987,[104] it appears that tactical operational doctrine in the early 1980s for French land–air forces in the Central Region called for the warheads of the 70 Pluton missiles, and air support from the Tactical Air Force (FATAC) with 15 warheads, to be used in FR Germany to destroy the first echelon of an invading Soviet Army before it could cross the Lorraine plateau, and to channel the enemy advance to obtain the maximum effect from nuclear weapons if their use were approved by the President. According to the document, if such approval were given, France would be restricted to fire only at military targets farther than 4 km from urban centres with populations of 5000 or more.

Air Force programmes

On 19 February 1987 the French manufacturer Dassault-Breguet delivered the first nuclear version of its Mirage 2000 combat aircraft, the 2000N, to the French Air Force training base at Bordeaux-Merignac.[105] The Mirage 2000N is due to replace the nuclear-armed Mirage IIIE and Jaguar A aircraft of the tactical air force (FATAC).

The Dauphiné Squadron (EC 1/4) of the Fourth Fighter Wing at Luxeuil will be the first to receive the nuclear-capable Mirage 2000N aircraft, in July 1988, replacing their Mirage IIIE nuclear-armed aircraft.[106]

France plans to build 112 Mirage 2000Ns for the FATAC, at an overall cost of 30.3 billion francs for the aircraft and 3.2 billion francs for the nuclear Air-Sol-Moyenne-Portée (ASMP) missile it will carry. Although all 112 Mirage 2000N aircraft will be able to carry nuclear or conventional weapons, 70 of them will now be dedicated to nuclear roles and armed with the ASMP. The remaining 2000Ns will be equipped to fire either the ASMP, or conventional weapons for non-nuclear strike missions.[107]

The Super Etendard carrier-based aircraft will also be equipped with the ASMP missile in 1988, replacing ANT-52 gravity bombs. This modification began in 1985 with Squadron 11F based at Landivisiau. Modification of all aircraft of Squadrons 11F and 17F (based at Hyères) will be completed in 1988. The remaining Squadron, number 14F (also at Landivisiau), will be modified to carry the ASMP after 1988.

The ASMP, now operational on Mirage IVP aircraft and soon to be deployed on the Super Etendard and Mirage 2000N aircraft, is a wingless air-to-surface nuclear missile, programmed to fly at a constant angle of attack of 1 degree (i.e., almost horizontal),[108] with a cruise speed of Mach 2.5–2.7 (under ramjet power) and a maximum range of 300 km. Propulsion is by solid-fuel rocket booster followed by a liquid-fuel ramjet which ignites when the rocket propellant is expended. Compared to the US air-launched cruise missile, the ASMP is slightly smaller, has about half the weight, has almost one-tenth the range, but has twice the yield at 300 kt.[109]

Concerning the British–French joint ALCM development plan, France has not only interest but also experience in nuclear-armed ASMs. The French ASMP missile has provided France with more than five years of knowledge of various aspects of air-launched, guided nuclear missile systems and related technologies. In addition, the French company Aérospatiale is already working on a longer-range supersonic variant of the ASMP missile, the Air-Sol-Longue-Portée (ASLP), which would have a maximum range of 480 km.[110] The joint cruise missile would replace the ASMP on such aircraft as the Mirage 2000N and the Rafale model being developed.

France also has experience in ALCM-compatible warheads and might use some future variant of its TN-80 series of warheads. The TN-81, an improved warhead for the ASMP, is now under development by the French Commissariat à l'Energie Atomique (CEA) and is expected to be deployed in 1988 on the Mirage 2000N and Super Etendard aircraft.[111]

Force Océanique Stratégique

It is estimated that six submarines of the Force Océanique Stratégique (FOST) have to date (March 1988) completed some 205 operational patrols since the first SSBN entered active service in 1971.[112]

At the end of 1987 the submarine *Le Tonnant* was put into operation. It is the first submarine to carry the TN-71 warhead on its newly installed M-4 missiles, and is the last of the Redoubtable Class submarines to be modified before new SSBNs join the fleet. The TN-71 warhead configuration permits an extended range of 6000 km. It is unclear how many warheads would be placed on each missile, but it could be fewer than the standard six. The TN-71 is known to be lighter and to have a smaller 'surface-equivalent' radar image than the original TN-70.

The first submarine of a new class, *Le Triomphant*, is expected to enter service with the French Navy in 1994. It will displace 14 200 tonnes submerged and have a length of 138 m and a crew of 100 (compared to 138 men on current Redoubtable Class SSBNs).[113] A second model, called the new-generation submarine and abbreviated SNLE-NG, is expected to be extended to 16 000 tonnes and 170 m, possibly to accommodate the larger M-5 SLBM.[114] In preparation for the future generation of SSBNs, France has opened new shipbuilding facilities at the Cherbourg naval dockyard, which will allow the construction of new and larger SSBNs.[115]

Le Triomphant, the seventh French SSBN, will carry 16 modified M-4 missiles, armed with the new TN-75 warhead. According to French officials, the TN-75, now in development, is an 'almost invisible' miniaturized warhead.[116] The first M-5 missiles are expected to appear on board the third submarine in the SNLE-NG programme that should be operational in 1999. The M-5 will be equipped with 8–12 very light and compact MIRV TN-76 warheads with a range exceeding 6000 km.[117]

Strategic communications

Recently France has taken an interest in redundant and survivable nuclear weapon communications. The ASTARTE (Avions Station Relais de Transmissions Exceptionelles) strategic communications programme entered operational service in early 1988. ASTARTE consists of four airborne communications aircraft derived from the French TRANSALL C 160 Nouvelle Génération aircraft. These are to be used for airborne VLF (very-low-frequency) communications with submerged ballistic-missile submarines and other strategic forces. The ASTARTE programme was launched in 1981, with the first experimental flight with VLF transmitters in 1986.[118] All four aircraft are expected to be operational in 1989.

The success of the ASTARTE programme has depended upon equipment from companies in the United States. The Rockwell Collins company has sold France four improved versions of the VLF transmitters used in US Navy/Lockheed EC-130Q TACAMO nuclear communications aircraft for $97 million. In addition, Rockwell International provided electromagnetic pulse (EMP) hardening for the aircraft, bringing the total cost for US involvement in ASTARTE to $120 million.[119] Rockwell has provided spares, training and support to France for the ASTARTE programme; for this purpose Rockwell has established 10 offices in France.

The CERTEL (Centre d'Études et de Recherches en Télécommunications) of the French Ministry of Armaments (DGA) is responsible for the elaborate and redundant forms of communication with French SSBNs. In a military crisis, or a situation in which the French land-based VLF system were threatened or destroyed, the ASTARTE plan would be put into action.[120] One of four aircraft would rise from an underground shelter at the Evreux Air Base

(Eure), take off, unroll 'several kilometres of antenna',[121] and be able to remain in flight for 10 hours without refuelling (although the aircraft are capable of being refuelled).

Future nuclear programmes

Development of the new French lightweight S4 land-based ballistic missile continued in 1987. When the S4 becomes operational in 1996 it will carry the new TN-75 warhead. The TN-75, now in development, is a miniaturized warhead using stealth techniques. This is the same warhead that will be carried by the M-4 missiles on the seventh French SSBN, *Le Triomphant*.[122]

Over the past decade the French Navy has debated the value of tactical nuclear weapons at sea. Unlike the USA, the UK and the USSR, France does not possess nuclear anti-submarine warfare (ASW) and anti-surface warfare (ASUW) weapons.[123] France's two Clemenceau Class aircraft-carriers were the first and only French vessels to have a nuclear capability: the Super Etendard strike aircraft, armed with the ANT-52 gravity bomb and from 1988 with the ASMP air-to-surface missile. Both the ANT-52 and the ASMP could be used against enemy surface ships, although it is more likely that they would be used to attack land targets.

Recently the debate has been revived by an article by the Commander of the French Navy, Admiral Louzeau, in the journal *Défense Nationale*. Admiral Louzeau cites the need for a French nuclear ASW weapon, while claiming the inadequacies of conventional ASW weapons against modern Soviet nuclear submarines.[124] It is unclear whether such a weapon would be intended for launch from a ship, submarine, helicopter or aircraft.

VI. Chinese nuclear weapon programmes

During 1987 China continued its programme of reform with the main emphasis on economic modernization. The military, which has been accorded last place in the 'four modernizations', is undergoing a major reform that will reduce its size but eventually increase its combat capabilities. The armed forces are also contributing to civilian production and economic improvement. A decision was taken in 1985 by the Central Military Commission of the Communist Party, which is the highest-level decision-making body on military affairs in China, that a major war is highly improbable for the rest of this century, and that China can concentrate on its economy while modernizing its military in a limited way.

Consequently, China's nuclear weapon programmes have generally stressed qualitative, rather than quantitative, improvements. China has an interest in appearing to have a minimal, yet credible, nuclear force. None the less, the US intelligence community predicted in 1986 that China's nuclear arsenal will double by 1996.[125] This could mean that China would have some 600-700 warheads, possibly including MIRVed missiles. China's existing nuclear forces are being modernized while kept at roughly the same overall number. Since China has neither the desire nor the resources to engage in a costly nuclear buildup, it is satisfied to carry out R&D efforts on a number of nuclear weapon

NUCLEAR WEAPONS 53

programmes and to keep as many options as possible open for the future. The current programmes are described below (see table 2.8).

Land-based missile programmes and technology

China is developing a new short-range ballistic missile (SRBM) called the M-9, or simply the M missile, which it is advertising for sale.[126] This missile, which is expected to be introduced into Chinese missile units before any versions are sold abroad, uses solid fuel, has a maximum range of 600 km and is mounted on a truck for transport and launching.[127] A full-scale model was displayed at a defence exposition in 1987 along with a list of the missile's characteristics. Its advertised high degree of mobility, use of solid fuel and consequent rapid reaction time—30 minutes—would represent considerable advances in Chinese missile technology and capability. It is unclear what effect, if any, the US–Soviet INF Treaty will have on China's interest in deploying the short-range nuclear M-9. Under the terms of the Treaty, the USSR will eliminate all its ground-launched ballistic missiles with ranges between 500 and 5500 km, including hundreds of nuclear missiles deployed within range of Chinese targets.

All Chinese land-based nuclear ballistic missiles currently use liquid fuel. China's newest nuclear missiles, CSS-N-3 SLBMs, use solid fuel, which is safer and more reliable than liquid fuel. By developing the M-9 missile with solid fuel, China may be starting a programme to convert all its land-based missiles from liquid to solid fuel. This would represent a considerable increase in Chinese nuclear capabilities for several reasons. First, liquid fuel imposes limits and dangers on missile operations. Liquid-fuelled missiles must be kept still in a vertical position when fuelled. They cannot be placed or transported in a horizontal position: the weight of the fuel would rupture the missile. As several liquid fuel accidents have proved, even small leaks can be disastrous.[128]

All of China's land-based missiles can be transported on or launched from trailers, but they must travel without fuel. To launch a missile, it must first be raised from a horizontal (travelling) to a vertical position and then fuelled. The fuelling process is dangerous, slow and cumbersome, requiring a large fuel crew, a fleet of special fuel trucks and pumping equipment. It generally takes hours to prepare a liquid-fuelled missile for operation, compared to 30 minutes claimed for the M-9 missile.[129]

Second, if China were to use solid fuel it would not only avoid the liquid fuel problems, but it could increase the mobility and survivability of its land-based missile force, both important qualities for China. In addition, the relative ease of maintaining communication with and control of land-based missile forces would increase Chinese incentives to convert them to solid fuel.

During 1987 China continued to work on the effectiveness of its land-based nuclear missiles by such measures as: modernizing and computerizing communications networks, improving the nuclear support and logistics system, preparing pre-surveyed launch sites for various kinds of missiles and launchers, training for nuclear war in all weather and geographic conditions, and generally improving and expanding the Chinese capability to launch nuclear weapons all

54   WEAPONS AND TECHNOLOGY

year round.[130] There were no public official reports of further tests of MIRVed systems during the year.

Other programmes

China continues to modernize its strategic submarine forces. There were prominent announcements that one of the Xia Class SSBNs had completed its training programme and had joined active service.[131] In 1987 the Chinese Navy announced the improvement of a VLF communications station with world-wide range, probably at Changde, that has been in operation since 1980. According to an article from the official news agency Xinhua, the station 'has been successfully communicating with submarines', and 'can transmit information . . . pertinent to the launching of carrier rockets', which means SLBMs.[132] The same article states that VLF 'is used for transmission through deep-water', and 'is not influenced by the ionosphere or atomic explosions'. China also has several VLF stations capable of regional transmission.[133] All five nuclear weapon nations use VLF as the primary means of communicating with their submerged submarines; it is an essential means for China to maintain control of its submarine forces. Other naval communications developments were also reported during the year.[134]

China is producing only a few, perhaps three, medium bombers per year at the Xian aircraft plant.[135] These are naval variants of the B-6 bomber designed for anti-shipping missions but potentially capable of using nuclear weapons. Given China's drive for economic modernization, there is a strong need to expand the civil air transport capacity throughout the country, thus subordinating military to civilian programmes. China has undertaken several joint ventures to build modern passenger aircraft, is reorganizing its civil air traffic management system and has converted a number of former military air bases into civilian airports. There are, however, several R&D programmes reported for new military aircraft, including a bomber, but these are a lower priority than the expansion of civilian air traffic service, and apparently do not yet involve any testing.

Modern bombers would be one option for China to increase its nuclear capabilities if the superpowers, particularly the USSR, proceed to develop nation-wide ballistic missile defences (BMD). Nuclear-armed cruise missiles would be another option as a countermeasure to BMD systems. China has considerable experience with non-nuclear anti-ship cruise missiles, but large nuclear weapon development and production programmes would be very costly, and the deployment of superpower strategic defences would undermine China's limited nuclear force. China hopes to avert such a situation and has been campaigning hard to dissuade the further development of strategic defence systems.

VII. Developments in nuclear proliferation[136]

In considering nuclear weapon developments it is important also to consider the situation of the so-called nuclear threshold countries, that is, states which have neither acknowledged the possession of nuclear weapons nor joined the 1968 Non-Proliferation Treaty (NPT), but conduct significant nuclear activities and operate nuclear plants not under safeguards but capable of making weapon-usable material. There is a constant danger that some of them might cross the threshold to become fully-fledged nuclear weapon states. This would be a serious blow to the non-proliferation regime, which has been laboriously developed over several decades, and a set-back to the cause of regional and international stability and security. The most important developments that became clear or took place in 1987 for the six states in this category are described in this section.

Israel

The information provided in 1986 by a former technician in an Israeli nuclear facility that Israel has a substantial nuclear arsenal may, if proved correct, mean that there actually exist six states in the world which are in possession of nuclear weapons rather than five, as had been previously believed. Actions taken against the author of these revelations—his prompt abduction, arrest, trial and conviction of treason for disclosing secret data—confirm the seriousness with which Israeli authorities treat this affair, but the official position of Israel on nuclear matters remains unchanged. It continues to affirm, somewhat ambiguously, that it will not be the first country to introduce nuclear weapons into the Middle East.[137]

Israel imported heavy water from Norway and the United States from 1959 to 1963 with the agreement to use it solely for peaceful purposes; it also agreed to accept on-site inspection of the heavy water supply. In September 1987, Norway made a formal demand to check the use made of its heavy water supply, but this was refused, adding to the suspicion that it was used for other than peaceful purposes. While the USA holds the same inspection rights, it has not taken any such action.

In addition to possessing the technology and materials for nuclear weapons, Israel also has a nuclear-capable ballistic missile. In May 1987 it was reported that Israel successfully tested a longer-range version of its Jericho missile, dubbed the Jericho II. It flew 510 miles (816 km) across the Mediterranean Sea.[138] The report estimates the maximum range to be about 900 miles (1440 km).

The establishment of a zone free of nuclear weapons in the Middle East has been repeatedly proposed in recent years, but the realization of this proposal is conceivable only within the framework of an overall political settlement of the Middle Eastern imbroglio and the consequent significant cuts in all categories of weapons. Given Israel's precarious security situation, the International Atomic Energy Agency (IAEA) or UN resolutions on 'Israeli nuclear capabilities and threat', requesting Israel to place all its nuclear facilities under IAEA safeguards,[139] apparently have no chance of being complied with.

Pakistan and India

Evidence has accumulated in the past few years that both countries possess all the essential elements for the manufacture of nuclear weapons. It is thus now an established fact that, owing to the technology and hardware clandestinely obtained from abroad,[140] Pakistan is producing highly enriched, weapon-grade uranium and is probably testing a high-explosive 'triggering package' for a nuclear device.[141] It may not yet have assembled a complete nuclear explosive device but, according to independent experts, its unsafeguarded enrichment plant has the capacity to produce enough fissile material for one to four weapons annually.[142] There have been reports that Pakistan is building one more plant, which will increase this capacity.[143]

India tested a nuclear device in 1974 and has greatly increased its plutonium production capacity in unsafeguarded facilities; it is considered by some analysts to be able to produce about 15 nuclear weapons per year.[144] Moreover, its nuclear weapon delivery capability by far exceeds that of Pakistan, its rival neighbour. On 4 May 1987 Radio Delhi announced that India had successfully launched a short-range missile, the RH-560. A Defence Ministry spokesman said that other missiles 'at an advanced stage of development' will be ready by 1993, including a medium-range missile.[145] In fact, since India has an indigenous space launch capability (and has launched its own satellite), it has a latent ICBM capacity.

In spite of these developments, in recent years international attention has been diverted from India's nuclear potential to that of Pakistan, even though the Pakistani posture can be regarded as primarily a reaction to India's nuclear ambitions. If attempts by the US Administration to restrain Pakistan's nuclear activities have not succeeded, and if the Pakistani Government continues with its unsafeguarded nuclear programme, it is mainly for the following reason. Pakistan's proposals for signing the NPT simultaneously with India, or declaring the denuclearization of the South Asian region, or at least accepting reciprocal inspections of nuclear facilities, have been repeatedly rejected by India, and political relations between the two countries have again deteriorated.

It has been suggested in the UN that a bilateral Indian–Pakistani comprehensive nuclear test ban might be more acceptable to India than the nuclear weapon-free concept. Significantly, this suggestion was also made by Pakistan,[146] even though, by precluding further development of nuclear capabilities, a test ban would freeze India's advantage in the nuclear field.[147]

South Africa

Accusations have been repeatedly made, mainly in the United Nations, that South Africa has clandestinely manufactured and tested a nuclear weapon. The suspicion is compounded by South Africa's refusal to submit to IAEA inspection its uranium enrichment facility which has the capacity of producing weapon-grade uranium. (The South African nuclear power reactors and a research reactor are under non-NPT safeguards.)

The attitude of South Africa towards the NPT has been ambivalent. Unlike India, Pakistan or Israel, South Africa has no obvious military incentives to build a nuclear arsenal. Its conventional armed forces are stronger than those of its possible regional adversaries. Nuclear weapons would also be useless in dealing with a possible internal insurgency against the apartheid regime. This may be one reason why South Africa has never expressed hostility to the NPT. In 1968 it voted for the UN General Assembly resolution which 'commended' the Treaty, and the South African representative subsequently took part in discussions at the IAEA of the model-NPT safeguards agreement.

On 21 September 1987 the South African President stated that his government was prepared to commence negotiations with each of the nuclear weapon states on the possibility of 'signing' the NPT and would consider including, in these negotiations, safeguards on its installations subject to the NPT conditions. The statement went on to express the hope that South Africa would soon be able to sign the NPT but added that any safeguards agreement which might subsequently be negotiated with the IAEA would have to be along the same lines as, and in conformity with, agreements with other NPT signatories.[148] The South African statement may carry significance, but it is unclear in several respects. First, the Treaty is not subject to signature because it is already in force; it can only be acceded to by a state willing to join it. Second, to become a party to the NPT, a state need not conduct negotiations with other states, be they nuclear or non-nuclear weapon states; deposit of the instrument of accession with all or any of the three depositaries (the USA, the UK or the USSR) would suffice. And third, the question of safeguards under the NPT must be discussed with the IAEA, not with individual parties; and it goes without saying that an agreement to safeguard South African nuclear activities would have to be similar to those concluded with other non-nuclear weapon parties to the NPT, that is, it would have to be comprehensive. If by that time South Africa had acquired nuclear weapons, it would have to dismantle them, and the IAEA would have to ensure that *all* fissionable material in the territory of South Africa was used exclusively for peaceful purposes.

The preparedness of South Africa to negotiate adherence to the NPT was made conditional on the outcome of the 1987 IAEA General Conference, which opened in Vienna on the same day the South African statement was made. The obvious aim of this diplomatic manoeuvre was to stave off an effort by several Third World states, led by Nigeria, to expel South Africa from the IAEA. The manoeuvre proved to be successful, at least in part: the view prevailed that for the time being it was better to have South Africa inside the Agency rather than outside it. None the less the General Conference resolved to consider, at its 1988 session, the June 1987 recommendation by the IAEA Board of Governors to suspend South Africa from the exercise of the privileges and rights of membership. It also requested the Director-General to take measures to ensure the implementation of its 1986 resolution which *inter alia* demanded that South Africa submit all its nuclear installations and facilities to Agency safeguards.[149]

Brazil and Argentina

It was revealed in 1987 that Brazil had mastered the centrifuge technology for uranium enrichment (a process used by only a few developed countries) and had begun the construction of a large enrichment plant soon to be put into operation.[150] This was achieved, presumably without outside help, in a secret, so-called parallel nuclear programme centred at an institute in São Paulo.[151] The enrichment plant, to be run by the Brazilian Navy, is not to be covered by international safeguards and can therefore be used for the manufacture of uranium for weapon purposes. Brazil can even make its own special steel needed for the centrifuges.

In announcing this technological breakthrough, Brazil reiterated its commitment to using nuclear energy exclusively for peaceful purposes.[152] However, of the three reactors now possessed or being built by Brazil, one—constructed by the US Westinghouse company—barely functions owing to constant breakdowns, and the construction of the other two reactors—following the co-operation agreement between FR Germany and Brazil—is almost at a standstill; the cost of the operation has proved to be unbearable.[153] The planned building of a Brazilian nuclear-powered submarine is even more remote; according to the Brazilian Minister of the Navy, the submarine could not be completed before the turn of the century, and the cost would exceed US $300 million.[154] In this situation, it is questionable what peaceful purposes can be served by the production of enriched uranium, which is expected to start in 1988,[155] if there are no power reactors or submarine reactors to use it. The prospects for exporting substantial quantities of enriched uranium to other countries are not bright either, considering the competition among the established suppliers on a saturated world market.

Given this situation, the production of enriched uranium could—in the opinion of José Goldemberg, rector of the University of São Paulo—enable Brazil to manufacture a nuclear weapon within five years.[156] Indeed, in the light of Brazil's adamant refusal to join the NPT or to assume unreservedly the obligations under the Treaty of Tlatelolco, the discovered preparatory work on what was presumed to be a Brazilian nuclear test site[157] and the development of rockets capable of delivering nuclear weapon payloads have both raised doubts regarding the intentions of the Brazilian military.

Argentina, which operates an unsafeguarded uranium enrichment plant using gaseous diffusion technology, does not appear to be able as yet to produce weapon-grade uranium. But as regards reprocessing—that is, the technique for separating plutonium from spent reactor fuel—Argentina is more advanced than Brazil.[158] It is noteworthy, however, that the role of the Argentine military in directing nuclear affairs has been reduced. The National Atomic Energy Commission of Argentina is now, after years of monopolistic military rule, responsible only for technical matters, whereas the Foreign Ministry takes all the relevant political decisions, including the choice of recipients of Argentine nuclear supplies.

The danger of nuclear weapon proliferation in Latin America has been somewhat dampened by a considerable improvement of political relations between Brazil and Argentina. A regional policy centred on economic co-operation, in particular in the nuclear field, seems to be replacing the traditional rivalry between the two countries, based on nationalistic military considerations. The July 1987 visit by the President of Brazil to Argentina's uranium enrichment facility—never before visited by a foreign official—and the planned visit by the President of Argentina to a similar facility in Brazil symbolize the changes.

Other countries

In addition to these threshold countries, there are three parties to the NPT—Iran, Iraq and Libya—whose commitments to the Treaty have been publicly questioned even though their nuclear activities are safeguarded. However, all three countries are at a very early stage of nuclear development and lack the industrial infrastructure to support a significant indigenous programme.

Notes and references

[1] 'Nuclear Notebook', *Bulletin of the Atomic Scientists*, Mar. 1988, p. 55.

[2] See Norris, R. S., Arkin, W. M. and Cochran, T. B., 'US–USSR strategic offensive nuclear forces 1946–1987', *Nuclear Weapons Databook* Working Paper 87-1 (Rev. 1), Dec. 1987.

[3] Congressional Budget Office, *Modernizing U.S. Strategic Offensive Forces: Costs, Effects, and Alternatives*, Nov. 1987.

[4] House Armed Services Committee (HASC), *The MX Missile Inertial Measurement Unit: A Program Review*, Committee Print no. 11, Aug. 1987; Moore, M., 'MX reliability in question', *Washington Post*, 28 Dec. 1987, p. A1.

[5] This was in response to the FY 1986 legislation which required a report from the President on future survivable basing modes for an additional 50 MX missiles to be deployed.

[6] Ballistic Missile Office, 'Peacekeeper in rail garrison', briefing by Colonel Glenn H. Vogel, 9 Apr. 1987; *Aviation Week & Space Technology*, 5 Jan. 1987, pp. 20–21; *Aviation Week & Space Technology*, 6 Apr. 1987, pp. 18–9; Senate Armed Services Committee (SASC), *Hearings on DOD Authorization for Appropriations for FY 1988* (hereafter cited as SASC, FY 1988 DOD), Part 4, pp. 1899–903.

[7] Blytheville AFB, Arkansas; Little Rock AFB, Arkansas; Barksdale AFB, Louisiana; Wurtsmith AFB, Michigan; Whiteman AFB, Missouri; Malmstrom AFB, Montana; Grand Forks AFB, North Dakota; Minot AFB, North Dakota; Dyess AFB, Texas; and Fairchild AFB, Washington; US Department of Defense, OSD(PA) News Release No. 73–87; Senate Appropriations Committee (SAC), *Hearings on Department of Defense Appropriations for FY 1988* (hereafter cited as SAC, FY 1988 DOD), Part 1, pp. 223–46.

[8] 15 Jan. 1987, 4 Mk 5 RVs; 17 Mar. 1987, 8 Mk 5 RVs; 30 Apr. 1987, 4 Mk 5 RVs; 12 June 1987, 4 Mk 5 RVs; 21 July 1987, 4 Mk 5 RVs; 8 Sep. 1987, 9 Mk 4 RVs plus one instrumentation package; 6 Oct. 1987, 8 Mk 5 RVs; and 11 Dec. 1987, number of RVs unknown.

[9] Gordon, M. R., 'U.S plans to test submarine missile with 12 warheads', *New York Times*, 7 Oct. 1987, p. A1; Congressional Budget Office, *The Trident II Missile Test Program: Implications for Arms Control*, Nov. 1987; Pincus. W., 'Test of 12-warhead missile delayed', *Washington Post*, 7 Nov. 1987, p. A11; Pincus, W., 'U.S. delays test of 12-warhead sub missile', *Washington Post*, 10 Nov. 1987, p. A3.

[10] Each test will cost upwards of $50 million, approximately $45 million for the missile and $5 million for conducting each flight-test.

[11] *Aviation Week & Space Technology*, 30 Sep. 1985, pp. 76–79; *Aviation Week & Space Technology*, 27 Aug. 1984, pp. 60, 65–6.

[12] The Navy could prolong the FOT programme by testing fewer missiles per year before the year 2012 and/or using the missiles from the first Trident II carrying SSBNs which will probably be retired between the years 2015 and 2020.

[13] The two RVs will have different masses, drag coefficients and ablation characteristics, all of which affect the performance of the RVs when they re-enter the atmosphere.

[14] Silber, H., 'B-1Bs begin to swell ranks of N-arsenal', *Omaha World Herald*, 16 Aug. 1987, p. 12.

[15] House Armed Services Committee, *Review of the Air Force B-1 Program*, House Report 100–8; House Armed Services Committee, *The B-1B: A Program Review*, Committee Print No. 2, 30 Mar. 1987; General Accounting Office (GAO), *Supportability, Maintainability, and Readiness of the B-1B Bomber*, GAO/NSIAD-87-177BR, June 1987; Marshall, E., 'Bomber number one', *Science*, 29 Jan. 1988, pp. 452–5.

[16] General Accounting Office, *Estimated Costs to Deploy the B-1B*, GAO/NSIAD-88-12, Oct. 1987.

[17] See Section 121 of the *National Defense Authorization Act for Fiscal Years 1988 and 1989*, Conference Report, House Report 100–446, pp. 23–4; Vartabedian, R., 'Bomber costs soar', *Los Angeles Times*, 8 July 1987, p. IV-1; Morrocco, J. D., 'Management problems delay first flight of Northrop B-2', *Aviation Week & Space Technology*, 11 Jan. 1988, pp. 16–7. One financial analyst estimated that ATB bomber funding for the period FY 1983–88 is $12.64 billion; Schemmer, B. F., 'Financial analysts estimate Stealth bomber costs within 4% of each other', *Armed Forces Journal International*, Oct. 1987, pp. 26–8.

[18] Read, E. W., 'Northrop gets stealth award, sources say', *Wall Street Journal*, 25 Jan. 1988, p. 7; *Aviation Week & Space Technology*, 1 Feb. 1988, p. 18.

[19] House Appropriations Committee (HAC), *Hearings on Department of Defense Appropriations for 1988* (hereafter cited as HAC, FY 1988 DOD), Part 6, p. 700.

[20] Silber, H., 'SAC preparing for advanced cruise missile', *Omaha World Herald*, 13 Sep. 1987, p. 9-B.

[21] Halloran, R., 'Plan to re-equip B-52's is proposed', *New York Times*, 18 Sep. 1987, p. 7.

[22] 'Deployed missiles' are defined in Article 11, para. 11 of the INF Treaty (see appendix 13A).

[23] *Air Force Magazine*, Feb. 1987, pp. 74–6.

[24] Hoagland, J., 'Spain tells U.S. to remove F16s', *Washington Post*, 24 Dec. 1987, p. A1.

[25] The Defence Planning Committee of NATO consists of the Defence Ministers under the chairmanship of the NATO Secretary-General.

[26] See Secretary of Defense James R. Schlesinger, *The Theater Nuclear Force Posture in Europe*, A Report to the United States Congress in compliance with Public Law 93–365, 1975, p. 26.

[27] These procedures recognized that 'special weight should be given in the consultation process to the country on or from whose territory the weapons would be employed; to the country providing the delivery system concerned; and to the country providing the warhead'; Legge, J. M., *Theater Nuclear Weapons and the NATO Strategy of Flexible Response*, Apr. 1983 (Rand Corporation R-2964-FF), p. 22. The procedures are regularly practised in the biennial NATO 'Wintex' command post exercises.

[28] As a result of a 1980 study of the role of Defensive Nuclear Forces (DNF) in NATO strategy by the High Level Group of the Nuclear Planning Group, Nike Hercules missiles and atomic demolition munitions (ADMs) were earmarked for withdrawal. All ADMs were withdrawn from Europe in 1985.

[29] NATO flexible response strategy is contained in the NATO document *Overall Strategic Concept for the Defense of the North Atlantic Treaty Organization Area* (MC 14/3).

[30] See Ruehl, L. (State Secretary of the Ministry of Defence, FR Germany), 'The nuclear balance in the Central Region and strategic stability in Europe', *NATO's Sixteen Nations*, Aug. 1987, p. 19. This is the only known public discussion or mention of the GPG by a NATO or US official.

[31] Ruehl (note 30), p. 19.

[32] Legge, J. M., *Theater Nuclear Weapons and the NATO Strategy of Flexible Response*, Apr. 1983 (Rand Corporation R-2964-FF), p. 20.

[33] For background on how the Administration came to reinterpret the ABM Treaty, see Garthoff, R. L., *Policy vs. the Law: The Reinterpretation of the ABM Treaty* (Brookings Institution: Washington, DC, 1987); Joint Hearings before the Committee on Foreign Relations and the Committee on the Judiciary, United States Senate, *The ABM Treaty and the Constitution*, Senate Hearing 100–110; Senate Foreign Relations Committee, *The ABM Treaty Interpretation Resolution*, Report 100–164, 22 Sep 1987; and chapter 14.

[34] *Congressional Record*, 11 Mar. 1987, pp. S2967–86; *Congressional Record*, 12 Mar. 1987, pp. S3090–5; *Congressional Record*, 13 Mar. 1987, pp. S3171–3. A fourth installment was published in the *Congressional Record*, 19 May 1987, pp. S6623–91.

[35] Smith, R. J., 'Dispute threatens INF Treaty', *Washington Post*, 6 Feb. 1988, p. A1; Smith, R. J., 'State Dept. uneasy over INF dispute', *Washington Post*, 7 Feb. 1988, p. A1.

NUCLEAR WEAPONS 61

36 Senators Dale Bumpers, John Chafee and Patrick Leahy, 'Salvaging SALT: the new congressional compromise', *Arms Control Today*, Dec. 1987, pp. 3–6.
37 National Defense Authorization Act for Fiscal Years 1988 and 1989 (note 17), p. 630.
38 Blechman, B. M. and Krepon, M., *Nuclear Risk Reduction Centers* (Georgetown University Center for Strategic and International Studies: Washington, DC, 1986).
39 See the communiqué of the 1985 Geneva summit meeting.
40 US Department of Defense, *Report of the Secretary of Defense Frank Carlucci to the Congress for FY 1989* (annual report), (hereafter cited as DOD FY 1989), p. 113.
41 See note 1. The totals count MRVs separately.
42 Ulsamer, E., 'Intelligence update on Soviet power', *Air Force Magazine*, Dec. 1986, p. 91.
43 Joint Chiefs of Staff (JCS), *Military Posture of the United States, FY 1988* (annual report), (hereafter cited as JCS, FY 1988).
44 Taubman, P., 'Soviet confirms new missile but denies violation', *New York Times*, 12 Aug. 1987; Diehl, J., 'Soviet defends new mobile missile system as step to "increase stability"', *Washington Post*, 12 Aug. 1987.
45 *Congressional Record*, 7 Aug. 1987, pp. S11561–5.
46 Gordon, M. R., 'New Soviet missile fuels U.S. dispute on compliance', *New York Times*, 9 Aug. 1987; Smith, R. J., 'Soviets said to deploy mobile ICBMs', *Washington Post*, 8 Aug. 1987; JCS, FY 1989, p. 39.
47 Compare US Department of Defense, *Soviet Military Power 1984* (hereafter cited as DOD, SMP 1984), p. 23; DOD, SMP 1987, p. 29. See also *National Journal*, 20 July 1985, p. 1692.
48 *Report of the Secretary of the Air Force to the Congress on the Air Force* (annual), p. 15.
49 Gertz, B., 'Soviets successfully test missile that will be largest in arsenal', *Washington Times*, 7 Jan. 1987; 'Failure of Soviet missile report by U.S. experts', *Baltimore Sun*, 18 Sep. 1986; Cannon, L., 'Missile test by Soviets goes astray', *Washington Post*, 16 Sep. 1986.
50 DOD, FY 1988, p. 25.
51 Senate Armed Services Committee/Senate Appropriations Committee, *Soviet Strategic Force Developments*, Joint Hearings, Senate Hearings 99–335, 26 June 1985.
52 Gordon, M. R., 'U.S. protests test of Soviet missiles north of Hawaii', *New York Times*, 2 Oct. 1987, p. A1; Moore, M., 'U.S. protests Soviet Pacific missile tests', *Washington Post*, 2 Oct. 1987, p. A1; Bunn, M., 'Soviet missile tests near Hawaii arouse controversy', *Arms Control Today*, Nov. 1987, pp. 22–3.
53 Senator Jesse Helms, *Congressional Record*, 7 Aug. 1987, p. S11562.
54 JCS, FY 1988, p. 35.
55 See, for example, DOD, SMP 1987, p. 33, which reports that the SS-N-23 missile carries 10 MIRV warheads.
56 JCS, FY 1988, p. 35.
57 DOD, FY 1988 *Annual Report*, p. 26; DOD, SMP 1987, p. 35.
58 DOD, SMP 1987, pp. 27, 34.
59 JCS, FY 1988, p. 36.
60 'Blackjack bomber crashes in USSR', *Aviation Week & Space Technology*, 25 May 1987, p. 19.
61 JCS, FY 1989, p. 41.
62 Broad, W. J., 'The secrets of Soviet star wars', *New York Times Magazine*, 28 June 1987, pp. 22–8.
63 Markham, J. M., 'Shultz declares missile pact needs no summit meeting', *New York Times*, 25 Oct. 1987, p. 1.
64 The SA-12A 'Gladiator' variant, intended for deployment in non-strategic forces, is already being fielded.
65 For example, Moscow Air Defence Commander Anatoly U. Konstantinov was replaced by Col. Gen. V. Tsarkov, although there were also reports that this replacement may have occurred before the flight. More importantly, Defence Minister Sergei L. Sokolov was replaced by General Dimitri Yazov, who supports Gorbachev. The Commander of Soviet air defence forces, Aleksander I. Koldunov, was also dismissed.
66 MOU of the INF Treaty (see appendix 13B).
67 DOD, SMP 1987, p. 66.
68 DOD, SMP 1987, p. 41.
69 JCS, FY 1989, p. 40.
70 DOD, SMP 1987, p. 38.
71 JCS, FY 1989, p. 54.
72 See note 71.
73 HAC, FY 1988 DOD, Part 2, p. 296.

[74] Toth, R., 'Moscow downgrades new aircraft carrier', *International Herald Tribune*, 23 Oct. 1987.

[75] 'Britain, France to assess joint development of cruise missile', *Aviation Week & Space Technology*, 21 Dec. 1987, p. 25; DeYoung, K., 'France, Britain consider joint nuclear weapon', *Washington Post*, 22 Dec. 1987, p. A-16.

[76] 'Britain, France to assess joint development of cruise missile', *Aviation Week & Space Technology*, 21 Dec. 1987, p. 25.

[77] Urban, M., 'UK in cruise missile talks with France', *The Independent*, 21 Apr. 1987.

[78] Arkin, W. M., Norris, R. S. and Cochran, T. B., 'Implications of the INF Treaty', NWD 87-3, *Nuclear Weapons Databook* Working Paper 87-3, 1 Dec. 1987, p. 27.

[79] Urban, M., 'RAF seeks new missile to beat Soviet defences', *The Independent*, 10 Nov. 1986, cited in SIPRI, *SIPRI Yearbook 1987: World Armaments and Disarmament* (Oxford University Press: Oxford, 1987), p. 28.

[80] See SIPRI, *World Armaments and Disarmament: SIPRI Yearbook 1986* (Oxford University Press: Oxford, 1986), p. 61.

[81] Daly, M., 'Chevaline refurbishment to begin this month', *Jane's Defence Weekly*, 16 Jan. 1988. p. 54.

[82] A total of 133 Polaris missiles were ordered; all have been delivered.

[83] Authors' estimates: $1.816 billion for Polaris and Chevaline (87%) and $280 million for Trident (13%).

[84] Authors' estimates.

[85] Webb, A., 'Thatcher reelection puts Trident back on track in United Kingdom', *Armed Forces Journal International*, Aug. 1987, p. 42.

[86] British Ministry of Defence, *Statement on the Defence Estimates 1987* (HMSO: London, 1987), Cmd 101-I, p. 41.

[87] Urban, M., 'Warheads shortage threatens Trident', *The Independent*, 26 Jan. 1988; see also articles of 27 and 28 Jan. 1988 in *The Independent*.

[88] However, it is also true, as the MOD has stated, that the deployment of Trident will result in 'an increase of up to two and a half times the payload of the Polaris boats, when they entered service in the 1960s each carrying 48 warheads'; see note 86. This translates to a fourfold increase over the present two-warhead Chevaline missile.

[89] See note 86.

[90] Freedman, L., 'British nuclear targeting', in eds. D. Ball and J. Richelson, *Strategic Nuclear Targeting* (Cornell University Press: Ithaca, N.Y., 1986), pp. 109-26.

[91] As of Aug. 1987, $280 million was expended and $713.31 million committed on Trident through SSPO; authors' estimates. Comptroller and Auditor General, National Audit Office, *Ministry of Defence and Property Services Agency: Control and Management of the Trident Programme* (HMSO: London, 14 July 1987), p. 3.

[92] Authors' estimates.

[93] See note 91, p. 8.

[94] See note 91.

[95] See note 91, p. 10.

[96] The latest such statement was made by British Defence Minister George Younger on 6 Nov. 1987 in Washington, DC, in response to questions by the press. When asked about British Trident production and development costs incurred in the USA, Younger stated that the 'warheads are totally British, in every way, including service, manufacture, etc.'. Transcript of press conference, National Press Club, mimeo.

[97] For FY 1982 these were $27 million; Office of the Inspector General, US Department of Energy, *Audit Report of Revenues Derived from Work Performed for Non-Federal Entities by the Nevada Operations Office Las Vegas, Nevada*, Report no. WR-O-84-4, 15 May, 1984, p. 8.

[98] 'Washington roundup', *Aviation Week & Space Technology*, 6 Apr. 1987, p. 17.

[99] 'France/nuclear weapons', Pentagon review of the press in the DOD press clipping service *Current News*, 23 Oct. 1987.

[100] Isnard, J., 'France considers the cost of neutron warheads', *Jane's Defence Weekly*, 12 Nov. 1987, p. 1163.

[101] *Aviation Week & Space Technology*, 10 Aug. 1987, p. 13.

[102] See note 100.

[103] McCartney, R. J., 'Mitterrand, ending visit to Bonn, seeks to calm German fears about French missiles', *Washington Post*, 23 Oct. 1987, p. A-26.

[104] Berry, J. A., 'French Land-Air Forces in the Central Region', Army War College Study Project, 20 May 1982 (secret, partially declassified under the Freedom of Information Act), pp.

33–34. This is based on instructional material used at the French War College, specifically the War College's 'Lorraine' Plan.

[105] 'Nuclear Notebook', *Bulletin of the Atomic Scientists*, July/Aug. 1987, p. 63.

[106] 'Unit name for nuclear capable Mirage 2000Ns', *Jane's Defence Weekly*, 24 Oct. 1987, p. 929.

[107] See note 106.

[108] As the missile is wingless, sufficient lift is provided by the air intakes. DIA, 'Super Etendard weapon system (U)', DST-1320S-712-85 (secret, partially declassified), 21 Feb. 1985, p. 40.

[109] ASMP specifications: length, 5.380 m; diameter, 0.420 m; weight, 850 kg.

[110] De Young, K., 'France, Britain consider joint nuclear weapon', *Washington Post*, 22 Dec. 1987, p. A-16.

[111] Commissariat à l'Énergie Atomique (CEA), *Rapport Annuel 1986*, p. 19.

[112] The 172nd patrol of the FOST was commenced at the end of February 1986 by the SSBN *Le Terrible*. See SIPRI (note 79), p. 32.

[113] 'France opens new shipyard for next-generation SSBN's', *Jane's Defence Weekly*, 7 Nov. 1987, p. 1024.

[114] See note 113.

[115] See note 113.

[116] See SIPRI (note 79), p. 34.

[117] See SIPRI (note 79), p. 34.

[118] 'Avions Station Relais de Transmissions Exceptionnelles', document received by NRDC from the NASC under the Freedom of Information Act.

[119] See note 118.

[120] This system has its main transmitter at Rosnay; however, other back-up land-based, low frequency (LF) and VLF communication transmitters are known to exist, including two VLF stations and at least eight LF stations. See Arkin, W. M. and Fieldhouse, R. W., *Nuclear Battlefields: Global Links in the Arms Race* (Ballinger: Cambridge, Mass., 1985), pp. 282–8.

[121] 'Les sous-marins sont au bout du fil', *DGA Info*, no. 9, May 1987, p. 17.

[122] Assemblée Nationale (Commission des Finances, de l'Économie Générale et du Plan), *Rapport sur le Project de loi de Finances pour 1988 (Annexe no. 39: Défense Titre V et VI)*, document no. 960, 9 Nov. 1987, p. 19.

[123] In the late 1970s France was purportedly researching a sea-to-sea nuclear missile to be mounted on French surface warships. Work concerned the miniaturization of warheads, so that they could be launched by a missile the size of the MM 38 Exocet or Otomat missiles. The programme was low-scale, and it is unsure if it still exists. See 'Work on the French Navy's ships', *Aviation & Marine International*, Feb. 1979, p. 19; 'Army chief says France ponders making neutron bomb', *New York Times*, 12 June 1978.

[124] Louzeau, B. (Adm.), 'Reflection pour la marine de 2007', *Defense Nationale*, July 1987, pp. 7–21.

[125] US Congress, Joint Economic Committee, *Allocation of Resources in the Soviet Union and China—1985*, Hearing, 99th Cong., 2nd sess., Senate Hearing 99–252, Part 11 (US Government Printing Office: Washington, DC, 1986), p. 123.

[126] See *Interavia Air Letter*, 16 Dec. 1986.

[127] US Defense Intelligence Agency (DIA), 'A Guide to Foreign Tactical Nuclear Weapon Systems Under the Command of Ground Force Commanders', DST-1040S-541-87, 4 Sep. 1987 (secret, partially declassified), p. 79.

[128] In 1986 a Soviet Yankee II class SSBN suffered a fire and explosion in a missile launch tube. The liquid fuel of the SS-N-6 SLBM apparently exploded after an accident, causing several deaths and sinking the submarine. In 1980 a US Titan II ICBM was blown out of its silo because of a fuel accident. A technician dropped a large socket which hit the missile and caused a leak in a fuel tank. Several hours later the leaking fuel vapour exploded. The silo cover, which weighed 740 tons, was blown off by the force of the explosion, and the warhead was found more than 180 m away. One person was killed and several were injured.

[129] DIA (note 127).

[130] See British Broadcasting Company (BBC), *Summary of World Broadcasts* (SWB), Part 3, 30 May 1987, reprinted by the Institute for Defense Studies and Analyses (IDSA, New Delhi) in *News Review on East Asia*, July 1987, p. 670; and SWB, Part 3, 1 Aug. 1987, reprinted in *News Review on East Asia*, Sep. 1987, p. 892.

[131] See, for example, 'Nuclear submarine ends maiden voyage', *Beijing Review*, 12 Jan. 1987, p. 8.

[132] 'Navy now using ultra-longwave information system', Xinhua, 15 July 1987, reprinted by the

Institute for Defense Studies and Analyses (IDSA, New Delhi) in *News Review on East Asia*, Aug. 1987, p. 784.

[133] See Arkin and Fieldhouse (note 120), pp. 290–1.

[134] See *Renmin Ribao*, 28 May 1987, reprinted in US Department of Commerce, *Foreign Broadcast Information Service—China* (FBIS-China), 3 June 1987.

[135] O'Lone, R. G., 'China reshaping industry to meet extensive needs', *Aviation Week & Space Technology*, 16 No. 1987, pp. 16–21.

[136] For an extensive discussion of the problem of nuclear threshold countries, see also Goldblat, J. (ed.), SIPRI, *Non-Proliferation: The Why and the Wherefore* (Taylor & Francis: London, 1985); and Goldblat, J. and Lomas, P., 'The threshold countries and the future of the nuclear non-proliferation regime', in ed. J. Simpson, *Nuclear Non-Proliferation: An Agenda for the 1990s* (Cambridge University Press: Cambridge, 1987).

[137] Cohen, A. and Frankel, B., 'Israel's nuclear ambiguity', *Bulletin of the Atomic Scientists*, Mar. 1987.

[138] *International Defence Review*, 21 July 1987, p. 857.

[139] IAEA Press Release PR 87/28.

[140] *New York Times* and *Los Angeles Times*, 15 July 1987.

[141] Testimony of Amb. Richard T. Kennedy, *Hearings on US Aid to Pakistan before the Subcommittee on Asian and Pacific Affairs of the Committee on Foreign Affairs*, US House of Representatives, 22 Oct. 1987; *International Herald Tribune*, 7–8 Nov. 1987.

[142] *Nuclear Weapons and South Asian Security*, Report of the Carnegie Task Force on Non-Proliferation and South Asian Security, Carnegie Endowment for International Peace, Washington, DC, 1988.

[143] *Financial Times*, 11 Dec. 1987.

[144] See note 142.

[145] Reported in US Department of Defense, *Current News*, 7 May 1987, p. 5.

[146] UN document A/C.1/42/4.

[147] *New York Times*, 25 Sep. 1987.

[148] IAEA document GC (XXXI)/819 with Attachment.

[149] IAEA Press Releases PR 87/17 and PR 87/29.

[150] *Financial Times*, 7 Oct. 1987.

[151] *Washington Post*, 10 Sep. 1987.

[152] *International Herald Tribune*, 7 Sep. 1987.

[153] *Frankfurter Rundschau*, 11 Sep. 1987.

[154] *International Herald Tribune*, 8 Dec. 1987.

[155] *Le Monde*, 15 Oct. 1987.

[156] See note 155.

[157] *Folha de São Paulo*, 8 and 9 Aug. 1986.

[158] See note 150.

3. Nuclear explosions

RAGNHILD FERM

I. Introduction

The USSR resumed its nuclear explosion programme in 1987, and the weekly average of nuclear explosions thus returned to the same level as during the decade before the Soviet moratorium was introduced: the five nuclear weapon states again conducted an average of almost one explosion per week. The problem of determining the actual yield of the tests, which has been an obstacle to verification, seems now to be on the way to solution as US and Soviet experts have been able to visit each other's test sites to prepare for calibration experiments. The Soviet Union, which had previously kept secret virtually all information about its nuclear testing, showed greater openness after the moratorium and has announced all its nuclear explosions since it resumed testing. During 1987 a re-examination of seismic data revealed dozens of unannounced low-yield US nuclear tests that were conducted from 1963 to 1986. This indication that many tests have gone unnoticed may also point to a need to improve the means of detecting and identifying other nuclear explosions, including possibly an international seismic network.

The total number of nuclear explosions conducted by all nuclear weapon countries in 1987 was 47. This is a higher figure than for the two previous years, owing to the resumption of testing by the Soviet Union. The USSR carried out 23 of these explosions, the USA 14, France 8, and China and the UK 1 explosion each.

II. Information on nuclear explosions

US and Soviet tests

When the United States exploded its first nuclear test of 1987, on 3 February, the Soviet Union stated that it no longer considered itself bound by its 1985 unilateral moratorium on nuclear explosions. It said, however, that it was still prepared to stop the implementation of its test programme if the USA halted its nuclear testing.[1] The moratorium had then been in effect for 18 months. The USA had refused to join the moratorium, stating that it regarded a ban on nuclear testing as a long-term objective and that such a ban would be possible only if there were no need to rely on nuclear weapons for deterrence.[2] According to preliminary figures the USA conducted at least 23 nuclear tests during the period of the Soviet moratorium.

The US Administration's attitude to the nuclear test issue is controversial; it is opposed by many members of Congress and nuclear experts. Several alternative policy suggestions have been made by various groups, both within and outside the Congress, some in response to Soviet test-ban proposals. These included limitations on the yield and on the frequency of tests as well as proposals for improved verification.

US practice has been not to announce its smallest nuclear tests. Indeed, unannounced nuclear explosions are known to have been conducted at least since 1963. In a report based on an analysis of the past two decades of seismic records and published in January 1988,[3] US scientists showed that over 115 tests had been kept secret. The US Administration has neither confirmed nor denied the findings of the report. The unannounced explosions were all very small, usually of less than 1-kt yield. Such tests have no direct use in developing powerful nuclear warheads for strategic weapons but may be conducted to probe the basic physics of nuclear reactions or to test the effects of nuclear radiation on military equipment.

On 26 February 1987, when the Soviet Union resumed its nuclear explosions, a press conference was held in Moscow. The Soviet Union expressed regret that it had been 'forced' to resume testing and again declared that it was prepared to stop testing in the event the USA ceased its nuclear testing. It was announced that the yield of this first test had been less than 20 kt and that the purpose of the test had been to check the results of research on the physics of a nuclear explosion.[4] The Soviet Union stated its intent to limit the number and yield of future tests and conduct only those deemed necessary for basic research and national security.[5] Subsequent Soviet tests which were recorded during the year were also announced.

Of the Soviet explosions in 1987, six were conducted outside the main weapon test sites and were announced as having been carried out 'in the interest of the national economy'. This is an indication that they were conducted for non-military purposes. So-called peaceful nuclear explosions (PNEs) may serve a variety of purposes such as excavation for the diversion of rivers, creation of underground storage areas for gas, and stimulation of gas and oil production. Deep seismic sounding is another PNE technique whereby seismic waves generated from a nuclear explosion are recorded at stations distant from the source. Analysis of the data enables accurate mapping of geological structures, which is of value for the exploration of mineral resources.[6] The Soviet PNE programme has been carried out for more than 20 years; by 1 January 1988 more than 100 PNEs had been conducted. The Soviet Union has declared, however, that it is prepared also to renounce PNEs if an agreement on a comprehensive test ban is reached.

The United Kingdom

Since 1962 the United Kingdom has conducted its nuclear tests jointly with the United States at the US Nevada Test Site (NTS). Usually one or possibly two such tests are carried out per year; in 1987 one explosion was conducted on 16 July. A number of tests will be required before the nuclear warhead for the British Trident D-5 missile system is completed. Concerning test limits, the UK argues that there are substantial disagreements with the USSR on the verification issue[7] and maintains essentially the same position as the USA as regards a comprehensive test ban.

France

In spite of world-wide criticism and strong protests from neighbouring countries, France continues its nuclear testing activities on the Mururoa atoll in the Tuamotu archipelago in French Polynesia. The first nuclear test at this test centre was carried out in 1966, and by 1 January 1988, 134 tests had been conducted there and on the nearby Fangataufa atoll (41 of them in the atmosphere). On the average five to eight tests are conducted per year; the figure for 1987 was eight. France does not participate in the discussions concerning a test ban as it considers that a test ban would become significant only at the end of a long process resulting in real and effective nuclear disarmament.[8]

The countries of the South Pacific region have long complained about French testing. Australia and New Zealand have repeatedly urged France to stop nuclear testing in the area and are unified with the other South Pacific nations in their opposition to tests, as reflected in the 1985 South Pacific Nuclear-Free Zone Treaty (Treaty of Rarotonga). Under Protocol 3 of the Treaty the nuclear powers undertake not to test any nuclear explosive device within the zone. The Soviet Union and China have signed this Protocol, but the USA, the UK and France have not.

In 1987 Peru sought the support of Chile, Colombia and Ecuador to approach France about the possibility of sending a new scientific mission to Mururoa and the neighbouring areas to determine whether, as France alleges, the nuclear testing there has had no ill effects, and to certify that levels of radioactivity are within tolerable limits. The work was to be carried out in the manner of the New Zealand–Australia–Papua New Guinea mission of 1983.[9]

It has been claimed that the geological condition of the Mururoa atoll is currently very poor as a result of the explosions, and that it is impossible to continue testing there indefinitely. Rumours have circulated that France is planning to move its test facilities to the Kerguelen Islands in the French southern and Antarctic territories. France has denied that such plans exist. However, in March 1988 the Commander-in-Chief of the French Navy in the Pacific revealed that, in order to prevent serious fractures in the rock of Mururoa that might be caused by repeated underground explosions, the most powerful blasts in the test programme will in the future be conducted on Fangataufa. (This atoll has not been used for nuclear explosions since 1975.) He acknowledged that the tests on Mururoa may have contributed to underwater landslides of sections of coral limestone on the flanks of the atoll.[10]

In May 1987 Australia and New Zealand signed an intergovernmental agreement on seismic monitoring of underground nuclear tests. It was explicitly pointed out that the Australian–New Zealand agreement was concluded against the background of continued French nuclear testing on Mururoa.[11] Australia has played an active role in the work of establishing an international seismic monitoring network for world-wide registration of nuclear explosions and operates a seismic station in co-operation with the USA. New Zealand also has expertise in seismic work and maintains a seismological station in Rarotonga, which gives good recordings of the French nuclear tests in the Pacific.

China

China carried out one underground nuclear test during 1987, on 5 June. According to estimates of the Swedish Hagfors Observatory, the blast was rather large—6.8 on the Richter scale—which in this case would indicate a yield of almost 150 kt. This was the first Chinese test since 1984. The last Chinese atmospheric test was conducted in 1980. Although China, like France, is not party to the Partial Test Ban Treaty (PTBT), it discontinued atmospheric testing in 1986. The Chinese Government has also declared that it is prepared to participate in discussion of a test ban within the framework of the Conference on Disarmament.

III. Violations and verification

In his March 1987 report on Soviet non-compliance with arms control agreements,[12] President Reagan again accused the USSR of having violated the US–Soviet 1974 Threshold Test Ban Treaty (TTBT) and the 1976 Peaceful Nuclear Explosions Treaty (PNET) under which the USA and the USSR have undertaken not to carry out nuclear explosions having a yield in excess of 150 kt. The treaties are not yet in force because the USA has not ratified either treaty, but both states have agreed to observe the basic yield restrictions. The verification provisions, including considerable exchanges of information and calibration explosions, are not, however, in effect. According to the Reagan report, the USSR exceeded the yield limit on several occasions. These accusations were rejected by the Soviet Union. Some US scientists assert that because of uncertainties about the geologic formation of Soviet test sites it is impossible to give accurate estimates of the yield of Soviet tests. The Soviet Union, on the other hand, alleged that the USA had conducted numerous nuclear weapon tests (the one on 13 August 1987 was explicitly mentioned) that exceeded the yield limit set by the treaties.[13] The USA argued that the accusations were false. It should be noted that because of difficulties in predicting the size of the explosions the parties have reached an understanding that one or two slight unintended breaches per year would not be considered a violation, but would be the subject of consultations at the request of either party.[14]

The USA has stated that it is prepared to ratify the treaties if verification methods are improved. Indeed, in January 1987 President Reagan asked the US Senate to consent to ratification, provided the Soviet Union accepted improved verification methods. One such method would be on-site yield measurement of nuclear explosions, the CORRTEX (Continuous Reflectometry for Radius versus Time Experiments) method, which involves placing underground cables next to the test hole. Soviet experts were invited to observe the performance of this system at the US NTS, but the Soviet Union repeatedly refused the invitation, arguing that CORRTEX allows for a high probability of error and is virtually useless for measuring small explosions. The USSR views the seismic method of verification—measuring earth tremors generated by explosions—as a more reliable method.[15] Nevertheless, in August 1987 Colonel-General Nikolai Chervov, head of a Soviet delegation visiting the USA, declared that the USSR was prepared to accept any type of verification of a test ban agreement including the CORRTEX method.[16]

Violations of the 1963 PTBT have also been reported. In addition to atmospheric tests, the Treaty forbids nuclear explosions in any environment 'if such explosion causes radioactive debris to be present outside the territorial limits of the State under whose jurisdiction or control such explosion is conducted' (Article I). The USSR claimed that US tests on 3 and 11 February and 18 March caused dissemination of radioactive particles outside the frontiers of the USA.[17] This allegation was denied.

According to the USA, Soviet tests on 26 February and 2 August released radiation beyond the boundaries of the USSR.[18] In the first instance, the accusation was rejected;[19] in the second, the Soviet Union acknowledged that gas had leaked but asserted that no radioactive fall-out had occurred, and that consequently there had been no violation of the PTBT.[20] A week after the 2 August Soviet nuclear test on Novaya Zemlya, Iodine 131 was detected in Scandinavia and, according to the Swedish National Defence Research Institute (FOA), short-lived fission products were detected in ground-level air all over Sweden. Concentration over the extreme north of Sweden was the highest in at least 15 years, except for during the 1986 Chernobyl nuclear reactor accident. After radionuclide analysis, it was stated that the most probable source of the fresh fission products was a quick release from the Soviet nuclear explosion.[21]

It should be noted that in the Russian-language version of the PTBT the term used for 'debris' is *osadki* which means 'deposited on the ground as fall-out'. The Soviet statement may, therefore, be a reflection of a different and less restrictive interpretation of the Treaty.[22]

The Director of the US Arms Control and Disarmament Agency (ACDA) reported that an interesting and unusual proposal was made by the Soviet Union during the April 1987 visit of the US Secretary of State to Moscow.[23] It was suggested that a US nuclear device be exploded at a Soviet test site and a Soviet nuclear device be exploded at the US test site. The exchange of tests would enable both states to develop a data base on the characteristics of the other's test site and to calibrate a seismic monitoring system. The proposal was renewed in August when the Soviet Union offered to accept the CORRTEX system.

In May 1986 representatives of the Natural Resources Defense Council (NRDC), a private US environmental protection organization, signed an agreement with the Soviet Academy of Sciences on mutual monitoring of test sites. Under the agreement US scientists were allowed to install seismic monitoring stations approximately 200 km from the Semipalatinsk test site; Soviet scientists were permitted to place seismic stations around the US NTS.

Owing to the moratorium, no nuclear testing took place in the Soviet Union during the first seven months after the installation of US monitoring devices, but even without Soviet tests the data obtained were judged by US scientists to have significant research value. The equipment was capable of detecting earthquakes and underground nuclear tests outside the Soviet Union, as well as chemical explosions, and scientists were able to study how the geological features of the area transmit shock waves. Before Soviet testing was resumed, the NRDC scientists were asked to turn off the equipment during the tests. However, a new agreement was signed in June 1987,[24] extending the joint monitoring project through August 1988. Under this agreement, three seismometers were to be relocated to distances greater than 1000 km from the test site, and a few chemical explosions of known yield were to be conducted to permit measurement of signal transmission. This would enable seismologists to estimate more accurately the size of past and current Soviet tests.

IV. Talks and negotiations

During 1986 and 1987 representatives of the USA and the USSR met on several occasions for expert-level discussions 'on the entire scope of issues relating to nuclear testing'.[25] No detailed reports were issued from these meetings. According to the USA the primary objective of the discussions was to achieve agreement on effective verification regimes for the TTBT and the PNET, while the USSR stressed the problems associated with the cessation of all nuclear testing.

In the announcement, on 17 September 1987, of the forthcoming INF Treaty it was also made known that US–Soviet full-scale, stage-by-stage negotiations regarding nuclear testing would start.[26] Both states declared that they would, as a first step towards ratification, agree on verification measures for the TTBT and the PNET and later proceed to the negotiation of further limitations on nuclear testing, leading to a complete cessation of nuclear testing as part of an effective disarmament process. The negotiations opened on 9 November in Geneva. In a joint statement on 9 December US Secretary of State Shultz and Soviet Foreign Minister Shevardnadze announced that a US–Soviet joint verification experiment (JVE) was being designed to take place at the Semipalatinsk and Nevada test sites. During the experiment each side was to be given the opportunity to measure yields using teleseismic methods and hydrodynamic yield measurements. The results of the experiments were to provide the basis for the designing and conducting of JVEs to be held at the US and Soviet test sites. The experiment would enable the sides to agree on verification of compliance with the TTBT and the PNET.[27] In accordance with this, US experts visited the Semipalatinsk test site in the beginning of January 1988 and a corresponding visit was made by Soviet representatives to the US NTS at the end of the month.[28]

Notes and references

[1] Conference on Disarmament document CD/PV.386, 5 Feb. 1987.
[2] US Information Service, EUR–205 (US Embassy, Stockholm), 13 Oct. 1987.
[3] Norris, R. S., Cochran, T. B. and Arkin, W. M., 'Known US nuclear tests July 1945 to

31 December 1987', *Nuclear Weapons Databook*, Working Paper no. 86–2 (Rev. 2A) (Natural Resources Defense Council: Washington, DC, Jan. 1988).

[4] *Krasnaya Zvezda*, 27 Feb. 1987.

[5] *Pravda*, 27 Feb. 1987.

[6] Borg, I., 'Nuclear explosions for peaceful purposes', eds J. Goldblat and D. Cox, SIPRI, *Nuclear Weapon Tests: Prohibition or Limitation?* (Oxford University Press: Oxford, 1988), p. 69.

[7] *Guardian*, 6 Feb. 1987.

[8] Conference on Disarmament document CD/PV.390, 19 Feb. 1987.

[9] See SIPRI, *World Armaments and Disarmament: SIPRI Yearbook 1985* (Taylor & Francis: London, 1985). The Peruvian proposal was presented in Conference on Disarmament document CD/PV.428, 6 Aug. 1987.

[10] *International Herald Tribune*, 28 Mar. 1988.

[11] Press release of 30 May 1987 by R. J. L. Hawke, Prime Minister of Australia (Australian Embassy, Stockholm).

[12] *Department of State Bulletin*, June 1987.

[13] *Pravda*, 22 Aug. 1987.

[14] *Arms Control and Disarmament Agreements: Texts and Histories of Negotiations*, 1982 edn, US Arms Control and Disarmament Agency (US Government Printing Office: Washington, DC, 1985), p. 166.

[15] Conference on Disarmament document CD/PV.408, 23 Apr. 1987.

[16] *Atlantic News*, no. 1945, 4 Sep. 1987.

[17] *Soviet News*, 13 May 1987.

[18] *Department of State Bulletin*, May 1987 and Oct. 1987.

[19] APN, *Military Bulletin* (Moscow), Mar. 1987.

[20] *Pravda*, 16 Aug. 1987.

[21] Bjurman, B. *et al.*, *The Detection in Sweden of Short-Lived Fission Products Probably Vented from the Underground Nuclear Test at Novaya Zemlya on 2 August 1987*, FOA Rapport C 20673–9.2 FOA, Stockholm, Sep. 1987.

[22] Goldblat, J., 'The nuclear explosion limitation treaties' (see note 6), p. 122.

[23] *Washington Post*, 18 Apr. 1987.

[24] 'USA–USSR Nuclear Test Ban Verification Project: Agreement', Text of an agreement between the National Resources Defense Council and the Soviet Academy of Sciences signed on 25 June 1987, mimeograph copy.

[25] US Information Service, EUR–406 (US Embassy, Stockholm), 31 July 1986.

[26] 'US–Soviet Joint Statement: Nuclear Testing', 17 Sep. 1987 (Swedish Embassy, Washington, DC).

[27] Federal News Service 202–347–1400, 1987.

[28] US Information Service, EUR–203 (US Embassy, Stockholm), 5 Jan. 1988.

Appendix 3A. Nuclear explosions, 1945–87

Table 3A.1. Observed nuclear explosions in 1987

Date	Origin time (GMT)	Latitude (deg)	Longitude (deg)	Region	Body wave magnitude[a]
USA					
3 Feb.	152000.0	37.181 N	116.048 W	Nevada	
11 Feb.	164500.0	37.011 N	116.045 W	Nevada	
18 Mar.	182800.0	37.210 N	116.209 W	Nevada	4.5
18 Apr.	134000.6	37.248 N	116.509 W	Nevada	5.5
22 Apr.	220000.0	36.983 N	116.005 W	Nevada	
30 Apr.	133000.0	37.233 N	116.423 W	Nevada	5.7
18 June	152000.0	37.194 N	116.035 W	Nevada	
20 June	160000.1	37.220 N	116.178 W	Nevada	
30 June	160500.1	36.999 N	116.043 W	Nevada	
13 Aug.	140000.0	37.061 N	116.045 W	Nevada	6.1
24 Sep.	150000.0	37.228 N	116.375 W	Nevada	5.9
23 Oct.	160000.0	37.142 N	116.079 W	Nevada	5.2
1 Dec.	163000.0	37. N	116. W	Nevada	
2 Dec.	163000.0	37.235 N	116.163 W	Nevada	
USSR					
26 Feb.	045822.0	49.839 N	78.122 E	Semipalatinsk	5.4
12 Mar.	015717.2	49.939 N	78.823 E	Semipalatinsk	6.6
3 Apr.	011708.1	49.902 N	78.808 E	Semipalatinsk	7.3
17 Apr.	010304.7	49.851 N	78.690 E	Semipalatinsk	7.2
19 Apr.	040001.8	60.781 N	56.220 E	Ural Mountains[b]	4.5
19 Apr.	040501.2	60.674 N	56.295 E	Ural Mountains[b]	4.5
6 May	040205.6	49.830 N	78.125 E	Semipalatinsk	6.1
6 June	023706.9	49.865 N	78.143 E	Semipalatinsk	
20 June	005304.8	49.901 N	78.726 E	Semipalatinsk	
6 July	235956.6	61.490 N	112.784 E	Siberia[b]	5.6
17 July	011707.0	49.779 N	78.128 E	Semipalatinsk	6.4
24 July	015956.7	61.466 N	112.721 E	Siberia[b]	5.3
2 Aug.	005806.7	49.841 N	78.886 E	Semipalatinsk	
2 Aug.	015959.6	73.314 N	54.709 E	Novaya Zemlya	
12 Aug.	012956.8	61.426 N	112.708 E	Siberia[b]	5.5
16 Sep.	073001.0	49. N	78. E	Semipalatinsk	5.0
18 Sep.	023157.0	49. N	78. E	Semipalatinsk	3.9
3 Oct.	151457.5	47.633 N	56.218 E	W. Kazakhstan[b]	5.0
16 Oct.	060600.0	49. N	78. E	Semipalatinsk	4.4
15 Nov.	033118.0	49.879 N	78.836 E	Semipalatinsk	7.1
13 Dec.	032104.7	49.969 N	78.880 E	Semipalatinsk	7.1
20 Dec.	025512.0	50.1 N	77.5 E	Semipalatinsk	5.2
27 Dec.	030508.0	49.9 N	78.5 E	Semipalatinsk	7.4
UK					
16 July	190000.0	37.104 N	116.023 W	Nevada	5.0
France					
5 May	165757.7	21.90 S	139.10 W	Mururoa	4.8
20 May	170458.2	21.893 S	138.964 W	Mururoa	5.4
6 June	180000.0	22. S	139. W	Mururoa	4.5
21 June	175458.4	21.984 S	138.844 W	Mururoa	5.2
23 Oct.	164958.6	21.870 S	139.009 W	Mururoa	5.6
5 Nov.	172959.0	21.786 S	139.003 W	Mururoa	5.2
19 Nov.	163058.5	21.878 S	139.037 W	Mururoa	5.7
29 Nov.	175900.0	22. S	139. W	Mururoa	4.6

Table 3A.1 *cont.*

Date	Origin time (GMT)	Latitude (deg)	Longitude (deg)	Region	Body wave magnitude[a]
China					
5 June	045958.4	41.580 N	88.754 E	Lop Nor	6.8

[a] Body wave magnitude (m_b) indicates the size of the event. m_b data for the US, Soviet and British tests were provided by the Hagfors Observatory of the Swedish National Defence Research Institute (FOA); data for the French tests were provided by the New Zealand Seismological Observatory.

[b] Announced as having been carried out 'in the interest of the national economy', which may be taken to mean that it is conducted for non-military purposes.

Table 3A.2. Estimated number of nuclear explosions 16 July 1945–5 August 1963 (the signing of the Partial Test Ban Treaty)

a = atmospheric
u = underground

	USA		USSR		UK		France		
Year	a	u	a	u	a	u	a	u	Total
1945	3	0							3
1946	2[a]	0							2
1947	0	0							0
1948	3	0							3
1949	0	0	1	0					1
1950	0	0	0	0					0
1951	15	1	2	0					18
1952	10	0	0	0	1	0			11
1953	11	0	4	0	2	0			17
1954	6	0	7	0	0	0			13
1955	17[a]	1	5[a]	0	0	0			23
1956	18	0	9	0	6	0			33
1957	27	5	15[a]	0	7	0			54
1958	62[b]	15	29	0	5	0			111
1949–58, exact years unknown			18						18
1959	0	0	0	0	0	0			0
1960	0	0	0	0	0	0	3	0	3
1961	0	10	50[a]	1	0	0	1	1	63
1962	39[a]	57	43	1	0	2	0	1	143
1 Jan.– 5 Aug. 1963	4	25	0	0	0	0	0	2	31
Total	**217**	**114**	**183**[c]	**2**	**21**	**2**	**4**	**4**	**547**

[a] One of these tests was carried out under water.

[b] Two of these tests were carried out under water.

[c] The total figure for Soviet atmospheric tests includes the 18 additional tests conducted in the period 1949–58, for which exact years are not available.

WEAPONS AND TECHNOLOGY

Table 3A.3. Estimated number of nuclear explosions 6 August 1963–31 December 1987

a = atmospheric
u = underground

Year	USA[a] a	USA[a] u	USSR a	USSR u	UK[a] a	UK[a] u	France a	France u	China a	China u	India a	India u	Total
6 Aug.–31 Dec. 1963	0	15	0	0	0	0	0	1					16
1964	0	40	0	6	0	1	0	3	1	0			51
1965	0	37	0	9	0	1	0	4	1	0			52
1966	0	43	0	15	0	0	5	1	3	0			67
1967	0	34	0	17	0	0	3	0	2	0			56
1968	0	45[b]	0	13	0	0	5	0	1	0			64
1969	0	38	0	16	0	0	0	0	1	1			56
1970	0	35	0	17	0	0	8	0	1	0			61
1971	0	17	0	19	0	0	5	0	1	0			42
1972	0	18	0	22	0	0	3	0	2	0			45
1973	0	16[c]	0	14	0	0	5	0	1	0			36
1974	0	14	0	19	0	1	7	0	1	0	0	1	43
1975	0	20	0	15	0	0	0	2	0	1	0	0	38
1976	0	18	0	17	0	1	0	4	3	1	0	0	44
1977	0	19	0	18	0	0	0	6	1	0	0	0	44
1978	0	17	0	28	0	2	0	7	2	1	0	0	57
1979	0	15	0	29	0	1	0	9	0	0	0	0	54
1980	0	14	0	21	0	3	0	11	1	0	0	0	50
1981	0	16	0	22	0	1	0	10	0	0	0	0	49
1982	0	18	0	31	0	1	0	5	0	0	0	0	55
1983	0	17	0	27	0	1	0	7	0	1	0	0	53
1984	0	17	0	28	0	2	0	8	0	2	0	0	57
1985	0	17	0	9	0	1	0	8	0	0	0	0	35
1986	0	14	0	0	0	1	0	8	0	0			23
1987	0	14	0	23	0	1	0	8	0	1	0	0	47
Total	**0**	**568[d]**	**0**	**435**	**0**	**18**	**41**	**102**	**22**	**8**	**0**	**1**	**1195**

[a] See note a below.
[b] Five devices used simultaneously in the same test are counted here as one explosion.
[c] Three devices used simultaneously in the same test are counted here as one explosion.
[d] The increase in this figure as compared with the figure in the *SIPRI Yearbook 1987* is the result of new information about unannounced US nuclear tests published by the Natural Resources Defense Council (NRDC) in January 1988.

Table 3A.4. Estimated number of nuclear explosions 16 July 1945–31 December 1987

USA[a]	USSR	UK[a]	France	China	India	Total
899	620	41	151	30	1	**1742**

[a] All British tests from 1962 have been conducted jointly with the United States at the Nevada Test Site. Therefore, the number of US tests is actually higher than indicated here.

Sources for tables 3A.1–3A.4

Swedish National Defence Research Institute (FOA), various estimates; Norris, R. S., Cochran, T. B. and Arkin, W. M., 'Known US nuclear tests July 1945 to 31 December 1987', *Nuclear Weapons Databook*, Working Paper no. 86-2 (Rev. 2A) (Natural Resources Defense Council: Washington, DC, Jan. 1988); Department of Scientific and Industrial Research (DSIR), Geophysics Division, New Zealand; and various estimates.

4. Military use of outer space

BHUPENDRA JASANI*

I. Introduction

The military use of outer space is devoted mainly to applications of artificial earth satellites to increase the efficiency of the fighting forces on earth. In 1987, 85 satellites or some 75 per cent of all the satellites orbited during the year were launched for various military purposes. A second use of the space environment is in preparation for actual warfare in space; space weapons to destroy either earth-orbiting spacecraft or missiles and nuclear warheads in their flight trajectories are being investigated. Such weapons could be earth-, air- or space-based. While only the United States and the Soviet Union have developed anti-satellite (ASAT) weapons, they and the People's Republic of China, France and the United Kingdom have used military satellites extensively.

In about 1975, the USA decommissioned its ground-based ASAT Thor missiles, which were mounted with nuclear warheads. In contrast, between 1968 and 1982, the Soviet Union carried out 20 tests of its ASAT weapon, which used a non-nuclear method of satellite destruction. However, since mid-1982, the USSR has refrained from further testing of its ASAT system against targets in space. In spite of this unilateral moratorium on ASAT tests, there is some evidence that the USSR is developing a new generation of ground-based laser ASAT weapons.[1]

In this chapter a brief overview is made of some of the military satellites launched or used in 1987. Some of these satellites—for instance, reconnaissance, early-warning, communication and navigation satellites—are expected to be useful in the new strategic defence (SD) systems of both the superpowers. This chapter describes briefly the current progress in research and development (R&D) in the SD systems being developed under the Strategic Defense Initiative (SDI). Similar information about the USSR is not available, although it is known to be conducting an SDI-type research programme.[2]

II. Military satellites

The first satellite of 1987 was a Soviet weather satellite, Meteor 2–15, launched on 5 January. Thus the Soviet Union held its record of over a decade of launching the 'first military satellite of the year'. In the following sections, other records set by the USSR are also reported. But it is worth noting that three Soviet satellites malfunctioned in space and that there were four unsuccessful Soviet launches involving a further six satellites. In contrast, 1987 saw the end of a long spell of unsuccessful US and French launches. The US space shuttle—grounded in 1986—has, however, continued to have problems.

SIPRI Yearbook 1988: World Armaments and Disarmament

Military-oriented satellites launched in 1987 by the USA, the USSR and China are listed in tables 4A.1–4A.9 in appendix 4A.

US military satellites

Because of problems with a seal on one of its boosters, the space shuttle launch planned for June 1988 was postponed until August. The current space shuttle plans are to launch only three of the five planned flights in 1988 and seven flights in 1989. Because of these launch delays the development of expendable launch vehicles (ELVs) has obtained momentum. As part of the recovery plan, by 1989 or 1990, the USA envisages an annual launch rate of 4–8 Titans, eight or nine Delta 23s and 8–10 space shuttles. All will be carrying military and commercial payloads. Of 16 space shuttle missions planned, four will belong to the Department of Defense (DOD).[3]

Reconnaissance satellites

On 26 October 1987 the USA launched its first KH-11 photoreconnaissance satellite since 1984. At this time, it had only an ageing KH-11 in orbit, launched on 17 April 1984. The lifetime of the electronic systems of the old KH-11 has been prolonged by recording the images of only the most important targets. This has enabled the USA to maintain its ability to verify arms control treaties and obtain essential targeting information, despite launch failures.

Two attempts were made to launch photographic surveillance satellites using Titan-34D rockets. One was on 28 August 1985, when a KH-11 was destroyed; and in another attempt, on 18 April 1986, a KH-9 (Big Bird) spacecraft was lost in a launch accident. The latter was the last in the KH-9 series of US spacecraft.[4]

The new KH-11 may be placed in an orbit with its plane 47° away from that of the old KH-11. This has been the US practice so as to increase the frequency of observation and also to increase the coverage.[5] It has been reported that the positions of the two KH-11s in their orbits are such that the new KH-11 can observe an area of the earth's surface in the afternoon while the old KH-11 surveys the same area in the morning.[6] The data from such satellites are relayed to the ground stations via communications satellites so that the information is available within one or two hours. There was an emergency plan to launch either an electronic-reconnaissance or an early-warning satellite instead of another KH-11, should the existing, ageing KH-11 cease to function.[7]

The DOD is beginning a new classified reconnaissance satellite programme called Vortex, which will use an imaging radar.[8] This will be the highest-resolution radar used on a satellite so far, and will improve reconnaissance over cloud-covered areas. The main purpose of the satellite will be to monitor, detect and track Warsaw Treaty Organization (WTO) armour and possibly military manoeuvres. The spacecraft could also be used as an ocean-surveillance satellite to provide intelligence on Soviet fleet movement. Under another programme called White Cloud the USA launched a classified payload on 15 May 1987, using an Atlas-H rocket. These are US Navy Ocean Surveillance Spacecraft (see table 4A.3).[9]

Communications satellites

After nearly 18 months, the first successful US launch, on 12 February 1987, was that of a Titan-3B rocket carrying a communications satellite. The satellite weight—just over 3000 kg—indicates that this was probably a Satellite Data System (SDS) satellite.[10] In the past, Titan-3B launchers have been used to orbit SDS relay spacecraft as well as some photoreconnaissance satellites. No SDS had been launched since February 1985. These satellites are used to relay data to ground facilities from such spacecraft as the KH-11 satellite.

On 25 March 1987, an attempt to launch an $83-million Fleet Satellite Communications (FltSatCom) satellite failed. The satellite would have been used by the US Navy, Air Force and other DOD agencies to link armed forces in the field with Strategic Air Command and National Command authorities. The Atlas-Centaur rocket was damaged in a thunderstorm 51 seconds after launch.[11] The rocket may have been struck by lightning since soon after launch the telemetry from the vehicle indicated problems and ceased being transmitted. The range safety officer then sent a destruct command. This was the second Atlas-Centaur failure in the last three launch attempts; FltSatCom 5 was damaged on 6 August 1981 because the rocket failed. However, FltSatCom 7 was successfully orbited on 4 December 1986. There were five FltSatCom satellites in orbit in early 1988, and all were functioning. The first of these was launched in February 1978. It is useful to note that of the total of 60 operational Atlas-Centaur missions only six have resulted in failures, which is not a high failure rate.

Meteorological satellites

The US Air Force launched a Defense Meteorological Satellite Program (DMSP) spacecraft on 19 June 1987. The satellite, the third in the Block 5D-2 series, will replace the first Block 5D-2 satellite launched in October 1982. Such satellites are usually kept in the polar orbit. The latest one will join an earlier one launched in November 1983.[12] On the civilian side, the USA launched a GOES-H weather satellite on 26 February 1987 using a Delta rocket. The satellite will be operational together with a four-year-old GOES-6 spacecraft. GOES-H also carries a Search and Rescue Satellite, SARSAT/COSPAS payload.

Navigation satellites

While no US navigation satellite was launched in 1987, the Navstar 15 satellite was damaged in the laboratory during its test phase. The fault occurred in the electrical system. There were three other Navstar satellites in the same area but they escaped damage. After the Challenger accident in 1986 construction of these three Navstar satellites was halted. But with the damage of Navstar 15 construction of one of the three satellites has been resumed.

On 22 September 1987, a Scout booster orbited a spacecraft as part of the Navy Navigation Satellite System, which includes the improved NOVA-1 and NOVA-3 satellites. The accuracy of position determination is reported to be about 185 metres.[13]

Early-warning satellites

An early-warning satellite, launched on 28 November using a Titan-34D launcher, was the first such spacecraft orbited since 1982. The satellite, developed under a programme called the Defense Support Program (DSP), will warn the US authorities of the launch of a missile or a spacecraft by observing the exhaust plume of the missile or spacecraft launcher.

This spacecraft was scheduled to be launched by the space shuttle in 1986. The next generation of early-warning satellites will orbit telescopes capable of withstanding laser jamming or damage. Because of the weight of the telescope, the satellites must be launched by the space shuttle.

The USA keeps three or more early-warning satellites in the geostationary orbit so as to get full coverage of the earth's surface for observation of land- and sea-launched ballistic missiles and space launches. The data from such satellites are transmitted to the earth-receiving stations via satellite. The first US early-warning satellite was launched in May 1971.

Soviet military satellites

The USSR launched 72 satellites in 1987, somewhat less than the usual annual figure. It suffered eight setbacks in its space programme, including four launch failures. Cosmos 1866 broke up in outer space; Cosmos 1813 had to be destroyed in orbit; Cosmos 1817, intended for geosynchronous orbit, had to be returned to earth after the fourth stage of its Proton launcher malfunctioned; Cosmos 1821 intended as a replacement for Cosmos 1725, a military navigation satellite, failed soon after it reached orbit; Cosmos 1825 had to be reactivated; Cosmos 1838, 1839 and 1840, the triple navigation satellites launched by a Proton launcher, did not achieve their required orbits because the apogee motor of the Proton failed; the large payload carried by the Energiya failed to achieve its orbit; Cosmos 1860 ceased to operate on the 39th day; and on 30 July cosmonaut Aleksander Laveikin, one of two on board the Mir space station, returned to earth for health reasons.[14]

1987 marked the beginning of a new Soviet expendable space launch vehicle. On 15 May 1987, the USSR, for the first time, flight tested its heavy-lift rocket called the Energiya.[15] The core of the rocket carried four engines which use O_2/H_2 fuel, making the USSR the fifth to use such a fuel, the others being the USA (in 1962), the European Space Agency (in 1979), China (in 1984) and Japan (in 1986).

It was reported that Energiya's first and second stage (the core vehicle) functioned as planned, but an attempt to orbit a full mock-up of a payload was unsuccessful. The engines on the payload did not function.[16] The payload was a mock-up of a heavy satellite, indicating that the satellite would be of a complex nature. Apparently, the re-entry of the payload was observed by a US early-warning satellite.[17]

The launcher is capable of orbiting payloads of 100 000 kg in low earth orbits. Thus, it will be capable of launching the Soviet re-usable space vehicle, which is similar to the US space shuttle. It is also known that the Soviet Union has been testing a small manned spacecraft.[18] Such a spaceplane could, for example, be used for quick-reaction, real-time reconnaissance, transportation of cosmonauts and satellite repairs and maintenance.

Reconnaissance satellites

On 9 January 1987, the Soviet Union launched Cosmos 1811, its first photoreconnaissance satellite of 1987. A total of 32 satellites were launched on photographic missions. The last such satellite launched in 1986 set a new Soviet record for such satellites by remaining in space for 259 days. Another interesting launch was that of Cosmos 1813 on 15 January 1987. The satellite carried a low-resolution photoreconnaissance payload into an orbit of 73°, 200 × 364 km with a period of 92.31 min. However, when after 14 days (its normal lifetime) the satellite was to return to earth, it failed to respond to commands from the ground. The satellite was destroyed in orbit on 29 January in order to prevent its film payload from falling into the wrong hands.[19] The explosion was powerful enough to send some of the debris into higher orbits at altitudes of some 800 km. Unfortunately, at such altitudes debris tends to remain in orbit for several tens, if not hundreds, of years.

A second such failure was observed on 26 July when Cosmos 1866, a possible fourth-generation photoreconnaissance satellite, failed to re-enter the earth's atmosphere. Instead, it broke up into several pieces, much before its normal 56-day lifetime.[20] The satellite was launched on 9 July 1987. Some five pieces of debris, including the main body of the satellite, are still in orbit and being tracked. However, there may be up to 40 more pieces which cannot be tracked. This spacecraft may also have been destroyed deliberately.[21] This was the eighth setback suffered by the Soviet Union in 1987.

Ocean-surveillance satellites

Two types of ocean-surveillance satellite have been launched by the Soviet Union; one was an Electronic Ocean Reconnaissance Satellite (EORSAT) and the other a Radar Ocean Reconnaissance Satellite (RORSAT). Both these are used to monitor the movement of surface naval ships. The EORSATs track ships and characterize them by listening to their radio transmissions, while the RORSATs carry a radar sensor to detect and track surface ships. The radars are powered by small nuclear reactors. Cosmos 1834, launched on 8 April 1987, was the first EORSAT of the year. The satellite is performing its mission in conjunction with Cosmos 1735, launched on 27 February 1986.[22] With these two spacecraft, ship movements can be observed every three days and the frequency would have been increased once the two spacecraft combined their reconnaissance with Cosmos 1775, which was launched in 1986.

Cosmos 1960 was the first RORSAT of 1987. After operating for about three months, such satellites are transferred to higher orbits where the radioactivity generated in the nuclear reactor is allowed to decay to a safe level.

It is worth noting that the Soviet Union is planning to place an ocean-monitoring satellite permanently in orbit, for the first time.[23] This indicates the importance it accords to US naval movements. Such satellites would carry a side-looking radar to monitor the oceans for civil and military purposes. The programme for such spacecraft began in 1976 with the launch of Cosmos 1076. An operational side-looking radar was first installed on Cosmos 1500.

Navigation satellites

On 24 April, the Soviet Union launched three navigation satellites in its Glonass series using its commercial Proton launcher. However, the launcher failed to place the satellites in their correct orbits. The spacecraft were Cosmos 1838, 1839 and 1840.[24] This was the second time the Proton launcher failed; the first failure was on 30 January. In both cases, the fourth stage malfunctioned. While Glonass satellites are for civil use, the USSR orbits navigation satellites for military purposes also. These are listed in table 4A.7 in appendix 4A.

Military satellites of other nations

An interesting trend is the development of military reconnaissance capabilities based on civilian technology. This emerges from the French decision to go ahead with its military reconnaissance satellite based on the civilian satellite SPOT. The French reconnaissance programme, which is to be partially funded by Italy, emphasizes a desire to become independent of US reconnaissance information. Apart from the countries mentioned above, the only other nation with its own military space programme is China. The UK seems to have dropped its Zircon satellite programme. While Canada does not have a military satellite programme it has plans to develop an arms control satellite.

China

During 1987, China launched two satellites. China-20, launched on 5 August, also carried a French experimental package. The satellite was recovered five days later.[25] China-21 was launched on 9 September. The satellite was in a higher orbit than usual, probably indicating improved sensors. It is reported that this may have been a new type of satellite since its lifetime was eight days rather than the usual five days.[26] Its ground tracks were closer compared with those of the other satellites, and the telemetry transmission was also different.

China is now also offering its recoverable satellite services. Two kinds of platform are offered, on which either a dedicated payload or a piggyback payload could be carried, as was the case with China-21.[27] The satellite could carry 150 kg for recoverable experiments and 300 kg for non-recoverable ones.

NATO

The NATO 3C communications satellite which was launched by the USA in November 1978 was reactivated. The satellite was placed in a storage orbit. It replaced NATO 3B, which is still operating but at a reduced capacity.[28] Another satellite, NATO 3D, was launched by the USA in November 1984 and is stored in an orbit for future use.

France

The 1987 French defence budget includes an authorization of 1545 million francs (0.91 per cent of the total) and an appropriation of 473 million francs (0.28 per cent of the total) for its military space programme.[29] This is a considerably smaller proportion of the budget than the superpowers assign to space. The French space programme is devoted mainly to the development of reconnaissance and communications satellites.

Reconnaissance satellites. While France has not yet launched a photoreconnaissance spacecraft, it has begun work on the Helios reconnaissance satellite. France receives most of its space-based intelligence information from the USA. With the development of Helios—with a resolution of 1 m from 800 km altitude—France will become independent of the USA regarding targeting information for nuclear weapons.

While the FRG has declined to participate, Italy and Spain have expressed interest in participating in the Helios programme. In fact, Italy has agreed to assume a 14 per cent share in the programme. This will be mainly for the ground segment, consisting of receiving and processing systems.[30] Four Helios satellites are to be built and launched over a period of 10 years using the Ariane 5 rocket. The first satellite will be orbited in about 1992. Helios will weigh 2000 kg and will use the basic civil SPOT satellite platform.[31]

French Defence Minister André Giraud recently announced that the Helios will carry on board electronic intelligence (ELINT) equipment as well as optical sensors. The satellite is expected to have similar ELINT capability to that of the now-abandoned British Zircon satellite.[32]

As a next project, France has initiated a study of a synthetic aperture radar (SAR) satellite for both military and civil uses.[33] The satellite is called RadarSAR and may deploy a SAR with peak power of either 7.5 kW or 30 kW, depending on the resolution required.

Communications satellites. France has been interested in military communications spacecraft for a long time. It has been developing satellite payloads under a programme called Syracuse. However, the military satellite Syracuse 2 has been considerably modified, and it has recently been decided to orbit the Syracuse 2 payload on the Telecom 2 civil satellite. This is not a new development, since a military payload is already orbited on board Telecom 1.[34] This policy has been dictated by financial considerations.

III. Space weapons

The discussion here on strategic defences is confined almost entirely to the US SDI programme since the Soviet Union has yet to release information on its SD programme. However, it might be noted that General Secretary Mikhail Gorbachev in an interview on US television said '. . . it's really hard to say what the Soviet Union is not doing. Particularly the Soviet Union is doing all that the United States is doing. I guess we are engaged in research, basic research, which relates to these aspects which are covered by SDI in the United States. But we will not build SDI, we will not deploy SDI, and we call on the United States to act similarly'.[35]

When considering space weapons, it is useful to bear in mind the similarities between technologies used in strategic defence, air defence, anti-tactical ballistic missile (ATBM) defence and ASAT systems. Because of this technology overlap, work in any one of the above areas can boost developments in the other areas. For example, the SDI Organization (SDIO) has stated that 'some of the elements of the terminal tier of a defense system against longer-range missiles could be adapted to antitactical ballistic missile (ATBM) systems'.[36] These technologies could also be applied to defensive systems against conventional weapons.

Sensors are important elements of air and ATBM defence systems, as is the case in SD, to detect an air and missile attack. In fact, sensors can be developed that are applicable to all three types of defence system and to ASAT weapons. Furthermore, all would have systems to process and communicate information from the sensors to battle management and weapon systems. Thus work on communication systems and computers could also be applied in all the above-mentioned areas. There is, however, a difference in the time scales. In the case of SD, space weapons would need to perform most of their tasks within minutes, while those with an air defence mission could do so over a period of some hours. Thus it would be easier to develop command and control systems and data management for air defence.

Sensor technology

While the Soviet Union has an extensive air defence programme, the US Air Defense Initiative (ADI) was first conceptualized in 1983 in order to counter ground- and submarine-launched cruise missiles and bombers.[37] Thus, the initial research was focused on developing ocean, space and air surveillance systems such as the sensor being developed under the Vortex programme mentioned above. It is estimated that a satellite carrying such a radar could cost $1 billion and, depending on the extent of coverage required, 6–12 satellites may have to be deployed.

Another sensor is the so-called infra-red focal plane sensor, which could be used in both missile and air defence. Instead of obtaining photographs, the images would be converted into electric signals and transmitted to ground stations in digital format. This would enable reconnaissance in near real time and would allow for manipulation of data so as to extract more information while maintaining the quality of the original data. One of the basic advantages of focal plane array detectors is the elimination of heavy mechanical gimbal systems. Such sensors are usually arranged in arrays which are of two types. In one, the so-called monolithic focal plane array, sensors are fabricated with detectors, preamplifiers and readout systems all in the same piece of material. The second one is called the hybrid focal plane array, which is constructed from more than one chip. For example, the detector array is made from one material while the readout chip may be a charge-coupled device (CCD) or a silicon charge transfer device.[38]

Arrays of 64 × 64 have been constructed in the case of the hybrid focal plane sensor. The more elements in a given array, the higher will be the resolution of the device. Up to 12 000 sensors in a focal plane detector array have been constructed using mercury-cadmium-telluride detectors.[39] An advantage of this material over the silicon-based sensor is that the detector can spot objects in both the near- and far-infra-red regions of the electromagnetic spectrum.

Some advances in computer technology

Another area common to ADI, ATBM and SD comprises battle management systems. Computers are an important element of such systems. Recently considerable advances have been reported. For example, a computer used for handling guidance and control information on board a missile interceptor would need to process over two million operations per second.[40] A computer with this capability has been developed which is only 25 cm in diameter and weighs just over 500 g. Designs are now under way to accommodate such capabilities on 15 computer chips weighing only 200 g and consuming 10 watts of power. A decade ago, for example, gyroscopes, accelerometers and associated electronics for inertial guidance systems weighed just under 20 kg. Such devices used, for example, laser gyroscopes. Today, with the use of fibre optics, the weight has been reduced to some 300 g; there is a possibility that this will be halved. Many of these techniques are being developed under the SD programme of the USA and perhaps even the USSR. In strategic defence systems there is a need for speed, compactness and lightness.

Interceptor technology

Two types of interceptor technology are being investigated; in one, the directed-energy weapon (DEW), the destructive energy is itself projected towards the target at the speed of light and in the other, the kinetic-energy weapon (KEW), guided or unguided projectiles destroy targets on impact. It is in the latter field that some advances have been reported in the USA.[41] In fact, certain KEWs could be ready for deployment in the near future. The kinetic-kill vehicles (KKV) could be propelled using conventional chemical rockets or using electromagnetic forces.

During the past couple of years the emphasis in the US SDI programme has been considerably changed. This is mainly because of budget constraints imposed by Congress. The planned FY 1989 budget of $5 billion—although more than the $3.6 billion approved for FY 1988—is considerably less than the $6.5 billion envisaged in 1987. As a result, the neutral particle beam experiment to discriminate between ballistic missile warheads and decoys has been terminated. More emphasis has been given to space-based lasers and kinetic-energy weapons. For example, the budget for the Surveillance, Acquisition, Tracking and Kill Assessment (SATKA) programme has been reduced from $1859.5 million to $1125 million, a reduction of about 40 per cent, while the budgets for DEW and KEW programmes have been reduced by about 20 per cent. The actual reductions were from $1245.8 million to $1030 million for DEWs and from $1199.7 million to $936 million for KEWs.[42]

The SDI programme is divided into three phases. Phase 1 would be based mainly on existing technology consisting of KEWs which are being developed and even tested. During phases 2 and 3, more exotic systems, on which research is continuing, would be tested and possibly deployed.

Among the DEWs the free-electron laser (FEL) operating at microwave wavelengths appears to be the most feasible. However, budget cuts may affect the test programme.

Kinetic-energy weapons

SDI. The US KEW programme under SDI consists of:

(1) space-based rocket-launched kinetic-kill vehicles for ballistic missile interception and satellite defense; (2) ground-launched exoatmospheric interceptor development; (3) ground-launched endoatmospheric interceptor development; (4) miniature-projectile development for ground- or space-based modes; (5) test and evaluation of initial concepts, using hardware for functional technology validations; and (6) technology development related to allied defense and antitactical ballistic missile.[43]

The space-based interceptors would consist of a number of spacecraft with multiple non-nuclear interceptors designed to destroy missiles and nuclear warheads in their mid-course phase as well as the opponent's satellites in their orbits. The destruction of targets would occur on collision at relative speeds of between 6 and 13 km/s. It has been stated that up to 300 spacecraft, each with 10 to 12 KEWs, would orbit the earth and about 100 would be over Soviet missile sites.[44] Those warheads that escape space-based interceptors would be destroyed by ground-based KEWs. Deployment of phase 1 weapons was expected to occur in the early 1990s at an estimated cost of $80 billion. No nuclear interceptors would be deployed during this phase.

Some successful tests have been reported using rocket-propelled KKV technology. For example, under a US Army programme called the Flexible Lightweight Agile-Guided Experiment (FLAGE), a radar-guided missile intercepted and destroyed a Lance tactical missile on 21 May 1987. The Lance missile was launched towards the test area some 50 km away in a ballistic trajectory and reached an altitude of about 15 km before plunging towards the earth. The 3.5-m FLAGE missile was launched 100 seconds after the Lance and intercepted the latter 7 seconds later at an altitude of under 4 km.[45] Both the FLAGE and the Lance missiles were travelling at just below 1 km/s. Initially the FLAGE missile flew for 5 seconds under its inertial guidance system. Its radar then acquired the target and guided the missile during the final terminal phase. The test showed the effectiveness of the missile's guidance control system for accurate interception and destruction of tactical ballistic missiles within the atmosphere.

Earlier, six tests were carried out to demonstrate the guidance capability of the FLAGE missile against large targets such as ballistic missile re-entry vehicles (RVs). The last of these six tests in June 1986 was against an air-launched target that simulated a ballistic missile RV travelling at Mach 5 within the atmosphere.

Because of the level of success of the FLAGE tests the US Army decided to cancel the remaining two follow-on tests of the FLAGE experiment.[46] The funds and the target vehicles will be used for the Extended Range Interceptor (ERINT) programme, which is aimed at the development of defence against tactical ballistic missiles.[47]

It should be kept in mind that the development of the Airborne Optical Adjunct (AOA) sensor, for use in the ERINT programme, for example, is expected to be tested in late 1988 or early 1989.

In the AOA system infra-red sensors are placed on board aircraft. Under a programme called Queen Match, a probe containing a long-wavelength infra-red sensor will be flown above the atmosphere sometime in 1988.[48]

On 4 November 1987, the US Army tested a Patriot missile as an interceptor against another Patriot, which was successfully destroyed.[49] The interception occurred at an altitude just below 8 km. The test was a part of the programme called Patriot Anti-Tactical Missile (ATM) Program Capability 2 (PAC-2). The target destruction is achieved by the use of enhanced explosives. The previous test under PAC-1 was carried out in 1986. It is expected that the Patriot missile will be useful in an extended air defence system, both for air defence and anti-tactical missile defence.

On 8 February 1988, the second in the Delta series of KEWs was tested. This was the Delta 181 test costing $200 million.[50] The Delta rocket carried 14 test objects and a number of sensors to monitor the behaviour of the test objects once deployed in space. The 3.5-m long sensor module remained attached to the second stage of the Delta throughout the test.

The 14 test objects included four rockets which were fired in space to simulate the plume characteristics of Soviet intercontinental ballistic missiles (ICBMs). Some of the other test objects simulated Soviet warheads and decoys. Some 250 air- and ground-based radars and optical sensors deployed in various parts of the world participated in the nine-hour experiment. A number of communications satellites relayed the data generated in the test to ground control facilities. In addition, microwave and submarine cables were probably used. The sensors included infra-red imaging systems, an infra-red spectrometer, ultra-violet and visible wavelength systems, a pulsed laser radar, a continuous beam laser radar and a continuous wave radar. While in orbit, the sensors remained on the second stage of the Delta and during the first two revolutions around the earth the 14 test objects were released from the Delta. The information will enable the designers to build operational space-based sensors to detect Soviet ICBMs during their mid-course trajectory and subsequently to detect and discriminate warheads from decoys soon after they are released.[51] The Delta 181 sensors examined the characteristics of the earth and space backgrounds against which missiles would have to be surveyed. The space-borne sensors observed the launch of a Strypi-II sounding rocket which simulated the plume characteristics of a Soviet ICBM in the atmosphere. Finally, the Delta 181 also assessed some of the requirements for battle management. This required detecting and tracking objects in space using the two laser radars and a continuous-wave radar. The Delta 181 manoeuvred to track the test objects. However, the test was not trouble free. The computers on board the Delta could not compute fast enough to keep complete track of the test objects.[52]

All the above-mentioned KEW technologies are considered to be mature enough to begin field testing or even deployment in the near future. Thus during the first phase, an SDI system would emphasize surveillance and tracking, kinetic-kill and command and control technologies.

Other tests include an investigation of the feasibility of acquisition and tracking with long-wavelength infra-red sensors from an aircraft. Another experiment involves a network of existing surveillance techniques on various platforms with the objective of continuous tracking of strategic ballistic missiles. Another in this series of tests is the continuation of the Delta experiment. For example, the Janus experiments are designed to gather signature data on objects at close ranges. Lastly, an experimental space-tracking and pointing system including space- and ground-based sensors is also being considered. Experiments will be carried out using the space shuttle and the free-flier experiment, which is a part of the Columbus manned space station.[53] Testing of fixed ground-based ABM systems as allowed by the ABM Treaty will also be carried out.

ASAT weapons. The Soviet Union has not conducted any tests of its ASAT KEW since 1982; and the USA has now terminated its F-15 aircraft-based ASAT programme. This is mainly because of constraints placed by Congress on testing against targets. Congress put a ban on tests against targets of the US Air Force's air-launched ASAT weapon during FY 1986 and extended it through FY 1987. While the Senate Armed Services Committee (SASC) recommended $236.8 million (reduced from the requested budget of $402.6 million), the House Armed Services Committee recommended only $50 million for the FY 1986 budget for the ASAT programme.[54] The SASC suggested that if the ban on testing continued the F-15 ASAT programme should be terminated. The programme was terminated in the FY 1989 budget.

However, the USA is considering the development of ASAT ground-launched miniature homing vehicles based on the Exoatmospheric Reentry Interceptor Subsystem (ERIS), which is being developed under the SDI programme. The ERIS would intercept and destroy nuclear warheads in the mid-course phase of their flight trajectory.[55] The SDIO is also considering the use of sensors for mid-course interception of ballistic missiles for ASAT purposes. This is for possible deployment during the first phase of SDI to observe the Soviet direct-ascent ASAT weapon.[56] In addition, the SDIO is considering the development of a ground-based ASAT laser weapon (see the section below).[57]

Directed-energy weapons

Among the first laboratory experiments to be conducted under the recently adopted US test programme[58] are two experiments called Alpha and Lode. Alpha is a ground-based chemical laser with orbiting mirrors, designed to demonstrate the feasibility of a high-power chemical infra-red laser for destroying targets in outer space. Lode is the Large Optics Demonstration Experiment, including the Large Advanced Mirror Programme (Lamp). Both of these are to demonstrate beam control and large lightweight space optics technologies. It has been reported that a laboratory test of Alpha was conducted on 23 December 1987.[59] Not much information is available at present but it involved a test of the energy conversion in the fuel at high temperatures. It is important to achieve efficient conversion of fuel into laser energy. But the main problem with an infra-red laser is transmitting a high-energy laser beam through the atmosphere.

Another area of development is the Skylite experiment which involves the MIRACL laser (Mid-Infra-Red Advanced Chemical Laser). On 18 September 1987, the MIRACL was tested against a drone, an unpiloted vehicle, flying at a speed of about 260 m/s at an altitude of about 0.5 km.[60] This particular test was to investigate how the technology could be used to defend against conventional weapons as a part of the US Conventional Defense Initiative (CDI) programme. The objective of this programme is to determine the characteristics of the laser, the beam director and the associated adaptive optics. Such data would then be useful for the free-electron laser programmes. The September test was successfully repeated on 2 November 1987. This time the drone was about one kilometre away.[61] It is claimed these tests do not violate the ABM Treaty because this chemical laser has, at present, neither the power nor the optics for atmospheric propagation of the laser light to ranges useful for ABM applications. Again it is claimed that all the other DEW tests will be in compliance with the terms of the ABM Treaty.

In an FEL, a beam of electrons passes through a magnetic field in a device called a 'wiggler'. By varying the speed of electrons in the magnetic field, the frequency of vibration of the electrons can be controlled, resulting in a laser light with a wavelength which could be varied from infra-red through the visible, to the near ultraviolet. This tunability of the FEL makes it a potential weapon because it could be earth- and/or space-based. The possibility of high efficiency also exists.

Both the USA and the USSR are considering developing free-electron lasers as DEWs.[62] There are two types of FEL being investigated in the USA. They differ essentially in the way the electrons are accelerated in the pre-accelerator device. In one a so-called radio-frequency quadrapole (RFQ) is used. The RFQ, first developed by the Soviet Union, uses radio-frequency power to accelerate the electrons. An advantage of this method is the compact size of the RFQ, which uses a device called klystron. A klystron recently developed and produced by France weighs about 2500 kg. Eventually the prototype will weigh 3500 kg and will be 7 m long.[63]

The second type is called the induction FEL. In this case the electrons are accelerated in a conventional linear accelerator which tends to be long. Also in an induction FEL a beam of laser light has to be injected into the wiggler together with the beam of electrons. The laser stimulates the electrons to lose their energy in the form of more laser light. However, while such a device is efficient, it tends to be about 1 km long, and could thus not be based in space. An experimental induction FEL is being tested at a wavelength of 10 micron. For a device to be useful as a defensive weapon against a missile or a warhead, its wavelength needs to be of the order of 1 micron. The RFQ FEL is designed to operate at 0.5 microns.[64]

Some recent theoretical studies renew old fears that the laser light from ground-based free electron lasers will also encounter problems with propagation through the atmosphere.[65] This problem is reduced if the FEL is operated at microwave wavelengths. Such long-wavelength FELs would be more suitable for boost-phase defence: missiles at this stage are softer targets because the antenna for command and control is still exposed. The FEL for mid-course applications would have to be of short wavelength because of the hardness of the target. This presents a problem. Although a ground-based laser with short wavelength has better kill properties, it has poorer transmission properties.

Essentially the problem of transmission through the atmosphere arises because of turbulence in the atmosphere and so-called thermal blooming. The former causes distortions of the light wave front resulting in the defocusing of the laser beam. Thermal blooming again defocuses the laser beam but due to a different phenomenon. As the beam passes through the atmosphere it heats it up, causing its refractive index to change. This will cause the light beam to refract differently thus destroying its sharp beam quality. Tests have already been conducted to show that so-called adaptive optics could correct for the above-mentioned effects. However, in these tests, laser beams of relatively low energies have been used. Both these effects become prominent with high-energy lasers. The degree of distortion will depend on the wavelength of lasers—the shorter the wavelength the worse the distortion.

To ensure kill of an ICBM, a laser would need to deliver an energy of 50 kJ/cm^2 or focus one-tenth this energy in a beam spot size 30 cm in diameter. For short pulses this would correspond to peak power levels of 1000 GW per pulse.[66]

Much of the data on kill mechanism is obtained from experiments conducted in the UK using a krypton-fluoride laser called Sprite.[67] Behaviour of laser light of wavelengths of about 0.24–1.06 micron showed that the impulse coupling in outer space to an aluminium target would be only one-tenth the effect at normal atmospheric conditions. The atmospheric conditions varied from normal to near vacuum of space. Pulse lengths were one microsecond and longer, and energies ranged from 10 kJ to 1 MJ (power levels of 100 MW to 1000 GW/cm^2). Another problem highlighted was the fact that the plasma emitted by the target absorbs energy from the laser beam, effectively blocking or decoupling the beam from the target surface. However, the pressure built up during this process is such that the plasma direction is eventually reversed and travels back towards the target, thus delivering a second impulse to the target. None the less, the force of impulses delivered to the target reached 8000 $dyne/s/cm^2$ with laser energy of 2 kJ/cm^2. Continuous-wave chemical lasers with power levels of 5 kW have been demonstrated. However, this has to be increased to at least two orders of magnitude if the laser is to be an effective weapon. Pulsed lasers with power levels of 10 kJ in one-millionth of a second have also been demonstrated. For such a laser to be an effective weapon its power has to be increased by four to five orders of magnitude. Lasers with such capabilities are not yet available.

The Soviet Union does not release any information on its DEW programmes, although the USSR has recently acknowledged that it is also engaged in its own SD research programme.[68] Several satellite images taken from earth resources satellites indicate that the Soviet Union is conducting a space weapons research programme. An example of this is the Soviet laser facility along the Soviet–Afghan border.[69] This facility is reported to be an ASAT weapon system, the technology of which could be applied for missile defence. The USSR has denied that the laser has weapon applications.[70] None the less, satellite imagery indicates heavy fencing around the laser facility.

The USA is also considering the development of ground-based lasers for ASAT applications. Two types of laser are being considered: the FEL and an excimer moderate-level raman-shifted laser device (EMRLD).[71]

IV. Conclusions

For the first time the Soviet Union has reported setbacks under its military programme. There were four launch failures in 1987, and three other satellites malfunctioned. Thus the USSR had a bad year, while the USA—with two launch failures—appeared to be recovering from its period of launching accidents. The Soviet failures were mainly due to the fact that it is developing new launchers. Despite the unsuccessful launches by the superpowers their capabilities for reconnaissance, navigation, communication and so on could still be considered adequate.

Setbacks for the space shuttle have given considerable impetus to the revival of expendable launch vehicles in the USA. This ELV revival has further underlined the importance the USA attaches to artificial earth satellites. The Soviet Union attaches equal importance to its military spacecraft. The USSR is beginning to regularly launch sophisticated satellites such as long-lived photographic reconnaissance satellites. Other nations, such as France, are also making a considerable effort to develop military satellites.

In this context, it is worth noting that the boundary between the civil and military uses of outer space is becoming indistinguishable. For example, France will use its SPOT satellite platform for its military reconnaissance satellite. This points to a new trend: the development of military reconnaissance capabilities based on civilian ones rather than vice versa, as has been the case with the superpowers. It also indicates the advanced level of development of civilian sensor technology. On the basis of such advances Canada has decided to develop an arms control satellite under its PAXSAT programme.

With regard to space weapons, it appears that the aims of SDI have been considerably lowered. The focus now seems to be on point defence of such targets as command and control systems and missile silos against strategic ballistic missiles, as well as defence against missiles launched accidentally. The development and deployment of such a defence are finding some acceptance. For example, recently Senator Nunn said that he envisages 'certain defensive deployments that could be in the interest of both our nation and the Soviet Union. If carefully directed our research efforts could produce options for limited deployments to deal with the frightening possibility of an accidental or unauthorized missile launch. Such defensive deployment might be possible within the terms of the ABM treaty or, at most, require a modest amendment'.[72]

In December 1987 the USA and the USSR signed the INF Treaty to eliminate their intermediate- and shorter-range land-based nuclear missiles. The superpowers are also considering reducing their long-range nuclear weapons to about half. Should significant reduction be achieved in strategic nuclear forces, it may become easier, from a technical point of view, to create an effective strategic defence because of the smaller numbers of warheads that would be encountered. The INF Treaty, on the other hand, has removed one of the major rationales for ATBM systems in Europe. It remains to be seen whether the two superpowers will apply this thinking to strategic defence: once an offensive threat is reduced, the need for defences against it diminishes.

Notes and references

* 41 Tenterden Drive, Hendon, London NW4 1EA, UK.

[1] Jasani, B., 'Military use of outer space', in SIPRI, *SIPRI Yearbook 1987: World Armaments and Disarmament* (Oxford University Press: Oxford, 1987), pp. 67–8.

[2] This has been admitted by General Secretary Gorbachev, as discussed under 'Directed-energy weapons'.

[3] 'Space shuttle plans revised', *Interavia Air Letter*, no. 11253 (22 May 1987), p. 7.

[4] Covault, C., 'U.S. Air Force Titan launch restarts heavy booster flights', *Aviation Week & Space Technology*, vol. 127, no. 18 (2 Nov. 1987), p. 24.

[5] Jasani, B., 'Military use of outer space', in SIPRI, *World Armaments and Disarmament: SIPRI Yearbook 1983* (Taylor & Francis: London, 1983), pp. 427–56.

[6] 'Titan launches spy satellite', *Flight International*, vol. 132, no. 4087 (7 Nov. 1987), p. 2.

[7] 'USAF plans launch of KH-11 replacement', *Aviation Week & Space Technology*, vol. 126, no. 5 (2 Feb. 1987), p. 22.

[8] *Aviation Week & Space Technology*, vol. 126, no. 23 (8 June 1987), p. 13.

[9] *Aviation Week & Space Technology*, vol. 126, no. 22 (1 June 1987), p. 13; and 'DoD spacecraft launched', *Interavia Air Letter*, no. 11253 (22 May 1987), p. 5.

[10] 'Relaunch of the Titan', *Interavia Air Letter*, no. 11186 (13 Feb. 1987), p. 1.

[11] 'FltSatCom lost when Atlas Centaur launch fails', *Aviation Week & Space Technology*, vol. 126, no. 13 (30 Mar. 1987), p. 20; and 'FLTSATCOM launch failure', *Interavia Air Letter*, no. 11216 (27 Mar. 1987), p. 5.

[12] 'Air Force launches DMSP spacecraft', *Aerospace Daily*, vol. 142, no. 59 (23 June 1987), p. 408.

[13] 'Navy Navigation Satellites orbited by Scout booster', *Aerospace Daily*, vol. 143, no. 58 (22 Sep. 1987), p. 462.

[14] 'Soviets in space: impressive, but less than perfect', *Aerospace Daily*, vol. 143, no. 34 (18 Aug. 1987), p. 269.

[15] Johnson, N., 'Soviet space maiden launch of Energiya', *Jane's Defence Weekly*, vol. 7, no. 25 (27 June 1987), p. 1384.

[16] 'Soviets launch large booster, plan more tests', *Aerospace Daily*, vol. 142, no. 35 (19 May 1987), p. 274.

[17] Covault, C., 'Soviets test massive new booster for station, shuttle missions', *Aviation Week & Space Technology*, vol. 126, no. 21 (25 May 1987), pp. 8–20.

[18] Covault, C., 'Soviet near flight test of small manned spaceplane', *Aviation Week & Space Technology*, vol. 126, no. 13 (30 May 1987), p. 23.

[19] 'Soviets fail in geosynchronous satellite mission', *Aerospace Daily*, vol. 141, no. 23 (4 Feb. 1987), p. 180.

[20] 'US notes breaking-up of Soviet reconnaissance satellite', *Aerospace Daily*, vol. 142, no. 32 (14 Aug. 1987), pp. 250–51.

[21] See note 20.

[22] 'Soviet spacecraft improve naval targeting', *Aviation Week & Space Technology*, vol. 126, no. 17 (27 Apr. 1987), p. 34.

[23] 'Soviets plan permanent satellite system to monitor oceans', *Aviation Week & Space Technology*, vol. 127, no. 6 (10 Aug. 1987), p. 133.

[24] 'Soviets lose Proton booster payload in launch failure', *Aviation Week & Space Technology*, vol. 126, no. 17 (4 May 1987), p. 24; and 'Soviets queried on reports of Proton loss', *Aerospace Daily*, vol. 142, no. 23 (1 May 1987), pp. 178–9.

[25] 'Chinese satellite with French experiment is recovered', *Aerospace Daily*, vol. 143, no. 29 (11 Aug. 1987), p. 228.

[26] 'Chinese recover new type of satellite after eight-day orbit', *Aerospace Daily*, vol. 143, no. 57 (21 Sep. 1987), p. 454.

[27] 'China promotes recoverable satellite utilization', *Aerospace Daily*, vol. 143, no. 24 (4 Aug. 1987), p. 191.

[28] 'NATO-IIIC reactivated after $7\frac{1}{2}$ years on-orbit storage', *Aerospace Daily*, vol. 141, no. 20 (30 Jan. 1987), p. 54.

[29] 'French 1987 defence budget—defining the affordable', *Interavia*, vol. 61 (Dec. 1987), p. 1358.

[30] *Aviation Week & Space Technology*, vol. 126, no. 13 (30 Mar. 1987), p. 13; and 'Italy to share in French satellite system', *Aviation Week & Space Technology*, vol. 126, no. 25 (22 June 1987), p. 66.

[31] 'France begins work on Helios reconnaissance satellite', *Aerospace Daily*, vol. 141, no. 34 (20 Feb. 1987), p. 270.

[32] 'ELINT for Helios', *Interavia Air Letter*, no. 11215 (26 Mar. 1987), p. 8.

[33] 'France studying synthetic aperture radar satellite', *Aviation Week & Space Technology*, vol. 126, no. 19 (11 Aug. 1987), p. 34.

[34] See *Interavia* (note 29).

[35] 'Mikhail Gorbachev's interview with NBC', *Soviet News*, no. 6403 (2 Dec. 1987), p. 430.

[36] *Report to the Congress on the Strategic Defense Initiative*, Strategic Defense Initiative Organization, Department of Defense, Apr. 1987, p. A-13.

[37] Beyers, D., 'Study results to shape future of continental air defense initiative', *Defense News*, vol. 2, no. 22 (1 June 1987), p. 32.

[38] Walter, G. A., and Dereniak, E. L., 'Photodetectors for focal plane arrays part 1: extrinsic silicon', *Laser Focus/Electro-optics*, vol. 22, no. 3 (Mar. 1986), pp. 108–18.

[39] 'Sensor technology yields $500 million in contracts', *Aviation Week & Space Technology*, vol. 129, no. 3 (18 Jan. 1988), p. 66.

[40] Gilmartin, T., *Defense News*, vol. 2, no. 1 (June 1987), p. 32.

[41] *Report to the Congress on the Strategic Defense Initiative* (note 36), pp. VI-D-1 and VI-D-3.

[42] Foley, T. M., 'Slow down in SDI growth delays development decision', *Aviation Week & Space Technology*, vol. 128, no. 8 (22 Feb. 1988), p. 16.

[43] *Report to the Congress on the Strategic Defense Initiative* (note 36).

[44] *Report to the Congress on the Strategic Defense Initiative* (note 36).

[45] Gilmartin, T., *Defense News*, vol. 2, no. 21 (25 May 1987), p. 11; 'Second SDI test', *Interavia Air Letter*, no. 11256 (27 May 1987), p. 4; and 'US Army FLAGE missile proves highly accurate', *Jane's Defence Weekly*, vol. 7, no. 22 (6 June 1987), p. 1109.

[46] *Aviation Week & Space Technology*, vol. 127, no. 6 (10 Aug. 1987), p. 13.

[47] 'Interceptor destroys Lance missile as FLAGE tests resume', *Aerospace Daily*, vol. 142, no. 39 (26 May 1987), p. 307; and Morocco, J. D., 'Army missile test demonstrates FLAGE guidance,' *Jane's Defence Weekly*, vol. 7, no. 22 (6 June 1987), p. 1109.

[48] 'Flight projects, Discrimination tests support sensor development in 1988', *Aviation Week & Space Technology*, vol. 128, no. 5 (1 Feb. 1988), p. 44.

[49] 'Patriot missile with new fuze, warhead tested against another Patriot target', *Aviation Week & Space Technology*, vol. 127, no. 20 (16 Nov. 1987), p. 28.

[50] Covault, C., 'Delta 181 mission has key SDI flight test objectives', *Aviation Week & Space Technology*, vol. 128, no. 5 (23 Nov. 1987), pp. 30–31; and 'Cape Canaveral finishes preparations for SDI Delta sensor development test', *Aviation Week & Space Technology*, vol. 128, no. 5 (1 Feb. 1988), p. 21.

[51] See note 50.

[52] Covault, C., *Aviation Week & Space Technology*, vol. 128, no. 7 (15 Feb. 1988), p. 14.

[53] The Columbus international space station consists of a pressurized man-tended space platform. To this could be attached extension modules, some of which are designed to be operated detached from the main space station for short periods for special experiments. Such modules are called free-fliers.

[54] 'Reagan asks Congress to end ASAT test restrictions', *Aerospace Daily*, vol. 142, no. 31 (13 May 1987), p. 121.

[55] Foley, T. M., 'USAF studies ground-based Asat systems to replace F-15 missile', *Aviation Week & Space Technology*, vol. 128, no. 10 (7 Mar. 1988), p. 213.

[56] 'SDIO sees ASAT self-protection in midcourse sensors, SDI', *Aerospace Daily*, vol. 143, no. 55 (22 Sep. 1987), p. 457.

[57] See Foley (note 55).

[58] 'SDIO sees up to nine flight tests in GST DEM/VAL', *Aerospace Daily*, vol. 143, no. 27 (7 Aug. 1987), p. 210; Mann, P., 'Nine SDI tests planned in 1988–89 amid ABM debate over "exotic" weapons', *Aviation Week & Space Technology*, vol. 126, no. 14 (6 Apr. 1987), p. 20; and Foley, T. M., 'Six SDI programs win approval of Defense Acquisition Board', *Aviation Week & Space Technology*, vol. 127, no. 6 (10 Aug. 1987), pp. 28–9.

[59] Tran, M., 'Laser test succeeds in Star Wars programme', *The Guardian*, 4 Jan. 1987, p. 8.

[60] 'Chemical laser destroys target drone', *Aviation Week & Space Technology*, vol. 127, no. 14 (5 Oct. 1987), p. 22.

[61] 'MIRACL laser destroys target drone', *Aviation Week & Space Technology*, vol. 127, no. 21 (23 Nov. 1987), p. 31.

[62] *Aviation Week & Space Technology*, vol. 127, no. 23 (7 Dec. 1987), p. 85.

[63] 'Boeing evaluates French klystron for SDI laser', *Aviation Week & Space Technology*, vol. 128, no. 5 (1 Feb. 1988), p. 45.

[64] 'SDIO explores range follow-on technologies for missile defense', *Aviation Week & Technology*, vol. 127, no. 21 (23 Nov. 1987), pp. 77–81.

[65] 'Scientists discover potential problems with ground-based free-electron lasers', *Aviation Week & Space Technology*, vol. 126, no. 17 (4 May 1987), p. 28.

[66] 'Science and technology of directed energy weapons', Report of the American Physical Society. The report describes at length the way in which laser light interacts with materials destructively. There are two ways in which high-energy lasers can cause damage to materials. In one, melting of material is brought about by heating it to high temperatures. This effect is prominent when a continuous-wave laser such as a chemical laser fuelled with hydrogen or deuterium and fluorine is used. If, on the other hand, a pulsed laser such as the FEL is used, it causes very rapid heating and vaporization of the surface of the material. The vaporized metal or composite material is ejected outward delivering a shock wave or momentum to the surface of a missile or a nuclear warhead. Repeated pulses shorter than microsecond duration can cause mechanical shearing or buckling of the surface of the target.

[67] Klass, P. J., 'Physicists assess laser lethality for ballistic missile defense role', *Aviation Week & Space Technology*, vol. 126, no. 20 (15 May 1987), pp. 104–5.

[68] Interview with Gorbachev by Tom Brokaw on NBC.

[69] See note 1.

[70] TASS, Moscow, 29 Oct. 1987.

[71] Foley (note 55).

[72] Mann, F., 'Nunn redirects antimissile debate, proposing accidental launch shield', *Aviation Week & Space Technology*, vol. 129, no. 4 (25 Jan. 1988), p. 18.

Appendix 4A. Tables of satellites launched in 1987

Tables 4A.1–4A.9 were prepared in collaboration with G. E. Perry, MBE, and members of the Kettering Group.

Table 4A.1. Photographic reconnaissance satellites launched in 1987

Country, satellite name and designation	Launch date and time (GMT)	Orbital inclination (deg) and period (min)	Perigee and apogee heights (km)	Comments
USA				
USA 27/KH-11 (1987–90A)	26 Oct. 2136	— —	— —	Orbital parameters not published but probably similar to 1982–111A; probably the first KH-11 photoreconnaissance satellite to be successfully launched since Apr. 1984; rocket decayed in less than one day, implying new launch profile
USSR				
Cosmos 1811 (1987–02A)	9 Jan. 1243	65 90	172 344	Lifetime 35 days; fourth generation; high resolution
Cosmos 1813 (1987–O4A)	15 Jan. 1131	73 92	356 416	Lifetime 14 days; medium resolution; deliberately destroyed on the 14th day
Cosmos 1819 (1987–14A)	7 Feb. 1034	73 89	209 256	Lifetime 11 days; high resolution
Cosmos 1822 (1987–19A)	19 Feb. 1019	73 90	228 287	Lifetime 14 days; high resolution
Cosmos 1824 (1987–21A)	26 Feb. 1341	67 90	167 345	Lifetime 55 days; fourth generation; high resolution
Cosmos 1826 (1987–25A)	11 Mar. 1034	73 92	356 414	Lifetime 14 days; medium resolution
Cosmos 1835 (1987–32A)	9 Apr. 1146	65 90	171 340	Lifetime 56 days; fourth generation; high resolution
Cosmos 1836 (1987–33A)	16 Apr. 0614	65 90	241 293	Lifetime 230 days; fifth generation
Cosmos 1837 (1987–35A)	22 Apr. 0922	82 89	226 247	Lifetime 6 days; high resolution
Cosmos 1843 (1987–39A)	5 May 0922	70 92	347 415	Lifetime 14 days; medium resolution; TF
Cosmos 1845 (1987–42A)	13 May 0600	70 90	207 376	Lifetime 14 days; medium resolution
Cosmos 1846 (1987–45A)	21 May 0741	82 91	323 342	Lifetime 14 days; medium resolution; earth resources
Cosmos 1947 (1987–46A)	26 May 1341	67 90	162 346	Lifetime 57 days; fourth generation
Cosmos 1848 (1987–47A)	28 May 1243	73 92	356 414	Lifetime 14 days; medium resolution; TF
Cosmos 1863 (1987–56A)	4 July 1229	73 92	357 416	Lifetime 14 days; medium resolution
Cosmos 1865 (1987–58A)	8 July 1102	65 89	209 268	Lifetime 37 days; fourth generation
Cosmos 1866 (1987–59A)	9 July 1619	67 90	166 358	Lifetime 17 days; fourth generation; satellite broke up on 26 July 1987

Table 4A.1 *cont.*

Country, satellite name and designation	Launch date and time (GMT)	Orbital inclination (deg) and period (min)	Perigee and apogee heights (km)	Comments
Cosmos 1870 (1987–64A)	25 July 0853	72 89	237 249	In orbit on 18 Feb. 1988; launched by Proton; earth resources satellite; orbit manoeuvres approximately every 11 days
Cosmos 1872 (1987–69A)	19 Aug. 0658	73 89	225 252	Lifetime 11 days; high resolution
Cosmos 1874 (1987–72A)	3 Sep. 1034	73 90	226 288	14 days; high resolution
Cosmos 1881 (1987–76A)	11 Sep. 0210	65 90	231 276	In orbit on 18 Feb. 1988; fifth generation; high resolution
Cosmos 1882 (1987–77A)	15 Sep. 1034	82 90	256 278	Lifetime 21 days; high resolution; earth resources; data received by Priroda (Nature) Station
Cosmos 1886 (1987–81A)	17 Sep. 1507	67 90	167 356	Lifetime 46 days; fourth generation; high resolution
Cosmos 1889 (1987–85A)	9 Oct. 0824	70 92	348 415	Lifetime 14 days; medium resolution
Cosmos 1893 (1987–89A)	22 Oct. 1424	67 90	167 340	Lifetime 55 days; fourth generation; high resolution
Cosmos 1895 (1987–92A)	11 Nov. 0907	90 90	228 288	Lifetime 15 days; high resolution
Cosmos 1896 (1987–93A)	14 Nov. 0936	65 89	209 267	Lifetime 41 days; high resolution
Cosmos 1899 (1987–99A)	7 Dec. 0853	70 90	208 302	Lifetime 14 days; high resolution
Cosmos 1901 (1987–102A)	14 Dec. 1131	65 90	173 345	Lifetime 51 days; fourth generation
Cosmos 1905 (1987–107A)	25 Dec. 0853	70 89	206 261	Lifetime 14 days; high resolution
Cosmos 1906 (1987–108A)	26 Dec. 1131	83 90	257 277	New generation, earth resources; Priroda (Nature) Station; data intended for sale through Soyuzkarta; destroyed on 36th day
Cosmos 1907 (1987–110A)	29 Dec. 1146	73 92	356 415	Lifetime 14 days; medium resolution
China				
China-20 (1987–67A)	5 Aug. 0643	63 90	171 396	Lifetime 5 days
China-21 (1987–75A)	9 Sep. 0712	63 90	206 310	Lifetime 8 days; orbit high and more circular indicating a different mission from earlier ones

Table 4A.2. Electronic reconnaissance satellites launched in 1987

Country, satellite name and designation	Launch date and time (GMT)	Orbital inclination (deg) and period (min)	Perigee and apogee heights (km)	Comments
USSR				
Cosmos 1812 (1987–03A)	14 Jan. 0907	83 98	635 664	Lifetime 60 years; seems to transmit on a different frequency from two other satellites; in the same plane as Cosmos 1726[a]
Cosmos 1825 (1987–24A)	3 Mar. 1507	83 98	633 664	Lifetime 60 years; same plane as Cosmos 1743
Cosmos 1833 (1987–27A)	18 Mar. 0838	71 102	849 852	Lifetime 60 years; third generation ELINT; launched by SL-16
Cosmos 1842 (1987–38A)	27 Apr. 0000	83 98	633 665	Lifetime 60 years; same plane as Cosmos 1707
Cosmos 1844 (1987–41A)	13 May 0546	71 102	849 853	Lifetime 60 years; third generation ELINT; launched by SL-16
Cosmos 1862 (1987–55A)	1 July 1926	83 98	633 667	Lifetime 60 years; similar to Cosmos 1703
Cosmos 1892 (1987–88A)	20 Oct. 0907	83 98	635 664	Lifetime 60 years; new orbital plane

[a] Ranft and Perry have shown that more than one satellite can be operational in each plane so it is therefore no longer advisable to speak of direct replacement. Ranft, C. and Perry, G. E., 'Capability of Soviet spy satellite', *Jane's Defence Weekly*, vol. 5, no. 17 (3 May 1986), p. 815.

Table 4A.3. Ocean surveillance satellites launched in 1987

Country, satellite name and designation	Launch date and time (GMT)	Orbital inclination (deg) and period (min)	Perigee and apogee heights (km)	Comments
USA				
NOSS 8/USA 22 (1987–43A)	15 May 1550	— —	— —	Orbit similar to NOSS 6 (1980–19A); probably part of the White Cloud ocean surveillance satellite programme
USA 23 (1987–43E)	15 May 1550	— —	— —	
USA 24 (1987–43F)	15 May 1550	— —	— —	
USA 25 (1987–43H)	15 May 1550	— —	— —	
USSR				
Cosmos 1818 (1987–11A)	1 Feb. 2331	65 101	786 800	New generation EORSAT in higher orbit
Cosmos 1834 (1987–31A)	8 Apr. 0350	65 93	404 418	EORSAT
Cosmos 1860 (1987–52A)	18 June 2122	65 90	250 264	RORSAT carrying a nuclear reactor; 1987–52D is probably uranium fuel core ejected from nuclear reactor in 104 min orbit; moved into higher orbit on 28 July 1987
Cosmos 1867 (1987–60A)	10 July 1536	65 101	786 801	EORSAT; orbit similar to Cosmos 1818 but 120° out of plane
Cosmos 1869 (1987–62A)	16 July 0419	83 98	634 667	Radar oceanographic; similar to Cosmos 1766; radar failed to deploy
Cosmos 1890 (1987–86A)	10 Oct. 2136	65 93	403 417	EORSAT
Cosmos 1900 (1987–101A)	12 Dec. 0546	65 90	256 271	RORSAT, carrying a nuclear reactor; possibly new generation

Table 4A.4. Early-warning satellites launched in 1987

Country, satellite name and designation	Launch date and time (GMT)	Orbital inclination (deg) and period (min)	Perigee and apogee heights (km)	Comments
USA				
USA 28 (1987–97A)	29 Nov. 0322	— —	— —	Orbital data not available
USSR				
Cosmos 1849 (1987–48A)	4 June 1843	63 718	627 39728	Replaced Cosmos 1661
Cosmos 1851 (1987–50A)	12 June 0741	63 710	599 39379	Replaced Cosmos 1658
Cosmos 1903 (1987–105A)	21 Dec. 2234	63 718	588 39757	Replaced Cosmos 1701

Table 4A.5. Meteorological satellites launched in 1987

Country, satellite name and designation	Launch date and time (GMT)	Orbital inclination (deg) and period (min)	Perigee and apogee heights (km)	Comments
USA				
GOES 7 (1987–22A)	26 Feb. 2302	0.6 1344	31839 36082	Carries SARSAT/COSPAS equipment; together with GOES 6, complete coverage of the earth would be achieved; location 75°W
DMSP 2–03/ USA 26 (1987–53A)	20 June 0238	99 102	840 859	Third in a Block 5D-2 series; will replace the first Block 5D-2 launched in Oct 1982; two maintained in orbit; the second was launched in Nov. 1982
USSR				
Meteor 2–15 (1987·01A)	5 Jan. 0015	83 104	942 961	Lifetime 1200 years
Meteor 2–16 (1987–68A)	18 Aug. 0224	83 104	944 960	Lifetime 1200 years

Table 4A.6. Communications satellites launched in 1987

Country, satellite name and designation	Launch date and time (GMT)	Orbital inclination (deg) and period (min)	Perigee and apogee heights (km)	Comments
USA				
SDS11/USA21 (1987–15A)	12 Feb. 0643	— —	— —	Orbital data not available but probably similar to 1985–14A
FLTSATCOM —	25 Mar. —	— —	— —	Launcher failed 51 sec. after lift-off during a thunderstorm; this was a second Atlas Centaur failure in the last three FLTSATCOM launch attempts
USSR				
Molniya 3–31 (1987–08A)	22 Jan. 1605	63 736	438 40807	Replaces Molniya 3–22
Cosmos 1814 (1987–06A)	21 Jan. 0907	74 101	771 810	Store dump; same plane as Cosmos 1680
Cosmos 1817 (1987–10C)	30 Jan. 0922	52 89	212 254	Mission unknown; failed to enter geosynchronous orbit
Cosmos 1850 (1987–49A)	9 June 1453	74 101	783 807	Store dump satellite; replaces Cosmos 1763
Cosmos 1852–59 (1987–51A–H)	16 June 1800	74 115	1388–1473 1477–1501	Octuple launch; tactical communications satellites
Cosmos 1888 (1987–84A)	1 Oct. 1702	1.4 1436	35765 35505	Mission unknown
Cosmos 1894 (1987–91A)	28 Oct. 1522	1.4 1442	35833 35958	Mission unknown
Cosmos 1897 (1987–96A)	26 Nov. 1326	1.4 1435	35718 35820	Data relay satellite; similar to Cosmos 1700
Cosmos 1898 (1987–98A)	1 Dec. 1424	74 101	778 810	Store dump satellite; in the same plane as Cosmos 1777[a]

[a] Ranft and Perry have shown that more than one satellite could be operational in each plane so it is therefore no longer advisable to speak of direct replacement. 'Soviet satellite longevity', *Aviation Week & Space Technology*, vol. 125, no. 16 (20 Oct. 1986), p. 60.

Table 4A.7. Navigation satellites launched in 1987[a]

Country, satellite name and designation	Launch date and time (GMT)	Orbital inclination (deg) and period (min)	Perigee and apogee heights (km)	Comments
USA				
Transit 21/ SOOS 27 (1987–80A)	16 Sep. 1912	90 107	1017 1183	A pair of USN satellites; this was the second of 4 planned dual launches; first pair was launched on 2 Aug. 1985; Stacked Oscar On Scout (SOOS)
Transit 22/ SOOS 29 (1987–80B)	16 Sep. 1912	90 107	1017 1185	
USSR				
Cosmos 1821 (1987–17A)	18 Feb. 1355	83 105	963 1016	Replaces Cosmos 1725; no. 5
Cosmos 1864 (1987–57A)	6 July 2205	83 105	961 1006	Replaces Cosmos 1821; no. 5
Cosmos 1891 (1987–87A)	14 Oct. 1243	83 105	954 1027	Replaces Cosmos 1759; no. 6
Cosmos 1904 (1987–106A)	23 Dec. 2024	83 105	967 1008	Replaces Cosmos 1709; no. 2

[a] Glonass (Global Navigation Satellite System), Cosmos 1838–1840 failed; Cosmos 1883–1885 successfully launched; stabilized their ground tracks and transmitted successfully; replaced earlier failure. These and other Glonass satellites form the Civil Navigation System.

Table 4A.8. Possible geodetic satellites launched during 1987

Country, satellite name and designation	Launch date and time (GMT)	Orbital inclination (deg) and period (min)	Perigee and apogee heights (km)	Comments
USSR				
Cosmos 1823 (1987–20A)	20 Feb. 0448	74 116	1479 1526	Transmitted on 150.30 MHz; same inclination as that of Cosmos 1732; disintegrated on 17 Dec. 1987

Table 4A.9. Manned space flights in 1987

Country, satellite name and designation	Launch date and time (GMT)	Orbital inclination (deg) and period (min)	Perigee and apogee heights (km)	Comments
USSR				
Soyuz TM2 (1987–13A)	5 Feb. 2136	52 90	263 301	Docked with Mir on 7 Feb. 1987; Yuri Romanenko and Alexander Laveykin; recovered on 30 July with Viktorenko, Laveykin and Faris (Syria) after 174 days, 3 hrs and 26 min
Kvant (1987–30A)	31 Mar. 2400	52 91	298 344	Docked with Mir (rear part) on 9 Apr. 1987; astronomical module
Soyuz TM3 (1987–63A)	22 July 0155	52 90	236 300	Docked with Kvant on 24 July 1987 with Alexander Viktorenko, Alexander Alexandrov and Mohammad Faris (Syria); transferred from front port of Mir on 30 July; recovered on 29 Dec. with Romenkov, Alexandrov and Lavchenkov after 160 days, 7 hrs and 17 min
Soyuz TM4 (1987–104A)	21 Dec. 1117	52 90	255 295	Docked with Kvant on 23 Dec. 1987; transferred to Mir front port on 30 Dec. 1987; Titov, Manarov and Lavchenko

5. Chemical and biological warfare: developments in 1987

S. J. LUNDIN, J. P. PERRY ROBINSON and RALF TRAPP*

I. Chemical weapons

Proliferation aspects

The notion that chemical weapons are spreading to more and more countries continued to be expounded during 1987.[1] As in earlier years, however, substantiation was generally absent. Even so, the notion has now become deeply established as a cause of concern, and several governments have announced their adoption of special counter-proliferation measures.

During an interview published in Moscow in June 1987, the leader of the Soviet delegation to the Conference on Disarmament (CD) was asked how many countries then had arsenals of chemical weapons. A 1986 TASS release had spoken of 13–15 such countries,[2] but the ambassador replied as follows: 'Only the United States and the USSR have officially admitted the existence of such weapons. Various signs indicate, however, that there are between 9 and 15 such countries. The figure 20 was also mentioned recently'.[3] It is the British Government that has associated itself with 'the figure 20', as when, in December 1986, the House of Commons was told that 'there may be more than 20 nations which now either possess chemical weapons or are looking at the option of acquiring them'.[4] US officials, by contrast, are more precise: 'Fourteen nations have chemical warfare weapons and two other nations possibly have them', wrote General Wickham, US Army Chief of Staff, to the Congress in 1986; 'nations confirmed as having them are the United States, the Soviet Union, France, — [security deletion]'.[5] And from the Office of the Secretary of Defense very shortly afterwards came this rendering, subsequently much repeated by other US officials: 'We count 16 nations today with chemical weapons, 6 more as probable'.[6] An unclassified US Department of Defense intelligence document that had been released four months previously had stated: 'There are now 11 nations outside the NATO/Warsaw Pact that have chemical weapons in their arsenals and two more that are attempting to acquire them'.[7]

There is a variety of purposes that may be served by propagating reports of chemical-weapon proliferation. A still-expanding market in equipment to protect against chemical weapons, one that is reaching deeply into Africa, Asia and Latin America,[8] is being nurtured and competed for with aggressive sales techniques such as are common in the world armaments trade. General Wickham's statement to the Congress was part of the Administration's quest

---

* S. J. Lundin, SIPRI; J. P. Perry Robinson, Science Policy Research Unit (SPRU), University of Sussex, UK; and Ralf Trapp, SIPRI. Charles Mallory, SIPRI, and Priya Deshingkar, SPRU, assisted in the search for literature references.

for congressional support of the binary-munitions acquisition programme. He stated: 'The realization that US forces could be attacked by chemical weapons in Third World areas of strategic importance underlines the need for a US forcewide deterrent and retaliatory capability'. A certain scepticism towards reports of chemical-weapon proliferation thus seems prudent.

It seems that responsible government officials speaking attributably for the public record so far have actually identified no more than 6–9 states as being, in their view, significant possessors of chemical weapons: France,[9] Iraq,[10] North Korea,[11] Syria,[12] the United States and the USSR, perhaps with Afghanistan[13] as a seventh, Iran[14] as an eighth and Viet Nam as a ninth state.[15] Other states have been mentioned by officials, but only in off-the-record or unattributable (and therefore deniable) statements. The device of the 'leaked' document has plainly been used as well to lend substance to proliferation stories, as when what was purportedly a secret Special National Intelligence Estimate (SNIE) by the US intelligence community[16] appeared on television screens in several countries in the course of a BBC *Panorama* documentary on chemical-weapon proliferation first shown in October 1986. The SNIE, which dated from September 1983, had several times surfaced in the print media,[17] and is said to have identified, with varying degrees of confidence, Burma, China, Egypt, Ethiopia, Iraq, Israel, Libya, North Korea, Syria and Taiwan as possessor states.

In such 'public information processes' there is obviously much opportunity for disinformation. The risk of misinformation is also high, for nuances, qualifications and reservations are unlikely to survive passage from the secret intelligence world into the open domain. Grappling with this problem, the *SIPRI Yearbook 1987* reported[18] that a search of the relevant literature had shown that at least 37 different countries had, at one time or another over the past 20-odd years, been identified on purportedly good authority as possessors of chemical weapons. Clearly, if those official US, British and Soviet numbers are to be even partly believed, the reports in respect of at least 16–29 of the 38 countries mentioned in 1987[19] must be disregarded. But which ones? And if the grounds are good for Washington to disregard 16 or more of them, why are they not also good for disregarding 29, as Moscow seems to be suggesting? Or 34?

The space allotted here does not allow a closer analysis of the available reports than the one given in the *SIPRI Yearbook 1987*. Such an analysis will appear elsewhere.[20] It can be pointed out that few reports of alleged possession address the question of whether the chemical weapons are of types or in quantities having immediate military significance. Attention should nevertheless be given to reports concerning states in areas of currently or potentially high political tension such as in the Middle East, including the Gulf states and the Korean peninsula.

Table 5.1 lists countries which, regardless of whether they do or do not possess significant stocks of chemical weapons today, are reliably known to have done so in the past. This category also includes countries that were once either repositories of foreign-owned chemical weapons or, as formerly dependent territories, were once the location of chemical weapons or chemical-weapon factories owned by colonial powers.

Table 5.1. States known to have been past possessors or repositories of chemical weapons[a]

Australia	Italy
Canada	Japan
China	Kenya
Czechoslovakia	Nigeria
Egypt	Poland
France	Singapore (Straits Settlements)
Germany	South Africa
Hungary	Soviet Union
India	United Kingdom
Indonesia (Netherlands East Indies)	United States

[a] Meaning, roughly, 1940–60. In some cases stocks of chemical weapons remain but have most probably deteriorated to the point of uselessness. This list is, in all probability, incomplete.
Source: SPRU, Sussex/Harvard Information Bank on CBW.

To be sceptical about proliferation reports is not to deny that they may be true. The use of chemical weapons by Iraq in the Gulf War is unquestionable evidence of proliferation; and the now-accepted fact that chemical weapons of Iraqi manufacture were employed indicates that motors of proliferation are at work other than those of the international arms trade or of state-to-state arms transfer such as the trade in precursor chemicals, those which react to form chemical-warfare agents, and applicable technology. But the now rather widely disseminated picture of advanced and still accelerating proliferation, though not demonstrably untrue, cannot be accepted on the evidence available as unquestionable fact.

Cause for concern, however, is very much present, as well as severely practical lessons for the negotiators of the projected chemical weapons convention (CWC). Above all, there is now indisputable evidence that, in the case of the Iraqi acquisition of chemical weapons, there was unwitting involvement on the part of private industry and traders in several countries; perhaps there was witting involvement, too.[21] In addition to firms in FR Germany and the Netherlands, companies in Britain, France, Italy and Switzerland have also, rightly or wrongly, been implicated in the supply of essential chemical intermediates, special materials and plant, or know-how. It is said, moreover, that similar involvements characterize the putative chemical-weapon programmes of other countries.

It is primarily in response to such evidence that express counter-proliferation measures, in the form of special export controls, have been adopted by many states. The Organization for Economic Co-operation and Development (OECD) states soon sought to concert their respective controls via the so-called Brussels Club, or Australian Group as it now prefers to be known,[22] and in 1987 the relevant Council for Mutual Economic Assistance (CMEA) states discussed similar measures in Leipzig.[23] One may perhaps suppose that a linkage between these two groups developed at the US–Soviet Bilateral Discussions on Spread of Chemical Weapons—the private superpower forum created in furtherance of an explicit commitment in the November 1985 Geneva summit communiqué, and of which the 1987 session was held in Bern on 7–8 October. Outside the two groups are other countries that have also adopted counter-proliferation export controls. They include Finland and Pakistan.

The Australian Group grew out of the Gulf War-related export controls which various Western governments began to impose upon their chemical industries in the spring of 1984 in the wake of evidence about the routes of supply for the Iraqi chemical-weapon programme.[24] At its January 1987 meeting, the Group comprised the 12 member states of the European Community, plus Australia (in whose Paris embassy the Group meets), Canada, Japan, New Zealand, Norway and the USA. By the time of its next meeting, in September 1987, its membership had grown to 20, the two newcomers being Switzerland and the European Commission itself. The list of chemicals which the Group has agreed are to be subject to certain formal export-licensing requirements in each and every member country now comprises eight chemicals (see table 5.2). Several individual member states are, in addition, applying export controls—either *erga omnes* or in respect only of named recipient states such as Iran, Iraq or Syria—to longer lists of chemicals. These longer lists are drawn from the Group's 'warning list', a specification of 30-odd chemicals (see table 5.2) potentially useful as chemical-warfare agent precursors which is circulated to the chemical industry to enable it to take action on a voluntary basis, including the information of governmental agencies regarding any attempts to acquire chemicals on the warning list.

The counter-proliferation measures in the chemical field, as in the nuclear, rest on the proposition that the relevant technologies are so highly developed, or rare, that they can be controlled by a relatively small number of governments through their export-control policies. The growing number of chemicals on the warning list,[25] the increase in the number of countries participating in the regulations in the Australian Group and also the 1987 CMEA meeting indicate that the measures have some effect. However, the relevant technologies have perhaps become so available that the only constraint may consist in some increased expenditure for countries which wish to acquire chemical weapons. Remaining benefits of counter-proliferation measures perhaps include increased warning possibilities concerning proliferation developments. Thus, even if export-control measures do have some effect, and may be the only currently practical measures that can be taken, they do not substitute for a CWC. Possibly they facilitate its coming into being. They certainly demonstrate the will of numerous governments to stop the proliferation of chemical weapons.

Developments in chemical-warfare armament

No new information appears to have been published during 1987 that would justify increasing the list of states definitely known to possess chemical weapons beyond that of 1986.[26]

Concerning some of the alleged possessor states, certain publications during the year should, nevertheless, be mentioned. As noted in table 5.3, governmental officials in *Iran* have stated that a production capacity for

Table 5.2. The chemicals on the Australian Group lists

Chemical Abstracts Service registry number and name		Applicable schedule under the CWC[a]
Core export control list		
111–48–8	Thiodiglycol	(Schedule 2)
10025–87–3	Phosphoryl chloride	Schedule 3
756–79–3	Dimethyl methylphosphonate	Schedule 2
676–99–3	Methylphosphonyl difluoride	Schedule 1
676–97–1	Methylphosphonyl dichloride	Schedule 2
868–85–9	Dimethyl hydrogen phosphite	Schedule 3
7719–12–2	Phosphorus trichloride	Schedule 3
121–45–9	Trimethyl phosphite	Schedule 3
Warning list		
7719–09–7	Thionyl chloride	Not listed
3554–74–3	N-methyl-3-piperidinol	(Schedule 2)
96–79–7	2-N,N-diisopropylaminoethyl chloride	Schedule 2
5842–07–9	2-N,N-diisopropylaminoethyl mercaptan	Schedule 2
1619–34–7	3-quinuclidinol	Schedule 2
7789–23–3	Potassium fluoride	Not listed
107–07–3	2-chloroethanol	Not listed
124–40–3	Dimethylamine	Not listed
78–38–6	Diethyl ethylphosphonate	Schedule 2
2404–03–7	Diethyl N,N-dimethylphosphoramidate	Schedule 2
762–04–9	Diethyl hydrogen phosphite	Schedule 3
506–59–2	Dimethylammonium chloride	Not listed
1498–40–4	Ethylphosphonous dichloride	Schedule 2
1066–50–8	Ethylphosphonyl dichloride	Schedule 2
753–98–0	Ethylphosphonyl difluoride	Schedule 1
7664–39–3	Hydrogen fluoride	Not listed
76–89–1	Methyl benzilate	(Schedule 2)
676–83–5	Methylphosphonous dichloride	Schedule 2
96–80–0	2-N,N-diisopropylaminoethyl alcohol	Schedule 2
464–07–3	Pinacolyl alcohol	(Schedule 2)
57856–11–8	Substance QL[b]	Schedule 1
122–52–1	Triethyl phosphite	Schedule 3
7784–34–1	Arsenic trichloride	Schedule 2
76–93–7	Benzilic acid	Schedule 2
15715–41–0	Diethyl methylphosphonite	Schedule 2
6163–75–3	Dimethyl ethylphosphonate	Schedule 2
430–78–4	Ethylphosphonous difluoride	Schedule 2
753–59–3	Methylphosphonous difluoride	Schedule 2
3731–38–2	3-quinuclidone	Not listed
10026–13–8	Phosphorus pentachloride	Not listed
75–97–8	Pinacolone	Not listed
151–50–8	Potassium cyanide	Not listed

[a] According to the 'rolling text' in Conference on Disarmament document CD/782, 26 Aug. 1987.
[b] 2-N,N-diisopropylaminoethyl ethyl methylphosphonite.
Source: SPRU, Sussex/Harvard Information Bank on CBW.

chemical weapons has been developed in that country, but without, as of April 1987, having yet been used. There continued to be reports of Syria assisting the Iranian production effort.[27] On 27 December 1987, the Iranian Prime Minister announced that Iran was now producing chemical weapons.[28] *Libya* continued to be the subject, in various Western countries, of contradictory press reports

Table 5.3. Allegations of CBW arms control violations during 1987

Implicated state	Activity alleged	Source of allegation
Activities prohibited by the 1972 Biological Weapons Convention		
USSR	Continuing 'to maintain a prohibited offensive biological warfare capability' and 'to expand toxin warfare capabilities'	President of the United States[a]
USA	Continuing 'with an extensive biological program' including 'the further qualitative developments of the existing types of biological weapons'[b]	USSR Ministry of Defence;[b] Novosti Press Agency[c]
Use of CBW weapons		
Viet Nam	Repeated poisoning of water supplies and use of toxic weapons by Vietnamese forces in Kampuchea during Mar. through Aug., killing several hundred people. Purported descriptions of allegedly used Chinese, Cuban, North Korean, Soviet and US toxic weapons have been published,[d] with attribution to Kampuchean deserters in Thailand. Viet Nam has denied these charges.	Voice of the National Army of Democratic Kampuchea[e]
Iran	In the Gulf War, use of mustard and phosgene in artillery shell against Iraqi forces on the southern front in mid-Apr. causing 385 casualties. But Iran stated that its production capacity for CW weapons had not yet been utilized,[f] and suggested that Iraqi forces had once again suffered from their own weapons.[g]	Iraqi Foreign Ministry;[h] the UN investigated but did not verify this Iraqi allegation[i]
Iraq	In the Gulf War, the use of blister, blood and nerve gas weapons on the southern front on many occasions during Jan. through May; on the northern front during Apr. through June, including many attacks on Kurdish towns and villages; and the central front during Oct.	Iranian Government;[j] Kurdish leaders;[k] alleged attacks in Apr. were verified by the UN[i]
Libya	In Chad during the spring, the use of air-delivered toxic gas, as well as napalm, against Chadian forces	President of Chad[l]

[a] President Reagan, report submitted to the Congress as required by US Public Law 99–145, 'Soviet noncompliance with arms control agreements', 10 Mar. 1987.
[b] USSR Ministry of Defence, *Whence the Threat to Peace*, 4th edn (Military Publishing House: Moscow, 1987), p. 60.
[c] 'Fifteen years after the signing of the Biological Convention of 1972 the preparations for bacteriological war are going on in the USA', *APN Military Bulletin*, no. 4 (Feb. 1987), pp. 9–12.
[d] Sola, R., 'Cambridge: la guerre chimique', *L'Impact*, June 1987, p. 16.

CHEMICAL AND BIOLOGICAL WARFARE 107

Notes to table 5.3 *cont.*

ᵉ Voice of the National Army of Democratic Kampuchea, broadcasts of 6 Apr., 28 Apr. and 4 May 1987, as quoted via *FBIS-AP* of 7 Apr., 30 Apr. and 5 May 1987, in *Arms Control Reporter*, May 1987, p. 704.B.220; and as quoted in 'Vietnam using chemical weapons, says Kampuchea', *Jane's Defence Weekly*, vol. 8, no. 8 (29 Aug. 1987), p. 367.

ᶠ Statement by Kamal Kharrazi, Director of the War Information Headquarters in Tehran, as quoted in 'UN starts chemical warfare investigation in Gulf War', *Jane's Defence Weekly*, vol. 7, no. 17 (2 May 1987), p. 807.

ᵍ Tehran domestic radio, 21 Apr. 1987 broadcast as quoted via *FBIS-ME* of 22 Apr. 1987, in *Arms Control Reporter*, May 1987, p. 704.B.225.

ʰ Iraq, Foreign Minister Tariq Aziz, letter dated 16 Apr. 1987 addressed to the UN Secretary-General; and letter dated 18 May 1987 from the Permanent Representative of Iraq to the United Nations addressed to the Secretary-General, UN document S/18870 of 18 May 1987.

ⁱ *Report of the Mission Dispatched by the Secretary-General to Investigate Allegations of the Use of Chemical Weapons in the Conflict between the Islamic Republic of Iran and Iraq*, UN document S/18852, 8 May 1987.

ʲ See, especially, the Iranian submission to the CD reproduced in Conference on Disarmament document CD/740, 13 Feb. 1987 and the Iranian statements to the CD in plenary session in Conference on Disarmament documents CD/PV.404, 9 Apr. 1987, pp. 4–8; CD/PV.406, 6 Apr. 1987, pp. 30–2; and CD/PV.425, 28 July 1987, pp. 2–6.

ᵏ Especially the *Appeal to the World Public Opinion on the Use of Poison Gas and Chemical Weapons in Iraqi Kurdistan* issued by the Secretary-General of the Patriotic Union of Kurdistan, 22 Apr. 1987.

ˡ As reported by Sciolino, E., 'US sends 2000 gas masks to the Chadians', *New York Times*, 25 Sep. 1987, p. 6. The charge is not, however, repeated in the 'Blue Book', *Kadhafi/Tchad: Ingérence, Aggression, Occupation*, which the Permanent Representative of Chad to the United Nations submitted to the President of the UN Security Council by letter dated 20 Aug. 1987; see UN document S/19066 of 21 Aug. 1987.

about its purported chemical-warfare armament. Most prominent were the allegations during the summer of Libya having agreed to provide Iran with Soviet-made sea-mines in return for Iranian-manufactured chemical weapons. The Libyan leader, Colonel Qadhafi, vigorously denied these allegations. Publicizing them, US officials said that 2000 gas masks had been sent to Chad in August.[29] In Israel, the chemical-warfare capabilities of *Syria* continued to be the subject of much parliamentary and press concern, and civil-defence exercises to protect against chemical warfare had begun to reach even into children's schools.[30] It was said that Israeli intelligence reports on Syria showed 'an army which is developing and stockpiling very advanced chemical agents, including nerve agent munitions capable of being delivered by aircraft and SCUD missiles'.[31] There was talk, as in 1986, of chemical-weapon warheads for Syrian Scarab (SS-21) missiles.[32] But an Israeli authority dismissed as 'nonsense' a report that Libya had been supplying Syria with chemical-weapon missile warheads.[33]

For those states which declare current possession of chemical weapons or future plans to possess them, the most conspicuous developments of 1987 regarding their chemical-warfare armament were the following. *France* is probably advancing with the chemical-weapon rearmament programme which the Chirac Administration announced in November 1986. *Iraq* appears to have increased its consumption of chemical weapons in the Gulf War. There were reports that, in order to nullify the effects of the export controls which many governments have been placing on precursor chemicals for nerve and mustard gases, Iraq has been establishing indigenous production capacity for certain of these intermediates as well, thus moving its overall chemical-warfare agent production capability further back towards basic raw materials that occur naturally in Iraq. Such exploitation does, however, place heightened demands upon the country's technological resources.

For the *Soviet Union*, 1987 was distinctive as being the first time since 1938 that the existence of Soviet chemical weapons was publicly acknowledged in official statements. The most prominent occurred during a speech which General Secretary Gorbachev made in Prague on 10 April 1987:

I can tell you that the Soviet Union has stopped making chemical weapons. As you know, the other Warsaw Treaty countries have never produced such weapons and never had them on their territory. The USSR has no chemical weapons outside its own borders and, as far as stocks of such weapons are concerned, I should like to inform you we have started building a special plant to destroy them. Its commissioning will enable us rapidly to implement the process of chemical disarmament once an international convention is concluded.[34]

In August the Soviet Government went one striking step further when its Foreign Minister spoke as follows to the CD: '. . . the Soviet side invites the participants in the chemical weapons negotiations to the Soviet military facility at Shikhany to see standard items of our chemical weapons and observe the technology of destroying chemical weapons at a mobile facility'.[35] At the end of the year, the Foreign Ministry of the USSR declared that the Soviet stock of chemical weapons does not exceed 50 000 tons of chemical-warfare agent in the USSR, that is, corresponding to the amount possessed by the USA.[36]

In the *United States*, chemical-weapon rearmament (or the Chemical Modernization Program) entered the phase at the end of the year of full-scale production of the first of the new 'binary' nerve-gas munitions, the M687 155-mm howitzer projectile. The funding needed to start production had been authorized at the end of 1985, but the Congress had stipulated that no funds be spent on 'final assembly' before 1 October 1987, and then only if 60 days had elapsed from a presidential certification to Congress about certain specific matters[37] (see table 5.4). This certification was made on 16 October 1987.[38]

The future of the programme, including procurement of the next two binary munitions that are being readied for production, is uncertain, irrespective of what happens in the Geneva negotiations. The Administration seems confident, however, that only a CWC will now stop it. According to a chart released in former Secretary of Defense Weinberger's report to Congress on the FY 1988/FY 1989 defence budget, the binary stockpile will have grown to a (still increasing) level of about 20 per cent of the present non-binary stockpile by the end of FY 1995, with the sharpest increase set to occur during FY 1991.[39] By the end of 1987, Bigeye had not yet received the certifications required under the 1987 Defense Authorization Act in order for the 1986 facilitation appropriations to be released (a circumstance which does not, however, appear to have prevented the award of a contract for the construction of a Bigeye production facility[40]). (See table 5.5.)

Table 5.4. US production of binary munitions: start-up schedule as of May 1987

Munition	Agent dispensed	Using weapon	Full-scale production start-up
Projectile, M687	Sarin	155-mm howitzers: M114 & M198 and SP how. M109	Dec. 1987[a]
500-lb spraybomb, BLU-80/B Bigeye	VX	Strike aircraft, including A–6E, AV–8B, F–4, F–16, F/A–18 and F–111E	Apr. 1989[b]
Rocket warhead, XM135	Thickened Soman (?)	MLRS, the new 40-km range SP 227-mm/ 12 multiple rocket launcher	FY 1991[c]

[a] Prepared statement of Brigadier P. D. Hidalgo (Deputy Chief of Staff for Chemical and Nuclear Matters, US Army Materiel Command) before the House Armed Services Committee on 12 Mar. 1986. According to Ambassador L. M. Hansen (Acting Representative of the United States to the CD), speaking on 27 May 1987 at the Holmenkollen Symposium in Norway, the actual start-up date would be 2 Dec. 1987. He must have presupposed that President Reagan would, on 1 Oct. 1987, have satisfied Section 1411(c) of the 1986 Defense Authorization Act, requiring the President to certify to the Congress that, among other things, 'final assembly of such complete munitions is necessitated by national security interests of the United States and the interests of other NATO member nations'; and that 'the plan of the Secretary of Defense for destruction of existing United States chemical warfare stocks by 30 Sep. 1994 . . . is ready to be implemented'.

[b] Prepared statement of Dr R. B. Barker (Assistant to the Secretary of Defense for Atomic Energy) before the Subcommittee on Procurement and Military Nuclear Systems of the House Armed Services Committee on 4 Mar. 1987, repeated before the Strategic and Nuclear Systems Subcommittee of the Senate Armed Services Committee on 23 Mar. Full-rate production of Bigeye was to be preceded by low-rate initial production, at first of unfilled bombs, beginning in Nov. 1987. This presupposed that President Reagan would beforehand have been able to make the certifications required by Section 152(c) of the 1987 Defense Authorization Act that: '(1) production of the Bigeye binary chemical bomb is in the national security interests of the United States; and (2) the design, planning, and environmental requirements for such facilities have been satisfied'.

[c] Dr R. B. Barker (see note b). A procurement expenditure of US $631 m. was reportedly envisaged; see Capaccio, T., 'New nerve agent for Army's mobile missile', *Defense Week*, 20 July 1987, p. 5, this suggesting a production target of about 60 000 rockets.

Visits to destruction sites

In his speech to the CD on 6 August 1987,[41] Soviet Foreign Minister Shevardnadze announced the invitation of the Soviet Government to governmental experts of countries participating in the CD and journalists to visit the Soviet chemical-weapon testing ground at Shikhany in the central part of the USSR. In the same speech, it was also stated that a further invitation would follow to visit a facility for industrial-scale destruction of chemical weapons, now under construction in the city of Chapayevsk in Kazakhstan.

The visit took place on 3–4 October 1987; 130 representatives and experts from 51 countries and 56 journalists from all over the world participated.[42] The information provided during the visit comprised data on chemical-warfare agents used in Soviet chemical weapons, technical details of different standard types of chemical weapons in the Soviet stockpile, and information regarding a mobile-destruction complex. Based on this information, agents in the Soviet stockpile are given in table 5.6 together with some other data.

At the time of the visit it was also stated that the ammunition displayed represented all ammunition types present in the stockpile, and that beyond

Table 5.5. US CBW expenditure as of March 1987: programme for FYs 1987–89
Figures are in US $m.

Item	1987	1988	1989
Anti-CBW protection			
RDT&E	324	297	304
Equipment and operations[a]	337	613	747
Chemical destruction programme			
RDT&E	9.6	3.5	0.7
Equipment and operations[b]	609	84	211
Binary munitions programme			
M687 155-mm projectile: procurement	86.3[c]	59.3[d]	65.6[d]
Bigeye spraybomb: RDT&E	5.0	—	—
Bigeye spraybomb	34.4	25[e]	99.4
MLRS warhead: RDT&E	25.3	30.7	29.3
MLRS warhead: production-facility construction	—	—	—
MLRS warhead: production-facility procurement	—	—	—
Other and follow-on systems: RDT&E	6.8	9.5	6.5

[a] Including procurement, operations & maintenance, war reserves, military construction and ship construction.
[b] Including procurement, operations & maintenance and military construction.
[c] The 1987 appropriation provided US $60.6 m. for initial production of M687 rounds, US $21.1 m. for the DC facility needed to provide feedstock for the DF facility at Pine Bluff Arsenal and US $4.6 m. to expand the metal-parts production line at Louisiana Army Ammunition Plant.
[d] According to the US Army's statement to the Congress on its FY 1988/89 procurement appropriations [*Equipping the United States Army*, 27 Feb. 1987, p. 59], procurement of the M687 as programmed by the US Army is: FY1986: US $20.6 m., FY1987: US $59.3 m., FY1988: US $0.0 m. and FY1989: US $0.0 m. Presumably, then, the FY1988/89 programmed procurements shown here are for a service other than the US Army—perhaps the US Marine Corps or some other service? The FY1986/87 funding is said to have provided 80–90 000 rounds [*Arms Control Reporter*, Jan. 1987, p. 704.E.3].
[e] US $14.8 m. from US Air Force procurement funding, US $10.2 m. from US Navy.
Source: Open US Defense Department data in the SPRU Sussex/Harvard Information Bank on CBW.

minor technical modification no other types of Soviet chemical weapons exist.[43] Landmines, mortar ammunition and warheads for cruise missiles or medium- or long-range ballistic missiles for chemical warfare were not displayed; neither was there any display of phosgene, hydrogen cyanide, tabun or psychochemical fillings, all items which were cited by the US Defense Intelligence Agency (DIA) report of 1985[44] and by sources quoted in previous *SIPRI Yearbooks*.

In the second part of the demonstration, a mobile complex for destruction of chemical weapons was displayed and its application demonstrated. The complex was described as suitable for small-scale destruction tasks only, and is used on a routine basis at the Shikhany testing ground.

No detailed information was given about the actual size of the Soviet chemical-weapon stockpile. However, during a press briefing that concluded the visit, the commander of the Soviet chemical troops, General Pikalov, explained that the Soviet stockpile had been built up to meet the threat posed by stocks of chemical weapons kept by other nations and would, consequently, roughly match that of the USA. This was immediately rejected by the head of the US delegation present who claimed that there was a 6 : 1 Soviet advantage in size of the chemical-weapon stockpile. The Soviet Union stated immediately

CHEMICAL AND BIOLOGICAL WARFARE   111

Table 5.6. Soviet chemical weapons as displayed during the visit to the Shikhany testing facility

Type/calibre	Agent	Ammunition (kg)	Agent fill (kg)
Tube artillery			
122 mm	Sarin	22.2	1.3
122 mm	Thickened Lewisite	23.1	3.3
130 mm	Sarin	33.4	1.6
130 mm	VX	33.4	1.4
152 mm	Sarin	40	2.8
152 mm	VX	42.5	5.4
Rocket artillery			
122 mm	Sarin	19.3	3.1
122 mm	VX	19.3	2.9
140 mm	Sarin	18.3	2.2
240 mm	Sarin	44.3	8.0
Close combat weapon			
Hand grenade	CS	0.25	0.17
Chemical bombs			
100 kg	Mustard/Lewisite	80	28
100 kg	Mustard/Lewisite	100	39
250 kg	Sarin	233	49
Tactical missile warheads			
540 mm	VX	436	216
884 mm	Thickened VX	985	555
Spray tanks			
250 kg	Thickened Soman	130	45
500 kg	Mustard/Lewisite	280	164
1500 kg	Mustard/Lewisite	963	630

Source: Conference on Disarmament document CD/789, 16 Dec. 1987.

after the visit that it was still only prepared to declare its stockpiles 30 days after entry into force of the CWC.[45] However, a Soviet Foreign Ministry statement issued in December 1987 stated that the Soviet stockpile did not exceed 50 000 tons.[46]

Beyond the technical data provided during the visit to Shikhany, the most important aspect of this endeavour was political. The invitation met a long-held demand from the West to open up the chemical-warfare establishments of the East. Certainly, it may not have revealed all the secrets of the Soviet chemical-weapon stockpile. However, taken together with the experience gathered in the implementation of the Stockholm Document and its verification on-challenge clause, as well as that of the confidence-building measures (CBMs) agreed at the second Review Conference of the Biological Weapons Convention, the visit certainly had a positive impact on the political climate in the CWC negotiations.

During the autumn of 1987 visits were also made by Soviet representatives to the Munster facility in FR Germany[47] and to the Tooele base in the state of Utah in the USA.[48] Speaking in regard to the Tooele visit, the present head of the Shikhany facility, General Razuvanov, formerly of the chemical service of the Soviet Pacific fleet,[49] commented that the US visit had not resulted in any information about US chemical weapons for its naval forces.[50]

II. Developments related to the Biological Weapons Convention

In 1987 the three main developments related to the Biological Weapons Convention (BWC) concerned continued work on CBMs, which were decided upon during the 1986 Review Conference, allegations regarding the origin of AIDS, and rapid developments in the application of genetic-engineering techniques.

The agreed CBMs are to be voluntary and comprise information and activities as described below:

1. Exchange of data concerning high-safety research facilities performing research relevant to the BWC.
2. Exchange of information on all outbreaks of infectious diseases which seem to deviate from the normal pattern.
3. Encouragement of publication of biological research directly related to the BWC and promotion of its use for permitted purposes.
4. Active promotion of contacts between and exchange of researchers engaged in biological research directly related to the BWC.

The modalities for reporting of information were worked out during a meeting with scientific and technical experts from the parties to the BWC in Geneva on 31 March–15 April 1987 and reported to the parties to the Convention.[51] The high-safety research facilities concerned are the so-called P4 and P3 laboratories, that is, those with the highest degree of safety measures and containment. As regards exchange of information on infectious diseases, it is the intention that the parties shall report outbreaks of infections and epidemics which do not follow normal patterns, or which might be difficult to diagnose. Reports on plant and animal diseases may be provided voluntarily but are not yet included in the modalities. Information on the results of basic biological research of relevance to the BWC are, as far as possible, to be published in generally available scientific journals. Increased contacts among researchers in fields related to the BWC should be among the aims of international conferences, symposia and seminars. The CBMs will be evaluated at the next review conference to take place not later than 1991.

The information yielded by the parties to the UN Secretary-General as of 15 October 1987 can be summarized thus: 16 parties have responded as of 31 December 1987. They are Australia, Canada, Czechoslovakia, Denmark, Finland, FR Germany, Hungary, the Netherlands, New Zealand, Norway, Poland, Spain, Sweden, the UK, the USA and the USSR. All have provided information according to the agreed modalities. As can be expected the amount of information varies in the different answers. The longest contribution, consisting of 33 typewritten pages, was given by the USSR.[52]

New and continued information is to be delivered by 30 April 1988. It is still too early to evaluate the importance of the information given, but a SIPRI study on the issue is under way and will be published before the next date for information to the UN Secretary-General, that is, by 1989.

A number of misgivings have been expressed that new 'genetic-engineering' techniques could constitute a threat to the BWC.[53] Rapid biotechnological developments might allow development of more specific and effective biological-warfare agents or toxin weapons. The risk that this may happen must, of course, not be disregarded. Such misgivings were not, however, subscribed to in the technical background papers which were prepared for the 1986 BWC Review Conference.[54] The *possibility* of misuse of this technique does not, in itself, constitute a violation of the Convention, and it is to be hoped that the agreed CBMs will, in the long run, contribute to increased confidence in the BWC.

III. Allegations of non-compliance with the CBW treaties

Allegations of violations or failures to comply with commitments under the treaties dealing with chemical and biological warfare (CBW) and CBW weapons were less numerous in 1987 as compared with earlier years. A summary is presented in table 5.3. Only in the case of the alleged use of chemical weapons by Iraq was there conclusive international verification.

Various allegations from earlier years were repeated in 1987. In particular, the equation of the South-East Asian 'yellow rain' phenomenon with Soviet-supported mycotoxin warfare in that region continued to be asserted by US Government officials, most notably in the March and December 1987 versions of the report on 'Soviet Noncompliance with Arms Control Agreements' which the Congress has obliged the President to make each year. Very probably the authors of those official statements simply proceeded as in earlier years, unaware or uninformed of any compelling reason for emending a position enunciated at Cabinet and then Presidential level.[55] An alternative explanation—that 'yellow rain' was due, not to CBW attack, but to mass-defaecation flights by wild honey-bees—had been further substantiated, which came to light in an academic study, utilizing information provided via the US Freedom of Information Act, that was published in September 1987.[56]

The March 1987 'Noncompliance Report' also reiterated the charge of Soviet use of mycotoxin weapons in Afghanistan prior to 1985. US officials were, however, on the record as being less confident that mycotoxin warfare had been used there than they were of its use in South-East Asia.[57] A US Defense Science Board panel, for example, reviewed the (secret) evidence and reportedly concluded that some unspecified type of chemical warfare, not mycotoxin warfare, had occurred in Afghanistan.[58] But in the 'Noncompliance Report' there was no accusation of Soviet use of lethal chemicals in violation of international law. This seems to suggest that the evidence the US Government may have had for Soviet chemical warfare in Afghanistan related to 'nonlethal' chemicals such as those used by US forces, sometimes with fatal consequences, during the Viet Nam War. This, perhaps, explains why in January 1987 the British Government spoke as follows to the House of Commons: 'We are unaware of reports of use of chemical weapons by the Soviet Union in Afghanistan. We regret that independent investigation of reports of use of chemical weapons in that country has not proved possible, but we believe that at least some form of incapacitating agent has been used by Soviet forces there.'[59]

In January 1987, the Secretary-General of the United Nations issued a statement expressing dismay at the resumption of reports of chemical warfare in the Gulf War. He recalled the condemnation of Iraqi use of chemical weapons which the Security Council had issued on 21 March 1986 following a report from the team of investigators which he had sent out earlier—the same team that had verified reports of Iraqi chemical warfare in 1984.[60] It appears that his action had been stimulated by reports of heavy Iraqi chemical warfare during the last week of December 1986 on both the southern and the central fronts.

From the southern front, the reports persisted throughout January and February 1987. Still more Iranian casualties that seemed to be victims of chemical weapons were arriving in European hospitals,[61] and Tehran was reiterating requests for a new UN investigation. By 8 April there had, according to the Iranian Government, been 3893 chemical-warfare casualties during 1987 alone, bringing the total for the war up to 27309 (of which more than 262 were fatalities).[62] Then, on 10 April, residential sections of the town of Khorramshahr were reportedly subjected to chemical-weapon bombardment; if so, this was (according to the Iranian Foreign Minister[63]) the first occasion in the war of civilian areas becoming deliberate targets of attack with chemical weapons. Shortly afterwards, the UN Secretary-General arranged for his four-man team of investigators to return to the war zone. They had access to Iraqi as well as Iranian sectors of the front because, in a letter to the UN Secretary-General on 16 April, the Iraqi Government had complained of Iranian resort to chemical warfare. By this time reports had begun to come in of Iraqi air attacks with chemical weapons on a succession of Kurdish villages, in Iraqi as well as Iranian Kurdistan, with many hundreds of civilian casualties.[64]

The UN team conducted its field inquiries from 22 April to 2 May 1987; its report was published on 8 May, with this conclusion: 'There has been repeated use of chemical weapons against Iranian forces by Iraqi forces, employing aerial bombs and very probably rockets. The chemical agents used are mustard gas and probably, on some occasions, nerve agents. A new dimension is that civilians in Iran have also been injured by chemical weapons.'[65]

Chemical-warfare operations by Iraq nevertheless continued to be reported. There were appalling stories of poison-gas suffering among noncombatant Kurdish civilians,[66] intensifying after what was said to have been an unprecedentedly heavy chemical-weapon air attack on the town of Sardasht on 28 June that caused many hundreds (thousands, according to some accounts) of casualties.[67] Seven of them, including one child, were flown by Iran to Austria for hospital treatment.[68] Reports of chemical-warfare raids on Kurdish villages were still being heard in September.[69] During October, according to Iranian reports which were denied[70] by Iraq, the Iranian town of Sūmar suffered large-scale Iraqi chemical bombardment.[71]

A critical and well-based military assessment of Iraq's use of chemical weapons in the war has yet to be published in the open literature. But a recent general military analysis of the fighting has concluded that the employment of chemical weapons 'has had a negligible impact on the course of the war'.[72]

It is noteworthy that even Iraq's use of chemical weapons was incremental and heavily circumscribed. Iraq did not employ lethal gas before it had indicated its intentions both by using tear gas first and by issuing continuous and persistent warnings about it so as to leave the door open for an Iranian retreat. When Iran failed to heed these warnings, Iraq employed this weapon only in vital segments of the front and only when it saw no other way to check the Iranian offensives.[73]

But after the events of 1987, one may suspect that at that time (1986) supply, at least as much as scruple, had been a substantial constraint on Iraqi resort to these prohibited weapons.

At the end of 1987 the press reported conflicting official statements by Iran as to whether or not it had then begun producing chemical weapons.[74] The implications of possible future use of chemical weapons by Iran are difficult to evaluate at present. Iran has stated that it will not violate existing international agreements unless necessary. In any case, the announcements may imply a further proliferation of chemical weapons. It remains to be seen whether the new situation might induce a cessation or escalation of chemical warfare in the Iran–Iraq War, in view of the capability, which Iran may now possess, to retaliate with chemical weapons.

The continued use of chemical weapons by Iraq constitutes one of the most serious current threats to the conclusion of a CWC. It may constitute an incentive to other states to acquire chemical weapons. Danger emerges also from the lack of international condemnation and from the absence of effective countermeasures to obstruct acquisition and production of Iraqi chemical weapons.

IV. Chemical weapon-free zones

Because of the progress of the negotiations on chemical weapons at the CD, regional initiatives received less attention in 1987 than in previous years. Calls for a chemical weapon-free zone (CWFZ) in Europe were nevertheless emphasized in a number of WTO declarations during the year.[75] The trilateral talks from Czechoslovakian, East German and West German representatives continued. In the view of the socialist countries, all that remained to be negotiated was the implementation of the zone.[76] High-level consultations on the issue of a CWFZ in the Balkans were initiated, involving Bulgaria, Greece, Romania and Yugoslavia.[77] These consultations were linked to other proposals for regional security arrangements, for example, a nuclear weapon-free Balkan region. It seems that in 1987 talks on the CWFZ concept were instrumental in initiating much broader consultations between leading political parties of the two German states on regional security matters.[78] Clearly, the talks have established new channels for the discussion of highly sensitive issues. By precedence of their positive outcome, they have produced positive political pressure on follow-up talks. It may well be that one intention of negotiating such regional arrangements for other regions, for example the Balkans, is the same.

However, even at the present state of negotiation regional concerns have in no way diminished. The current French position, as discussed below, may serve to highlight this. It may well be that the concept will re-emerge in more practical terms at the time of implementation of the world-wide ban. It may serve to allay security concerns during the 10-year transition phase of chemical-weapon destruction, by arranging the order of destruction so as to meet concerns about regional instability. However, the greater emphasis put on the CWC may be taken as a sign of the seriousness with which the USSR and other members of the WTO consider the successful conclusion of the CWC.

V. Developments influencing the CWC negotiations

The possibility of achieving a CWC increased substantially during 1987. But, unfortunately, so did the risk that a convention may not be universally ratified in the foreseeable future because of events outside the negotiations. This paradox is analysed below.

Progress at the negotiations was marked by a series of substantive Soviet moves, to which reference was made above, and included:

1. The announcement by General Secretary Gorbachev that the USSR had stopped production of chemical weapons.

2. The expressed willingness of the USSR[79] to accept the British proposal for mandatory on-site inspection, which also provided a possibility for the challenged party to demonstrate compliance by interim alternative inspection measures.[80]

3. The announcement that the Soviet Union was ready to accept, in principle, the US proposal in its draft convention CD/500[81] of mandatory on-site inspection at any site within 48 hours.[82]

4. The declaration, made in advance of future obligations under a CWC, that Soviet stockpiles do not exceed 50 000 agent tons.

A number of political endorsements were also made during 1987 which indicate the interest of the USA and the USSR in achieving a CWC. General Secretary Gorbachev particularly expressed his interest in a number of statements.[83] This must be seen as an indication that the chemical-weapon issue has been dealt with on the highest possible level in the USSR. The WTO also issued a number of declarations in which the desire to achieve a CWC was underlined.

It must be emphasized that the principal agreement between the USA and the USSR has not eliminated the practical problems of how to implement on-site inspections, whether by routine or by challenge, and through which procedures. On the contrary, much work probably remains to be done before an agreement can be reached in these areas. This need not result in insurmountable difficulties for the conclusion of the CWC unless—owing to political circumstances—they are used as pretexts for halting the work on the convention. The INF Treaty on intermediate-range nuclear forces[84] is a positive example of how solutions to such problems can quickly be agreed upon when political will exists.

French emphasis on a more security-directed attitude to the future CWC gave rise to concern.[85] Their document expressed a need for countries with stockpiles of chemical weapons to keep 'security stocks' until the end of the 10-year period during which chemical weapons are to be destroyed under the CWC. It also suggested that the locations of stockpiles should not be declared until the time of destruction, and further that production of chemical weapons could take place during the destruction period to substitute for destroyed weapons permitted as 'security stocks'. While there are those who see some logic in this reasoning from a security point of view, it is not in conformity with the approach of the draft CWC. It is difficult to imagine the French approach substituting for the well-established ideas of declaration and destruction of weapons and production facilities. The French ideas for the convention are quite in line with their announcement, on 5 November 1986,[86] of a decision to begin production in 1987 of chemical weapons for deterrence purposes. French Foreign Minister Raimond announced that France also intended to acquire a chemical-weapon retaliation and deterrence capacity during 1987–92.

The formal voicing of these concerns at a point when the CWC appears to be rapidly becoming a reality must have some underlying reasons. There are several different explanations for the French position, one being the mere fact that the agreement on chemical weapons seems much closer today than a year ago. Further, and somewhat contradictory to the previous explanation, France might suspect a new escalation in chemical-weapon acquisition programmes. France—also a Mediterranean state—may have serious concerns regarding chemical-weapon proliferation. Long-term problems may also result owing to possible stockpiles of chemical weapons in other parts of the world, which may be a problem for the superpowers even if a CWC is achieved within the next few years. Since an agreed CWC is probably a prerequisite to the solution of these problems, it could be considered useful for France to adhere ultimately to a CWC formed along the present lines.

Another reason why France might consider it useful to abandon its present position—after it has served its purpose—is the unfortunate effect it would have upon world-wide proliferation of chemical weapons. Should the French ideas be accepted, this would serve as a strong signal for further proliferation of chemical weapons. Increased chemical-weapon proliferation would have a negative impact on the negotiating climate. It would also considerably increase the difficulties of verification of the destruction and could possibly lead to diminished trust in the CWC. If this analysis is correct, one must hope for alteration in the current French position. This is not to disregard France's purported concerns; indeed, the guarded comment which the USA has provided through its CD delegation shows that they are not being disregarded.[87]

The US desire to start production of binary chemical weapons had been the subject of much concern for many years. The simultaneous start of production of binary chemical weapons and the delay in destroying old ones in the USA could have a negative impact on the conclusion of a CWC. Such production had been viewed both as completely jeopardizing the prospects for a CWC and as the only way to induce the Soviet Union to start serious discussions on the convention. It is important to remember that the USA, in fact, had maintained a moratorium on chemical-weapon production since 1969. The USSR announced the cessation of production in 1987. When US production of binary weapons did start, official Soviet statements made clear that the Soviet approach to conclusion of a CWC would not be affected by the US action.[88] This probably will be taken as positive evidence by those who support the view that the Soviet Union would be unwilling to conclude a CWC before production of binary weapons was actually imminent. The Soviet position has always been that such a move would complicate verification of a CWC.[89] Technically, this is certainly true. However, this complication is not new. The difficulty had to be taken into account from the very earliest stages of the negotiations since the concept of binary chemical weapons was known at that time.[90] Whether or not binary weapons were to become a reality, provisions for that theoretical possibility would nevertheless have had to be made in the convention. The question of binary weapons has, however, a considerable political impact. US production of binary chemical weapons in advance of the conclusion of a CWC implies that within several years (that is, within the time required for finalization of a CWC) the USA will acquire a force-wide retaliatory capacity and that the hazard of transporting these weapons will have diminished or even ceased. Thus the 10-year period of destruction and—above all—confidence building under the CWC would, from the US point of view, imply less risk for the USA in the event a party chose to violate the convention during that period.

In 1987 the bilateral discussions between the USA and the USSR continued, and seven meetings, described as useful,[91] were held. The bilateral meetings addressed the issues of mutual invitation, CBMs, proliferation problems and verification problems. A particularly important CBM, which appears to have been agreed upon during the meeting in November 1987 between the foreign ministers of the USA and the USSR, is the mutual exchange of information about stockpile sites, types of chemical weapons and amounts of chemical weapons possessed.[92] This was achieved in part by the Soviet declaration of 27 December 1987 quoted above. Should this be fully realized, it will represent an unprecedented breakthrough in the negotiations on chemical weapons. It would also set an important example for other states possessing chemical weapons. Such 'pre-convention' CBMs in order to facilitate the conclusion of the CWC were suggested long ago, when, however, the political climate was another.[93]

Bilateral consultations were held not only between the superpowers themselves. The USSR had consultations with FR Germany. This resulted in acceptance of the 1984 invitation to members of the CD to visit the Munster destruction site for old (World War II and earlier) chemical munitions, and a visit was made by Soviet experts. Other members of the CD had accepted the invitation although the USSR had not. The results of that visit were published as a CD Working Paper.[94]

Discussions were also held between the UK and the USSR about the possibility of a visit by Soviet military experts to the British chemical defence research institute at Porton Down.[95]

It seems fair to conclude that these bilateral consultations during 1987 contributed positively to the Geneva negotiations and appeared to set a trend of widening the forum to venues outside the CD. Such development will probably help to speed up negotiation by clarifying issues between countries, which are of a more pronounced bilateral character and which therefore need not complicate the multilateral negotiations.

In the report of the 1987 CD summer session[96] containing (at the time of writing) the latest version of the rolling text of the CWC, substantial progress could be reported on some important technical and procedural matters. Work continued in consultations with the Committee on Chemical Weapons during 23–27 November and 30 November–16 December 1987. (See also chapter 12.)

Matters which remain unresolved at the end of 1987 concern, among others, some aspects of the definition of chemical weapons, the problem of some super-toxic chemicals which may be produced in small amounts for civilian purposes, the definition of production facilities, and, not least, the international organization for the CWC and detailed procedures for different verification purposes.

Although much work has been done to define the goals for different verification measures, it is obvious that the negotiations are now approaching the point when it will be necessary to examine the technical methods to be used for this purpose.[97] Two questions must be treated in this context: (*a*) Which of the necessary methods are currently available? and (*b*) What efforts may have to be begun in the near future to find methods which are not now available? One may ask whether the CD is the right forum for this work which must, of necessity, be exploratory. Alternative options may have to be presented, depending upon the political results of the negotiations, and it is possible that much work will be required on national levels, which might be politically difficult to accept at the Geneva negotiations. It thus seems necessary to find an additional forum in which to deal with these technical questions.

Two possibilities present themselves. First, it could be agreed that the Preparatory Commission should start its work. Formal agreement upon the commission would be needed, perhaps in the form of a particular document, signed by the CD negotiating delegations. Such a measure would also constitute a powerful political signal that the CWC would soon be a reality. Without such a sign, and if technical difficulties cause the work to be drawn out, the present positive outlook may soon change for the worse. Second, a technical group might be instituted as soon as possible similar to the test-ban group of seismic experts, the existence of which constitutes a precedent. Additionally, the tasks for a group of chemical experts could easily be regulated by directives from the Committee on Chemical Weapons in the CD. Suggestions to this effect, together with other means of improving the work at the Committee on Chemical Weapons of the CD, were in fact put forward by the UK and the WTO.[98]

From the work done during 1987 on outlining three (actually four) lists of chemicals, which would be subject to different verification measures under the CWC, it is clear that many technical problems currently remain in this context and will remain even after entry into force of the convention. One important area which will require further work is the international organization for the CWC. Important political decisions will need to be taken on its procedures, size and detailed functions. The history of the negotiations shows how complicated this matter will be.[99]

The questions of definition of chemical weapons have been reported upon in earlier SIPRI publications and concern mainly riot-control agents, herbicides and formulations needed for binary chemical weapons. They do not seem to constitute major political problems, although the actual concerns behind them are real enough.

The verification concepts of the INF Treaty concluded between the USA and the USSR most probably will influence the corresponding provisions in the CWC.

VI. Conclusions

In 1987 a number of important events took place in the fields of chemical and biological warfare. They lead to contradictory conclusions.

With respect to biological warfare, new efforts were made to increase confidence in the BWC by asking parties to provide information on their activities related to it. Allegations of violation of the BWC continued but were moderated. Concerns were expressed that new technologies, including so-called genetic engineering, might be utilized to construct new biological weapons or even weapons which may not be covered by the BWC or a new CWC. These concerns did not, in general, take the form of official positions. Efforts to strengthen the BWC with CBMs have started, but there is a continued need to watch future developments in relation to the Convention.

In the case of chemical weapons, the work on the CWC proceeded rapidly although much technical work remains to be done. The need for rapid conclusion of a convention was generally supported. During 1987 the USSR acceded to the concept of obligatory on-site inspection as a verification measure of the CWC, and unprecedented openness was shown by the USSR in inviting members of the CD and others to a demonstration of Soviet chemical weapons. The USSR also announced that it had ceased to produce chemical weapons; this was the first official Soviet admission of possession of chemical weapons since World War II. At the end of 1987 the USSR officially declared its total amount of chemical weapons, and Soviet representatives visited US and West German chemical-weapon destruction facilities for the first time. Further exchanges of information between the USA and the USSR, as well as between other states, seemed to increase confidence in the eventual conclusion of the convention.

However, a number of developments took place which caused concern about the rapid finalization of the convention and about the development of new interest in chemical warfare. There was repeated Iraqi use of chemical weapons. Proliferation of chemical weapons may even have continued in the area if Iran actually started production of chemical weapons. The USA started production of binary chemical weapons while France proposed that, under a future convention, parties be allowed to keep 'security stocks' during the proposed 'destruction period'. If agreed to, such a provision would constitute a strong incentive for accelerated proliferation of chemical weapons before entry into force of a CWC.

The conclusion of the INF Treaty gave hope for continued disarmament measures. Some of the provisions in the Treaty may influence the work on the CWC. However, official statements from the USA and the USSR appear to indicate that a CWC now has only third priority after agreements on strategic nuclear weapons and conventional weapons. If so, conclusion of a CWC may be postponed for a long time. It would seem to be an enormous waste of opportunity if rapid conclusion of the convention cannot be obtained. Only a finalized global CWC can possibly constitute an effective basis to hinder the further development and proliferation of both biological and chemical weapons.

Notes and references

[1] See especially the section on 'Chemical weapons proliferation' in Roberts, B. (ed.), *Chemical Warfare Policy: Beyond the Binary Production Decision*, Significant Issue Series, vol. 9, no. 3 (Center for Strategic and International Studies, Georgetown University: Washington, DC, 1987), pp. 36–40.

[2] TASS (Abarenkov, V.) in English from Moscow, 9 Apr. 1986, as reproduced (LD090649) by *Foreign Broadcast Information Service (FBIS)*.

[3] Novikov, A., ['Topical interview'], *Komsomol'skaya Pravda*, 16 June 1987, p. 3 (in Russian).

[4] 'Written answers: Mr Stanley responding for the Secretary of State for Defence to a written question from Sir David Price', *Hansard* (Commons), vol. 107, no. 25, col. 500 (16 Dec. 1986); and Statement of Minister T. Renton, 15 July 1986 in Committee on Disarmament document CD/PV.370, pp. 2–9, at p. 4.

[5] General Wickham (US Army Chief of Staff), written response to a question put by Congressman Miller during a hearing before the House Defense Appropriations Subcommittee (HDASC) on 25 Feb. 1986 (see *Fiscal Year 1987 Hearings*, part 1, p. 114). An 'unsanitized' version of this submission, reportedly listing North Korea among those 14 possessors, was apparently leaked to the press. See, for example, Vinch, C., 'US: North Korea has chemical arms', *Pacific Stars and Stripes*, 30 June 1986, p. 1.

[6] Dr Welch, statement before the Senate Armed Services Committee (SASC) on 10 Apr. 1986, *Fiscal Year 1987 Hearings*, part 4, p. 1730. See also his statement before the HDASC on 22 Apr. 1986, *Fiscal Year 1987 Hearings*, part 3, p. 725.

[7] US Defense Intelligence Agency, *Soviet Chemical Weapons Threat 1985*, report no. DST–1620F–051–85, released 28 Oct. 1985.

[8] *NBC Defense & Technology International*, vol. 2, no. 1 (1987).

[9] See General Wickham (note 5). This is the latest in a succession of public statements by US officials that France has continued to maintain a stockpile of chemical-warfare weapons. In contrast, French officials, when speaking publicly, say no such thing, and often seem to be denying the existence of the stockpile.

[10] Prime Minister Shimon Peres, before Israel's National Defence College on 7 August 1986: '[Syria] is spending large sums to acquire surface-to-surface missiles and to develop chemical warheads, as if these weapons could decide the outcome of a war'. (See, for example, Reuter, as in 'Syria plans "poison gas warheads"', *Daily Telegraph*, 8 Aug. 1986.) In 1986, then US Deputy Assistant Secretary of Defense, Douglas Feith, told a journalist: 'The Syrians have been interested

in chemicals for years. They do have a production capability for nerve agents.' (See Diaz, T., 'Syria said to have offered chemical weapons to Iran', *Washington Times*, 9 Dec. 1985, p. 4.)

[11] General Wickham to the HDASC, *Fiscal Year 1986 Hearings*, part 2, p. 85: '[Soviet] doctrine calls for use of [CW offensive capability], they are fielding defensive equipment and producing chemical weapons. So are the North Koreans, for example.' See also note 5.

[12] See note 10.

[13] Then US Secretary of State, Alexander Haig, in a report to Congress of 'some evidence that Afghan Government forces may have used Soviet supplied chemical weapons against the *mujahidin* even before the Soviet invasion'. US State Department, 'Chemical warfare in South-East Asia and Afghanistan', *Special Report*, no. 98 (22 Mar. 1982), p. 6.

[14] US State Department spokesman, Bernard Kalb, 24 Apr. 1985: 'We are aware that Iran has been seeking to develop a chemical weapons capability, and it may now be in a position to use such weapons'. See 'US fears Iran may use chemical arms', *New York Times*, 25 Apr. 1985, p. A3.

[15] For a discussion of the credence still attached in US Government circles to the CBW explanation of 'yellow rain', see section III.

[16] Director of Central Intelligence, William Casey, 'Implication of Soviet use of chemical and toxin weapons for US security interests', *Special National Intelligence Estimate* 11–17–83, 15 Sep. 1983.

[17] For references, see SIPRI, *World Armaments and Disarmament: SIPRI Yearbook 1985* (Taylor & Francis: London, 1985), pp. 170–3.

[18] SIPRI, *SIPRI Yearbook 1987: World Armaments and Disarmament* (Oxford University Press: Oxford, 1987), p. 104.

[19] The RENAMO (MNR) leader Alfonso Dhlakama as reported by Morrison, J., 'Mozambique accused of chemical warfare', *Washington Times*, 31 Dec. 1986, p. 8; and *SIPRI Yearbook 1985* (note 17).

[20] Perry Robinson, J. P., *Chemical and Biological Warfare Developments: 1986 and 1987*, SIPRI Chemical & Biological Warfare Studies (Oxford University Press: Oxford, forthcoming).

[21] Harris, R. and Woolwich, P., 'The secrets of Samarra', a 40-minute BBC *Panorama* television documentary aired in Britain on 27 Oct. 1986 at 2130 hours.

[22] 'The US tightens exports of warfare chemicals', *Chemical and Engineering News*, 10 Aug. 1987, p. 8.

[23] ADN, ['Consultations on export regulations for chemicals'], *Neues Deutschland*, 24 June 1987, p. 8 (in German).

[24] Some particulars of these early controls are collated in *SIPRI Yearbook 1985* (note 17), pp. 174–6.

[25] Australia has 30 chemical-weapon related chemicals on its Export Control List. See the statement of Mr Butler to the Conference on Disarmament in plenary session on 3 Feb. 1987 in Conference on Disarmament document CD/PV.384, p. 37. It is second in this particular league table, preceded by Ireland and followed by the Netherlands. FR Germany is in the lower range. Britain and the United States are mid-range.

[26] SIPRI, *World Armaments and Disarmament: SIPRI Yearbook 1986* (Oxford University Press: Oxford, 1986).

[27] Abramowitz, J., 'CW changes the rules of Middle East war', *Jane's Defence Weekly*, vol. 8, no. 18 (7 Nov. 1987), pp. 1063–9.

[28] Hirst, D., 'Iran admits making chemical weapons', *Guardian*, 28 Dec. 1987, p. 1.

[29] Sciolino, E. (from Washington, 24 Sep.), 'US sends 2,000 gas masks to the Chadians', *New York Times*, 25 Sep. 1987, p. 6.

[30] Lustig, R., 'Israel under a pall of chemical fear', *Observer* (London), 4 Jan. 1987, p. 14.

[31] See note 27.

[32] O'Dwyer-Russell, S., 'Missile horror predicted', *Sunday Telegraph* (London), 18 Jan. 1987, p. 7.

[33] Brigadier Aharon Levran, as quoted by Abramowitz (see note 27). The report which he dismissed was a front-page story: O'Dwyer-Russell, S., 'Gaddafi arms Syria with gas warheads', *Sunday Telegraph*, 23 Nov. 1986.

[34] The full text of the speech is available in Conference on Disarmament document CD/751, 13 Apr. 1987.

[35] Statement of Soviet Foreign Minister Shevardnadze before the Conference on Disarmament in plenary session in Conference on Disarmament document CD/PV.428, 6 Aug. 1987.

[36] Permanent Mission of the Soviet Union (Geneva), 'Statement of the Soviet Foreign Ministry', *Press Bulletin*, 31 Dec. 1987, p. 5. For a discussion of the different estimates of the amounts of chemical weapons in the USSR, see also Assembly of Western European Union, 33rd Ordinary

Session, 2nd part, *Threat Assessment: Report submitted on behalf of the Committee on Defence Questions and Armaments*, document 1115, 2 Nov. 1987.

[37] The 1986 Defense Authorization Act, section 1411(c).

[38] 'Executive messages referred', *Congressional Record*, 20 Oct. 1987, p. S145 97, as quoted in 'Reagan letter of certification to the Senate on [sic] to proceed with production of binary weapons 16.10.87', *Arms Control Reporter*, Nov. 1987, p. 704.E.4.

[39] US Defense Secretary Caspar W. Weinberger, *Annual Report to the Congress, Fiscal Year 1988*, 12 Jan. 1987, p. 292.

[40] The contract, between the US Army and the Charles N. White Construction Company and worth US $6 m., was reported in 'Contracts', *Jane's Defence Weekly*, vol. 7, no. 1 (10 Jan. 1987), p. 38.

[41] See note 35.

[42] USSR, 'Information on the presentation at the Shikhany military facility of standard chemical munitions and of technology for the destruction of chemical weapons at a mobile unit', Conference on Disarmament Working Paper CD/789, 16 Dec. 1987. Information was also compiled in a brochure entitled *Information on Demonstration at Shikhany Military Area* which was provided to the participants of the Shikhany workshop.

[43] General-Colonel Pikalov at a press conference said that all chemical-delivery methods, chemical agents and munition, with the exception of certain modified models were displayed. Gorokhov, A. and Serbin, A., 'Hope: reporting from the Soviet military installation Shikhany', *Pravda*, 4 Oct. 1987.

[44] See note 7.

[45] See Gorokhov and Serbin (note 43); and USSR, Conference on Disarmament document CD/PV.389, 17 Feb. 1987.

[46] See Permanent Mission of the Soviet Union (note 36).

[47] ['Soviet chemical weapon experts in the FRG'], *Neue Zürcher Zeitung*, 18 Nov. 1987, p. 4 (in German).

[48] Knudson, T. J., 'Russians tour U.S. chemical arms stockpile', *New York Times*, 20 Nov. 1987, p. 4.

[49] Gorokhov, A. and Serbin, A., 'Confidence: reporting from the Soviet military installation Shikhany', *Pravda*, 4 Oct. 1987. 'Its [Shikhany's] director General Major R. Razuvanov . . . in the not too distant past a navy man, with a chemical bent, though, in so far as he graduated in chemistry and served in the chemical service of the Pacific Fleet.'

[50] Permanent Mission of the Soviet Union (Geneva), 'General Razuvanov on visit to Tooele chemical facility', *Press Bulletin*, no. 214 (25 Nov. 1987), p. 3.

[51] *Ad Hoc Meeting of Scientific and Technical Experts from States Parties to the Convention on the Prohibition of the Development, Production and Stockpiling of Bacteriological (Biological) and Toxin Weapons and on their Destruction*, BWC/CONF.II/EX/2, 21 Apr. 1987.

[52] APN, ['Information by the USSR in Pursuance of the Accords Reached at the 2nd Review Conference on the Prohibition of the Development, and Stockpiling of Bacteriological (Biological) and Toxin Weapons and on Their Destruction, and in Keeping with the Decisions and Recommendations of the Special Meeting of Scientific and Technical Experts from the Participating States'], *Military Bulletin*, no. 21(27), (Oct. 1987), p. 2 (in German).

[53] ['Genetic techniques: viruses in the grey zone'], *Der Spiegel*, 9 Mar. 1987, pp. 221–7 (in German); Rose, S., 'Biotechnology at war: stop worrying about the bomb & start worrying about nerve gas . . .', *New Scientist*, 19 Mar. 1987; Geissler, E. (ed.), SIPRI, *Biological and Toxin Weapons Today* (Oxford University Press: Oxford, 1986); and Douglass, J. D. and Livingstone, N. C., *America the Vulnerable: the threat of chemical and biological warfare* (Lexington Books: Lexington, Mass., 1987).

[54] *Prohibition of the Development, Production and Stockpiling of Bacteriological (Biological) and Toxin Weapons and on their Destruction, Final Document*, 13, 30 Sep. 1986, Annex I, BWC/Conf. II/4 and Addenda 1 and 2.

[55] Harris, E., 'Sverdlovsk and yellow rain: two cases of Soviet noncompliance?', *International Security*, vol. 11, no. 4 (spring 1987), pp. 41–95.

[56] Robinson, J., Guillemin, J. and Meselson, M., 'Yellow rain: the story collapses', *Foreign Policy*, no. 68 (fall 1987), pp. 100–17.

[57] *The President's Unclassified Report on Soviet Noncompliance with Arms Control Agreements*, The White House: Office of the Press Secretary, 3 Oct. 1987.

[58] US Defense Department, for example, in the foreword of a report to the Congress: 'The use of potent, previously unknown biological weapons (toxins) in southeast Asia and perhaps Afghanistan has underscored the need to develop effective biological defenses . . .', *Department of Defense Biological Defense Program*, May 1986, p. i.

[59] *Hansard* (Commons), vol. 108, no. 35, col. 880 (21 Jan. 1987).
[60] Details are given in *SIPRI Yearbook 1985* (note 17), pp. 181–3, 206–19.
[61] See, for example, Mäder, S. (from Recklinghausen), ['Iranian with mustard burns begs the doctors: "Don't hurt me!"'], *Westdeutsche Allgemeine*, 31 Jan. 1987 (in German).
[62] The 'chronological table ... provided in the annex' referred to by the Iranian Foreign Minister, Dr Ali Akbar Velayati, in his statement to the CD in plenary session on 9 Apr. 1987; see Conference on Disarmament document CD/PV.404, p. 5.
[63] As quoted by Iran in Conference on Disarmament document CD/PV.406, 16 Apr. 1987, p. 31.
[64] See especially, Graham, H., 'Kurds accuse Iraq of chemical attack', *Independent* (London), 21 Apr. 1987, p. 10; *Appeal to the World Public Opinion on the Use of Poison Gas and Chemical Weapons in Iraqi Kurdistan*, Patriotic Union of Kurdistan, Foreign Relations Committee, 22 Apr. 1987; Jenkins, L. (from Baneh), 'Iranians detail charges of gas warfare', *Washington Post*, 11 May 1987, p. 1; and Lancaster, P., 'Fighting guerrillas with gas', *Middle East*, June 1987, p. 17.
[65] *Report of the Mission Dispatched by the Secretary-General to Investigate Allegations of the Use of Chemical Weapons in the Conflict Between the Islamic Republic of Iran and Iraq*, UN document S/18852, 8 May 1987.
[66] Kaidi, H., ['Iraq: blind chemical bombing'], *Jeune Afrique*, no. 1382 (1 July 1987), p. 27 (in French).
[67] See, especially, Alexander, A. (from Tabriz) 'Iraq continues chemical war against Iran; UN looks other way', *Atlanta Constitution*, 9 July 1987, p. 22.
[68] AP from Vienna, in 'Chemical claim', *Guardian*, 15 July 1987, p. 6.
[69] Graham, H., 'Iraq confronts Kurdish gains', *Independent*, 18 Sep. 1987, p. 9.
[70] By an Iraqi military spokesman reported in an INA release of 10 Oct. 1987, as cited via *FBIS-ME* of 13 Oct. 1987, in *Arms Control Reporter*, Oct. 1987, pp. 704.B.246–7.
[71] Letter from the Minister of Foreign Affairs of the Islamic Republic of Iran addressed to the UN Secretary-General, in UN Security Council document S/19193, 9 Oct. 1987.
[72] Karsh, E., 'The Iran–Iraq War: a military analysis', *Adelphi Papers*, no. 220 (IISS: London, spring 1987), p. 56.
[73] See note 72.
[74] Hirst (see note 28). See also Morris, H., 'Iran military wants to use chemical arms', *Independent*, 28 Dec. 1987; and AP from Manama, in 'Iranians back off claim for weapons', *Washington Times*, 31 Dec. 1987, p. 9.
[75] 'Warsaw Treaty Foreign Ministers' statement of 25 March 1987', *Soviet News*, no. 6368 (1 Apr. 1987), p. 114; and 'Warsaw Treaty Member-States statement on the issue of a ban on chemical weapons, adopted during the WTO Foreign Ministers' meeting in Moscow 24–25 March 1987', *Soviet News*, no. 6368 (1 Apr. 1987), pp. 113, 115. See also Trapp, R. (ed.), *Chemical Weapon Free Zones?*, SIPRI Chemical & Biological Warfare Studies no. 7 (Oxford University Press: Oxford, 1987).
[76] Statements of the Foreign Ministers of the GDR and Czechoslovakia on the occasion of the visit of Czechoslovakian Foreign Minister Chňoupek to the GDR in April 1987, *Neues Deutschland*, 14 Apr. 1987, p. 2.
[77] *Neues Deutschland*, 25–25 Jan. 1987, p. 6.
[78] Talks between SED General Secretary E. Honecker and SPD Parliamentary Group Chairman H.-J. Vogel on 15 May 1987, as reported by *Neues Deutschland*, 16–17 May 1987.
[79] 'Nazarkin described the state of negotiations in Geneva', *Arms Control Reporter*, July 1987, pp. 704.B.229–30; and Novikov, A., *Komsomolskaya Pravda*, 16 June 1987, cited by *FBIS-SU*, 22 June 1987.
[80] UK, Conference on Disarmament document CD/715, 15 July 1986.
[81] USA, Conference on Disarmament document CD/500, 18 Apr. 1984.
[82] USSR, Conference on Disarmament document CD/PV.429, 11 Aug. 1987, p. 5.
[83] See, for example, USSR, Conference on Disarament document CD/751 of 13 Apr. 1987.
[84] Text of *Treaty between the United States and the Union of the Soviet Socialist Republics on the Elimination of their Intermediate-Range and Shorter-Range Missiles*, concluded in Washington on 8 Dec. 1987, United States Information Service, press section, SM–0011208, Stockholm, 10 Dec. 1987.
[85] France, Conference on Disarmament document CD/PV.390, 19 Feb. 1987.
[86] French Cabinet announcement, *Le Monde*, 8 Nov. 1987.
[87] USA, Conference on Disarmament document CD/PV 432, 20 Aug. 1987.
[88] See, for example, Permanent Mission of the Soviet Union (Geneva), 'Statement of the Foreign Ministry', *Press Bulletin*, no. 273(1500), (31 Dec. 1987).

[89] Mamedov, E., 'Who is obstructing talks on banning chemical weapons', *International Affairs* (Moscow), no. 8 (Aug. 1987), p. 102.

[90] SIPRI, *Chemical Disarmament: New Weapons for Old*, (Almqvist & Wiksell: Stockholm, 1975).

[91] 'A fifth round of Soviet–American bilateral consultations on the CW Convention began', *Arms Control Reporter*, Mar. 1987, p. 704.B.214; 'Chemical weapons: progress in Soviet–American bilateral talks', *Atlantic News*, 13 Mar. 1987, p. 18; 'The USSR and the US agreed to exchange visits to destruction facilities', *Arms Control Reporter*, May 1987, p. 704.B.221; United States Mission (Geneva), 'US invites USSR to US chemical weapons destruction site', *Daily Bulletin*, 23 Apr. 1987, p. 4; TASS, 'The sixth round of Soviet–US consultations in Geneva on banning chemical weapons has come to a close', 10 Aug. 1987; 'US Soviets agree on chemical plant visits', *Washington Post*, 11 Aug. 1987, p. 21; and Statement by the US Delegation to the CD, 'US–USSR talks on chemical weapons end', United States Information Service, press section, EU4101217, Geneva, 17 Dec. 1987.

[92] TASS, report of a statement by Deputy Foreign Minister V. Petrovsky at a press conference in Moscow on 10 Nov. 1987.

[93] Lundin, S. J., 'Confidence-building measures and a chemical weapons convention', SIPRI, *Chemical Weapons: Destruction and Conversion* (Taylor & Francis: London, 1980), pp. 139–53.

[94] FR Germany, Conference on Disarmament document CD/518, 17 July 1984.

[95] Baberdin, Lt-Col V., ['Shikhany: two days in October'], *Krasnaya Zvezda*, 16 Oct. 1987 (in Russian); and Walker, C., 'Angry clash as chemistry of glasnost goes awry', *Times*, 6 Oct. 1987, p. 1.

[96] Report of the Ad Hoc Committee on Chemical Weapons, appendix I, Conference on Disarmament document CD/782, 26 Aug. 1987.

[97] '12th workshop of the Pugwash study group on chemical warfare: verification of non-production', *Pugwash Newsletter*, vol. 24, no. 4 (Apr. 1987), pp. 106–10; and Lundin, S. J., Working group 4, 'Chemical weapons: build-up or elimination', *Pugwash Newsletter*, vol. 25, no. 2 (Oct. 1987), pp. 80–2.

[98] UK, Conference on Disarmament document CD/769, 10 July 1987; and ADN, ['On improving the effectiveness of the Geneva Conference on Disarmament: document of the meeting of the Foreign Ministers Committee of the Warsaw Treaty Member States'], *Neues Deutschland*, 31 Oct. 1987, p. 6 (in German).

[99] Sims, N. A., *International Organization for Chemical Disarmament*, SIPRI Chemical & Biological Warfare Studies no. 8 (Oxford University Press: Oxford, 1987).

Part II. Military expenditure, the arms trade and armed conflicts

Chapter 6. SIPRI military expenditure data

Chapter 7. The trade in conventional weapons

Chapter 8. The naval arms trade and implications of changes in maritime law

Chapter 9. Major armed conflicts in 1987

6. SIPRI military expenditure data

RITA TULLBERG and GERD HAGMEYER-GAVERUS

I. Introduction

The subject of military expenditure data is responding slowly to demands for more complete and standardized information. Various United Nations forums have called for an improved and comprehensive data base which would help the analysis of the impact of global defence spending on the international economy. In addition, it is recognized that the exchange of military data can help as a confidence-building measure in areas of tension. It can also facilitate plans involving the limitation of military expenditure as a means of arms control, though of course political will and economic constraints are far more important and necessary conditions for disarmament. The UN Reduction of Military Budgets project is also seeking to construct standardized methods for defining and comparing national defence budgets.[1] In 1987, General Secretary Gorbachev announced the intention of publishing Soviet military spending data in a form comparable to that of Western budget data. Though this will take time, given the differences in economic-accounting structures and procedures, it must be considered a welcome move.

Military expenditure data are collected to provide information on the size and economic burden of military spending not only to meet these international requirements but also for the purposes of domestic discussion and analysis. At the domestic level, accountability of those responsible for public spending is a fundamental element of the democratic process. Public control presupposes a reasonably accurate knowledge of the amount of resources allocated to various areas of government spending—roads, hospitals and schools, for example—as well as to the military. Rational choices in public spending cannot be made on the basis of incomplete or misleading information.

SIPRI provides military expenditure data in forms which can be used for many purposes: simple comparative statements; analyses of time trends; measurements of the burden of military spending; evaluations of the relationship between military and socio-economic variables; and so forth. They can also be used as a basis from which more complex information on different elements of the military budget can be examined: how these budgets are financed; how the money is spent; and the relative importance of procurement, personnel or research and development (R&D) expenditures. All these methods of financing and spending military allocations have different macroeconomic, public-finance and inter-industrial implications for the economy in the short, medium and long term. For a discussion of the economic aspects of military expenditure, see chapter 16.

SIPRI aims to identify, record and monitor military-related expenditure in accordance with a standard definition for as many countries and for as many years as are possible or relevant. Countries not included in the military expenditure data base are small (often island) states which have only recently gained their independence and/or which are known to have very small or non-existent armed forces. For some countries at war, under occupation or otherwise isolated, no adequate information is available.[2]

Ten-year military expenditure series are published annually in the *SIPRI Yearbook* in local currencies at current prices, in US dollars at constant prices and as a percentage of gross domestic product (GDP). Every effort is made to standardize data on the basis of the NATO definition of military spending (given in the notes, definitions and sources for the tables of world military expenditure in appendix 6A). The definition is a functional one and covers all spending by central or federal governments on resources which serve a military purpose. SIPRI data are gathered independently of any government or political organization. Only open sources are used.

Wherever possible, primary sources—the budgets and accounts of the countries concerned—are examined, so that data can be brought in line with the standard NATO definition. This is because figures cited by countries as 'defence spending' often cover only the amount spent by the armed forces on manpower and equipment or in some cases only on manpower. However, significant sums can be spent on such items as central administration, service pensions, education in military schools and academies, military R&D undertaken in military and civilian establishments, military elements of atomic energy and space programmes, health services, geological and meteorological services, financial support to military industries, military housing, military lawyers and paramilitaries, all of which may be included in the budgets of other ministries or in off-budget accounts.[3] An examination of government accounts and budgets, where available, permits a more informed assessment of the total volume of resources devoted to military ends.

Emphasis in this chapter is therefore placed on descriptions of the data provided in the military expenditure tables (tables 6A.1–6A.3). Sections II–XI examine the sources and content of recent data, within the familiar framework of the major alliances and regions of the world. The chapter concludes with a description of the economic data used to construct two special SIPRI series: military expenditure in constant prices and dollars, and military spending as a share of national resources.

II. NATO

Among the more closely monitored events of the year has been the progress of the US defence budget for fiscal year (FY) 1988 (1 October 1987–30 September 1988) through Congress. The Reagan Administration had asked for US $312 billion. Insisting that the Pentagon must bear its share of the general cut-back in government spending, Congress finally agreed on a budget authority of $291.5 billion for national defence. This represented a 4 per cent real reduction in national defence authority, cutting spending for the third fiscal year in succession. Overall, the real increase during President Reagan's seven years of office has been 28 per cent. The budget request for FY 1989 proposes $299.5 billion in budget authority for national defence, $33 billion lower than the amount proposed in earlier plans. Heavy cuts are inevitable in the programmes of the three services and in the Strategic Defense Initiative (SDI) programme.

The NATO governments all felt, in some degree, the need to maintain tight control of their military expenditure, as pressure mounted on other areas of public spending. However, the final communiqué of the NATO Planning Committee, meeting in Ministerial Session in Brussels in May 1987, did not reflect these fiscal worries. The Ministers welcomed the progress which was being made in the field of arms control between East and West. None the less, the need was felt to retain and strengthen the NATO strategy of flexible response and forward defence. The Ministers therefore reaffirmed the 3 per cent annual real increase in the defence expenditure of member countries as part of the broad guidelines for the development of NATO's deterrence and defence requirements. Continued emphasis on this 3 per cent figure is surprising since the Ministers clearly understand that it is the use made of available resources rather than the rate of growth of overall resources that determines whether policy objectives can be met. As a planning tool the figure is of little value, not only because it is not very meaningful to make a statistic a goal in itself, but also because its fulfilment can be established only years after the event. Its propaganda value is weakened by an examination of the problems involved in its measurement even when the data are produced in a standardized form by NATO itself.

Military expenditure data are collected and collated for 14 NATO countries and published annually by NATO at the beginning of December.[4] Iceland has no armed forces and data are still not available for Spain, although that country became a member of NATO in 1982. When given, Spanish data, like those of France, will be 'indicative only' since neither country belongs to the integrated military structure of NATO.[5] Tables currently published by NATO cover military expenditure in local currencies at current prices and, since 1986, in dollars at constant prices, together with both current and constant dollar aggregates. Tables are published on military expenditure as a percentage of GDP; military expenditure and GDP per capita in constant prices and dollars; equipment expenditure as a percentage of total military expenditure; and numbers of armed forces personnel and total armed forces as a percentage of the labour force.

The notes accompanying the NATO tables are brief and the picture is further complicated by recent changes in presentation. Prior to December 1986, the figures given in the military expenditure tables represented payments actually made or to be made during the course of the calendar year. Since 1986, the payments are given on a fiscal year basis. In the column headed '1985', for example, data are given for France for the calendar year 1985, for the UK for the fiscal year 1985/86 and for the USA for the fiscal year 1984/85.[6]

The data are described as being based on the NATO definition of military expenditure which, however, is not given. The figures for Canada, FR Germany and the USA are mentioned as including expenditures for military aid programmes. It is not clear whether this means that the military aid programmes of other countries, such as France and the UK, are excluded. The

132 MILITARY EXPENDITURE, ARMS TRADE, CONFLICTS

confusion is compounded by the inclusion of military aid in the British presentation of the military expenditure budget for the UK according to the NATO definition (see table 6.1). The British budget also affords a good example of different concepts of defence spending. Three are given—defence votes, defence budget and defence expenditure (NATO definition)—and any one of the three may loosely be referred to as 'defence spending'. Furthermore there are discrepancies in the two versions of defence spending according to the NATO definition (A and B in table 6.1). These differences are in some cases small but can amount to +/−£0.5 billion.

Table 6.1. The British defence budget: domestic and NATO definitions

Figures are in £m.

	Fiscal years					
	1979	1980	1981	1982	1983	1984
Defence Votes	8 463	10 668	12 138	13 945	15 792	16 818
Attributions from other votes[a]	89	109	127	138	173	204
Other adjustments[b]	6	7	9	7	8	11
Defence Budget	8 558	10 785	12 274	14 091	15 973	17 033
Military aid to overseas countries	14	7	11	15	15	13
Supporting services[c]	347	362	422	450	426	428
Meteorological services in defence budget	−29	−37	−34	−37	−35	−41
Other adjustments	−4	−4	−4	15	14	−2
Defence Expenditure (A) (NATO definition)	8 885	11 113	12 668	14 534	16 394	17 431
Memorandum item NATO data (B)[d]	9 029	11 542	12 144	14 870	15 830	17 511
Difference between NATO data (B) and British data (A)	144	429	−524	336	564	80

Numbers may not add up to totals because of rounding.

[a] Property Service Agency (PSA) staff costs and other PSA expenditure.
[b] Appropriations-in-aid and expenditure included in Defence Votes but not classified as public expenditure.
[c] Accommodation (maintenance and rental); stationery and printing; home publicity; civil superannuation (by far the largest item); computers and telecommunications; rates; services by the National Audit Office; services by the Treasury Solicitor; valuations services by the Inland Revenue; various other services.
[d] As published by NATO.

Source: UK, Statement on the Defence Estimates 1985–86 (HMSO: London, 1985), Cmnd 9430–II, table 2.4, p. 10. NATO data are taken from NATO Press Release, 1 Dec. 1987 and Defence and Economy World Report (Washington, DC), no. 1072 (18 Jan. 1988).

NATO data published in early December each year include figures for current-year spending. Recent-year figures involve a high degree of estimation[7] and cannot be used to establish growth rates for military spending. As in all compilations of statistics, revisions must be made as data are finalized, in some cases several years after the end of the fiscal year in question. For example, the real growth of US spending in 1985, as estimated by NATO in December 1986, was 2.5 per cent—a dramatic decline over the 1984 growth rate. However, the data when revised and published in December 1987 showed a growth of 6.5 per cent for the same period, a far less significant fall in the rate of growth of military spending. It can be assumed that further, though probably minor, adjustments will be made to the data before publication in December 1988.

These statistical problems—inconsistencies of definition, confusion over fiscal years and the inevitable revision of data—take on a special significance in the light of the commitment to the goal of 3 per cent annual real growth of military expenditure, first made in 1978 and adopted as part of the Long Term Defence Programme (LTDP) for the 1980s, reaffirmed in 1985 and again in 1987. This was an expression of political will, which had little to do with economic—and even less with statistical—realities. It is problematic to determine whether Alliance members have lived up to the 3 per cent real-growth goal. Current and future growth rates can only be, at best, rough estimates. Clearly, whether the exercise is to increase military spending or to reduce it, the statistical issues involved in measuring the change are important.

III. The WTO

Soviet military expenditure

The economic reforms currently under way in the Soviet Union will gradually have an impact on the Soviet military sector and on Soviet defence spending. Since the beginning of 1988, Soviet factories are obliged to be self-financing and have full responsibility for their own accounts.[8] This will result in a change of the price structure towards more market-oriented prices, which may also influence the prices of military goods and hence military spending. Restructuring an economy is a process that takes a long time, yet demand in the consumer sector is very great and the reforms need some fast, visible results. General Secretary Gorbachev therefore wants the capacity of the military sector to be used to build up the food industry.[9]

The official Soviet defence budget for 1987 was 20.2 billion roubles. In October 1987 Soviet Finance Minister Boris Gostev confirmed that this figure covers only the upkeep of the army's personnel, their pensions and infrastructure costs.[10] However, General Secretary Gorbachev had announced a month earlier that the Soviet Union might publish defence budget figures comparable to those of Western budgets—but only after two or three years, because a thorough reform of the Soviet pricing system is necessary before the figures can be calculated.[11] In January 1988 Marshal Sergei Akhromeyev stated that in the near future the Soviet Union would publish a defence budget that included all military-related expenditures.[12] The official statements made in 1987 and 1988 clearly confirm what was known before, that the official budget figure only describes the operational costs of Soviet military defence and does not include military R&D and procurement. Until more detailed information about military spending is disclosed—as announced—Soviet military expenditure will have to be estimated in one way or another.

How much the Soviet Union really spends on the military is the subject of much discussion and debate. The difficulties encountered in getting a clear picture of Soviet military efforts in economic terms are illustrated by the wide range of estimates on Soviet military expenditure and the Soviet military burden to be found in the open scientific literature. SIPRI has in the past frequently published on the subject, most recently in 1987.[13]

The interested world often focuses on the estimates put forward by the US Central Intelligence Agency (CIA) as the 'reliable' estimates, although the sources and methods used for the compilation of these estimates are not disclosed other than in a very general way. Alternatively, experts from the scientific community produce their own estimates, using Soviet statistical material and econometric models. However, the assumptions underlying these models are discussed and disputed at length.

Intelligence agency approaches

Since a great deal of interest focuses on CIA estimates of Soviet military expenditure, it may be useful to evaluate these numbers for the 1980s. Three major revisions have been made in the way the Agency calculates its time series data, in constant roubles and dollars. The first, and most controversial, was made in 1976. Soviet rouble defence spending was doubled, relative to earlier estimates, on the assumption that defence industries in the USSR were less productive (by half) than earlier assumed. The second revision (in 1983) lowered the previously reported growth rate of Soviet defence spending for the late 1970s. In particular, the growth rate of total spending, in constant 1970 roubles, was measured at 2 per cent per year starting from 1976.[14] The most recent methodological change rebased the constant price series from 1970 to 1982 price levels in roubles.[15] It is also thought that the proportions of the major resource categories (investment, operating costs and R&D[16]) in the total will now change to reflect the current price structure.

The CIA uses the so-called building-block method to arrive at a Soviet defence-expenditure figure in both roubles and dollars. It puts an estimated Soviet price and a US dollar price on all items of the defence sector. To obtain a rouble price the cost of producing the item in the Soviet Union is estimated. For the dollar estimate the CIA calculates the cost of producing an identical item in the USA. Information on military items is not taken from Soviet statistics but from various intelligence sources. R&D costs, however, are estimated from Soviet statistics.

To calculate the burden of defence, the CIA constructs Soviet end-use gross national product (GNP) on the basis of a large amount of Soviet statistical and budget data.[17]

The US Defense Intelligence Agency (DIA) presents Soviet defence expenditure as a rouble estimate in current roubles (unadjusted for inflation). Unlike the CIA, the DIA makes considerable use of Soviet statistics. The DIA's basic assumption is that the defence portion of the Soviet state budget has remained constant (at 31–34 per cent).[18]

Other approaches

In the absence of intelligence sources, other approaches depend on statistics collected and provided by the Soviet administration: official national accounts, input–output accounts, demographic and other statistics. It is assumed that by combining all these statistics an overall quantified picture of Soviet society is obtained. Input and output must balance as well as income and expenditures. Subtracting identifiable uses of output from Soviet national income or budget statistics, one is able to discover 'gaps' or hidden accounts, which many conclude must belong to the military sector. Finding and assigning those gaps is called the 'residual approach', which in one or another form has been applied by the following authors.

1. Dmitri Steinberg uses the concept of extra-budgetary funding for defence production and other defence sectors, tracing such funding from the gaps revealed by comparing national accounts with other Soviet statistics.[19]

2. Gerard Duchêne estimates the defence burden using the framework of material product accountancy (MPA). He seeks 'to determine which part of the production of the so-called productive sectors is used by the military non-productive institution'.[20] He uses current prices without any factor cost adjustments. Pensions are not included in his estimates.

3. Kiichi Mochizuki derives an estimate from the Soviet national accounts by examining the production data and the demand categories.[21]

4. The Arms Control and Disarmament Agency (ACDA) uses CIA figures and converts them to current dollar figures.[22]

5. Bill Lee calculates Soviet national security expenditures as the sum of three components: durables, personnel and construction, as well as R&D. The estimates of the first component have come in for particular criticism.[23] The fundamental assumption was that all unaccounted for and unspecified production of machine-building and metal-working (MB&MW) went to defence. Military procurement is calculated as a residual of MB&MW industries' net output—minus consumption and investment. The method has been criticized[24] for various reasons. The most important is that there is little evidence about the machine-building sector's use of its own output; hence the residual does not give an accurate picture of military demand.

6. Steven Rosefielde concludes from his analysis that the USSR has a very productive machine-building sector for military purposes; it acquired this by rapid introduction of expensive technology at the expense of consumer goods production. He concludes that, accounting for this, military expenditure and military burden are much higher than the CIA assumes. The framework of his analysis is Soviet production and national account statistics, using an input–output model on the basic data. Additionally he cannot find any proof for inflation in the Soviet productive sector, as others do. He arrives, therefore, at a very high and controversial growth rate for military expenditure.[25]

Estimates resulting from these different approaches are summarized in table 6.2.

The *SIPRI Yearbook 1987* explains why SIPRI has not continued to publish

Table 6.2. Estimates of Soviet military expenditure.

Figures are in billion current roubles.

Proponent	Limits	Value terms	1970	1972	1975	1980	1982	1984
USSR, official[a]		Current	17.9	17.9	17.4	17.1	17.0	17.0
CIA[b]	Lower limit	Current	..	..	..	99	108	111
	Upper limit	Current	..	..	..	112	122	125
Duchêne[c]		Current	..	..	43	59	65	72
Lee[d]	Lower limit	Current	42.5	51.0	66.5	..	..	..
	Upper limit	Current	49.0	58.5	76.0	..	..	..
Mochizuki[e]	Lower limit	Current	..	..	49.5	58.2	64.7	80.8
	Upper limit	Current	..	..	61.4	73.9	81.2	113
Rosefielde[f]		1970 constant	43.5	50.2	64.7	..	..	..
Steinberg[g]		Current	54.3	61.5	73.8	97.2	108.1	118.6

.. Information not available or not applicable.

Sources:

[a] IISS, *Military Balance 1987–88* (IISS: London, 1987), p. 29.

[b] The actual CIA estimates for the 1980s are still unpublished and are presumably classified. However, despite the paucity of open information available, specifically in the US Congress Joint Economic Committee (JEC) reports, it is possible to get a fair idea of a constructed time series which reflects the 'true' Agency values. Given SIPRI's interest in current price local currency values, the figures here are confined to the current rouble price reconstructed military expenditure figures for the Soviet Union.

Evidence from the 1986 JEC report claims that the share of GNP devoted to the military, *in current rouble prices*, was between 15 per cent and 17 per cent in the early 1980s. (See note 14, p. 31.)

The GNP series is given in 1982 roubles. Hence for 1982 the current and constant price figures coincide and the upper and lower limits of Soviet military expenditure can be estimated. These turn out to be 122 b. and 108 b. roubles, given a GNP of 719.7 b. roubles. The report also states that between 1975 and 1984 overall defence growth, *measured in dollars*, was around 2 per cent (note 14, p. 33). The 2 per cent growth rate is also used for SIPRI's reconstructed rouble series. First, the previous revision had already suggested, in very definitive terms, that the rate of growth of rouble military expenditure, in 1970 prices, was 2 per cent. Second, the updating of the base year (from 1970 to 1982) would certainly lower the rate of growth. (A Laspeyre index was used to calculate the base 1970 data and a Paasche index to calculate the base 1982 data.) Finally, the rouble prices are often determined by US dollar prices since precise monetary values of Soviet procurements are known for only a small fraction of total products used (*SIPRI Yearbook 1987*, p. 130). Thus, on the balance of probabilities, the 2 per cent 'rule' is applied to derive military expenditure values for 1980, 1981, 1983 and 1984. A correction is made for inflation by using the consumer price index (from *United Nations Statistical Yearbook*).

[c] Duchêne, G., 'How much do the Soviets spend on defence?', in Jacobsen (note 13), p. 110.

[d] Lee, W. T., *The Estimation of Soviet Defense Expenditures, 1955–75* (Praeger: New York, 1977), p. 141.

[e] Mochizuki, K., 'Estimating Soviet defence expenditures from national accounts', in Jacobsen (note 13), p. 133.

[f] Rosefielde, S., *False Science, Underestimating the Soviet Arms Buildup* (Transaction Books: New Brunswick, 1982), p. 186.

[g] Steinberg, D., 'Estimating total Soviet military expenditures: an alternative approach based on reconstructed Soviet national accounts', in Jacobsen (note 13), p. 32.

its own estimates: principally for lack of official data from the Soviet Union. However, in the interim, SIPRI is working on refining its methods of estimating Soviet defence expenditure in order to facilitate the provision of a SIPRI estimate again at a future date.

The rest of the WTO

Economic difficulties such as high inflation, trade deficits and severe debt problems are mirrored by the defence spending of most non-Soviet Warsaw Treaty Organization countries (referred to here as the non-Soviet WTO). Romania and Hungary have shown a real decrease in defence spending of 2.8 per cent and 1.3 per cent respectively over the past five years. Only slight increases were shown by Poland (1.8 per cent) and Czechoslovakia (2.3 per cent), while the German Democratic Republic increased its defence budget by an average of 5.4 per cent a year in real terms over this period, probably as a result of its strong economic performance.

SIPRI uses official aggregated budget data and actual expenditure data when available for these countries. Although these data do not represent total military outlay, the consistency of the figures with developments observed in the military sector and the economy in general indicates that they roughly reflect the current trends in total military spending.[26] While these data are the most detailed available, there are some problems: it is often unclear what is included under the budget heads; some heads may mean different things or include different items from one country to the next; and so on.

Budgeted aggregated military spending and actual expenditure are usually reported, except for the GDR—which has only reported budgeted figures since 1977. However, there are some other exceptions:

1. Czechoslovakia breaks spending down into expenditures by Czech lands, Slovakia and the central government. Alton argues that border guards may be included.[27]

2. Hungary publishes figures for defence expenditure and military earnings from activities such as work on construction projects, help with harvests, and so on.

3. Poland reports budget figures for current defence spending and for military investments which are presumably limited to military construction. Poland also reports on military earnings.

4. Romania reports budget figures and actual spending. Romania has started to submit more specific data to the United Nations,[28] disaggregated under the subheads: personnel costs, operations and maintenance costs, procurement and construction, administrative facilities and R&D.

5. Bulgaria is the only nation that currently does not publish a defence budget. From 1946–62 it reported total defence budget figures, and from 1963–70 the percentage share of defence in the state budget was announced. SIPRI made estimates for the years after 1970 using a percentage share of the total budget outlays as military expenditure.[29]

Operational costs and procurement of military durables by non-Soviet WTO economies may fall under 'social consumption', that is, consumption by state institutions and organizations satisfying common and collective needs.[30] Arms procurement and/or production are probably kept under the different heads of general consumption and centrally funded investment accounts. As in the estimation of Soviet military production and procurement, the input–output statistics of non-Soviet WTO countries could serve as a basis for tracing the production of military durables.

According to the NATO definition, border guards are included in military expenditures when militarily equipped and trained. In the case of the GDR, border guards are excluded and put under the heading of expenditures of the Ministry for the Interior.

Payments for the support of Soviet troops are probably also excluded from the defence budgets of the non-Soviet WTO countries. These costs are based upon agreements between the countries and are included in general accounts. They cover at least the provision of barracks, housing, services, warehouses, airfields and other facilities, but there is no evidence that any of the operational costs of the Soviet troops are met by the host countries. Domestic investments for strategic stockpiles and price subsidies for military equipment are also centrally funded.

SIPRI reports the defence budgets announced by the East European governments and converts them to dollars using conversion rates based on purchasing-power-parities (PPP) from 1978, extrapolated to 1986.[31]

IV. Other Europe

From 1982 to 1987, the countries in the 'other Europe' category have increased their military expenditures nominally by about 5 per cent a year. In real terms, however, the picture looks different when examining the annual average growth rate for the same period: Ireland decreased military spending by about 1.5 per cent; Switzerland and Sweden stayed at the same level; while Austria, Finland and Yugoslavia increased their military budgets by about 2 per cent.

Data from these countries are easily accessible, and in the case of Austria, Finland, Ireland and Sweden they are reported to the United Nations. Data from Albania and Yugoslavia are problematic. Albanian budget data are available through a domestic publication *Probleme Ekonomike*, from *Statistik des Auslandes* (SAUS) and from the *Europa Yearbook*. Yugoslavia's military expenditure is divided up into the expenditure of the central government—which finances the majority of the defence expenditures—and that of the states and local authorities—which pay some operational costs.

Ireland's Statistical Office publishes an annual figure of actual military expenditure adjusted for expenditures by departments other than the Defence Department. The figure covers personnel costs, including reserve force payments, civilian payments and pensions, and operation and maintenance costs such as transportation and travel, general service, provision of equipment, maintenance of buildings, military education and fuel storage. Procurement and construction are reported in detail. The figure also includes civil defence.

Switzerland[32] keeps a small number of professional military personnel for military training and education. During their 17-week military service, conscripts continue to be paid by their civilian employers: both salaries and social security costs are paid during their absence. Swiss defence expenditure figures include the cost of the defence administration, construction, transportation, stockpiling for military purposes and R&D. UN peacekeeping troops and military insurance are not included. The Defence Department only pays the social costs for its own employees, such as educational and training personnel, and administrative staff.

Sweden's military expenditure, as reported in a special statistic by the Department of Defence,[33] includes operational costs, administrative costs, R&D, transportation, maintenance and construction of buildings, stockpiling of military goods and operational costs for UN troops overseas. Civil defence costs and military pensions, which are paid out of the Swedish social security fund, are not included. However, a part of the military wages is regularly paid into the fund for these purposes.

Finland's military expenditure data are in line with the NATO definition, including defence force costs, administration, construction and procurement, medical care, transportation of military personnel and other social-related costs. Military costs in Finland, as in many other countries, are financed not only by the Ministry of Defence but also by other ministries. The data which the Finnish Defence Ministry provides to SIPRI include expenses for pensions, border guards, UN peacekeeping troops and military-related expenditures from the Ministry of Labour, the Ministry of Social Affairs and Health and the Ministry of Justice.

Austria's military expenditure data as published by the Defence Ministry[34] exclude costs for military pensions but cover all other military-related spending, even that financed from outside the Defence Ministry.

V. The Middle East

The *SIPRI Yearbook 1987* includes a discussion of the trends in military spending for countries of the Middle East and Africa over the past decade. Patterns of spending in 1987 were consistent with these trends. The political and economic situation is largely unchanged. The major war in the Middle East between Iran and Iraq still creates instability in the region, which is reflected in the military spending of their neighbouring countries. In 1987 the region's economic performance decreased—gross domestic product fell by 1.5 per cent.

With ongoing conflicts in the region, countries are very reluctant to provide information about their military spending. The war-fighting nations Iran and Iraq have not recently reported any reliable figures. Until 1981, Iranian military expenditures were reported by the International Monetary Fund (IMF). However, Iraqi data were available up to 1981 from SAUS and original budget publications, in an aggregated account for 'national defence and security'. Many countries in the region publish military expenditure in an account labelled national defence, internal order and security, or national defence, justice and security.

Saudi Arabia's defence spending—one of the biggest in the region—has been decreasing in recent years because of falling oil incomes. In the past, data have been reported in a very general way by journals and newspapers and for the years 1982–86 by the *Europa Yearbook*. Budget figures even on an aggregated level have not been available.

Israel and Egypt report their military expenditure budget data and actual spending. SIPRI deducts military grants from military expenditure and adds military loans made to the countries. The defence expenditure data released, however, could very well be an understatement of real military spending if the entire military debt burden is not captured.

Lebanon's national defence spending is reported by SAUS from national budgets, and it is also reported to the United Nations,[35] but it is difficult to ascertain real military spending in view of the conflict situation and the numerous groups it involves. Lebanon's national forces may be the smallest of the groups involved in the conflict. The value of a reported budget figure in such a situation is very open to question and, in a shattered war economy like that of Lebanon, economic data are difficult to obtain. For inflation and GDP a reasonable figure has not been obtainable for recent years; even estimates are almost impossible to achieve.

Jordan reports no defence spending on procurement for recent years, which, considering their extensive arms imports, is not realistic; however, these investments may be financed by assistance from other Arab states such as Saudi Arabia.

Oman is one of the few countries for which recent annual domestic statistics are available in a *Statistical Yearbook*. However, it publishes only a highly aggregated figure for defence and national security, which includes civilian-related security expenditures.

One of the big problems in determining military expenditures for the 'rich' oil-producing states is in identifying the extent to which they provide financial military assistance to other Arab states and especially Iraq. According to the NATO definition these expenditures are part of the military spending of the donor country. However, the level of aggregation of budget data means that they cannot be assigned to military spending.

VI. Africa

Africa's economic problems remain unsolved: in 1987 the low economic growth—estimated at 1.5 per cent[36]—did not keep pace with the rapid increase of the population. Total debt was estimated to be $233 billion[37] in 1987, which is an increase of 25 per cent since 1985. Many countries were therefore forced to introduce austerity packages. The major armed conflicts continued, causing more human tragedy, further disruption of the economies and an increasing diversion of scarce resources to military ends. Zimbabwe, Angola and Mozambique have to spend between 40 and 60 per cent of their total budgets on the military in order to fight wars against South African-supported guerrillas. To secure the continuation of its policy of apartheid, South Africa increased its military budget by 21 per cent in 1987 and continued its efforts to destabilize the region and to control internal opposition.

In recent years it has been increasingly difficult to obtain data for African states. Involvement in regional conflicts and civil wars and the security problems of military regimes are some of the reasons why governments do not want to disclose military spending figures. Domestic statistics, where available, and IMF data, *Statistik des Auslandes*, the US Agency for International Development (USAID) and the *African Research Bulletin*, are the major sources used.

In North Africa, Morocco and Tunisia spend major sums on the military, but a decline in spending can be seen in recent years. Budget data on current and capital expenditure are available from domestic statistics and publications. Libya reports an administrative budget figure for national defence which does not include expenditure for the extensive procurement of weapon systems. To arrive at a reasonable figure for Libya's defence spending, adjustment has to be made using information about the arms trade to Libya. SIPRI therefore adds to the given budget figure a value that represents Libya's arms purchases.

The military expenditure of South Africa is published annually in the government budget, but military-trained and -equipped police forces are not included. South Africa's defence spending is presumably much higher:

The Department of Public Works pays for expenditure on SADF (South African Defence Forces) construction, the Department of Finance covers the considerable cost of the SWA (South-West Africa/Namibia) Territory Force, and the Department of Community Development covers the cost of housing military personnel. Examples of additional expenditure are the capital expansion of ARMSCOR projects, the military R&D carried out by the Council for Scientific and Industrial Research (CSIR) and university departments and institutes, support for SADF Medical Services from the Department of Health and Welfare. South Africa's real defence expenditures are probably 30–35 per cent higher than the official budget figure.[38]

The Recurrent and Capital Estimate of the Republic of Nigeria is an annually published statistical volume of the Nigerian Ministry of Defence. It includes under the heading 'recurrent expenditure' the operational costs for the army, navy and air force as well as costs for the administrative and civilian staff. Medical services, costs of the defence academy, transportation, building maintenance, petrol, oil and lubricants are also included. Capital expenditure is very much dependent on national development plans. It includes procurement of weaponry, construction, provision of transport facilities, medical service and some R&D. Pensions are paid by different bodies. The civilian staff of the military sector receive their pension from a civilian account, which is not part of the budget of the Ministry of Defence. Military personnel receive their pension from an account of the Defence Ministry.[39] The published data of Nigerian defence expenditures are to a great extent compatible with military expenditure data under the NATO definition.

Angola is an example of the wartime economies of Africa. Data on Angola are difficult to obtain; the main sources are special country reports. A report on Angola from the Economic Intelligence Unit in London was presented in 1987. The report includes a series of valuable data which were collected from the Angolan authorities and via personal interviews during a visit to Angola by the author. Expert studies of this kind are sometimes the only valuable source of information.

VII. South Asia

Military expenditure in the sub-continent continues to rise. Tension between India and Pakistan remains high and border skirmishes during the year have exacerbated the problems. Though Pakistan is preoccupied with the prospective end to the Afghanistan problem, and India is concerned with its relations with China, the arms race between them has not abated. Domestic security problems and civil war have forced the Sri Lankan Government to increase defence budgets successively, sometimes more than once in the same year. Socio-economic entitlements have suffered as the government budget is diverted towards defence. In October 1987, Indian peacekeeping forces in Sri Lanka were involved in a major offensive against the Tamil separatists. Bangladesh continues to have serious political and economic problems. The restoration of democracy, following military rule, remains problematic, and economic aid from Western and Islamic donors is essential for survival.

Despite the great poverty of this region in terms of per capita incomes, the five countries given in the SIPRI tables have functioning statistical services. These, combined with an inherited tradition of parliamentary democracy and the frequent use of the English language in South Asia, afford good opportunities for the study of military spending in the region. On the other hand, military governments, civil unrest involving military participation and attempts to promote national identity by the use of local languages to the exclusion of English serve to make the task more difficult.

The degree to which SIPRI data conform with the NATO definition varies within the region. More is known about India, Nepal and Sri Lanka, and much less about Pakistan and Bangladesh. Nothing is known about Afghan military expenditure since 1980 and so Afghanistan has been omitted from the tables. It is clear that in the case of India and Pakistan some part of their nuclear programmes could be considered as military expenditure, as could India's space programme and Pakistan's production of rocket fuel and participation in the space programmes of other countries. This has not been done here.

Expenditure data on India have been taken from the *Defence Service Estimates* since FY 1980. Amounts allocated to R&D and the defence ordnance factories are included in totals given in the *Estimates*. Data on expenditure for medical services have been added by SIPRI to these totals to bring them in line with the NATO definition. Pensions were included in the *Estimates* until FY 1984; after that date the *Estimates* do not include expenditure on pensions.[40] Where necessary, estimates have been made for medical services and pensions on the basis of previous years' payments. Other military expenditure which does not seem to be included in the *Estimates*, and for which no provision is made in the SIPRI tables, is the administrative cost of the Ministry of Defence and of the Ministry of Finance (defence).[41] Back-dated and 'significantly improved' pay-scales for commissioned officers were announced by the Defence Minister in June 1987 which may not have been fully covered in the original budget of 1987 and would therefore require the voting of supplementary funds during the year.[42]

Information on Nepalese military expenditure is taken from budget speeches, where it is given in a highly aggregated form. After 1984, estimates have had to be made from total current expenditure of the central government. Expenditure on the police force, described by the International Institute for Strategic Studies (IISS) as paramilitary,[43] has been included. Pensions are given under the main budget head 'Miscellaneous', but it is not clear what part, if any, relates to military pensions.

Characteristic of the Sri Lankan budget in recent years, with the escalation of domestic disturbances, is the frequent announcement of supplementary military budgets. These tend to be large—up to 40 per cent or more of the original budget—and may account for discrepancies in reported spending. The military budget is known to cover the armed forces and the police, as well as such units as special security operations, the Home Guard, the Police Task Force and National Auxiliary Forces. The Sri Lankan Minister of State announced in late 1987 that India was spending about $1 million daily on its peacekeeping force of 25 000–30 000 men in Sri Lanka.[44] It was not made known, however, whether this is the additional cost of keeping the Indian contingent in Sri Lanka, nor whether Sri Lanka is making any contribution to their presence.

Bangladesh is reported to be increasing the size of its paramilitary forces; announced spending on the police in FY 1987 showed an allocation increase of over 40 per cent on the previous year. The details of recent military expenditure in Pakistan are not known, only its overall size. It has been suggested that many items of military spending are covered by the budgets of civilian ministries.[45] The FY 1987 budget contained a proposal for a defence tax in an attempt to cover more of the military budget from domestic revenue rather than from domestic and foreign borrowing.[46] The proposal was strongly opposed and quickly withdrawn, but the debate led to repeated calls for more openness on military spending. An opposition member complained that the National Assembly was informed about the defence budget 'in two lines'; he asked the Minister of Finance to give a breakdown of defence expenses, at least for that part of the budget which was not secret.[47]

VIII. The Far East

Some countries of the Far East continue to enjoy economic growth despite the slow-down of the world economy. Economic problems remain, however, for others, particularly those like Malaysia and Indonesia, which suffer from the decline of commodity prices. This is reflected in their military expenditure figures; the boom in defence spending witnessed in the early 1980s seems to be over. The arms race between South and North Korea continues. In spite of domestic unrest, the South Korean economy now has a very healthy trade surplus through export growth. Military expenditure there increased by over 30 per cent during the five-year period 1982–87. A similar trend is observable in Singapore, which has a strong economy coupled with an expanding defence capability. Economic reforms in socialist countries world-wide will, no doubt, affect Viet Nam, but the implications for defence cannot be predicted. In 1987

Japan's military burden was once again over 1 per cent, its historical upper limit.

Far Eastern countries are characterized not only by a wide variety of economic development levels but also by different politico-economic systems. They include capitalist, socialist and centrally planned economies, two world powers and many ex-colonies. Methods of presenting government expenditure data and degree of openness also vary greatly. The multiplicity and complexity of languages used in the region are a further obstacle to understanding the countries' public finance statistics.

Data are not given in the SIPRI tables for four of the countries in the region—China, Kampuchea, Laos and Viet Nam. SIPRI will put special effort into producing data on China and Viet Nam in the near future. Official figures for Chinese military expenditure are usually announced in the annual budget and expenditure reports to the National People's Congress. The amount has been falling in real terms since 1982, a reflection, most probably, of the reductions in personnel which have been made in the People's Liberation Army in recent years. It is believed, however, that the sums announced cover only manpower costs, while procurement and R&D are financed within the budgets of the Ministries of Machine Building. The composition of the Chinese national budget is such that it can also be assumed that certain investment takes place through off-budget accounts.[48]

Reliable data on Japanese military spending are published annually in the English-language version of the defence White Paper.[49] It includes tables which show military expenditure in relation to national income and other government spending, and gives a breakdown of outlays into personnel, equipment and R&D costs, as well as costs for major items of equipment. A special feature of the Japanese fiscal system is that budgeted amounts may not, by law, be exceeded. Adjustments to the original allocation are covered by supplementary budgets and contingency funds. As a result, the Defense Agency publishes data on budgeted spending only. The small differences which do arise are recorded in more general statistical sources.[50] Japanese military spending data do not completely match the NATO definition in that they do not include expenditure on pensions.

Military spending is included under at least three heads in the Singapore budget—the Ministry of Defence, the Ministry of Home Affairs, and Pensions—and in both the recurrent and the development estimates.[51] A functional classification of budget spending is also published, but the amount given for defence spending does not differ from that given in the budget of the Ministry of Defence. Total defence estimates are disaggregated into expenditure on manpower, other operating expenditures, grants, subsidies and other transfers, and development expenditure. Equipment costs appear to fall under both main and development expenditure heads. There is a separate security programme within the Ministry of Home Affairs, the objective of which is to ensure the security of Singapore and its territorial waters.[52] In 1985 the development budget of this security programme was devoted to the purchase of equipment for the Police Task Force and the Gurkha Contingent stationed in Singapore, numbering approximately 700 men. It can be deduced from the pensions budget that current and development expenditure on certain paramilitary forces are missing from SIPRI data.[53]

The 'Security Services' classification of the Hong Kong budget covers immigration, law and order, and internal security. Expenditure on internal security covers the cost of maintaining a garrison of British forces in Hong Kong, capital works related to accommodation for the garrison and internal security installations, and the auxiliary services which are available to assist the armed forces and the civil power in times of emergency. These latter are the Royal Hong Kong Auxiliary Air Force and the Royal Hong Kong Regiment (the Volunteers). Under the Defence Costs Agreement, effective for seven years from 1 April 1981, the Hong Kong Government contributes 75 per cent of the total costs of British troops in the colony and provides for a programme of capital works and maintenance associated with the garrison and other military facilities. Outside the Agreement, the Hong Kong Government is contributing to the capital cost of the replacement of five Royal Navy patrol craft. Since 1985 the size of the garrison has been somewhat reduced, as the local police force has expanded to deal with the problems of illegal immigration from China.[54]

Information on military spending in the Philippines during the Marcos era is confusing, with one government publication seeming to contradict another.[55] The objective of the Ministry of National Defence (MND) was at that time 'to upgrade national defence capability and to maintain peace and order throughout the nation'.[56] Three-quarters of the estimated spending was for the Philippine Armed Forces (AFP) and covered logistical services, training, intelligence, medical and dental services, and home defence and civilian relations activities. Most of the remainder was for the paramilitary Integrated National Police. No mention is made of the budget of the Civilian Home Defence Force (CHDF) which numbered over 60 000 at the time of Marcos' downfall.[57] The budgets of President Aquino have not been examined but it seems probable that allocation for 'peace and order' are no longer included in the defence budget *per se*, which would explain why SIPRI's current estimates are so low. Amounts budgeted for the police and paramilitary forces must be included in any assessment of overall military spending. President Aquino announced plans in June 1987 to disband the much-criticized CHDF, replacing it with a citizen's army, and to expand the military forces.[58] During the year, two major pay and pension increases were announced for the AFP, which will be a heavy charge on future budgets.[59]

Indonesia is an example of a country in which the military, through the official doctrine of 'dual function', play a central role in the development of the country's economic and social life and in maintaining political stability and internal order. The armed forces are said to control, directly or indirectly, the majority of seats in the two legislative assemblies. Regional and local government are heavily militarized, as is the state bureaucracy.[60] Military personnel can also be found holding a variety of civil and industrial posts. With such a degree of integration of the military into what normally would be considered civilian domains, it is very difficult to draw clear boundaries between military and civilian spending. When oil revenues were high and Indonesia was in the market for new and advanced military equipment, it was believed that some of this procurement was financed over the budgets of certain state enterprises which were under direct military control.[61] SIPRI data are adjusted to account for the 30–40 per cent of military expenditure believed to be financed outside the budget during that period. Items in both the routine and development budgets cover 'National Defence and Security', but the amounts spent are not announced in the budget speech.[62]

English-language reports on the Thai budget give basic information on military spending, both budgeted and actual. In some cases the budget is presented both by ministry and by functional category. Military spending includes the two categories 'internal security' and 'national defence'. Paramilitary forces, such as the National Defence Volunteers and other groups, are organized by the Internal Security Operations Command (ISOC) which is an army-affiliated agency. Through ISOC, the army is reported to be taking a leading role in plans to develop the north-eastern region for both economic and security reasons.[63] Included in SIPRI data are known or estimated amounts for the army's 'secret fund'. Amounts budgeted for this fund are made public, and include transfers from regular army allocations. The uses to which they are put, however, remain a secret, though the army in its request for funds in 1987 said that they were needed for speedy and covert border operations co-ordinated by the police and the armed forces.[64]

SIPRI uses the official North Korean military expenditure data monitored in Seoul. The North Korean budget is presented to the Supreme People's Assembly under functional categories; official military spending represents about 14 per cent of the government budget. It is believed, however, that other military outlays occur in the people's economic and socio-cultural sectors of the budget; in particular, that arms production falls under the commission of Metal and Machine Industry.[65] Military spending takes approximately 30 per cent of the national budgets of both South Korea and Taiwan. Single budget figures for annual military spending are given wide publicity, but are not disaggregated. In the case of Taiwan, 'defence and foreign affairs' are grouped together, though it is assumed that the bulk of this spending is for military purposes. Both countries have rapidly developing arms-production capabilities. It is not known whether R&D costs and subsidies to military industries are included in the announced military spending. Very little is known about recent military spending in Brunei, Burma and Mongolia, and the budget of Malaysia has not yet been examined.

Economic data for this region present no major problems, although data on North Korea, Mongolia and Taiwan are not included in IMF sources. Mongolian dollar exchange-rates are taken from *Statistik des Auslandes*.[66] North Korea claims to have no inflation. Data for Taiwan are drawn from the official *Statistical Yearbook*.[67]

IX. Oceania

The Australian Government, in an effort to reduce the federal deficit below 1 per cent of GDP, made cuts in military spending in real terms in 1987. This is believed to be only a temporary slow-down in the flow of resources to the military. In a policy statement published in a 1987 Defence White Paper, New Zealand announced its intention of adopting a more self-reliant defence strategy. Although it was held that the new objectives could be achieved at about the current level of spending, substantial increases were made in the FY 1987 military budget overall and in the procurement allocation. From Fiji it was reported in the autumn that Army pay was being cut by 18–25 per cent to help the country out of the economic difficulties resulting from the constitutional crisis on the island.[68]

The data on Australia, Fiji and New Zealand given in the SIPRI tables are in close agreement with the NATO definition used by SIPRI. In all three cases budget material has been examined; Australia and New Zealand have participated in the UN Reduction of Military Budgets project. The availability of economic data for the three countries is generally good.

For Australia, outlay figures are used from the Departments of Defence and Defence Support, as published in the latest *Defence Report*.[69] The items covered include R&D, outlays on military pensions, medical services and military industries. Totals are corrected for minor outlays on civil defence. In a reply to the UN budget project, Australia pointed out that its civil defence service is more oriented to national disaster than conflicts.[70] Newspaper reports of the FY 1987 military budget note that a reduction of 1 per cent in real terms is planned and that there will be further adjustment in the final figures for FY 1986.

Fijian data have been supplied for a number of years in considerable detail by the Fijian Bureau of Statistics. SIPRI has published the data supplied, net of spending reimbursed by the UN in respect of Fijian units attached to the UN peacekeeping troops in the Lebanon and Sinai. A recent exmination of published budget accounts suggests, however, that military pensions are not included in this supplied material.[71] Political unrest in 1987 has disrupted the flow of information from Fiji.

New Zealand data are taken from the government expenditure estimates.[72] R&D is included each year. Unfortunately the FY 1985 expenditure includes an amount for civil defence and disaster relief, which it has not been possible to subtract. New Zealand data do not include superannuation payments for ex-servicemen or civilian employees of the Ministry of Defence.[73]

X. Central America

With the exception of Costa Rica, the countries of the Central American isthmus remained embroiled to varying degrees in domestic and border strife, exacerbated by superpower interference. The economic realities of poor growth, high inflation (with the exception of Honduras) and debt servicing problems left little room for constructive policies to redress the poverty and social inequalities which fuel the militant opposition. Having failed to suppress the various insurgent groups by military means, or to achieve the economic growth which might have mitigated popular grievances, the countries of the region sought in 1987 to reach negotiated settlements of their domestic and intra-regional problems. In particular, the economic difficulties of Nicaragua became critical by the end of the year. Risking a serious loss of popular domestic support in the face of hyperinflation and acute shortages of fuel and other necessities, the Nicaraguan Government felt obliged to adopt a flexible approach to reaching a *modus vivendi* with the Contra rebels. The performance of the Mexican economy was mixed, with some growth, very high inflation and an expansion of export earnings. These earnings, however, were needed to meet repayments of Mexico's foreign debt of over $100 billion. More than half the central government budget is spent on servicing government debt, both domestic and external, and with a budget deficit of about 17 per cent of GDP, there is criticism of the government's reluctance to cut public spending more severely. The Cuban economy was badly hit in 1987 by a poor sugar harvest and the curtailment of imports as a result of external debt problems and the continuing US economic embargo.

Primary source material for this region is fairly readily available, but its quality is very varied. Some expenditure estimates give not only spending on each programme but also a description of the objectives of the programmes in considerable detail. In other cases, 'national defence' is simply a one-line item, requiring much deeper research into official documents, should these become available.

SIPRI data on Costa Rica cover spending on the Guardia de Assistencia Rural (the Rural Guard), which forms part of the police service, expenditure within the Ministry of Public Security and pensions for its personnel, unspecified works, and the central administration of the security services where relevant. Costa Rica abolished its armed forces in 1948 but the security services have a military function, that is, the maintenance of the country's territorial integrity.[74] The Guardia de Assistencia Rural is generally considered a paramilitary force and has an important role to play in the unsettled border area with Nicaragua. President Oscar Arias announced in July 1987 that he wished to eliminate the 'military look' of the police by abolishing military ranks within the police forces, housing them outside the barracks, changing their uniforms and concentrating their attention on the protection of citizens from criminals.[75]

Good functional and programme budgets are given for the Dominican Republic in the official reports on government spending.[76] Expenditure on the armed forces can be found under the national defence, internal relations, education, health, social assistance and municipal and community service budgets. Expenditure on pensions took 14 per cent of total spending in 1985.[77] Jamaican data given in the annual *Estimates*[78] cover recurrent and capital expenditure on the Jamaican Defence Force, the Combined Cadet Force and their central administration within the Ministry of National Security. Although falling within the budget of the same ministry, the police force does not seem to have any paramilitary functions. Some small allocations for the justice department may be included in the national security data for the 1970s. It seems likely that pensions are covered elsewhere in the central government budget.

Official Cuban budget and expenditure data on military spending are used in the SIPRI tables for that country.[79] No information is supplied as to what these data cover and, since the Cuban military forces are made up of a number of paramilitary and reservist groups as well as regular forces and forces serving abroad, a disaggregated budget would be of particular interest. Cuba claims that it receives its military assistance from the USSR in the form of gifts rather than loans and in consequence does not incur any military debts.

The true levels of military spending in El Salvador and Guatemala are very difficult to estimate since political and economic life in the two countries is so thoroughly militarized. There have also been big differences between budgeted amounts and final expenditure in recent years, although inflation has not been remarkable. El Salvador, for example, submitted its actual spending in 1986 to the UN Reduction of Military Budgets project;[80] the amount reported was 70 per cent higher than the amount budgeted for overall defence in 1986,[81] far in excess of inflation for that year. Another difficulty in estimating military spending in these countries is the extent to which internal security should be included. It is quite clear that paramilitary forces exist in El Salvador, but nothing has been entered under this head on the UN project matrix. SIPRI data include estimates for internal security expenditure for all years except 1986. The functional budget for Guatemala[82] covers both defence and internal security, but budgeted amounts fall far below estimated expenditure. Estimates of military spending as a share of the central government budget range from 13 to 33 per cent.[83] A certain amount of confusion may arise from the fact that both these countries are receiving US security assistance which swells the funds available for military spending. However, under the NATO definition, security assistance is not included in the military expenditure of the recipient.

Most recent data for Honduras are contradictory. For example, the amount given as final expenditure for 1981 is identical with the amount given for final expenditure in 1982, the preliminary estimate of spending in 1983 and the budget for 1984.[84] The war in Nicaragua makes it impossible to give sensible estimates of military expenditure in that country. In recent years it has been reported that military spending took 40 per cent of central government expenditure. This estimate has now risen to 50 per cent.[85] In addition, annual inflation is currently between 1000 and 1500 per cent.

Mexican military expenditure accounts have not yet been examined in detail. However, the functional definition of spending used in the 1970s covers personnel and operational costs, procurement, medical and educational services, pensions, military construction and military industries.[86] Inflation has been high for many years, often greatly in excess of the expected rate of inflation on the basis of which expenditure plans are drawn up.

XI. South America

Many of the countries of this region are, to a greater or lesser extent, victims of the debt trap—that is, the paradoxical situation by which net transfers of funds are negative, flowing from the developing to the developed world. South American economies are forced to cut imports and boost exports. In doing so, they contribute to US trade problems, making it harder for the USA in turn to service its external debt. Military spending and debt are closely connected. A significant proportion of South American debt can be traced to arms purchases in the 1970s and strong links exist, via the budget deficit, between US foreign debt and the Reagan military buildup. Faced with an export imperative in a situation of generally depressed world trade, some South American countries are increasing their efforts to sell domestically produced arms.

Argentina ended the year critically short of foreign reserves and was forced to piece together bridging loans from governments and the IMF to cover arrears on interest payments to commercial banks which had built up during 1987. Part of the new agreement with the IMF was to hold the fiscal deficit at 3 per cent of GDP as opposed to the 7 per cent level of 1987. However, the military demonstrated on several occasions in 1987 that their claims for higher salaries were not to be ignored, and the government is not yet able to exercise tight control over military spending. A similar situation prevails in Brazil. This is a country of great wealth, very unequally distributed, and massive external debt. After 20 years of authoritarian military rule, democracy was restored in 1985. However, the new government, in the face of enormous economic difficulties inherited from the previous regime, has not been able to cope quickly enough with the challenge of poverty. Meanwhile, the military have been able to secure significant salary increases, major investment programmes and a budget for 1988 which is ahead of important social programmes. The Chilean economy is currently experiencing a period of solid growth and forecasts for the coming years are favourable. Irrespective of the outcome of economic policies—and there have been periods of severe recession over the decade—Chile, in the Latin American context, devotes an exceptionally high proportion of its national resources to military ends.

Several countries in this region give their government expenditure data in some considerable detail. The estimation of total military spending involves two main problems: first, in view of the central role of the armed forces in meeting domestic unrest and subversion in some countries, budgets of paramilitary and internal security forces must be identified and included in overall military spending; second, the adjustments made to budgeted amounts during the year because of high inflation must be carefully monitored. Examples of these problems are given below. In addition, in the case of Argentina, Brazil and Chile, some commentators would argue that part of their nuclear power programmes should be included under military spending.

Argentina publishes a functional budget for the Ministry of Defence which includes spending under a number of heads and conforms well with the NATO definition of military expenditure used by SIPRI. In addition to *Defensa*, which covers direct spending on the armed forces, these heads in 1986 were: general administration (General Staff); health, culture and education; economic development; social security; and science and technology. Those police units which are the responsibility of the Ministry of Defence rather than the Ministry of the Interior are regarded as paramilitary and have been included in SIPRI's data. Small amounts of civilian spending may be covered by this functional budget, as, for example, in the case of air traffic controllers who provide services for both civilian and military aircraft. On the other hand, the full amount of pension payments is probably not covered by the budget and service payments on the military debt have not been identified. No part of the budget of the National Commission for Atomic Energy has been included.[87]

The 1987 Argentine expenditure plans were drawn up on the assumption that inflation would not exceed 42 per cent during the year.[88] Despite a wages and prices freeze for three months from February and a similar measure introduced in October, annual inflation reached 180 per cent, far in excess of the government's goal. This most certainly meant that the military budget had to be supplemented. Major pay rises for the military were reported on three occasions during the year, in addition to increases granted to all civil servants.[89]

The problems of estimating Brazilian military spending are particularly vexing since published data do not seem to match the size and activity of the Brazilian forces. Military spending falls under a number of budget heads beyond those of the army, navy and air force.[90] These include the Presidential budget, the Ministry of Justice (which is responsible, among other things, for the paramilitary federal police), some part of the nuclear energy budget and a pension commitment which is presumably large in view of the numbers of professional personnel employed by the armed forces. Even when adjustments are made to cover some of these items, the very high annual rate of inflation in Brazil in recent years—not less than 100 per cent annually since 1980—makes the estimation of final expenditure very difficult. An inflation rate of 340 per cent in 1987, for example, was countered by substantial pay rises for military personnel. Until the picture of Brazilian spending becomes clearer, SIPRI has chosen to print the IMF *Government Finance Statistics* data in its military expenditure tables. Data beyond 1984 are not available from that source.

The increasingly unstable situation in Colombia does not permit any exact estimate of total military expenditure. Colombian congressmen rejected a suggestion in September 1987 that details of the armed forces finances should be discussed in congress on the grounds that publication of the critical financial situation of the military would threaten national security. Congress was asked to approve additional funds to the military of $400 million over the next five years to be spent on 'arms and equipment to help them overcome serious deficiencies and operate more effectively against terrorism, subversion and drug trafficking'.[91] Only $40 million of this will be raised through domestic taxation; the remainder will be financed through foreign loans. The Minister of Defence also announced that the number of professional soldiers—mainly anti-guerrilla troops—had been increased by 50 per cent during the year.[92] SIPRI data, which cover spending on defence, the police, the security police (DAS) and the administrative department of national security, show an increase of real spending of 5 per cent since 1986, but spending is normally revised upwards during the year.

Military spending in Chile is fuelled by the rivalry between two philosophies—armed forces as a safeguard against internal subversion and armed forces whose chief concern is external defence. The military budget contains two major elements which reflect this: the Forces of Order and Public Security (*carabineros* and *investigaciones*) and National Defence (army, navy and air force).[93] Allocations under these heads, together with supporting services, military industries and a heavy pensions commitment form the most easily identifiable elements of military spending. No estimate has been made of any military interest in the nuclear programme nor of military involvement in the civilian administration.

XII. Economic data used by SIPRI

In producing the constant dollar series of military expenditure data, SIPRI makes use of a consumer price index and a dollar exchange-rate for each country. The table showing military expenditure as a percentage of GDP (table 6A.3) utilizes data on gross domestic products or their equivalents. These variables are chosen not only because they are familiar, well understood and readily available; they also interpret military expenditure in a way which illustrates its opportunity cost in terms of consumer goods and services.

For a large number of countries, economic variables are available from the International Monetary Fund's *International Financial Statistics*, published monthly. In two sets of cases, first, where countries are not members of the International Monetary Fund (IMF) and second, where the relevant information has not been published by the IMF, other sources must be used. In the first case it is often possible to use another regular, reliable source of information, such as the UN or a central bank, to produce consistent series. The second case creates more serious problems. Since SIPRI finalizes its military expenditure tables in January in order to meet its publication date, very special difficulties are faced in estimating missing economic variables, in particular the change in average consumer prices for the year that has just ended. In earlier years it was possible to make a good estimate of price changes on the basis of monthly data reported by the IMF. This is no longer the case, in part due to slowness in reporting, in part due to the wide swings in inflation rates as governments, often at the behest of the IMF, struggle to gain control of their economies. In some cases reliable price index data are unavailable for the most recent two or three years. SIPRI's own estimates of price changes are based on information gathered throughout the year from as many sources as possible. It must be understood, however, that over and above the statistical problems involved in choosing a suitable deflator (which are discussed below), there are practical difficulties involved in finding *any* deflator which correctly reflects price rises in the most recent period. Little weight should therefore be given to real changes in military expenditure for the latest year(s).

The annual average dollar exchange-rate data involve fewer problems since the base year used in the SIPRI constant dollar series is chosen so that IMF or equivalent official exchange-rate data are available. Some exceptions to this are discussed in the notes, definitions and sources at the end of appendix 6A. Data on recent year GDP or its equivalent are no longer readily available even for countries with highly developed statistical services.[94] Missing data must therefore be estimated from newspaper and journal reports and the Organization for Economic Co-operation and Development (OECD), UN economic commissions and central bank sources. Net material product (NMP) figures are normally used for those centrally planned economies which do not supply GDP data.

Aside from the practical problems involved in the collection of price-index, exchange-rate and GDP data, some commentators propose the use of other statistics to describe inflationary/deflationary changes in prices and the relative values of currencies.[95] In particular it is suggested that use should be made of military price indices and purchasing-power-parities.

It is widely believed that the prices which the military must pay for 'military' goods and services rise more rapidly than the prices which consumers must pay for a typical 'basket' of consumer goods and services and that deflating a military expenditure series with a consumer price index overestimates the real growth of military spending. Recent research has cast doubt on this viewpoint[96] and it is likely that military price rises which are due to technical improvements and 'gold plating' are mistaken for inflationary movements. However, a number of countries construct military price indices for domestic budgeting purposes so that trends in military purchasing power can be monitored. The UN Reduction of Military Budgets project is also seeking to construct standardized military price indices so that real increases in military spending can be identified for the purposes of international comparison. In these two cases, the concern is to examine current military spending within the context of past or future military spending. SIPRI is concerned to measure increases in military expenditure in terms of forgone civil expenditure, in particular in terms of forgone consumer expenditure. The choice of the civil price index to be used is determined by convenience and availability. A GDP deflator could be used, thereby measuring increases in military expenditure in terms of resources lost to the economy as a whole.[97]

Military expenditure data are often converted into a common currency, usually the US dollar. Flexible exchange-rates and the fluctuation of the dollar have made it more difficult to use the dollar as an international standard of comparison.[98] Other exchange-rates, such as the European Community's European Currency Unit or the IMF's Special Drawing Rights, use a basket of currencies to determine the value of a monetary unit. These provide more stable standards of comparison but do not necessarily measure relative purchasing power.

While one US dollar may be the price of a loaf of bread in the USA, the exchange equivalent of a dollar might buy half a loaf or four loaves in another country. In theory, exchange-rates should reflect the relative purchasing power of currencies. This is not the case in the real world, where exchange-rates are controlled or manipulated by governments to further their trade and monetary policies. Exchange-rates which more accurately reflect the purchasing power of a country's currency, compared to dollars, have been calculated for some countries for some years. It is sometimes held that it would be better to use these 'purchasing-power-parities' when converting military expenditure into dollars. SIPRI has chosen not to do so for a number of reasons.

First, PPP rates are neither readily available nor well understood. Second, while part of a military budget is spent domestically, part—and in many cases a large part—is spent on buying goods and services abroad for which foreign exchange must be paid and for which, therefore, the dollar exchange-rate is the relevant one to use. Third, PPP rates are of interest when comparisons are made between two or more countries or when aggregating their economic indicators. But it is not always relevant or enlightening to compare the absolute level of military expenditure of different countries. However, the use of PPP rates has a pedagogical value and SIPRI will continue to monitor the possibility of producing military expenditure tables in terms of purchasing-power-parities as well as in US dollars.

Notes and references

[1] A discussion of the UN Reduction of Military Budgets project can be found in the relevant UN documents: A/9770 (1974); A/9770/Rev. 1 (1974); A/31/222 (1976); A/35/479 (1980); A/36/353 (1981); A/38/434 (1983); A/S–12/7 (1983); A/40/421 (1986); A/42/573 (1987).

[2] Countries not included in the military expenditure tables are: Andorra; Antigua & Barbuda; Bahamas; Barbados; Belize; Bhutan; Cape Verde; Comoros; Djibouti; Dominica; Equatorial Guinea; The Gambia; Grenada; Guinea; Guinea-Bissau; Iceland; Kiribati; Lesotho; Maldives; Monaco; Namibia; Nauru; Papua New Guinea; Qatar; Saint Christopher & Nevis; Saint Lucia; Saint Vincent & the Grenadines; San Marino; Sao Tome & Principe; Seychelles; Solomon Islands; Suriname; Swaziland; Tuvalu; Vanuatu; Vatican City; and Western Samoa. Countries currently excluded in the absence of adequate data are: Afghanistan, Kampuchea, Laos and Viet Nam.

[3] Many of these items, and especially paramilitary forces, involve difficult problems of definition. It should also be remembered in this context that military aid (narrowly defined) is included in the budget of the donor and not the recipient country. For a discussion of the size and significance of security assistance, see Tullberg, R. and Millán, V., 'Security assistance: the case of Central America', in SIPRI, *World Armaments and Disarmament: SIPRI Yearbook 1986* (Oxford University Press: Oxford, 1986), chapter 16, pp. 309–22.

[4] The data are first published in a press release in December each year and then later in *NATO Review*. The data are also given in Jan./Feb. by *Defense and Economy World Report* (Washington). This latter source is to be preferred for details of spending in local currency since it gives a military expenditure series from 1949 and gives full details of fiscal years and the changes which have been made in them.

[5] Spanish military spending, when calculated on a functional basis similar to the definition used by NATO, is approximately 50 per cent higher than the amount budgeted by the Ministry of Defence. See Tullberg, R. and Hagmeyer-Gaverus, G., 'World military expenditure', in SIPRI, *SIPRI Yearbook 1987: World Armaments and Disarmament* (Oxford University Press: Oxford, 1987), p. 127; and Fisas Armegol, V., in *Derechos Humanos* (Madrid), no. 18 (Nov./Dec. 1987).

[6] In the *NATO Press Service Release*, 1 Dec. 1987, Canada, the UK and the USA are mentioned as countries having fiscal years which differ from calendar years. However, Denmark (prior to 1979), the FRG (prior to 1961), Italy (prior to 1965), Norway (prior to 1961) and Turkey (between 1965 and 1981) all used fiscal years which did not coincide with calendar years. The attribution of US military expenditure to the year in which the fiscal year ends rather than to that in which it starts has created confusion for the NATO statistical analysis service itself; in the 1986 press release, US data were attributed to the wrong year.

[7] In the 1986 and 1987 press releases, NATO describe their latest year figures as 'estimates'.

[8] *Neue Zürcher Zeitung*, 30 Dec. 1987, p. 11.

[9] *Neue Zürcher Zeitung*, 17 Oct. 1987, p. 17.

[10] *The Independent*, 20 Oct. 1987, p. 12.

[11] *Newsweek*, 21 Sep. 1987, p. 12.

[12] *Frankfurter Rundschau*, 18 Jan. 1988.

[13] Jacobsen, C. G. (ed.), SIPRI, *The Soviet Defence Enigma: Estimating Costs and Burden* (Oxford University Press: Oxford, 1987).

[14] Statement by Robert Gates, Deputy Director of Intelligence, CIA, before the Joint Economic Committee (JEC), US Congress, *Allocation of Resources in the Soviet Union and China* (US Government Printing Office: Washington, DC, 1986), 21 Nov. 1986, p. 12.

[15] JEC 1986 (note 14).

[16] Definitions of these categories can be found in CIA, *Soviet and US Defence Activities, 1971–80: A Dollar Cost Comparison*, a research paper (CIA: Washington, DC, Dec. 1980).

[17] Duchêne, G., 'How much do the Soviets spend on defence?', in Jacobsen (note 13), p. 99.

[18] JEC, *Soviet Defense Trends*, a staff study, subcommittee on international trade finance and

security economics of the Joint Economic Committee, US Congress (US Government Printing Office: Washington, DC, Sep. 1983), p. 13.

[19] Steinberg, D., 'Estimating total Soviet military expenditures: an alternative approach based on reconstructed Soviet national accounts', in Jacobsen (note 13), pp. 27–57.

[20] Duchêne, G., 'How much do the Soviets spend on defence?', in Jacobsen (note 13), p. 105.

[21] Mochizuki, K., 'Estimating Soviet defence expenditures from national accounts', in Jacobsen (note 13), p. 116.

[22] ACDA, *World Military Expenditures and Arms Transfer 1986* (ACDA: Washington, DC, 1986), p. 156.

[23] Nove, A., 'The defence burden—some general observations', in Jacobsen (note 13), p. 177.

[24] Jacobsen (note 13), p. 6.

[25] Rosefielde, S., *False Science, Underestimating the Soviet Arms Buildup* (Transaction Books: New Brunswick, 1982); see also Nove (note 23).

[26] Tullberg and Hagmeyer-Gaverus (note 5), p. 132.

[27] Alton, T., Lazarcik, G., Bass, E. and Znayenko, W., *Military Expenditures in East Europe, Post World War II to 1979*, OP-63 (LW International: New York, 1980).

[28] UN document A/42/573 (1987), pp. 108–11.

[29] 1970–75: 6% of the total budget outlays; 1976–77: 12% of total planned outlays, excluding outlays on the national economy; since 1977 a constant share of about 3.1% of the national material product (NMP).

[30] Crane, K., *Military Spending in Eastern Europe*, The RAND Corporation, R–3444–USDP, May 1987, p. 57.

[31] For the calculation of 1986 constant dollar figures for the WTO countries purchasing-power-parities published by Alton *et al.* were used, adjusted to 1986 levels using changes in the tourist exchange-rates; see Alton, T. P., *et al.*, 'East European defense expenditures, 1965–1978,' in *East European Assessment*, Part 2, a compendium of papers submitted to the Joint Economic Committee, US Congress (US Government Printing Office: Washington, DC, 1981).

[32] *Schweizer Armee* (Verlag Huber & Co AG: Frauenfeldt, annual).

[33] *Försvarsstatistik* (Planning and Budget Secretariat, Swedish Ministry of Defence: Stockholm, annual).

[34] Kropik, Obst., *WPOL Service*, no. 4 (Nov. 1987), Bundesministerium für Landesverteidigung, Vienna.

[35] Note 28, pp. 62–6.

[36] IMF, *World Economic Outlook* (International Monetary Fund: Washington, DC, Oct. 1987), p. 39.

[37] Note 36, p. 103.

[38] Landgren, S., SIPRI, *Embargo Disimplemented: South Africa's Military Industry* (Oxford University Press: Oxford, forthcoming).

[39] Adekanye, B., 'Sources and methods for Nigerian military expenditure data', a research note.

[40] *Defence Service Estimates* (Government of India Press: New Delhi, annual). The budget estimates for FY 1985 do not include the expenditure on defence pensions. These are included instead under Demand no. 19 of the Ministry of Defence. See *Defence Service Estimates 1985–86* (Government of India Press: New Delhi, 1985), p. 1.

[41] Organisation and Functions of the Raksha Mantralaya (Ministry of Defence) and Organisation and Functions of the Vitta Mantralaya (Raksha) Ministry of Finance (Defence), Appendices A & B, in *Defence Service Estimates* (note 40).

[42] *Times of India*, reprinted in *Asian Recorder*, 23–29 July 1987, p. 19566.

[43] IISS, *Military Balance 1987–1988* (IISS: London, 1987), entry on Nepal.

[44] *Far Eastern Economic Review*, vol. 138, no. 48 (26 Nov. 1987).

[45] Chopra, V. D. and Gupta, R., *Nuclear Bomb and Pakistan* (Patriot Publishers for Indian Centre for Regional Affairs: New Delhi, 1986).

[46] The Finance Minister told a press conference that 50% of the current military budget was being borrowed. *Muslim* (Islamabad), 6 June 1987.

[47] *POT* (India), 25 June 1987; *Nation* (Pakistan), 8 June 1987.

[48] Chinese spending is discussed in more detail in Tullberg, R., 'World military expenditure', in SIPRI (note 3), pp. 217–18.

[49] *Defense of Japan* (Defense Agency: Tokyo, annual), Reference Material and Statistical Data. English translation by *Japan Times*.

[50] See, for example, the annual *Statistical Survey of Japan's Economy* (Economic & Foreign Affairs Association: Tokyo).

[51] *Budget of Singapore for the Financial Year 1985–1986* (Government Printer: Singapore, 1985).

[52] Other police duties relating to crime, traffic, drugs and immigration are budgeted for separately.

[53] As well as pensions for the Singapore Armed Forces (SAF) and the police, amounts are mentioned for Singapore Defence Forces and Singapore Vigilante Corps. See note 51, Pensions Programme.

[54] Budget Speech by the Financial Secretary of Hong Kong, moving the Second Reading on the Appropriations Bill for 1984, 27 Feb. 1985 (Government Printer: Hong Kong, 1984).

[55] See, for example, *The 1982 National Budget, Jan. 1–Dec. 31, 1982* (Office of the President, Office of Budget & Management: Manila, 1982), p. 27; and *Primer on the National Budget 1982* (Office of Budget & Management: Manila, 1982), p. 35.

[56] *The 1982 National Budget* (note 55), p. 27.

[57] Tullberg (note 48), p. 223; and Tullberg and Hagmeyer-Gaverus (note 5), p. 142 and note 76.

[58] *Bangkok Post*, 6 June 1987.

[59] *Far Eastern Economic Review*, vol. 135, no. 20 (14 May 1987), p. 12; vol. 137, no. 37 (10 Sep. 1987), p. 19; and vol. 138, no. 48 (26 Nov. 1987), p. 36.

[60] Budiardjo, C., 'Militarism and repression in Indonesia', *Third World Quarterly*, vol. 8, no. 4 (Oct. 1986), pp. 1221–2; *Financial Times*, 10 Mar. 1986, special issue on Indonesia, p. vi, 'Armed forces'.

[61] *Financial Times*, 21 Dec. 1981; *Financial Times* (note 60); *Far Eastern Economic Review*, 24 Oct. 1985.

[62] Government statement on the draft state budget for 1983–84 to the House of the People's Representatives, delivered by the President of the Republic of Indonesia on 6 Jan. 1983 (Department of Information; Republic of Indonesia: undated).

[63] *Far Eastern Economic Review*, vol. 135, no. 8 (19 Feb. 1987); and vol. 137, no. 30 (23 July 1987).

[64] *FBIS (Asia & Pacific)*, 5 Mar. 1987 quoting *Bangkok Post* of the same date.

[65] *Vantage Point*, vol. 10, no. 5 (May 1987), p. 22.

[66] *Statistik des Auslandes: Mongolei 1987* (Statistisches Bundesamt: Wiesbaden, 1987).

[67] *Statistical Yearbook of the Republic of China 1987* (Taipei, 1987).

[68] *Pacific Islands Monthly*, vol. 58, no. 10 (Oct. 1987).

[69] *Defence Report 1986–7* (Australian Government Publication Service: Canberra, 1987), Appendix 2, p. 2.

[70] UN document A/35/479 (1980), p. 54.

[71] *Reports on the Accounts and Finances for the Year* (Suva, Fiji, various years).

[72] *Estimates of the Expenditure of the Government of New Zealand* (Government Printer: Wellington, annual).

[73] Note 72.

[74] *Ley de Presupuestos: Ordinario y Extraordinario de la República, Fiscal y por Programas para el ejercicio Fiscal de 1983* (Budget law for 1983), San José, Costa Rica, 28 Dec. 1982, p. 75.

[75] Announcement by President Arias in July 1987, report in *Latin American Regional Reports: Mexico & Central America*, RM-87-07 (20 Aug. 1987).

[76] *Informe de ejecución presupuestaria* (Oficina Nacional de Presupuesto, Secretariado Técnico de la Presupuesto: Dominican Republic, various years).

[77] Note 76, 1985.

[78] *Estimates of Expenditure as presented to the House of Representatives* (Kingston, Jamaica, various years).

[79] This figure is usually announced in a speech by President Fidel Castro and published in the Havana newspaper *Granma*, at the turn of the year.

[80] UN Document A/42/573 (1987).

[81] *Ley de Presupuesto 1986* published in *Diario Oficial*, vol. 289, no. 243 (San Salvador, 21 Dec. 1985).

[82] *Presupuestade Ingresos y Egresos del Estado 1982* (Ministerio de Finanzas Públicas: Republic of Guatemala, 31 Dec. 1981).

[83] See, for example, *Latin American Weekly Review*, WR-86-49 (18 Dec. 1986) and WR-87-37 (24 Sep. 1987); and *Latin American Regional Reports: Mexico & Central America*, RM-86-06 (17 July 1986).

[84] *Presupuesto general de ingresos y egresos de la República* (Dirección General de Presupuesto, República de Honduras: Tegucigalpa, various years).

[85] *Latin American Weekly Review*, WR-87-24 (25 June 1987) and WR-87-44 (12 Nov. 1987); *International Herald Tribune*, 21 Dec. 1987.

[86] *Información sobre Gasto Público 1970–80* (Instituto Nacional de Estadística, Geografía y Informatión: Mexico, no date).

[87] For a fuller discussion of the structure of the Argentine budget, see Tullberg and Hagmeyer-Gaverus (note 5), pp. 151-2.

[88] *Latin American Weekly Review*, WR-87-29 (30 July 1987), and *Latin American Regional Reports: Southern Cone*, RS-87-06 (6 Aug. 1987).

[89] In June, military personnel were reportedly given an extra 9% over and above a 6% rise given to all civil servants (*Jane's Defence Weekly*, vol. 7, no. 22 (6 June 1987)). A retroactive 22-23.5% wage increase was announced in October (*Jane's Defence Weekly*, vol. 8, no. 15 (17 Oct. 1987)) and a further increase of 16-18% for the last quarter of 1987 (*Latin American Regional Reports: Southern Cone*, RS-88-01 (4 Feb. 1988)).

[90] Budget and Finance Secretariat, Brazil, *Orçamento da União*, for 1982, 1984 and 1985.

[91] Colombian Defence Minister, Samundio Molina, cited in *El Espectador* (Bogotá) and given in *Latin American Regional Reports: the Andean Group*, RA-87-07 (3 Sep. 1987).

[92] *Latin American Regional Reports* (note 91).

[93] *Diario Oficial de la República de Chile* (Santiago), 2 Dec. 1986.

[94] For example, in the Nov. 1987 issue of IMF, *International Financial Statistics* (IMF: Washington, DC, 1987), preliminary information on 1986 GDP is not available for such statistically sophisticated countries as Belgium, Japan, the Netherlands and the UK, as well as a host of developing countries.

[95] See, for example, the UN Reduction of Military Budgets project, 'Construction of military price indexes and purchasing-power-parities for comparison of military expenditures', UN document A/40/421 (1986).

[96] Aben, J., et al., 'La défense nationale française face à l'inflation', Foundation pour les Etudes de Défense Nationale, Montpellier, France, cited in *Defence & Armament Héraclès International*, no. 61 (Apr. 1987), p. 18.

[97] See Sköns, E., 'Military prices', in SIPRI, *World Armaments and Disarmament: SIPRI Yearbook 1983* (Taylor & Francis: London, 1983), pp. 195-211; and UN documents A/31/222 (1976); A/S-12/7 (1983); and A/40/421 (1986).

[98] NATO Europe's military expenditure in current prices and dollar exchange-rates *fell* from US $107 930 m. in 1980 to $88 937 m. in 1985. In constant prices and 1980 exchange-rates, it *rose* from $107 930 m. in 1980 to $116 650 m. in 1985. There was no deflation in Europe in this period. On the contrary, the NATO Europe data expressed in current dollars and prices fell despite inflation, because of the increase in the value of the dollar. *NATO Press Release*, 4 Dec. 1986.

Appendix 6A. Tables of world military expenditure, 1978–87

Notes, definitions, sources and conventions for the military expenditure tables can be found on pp. 172–74

Table 6A.1. World military expenditure, in current price figures

Figures are in local currency, current prices.

		1978	1979	1980	1981	1982	1983	1984	1985	1986	1987
NATO
North America
Canada	m. dollars	4 528	4 784	5 547	6 164	7 474	8 562	9 519	10 188	10 811	11 295
USA	m. dollars	112 505	126 257	146 115	174 909	195 885	218 084	238 136	263 899	282 935	287 575
Europe
Belgium	m. francs	99 726	106 472	115 754	125 689	132 127	136 615	139 113	144 183	152 079	154 703
Denmark	m. kroner	7 066	8 049	9 117	10 301	11 669	12 574	13 045	13 344	13 333	14 547
France	m. francs	85 175	96 439	111 672	129 708	148 021	165 029	176 638	186 715	197 110	207 552
FR Germany	m. D. marks	43 019	45 415	48 518	52 193	54 234	56 496	57 274	58 650	60 131	61 551
Greece	m. drachmas	77 861	89 791	96 975	142 865	176 270	193 340	271 922	321 981	338 465	402 459
Italy	b. lire	5 301	6 468	8 203	9 868	12 294	14 400	16 433	18 584	20 071	21 797
Luxembourg	m. francs	1 154	1 242	1 534	1 715	1 893	2 104	2 234	2 265	2 390	2 824
Netherlands	m. guilders	9 146	10 106	10 476	11 296	11 921	12 149	12 762	12 901	13 035	13 174
Norway	m. kroner	6 854	7 362	8 242	9 468	10 956	12 395	12 688	15 446	16 034	17 736
Portugal	m. escudos	27 354	34 343	43 440	51 917	63 817	76 765	92 009	111 375	139 972	159 889
Spain[a]	m. pesetas	(302 566)	(367 042)	(471 850)	551 019	649 262	743 917	846 844	947 656	966 703	1 077 385
Turkey	m. lira	63 492	88 754	184 818	294 715	447 790	556 738	803 044	1 234 547	1 867 990	2 476 869
UK	m. pounds	7 415	8 676	10 914	11 994	14 189	15 590	17 091	18 142	18 567	19 200

SIPRI MILITARY EXPENDITURE DATA

WTO									
Bulgaria	m. leva	[650]	[700]	[820]	[870]	[901]	[932]	[969]	[1 010]
Czechoslovakia	m. korunas	20 808	21 380	22 900	23 099	24 560	25 261	26 276	(27 500)	[28 800]	[29 260]
German DR	m. marks	8 674	9 110	9 875	10 705	11 315	11 970	12 830	13 041	(14 045)	(15 141)
Hungary	m. forints	14 983	16 200	17 700	19 060	20 050	21 900	22 700	37 700	(53 150)	(53 340)
Poland	m. zlotys	65 653	70 780	74 285	84 450	175 800	191 000	(250 900)	[315 200]	[347 800]	[386 690]
Romania	m. lei	11 713	11 835	10 394	10 490	11 340	11 660	11 888	(12 113)	[12 208]	[11 597]
USSR	m. roubles	. .	. .	. .	. .	. .	. .	. .	. .	. .	. .
Other Europe										
Albania	m. leks	818	885	915	940	935	910	1 010	1 700	[2 300]	. .
Austria	m. schillings	10 767	11 693	12 423	12 864	14 140	14 845	15 843	17 875	18 768	18 295
Finland	m. markkaa	2 668	3 044	3 612	4 128	5 187	5 659	6 086	6 565	7 257	7 651
Ireland	m. punt	116	142	176	203	241	250	263	283	306	305
Sweden	m. kronor	13 011	14 493	15 977	17 515	18 553	19 603	21 204	22 506	23 735	25 291
Switzerland	m. francs	2 678	2 982	3 152	3 349	3 727	3 862	4 009	4 576	4 282	4 235
Yugoslavia	m. new dinars	42 590	55 090	76 270	100 990	118 260	154 590	246 600	459 610	[780 270]	[1 466 630]
Middle East										
Bahrain	m. dinars	40.5	53.9	59.2	80.7	106	(62.3)	55.6	(56.6)	(60.4)	[61.5]
Cyprus	m. pounds	8.9	12.6	10.9	17.5	17.9	19.1	19.9	18.5	13.7	. .
Egypt	m. pounds	[1 150]	[3 342]	[2 408]	[1 971]	[2 649]	(2 946)	[3 139]	[2 055]	[932]	. .
Iran	m. rials	586 800	386 650	363 625	[488 500]	[641 250]	[657 500]	. .	. .	. .	. .
Iraq	m. dinars	587	(788)	[990]	[1 350]	[2 400]	[3 200]	[4 300]	[4 000]	. .	. .
Israel	m. new shekels	(5.7)	(12.0)	(26.7)	(56.6)	(120)	(329)	(1 720)	(4 654)	(6 813)	. .
Jordan	m. dinars	102	133	136	160	179	196	197	(219)	[243]	[270]
Kuwait	m. dinars	215	244	257	291	370	416	434	(415)	. .	. .
Lebanon	m. pounds	491	738	980	(654)	(1 215)	[3 554]	[2 004]	[2 178]	[1 798]	[580]
Oman	m. riyals	265	269	407	522	581	671	728	745	665	. .
Saudi Arabia	m. riyals	(38 684)	(52 388)	(64 076)	(75 723)	(87 695)	(84 311)	(77 817)	(72 000)	. .	. .
Syria	m. pounds	4 777	6 226	8 884	9 653	10 703	11 309	12 601	13 673	14 220	[15 240]
United Arab Emirates	m. dirhams	3 019	4 394	6 330	7 672	7 268	7 042	7 093	[7 500]	[6 900]	[5 800]
Yemen Arab Republic	m. rials	766	2 616	1 978	2 677	3 701	3 146	2 733	2 747	2 852	. .
Yemen, People's Democratic Rep. of	m. dinars	30.8	36.1	42.6	56.0	[57.5]	[65.8]	[66.1]	[65.3]	[68.8]	. .

160 MILITARY EXPENDITURE, ARMS TRADE, CONFLICTS

		1978	1979	1980	1981	1982	1983	1984	1985	1986	1987
South Asia											
Bangladesh	m. taka	2 038	2 409	2 832	3 350	[4 134]	[4 840]	[5 450]	[6 011]	7 871	9 840
India	m. rupees	32 508	36 648	(39 024)	(45 371)	53 805	62 148	70 834	(79 348)	(98 271)	121 408
Nepal	m. rupees	190	217	244	274	342	432	496	[607]	(882)	[1 159]
Pakistan	m. rupees	(10 263)	(12 085)	(14 595)	(17 730)	(22 635)	(26 915)	(29 585)	(32 925)	(37 775)	(43 645)
Sri Lanka	m. rupees	560	804	971	1 051	1 500	1 800	2 600	4 280	[10 000]	(12 937)
Far East											
Brunei	m. dollars	203	372	410	416	(480)	(530)	[534]	. .	[700]	. .
Burma	m. kyats	1 247	1 324	(1 417)	(1 590)	(1 610)	1 630	[1 760]	(1 973)	(1 858)	. .
Hong Kong	m. dollars	536	628	1 353	1 521	1 478	1 537	1 523	(1 639)	(1 530)	1 589
Indonesia	b. new rupiahs	[1 130]	[1 300]	[1 708]	[2 153]	[2 613]	[2 858]	[3 106]	[2 856]	[3 089]	. .
Japan	b. yen	1 822	2 010	2 215	2 388	2 532	2 712	2 911	3 117	3 296	3 473
Korea, North	m. won	2 344	2 563	2 750	3 009	3 242	3 530	3 819	3 935	3 976	4 183
Korea, South	m. won	1 438	1 597	2 252	2 831	3 163	3 406	3 452	3 826	4 309	4 914
Malaysia	m. ringgits	2 183	2 547	3 389	4 693	4 975	(4 820)	(4 370)	(4 320)	(4 215)	. .
Mongolia	m. tugriks	(421)	(480)	(590)	(630)	[716]	(726)	(764)	(764)	(790)	(837)
Philippines	m. pesos	[4 863]	[5 240]	[5 829]	[6 746]	[7 778]	[8 554]	. .	. .	[7 600]	8 500
Singapore	m. dollars	(992)	(1 035)	1 259	1 507	1 659	1 640	2 204	2 516	(2 403)	(2 439)
Taiwan	m. dollars	70 000	80 500	96 500	117 000	135 500	138 500	137 500	151 650	160 650	167 960
Thailand	m. baht	(20 228)	30 250	34 625	37 375	41 250	45 875	49 500	52 275	51 825	53 125
Oceania											
Australia	m. dollars	2 495	2 813	3 252	3 772	4 376	4 998	5 616	6 304	6 939	7 308
Fiji	m. dollars	3.2	3.9	4.3	3.6	4.2	4.7	4.5	4.5	4.8	. .
New Zealand	m. dollars	288	334	421	557	638	668	735	842	1 022	1 228
Africa											
Algeria	m. dinars	2 490	2 742	3 417	3 481	3 893	4 477	4 631	4 793	(5 459)	(5 805)
Angola	m. kwanzas	. .	(15 150)	(15 060)	(15 060)	(15 060)	(23 370)	(29 520)	(34 410)	[38 000]	. .
Benin	m. francs	1 997	3 680	(4 700)	[5 400]	[6 800]	[9 300]	[10 200]	[10 600]	. .	. .
Botswana	m. pulas	14.4	22.3	26.9	28.5	25.2	28.2	[34.9]	[41.6]	. .	. .
Burkina Faso	m. francs	7 305	6 814	7 471	9 216	10 800	11 172	[11 784]	[11 709]	[10 870]	. .
Burundi	m. francs	(1 533)	(1 800)	[2 500]	[2 700]	[3 300]	[3 200]	[3 900]	[4 200]	[4 800]	. .

SIPRI MILITARY EXPENDITURE DATA

Cameroon	m. francs	16 120	18 795	19 540	21 300	40 900	63 105	[73 658]	[81 923]	[86 912]	. .
Central African Rep.	m. francs	2 289	3 061	2 816	4 029	(5 000)	[6 500]	(17 496)	[20 000]	[32 000]	. .
Chad	m. francs	5 186	5 890	. .	. .	. .	. .	[21 596]	[25 000]	[33 547]	. .
Congo	m. francs	10 000	9 450	10 050	[11 250]	[16 500]	[18 600]	(30 706)	[31 320]	[31 320]	[35 336]
Côte d'Ivoire	m. francs	19 579	21 854	26 643	[25 000]	[28 400]	[29 658]	[915]	[990]	. .
Ethiopia	m. birr	519	722	744	[789]	[811]	816	[35 100]	[42 400]	[47 100]
Gabon	m. francs	[12 160]	(12 036)	[18 600]	[25 600]	[29 100]	33 000	(1 605)	[3 432]	. .
Ghana	m. cedis	167	(190)	(175)	488	587	(673)	[2 550]	[2 469]	[2 820]	[3 120]
Kenya	m. shillings	1 669	2 176	2 016	2 182	2 662	2 778	25.2	24.4	[29.4]
Liberia	m. dollars	9.4	13.1	27.1	51.6	46.9	25.3	[900]	. .
Libya	m. dinars	[810]	[995]	[970]	[1 130]	[1 270]	[1 010]	[33 520]	[39 830]	[39 200]
Madagascar	m. francs	11 775	17 420	(19 315)	(23 500)	[27 200]	[29 600]	(31 730)	[28.1]	[35.0]
Malawi	m. kwachas	22.0	35.3	43.2	36.0	29.0	26.1	26.6	[12 500]	[12 900]	(18 313)
Mali	m. francs	14 080	15 331	16 295	17 217	19 302	20 486	[2 660]	[2 740]	[2 850]
Mauritania	m. ouguiyas	3 541	3 238	3 700	3 541	3 238	2 639	36.3	36.7	41.5
Mauritius	m. rupees	10.9	15.7	42.6	47.8	30.9	34.4	4 960	(5 245)	6 737	[7 192]
Morocco	m. dirhams	3 219	3 495	4 400	5 047	5 814	4 675	(10 300)	(11 000)	(12 400)	[42 000]
Mozambique	m. meticais	3 650	3 733	4 419	5 741	6 946	(8 327)	[4 688]	[4 703]	[4 948]
Niger	m. francs	2 862	3 430	3 867	4 286	4 232	[4 389]	[928]	[976]	[957]	[810]
Nigeria	m. nairas	1 218	1 142	1 352	1 319	1 113	1 179	2 500	2 760	(3 050)	[2 709]
Rwanda	m. francs	1 288	1 702	2 027	2 500	2 622	2 693	(27 046)	(28 235)	[28 490]	[28 784]
Senegal	m. francs	18 800	20 150	19 870	21 565	23 505	25 110	[22.4]	[29.4]	[40.1]	[48.0]
Sierra Leone	m. leones	8.3	10.0	14.1	17.5	17.9	18.6	(1 831)	[1 807]
Somalia	m. shillings	512	552	601	843	846	1 325	(3 922)	(4 414)	(5 487)	(6 721)
South Africa[b]	m. rands	(1 654)	(2 018)	(2 419)	(2 615)	(2 967)	(3 314)	[385]	[460]	[560]
Sudan	m. pounds	70.9	84.7	108	131	162	[248]	3 201	3 914
Tanzania	m. shillings	2 797	2 771	1 688	2 122	2 433	2 651	7 007	8 632	[8 500]
Togo	m. francs	10 088	4 786	5 155	6 202	6 138	6 328	(296)	(357)	[413]	[434]
Tunisia	m. dinars	61.8	65.4	78.6	113	(284)	(364)	27 574	53 560	94 300
Uganda	m. shillings	1 125	1 548	2 958	5 413	8 228	14 420	1 928	2 013
Zaire	m. zaires	181	330	430	316	873	723	[123]	[200]
Zambia	m. kwachas	[62.0]	[128]	[106]	[140]	[100]	[120]	398	436	[554]	[685]
Zimbabwe	m. dollars	145	171	243	284	296	353

Central America

Costa Rica	m. colones	220	291	316	367	711	1 071	(1 322)	(1 470)	(1 730)	. .
Cuba	m. pesos	784	814	759	931	1 109	1 133	1 386	1 335	1 307	1 300

		1978	1979	1980	1981	1982	1983	1984	1985	1986	1987
Dominican Republic	m. pesos	87.1	109	99.4	[126]	[128]	129	164	191	. .	. .
El Salvador	m. colones	159	(172)	254	322	395	442	574	. .	[964]	. .
Guatemala	m. quetzales	103	118	143	161	[208]	(231)	(270)	[400]	. .	. .
Haiti	m. gourdes	73.7	93.8	99.8	105	104	102	110	(132)	. .	. .
Honduras	m. lempiras	86.2	99.1	158	(198)	(216)	240	318	(317)	404	. .
Jamaica	m. dollars	30.0	41.0	67.0	86.0	[103]	[96.0]	(107)	[129]	. .	. .
Mexico	b. pesos	12	18	24	38	52	[128]	(186)	(279)	[520]	(1 383)
Nicaragua	m. cordobas	459	(456)	(961)	(1 300)	(1 760)	[3 420]	[4 930]	. .	[192 000]	. .
Panama	m. balboas	36.0	41.0	42.2	46.5	55.0	60.0	(88.0)	(92.0)	[94.0]	(101)
Trinidad and Tobago	m. dollars	195	208	296	371	563	(545)	(490)	[465]	[465]	. .
South America											
Argentina	m. australes	0.3	0.8	1.6	3.4	(8.8)	(31.0)	(229)	1 649	3 328	. .
Bolivia	t. bolivianos	2.7	3.2	4.8	8.0	(19.0)	(58.0)	[805]	105 707	. .	. .
Brazil[c]	m. cruzados	[31.0]	[44.0]	[88.0]	[171]	[452]	[996]	[3 058]	. .	. .	. .
Chile	m. pesos	34 144	53 300	71 964	94 252	117 386	124 439	181 492	193 833	. .	. .
Colombia	m. pesos	15 000	[20 530]	(29 950)	(36 980)	(46 090)	(71 760)	(94 690)	(108 450)	[270 000]	(182 650)
Ecuador	m. sucres	(4 097)	(4 638)	5 539	6 639	(6 870)	(8 833)	(12 086)	. .	(140 050)	. .
Guyana	m. dollars	67.0	67.2	98.0	96.0	108	(142)	(156)	(192)	[276]	. .
Paraguay	m. guaranies	4 892	5 793	7 644	10 581	11 687	15 000	. .	(15 790)	(21 360)	. .
Peru	m. intis	92.5	121	[265]	[515]	. .	[2 530]	[3 875]	[11 900]	[23 900]	[37 000]
Uruguay	m. new pesos	697	1 361	2 693	4 770	5 168	5 877	7 708	[12 831]	[19 800]	[33 500]
Venezuela	m. bolivares	3 500	4 991	6 899	8 952	9 905	(8 488)	(9 800)	[11 200]	[12 720]	[17 000]

SIPRI MILITARY EXPENDITURE DATA

Table 6A.2. World military expenditure, in constant price figures

Figures are in US $m., at 1986 prices and exchange-rates.

	1978	1979	1980	1981	1982	1983	1984	1985	1986	1987
NATO										
North America										
Canada	5 832	5 652	5 944	5 877	6 428	6 961	7 419	7 635	7 780	7 794
USA	189 071	190 747	194 479	210 873	222 650	240 091	251 355	269 157	282 935	275 190
Europe										
Belgium	3 537	3 615	3 686	3 720	3 596	3 453	3 306	3 268	3 404	3 236
Denmark	1 632	1 696	1 709	1 729	1 779	1 793	1 750	1 709	1 648	1 731
France	25 076	25 646	26 104	26 737	27 287	27 753	27 656	27 641	28 459	29 038
FR Germany	20 974	21 255	21 550	21 808	21 527	21 707	21 485	21 529	22 127	22 447
Greece	2 602	2 521	2 181	2 581	2 632	2 401	2 851	2 830	2 418	2 494
Italy	10 104	10 744	11 241	11 316	12 103	12 372	12 737	13 196	13 463	13 885
Luxembourg	40.6	41.8	48.6	50.3	50.8	51.9	52.2	50.9	53.5	63.2
Netherlands	5 084	5 390	5 247	5 302	5 283	5 236	5 326	5 266	5 320	5 372
Norway	1 778	1 821	1 841	1 860	1 933	2 017	1 943	2 238	2 168	2 231
Portugal	839	852	924	920	921	886	823	833	937	975
Spain[a]	(5 592)	(5 866)	(6 523)	6 647	6 846	6 996	7 156	7 360	6 903	7 195
Turkey	2 159	1 902	1 884	2 200	2 555	2 390	2 323	2 464	2 769	2 692
UK	21 371	22 027	23 497	23 076	25 142	26 408	27 583	27 603	27 304	27 019
WTO[d]										
Bulgaria	[662]	[680]	[700]	[739]	[763]	[778]	[800]	[828]	. .	[3 478]
Czechoslovakia	3 051	(3 019)	(3 142)	(3 144)	(3 179)	(3 242)	(3 342)	(3 463)	[3 534]	(5 388)
German DR	3 131	(3 278)	(3 539)	(3 829)	(4 047)	(4 273)	(4 566)	(4 641)	(4 998)	[936]
Hungary	516	512	513	528	519	528	506	785	1 026	[2 238]
Poland	2 408	(2 424)	(2 326)	(2 171)	(2 196)	(1 954)	(2 244)	[2 449]	2 353	[1 250]
Romania	1 844	1 829	1 582	1 562	1 445	(1 412)	(1 424)	(1 386)	1 356	. .
USSR	. .	. .	. .	. .	. .	. .	. .	. .	. .	. .

	1978	1979	1980	1981	1982	1983	1984	1985	1986	1987
Other Europe										
Albania[c]	117	126	131	134	134	130	144	243	329	. .
Austria	1 003	1 051	1 050	1 018	1 060	1 079	1 089	1 190	1 229	1 171
Finland	985	1 046	1 112	1 135	1 302	1 310	1 316	1 341	1 431	1 454
Ireland	386	416	438	420	425	398	386	394	411	395
Sweden	3 570	3 710	3 595	3 516	3 430	3 327	3 332	3 293	3 332	3 408
Switzerland	1 992	2 142	2 176	2 171	2 287	2 301	2 320	2 561	2 380	2 322
Yugoslavia	2 307	2 461	2 623	2 486	2 190	2 058	2 126	2 300	[2 058]	[1 921]
Middle East										
Bahrain	136	177	188	230	276	158	141	(147)	(161)	[162]
Cyprus	29.8	38.6	29.4	42.7	41.0	41.6	40.8	36.3	26.4	. .
Egypt	[5 214]	[13 782]	[8 232]	[6 103]	[7 142]	(6 842)	[6 228]	[3 599]	[1 331]	. .
Iran	26 892	16 031	12 498	[13 519]	[14 953]	[12 804]	. .	. .	. .	. .
Iraq	6 572	(8 319)	[8 620]	[9 810]	[15 377]	[20 031]	[22 129]	[16 468]	. .	. .
Israel	5 128	6 205	5 986	5 841	5 645	6 283	6 931	4 634	4 579	. .
Jordan	482	549	505	552	575	599	580	(626)	(694)	[775]
Kuwait	1 056	1 123	1 106	1 164	1 376	1 475	1 523	(1 435)	. .	. .
Lebanon	69.8	95.2	102	(58.8)	(96.0)	(262)	(106)	(82.6)	(46.9)	. .
Oman[c]	767	779	1 178	1 511	1 682	1 943	2 108	2 157	1 926	[1 679]
Saudi Arabia	(10 380)	(13 809)	(16 282)	(18 735)	(21 825)	(21 107)	(19 714)	(18 861)	. .	. .
Syria	3 797	4 722	5 665	5 199	5 045	5 022	5 122	4 741	3 623	[3 534]
United Arab Emirates	1 045	1 490	2 104	2 452	2 100	2 035	2 015	[2 077]	[1 880]	[1 554]
Yemen Arab Republic	290	785	(564)	727	977	787	609	484	386	. .
Yemen, People's Democratic Rep. of	164	169	181	230	[215]	[222]	[211]	[199]	[199]	. .
South Asia										
Bangladesh	170	175	182	185	[203]	[217]	[221]	[221]	259	293
India	5 177	5 491	(5 245)	(5 397)	5 932	6 128	6 446	(6 841)	(7 792)	8 821
Nepal	19.6	21.6	21.2	21.4	24.0	26.9	30.1	[34.0]	41.5	[48.3]
Pakistan	(1 099)	(1 195)	(1 290)	(1 400)	(1 688)	(1 890)	(1 949)	(2 050)	(2 269)	(2 521)
Sri Lanka	52.2	67.7	64.8	59.4	76.6	80.6	99.8	162	[357]	(428)

SIPRI MILITARY EXPENDITURE DATA

Far East

Brunei	128	222	232	216	(257)	[250]		
Burma	247	248	(264)	(295)	(272)	[280]	(294)	[322]
Hong Kong	141	149	275	272	226	207	(216)	(253)
Indonesia	[2 118]	[2 021]	[2 239]	[2 515]	[2 728]	[2 685]	[2 357]	196
Japan	13 942	14 851	15 152	15 578	16 886	17 738	18 613	[2 408]
Korea, North[e]	1 051	1 149	1 233	1 349	1 583	1 713	1 765	19 558
Korea, South	3 581	3 362	3 684	3 819	4 142	4 105	4 439	1 783
Malaysia	1 181	1 331	1 659	2 095	(1 960)	(1 710)	(1 686)	4 889
Mongolia[e]	(137)	(157)	(193)	(206)	(237)	(249)	(249)	(1 633)
Philippines	847	[777]	[731]	[748]	[783]			(258)
Singapore	(594)	(597)	669	740	766	1 003	1 140	[373]
Taiwan	3 141	3 294	3 317	3 458	3 921	3 893	4 302	(1 104)
Thailand	(1 310)	1 783	1 704	1 632	1 835	1 963	2 024	4 525

Brunei ... 196
Burma ...
Hong Kong 196
Indonesia 20 482
Japan 1 876
Korea, North[e] 5 310
Korea, South (273)
Malaysia [391]
Mongolia (1 108)
Philippines 4 656
Taiwan 1 965

Oceania

Australia	3 255	3 367	3 535	3 737	4 047	4 372	4 598	4 655	4 539
Fiji	4.9	5.6	5.4	4.1	4.6	4.2	4.0	4.2	
New Zealand	395	404	434	498	478	496	492	535	550

Africa

Algeria	1 124	1 111	1 264	1 123	1 180	1 222	1 146	(1 161)	(1 180)
Angola[e]	(344)	(506)	(503)	(503)	(503)	(987)	(1 150)	[1 270]	
Benin	11.0	19.0	(22.5)	[23.2]	[26.0]	[33.7]	[32.8]		
Botswana	18.1	25.1	26.6	24.2	19.2	[22.2]	[24.6]		
Burkina Faso	38.8	31.5	30.7	35.2	36.9	[35.4]	[32.9]	[31.4]	
Burundi	(31.1)	(26.7)	[33.9]	[32.7]	[37.8]	[36.1]	[37.5]	[42.0]	
Cameroon	96.8	106	100	98.9	168	[232]	[255]	[251]	
Central African Rep.	(15.6)	(19.1)	[15.0]	[19.0]	(20.9)				
Chad[e]	15.0	17.0				[24.0]	[50.5]	[57.8]	[92.4]
Congo	58.4	51.0	50.6	[48.4]	[62.9]	[43.3]	[67.8]	[74.0]	
Côte d'Ivoire	106	101	108	[93.0]	[98.4]	[65.8]	[96.3]	[96.9]	[98.0]
Ethiopia	395	474	467	[467]	[460]	[97.0]	[431]		
Gabon	[72.0]	(66.0)	[90.8]	[115]	[112]	[459]	[130]	[136]	
Ghana	49.1	(36.2)	(22.2)	28.6	28.1	[115]	(47.9)		

	1978	1979	1980	1981	1982	1983	1984	1985	1986	1987
Kenya	246	297	242	234	237	222	[185]	[158]	[174]	[184]
Liberia	14.7	18.3	33.1	58.6	50.2	26.3	25.9	25.2	[29.4]	:
Libya	[6 150]	[7 990]	[6 890]	[7 233]	[7 398]	[4 772]	[3 871]	:	:	:
Madagascar	67.0	86.9	(81.5)	(76.0)	[66.8]	[60.9]	(59.4)	[56.8]	[58.9]	[52.9]
Malawi	32.9	47.6	48.9	36.5	26.7	21.2	18.0	[17.2]	[18.8]	:
Mali	79.7	90.5	78.8	74.2	81.3	77.9	(89.8)	(39.7)	(37.3)	(48.2)
Mauritania	89.8	75.2	77.6	62.4	50.6	40.9	[38.5]	[38.6]	[38.3]	:
Mauritius	2.1	2.6	5.0	4.9	2.8	3.0	2.9	2.8	3.1	:
Morocco	729	731	841	857	893	676	638	(627)	740	[774]
Mozambique	89.4	91.4	108	141	170	(204)	(252)	(269)	(304)	[1 028]
Niger	13.6	15.2	15.5	14.0	12.4	[13.2]	[13.0]	[13.1]	[14.3]	559
Nigeria	2 764	2 321	2 498	2 017	1 580	1 359	766	763	711	[29.8]
Rwanda	24.7	28.2	31.3	36.3	33.8	32.6	28.7	31.1	(34.8)	[77.5]
Senegal	121	118	107	110	102	97.4	(93.9)	(86.7)	[82.3]	[3.4]
Sierra Leone	18.7	18.5	23.5	23.7	19.1	11.8	[8.5]	[6.3]	[4.8]	:
Somalia	122	106	72.5	70.4	57.2	65.8	(47.6)	[34.1]	:	:
South Africa	(2 144)	(2 312)	(2 436)	(2 287)	(2 261)	2 249	2 384	2 308	2 419	2 596
Sudan	260	236	242	235	230	[270]	[313]	[257]	[224]	:
Tanzania	627	546	255	256	227	195	174	[159]	:	:
Togo	50.5	22.3	21.4	21.5	19.1	18.0	20.7	26.0	[24.5]	:
Tunisia	154	151	165	218	(483)	(568)	(426)	(476)	[520]	[514]
Uganda	17.8	24.5	46.9	85.7	64.9	91.8	123	[103]	[67.4]	:
Zaire	81.1	70.8	65.0	35.4	71.7	33.5	58.7	49.5	:	:
Zambia	[39.9]	[75.1]	[55.7]	[64.5]	[41.0]	[41.1]	[35.1]	[41.5]	:	:
Zimbabwe	250	248	336	346	326	316	296	299	[333]	[368]
Central America										
Costa Rica	25.2	30.5	28.1	23.8	24.3	27.6	(30.4)	(29.4)	(30.9)	:
Cuba	1 205	1 252	1 155	1 265	1 431	1 402	1 648	1 540	1 452	1 444
Dominican Republic	88.8	102	79.6	93.8	88.3	85.1	85.3	72.2	:	:
El Salvador	112	(106)	133	147	161	159	185	:	(193)	:
Guatemala	133	137	150	151	[195]	(207)	(234)	[292]	:	:
Haiti	31.3	35.3	31.8	30.1	27.8	24.9	25.0	(27.3)	:	:
Honduras	81.7	85.3	115	(132)	(132)	136	171	(165)	202	:

Jamaica	22.3	23.6	30.3	34.5	38.8	32.4	28.3	27.1	..
Mexico	594	733	783	966	837	(1 018)	(893)	(850)	(850)
Nicaragua	947	(636)	(991)	(1 081)	(1 173)	[1 739]	[1 851]	..	[2 887]
Panama	51.8	54.7	49.5	50.8	57.6	61.6	(88.9)	(92.0)	(94.0)
Trinidad and Tobago	141	131	159	174	237	(199)	(158)	[139]	[129]

South America

Argentina	4 253	4 222	4 345	4 532	(4 418)	(3 507)	(3 565)	3 324	3 529
Bolivia	166	170	170	220	(225)	(186)	[187]	[207]	..
Brazil[c]	[1 486]	[1 380]	[1 510]	[1 427]	[1 906]	[1 736]	[1 795]	..	..
Chile	999	1 169	1 168	1 278	1 448	1 206	1 468	1 200	1 445
Colombia	999	[435]	(502)	(486)	(486)	(632)	(718)	(663)	(721)
Ecuador	1 008	(177)	187	193	(172)	(149)	(155)	..	..
Guyana	55.6	47.3	60.5	47.5	44.5	(51.6)	(45.3)	(48.5)	[64.6]
Paraguay	62.0	57.3	61.7	75.0	77.6	[87.8]	..	61.3	63.0
Peru	1 053	826	[1 137]	[1 260]	..	[1 782]	[1 299]	[1 514]	[1 709]
Uruguay	140	164	199	263	239	182	154	149	[130]
Venezuela	1 116	1 415	1 610	1 797	1 815	(1 464)	1 506	1 545	1 574

SIPRI MILITARY EXPENDITURE DATA 167

Table 6A.3. World military expenditure as a percentage of gross domestic product

	1978	1979	1980	1981	1982	1983	1984	1985	1986	1987
NATO										
North America										
Canada	1.9	1.7	1.8	1.7	2.0	2.1	2.1	2.1	2.1	2.1
USA	5.1	5.1	5.4	5.8	6.3	6.5	6.4	6.6	6.7	6.4
Europe										
Belgium	3.3	3.3	3.3	3.4	3.3	3.2	3.1	3.0	3.0	3.0
Denmark	2.3	2.3	2.4	2.5	2.5	2.5	2.3	2.2	2.0	2.1
France	3.9	3.9	4.0	4.1	4.1	4.1	4.0	4.0	3.9	4.0
FR Germany	3.3	3.3	3.3	3.4	3.4	3.4	3.3	3.2	3.1	3.1
Greece	6.7	6.3	5.7	7.0	6.8	6.3	7.1	7.0	6.1	6.3
Italy	2.4	2.4	2.1	2.1	2.3	2.3	2.3	2.3	2.2	2.2
Luxembourg	0.9	0.9	1.0	1.1	1.0	1.1	1.1	1.0	1.0	1.2
Netherlands	3.1	3.2	3.1	3.2	3.2	3.2	3.2	3.1	3.0	3.1
Norway	3.2	3.1	2.9	2.9	3.0	3.1	2.8	3.1	3.1	3.2
Portugal	3.5	3.5	3.5	3.5	3.5	3.4	3.3	3.2	3.2	3.2
Spain[a]	(2.7)	(2.8)	(3.1)	3.2	3.3	3.3	3.3	3.3	3.0	..
Turkey	5.4	4.5	4.9	5.0	5.6	5.2	4.9	4.9	5.2	(4.7)
UK	4.6	4.6	4.9	4.8	5.2	5.3	5.4	5.3	5.0	4.9
WTO										
Bulgaria[g]	[3.1]	[3.1]	[3.1]	[3.1]	[3.0]	[3.1]	[3.1]	..	..	..
Czechoslovakia[g]	3.3	3.3	3.3	3.4	3.5	3.5	3.5	(3.6)	[3.6]	..
German DR[g]	4.1	4.1	4.2	4.4	4.5	4.5	4.7	4.6	(4.8)	(4.8)
Hungary	2.4	2.4	2.5	2.4	2.4	2.4	2.3	(2.3)	(2.3)	..
Poland[g]	2.6	2.7	2.8	2.9	(2.7)	(2.4)	(2.7)	[3.0]	[2.9]	..
Romania[g]	2.1	2.0	1.7	1.6	1.5	(1.5)	(1.4)	(1.4)	[1.3]	..
USSR	..	..	..	..	..	..	..	..	..	..

SIPRI MILITARY EXPENDITURE DATA

Other Europe

Austria	1.3	1.3	1.2	1.2	1.2	1.2	1.3	1.2
Finland	1.9	1.8	1.9	2.1	2.1	2.0	2.2	2.0
Ireland	1.7	1.8	1.9	1.8	1.7	1.6	1.7	1.6
Sweden	3.0	2.9	2.9	2.8	2.6	2.6	2.5	2.4
Switzerland	1.8	1.9	1.9	1.8	1.8	1.8	1.8	1.7
Yugoslavia[h]	4.7	4.7	4.6	4.0	3.8	3.7	[3.1]	[3.0]

Middle East

Bahrain	4.2	5.1	4.0	4.8	6.2	3.6	3.1	(3.2)	(4.0)
Cyprus	1.7	2.0	1.4	2.0	1.8	1.7	1.5	1.3	0.9
Egypt	[10.3]	[23.7]	[14.7]	[10.5]	[11.7]	(11.2)	10.4	[5.8]	
Iran	10.6	6.3	5.4	[6.1]	[6.3]	[5.1]			
Iraq	8.1	(6.9)	[6.3]	[13.1]	[23.2]	[33.7]	[51.2]	[57.1]	[21.0]
Israel	(26.0)	(29.7)	(28.2)	(25.5)	(24.0)	(26.1)	(28.9)	(21.1)	[15.1]
Jordan	16.2	17.7	13.8	13.7	13.5	13.8	13.1	(13.9)	
Kuwait	3.9	3.4	3.5	4.5	6.0	6.5	6.9	(7.6)	
Lebanon	5.6	6.6				(18.1)	(11.7)		
Oman	28.0	20.9	19.8	20.6	21.1	23.3	22.9	20.8	28.4
Saudi Arabia	(17.3)	(21.1)	(16.6)	(14.5)	(16.7)	(20.3)	(20.9)	(21.8)	
Syria	14.6	15.8	17.3	14.7	15.6	15.4	16.7	17.2	17.7
United Arab Emirates	5.0	5.5	5.8	6.5	6.7	6.9	7.0	7.8	
Yemen Arab Republic	7.5	23.7	(16.6)	21.4	25.1	18.4	14.8	12.8	
Yemen, People's Democratic Rep. of	17.5	17.5	17.8	19.7	[18.7]	[19.1]	[17.5]	[16.7]	[16.7]

South Asia

Bangladesh	1.3	1.3	1.3	1.3	[1.5]	[1.5]	[1.4]	[1.3]	
India	3.4	3.5	(3.2)	(3.2)	3.3	3.3	3.4	3.4	
Nepal	0.9	1.0	1.0	0.9	1.1	1.2	1.2	[1.3]	
Pakistan	(5.5)	(5.6)	(5.7)	(5.9)	(6.6)	(6.9)	(6.6)	(6.5)	
Sri Lanka	1.3	1.5	1.5	1.2	1.5	1.5	1.7	2.6	

	1978	1979	1980	1981	1982	1983	1984	1985	1986	1987
Far East										
Brunei	4.6	6.1	3.9	4.5	(5.4)	(6.6)	[6.6]	. .	. .	. .
Burma	4.0	3.8	(3.7)	(3.8)	(3.5)	[3.3]	[3.3]	(3.6)	(3.2)	. .
Hong Kong	0.7	0.6	1.0	0.9	0.8	0.7	0.6	(0.6)	0.5	. .
Indonesia	[5.0]	[4.1]	[3.8]	[3.7]	[4.2]	[3.9]	[3.6]	[3.0]	[3.2]	. .
Japan	0.9	0.9	0.9	0.9	0.9	1.0	1.0	1.0	. .	. .
Korea, North[g]		10.1	10.4	10.7	11.5	11.8	12.3			
Korea, South	5.9	5.1	5.9	6.0	6.0	5.6	5.0	5.1	5.0	. .
Malaysia	5.8	5.5	6.4	8.1	7.9	(6.9)	(5.5)	(5.6)	(5.9)	. .
Philippines	[2.7]	[2.4]	[2.2]	[2.2]	[2.3]	[2.2]				
Singapore	(5.6)	(5.0)	5.0	5.1	5.1	4.5	5.5	6.5	6.4	. .
Taiwan	7.1	6.8	6.6	6.7	7.3	6.8	6.1	6.4	5.9	. .
Thailand	(4.3)	5.4	5.1	4.8	4.9	5.0	5.0	5.0	4.8	. .
Oceania										
Australia	2.5	2.4	2.6	2.6	2.7	2.9	2.8	2.8	2.8	. .
Fiji	0.5	0.5	0.4	0.3	0.4	0.4	0.4	0.3	. .	. .
New Zealand	1.8	1.8	1.9	2.1	2.1	2.0	2.0			
Africa										
Algeria	2.4	2.1	2.1	1.8	1.9	1.9	1.9	1.6	(1.7)	. .
Angola	. .	(14.0)	(12.8)	(13.8)	(11.9)	(16.5)	(20.4)	(28.5)	. .	. .
Benin	1.2	1.9	(1.9)	[1.8]	[1.7]	[2.1]	[2.2]	[2.1]	. .	. .
Botswana	3.3	3.7	3.6	3.7	2.8	2.4	2.5			
Burkina Faso	3.3	2.6	2.9	3.0	3.2	3.2	(3.2)	[2.4]	[2.4]	. .
Burundi	(2.8)	(2.6)	[2.9]	[3.0]	[3.6]	[3.2]	[3.3]	[3.0]	[3.2]	. .
Cameroon	1.5	1.5	1.2	1.1	1.7	2.2	[2.1]	[2.3]	[2.3]	. .
Central African Rep.	(1.7)	(2.0)	[1.7]	[2.1]	[2.3]	[2.8]				
Congo	5.0	3.7	2.8	[2.1]	[2.3]	[2.3]	[2.3]	[2.5]	. .	. .
Côte d'Ivoire	1.1	1.1	1.2	[1.1]	[1.1]	[1.2]	[1.1]	[1.0]	[1.0]	[1.2]
Ethiopia	6.8	8.8	8.5	[8.7]	[8.4]	[8.2]	[9.2]	[9.7]	[2.9]	. .
Gabon	[2.3]	(1.9)	[2.1]	[2.4]	[2.4]	[2.5]	[2.4]	[2.8]		
Ghana	0.7	(0.5)	(0.3)	0.6	0.4	(0.3)	(0.5)	[0.9]		
Kenya	3.9	4.4	3.6	3.4	3.7	3.5	[2.8]	[2.4]	[2.7]	[2.8]

SIPRI MILITARY EXPENDITURE DATA 171

Liberia	1.1	1.5	3.0	5.8	5.4	3.0	3.1	[3.1]	[3.5]	. .
Libya	[14.2]	[12.7]	[9.2]	[12.7]	[14.9]	[11.8]	[11.4]	. .	. .	. .
Madagascar	2.5	3.0	(2.8)	(3.0)	[2.7]	[2.4]	(2.3)	[2.1]	[2.2]	[2.0]
Malawi	2.8	4.3	4.5	3.3	2.4	1.9	1.6	1.4	1.6	. .
Mali	. .	. .	5.9	5.2	5.4	5.2	(5.6)	[2.7]	[2.7]	[3.1]
Mauritania	14.2	11.6	9.7	8.2	7.6	5.7	[6.0]	[6.6]	[6.6]	. .
Mauritius	0.2	0.2	0.5	0.4	0.3	0.3	0.2	[0.2]	[0.3]	. .
Morocco	5.8	5.6	6.3	6.6	6.5	4.9	4.7	4.4	5.0	. .
Mozambique	. .	. .	5.6	7.0	8.1	(10.7)	(12.1)	(12.4)	(11.5)	. .
Niger	0.9	0.9	0.8	0.7	0.7	[0.7]	[0.8]	[0.7]	0.7	. .
Nigeria	3.5	2.8	2.8	2.6	2.0	2.1	[1.6]	[1.5]	[1.4]	[1.5]
Rwanda	1.6	1.8	1.9	2.0	2.0	1.9	1.6	1.6	(1.6)	. .
Senegal	3.5	3.3	3.1	2.9	2.7	2.6	(2.5)	(2.3)	(2.2)	[2.2]
Sierra Leone	0.9	0.9	1.1	1.2	1.0	0.8	[0.6]	[0.5]	[0.4]	[0.4]
South Africa	. .	. .	(3.9)	(3.7)	(3.7)	3.7	3.7	3.7	3.9	[4.1]
Sudan	(4.2)	(4.3)	1.8	1.7	1.7	[2.5]	[3.4]	[3.1]	[3.0]	. .
Tanzania	2.3	2.0	3.6	3.8	3.8	3.7	3.5	[3.1]	. .	. .
Togo	8.0	7.0	2.2	2.4	2.3	2.2	2.4	2.8	[2.4]	. .
Tunisia	5.2	2.2	2.2	2.7	(5.9)	(6.6)	(4.7)	(5.2)	[5.8]	[5.4]
Uganda	2.5	2.2	2.1	2.5	2.1	2.6	2.7	[2.6]	. .	. .
Zaire	1.8	. .	2.1	1.3	2.8	1.2	1.9	1.4	. .	. .
Zambia	3.3	3.0	2.5	[4.0]	[2.8]	[2.9]	[2.5]	[2.8]	. .	. .
Zimbabwe	[2.8]	[4.8]	[3.5]	6.4	[2.8]	5.9	5.9	5.4	[5.9]	. .
	6.4	6.0	7.1		5.8					

Central America

Costa Rica	0.7	0.8	0.8	0.6	0.7	0.8	(0.8)	(0.8)	(0.7)	. .
Cuba[h]	8.3	8.5	7.7	8.1	9.1	8.8	10.1	9.6	. .	. .
Dominican Republic	1.8	2.0	1.5	1.7	1.6	1.5	1.5	1.3	. .	. .
El Salvador	2.1	(2.0)	2.8	3.7	4.4	4.4	4.9	. .	(4.8)	. .
Guatemala	1.7	1.7	1.8	1.9	[2.4]	(2.6)	(2.9)	[3.6]	. .	. .
Haiti	1.3	1.4	1.4	1.4	1.3	1.2	1.1	[1.2]	. .	. .
Honduras	2.3	2.3	3.1	(3.6)	(3.7)	4.0	4.9	(4.6)	5.4	. .
Jamaica	0.8	1.0	1.4	1.6	1.8	1.4	1.1	1.1	. .	. .
Mexico	0.5	0.6	0.6	0.6	0.6	(0.7)	(0.6)	(0.6)	(0.6)	. .
Nicaragua	3.2	(3.1)	(4.4)	(5.0)	(5.9)	[9.6]	[10.8]	[4.6]	[17.7]	. .
Panama	1.5	1.5	1.2	1.2	1.3	1.4	(1.9)	(1.9)	(1.9)	. .
Trinidad and Tobago	2.3	1.9	2.0	2.3	2.9	. .	[2.6]	[2.6]	[2.5]	. .

172 MILITARY EXPENDITURE, ARMS TRADE, CONFLICTS

	1978	1979	1980	1981	1982	1983	1984	1985	1986	1987
South America										
Argentina	5.8	5.4	5.6	6.2	(6.0)	(4.5)	(4.3)	4.2	4.5	..
Bolivia	3.4	3.5	4.0	5.3	(4.5)	(3.7)	[3.7]	[3.8]	..	..
Brazil[c]	[0.8]	[0.7]	[0.7]	[0.7]	[0.9]	[0.8]	[0.8]	..	..	..
Chile	7.0	6.9	6.7	7.4	9.5	8.0	9.6	7.6	(8.3)	..
Colombia	..	[1.7]	(1.9)	(1.9)	(1.8)	(2.3)	(2.5)	(2.2)	(2.2)	..
Ecuador	(2.1)	(2.0)	1.9	1.9	(1.7)	(1.6)	(1.5)	..	..	..
Guyana	5.3	5.1	6.5	6.0	7.5	(9.7)	(9.2)	(9.8)	[12.4]	..
Paraguay	1.5	1.3	1.4	1.5	1.6	[1.8]	..	(1.1)	(1.2)	..
Peru	5.5	3.9	[5.3]	[6.0]	..	[9.6]	[6.5]	[7.5]	[8.7]	..
Uruguay	2.3	2.4	2.9	3.9	4.0	3.2	2.6	2.5	[2.1]	..
Venezuela	2.1	2.4	2.7	3.1	3.4	(2.9)	2.8	3.0	[3.1]	..

Conventions
.. Information not available or not applicable
( ) Uncertain data
[ ] Estimates with a high degree of uncertainty
— Negligible or nil
t. Thousand
m. Million
b. Billion

Notes, definitions and sources for the tables of world military expenditure

[a] Spain became a NATO member on 30 May 1982. Military expenditure has been estimated on the basis of the NATO definition for the period 1980–87 and extrapolated to give estimates for 1978–79. For convenience, the whole series is presented here in the NATO section.
[b] The SIPRI estimate in square brackets is based on planned military expenditure in real terms.
[c] Recent evidence suggests that Brazilian military expenditure is considerably higher than the amount given here. The series is currently being revised.
[d] The SIPRI practice of using official consumer price indices, which tend to understate actual price changes in WTO countries, especially for recent years, results in overstated volume expenditure increases for the WTO countries, excluding the USSR.
[e] At current prices and 1986 exchange-rates.
[f] At current prices and an exchange-rate of 29.92 kwanzas per US dollar.
[g] Per cent of gross national product.
[h] Per cent of net material product.

SIPRI MILITARY EXPENDITURE DATA   173

Table 6A.1: Military expenditure figures are given in local currency at current prices. Figures for recent years are budget estimates.
Table 6A.2: This series is based on the data given in the local currency series, deflated to 1986 price levels and converted into dollars at 1986 period-average exchange-rates. Local consumer-price indices (CPI) are taken as far as possible from *International Financial Statistics* (IFS) (International Monetary Fund: Washington, DC). For the most recent year, the CPI is an estimate based on the first 6–10 months of the year. Period-average exchange-rates are taken as far as possible from the IFS.
Table 6A.3: The share of gross domestic product (GDP) is calculated in local currency. GDP data are taken as far as possible from IFS. For WTO countries (except Hungary), military expenditure is given as a percentage of gross national product (GNP) for 1978, and after 1978 as a percentage of net material product (NMP). For Romania, military expenditure is given as a percentage of GNP for the years 1978–86.

Definitions and sources

For more detailed information, readers are referred to previous editions of the *SIPRI Yearbook*.
The NATO definition of military expenditure is used as a guideline throughout. Where possible, the following items are *included*: all current and capital expenditure on the armed forces and on the running of defence departments and other government agencies engaged in defence projects; the cost of paramilitary forces and police when judged to be trained and equipped for military operations; military R&D, tests and evaluation costs; costs of retirement pensions of service personnel, including pensions of civilian employees. Military aid is included in the budget of the donor country.
Excluded: civil defence, interest on war debts and some types of veterans' payments.
Problems encountered when applying this definition include: the absence of disaggregated expenditure series; the non-disclosure of certain expenditure categories, especially procurement and R&D; uncertainty as to the amount of military aid included in recipients' budgets; and the degree to which police forces, border and coastguards and the like play a military role.
The data cover 127 countries for the calendar years 1978–87. *Calendar year* figures are calculated from fiscal year data where necessary, on the assumption that expenditure takes place evenly throughout the year. All series are *revised* annually.

General remarks on the data and data presentation

Changes in data published in successive Yearbooks may be due to the revision of any component of the data base, i.e., military expenditure, consumer price indices, exchange-rates and GDP/GNP/NMP data.
Primary sources are official publications.
Secondary sources are press information, specialist literature and other background information.
Uncertain data (with round brackets in the tables) are figures from secondary sources or figures from primary sources, adjusted for known inconsistencies with the time-series in use. Estimates with a high degree of uncertainty (with square brackets in the tables) are data with components of primary and secondary sources and SIPRI estimates based on other country background material.

Main sources of military expenditure data

NATO
Official NATO data published in *Financial and Economic Data Relating to NATO Defence*, annual press release (NATO: Brussels).

Other WTO
1978–79: Alton, T. P., Lazarcik, G., Bass, E. M. and Znayenko, W., 'East European defense expenditures, 1965–1978', in *East European Assessment, Part 2*, a compendium of papers submitted to the Joint Economic Committee, US Congress (US Government Printing Office: Washington, DC, 1981); Alton, T. P., Lazarcik, G., Bass, E. M. and Znayenko, W., *Military expenditure in Eastern Europe, Post World War II to 1979* (L.W. International Financial Research, Inc: New York, 1980). After 1979: domestic sources.

Others
Domestic budgets, defence appropriations and final accounts. Official publications such as *Government Finance Statistics* (International Monetary Fund: Washington, DC); *Statistical Yearbook* (United Nations: New York); *Statistical Yearbook for Asia and the Pacific* (United Nations: Bangkok); *Statistik des Auslandes* (Federal Statistical Office: Wiesbaden); *Europa Yearbook* (Europa Publications: London). Journals and newspapers are consulted for the most recent figures.

7. The trade in conventional weapons

AARON KARP*

I. Introduction

Since academic analysis of the international trade in arms and military equipment began in the mid-1960s, a weighty literature has emerged. Much has been done to illuminate basic facts, trends and relationships. None the less, understanding remains far from complete. Events in 1987 helped show the limits of insights about the arms trade. Old assumptions can no longer be taken for granted. Basic relationships are not as clear as they seemed to be just a few years ago. New aspects of the arms trade require extensive study.

1987 made it apparent that the international arms trade is evolving in ways that had not been anticipated. This chapter examines how the trade is evolving and offers tentative assessments. As in the past, government-to-government transfers of major weapons continue to form the largest part of the arms trade, but they tell less and less of the story. Small transactions are increasingly salient. The grey and black markets have matured into significant forces, and the trade in technology and parts is evolving into new forms. Once minor side-shows, they soon may emerge as the most significant aspect of the arms trade, militarily, politically and economically. Nations accustomed to relying on exports of major weapons to achieve myriad objectives may confront dramatic and painful adjustments. As arms sales change, the policy objectives they have served may have to change as well.

These changes necessitate extensive adjustments. Policies and approaches left from an era in which traditional transfers of major weapons were of overwhelming importance must be revised to cope with the emerging environment. Policy makers, industry and analysts must develop new tools if they are to remain informed and relevant.

This chapter concentrates primarily on the leading arms exporters. Many of the key disputes and controversies of 1987 arise from the special problems of arms suppliers discussed below. With telling frequency, their industries are in trouble, their sales violate laws or conscience, and their arms trade regulations are under sharp debate. The importer perspective is not ignored, but it is offered mostly as importers' interests influence the actions and policies of leading exporters. The issues facing arms importers are developed more thoroughly in chapter 8.

II. The trade in major weapons

The trade in major weapons remains the largest element of the international arms trade. Even if sales of complete naval vessels, military aircraft, armour, artillery, missiles and radars no longer dominate the arms trade as they did in

* This chapter could not have been prepared without the assistance of Agnès Allebeck, Ian Anthony and Evamaria Loose-Weintraub.

the 1970s, the trade is still very prominent. It remains the most important source of military hardware for most—if not all—nations. For the rest it is a prominent symbol of military power, diplomatic relations and economic priorities.

SIPRI arms trade statistics show that the global trade in major weapons rose in 1987. Total deliveries reached roughly $35 billion (all figures in 1985 US dollars), of which some $24.7 billion went to Third World nations. This increase was caused largely by sudden US and Soviet deliveries of fighter aircraft ordered in the early 1980s. The scarcity of new orders (analysed below) suggests that future deliveries will decline. If the wars in Afghanistan and the Persian Gulf end soon, the trade in major weapons could drop precipitously.

SIPRI arms trade statistics are constantly being revised as better information becomes available. Given the present methodology, SIPRI data are intended to provide a conservative estimate for the evaluation of general trends. Experience shows that SIPRI estimates of the trade in major weapons for the previous year are usually about 95 per cent complete. These figures typically rise over time. For example, table 7.1 shows that the value of deliveries of major weapons to the Third World in 1986 was worth $21.7 billion. This is 2 per cent higher than the figure published in the *SIPRI Yearbook 1987* ($21.3 billion). The figures published here for 1987 will probably be raised next year as well.

This statistical increase also reflects a change to improve the comprehensiveness of SIPRI's methodology for tracking the arms trade. SIPRI arms trade registers are compiled principally from publicly available, published sources. This ensures independence and improves accuracy, but sometimes results in the exclusion of some unpublicized deals. This oversight has been particularly

Table 7.1. The leading exporters of major weapons, 1983–87

Countries are ranked according to 1987 exports. Figures are in US $m., at constant (1985) prices.

	1983	1984	1985	1986	1987	1983–87
To the Third World						
1. USSR	6 889	7 310	7 754	8 065	9 697	39 714
2. USA	6 256	4 983	4 113	4 891	5 829	26 073
3. France	2 843	3 603	3 784	3 669	3 213	17 112
4. UK	579	1 139	942	1 263	1 641	5 564
5. China	961	1 180	872	1 302	1 040	5 356
6. FR Germany	1 175	1 835	520	613	630	4 773
7. Netherlands	—	57	38	132	495	722
8. Brazil	298	271	191	189	368	1 317
9. Sweden	20	49	39	145	302	555
10. Italy	970	811	539	325	228	2 873
11. Israel	384	252	152	179	201	1 168
12. Spain	545	400	119	202	177	1 442
13. Egypt	325	141	113	126	158	862
14. Czechoslovakia	99	122	37	89	133	481
15. Singapore	1	48	44	92	125	311
Others	1 293	756	511	405	487	3 452
Total	**22 638**	**22 957**	**19 768**	**21 687**	**24 724**	**111 775**

	1983	1984	1985	1986	1987	1983–87
To the industrial world						
1. USA	5 622	4 954	4 803	5 074	5 718	26 171
2. USSR	2 116	2 091	3 662	2 843	2 565	13 277
3. FR Germany	650	612	436	330	814	2 842
4. France	617	493	368	709	360	2 547
5. Czechoslovakia	213	213	187	187	187	988
6. UK	498	790	835	430	151	2 704
7. Saudi Arabia	—	—	—	39	125	164
8. Canada	89	63	50	707	102	1 010
9. Sweden	12	57	117	177	77	440
10. Israel	1	—	59	—	67	128
11. South Korea	—	—	—	—	40	40
12. Austria	29	42	42	—	34	147
13. Switzerland	2	13	72	65	32	184
14. Norway	27		36	9	22	94
15. Italy	4	54	12	2	19	91
Others	185	267	145	132	67	796
Total	**10 065**	**9 649**	**10 824**	**10 704**	**10 380**	**51 623**
To all countries						
1. USSR	9 004	9 401	11 416	10 908	12 262	52 991
2. USA	11 878	9 937	8 916	9 965	11 547	52 244
3. France	3 460	4 096	4 152	4 378	3 573	19 659
4. UK	1 077	1 928	1 777	1 693	1 792	8 268
5. FR Germany	1 826	2 447	956	943	1 444	7 615
6. China	973	1 227	943	1 302	1 040	5 486
7. Netherlands	87	98	88	240	497	1 011
8. Sweden	32	107	156	322	380	996
9. Brazil	363	296	191	189	369	1 408
10. Czechoslovakia	312	335	225	276	321	1 469
11. Israel	386	252	211	179	268	1 296
12. Italy	973	865	551	327	247	2 963
13. Spain	545	400	119	210	177	1 451
14. Egypt	325	141	113	126	158	862
15. Canada	239	86	84	746	139	1 293
Others	1 223	990	694	587	890	4 384
World total	**32 703**	**32 606**	**30 592**	**32 391**	**35 104**	**163 396**

Source: SIPRI data base.

obvious for Afghanistan, where large Soviet transfers sustain the Kabul Government. These transfers are included here for the first time, for the duration of the war which began in 1978. The process used to produce these estimates is described in appendix 7D. SIPRI welcomes comments on the procedure.

The market for major items of military equipment continues to be highly concentrated. The five largest exporters—the USSR, the USA, France, Britain and China (see table 7A.2, appendix 7A)—provide over 80 per cent of all global deliveries. The rest of the market is divided among a large number of smaller suppliers, including increasingly large numbers of Third World manufacturers.

The USSR

Among major arms exporters, the Soviet Union retains its role as the leading supplier to the Third World, a role it has had, with exceptions, since the late 1970s. The USSR's 39 per cent share of all transfers of major weapons to the Third World continues to be highly concentrated among a small number of leading clients, especially India, Iraq and to a lesser degree Syria and Angola. In 1987 the USSR made unprecedented efforts to recover its place as a supplier of technically sophisticated military equipment. Nevertheless, these efforts cannot conceal serious problems facing the Soviet arms sale programme.

The Soviet Union continues to favour India as its most important client. India can usually insist on the most advanced Soviet hardware, even more advanced than that which the USSR supplies to Eastern Europe. (For import statistics see table 7.2.) India's unique relationship with Moscow—comparable only to Israel's relationship with Washington—was symbolized dramatically by the revelation that the Soviet Union is leasing a nuclear-powered submarine to the Indian Navy (see also chapter 12). While it is not clear if this violates the Nuclear Non-Proliferation Treaty, it is the first time nuclear military technology has been transferred directly by a major government to a Third World nation. The submarine's precise designation was unclear at this writing (early 1988), but it probably relies on early-1960s reactor technology. In 1987 India also started licensed production of Soviet T-72 tanks and BMP armoured personnel carriers. After years of unexplained delay India began licensed production of the MiG-27 ground attack aircraft. India also became the first foreign recipient of the MiG-29 multi-role fighter.[1]

Table 7.2. The leading importers of major weapons, 1983–87

Countries are ranked according to 1987 imports. Figures are in US $m., at constant (1985) prices.

	1983	1984	1985	1986	1987	1983–87
Third World						
1. India	1 757	999	1 892	2 695	5 246	12 589
2. Iraq	3 003	4 157	2 935	2 100	3 541	15 736
3. Egypt	2 393	2 257	1 307	1 776	2 231	9 964
4. Saudi Arabia	1 121	970	1 526	2 495	1 753	7 865
5. Israel	357	290	192	406	1 632	2 877
6. Syria	1 868	1 598	1 634	1 782	1 301	8 183
7. Angola	443	568	444	720	1 126	3 300
8. Taiwan	592	378	574	664	607	2 815
9. South Korea	280	244	382	288	556	1 750
10. Peru	99	329	375	222	544	1 568
11. Thailand	360	309	310	91	520	1 590
12. Iran	347	277	535	618	519	2 297
13. Afghanistan	136	215	83	373	449	1 255
14. Brazil	24	22	21	293	428	788
15. Pakistan	321	656	675	864	424	2 940
Others	9 537	9 688	6 883	6 300	3 847	36 257
Total	**22 638**	**22 957**	**19 768**	**21 687**	**24 724**	**111 773**

	1983	1984	1985	1986	1987	1983–87
Industrial world						
1. Japan	1 551	1 516	1 514	1 640	1 331	7 552
2. Turkey	470	519	498	789	1 212	3 489
3. Czechoslovakia	946	867	1 461	1 161	1 191	5 627
4. Spain	136	28	88	865	1 111	2 228
5. Canada	517	459	790	759	677	3 204
6. Australia	809	463	345	867	654	3 139
7. Hungary	54	—	590	432	506	1 582
8. Poland	244	243	330	409	403	1 629
9. UK	406	790	379	372	402	2 350
10. FR Germany	469	470	422	395	328	2 084
11. Netherlands	1 083	907	777	676	311	3 754
12. German DR	776	847	851	492	281	3 247
13. Norway	220	228	103	153	271	975
14. Italy	315	176	179	190	204	1 063
15. USSR	202	195	195	195	199	987
Others	1 867	1 941	2 302	1 309	1 299	8 712
Total	**10 065**	**9 649**	**10 824**	**10 704**	**10 380**	**51 622**
All countries						
1. India	1 757	999	1 892	2 695	5 246	12 589
2. Iraq	3 003	4 157	2 935	2 100	3 541	15 736
3. Egypt	2 393	2 257	1 307	1 776	2 231	9 964
4. Saudi Arabia	1 121	970	1 526	2 495	1 753	7 865
5. Israel	357	290	192	406	1 632	2 877
6. Japan	1 551	1 516	1 514	1 640	1 331	7 552
7. Syria	1 868	1 598	1 634	1 782	1 301	8 183
8. Turkey	470	519	498	789	1 212	3 489
9. Czechoslovakia	946	867	1 461	1 161	1 191	5 627
10. Angola	443	568	444	720	1 126	3 300
11. Spain	136	28	88	865	1 111	2 228
12. Canada	517	459	790	759	677	3 204
13. Australia	809	463	345	867	654	3 139
14. Taiwan	592	378	574	664	607	2 815
15. South Korea	280	244	382	288	556	1 750
Others	16 460	17 293	15 010	13 384	10 935	73 077
World total	**32 703**	**32 606**	**30 592**	**32 391**	**35 104**	**163 395**

Source: SIPRI data base.

Other recipients of the MiG-29 include Iraq and Syria. Exports of some 96 MiG-29s pushed the value of Soviet arms exports up by 30 per cent in 1987. This aircraft is an exception among Soviet arms exports, which typically consist of large quantities of relatively low-technology items reflecting Soviet technological weaknesses and procurement doctrine. There is increasing evidence that Soviet arms transfers are technologically limited both in quality and, in the long run, in quantity. Recent analyses show that many top Soviet export items are manifestly second-rate, including armoured vehicles such as the BMP, artillery such as the D-30 122-mm, An-26/32 transport aircraft or Kilo diesel-powered submarines. Even the heralded MiG-29 which would have been breathtaking in 1975 (when similar Western aircraft were being introduced) was merely interesting in 1987. The Soviet Union is unable to provide its friends and allies with an AWACS (Airborne Warning and Control System) similar to the widely sold US E-2C Hawkeye or E-3 Sentry. Nor can its tanks match Western vehicles such as the Abrams, Leopard-2 or Merkava.[2]

Unless the USSR can develop newer and better weapon systems for export, it will continue to lose clients and influence. Leasing a nuclear-powered submarine to India is a clear attempt to regain influence by escalating to new kinds of technology. The traditional advantage of Soviet equipment was its low cost, but this asset is less important now that many Third World governments are willing to pay for superior Western hardware. Nations that once bought almost exclusively from the USSR now turn with increasing alacrity to the West for their most advanced equipment. This is certainly true for Soviet clients such as India, Iraq and Peru which give a growing share of their arms business to others.

India offers an important example. After almost 20 years of buying its most important equipment from the USSR, India now turns to the USSR for the bulk of its forces while it prefers Western suppliers for its most advanced items when possible. India has raised its defence budget by some 250 per cent in the past decade, greatly expanding procurement options.[3] Now India's best aircraft are generally British and French. In 1987 India turned to Britain for an aircraft-carrier, to the Netherlands for radar, and to France for design assistance on its new domestic fighter aircraft. Iraq also relies on Soviet equipment for the bulk of its forces in its war with Iran, but most of its more advanced items are French (see appendices 7B and 7C). Both nations are partially diversifying their purchases to avoid excessive political dependence. Their concern with quality, however, is unmistakable as well.

Unless the Soviet Union can reform its procurement bureaucracy to develop better quality arms—which seems unlikely—it may find itself becoming the world's largest marginal supplier. Like some Third World suppliers such as Brazil or China, it will have only a specific niche in the international arms market. Although the size of its arms exports is unlikely to shrink, their significance will tend to diminish. Unable to furnish all the needs of its most important clients, the USSR will probably lose political influence and military options.

Kremlin policy-makers developed arms sales into a major policy tool in the 1960s and into a principal hard-currency earner in the 1970s. Despite its significance, there is no evidence that Soviet arms sales policy has undergone a systematic re-evaluation under General Secretary Gorbachev.[4] *Glasnost* has not illuminated Moscow's arms sale decision-making process which remains almost completely unknown outside the Soviet Union. Nor have the Soviets been any more forthcoming with information about their arms exports. Very little is known about internal debates within the Soviet Union on specific arms transfers since the Khrushchev era. We have no insights about new sales agreements undertaken during 1987. Out of necessity, SIPRI data on Soviet arms exports are derived largely from Western sources.

There is evidence, however, pointing to some desire to reduce overseas commitments and risks. Soviet clients are sometimes not allowed to receive all the weapons that they would like to have. Nicaragua has taken delivery of considerably less Soviet equipment than it wants. Long sought MiG-21s remain in limbo. Nicaraguan leaders have made it clear they want the fighter aircraft, but Moscow is hesitant. Evidence suggests that the aircraft may be in Cuba, awaiting final Soviet approval. Attempts were made by Moscow to restrain Libya, leading Colonel Muammar Qadhafi to turn to China. Even an old Soviet favourite client such as Syria was unable to buy as many MiG-29s as it wanted and was refused SS-23 missiles. The latter may have been denied in anticipation of the INF Treaty, which specifically calls for their destruction. In other cases Kremlin decisions suggest concern with improving hard currency income. Angola has been forced to pay more for its Soviet equipment, and Iraq apparently was denied MiG-27 aircraft—in the middle of Iran's spring 1987 offensives—owing to payment problems.[5]

SIPRI arms trade statistics slightly exaggerate Soviet arms transfers by neglecting the role of *Czechoslovakia* and *Poland*. Both countries are sole suppliers to the Warsaw Treaty Organization (WTO) of jet trainers and some types of light transport aircraft and helicopters. Exports of these items are appropriately recognized in the registers. Both nations also manufacture large quantities of Soviet-designed armoured vehicles such as T-72 tanks. These vehicles seem to be primarily for export, either directly to the Third World or to the Soviet Union for subsequent re-export.[6] When deliveries of these vehicles to other WTO allies and Third World clients cannot be distinguished from Soviet deliveries, SIPRI lists them as Soviet exports. This diminishes the true significance of Czechoslovakia and Poland as suppliers of major weapons.

The United States

For the United States, 1987 was a painful year full of arms sales controversies. While the USA's position as a major arms exporter is not seriously challenged, only deals with formal allies and close friends such as Israel enjoy widespread support. Third World arms sales face increasingly hostile congressional scrutiny. Indeed, several proposed US arms deals of 1987 were killed, modified or delayed indefinitely. While the Congress failed in its efforts to strengthen its power to veto proposed deals, existing powers were used with unprecedented persistence and strength.

US deliveries of major weapons to the Third World totalled some $6 billion in 1987, second to the USSR. This figure was dominated by deliveries of high-technology items, principally E-3 AWACS aircraft to Saudi Arabia, E-2C AWACS to Egypt and F-16 fighters to Israel. (These and other deliveries of 1987 are listed in appendices 7B and 7C.) Like the Soviet Union, the United States is finding its arms exports to the Third World concentrated among a small number of recipients. Only those with state-of-the-art requirements and hefty defence budgets can afford the United States' principal weapon systems.[7] Consequently US arms transfers to the Third World are concentrated among a few key aid recipients, newly industrialized countries and oil powers. It is no wonder that the USA now sells more to its allies in Europe and the Pacific than to the Third World.

Advanced aircraft are the largest category of US arms exports. Foreign deliveries of General Dynamics F-16 fighters alone (123 in 1987) constituted over 25 per cent of all US arms exports for the year. The largest new order for the United States came from Italy, which will buy 20 Patriot air defence batteries worth about $3 billion. Britain and France followed NATO by ordering the Boeing E-3 Sentry AWACS in deals worth almost $1.5 and $1 billion, respectively. Italy is likely to follow suit in the near future. After a politically painful decision not to develop an indigenous aircraft for its FS-X strike fighter requirement, Japan elected to procure at least 130 copies of a new version of the General Dynamics F-16. South Korea is likely to make the same choice in 1988.[8] Variants of this ageing airframe (first flight in 1974) will probably be in production for foreign customers well into the next century.

Major Third World orders were more illusive. Cognizant of the difficulties of arms sales decision making in Washington, many Third World leaders have taken their business elsewhere, but the lure of US technology, political support and assistance cannot be ignored. Nevertheless, 1987 saw no multi-billion dollar US defence contracts with Third World nations.

Saudi Arabia, whose early 1980s buying spree temporarily made it the world's biggest arms importer, no longer buys US equipment with seeming abandon. The reasons are manifold. First, Saudi Arabia is struggling to integrate its previous purchases into its force structure. Second, decreasing oil revenue and the Gulf War have altered Riyadh's priorities. Third, repeated embarrassment at the hands of Congress (discussed below) encourages Saudi Arabia to buy from more appreciative suppliers such as Britain, France and even Brazil. Finally, even US defence industries are technically limited, but in the opposite way from the Soviet Union. The US problem is in supplying low-technology equipment for which its own armed forces have no need and which it rarely produces. A Saudi requirement for diesel-powered submarines will have to be satisfied elsewhere; the USA builds only nuclear-powered submarines. The Saudi Army would probably prefer the General Motors M-1 Abrams tank (now that FR Germany refuses to sell its Leopard-2), but the price may send them elsewhere in 1988.[9]

The same is not true for Egypt, which won White House approval for a licence to co-produce some 555 of the state-of-the-art armoured vehicles. As a signatory of the Camp David Peace Accords, Egypt can get almost any US item it wants. Even so, the M-1 tank licence raised eyebrows among observers who see it as a threat to US security interests and far beyond Egypt's weak economy. Others, noting that no production is scheduled until 1997, doubt that anything will ever come of it.[10]

Another licence was granted to Israel for purchase of 75–90 additional F-16 aircraft. This reward for Israel's decision to cancel the highly controversial Lavi fighter aircraft may lead to limited co-production. As part of the new US package, Israel is also becoming a preferential supplier to the US armed forces.[11]

Other major US arms deals came under the rubric of the Reagan Doctrine's support for insurgencies fighting Marxist governments. Stinger missiles continued to flow to the Afghan Mujahideen. Smaller quantities were probably delivered to the Union for the Total Independence of Angola (UNITA) in Angola and to the Chadian Government to aid its fight against Libya. The

Nicaraguan Contras received less capable Redeye missiles.[12] In a related move, Honduras is receiving 12 Northrop F-5 fighters as insurance against the possibility that Nicaragua will receive MiG-21s. All of these transfers were challenged in Congress. The Honduran F-5 deal was very nearly blocked until a heavy White House lobbying campaign saved it.[13]

In the spring and summer of 1987, the US Congress debated several proposals to alter the way in which the US Government makes arms sale decisions. Most consequential was the proposed Biden-Levine amendment to the 1976 Arms Export Control Act.[14] This sought to restore powers which Congress lost in 1983 when the Supreme Court invalidated the legislated veto provision under which Congress could stop arms sales. Instead the amendment would require positive congressional approval of most major arms deals. Unable to win consideration when submitted in 1986, the proposed amendment benefited from the November elections in which Democrats took Senate leadership. Hearings in March 1987 pitted advocates of congressional authority against critics who maintained that it would deprive the President of an essential policy instrument. Critics added that the bill would create an enormous congressional workload, resulting in an endless backlog of unapproved cases.

By the summer of 1987, the Biden-Levine bill had disappeared from the legislative agenda. Many congressmen were impressed by pleas from industry that it would create an unfair disadvantage for US defence exporters. Others doubted that Congress could responsibly undertake the workload. A cosponsor, Senator Joe Biden, devoted his energies instead to a presidential campaign and the nomination hearings of Judge Robert Bork. Despite this failure, new proposals to fully restore congressional power over US arms transfers are likely to appear in the near future. With important policy and constitutional issues at stake, this is not a matter that can be easily ignored.

Another proposal, championed by Senator David Pryor, aims to improve arms export licensing procedures by transferring the Office of Munitions Control (OMC) from the State Department to the Pentagon. This office, which decides upon all licence applications for arms sales, has been criticized for being too small to review thoroughly the 50 000 applications it receives annually. Moving it to the Defense Department could ensure better funding and expansion. The plan was fought successfully by the State Department and also by industry, which feared more stringent regulations.[15] The proposal may be revived in the near future.

Other than administrative changes in the arms export process and some tinkering with the Foreign Military Sales financing system, two changes in US arms trade law were actually enacted in 1987. One simply prohibits sales of special anti-tank shells made with depleted uranium to enemies of Israel. The other, a reaction to the Iran–Contra scandal, requires Congress to be notified of all sales of munitions and dual-use items to nations on the US 'terrorist list': Cuba, Iran, Libya, North Korea, Syria and South Yemen.[16]

One factor contributing to the lack of urgency in the debate on congressional oversight of US arms transfers is that Congress still has the ability to stop controversial arms deals. Since losing its veto authority, Congress has discovered other legal mechanisms to kill or change an arms deal. Specific legislation can be used to forbid an individual deal. Funding can be denied. Sometimes mere publicity is enough. In 1987 the Congress used all of these techniques to halt or modify a series of proposed transfers.

On 16 April 1987 then Pakistani Prime Minister Junejo urgently requested US AWACS aircraft. After a series of Soviet-Afghan air incursions and bombings on Pakistani soil, Junejo claimed that the aircraft were essential to contain the Afghan War. US officials initially reacted hesitantly, fearing that the aircraft could disrupt Pakistan's delicate balance with India. India and the USSR denounced the proposal as an 'unfriendly act'. Nevertheless, within a month the White House approved a plan to lease Grumman E-2C Hawkeye AWACS aircraft to Pakistan.[17] The Administration never showed great enthusiasm for the idea, especially when confronted with harsh congressional questioning. Pakistan damaged its own credibility when its nationals were caught trying to ship illegal nuclear weapon components. The fiscal year 1988 foreign aid bill now delays the whole issue by insisting upon further study.[18]

The White House was also faced with the never-ending US-Saudi arms sale crisis. Despite a decade of nasty confrontations between Congress and the President, the USA still has not found a solution to the raging passions ignited by proposed arms sales to Saudi Arabia. These disputes often seem unpredictable if not quixotic. Concerns for Israeli security lie at the heart of the matter. It may be that there is no way to reconcile absolute security for both Saudi Arabia and Israel.

A plan announced in March 1987 to sell transport helicopters to Saudi Arabia roused no serious opposition. A subsequent sale of attack helicopters and sophisticated electronic countermeasure packages for tactical aircraft received only passing criticism.[19] Not until June did the White House arouse congressional defiance with a plan to sell 12 F-15 C/D Eagle fighters to replace losses from training and 1600 AGM-65 D Maverick anti-tank missiles.[20] Israel's supporters in the US Congress saw grave danger in the Maverick sale and forced the Administration to withdraw the package. Saudi Arabia's failure to defend the *USS Stark* in May did not help its case.[21] In September the Administration tried again. When it was clear that congressional dissatisfaction had not abated, the White House abandoned the Maverick sale to save the aircraft. Congress went along, but forbade any sale to Saudi Arabia of a more advanced version of the aircraft, the F-15 E Strike Eagle.[22]

A related problem surrounded a proposal to sell Stinger anti-aircraft missiles to the Persian Gulf sheikdoms of Bahrain and Oman. This shoulder-fired missile was proposed for defence against Iran. Critics feared it could fall into terrorists' hands. Identical fears blocked previous proposed sales to Kuwait and Saudi Arabia. The critics' anxieties were illustrated fortuitously when—during the debate on the issue—Iran fired a Stinger taken from the Afghan Mujahideen at a US helicopter. Congress took no action in the spring when Bahrain bought F-16 fighters, but acted with alarm against the smaller Stinger sale in the autumn. Vigorous negotiating brought a compromise whereby Oman will receive no missiles, and Bahrain will receive 70 under rigorous controls.[23]

France

French exports of major weapons have much broader public and official support. This helped France to become the world's third leading exporter of major weaponry, but it has not saved the country from problems as an arms salesman. French defence industries and military procurement bureaucracy operated for 35 years under the assumption that arms exports complemented national security.[24] Guided by the belief that foreign sales made it possible for France to afford a completely independent arsenal, firms such as Avions Marcel Dassault relied on foreign orders for over 70 per cent of their business. Now that foreign orders are evaporating, France is having to re-think a major element of its defence policy.[25]

Dassault, symbolically the most important French defence firm even if it is not the largest economically, had no new foreign orders for its fighter aircraft in 1986 and sold only one in 1987. Unless the firm is to be radically restructured, it probably must build some 40 export fighters annually.[26] The firm has been able to delay restructuring through continual Iraqi replacement orders for Mirage F-1s (roughly 24 annually). This reprieve cannot outlast the Iraq-Iran War.[27] Other orders, from Greece and Jordan, will help sustain the firm in the short run, but its long-run prospects are not promising. Contraction is a possibility, but so is a major new sales campaign. Other French arms makers are in somewhat better health, not least because of France's role as Iraq's principal supplier of advanced weaponry. Aérospatiale's military helicopters—now France's biggest military export product—continue to sell well. In 1987 the company made large deliveries to the Brazilian armed services. French tactical missile sales also continue to be very strong. Armour and artillery manufacturers, however, subsist on small orders.[28]

Some observers believe that French defence firms have lost their place in the international arms market. Whereas France once was a neutral supplier of low-cost, high-performance items, it now offers systems like the Mirage-2000, suffering from high cost and disappointing capability. Others insist that the problem is not declining French technology but rising Third World industries combined with more restrained buying habits.[29] In either case France will be hard pressed to find an easy way to adjust.

The UK

In Britain, much was made of an announcement by the Ministry of Defence that Britain had become the world's second leading arms seller, reassuming a position it had lost in the early 1960s.[30] Using deliveries, the more reliable guide, Britain was still only the fourth largest exporter of major weapons. In either case Britain has emerged from the situation five years ago when its arms industries faced a serious export crisis.

The British recovery is more apparent than real. It is almost entirely due to a single deal, the sale of 72 Tornado tactical aircraft and trainers to Saudi Arabia in 1986. Britain will never see much of the proceeds, which must be shared with its colleagues in the multinational Tornado programme—FR Germany and

Italy—and with Switzerland.[31] While further export opportunities are still open, Turkey is a prominent prospect, the Tornado is beginning to show its age prematurely at 13 years, and its export outlook is growing dimmer.[32]

Other sectors of the British defence industry face troublesome prospects. Despite the possible sale in 1988 of Type 23 frigates to Pakistan, major foreign orders for British naval vessels have become few and far between. The aerospace industry is hoping to provide Hawk trainers to India, but no other large sales of military aircraft are in sight. British armoured vehicle production is centred around the 65-ton Challenger.[33] This vehicle is too heavy for use in many NATO scenarios and majestically overwhelming for prospective Third World buyers.

As in many other European nations, British industry has declining expectations for major Third World orders. Instead more emphasis is being directed at NATO collaborative projects and defence exports to the United States. British artillery and mortars won major contracts with the United States in 1987, as did British naval communications equipment. Other key US orders have been lost to harsh competition among Britain's other NATO allies.[34]

China

Since the late 1970s, China has developed a place in the international arms market, owing largely to its role in the Iraq-Iran War.[35] As the only nation consistently supplying major weapons to both sides, it has used the war to become a major supplier. China has found a few other clients for its major weapons, such as North Korea, Pakistan and Thailand, but China has no substitute for Iran and Iraq. Indeed, Beijing sells virtually nothing to industrial nations. When the Gulf War ends it will be difficult for China to retain its role in the arms market.

China's dilemma stems from its technical situation. Almost 30 years after the Sino-Soviet split, China is still working with a technological inheritance left from co-operation with the Soviet Union in the 1950s.[36] China's situation is not unlike that of the Soviet Union, but it is much more severe. Following the death of Chairman Mao Zedong, his successors steered the nation on a pragmatic course that allowed the country to become a genuinely neutral arms merchant. Political neutrality and low-cost weapons made China an appealing supplier to some, but few nations are interested in 1950s tanks and aircraft as they arm for the 1990s.

Several Latin American nations considered Chinese fighter aircraft in 1987 as a temporary solution to their own procurement dilemmas, but the lack of enthusiasm is palpable.[37] These MiG-21 copies are poor performers by every contemporary standard. Nor are they easy to maintain and operate. China's Hai Ying-2 (Silkworm) anti-ship missiles which Iran acquired in 1987 may have helped lead to the establishment of an enormous multinational peace-keeping fleet in the Persian Gulf. But other prospective buyers seem uninterested in this copy of a 1950s Soviet Styx missile. Newer missiles, such as the European Exocet, Sea Eagle or Penguin, are cheaper, more versatile and more effective.[38]

Ever mindful of the 60 Soviet divisions facing their borders, Chinese leaders are trying to modernize their armed forces. These efforts will also shape China's future role as an arms merchant. China's unwillingness to co-operate with United Nations peace efforts in the Persian Gulf in 1987 leaves little doubt but that it hopes to preserve its role as a large neutral supplier. These hopes will depend mainly on technical modernization. Large retrofit package deals with Italy to update A-5 (modified MiG-19) fighters and with Grumman to update F-8 (modified MiG-21) fighters were signed in 1986 and 1987, respectively. Technical co-operation with Britain, France and Israel also continues, demonstrating where China's leaders want to go.[39]

Other suppliers

After these five largest arms suppliers the international market for major weapons is a confusing welter of countries and firms. Their places as suppliers are very flexible. A single large deal or an individual delivery can make a nation into a high-ranking exporter overnight, a distinction it may lose entirely the following year. Most of these countries are niche suppliers with a handful of firms and key items which dominate their exports of major weapons.

Examples of these vicissitudes abound. *Spain* came out of nowhere in 1983–84 with deliveries of almost $1 billion. By 1987, however, its position had dropped dramatically with no expectation of sudden change. The most meteoric rise in 1987 belonged to the *Netherlands*, which jumped to seventh place in exports to the Third World by delivering just one submarine to Taiwan. The swiftest decline continues to affect *Italy*, now falling between *Israel* and *Spain* in total arms exports.

The case of *Libya* is most perverse of all, for Qadhafi made his biggest deal ever totally involuntarily. Catastrophic defeat in Chad resulted in an enormous loss of major weapons, many of them virtually unused. Although Libya has furnished small quantities of major weapons to allies such as Iran, Sudan, Syria and Uganda, these deals do not compare to the quantity and quality of those captured by Chad (see appendix 7B).[40] Most of this booty now belongs to Chad's central government although some fell into the hands of tribal chieftains. Key items such as Mi-24 helicopters and SA-13 surface-to-air missiles appear to have been purchased immediately by US and French intelligence agencies. The rest of this equipment may very well be used against Libya if hostilities with Chad resume. This event demonstrates the importance of captured weapons as a form of arms transfer.

For some secondary suppliers, SIPRI statistics are misleading. By concentrating exclusively on exports of complete major weapons, large contributions to co-operative programmes and through sub-contracting are missed. *FR Germany* would stand higher than sixth place among arms suppliers to the Third World if its 42 per cent contribution to every Saudi Tornado—officially sold by Britain—were recognized. It ranks higher as a supplier to other NATO allies, especially Turkey. None the less, West German arms sales to the Third World are in a period of decline, principally owing to the nation's inability to find new customers for its naval vessels and its unwillingness to sell its Leopard-2 tank to nations in regions of tension such as Saudi Arabia.

The second and third largest individual arms deals in 1987 were signed by firms from smaller nations. Kockums of *Sweden* initialled a contract estimated to be worth at least $2.7 billion to supply six Type 471 diesel-powered submarines to Australia. Oerlikon–Bührle of *Switzerland* won a US Army competition for a forward air defence system with its ADATS (Air Defence Anti-Tank System). The initial US requirement is for 166 ADATS systems worth $1.7 billion, although this may grow to over 500 systems worth $5 billion in the years ahead.[41] For both Sweden and Switzerland these contracts represent their largest foreign defence deals ever. It is unclear, however, whether they set precedents or merely establish exceptions.

Neither deal will propel the selling nation into the ranks of the major suppliers. They show how difficult it is for smaller suppliers to become major suppliers, even in a flexible arms market. Only a small proportion of the total contract values will translate into work for Sweden or Switzerland. The reasons are essentially twofold. First, neither weapon system is completely designed or built by the firm that signed the basic contract. With limited funds for development and marketing, both turned to US sub-contractors for essential support. These sub-contractors may actually gross more than the prime contractors. Second, both contracts are with recipients with large industrial facilities which will complete much of the actual production domestically. Since they have the capability to build much of the equipment at home, they have enormous incentives and domestic pressure to do so.

Sweden will probably see no more than 25 per cent of the value of the Australian submarines. Another 25 per cent will go to Rockwell in the United States, builder of the boats' weapon and sensor systems. Perhaps 50 per cent of the value will never leave Australia.[42] Over the next few years, Sweden will make considerably more money through Bofors' 1986 deal with India for 155-mm howitzers. Although the howitzer contract is worth less than half the value of the Australian submarines, $1.2 billion as opposed to $2.7 billion, most of this goes directly to Bofors in Sweden. The howitzer deal itself has become highly controversial in India (see below) but the Gandhi Government is continuing to go forward with it.

Oerlikon-Bührle is in similar straits with its ADATS, whose fire control system is built by Martin Marietta in the USA. For the US Army order the chassis, an FMC Bradley, will also come from the USA. Out of a total order for 166 missile systems, no more than 60 will come from Switzerland and these will feature a large US content.[43] The other 106 may be completely US-built. Because this situation is so common, even the largest deals may no longer make a nation into a large supplier.

III. The rising importance of smaller arms deals

Many of the most important and prominent arms transfers of the year were smaller deals. Major arms deals, involving large quantities of major weapon systems, will probably remain more significant in the long run since they alone can affect the international balance of power directly. Smaller deals, however, can be more significant in day-to-day politics. These transactions involve military equipment that is too small or inconspicuous to trace routinely. Often its existence is not revealed until it is publicly displayed or used in battle. In other cases minor deals may involve small quantities of major weapons, typically worth no more than a few million US dollars, whose significance is not immediately appreciated. Smaller deals will rarely alter equations of national power, but they may inflame passions and excite forceful reactions.

Small arms deals are not a single, uniform phenomenon. They are best defined in opposition to what they are not: large transfers of major weapons. A small deal usually involves only small arms, ammunition or non-lethal military supplies. Some may involve very small quantities of major weapons; an upper value of $25 million provides a useful threshold. While a sale of rifles worth millions of dollars may not seem small to the casual observer, it probably will be virtually invisible compared to the massive transactions that dominate the international arms trade. Even a transfer of a few artillery pieces or shoulder-fired surface-to-air missiles can be inconspicuous.

Smaller deals usually receive no publicity. Because they are small, few people are interested in them other than those directly involved. Consequently it is not possible to track them reliably and include them comprehensively in a data base such as SIPRI's. Even fundamental trends are difficult to identify. Indeed, most small deals are profoundly uninteresting. It is the exceptions that stand out.

1987 reminded the world that sometimes smaller arms deals can reveal much more about the contemporary international system than their largest counterparts. A leading example was Liberia's purchase of $4 million worth of armoured vehicles and artillery from Romania (see appendix 7B). Despite the deal's small size, it radically expands the Liberian Army and strengthens the military government. It is an important signal of Liberia's estrangement from its erstwhile mentor, the United States. Uganda's purchases from North Korea and Libya are similarly telling.

In addition to broadcasting political messages, small deals can have a direct impact on military events. The classic example is the 'secret weapon', the essential part or key scrap of knowledge. Such things are mostly the stuff of myth and legend. Wars are usually won through planning, leadership and commitment, not fancy gadgets. But small deals can be instrumental. The several hundred Japanese trucks that Chad received in winter 1986/87 were crucial in its victory over Libya.[44] And small deals, more so than major ones, provide the killing hardware of war. After all, what is more deadly, one $25 million fighter aircraft or $25 million worth of rifles and ammunition?

Smaller deals that became known in 1987 also make important statements about the nature of the arms trade itself. When Polish and Romanian arms were sold to the Nicaraguan Contras, the implication was not so much that these countries were changing their policy, but that policy was becoming irrelevant at the shadowy depths of the arms trade. Similarly, when Iran bought SA-7 missiles from the USSR (apparently in autumn 1986) and acquired US Stinger missiles a year later, policy was not out of control, only military technology.[45]

For smaller arms deals significance is often proportional to obscurity. Their impact can be directly related to their secrecy. This is especially true for the grey and black markets. While not all grey and black market deals are small, most seem to be. It is in the black market particularly that small deals become most significant, as small size and secrecy combined create success for arms sellers and buyers and a terrible policy problem for others.

IV. The rise of the grey and black markets

The hidden arms trade, with its covert and illegal transactions, is hardly new. Concern with the illegal and devious machinations of munitions makers and private dealers dominated discussion of the arms trade prior to World War II. But after the war arms transfers became an occupation for national governments. As contracts grew into billions of dollars, the arms trade ceased to be a private affair. It became instead an issue of public policy.[46] Decision makers and analysts paid little attention to the black market, which seemed to drift into irrelevance.

Not until the Iraq-Iran War did the black market regain its salience as an arms trade issue. This became abundantly clear in 1987 as virtually all Western nations found themselves embroiled in controversies over illegal arms sales. Small black markets developed to cater to North Korea, Libya, the Irish Republican Army (IRA) and others. Much larger illegal opportunities arose when the US-led embargo on Iran forced the Tehran Government to scavenge the planet in search of military hardware essential in its war with Iraq. The United Nations embargo on South Africa created another country dependent on illegally acquired arms technology. Together these countries, insurgencies and terrorist groups offer economic demands which an illegal market rose to satisfy (see table 7.3).

This market consists of two parts. First, there is the large *grey market* worth at least $2 billion annually. *The grey market includes officially approved exports from governments which do not want to be associated with their actions.* Grey deals need not be illegal, only covert or unacknowledged. These covert transfers are often very large and can include the full range of major weaponry. Because the shipments often are so large, they rarely can be kept permanently secret. It is virtually impossible to conceal big shipments of major weapons. Sooner or later, they become 'public secrets', covert in form only.

The ranks of prominent grey marketeers include most major arms exporters such as Argentina, China, France, Israel, Libya, North Korea, Portugal, Spain, the United Kingdom, the USA and the USSR. All of these countries covertly license transfers, often in huge quantities, to foreign causes they support or exploit. China and North Korea continue to sell large quantities of major weapons to Iran. In addition to the notorious Silkworm anti-ship missiles China supplies the bulk of Iran's military equipment. North Korea has supplied large quantities as well and is widely thought to be the source of mines used by Iran against merchant vessels in 1987.[47] A French Government report issued in September 1987 revealed that Paris permitted secret sales of artillery shells to Iran in order to help a failing company.[48] Portugal and Spain do nothing to stop large exports of munitions to Iran. Argentina also began to support Iran in 1987

Table 7.3. Some recently disclosed grey and black market arms deals

Delivery date	Item	Quantity	Source	Recipient	Value	Status
1981–84	Landmines	250 000	Valsella, Italy	Iran	$18 m.	Black
1981–86?	Chemical explosives	Thousands of tons	Schmitz, Sweden and others	Iran	$600 m.	Black[a]
1983–86	Artillery shells	470 000	Luchaire, France	Iran	$120 m.	Grey
1984–87	Speed boats	40–50	Boghammar, Sweden	Iran	$8–10 m.	Grey
1985	155-mm Artillery	140	Noricum, Austria	Iran	$200 m.	Black
1985	RBS-70 surface-to-air missiles	200?	Bofors, Sweden	Iran	$20 m.	Black
1985	AK-47 Rifle factory	1	Czechoslovakia	Iran	—	Grey
1985–86	TOW anti-tank missiles	2008	United States	Iran	$7 m.	Grey
1986	Hawk missile parts	238	United States	Iran	$8 m.	Grey
1986	SA-7 surface-to-air missiles	400	Soviet Union	Iran	$18 m.	Grey
1986	SA-7 surface-to-air missiles	50	Poland	Contras	$2.3 m.	?
1986–87?	Naval mines	1 000?	North Korea	Iran	—	Grey
1987	Silkworm anti-ship mines	72–96	China	Iran	$63–70 m.	Grey
1987	Acoustic naval mines	Dozens	Libya	Iran	—	Grey
1987	Mini-submarine	1?	France, N. Korea?	Iran	—	?
1987	Stinger surface-to-air-missiles	9	Afghan Mujahideen	Iran	$0.4 m.	Black[b]
1987	SA-7 surface-to-air missiles	20	Libya?	IRA	$0.9 m.	Grey[c]

[a] Co-ordinated by the European Association for the Study of Safety Problems in the Production of Propellant Powder (established in Brussels in 1975) and involving production and shipment through other nations including Belgium, Britain, France, Israel, Italy, Portugal, South Africa, FR Germany and Yugoslavia.
[b] The missiles were either captured or purchased by Iran from the Afghan Mujahideen.
[c] This shipment was intercepted by French authorities and impounded.

Source: SIPRI arms trade files.

with a $31 million munitions deal.[49] Israeli assistance for Iran, long rumoured, was finally documented in 1987 when a reporter uncovered proof of large munitions deals.[50] The Israeli arms trade with South Africa is discussed in the next section. Libya is suspected of supplying the IRA, including a 150-ton shipment featuring anti-aircraft missiles intercepted by France in October.[51] US and British missile shipments to the Afghan Mujahideen are still officially denied. Chinese, Cuban, Soviet and US assistance for revolutionaries of their choice also fit into the grey market.

The grey market poses a special problem for arms embargoes. Unless all major arms exporters support an embargo, its chances are poor. The US-led embargo on Iran, Operation Staunch, was inaugurated in 1983. It had some successes, most notably in enlisting Italy and South Korea. But its failures with the governments of Portugal and Spain, to say nothing of China and North Korea, vitiated its effectiveness. Although it slowed in 1985–86, Operation Staunch picked up new momentum following the Iran–Contra scandal in the United States.[52] A stronger embargo on Iran could be established by the United

Nations, if it grows frustrated in its peace efforts under Security Council Resolution 598 of 20 July 1987.

Second, there is *the black market, consisting mostly of small transactions that violate the laws of the nation from which they originate.* Black market deals need to be small and secret in order to succeed; otherwise they are intercepted and the perpetrators may be prosecuted. An unprecedented number of interceptions and prosecutions in 1987 revealed much about the black market but insights necessarily remain tentative. Ironically, we know the most about unsuccessful black marketeers. Insights about those who do not get caught are minimal.

Some enormous black market deals have been attempted in recent years. Most were either pipe-dreams or totally fraudulent. The few large black market deals that lead to actual deliveries invariably seem to backfire upon their perpetrators. The Damavand project, in which US and Israeli citizens hoped to sell Iran 50 M-48 tanks, 39 F-4 Phantom fighters and 25 attack helicopters, was an example of a pipe-dream; despite years of hard work, its organizers never had a serious chance of finding a nation willing to supply the arms for the deal. A plan in FR Germany offering 20 000 non-existent TOW anti-tank missiles to Iran was an example of simple fraud.[53] The largest black deals to approach success in recent years involved the transfer of 140 Austrian howitzers to Iran and the delivery of 72 US helicopters to North Korea.[54] In neither case could the deliveries be kept secret, however, and the organizers were prosecuted.

If the record of prosecutions is indicative, these deals were exceptional. Major arms dealers seem to avoid the black market: the profits—great as they can be—rarely seem commensurate to the risks. Most prosecutions involve first-time amateurs accused of dealings worth less than $1 million.[55] When major firms do make questionable sales they often do so behind a legal shield of false end-user certificates and intermediaries, making successful prosecution difficult. The black market is less of a threat to an arms embargo than the officially sanctioned grey market. Unlike the grey market, it cannot sustain Iran's war effort all by itself.

What the black market can do is to supply technology effectively, especially plans and know-how. South Africa has used the black market to circumvent the United Nations arms embargo by acquiring technology that greatly aids its large defence industries.[56] Since this technology is usually just paper or key parts, it is readily concealed and transported, making it ideal for secrecy. The black market in technology is much harder to control for this very reason. NATO's problems controlling illegal Soviet and East European acquisition of Western military technology have confounded the Alliance since the late 1940s. Now that some Third World nations can apply illegally acquired technology in much the same way, the problem can only get worse.

V. International implications

The impact of the growing grey and black markets can be seen not only in the recipient countries, but also among the nations where these deals originated. As a result of a wave of unhappy disclosures, more nations are debating their arms trade policies than at any other time since the 1930s. Many have taken remedial action. Others are weighing reforms. Some nations have responded to allegations with bitter denials of wrong-doing. These conflicting reactions made it impossible for the United Nations, despite rising concern, to establish an arms embargo on Iran in 1987.

Sweden was perhaps hit hardest of all by the arms scandals of 1987. A nation that long took pride in its restrictive arms export regulations learned that these restrictions were systematically undermined by greed and the needs of national welfare. Businessmen and government officials, it appeared, had encouraged or permitted questionable exports in order to make profits, strengthen local industry, remain competitive, sustain employment and subsidize domestic military procurement. The unexplained death of War Material Inspector Carl Algernon in January 1987 led to official investigations of charges that Bofors sold its RBS-70 missiles to Iran and other proscribed nations. Another scandal shook Bofors when it was revealed that a large sale of FH-77 howitzers to India involved substantial bribes. The bribery allegations have shaken the Indian Government and relations with Sweden. A third affair stemmed from revelations that a Swedish shipbuilder sold speedboats to Iran which were used to attack merchantmen. The company later was cleared of wrong-doing.[57]

At this writing Sweden's reaction to its arms scandals is unclear. Key investigations are incomplete, trials have not begun and the Government remains reticent. The War Material Inspectorate has been strengthened, and legislation to further restrict sales of explosives and third-party sales are pending. Critics maintain that no meaningful change in the laws is possible unless Sweden can wean itself off of arms exports.[58]

Another disclosure revealed a Swedish scandal that could more accurately be characterized as a European affair. In May the public learned that Karl-Erik Schmitz, a Swedish arms dealer, had illegally sold Swedish explosives to Iran through various intermediary nations. Upon his indictment, evidence was released showing that Schmitz was involved in a European cartel of explosives manufacturers with Iranian contracts worth $600 million. European explosives were shipped to Iran in enormous quantities. European arms trade laws, it emerged, are designed principally to control sales of major weapons, not explosives. Schmitz and his colleagues found a weak spot in the laws and took advantage of it. Few European nations were untouched by the Schmitz affair.[59]

Italy was implicated in the Schmitz affair as a centre for trans-shipping explosives to Iran. The Italian Government, which acted forthrightly in 1983–84 to stop exports to Iran, faced several new discoveries. An Italian firm, Valsella Meccanotecnica, was found exporting to Iran hundreds of thousands of anti-personnel mines made with French explosives between 1981 and 1984. Several arms dealers were indicted in this and other Italian cases. Official indignation was voiced uniformly. Some called for a total ban on Italian arms exports—virtually inconceivable—while the government said regulations would be tightened.[60]

In France a report by Armed Forces Inspector-General Barba charged that a French munitions maker, Luchaire, was permitted to sell artillery shells to Iran from 1983 to 1986 under Mitterrand's socialist government. Later it was revealed that these sales probably continued under Prime Minister Chirac. As in the Italian and Swedish cases the shells were falsely licensed for sales to other nations. Former Defence Minister Charles Hernu was held personally responsible. His successor, André Giraud, claims to have reorganized French administration of arms sales. A legislative reaction seems unlikely. Indeed, in December 1987 it was learned that the Chirac Government probably sent additional arms to Iran to win freedom for French hostages in Lebanon.[61]

Many other nations wrestled with arms sale controversies in 1987, although these were generally on a smaller scale or involved disputes continuing from previous years:

Austria is prosecuting the president of its largest artillery-maker for selling 140 howitzers to Iran in 1985 and offering Iran an artillery factory.[62]

In Belgium, which has weak arms trade regulations, stronger regulations have become a partisan issue paralysed by conflict between the Flemish and Walloons.[63]

Britain is investigating allegations that 50 British firms sold explosives and military parts to Iran. It has closed an Iranian military procurement office that was operating in London as well.[64]

Canadian opposition leaders criticized the government proposal to ease restrictions on arms sales to friendly nations.[65]

Denmark is debating legislation to forbid Danish ships from carrying arms to countries at war, in response to evidence that Danish vessels have been heavily used by arms dealers trading with Iran and Iraq.[66]

FR Germany completed an official investigation of charges that the HDW shipyard sold submarine plans to South Africa, amid growing allegations of high-level official involvement. The investigation reached no authoritative conclusions.[67]

Israel, under US pressure, agreed in March 1987 not to sign new defence contracts with South Africa. Debates surrounded allegations of secret arms sales to Muslim Malaysia and Indonesia.[68]

Japan suspended exports of lorries to North Korea that were being used to launch artillery rockets in violation of Japanese law.[69] Similar lorry sales to Chad, Iran, Iraq, Libya and other nations are not so controversial.

Norway refused to permit sales of anti-ship missiles to developing nations at the same time as the country was prosecuting individuals involved in the sale of key submarine technology to the Soviet Union.[70]

Polish Government spokesman Jerzy Urban denied reports that Poland had licensed armed shipments for the Nicaraguan Contras, prompting speculation that Poland is the home of a thriving black market.[71]

In Spain the government was criticized by its opposition for permitting arms sales to Iran and Iraq.[72]

The Soviet Union denied repeated and well-documented reports that it has delivered SA-7 missiles to Iran.[73]

The United States ordered major investigations of the Iran–Contra affair and is preparing for prosecutions. Criminal prosecutions of black marketeers became numerous.[74]

China's reaction to publicity of its arms sales to Iran is of particular moment to the establishment of an international embargo to end the war. As Iran's most important supplier, China must support such efforts if they are to succeed. Yet China consistently denies that it sells any arms to Iran. Its denials are upheld by Iran which claims to make most of its weapons itself, despite lacking the key industries. The USA pressured China to change its arms sales policies. Late in the year, Chinese Foreign Minister Wu Xueqian indicated that China was becoming more restrictive. Other Chinese officials said that support for a UN embargo was possible in the future. In the meantime there is evidence that China has continued arms deliveries to both antagonists in the Gulf War.[75]

The failure to pass an arms embargo to enforce compliance with Security Council Resolution 598 (on peace between Iran and Iraq) was a serious disappointment for the UN in the fall of 1987. The momentum which built up following Iranian mining of the Persian Gulf and the *USS Stark* incident culminated in September–October. Progress in the Security Council was blocked principally by China and the Soviet Union, which insisted that the voluntary recommendations of Resolution 598 be allowed more time.[76] The war has gone on for eight years, yet the international community still hesitates to use its most powerful tools (see also chapter 15).

VI. Will Third World arms sales return?

The depression of the Third World arms trade in the 1980s can no longer be dismissed as a temporary aberration. These countries are not buying major weapons as avidly as they did in the late 1970s. Is this a permanent transformation for international security? Will transfers of major weapons eventually grow back to surpass the peaks of the past? Or will smaller arms deals and sales of military technology increasingly characterize the arms trade?

These questions will be resolved only through experience, but several developments suggest that the arms trade is entering a period of profound change. Sales of major weapons tell progressively less of the arms trade story. Public officials, industrialists and analysts are finding that old assumptions about the arms trade no longer hold up. The international arms trade is evolving into new patterns and forms.

Many factors brought sales of major weapons down in the early 1980s. None appears to be abating. Third World nations have generally not found ways to recover the income they lost when oil prices collapsed and the debt crisis hit in 1982. Several nations that continued large arms purchases in the following years did so only by incurring crippling debt, as did Egypt (owing almost $5 billion in US military credits and $5 billion for arms purchases elsewhere), Iraq ($7 billion and $5 billion to France and the USSR, respectively) and Syria (total civil and military debt to the USSR of $15 billion).[77] Countries which want to buy often cannot find suitable arms which they can afford. This was illustrated in 1987 when the USA and the USSR both ended production of their cheap export fighters, the Northrop F-5 and Mikoyan MiG-21, respectively.[78]

Since their traditional clients cannot afford costly new systems such as the F/A-18, Mirage-2000, M-1 Abrams or Leopard-2, manufacturers have developed less expensive counterparts for the Third World. Potential buyers appear to be sceptical of such systems. Highly publicized low-cost fighters, such as the Brazilian-Italian AMX, the British Hawk 200 or the US Northrop F-20, have failed to find any export orders despite years on the market.[79]

Arms suppliers cannot assist prospective buyers as they once did. The large aid programmes that financed military assistance from the 1950s to the late 1970s are shrinking everywhere. The Soviet aid cuts have already been noted. US military aid was cut dramatically in 1987 and will fall more as US budgetary priorities shift. Other exporters such as Britain and China have virtually abandoned arms give-aways in favour of commercial sales.[80]

When Third World nations buy abroad, they tend to buy more carefully. Tales of huge arsenals rusting on the docks, a commonplace of the 1960s, are becoming rare.[81] Military officers the world over are better trained and informed. They can make much better use of their budgets and physical resources. Procurement funds are more likely to be invested with an emphasis on long-term requirements instead of bargain-hunting. Weapons are more likely to be properly supported and maintained, extending their useful lifetimes.[82] As a result, it will be many years before the arsenals purchased in the past decades must be replaced.

The increasing longevity of weapon platforms (ships, airframes and tank hulls) has inspired a quickly growing industry to keep old weapon systems serviceable and useful. Variously known as upgrading, updating, modernizing or retrofit, new components and sub-systems are substituted to replace original parts. This is possible because of technical advances in weapon platforms. In World War II, for example, a fighter plane might last only 70 flight hours (accumulated in a few months) before it was unserviceable. Today's fighters, such as the US F/A-18, are designed for service lifetimes of up to 6000 flight hours (20 years in normal service).[83]

Progressively more arms deals involve updating these long-surviving platforms. Individual parts and sub-systems are bought instead of major weapons. This process is aided by the rise of Third World arms industries capable of doing the work. These manufacturers are well understood as a challenge to traditional arms exporters.[84] That challenge is growing as they go from building new weapons to also improving old ones. Arms makers who once dismissed the upgrade market are racing to get into this business by offering an array of upgrade packages. Although the biggest upgrades still occur within industrial countries (such as the US Navy's Ship Life Extension Programme and FR Germany's F-4 modernization programme) major Third World upgrade contracts are becoming common. In 1987, China signed a $245 million design contract with Grumman to improve its F-8 fighter and Pakistan signed a $150 million contract for design of upgraded Chinese F-7 fighters for its own use. Israel helped South Africa rebuild its French Mirages and signed a $200 million deal to modernize Colombia's Mirages. For some time British and US firms have helped Egypt to rebuild its ageing fleet of Soviet tanks. Turkey may soon sign a similar contract to rebuild its fleet of 2700 US M-48 tanks.[85] The foreign contractors in these deals would prefer to sell new weapon systems. The upgrade business is, by consensus, a less attractive substitute.[86]

For the established arms exporters, changing Third World procurement habits have meant less business and smaller earnings. Many have begun long-term adjustments. In 1987, Dassault laid off workers—over 2000—for the first time in its post-war history. Losses and lay-offs also affected military manufacturers in Belgium, Brazil, Britain, Finland, Israel, Spain and the United States. The firms that showed profit for 1987 are bracing for future trouble, especially as declining exports coincide with contracting domestic procurement budgets. Few hold much hope for massive exports of new major weapon systems, since these promise to be even more costly than their predecessors.[87]

VII. Conclusion

In retrospect, the arms trade patterns of the 1960s and 1970s may come to be seen as anomalies in the history of international relations. The period may have been a brief interlude when a handful of supplier countries—Britain, France, the Soviet Union and the United States—dominated the international arms trade more than ever before or since.[88] It was a time when political power was unusually concentrated, and the arms trade reflected this. Yet the uniqueness of the period was not always apparent to the decision makers or analysts who tried to make sense of it. The theories and assumptions they developed to understand the arms trade simply appear to be out of date.

As has been shown, the international trade in military equipment and technology is becoming less tidy. It has diversified into many new forms, making the trade less predictable and harder to evaluate. While the trade in major weapons remains very significant, it tells consistently less of the story. Other forms of arms transfer—licensed production, technology transfer, retrofit and modernization, small transactions, and the grey and black markets—often rival the significance of orthodox sales of major weapons. Any theory of the arms trade that does not include these other forms is inherently misleading. Any policy that does not take them into account is doomed to fail.

These changes do not affect all nations the same way. For importers, this changing situation creates many new opportunities. They have more options in their military procurement. They are increasingly able to insulate themselves from the supplier influence traditionally associated with imported armaments. While they still must depend on foreign technology, the political consequences of the dependence are becoming very abstract.

For exporters, the changes are leading to a search for new products and markets. But they are not adapting easily. The increased deliveries that many saw in 1987 were not matched with increased sales, making recent increases seem ephemeral. All the major exporters are conscious of the weakness of their positions. None has ready solutions to restore the objectives that arms transfers once achieved. Nor are they ready to commit themselves to alternatives such as international arms trade control.[89] Even limited embargoes on countries at war (such as Iran) are controversial and poorly enforced.

The political factors that dominated the arms trade in the recent past are yielding to market forces. As this happens, the arms trade is returning to its patterns prior to World War II, when the trade in military equipment was not dramatically different from the trade in many other industrial products. As market forces become more powerful, national policy tends to become weaker. Individual nations will be less able to address their arms trade problems than in the past. Consequently, these transformations increase the need for multinational responses to arms trade problems.

Notes and references

[1] For a general review of Soviet military assistance to India, see Thakur, R., 'The Indo-Soviet military relationship', *Asian Defence Journal*, June 1987. On India's nuclear-powered submarine, see 'Indian navy has wider reach', *Times of India*, 12 Jan. 1988. Indian co-production of the MiG-27 is examined in Gunston, B., *MiG-23/27 Flogger* (Osprey: London, 1986).

[2] Current Soviet military equipment is examined in Grier, P., 'Acquisition: quantity over quality', *Military Logistics Forum*, Apr. 1987; Contin, R., 'MiG-29: a new step in the "Mirror Policy"', *Military Technology*, Apr. 1987; Zaloga, S. J. and Loop, J. E., *Soviet Tanks and Combat Vehicles* (Arms and Armour Press: Poole, Dorset, 1987). David Holloway explores the problems afflicting Soviet military procurement in his book, *The Soviet Union and the Arms Race* (Yale University Press: New Haven, 1983).

[3] 'Massive rise in Indian budget', *Jane's Defence Weekly*, 30 May 1987, p. 1040; US Arms Control and Disarmament Agency, *World Military Expenditures and Arms Transfers 1986* (US Government Printing Office: Washington, DC, 1987), p. 78.

[4] Simes, D. K., 'Gorbachev: a new foreign policy?', *Foreign Affairs*, vol. 65, no. 3 (1987) explores Moscow's new foreign policy flexibility with careful attention to its limitations.

[5] Chardy, A., 'U.S. intelligence says Sandinista pilots training at Cuban base on MiG-21 jets', *Philadelphia Inquirer*, 14 June 1987 p. 3; Chubin, S., 'Hedging in the Gulf: Soviets arm both sides', *International Defense Review*, no. 6 (June 1987); Hoagland, J. and Tyler, P. E., 'Reduced Soviet arms flow weakens Syrian military', *Washington Post*, 25 Sep. 1987, p. 1; Sciolino, E., 'Soviet tried to rein in Libya on mine deal', *International Herald Tribune*, 12–13 Sep. 1987, p. 1; Wilson, G. and Moore, M., 'Gadafy turns from Moscow to China for arms', *The Guardian*, 4 May 1987.

[6] Zaloga and Loop (note 2), pp. 25–27.

[7] This theme is developed by Ferrari, P. L., Knopf, J. W. and Madrid, R. L., *U.S. Arms Exports: Policies and Contractors* (Investor Responsibility Research Center: Washington, DC, 1987). A similar argument is advanced by Neuman, S. G., *Military Assistance in Recent Wars: the Dominance of the Superpowers, Washington Paper no. 122* (Center for Strategic and International Studies: Washington, DC, 1986).

[8] Yoder, S. K., 'Japan picks General Dynamics F-16', *Wall Street Journal*, 22 Oct. 1987, p. 34; 'Japan outlines F-16 selection criteria', *Flight International*, 7 Nov. 1987, p. 10.

[9] Foss, C. F., 'Saudi short lists Abrahams, Osorio MBTs', *Jane's Defence Weekly*, 6 Feb. 1988, p. 191.

[10] Silverberg, D., 'Briefing defuses Congress' opposition to Egyptian assembly of M1A1 tanks', *Defense News*, 13 July 1987, p. 7; 'Say no to the Pharaonic tank', *New York Times*, 6 July 1987, p. 30 (editorial).

[11] Levite, A., 'In the aftermath of Israeli's Lavi decision', *Armed Forces Journal International*, Oct. 1987, p. 40; 'Israeli arms sales to US to increase', *Interavia Air Letter*, no. 11, 397 (16 Dec. 1987); 'The wreck of the Lavi', *Jerusalem Post* (intl edn), 10 Oct. 1987, p. 9.

[12] Copson, R. W. and Cronin R., 'The "Reagan Doctrine" and its prospects', *Survival*, vol. 29, no. 1 (Jan./Feb. 1987); Karp, A., 'Stingers and blowpipes in Afghanistan: one year after', *Armed Forces Journal International*, Sep. 1987.

[13] Sciolino, E., 'White House to push sale of jets to Honduras', *New York Times*, 12 May 1987, p. 13; Preston, J., 'Nicaragua says it will proceed with plans to get MiGs', *Washington Post*, 3 Aug. 1987, p. 17.

[14] Cushman, Jr., J. H., 'Legislation would return control of arms sales to Congress', *New York Times*, 23 Nov. 1986, p. 18; Silverberg, D., 'Reagan advised to veto arms export reform bill', *Defense News*, 9 Mar. 1987, p. 7; 'Congress aims to run arms sales', *Insight*, 16 Mar. 1987, p. 23.

[15] Silverberg, D., 'Pentagon may absorb State Department's export licensing Office of Munitions Control', *Defense News*, 15 June 1987, p. 3; 'New dispute seen looming over DoD effort to take export review from State', *Inside the Pentagon*, 3 July 1987, p. 6; 'Don't rubber-stamp arms exports', *Hartford Courant*, 19 Sep. 1987, p. C10 (editorial).

[16] Kurtz, H., 'Panel would bar ammo sale to 3 Arab states', *Washington Post*, 20 Nov. 1987, p. 12; Silverberg, D., 'Amendments to U.S. Foreign Aid Bill would ease arms export restrictions', *Washington Post*, 6 Apr. 1987, p. 12.

[17] Mechman, M., 'Administration expected to back lease of E-2Cs to Pakistan', *Aviation Week & Space Technology*, 4 May 1987, pp. 27–8; Sciolino, E., 'U.S. aide hesitant on Pakistan request', *New York Times*, 7 May 1987, p. 3; *Radio New Delhi*, reported in *Current News: Early Bird Edition*, 12 May 1987, p. 4.

[18] Van Doren, C., 'Pakistan, Congress and the nonproliferation challenge', *Arms Control Today*, vol. 17, no. 9 (Nov. 1987), pp. 8–9.

[19] Shipler, D. K., 'Arab arms sales draw less protest', *New York Times*, 22 Mar. 1987, p. 3.

[20] Greenberger, R. S., 'U.S. is planning to sell missiles to Saudi Arabia', *Wall Street Journal*, 1 June 1987, p. 18.

[21] Ottaway, D. B., 'Reagan drops plan for Saudi arms sale', *International Herald Tribune*, 12 June 1987, p. 1; Ottaway, D. B., 'Saudi missile sale botched, Hill figures say', *Washington Post*, 15 June 1987, p. 1.

[22] Oberdorfer, D., 'U.S. pressing ahead on Saudi arms sale', *International Herald Tribune*, 1 Oct. 1987; Mecham, M., 'Congress warns Administration not to attempt Saudi arms sale', *Aviation Week & Space Technology*, 5 Oct. 1987, pp. 28–9; Sciolino, E., 'U.S. withdraws antitank arms from Saudi sale', *New York Times*, 9 Oct. 1987, p. 1; 'No F-15Es for Saudi Arabia', *Interavia Air Letter*, no. 11, 378 (19 Nov. 1987), p. 6.

[23] 'Afghan tells of Iran seizing 9 Stingers', *Washington Post*, 19 Nov. 1987, p. 17; Ottaway, D. B., 'Senate unit votes to ban Stinger sales to Bahrain in rebuff to Administration', *Washington Post*, 4 Dec. 1987, p. 24; Ottaway, D. B., 'Stinger sale to Bahrain survives try to reverse it', *International Herald Tribune*, 19–20 Dec. 1987, p. 2. The Bahraini missiles are to be stored under continual surveillance and will eventually be returned to the USA.

[24] Kolodziej, E., 'France and the arms trade', *International Affairs*, Jan. 1980.

[25] Isnard, J., 'Dassault-Breguet goes into a nosedive', *Guardian Weekly* (UK), 15 Nov. 1987, p. 14.

[26] Hooton, T. and Prince, B., 'French industry at the crossroads', *Defence Attaché*, no. 3 (1987).

[27] Deen, T., 'Iraq's battle for arms', *Jane's Defence Weekly*, 29 Aug. 1987. p. 396.

[28] Lenorovitz, J. M., 'French companies face increased competition in export sales', *Aviation Week & Space Technology*, 9 Mar. 1987, pp. 92–3.

[29] Changing market conditions are surveyed in Timmerman, K. R., 'Shrinking market, costs bring shift in fighter production', *International Herald Tribune*, 16 June 1987, pp. 9–10.

[30] 'Number two', *The Economist*, 4 July 1987, p. 31.

[31] Bloom, B., 'Saudi Arabia signs £5bn deal to buy UK military aircraft', *Financial Times*, 18 Feb. 1986.

[32] The Tornado's capabilities are reviewed in Taylor, J. W. R. (ed.), *Jane's All the World's Aircraft, (1987–88)* (Jane's: London, 1987), pp. 134–6.

[33] Described in Foss, C. F. (ed.), *Jane's Armour and Artillery, 1987–88* (Jane's: London, 1987), pp. 90–94.

[34] Buchan, D., 'Royal Ordnance makes $40m sales to US', *Financial Times*, 13 Oct. 1987, p. 6; Evans, M., 'Marconi win £2bn US defence deal', *The Times* (London), 16 Oct. 1987; Hooton, T., 'Europe's fight for US contracts', *Jane's Defence Weekly*, 3 Oct. 1987, pp. 753–4.

[35] Cordesman, A. H., *The Iran-Iraq War and Western Security, 1984–87* (Royal United Services Institute and Jane's: London, 1987), pp. 23–36.

[36] Gilks, A. and Segal, G., *China and the Arms Trade* (Croom Helm: Beckenham, 1985), especially ch. 2.

[37] For example, see the symposium, 'Aerospace in South America: Part 2—Military', *Aviation Week & Space Technology*, 24 Aug. 1987, pp. 40–79.

[38] The MiG-21 and its Chinese copies are thoroughly evaluated in Gunston, B., *Mikoyan MiG-21* (Osprey: London, 1986). Anti-ship missiles are described in *The Market for Anti-Ship Missiles and Defensive Systems through the Year 2000* (Forecast Associates: Newton, Conn., 1988).

[39] 'Aeritalia modernizing Chinese fighters', *Aviation Week & Space Technology*, 3 Aug. 1987, p. 85; 'Grumman wins major PRC contract', *Interavia Air Letter*, no. 11, 304 (6 Aug. 1987), p. 1.

[40] Brooke, J., 'Chadians describe victory over Libyans in desert', *New York Times*, 14 Aug. 1987, p. 1. Chad had publicized its military victory in *Le Heros: Glorieuses Victoire des Fant sur l'Armée Libyenne* (Organe de Liaison et d'Information des Forces Armées Nationales Tchadiennes), no. 8, which includes an accurate accounting of items captured from the Ouadi Doum air base.

[41] Done, K., 'Kockums in Australian submarine order', *Financial Times*, 19 June 1987; Chuter, A., 'Derungs: we thought ADATS had lost'. *Jane's Defence Weekly*, 12 Dec. 1987, p. 1341.

[42] Clark, G., 'Australia to order six Swedish-designed subs', *Defense News*, 25 May 1987, p. 3.
[43] Dean, S. D., 'Army locks onto ADATS', *Armed Forces Journal*, Jan. 1988, p. 17.
[44] Brooke, J., 'Chad's desert weapon: fast pick-up truck', *International Herald Tribune*, 15–16 Aug. 1987, p. 3.
[45] 'East bloc said to sell Contras arms', *International Herald Tribune*, 28 Apr. 1987, p. 2; McCaslin, J., 'Polish-Contra arms tie cited in Paris slaying', *Washington Times*, 25 June 1987, p. 1; Tagliabue, J., 'How $18 million got Soviet weapons to Iran', *New York Times*, 27 May 1987, p. 1.
[46] The best comparison of arms sale policies before and after World War II remains Harkavy, R. E., *The Arms Trade and International Systems* (Ballinger: Cambridge, Mass., 1975).
[47] Deen, T., 'Iran—meeting its arms requirements', *Jane's Defence Weekly*, 28 Nov. 1987, pp. 1276–77.
[48] Markham, J. M., 'Secret report says Mitterrand knew of illegal Iran arms sales', *International Herald Tribune*, 5 Nov. 1987, p. 2.
[49] DeYoung, K., 'Iran sales key to Portugal's arms trade', *Washington Post*, 16 Jan. 1987, p. 18: Cunningham, M. J., 'Iran-Iraq: who fuels the fire?, *Defence Attaché*, no. 1 (Jan. 1987), pp. 33–37; Morgan, J., 'Argentina in "arms deal" with Iran', *The Guardian*, 30 July 1987, p. 10.
[50] Elsner, A., 'Israel sold Iran large amount of explosives', *Reuters*, 2 Dec. 1987.
[51] Cooley, J. K., 'The long, violent history of the Libyan–IRA connection', *International Herald Tribune*, 20 Nov. 1987; Cooney, J., 'IRA weapons ship was loaded by the Libyans', *The Times* (London), 5 Nov. 1987.
[52] The history of Operation Staunch is explicated in Timmerman, K. R., *Fanning the Flames: Guns and Geopolitics in the Gulf War* (Pergamon: London, 1988), chs 9 and 13.
[53] Diamond, S. with Blumenthal, R., 'Huge illegal deal on arms for Iran was known to U.S.', *New York Times*, 2 Feb. 1987, p. 1.
[54] Swartz, R., 'Vapenexport splittrar' ['Weapon exports divide'], *Svenska Dagbladet* (Stockholm), 17 Sep. 1987; 'Brothers indicted in sale of copters to North Korea', *New York Times*, 22 Jan. 1987, p. 23.
[55] Laurance, E. J., 'The United States: blackmarketeers', in ed. A. Karp, SIPRI, *Shades of Grey: The Hidden Arms Trade Today* (Oxford University Press: Oxford, forthcoming).
[56] Brzoska, M., 'South Africa: arming under the UN embargo', in Karp (note 55).
[57] Elliott, J., 'Bofors admits it paid SKR 319 mn to win contract', *Financial Times*, 21 Sep. 1987, p. 5; Jonasson, T., 'The "Bofors Affair" and the peace movement in Sweden', *Inside Sweden*, Sep. 1987, pp. 3–5; Webb, S., 'Mystery death spotlights Swedish arms trade investigation', *Financial Times*, 30 Jan. 1987.
[58] 'Explosive goods', Swedish Peace and Arbitration Society, Jan. 1987; the opposite position is presented in Webb, S., 'Sweden needs Third World sales', *Financial Times*, 8 May 1987, p. 20; between these two is Ohlson, T., 'Swedish arms exports in an international perspective', *Inside Sweden*, Sep. 1987, pp, 6–9.
[59] 'Two Swedes charged in ammo sales', *International Herald Tribune*, 27 May 1987, p. 1; Brauchli, M. W. and Nelson, M. M., 'Iran's supply network for munitions involves web of European firms', *Wall Street Journal*, 3 Sep. 1987, p. 1; Timmerman, K. R., 'Europe's arms pipeline to Iran', *The Nation*, 18–25 July 1987, pp. 47–52.
[60] 'Italy arrests 32 suspects in Mid-East arms deals', *International Herald Tribune*, 7 Sep. 1987; Timmerman, K. R. and Krop, P., 'Un Comble: les mines de Khmoiny ont été fabriquées par France', *L'Evenement du Jeudi*, 13–19 Aug. 1987, pp. 10–13; Suttora, M. and Timmerman, G., 'Irangate all', *Italiana Europeo*, 19 Aug. 1987, pp. 116–121.
[61] Markham, J. M., 'Secret report says Mitterrand knew of illegal Iran sales', *International Herald Tribune*, 5 Nov. 1987, p. 5; Ibrahim, Y. M., 'Chirac made arms sales to Iran, paper asserts', *International Herald Tribune*, 24–25 Dec. 1987; Bulloch, J., 'France gives arms to Iran in hostage deal', *The Independent*, 1 Dec. 1987; 'Giraud announces tighter control of arms exports', *Jane's Defence Weekly*, 14 Nov. 1987, p. 1096.
[62] Dempsey, J., 'Austrian probe into arms charge', *Financial Times*, 8 Sep. 1987, p. 2; Dempsey, J., 'Voest-Alpine plans weapons plant in Iran', *Financial Times*, 17 Sep. 1987, p. 18.
[63] James, B., 'Belgium, some say, turns a blind eye to Gulf arms dealing', *International Herald Tribune*, 11 Dec. 1987, p. 2.
[64] 'UK inquires into weapons sale to Iran', *Financial Times*, 6 Aug. 1987, p. 1; Bremner, C., 'Howe closes Iran's London arms office', *The Times*, (London), 24 Sep. 1987, p. 7; Chancellor, A., 'Britain shuts Iran's London arms office', *The Independent, 24 Sep. 1987, p. 1.
[65] Matas, R., 'Ottawa must keep arms export curbs, defence critics say', *Toronto Globe and Mail*, 24 June 1987, p. 5.
[66] Clines, F. X., 'Danish seamen's union tells of arms shipments', *New York Times*, 9 Nov. 1987,

p. 12; Lohr, S., 'Arms operation made wide use of Danish ships', *New York Times*, 20 Feb. 1987, p. 1.

[67] 'Wunschgemäss geäussert', *Der Spiegel*, vol. 42, no. 3 (18 Jan. 1988), pp. 31–2.

[68] Frankel, G., 'Israel pledges to reduce military ties to South Africa', *Washington Post*, 20 Mar. 1987, p. 1; Inbar, E., 'Israel's arms exports', *Jerusalem Letter* (Jerusalem Center for Public Affairs), 7 May 1987.

[69] 'Japanese big-truck sales to North Korea suspended', *Wall Street Journal*, 17 June 1987, p. 22.

[70] 'Norway blocks sale of missiles', *Financial Times*, 18 Sep. 1987, p. 3.

[71] 'Keine Munitions aus Polen', *Frankfurter Rundschau*, 29 Apr. 1987.

[72] Wigg, R., 'Madrid arms inquiry', *The Times* (London), 12 May 1987, p. 6.

[73] 'Soviets deny they sold arms to Iran', *Defense News*, 1 June 1987, p. 22.

[74] *Report of the President's Special Review Board* (US Government Printing Office: Washington, DC, 26 Feb. 1987). Examples of US black marketeers are legion, but for typical cases see Bruske, E., 'Indicted in scheme to sell military gear to Syria', *Washington Post*, 27 May 1987, p. 8; Kaufman, M., 'Man fined, jailed for arms deals', *Hartford Courant*, 14 May 1987, p. 26; Kessler, R. E., 'Trial set for 17 in arms-sale plot', *Long Island News Day*, 19 May 1987, p. 7; 'Two cases involve illegal export of military goods', *Long Island News Day*, 27 Nov. 1987, p. 4.

[75] Sun, L., 'China strongly denies selling arms to Iran', *Washington Post*, 11 June 1987, p. 29; 'Display reveals "evidence" of growing Iranian defence industry', *Jane's Defence Weekly*, 31 Oct. 1987; Pauley, R., 'China promises strict controls of weapons sales', *Financial Times*, 27 Nov. 1987, p. 1.

[76] Tyson, A. S. 'China sees embargo on Iran as last resort in efforts to end Gulf War', *Christian Science Monitor*, 6 Oct. 1987, p. 12.

[77] *AAS Milavnews*, July 1987 and Aug. 1987.

[78] *AAS Milavnews*, vol. 26, no. 305 (Mar. 1987), p. 2324; Gunston (note 38).

[79] These programmes are surveyed in Salvy, R., 'Light combat aircraft projects proliferate', *International Defense Review*, no. 12 (Dec. 1987), pp. 1607–12.

[80] Silverberg, D., 'House panel slashes foreign military assistance', *Defense News*, 3 Aug. 1987; Edmonds, M., 'The domestic and international dimension of British arms sales', ed. C. Cannizzo, *The Gun Merchants* (Pergamon: New York, 1980), ch. 4; Gilks and Segal (note 36), ch. 2.

[81] Neuman, S. G., 'The role of military assistance in recent wars', eds S. G. Neuman and R. E. Harkavy, *Lessons of Recent Wars in the Third World: Comparative Dimensions*, vol. 2 (Lexington: Lexington, Mass., 1987), ch. 4.

[82] Cohen, E. A., 'Distant battles', in Neuman and Harkavy (note 81), ch. 2.

[83] Mann, P., 'New CF-18 fatigue tests raise more doubts about service life', *Aviation Week & Space Technology*, 17 Aug. 1987, pp. 18–20. The article reports that under Canadian conditions the lifetime of the aircraft may be only 12 years, not 20.

[84] Third World arms industries, another factor reducing sales opportunities for traditional arms exporters, are studied in Brzoska, M. and Ohlson, T. (eds), SIPRI, *Arms Production in the Third World* (Taylor & Francis: London, 1986); Katz, J. E. (ed.), *The Implications of Third World Military Industrialization* (Lexington: Lexington, Mass., 1986). The significance of Third World arms industries is disputed by Clare, J. F., 'Whither Third World arms producers?,' in US Arms Control and Disarmament Agency, *World Military Expenditures and Arms Transfers 1986* (US Government Printing Office: Washington, DC, 1987), pp. 23–8.

[85] Steinberg, G. M., 'Recycled weapons', *Technology Review*, Apr. 1985, pp. 28–38; symposium on retrofitting in *Jane's Defence Weekly*, 19 Dec. 1987, pp. 1417–36; Lachica, E., 'China will buy U.S. equipment for jet fighters', *Wall Street Journal*, 6 Aug. 1987, p. 21; 'Columbian/Israeli Mirage III agreement?', *Jane's Defence Weekly*, 25 July 1987, p. 126.

[86] Howarth, M., 'Combat aircraft upgrades for smaller air forces', *International Defense Review*, no. 2 (Feb. 1987), pp. 161–5.

[87] For examples, see Cody, E., 'Sale slump stings Western Europe's arms producers', *Washington Post*, 19 Apr. 1987, p. H-1; Levite, A., 'Rough sailing for Israeli arms industry', *Armed Forces Journal*, July 1987, p. 20; 'Further cut in Dassault-Breguet work force', *Interavia Air Letter*, no. 11, 347 (7 Oct. 1987), p. 1.

[88] I would like to thank my colleague Ian Anthony for this point.

[89] See Ohlson, T. (ed.), SIPRI, *Arms Transfer Limitations and Third World Security* (Oxford University Press: Oxford, 1988).

Appendix 7A. Aggregate tables of the value of the trade in major weapons with the Third World, 1968–87

Table 7A.1. Values of imports of major weapons by the Third World: by region, 1968–87[a]
Figures are SIPRI trend indicator values, as expressed in US $m., at constant (1985) prices.
A = yearly figures, B = five-year moving averages.[b]

Region[c]		1968	1969	1970	1971	1972	1973	1974
Middle East	A	3 634	3 240	4 893	5 601	5 339	10 269	6 760
	B	3 278	4 119	4 541	5 868	6 572	7 043	7 403
South Asia	A	817	865	798	1 208	1 734	1 049	936
	B	869	889	1 085	1 131	1 145	1 100	1 067
Far East	A	2 392	1 935	2 249	3 166	5 601	1 825	1 786
	B	2 133	2 414	3 069	2 955	2 925	2 766	2 426
South America	A	330	601	285	922	1 156	2 255	1 235
	B	357	488	659	1 044	1 170	1 408	1 586
Sub-Saharan Africa	A	161	126	357	393	266	468	841
	B	213	247	260	322	465	523	638
North Africa	A	167	343	185	224	373	340	591
	B	287	255	258	293	342	655	1 136
Central America	A	51	60	181	135	261	309	299
	B	105	91	138	189	237	241	261
South Africa	A	169	67	275	104	292	459	533
	B	209	185	181	240	333	324	378
Total[d]	A	7 721	7 238	9 223	11 752	15 023	16 974	12 982
	B	7 451	8 688	10 191	12 042	13 191	14 060	14 894

[a] The values include licensed production of major weapons in Third World countries (see appendix 7C). For the values for the period 1951–66, see Brzoska, M. and Ohlson, T., SIPRI, *Arms Transfers to the Third World, 1971–85* (Oxford University Press: Oxford, 1987).

[b] Five-year moving averages are calculated as a more stable measure of the trend in arms imports than the often erratic year-to-year figures.

[c] The regions are listed in rank order according to their five-year average values in the column for 1985. The following countries are included in each region:
Middle East: Bahrain, Egypt, Iran, Iraq, Israel, Jordan, Kuwait, Lebanon, Oman, Qatar, Saudi Arabia, Syria, United Arab Emirates, North Yemen, South Yemen.
South Asia: Afghanistan, Bangladesh, India, Nepal, Pakistan, Sri Lanka.
Far East: Brunei, Burma, Fiji, Indonesia, Kampuchea, North Korea, South Korea, Laos, Malaysia, Mongolia, Papua New Guinea, Philippines, Samoa, Singapore, Solomon Islands.
South America: Argentina, Bolivia, Brazil, Chile, Colombia, Ecuador, Guyana, Paraguay, Peru, Suriname.

1975	1976	1977	1978	1979	1980	1981	1982	1983	1984	1985	1986	1987
7 248	7 398	9 833	7 605	6 003	8 319	8 966	11 522	11 293	11 520	9 581	10 193	11 546
8 302	7 769	7 617	7 831	8 145	8 483	9 221	10 324	10 577	10 822	10 827	..	..
573	1 044	1 958	1 789	1 181	2 088	2 202	2 449	2 326	2 034	2 723	3 974	6 152
1 112	1 260	1 309	1 612	1 844	1 942	2 049	2 220	2 347	2 701	3 442	..	..
1 451	1 468	1 970	3 520	5 644	2 934	2 832	1 711	2 383	2 554	2 694	2 954	2 477
1 700	2 039	2 811	3 107	3 380	3 328	3 101	2 483	2 435	2 459	2 612	..	..
1 473	1 809	2 547	2 238	1 599	2 090	3 160	2 288	2 733	3 019	1 308	1 062	1 939
1 864	1 861	1 933	2 057	2 327	2 275	2 374	2 658	2 502	2 082	2 012	..	..
645	968	2.449	2 532	929	1 394	1 876	1 514	1 173	1 687	1 753	1 392	1 807
1 074	1 487	1 505	1 654	1 836	1 649	1 377	1 529	1 601	1 504	1 563	..	..
1 747	2 629	2 595	3 702	5 435	3 016	2 492	2 888	1 685	1 563	1 077	1 363	479
1 580	2 253	3 222	3 476	3 448	3 507	3 103	2 329	1 941	1 715	1 233	..	..
201	234	557	202	238	185	644	1 067	886	575	627	594	316
320	299	286	283	365	467	604	671	760	750	600	..	..
232	371	171	343	102	109	4	4	158	5	4	154	8
353	330	244	219	146	112	75	56	35	65	66	..	..
13 571	**15 921**	**22 082**	**21 932**	**21 130**	**20 135**	**22 176**	**23 444**	**22 638**	**22 957**	**19 768**	**21 687**	**24 724**
16 306	**17 297**	**18 927**	**20 240**	**21 491**	**21 763**	**21 904**	**22 270**	**22 196**	**22 099**	**22 355**	..	..

Sub-Saharan Africa: Angola, Burundi, Benin, Burkina Faso, Botswana, Cameroon, Cape Verde, Central African Republic, Chad, Comoros, Congo, Djibouti, Equatorial Guinea, Ethiopia, Gabon, Gambia, Guinea Bissau, Gambia, Guinea, Ivory Coast, Kenya, Lesotho, Liberia, Madagascar, Malawi, Mali, Mauritania, Mauritius, Mozambique, Namibia, Nigeria, Niger, Rwanda, Senegal, Seychelles, Sierra Leone, Somalia, Sudan, Swaziland, Uganda, Zaire, Zimbabwe.
North Africa: Algeria, Libya, Morocco, Tunisia.
Central America: Bahamas, Barbados, Belize, Costa Rica, Cuba, Dominican Republic, Dominica, Guatemala, Haiti, Honduras, Jamaica, Mexico, Nicaragua, Panama, El Salvador, St Vincent and the Grenadines.
    [d] Items may not add up to totals due to rounding.
.. Not applicable.

Source: SIPRI data base.

Table 7A.2. Values of exports of major weapons to regions listed in table 7A.1: by supplier, 1968–87[a]

Figures are SIPRI trend indicator values, as expressed in US $m., at constant (1985) prices.
A = yearly figures, B = five-year moving averages.[b]

Supplier[c]		1968	1969	1970	1971	1972	1973	1974
USSR	A	3 787	2 164	4 121	4 967	5 874	7 025	4 732
	B	3 398	3 871	4 183	4 830	5 344	5 094	5 076
USA	A	2 215	3 118	3 551	3 830	5 924	6 264	4 481
	B	2 442	2 906	3 728	4 538	4 810	5 515	6 200
France	A	580	274	693	677	786	1 643	1 263
	B	433	500	602	815	1 012	1 102	1 247
UK	A	518	1 038	472	1 212	1 195	1 307	1 071
	B	564	744	887	1 045	1 052	1 196	1 121
China	A	162	86	101	321	417	232	382
	B	159	177	218	232	291	335	313
FR Germany	A	36	56	3	86	108	—	408
	B	44	50	58	51	121	173	188
Italy	A	121	85	37	95	137	148	268
	B	75	87	95	100	137	157	171
Spain	A	12	6	—	—	10	—	—
	B	8	5	5	3	2	3	4
Brazil	A	—	1	—	—	—	—	11
	B	0	0	0	0	2	7	38
Israel	A	1	9	5	1	34	4	67
	B	3	3	10	10	22	45	57
Other Third World	A	13	15	26	48	134	30	184
	B	81	29	47	51	84	108	130
Other Industrialized, West[d]	A	105	241	68	223	327	254	83
	B	102	141	193	223	191	221	279
Other Industrialized, neutral[e]	A	7	6	3	232	5	10	13
	B	4	50	51	51	52	57	23
Other Industrialized, East[f]	A	163	139	143	60	72	56	19
	B	135	126	115	94	70	46	47
Total[g]	A	7 721	7 238	9 223	11 752	15 023	16 974	12 982
	B	7 451	8 688	10 191	12 042	13 191	14 060	14 894

[a] The values include licences sold to Third World countries for production of major weapons (see appendix 7C). For the values for the period 1951–66, see Brzoska, M. and Ohlson, T., SIPRI, *Arms Transfers to the Third World, 1971–85* (Oxford University Press: Oxford, 1987).
[b] Five-year moving averages are calculated as a more stable measure of the trend in arms exports than the often erratic year-to-year figures.
[c] The countries are listed in rank order according to their five-year average values in the column for 1985.
[d] Other NATO, Australia and Japan.
[e] Austria, New Zealand, Sweden, Switzerland and Yugoslavia.
[f] Other WTO.
[g] Items may not add up to totals due to rounding.
— Nil.
.. Not applicable.

Source: SIPRI data base.

TRADE IN CONVENTIONAL WEAPONS   205

1975	1976	1977	1978	1979	1980	1981	1982	1983	1984	1985	1986	1987
2 874	4 875	7 233	9 065	9 786	8 590	7 141	7 112	6 889	7 310	7 754	8 065	9 697
5 348	5 756	6 766	7 910	8 363	8 339	7 903	7 408	7 241	7 426	7 943	..	..
7 074	7 257	9 722	6 852	4 020	5 712	6 277	7 192	6 256	4 983	4 113	4 891	5 829
6 960	7 077	6 985	6 713	6 517	6 011	5 892	6 084	5 764	5 487	5 215	..	..
1 144	1 398	2 157	2 409	3 264	2 356	3 134	2 892	2 843	3 603	3 784	3 669	3 213
1 521	1 674	2 074	2 317	2 664	2 811	2 898	2 966	3 251	3 358	3 422	..	..
1 196	834	1 641	1 200	773	703	1 161	1 670	579	1 139	942	1 263	1 641
1 210	1 189	1 129	1 030	1 096	1 102	977	1 050	1 098	1 119	1 113	..	..
320	211	114	459	412	548	328	736	961	1 180	872	1 302	1 040
252	297	303	349	372	497	597	751	816	1 010	1 071	..	..
261	166	204	258	162	283	931	321	1 175	1 835	520	613	630
208	259	210	215	368	391	574	909	956	893	955	..	..
139	163	294	323	975	653	1 332	1 346	970	811	539	325	228
202	237	379	481	715	926	1 055	1 022	999	798	575	..	..
5	7	13	30	21	9	97	371	545	400	119	202	177
5	11	15	16	34	106	208	284	306	327	288	..	..
25	154	130	120	112	268	273	202	298	271	191	189	368
64	88	108	157	181	195	231	262	247	230	263	..	..
121	59	55	470	228	209	277	375	384	252	152	179	201
61	155	187	204	248	312	295	299	288	268	234	..	..
146	157	187	95	507	177	385	542	856	577	350	446	492
141	154	218	225	270	341	493	507	542	554	544	..	..
218	514	184	464	301	226	287	437	431	141	129	203	680
251	293	336	338	292	343	336	304	285	268	317	..	..
24	63	71	41	445	272	320	181	316	275	187	194	389
36	42	129	178	230	252	307	273	256	231	272	..	..
23	63	76	144	124	129	232	68	133	182	117	145	138
48	65	86	107	141	139	137	149	146	129	143	..	..
571	15 921	22 082	21 932	21 130	20 135	22 176	23 444	22 638	22 957	19 768	21 687	24 724
306	17 297	18 927	20 240	21 491	21 763	21 904	22 270	22 196	22 099	22 355	..	..

Appendix 7B. Register of the trade in major conventional weapons with industrialized and Third World countries, 1987

This appendix lists major weapons on order or under delivery during 1987. This year the column 'Year(s) of deliveries' includes aggregates of all deliveries since the beginning of the contract. This gives a better idea of the scale of the contract. The sources and methods for the data collection, and the conventions, abbreviations and acronyms used, are explained in appendix 7D. The entries are made alphabetically, by recipient and supplier.

Region code/ Recipient	Supplier	No. ordered	Weapon designation	Weapon description	Year of order	Year(s) of deliveries	No. delivered	Comments
I. Industrialized countries								
7 Australia	Italy	. .	HSS-1	Surveillance radar	1986			Unspecified number of air surveillance radars ordered; total cost: $20 m
	Sweden	(2)	Giraffe	Fire control radar	(1985)	1986-87	(2)	Follow-on order expected
		60	RBS-70	Port SAM	1985	1986-87	(60)	
	Switzerland	2	PC-9	Trainer	1985	1987	(2)	To be followed by assembly/production of 65
	UK	. .	Rapier	Landmob SAM	1975	1978-87	(500)	Final assembly in Australia from 1983
	USA	8	SH-60B Seahawk	Hel	1985	1988	(6)	First assembly due for completion in Aug 1988; for deployment on FFG-7 frigates
		8	SH-60B Seahawk	Hel	1986	1988	(4)	In addition to 8 ordered 1985; for Navy
		14	UH-60 Blackhawk	Hel	1986	1987-88	(14)	Followed by co-production of some 60 more Blackhawks/Seahawks
		7	AN/TPQ-36	Tracking radar	1982	1986-87	(7)	
		(8)	RGM-84A L	ShShM launcher	(1985)	1986	1	Variable launchers for FFG-7 Class frigates
		(25)	AGM-84A Harpoon	AShM	(1987)			Unspecified number for FFG-7 Class frigates
		. .	AIM-7M Sparrow	AAM	1984	1986	(50)	Arming F/A-18 Hornet aircraft
		. .	AIM-9M	AAM	1984	1986	(72)	Arming F/A-18 Hornet aircraft
		(32)	RGM-84A Harpoon	ShShM	1986			Some intended for FFG-7 frigates; deal worth $47 m
		(96)	RGM-84A Harpoon	ShShM	1987			
		(65)	RIM-67C/SM-2	ShAM/ShShM	(1987)			Order number unspecified
6 Austria	Jordan	12	Alouette-3	Hel	(1987)	1987	12	

TRADE IN CONVENTIONAL WEAPONS 207

	Sweden	24	J-35 Draken	Fighter	1985	1987	(1)	Offsets worth 130%; deliveries planned for 1988 may be delayed by technical problems
	USA	18	M-109-A2 155mm	SPH	1987			Deal worth $18 m incl spares, support and machine-guns
4 Belgium	Bolivia	3	SF-260C	Trainer/COIN	1987	1987	3	Sold back to Belgian distributor due to lack of spares
	Canada	1	Do-27	Transport	(1987)	1987	1	Canadian-registered; confiscated from drug smugglers, former Portuguese AF aircraft
	France	(1 000)	SATCP Mistral	Port SAM	1985			Order incl 150 launchers; total cost: approx $66 m; for delivery from 1988
	USA	(840)	AIM-9L	AAM	(1977)			Requirement only; deliveries delayed by financial problems
5 Bulgaria	USSR	..	SA-13 TELAR	AAV(M)	(1984)	1985-87	(12)	In service
		..	ZSU-23-4 Shilka	AAV	(1984)	1985-87	(36)	In service
		..	SA-13 Gopher	Landmob SAM	(1984)	1985-87	(864)	
4 Canada	France	..	Eryx	ATGM	(1987)			Agreement in principle; deal worth $187 m; licensed production probable
	Nicaragua	4	T-28A Trojan	Trainer	(1987)	1987	4	Sold by Sandinista AF to Victoria Air Maintenance
	Sweden	(12)	Giraffe	Fire control radar	(1985)			Shipborne version for Halifax Class destroyers
	Switzerland	(864)	ADATS	SAM system	1986			36 ADATS systems on M-113 vehicles; order incl 10 Oerlikon 35mm AA-guns and 10 Skyguard fire control systems; total cost: $145 m; possibly for licensed production
	UK	10	Skyguard SAMS	Mobile SAM system	1986			Part of ADATS contract
		..	EH-101	Hel	1987			Final order of 35-50 expected
	USA	138	F/A-18 Hornet	Fighter	1980	1982-87	(110)	Order incl 113 single-seat fighters and 25 two-seat operational trainers; delivery schedule: 1982-89
		4	Phalanx	CIWS	1987			Arming Tribal Class frigates
		12	Seasparrow VLS	ShAM/PDM launcher	1984			Arming 6 Halifax Class destroyers
		8	Seasparrow VLS	ShAM/PDM launcher	1986			Arming Tribal Class frigates; for delivery 1988-90
		408	AIM-7M Sparrow	AAM	1984	1985-87	(372)	Arming F/A-18 Hornets; total cost incl spares and training: $113 m
		184	AIM-7M Sparrow	AAM	1985			Arming F/A-18 Hornets
		96	AIM-7M Sparrow	AAM	(1987)			Arming F/A-18 Hornets; deal worth $31 m incl 24 Mk 48 torpedoes

Region code/ Recipient	Supplier	No. ordered	Weapon designation	Weapon description	Year of order	Year(s) of deliveries	No. delivered	Comments
		416	AIM-9M	AAM	1984	1985-87	(372)	Arming F/A-18 Hornets; total cost incl 40 training missiles: $41 m
		2 160	BGM-71D TOW-2	ATM	1985			For delivery 1988
		22	RIM-67C/SM-2	ShAM/ShShM	1987			Arming Tribal Class frigates
		(240)	Seasparrow	ShAM/ShShM/PDM	1984			Arming 6 Halifax Class destroyers; total cost: $92 m
		(128)	Seasparrow	ShAM/ShShM/PDM	1986			Arming 4 Tribal Class frigates; for delivery 1988-90
3 China	France	8	SA-342L Gazelle	Hel	1987	1988	(8)	For evaluation; licensed production or reverse engineering may follow
		2	Crotale Naval L	ShAM launcher	1987			Deal worth $91.5 m incl dummy missiles and support; probably arming Jiang Dong and Shanghai Class escort vessels under construction
		..	Rasit-3190B	Surveillance radar	1986			To use Castor 2-C fire control radar; deal worth $91.5 m; for delivery 1989
		(72)	Crotale Naval	ShAM	1987			Arming 8 SA-342L Gazelle helicopters
	Israel	(96)	HOT	ATM	1987			
		..	Mapats	Port ATM	1986			
		2	L-100-30	Transport	1987			
	USA	5	Learjet-35A	Mar patrol/trpt	1987	1987	5	For China Air Cargo; offsets probable Version unconfirmed; for recce
		4	AN/TPQ-37	Tracking radar	(1987)			Deal worth $62 m incl spares, support and ancillary equipment
		(2)	Phalanx	CIWS	(1987)			Arming new class of missile-armed frigate
		..	BGM-71A TOW	ATM	(1987)			Agreed in principle June 1984
6 Cyprus	France	4	SA-342L Gazelle	Hel	(1986)	1987	4	For Greek Cypriot Government
		16	AMX-30B	MBT	1987			Deal worth $250 m incl SA-342 helicopters and HOT ATMs
		84	VAB	APC	1984	1985-87	(84)	66 of the VII version and 18 of the VCI-type
		..	HOT-2	ATM	1987			Part of $250 m order: arming 4 SA-342 helicopters and VAB APCs; deal incl spares and training

TRADE IN CONVENTIONAL WEAPONS 209

5 Czechoslovakia	USSR		An-26 Curl	Transport	(1984)	1985-87	(30) Replacing Avia-14s and Il-14s
			Mi-17 Hip-H	Hel	(1985)	1985-87	(36) Replacing Mi-4s
		(60)	Su-25 Frogfoot	Fighter/grd attack	(1984)	1985-87	(60) Replacing MiG-17s
			BMP-1 Spigot	TD(M)	1979	1980-87	(192)
			BRDM-2 Gaskin	AAV(M)	1979	1980-87	(80)
			SA-13 TELAR	AAV(M)	(1984)	1984-87	(20) In service
		(24)	SA-8 SAMS	Mobile SAM system	(1986)	1987	(8)
			AT-4 Spigot	ATM	1979	1980-87	(1 920)
			SA-13 Gopher	Landmob SAM	(1984)	1984-87	(1 440) In service
		(96)	SA-8 Gecko	Landmob SAM	(1986)	1987	(32)
			SA-9 Gaskin	Landmob SAM	1979	1980-87	(1 600)
4 Denmark	Argentina	1	Lynx	Hel	(1987)	1987	1
	Australia	1	Lynx	Hel	(1987)	1988	1 Deal worth $3.5 m incl 3 spare engines; for fishery protection
	France	12	AS-350 Ecureuil	Hel	1987		Equipped with Helitow sight system incl TOW-2 ATMs; deal worth $50 m
	Germany, FR		RAM	ShAM/PDM	(1985)		Arming 3 Niels Juel Class frigates US approval granted 1987; ships originally built with US funds
	Norway	3	Type 207	Submarine	1985		
	Sweden	12	Helitow	Hel fire control	1987		Arming 12 AS-350 Ecureuil helicopters; total cost: $15.5 m
	UK	2	Lynx	Hel	(1986)	1987	2 Attrition replacement
	USA	8	F-16A	Fighter	1985	1987	(5) For delivery 1987-89; in addition to 58 in service; total cost incl spares and technical support: $210 m
		4	F-16B	Fighter/trainer	1985	1987	(2) For delivery 1987-89
		(196)	BGM-71D TOW-2	ATM	1987		Arming 12 AS-350 Ecureuil helicopters
		840	FIM-92A Stinger	Port SAM	(1987)		Final decision postponed
6 Finland	Italy	1	AB-412 Griffon	Hel	(1986)	1987	1 For Coast Guard; equipped with FLIR search radar
	Sweden	18	J-35 Draken	Fighter	1984	1984-87	(18) Arming Helsinki Class FACs
		4	RBS-15 L	ShShM launcher	1983	1987	(4) Arming Helsinki Class FACs
		6	RBS-15 L	ShShM launcher	1987		Arming Helsinki Class FACs; future order of coastal defence version likely
		(96)	RBS-15	ShAM/ShShM	(1987)		
	UK	4	Watchman	Surveillance radar	1988		Second order; deliveries to begin 1989
	USA		BGM-71C I-TOW	ATM	(1985)		Undisclosed number ordered
	USSR	(100)	MT-LB	APC	(1986)	1986-87	(20)
		(60)	T-72	MBT	(1986)	1986-87	(24) For delivery 1986-90
			AT-4 Spigot	ATM	(1986)	1986-87	(120) Part of $400 m 5-year agreement also incl T-72 tanks and MT-LB APCs

Region code/ Recipient	Supplier	No. ordered	Weapon designation	Weapon description	Year of order	Year(s) of deliveries	No. delivered	Comments
4 France	Brazil	..	SA-14 Gremlin	Port SAM	1984	1986-87	(105)	Unspecified number; modified in Finland; renamed 'Igla'
		(150)	EMB-312 Tucano	Trainer	(1987)			Negotiating; conditional upon reciprocal Brazilian helicopter purchase
	Chad	..	Mi-24 Hind-D	Hel	1987	1987	(1)	Captured by Chad from Libya
		..	SA-13 TELAR	AAV(M)	1987	1987	(2)	Captured from Libya with missiles
	Libya	..	SA-7 Grail	Port SAM	1987	1987	20	Confiscated by French police Oct 1987 from 150-ton shipment for IRA; no launchers; supplier unconfirmed
	Spain	5	C-212 Aviocar	Transport	1987			Offset for Spanish order for AS-332 helicopters
	USA	6	C-130H Hercules	Transport	1987	1987	3	Deal worth $128 m; requirement for 6 more
		4	E-3A Sentry	AEW	1987	1991	(2)	Ordered Feb 1987; 130% offsets in aerospace; option for 2 more
		51	MLRS 227mm	MRS	1987	1988	6	
5 German DR	Bulgaria	..	MT-LB	APC	(1982)	1984-87	(40)	Unconfirmed
	USSR	..	BRDM-2 Spigot	TD(M)	1978	1979-87	(146)	
		..	BTR-70	APC	(1982)	1983-87	(450)	Replacing BTR-60; also designated SPW-70
		..	SA-13 TELAR	AAV(M)	(1984)	1985-86	(20)	Unconfirmed
		..	T-72	MBT	(1978)	1979-87	(850)	May be from Czechoslovakian or Polish production
		..	T-74	MBT	(1981)	1982-87	(90)	Improved T-72 MBT
		..	SA-N-5 L	ShAM launcher	(1982)	1984-86	(4)	Arming Tarantul Class FACs
		..	SSN-2 Styx L	ShShM launcher	(1982)	1984-86	(4)	Arming Tarantul Class FACs
		..	AT-4 Spigot	ATM	1978	1979-86	(1 920)	
		..	SA-13 Gopher	Landmob SAM	(1984)	1985-86	(20)	Unconfirmed
4 Germany, FR	Canada	7	Challenger-601	Transport	1984	1986-87	7	
	France	3	AS-332	Hel	(1987)			For frontier police
		(23)	TRS-3050	Surveillance radar	(1986)	1986-87	(2)	Arming 20 S-148 Class FACs
	Malaysia	6	Do-27	Transport	(1986)	1987	6	Partial payment for Malawi Do-228 aircraft
		2	Do-28D-2	Transport	(1986)	1987	2	Partial payment for Malawi Do-228 aircraft

TRADE IN CONVENTIONAL WEAPONS

	Supplier	No.	Weapon designation	Weapon description	Year of order	Year(s) of delivery	(Nos delivered)	Comments
	UK	5	Lynx	Hel	1986			Arming new F-122 Class frigates; delivery 1988-89; offset value: 30%
	USA	(100)	Sea Skua	AShM	1986			Arming Sea King Mk 41 helicopters
		(80)	M-109-A2 155mm	SPH	(1987)			
		28	Patriot Unit	Mobile SAM system	(1983)			Order number refers to fire units; each unit has 8 launchers with 4 missiles per launcher and 32 reload missiles
		(4)	RGM-84A L	ShShM launcher	(1986)			Arming 2 Bremen Class frigates
		(2)	Seasparrow L	ShAM/PDM launcher	1986			Arming 2 Bremen Class frigates
		310	AGM-65B	ASM	1986	1987	(310)	In addition to 450 ordered 1981 and 120 ordered 1985; total value: $40 m
		368	AGM-88 Harm	ARM	1986			Arming Tornado fighters; option on 576 more
		180	AGM-88 Harm	ARM	1987			Arming Tornado fighters
		(1 792)	MIM-104 Patriot	Landmob SAM	1984			28 fire units with 64 missiles each; FRG will pay for 14 units and get the rest in exchange for Roland-2 air defence of West German and US air bases in FRG; total cost: $1000 m
		(150)	RAM	ShAM/PDM	(1985)			Prior to licensed production; probably for 20 S-143 Class FACs
		(48)	RGM-84A Harpoon	ShShM	(1986)			Arming 2 Bremen Class frigates
		110	RIM-66A/SM-1	ShAM/ShShM	1985			Deal worth $44 m incl 70 containers and spares
		(56)	Seasparrow	ShAM/ShShM/PDM	(1986)			Arming 2 Bremen Class frigates
4 Greece	France	40	Mirage-2000	Fighter	1985			36 fighters and 4 trainers; for delivery 1988-89
		..	Stentor	Battlefield radar	(1987)			Unconfirmed; includes agreement for licensed production
		(240)	Magic-2	AAM	(1986)			Arming Mirage-2000 fighters; severe domestic criticism because of high price of missiles compared to US Sidewinder
	Italy	4 000	Milan	ATM	1987			Deal worth $54 m incl 100 launchers
		25	A-109 Hirundo	Hel	(1987)			Negotiating
		5	C-47	Transport	(1986)		5	
		(30)	G-222	Transport	(1987)			Negotiating
	Netherlands	10	F-5A	Fighter	1987	1987		Deal includes supply of F-5s to Turkey
	USA	40	F-16C	Fighter	1985	1988-89	(40)	Includes 6 F-16D versions
		40	F-4E Phantom	Fighter	(1987)			LoO Apr 1987
		8	Model 209 AH-1S	Hel	1980	1986-87	(8)	Armed with TOW ATMs; total cost: $66 m
		300	M-48-A5	MBT	1986	1987	(50)	To be purchased from US surplus stocks; total cost: $103 m

212 MILITARY EXPENDITURE, ARMS TRADE, CONFLICTS

Region code/ Recipient	Supplier	No. ordered	Weapon designation	Weapon description	Year of order	Year(s) of deliveries	No. delivered	Comments
		(110)	M-60-A3	MBT	(1987)			US LoO Aug 1983; total cost: $186 m; competing with Leopard-1
		(54)	M-901 TOW	TD(M)	1984	1985-87	(54)	
		2	HADR	Air defence radar	1985			Part of NADGE air defence system
		2	Phalanx	CIWS	1986			US LoO July 1986; total cost: $28 m
		4	Phalanx	CIWS	(1987)			
		80	AIM-7F Sparrow	AAM	(1987)			Arming 40 F-4E Phantom fighters from US stockpiles
		80	AIM-9F	AAM	(1987)			Arming 40 F-4E Phantoms from US stockpiles
		(160)	BGM-71A TOW	ATM	(1983)	1986-87	(160)	Arming 8 Model 209 AH-1S helicopters
		1 097	BGM-71C I-TOW	ATM	1984	1985-87	(1 097)	
		32	RGM-84A Harpoon	ShShM	1986			Deal worth $43 m incl containers and spares; arming Elli (Kortenaer) Class frigates
5 Hungary	USSR	. .	SA-5 SAMS	Mobile SAM system	(1986)	1987	(6)	Unconfirmed
		(60)	SA-6 SAMS	Mobile SAM system	(1984)	1985-87	(60)	Unconfirmed
		(72)	SA-5 Gammon	SAM	(1986)	1987	(72)	
		. .	SA-6 Gainful	Landmob SAM	(1984)	1985-87	(540)	
6 Ireland	Italy	5	SF-260 Warrior	Trainer/COIN	(1987)			For Air Corps
4 Italy	Germany, FR	(6)	TF-104G	Jet trainer	1987	1987	(6)	Arming Tornado fighters
		. .	Kormoran-2	AShM	(1986)			
	Sweden	60	Helitow	Hel fire control	(1987)	1987-88	(60)	For A-129 Mangusta helicopters ordered by Italian Army; option on 30 more
	Switzerland	. .	Fledermaus II	Mobile AA system	(1970)	1973-87	(60)	Details unconfirmed
	USA	1	Model 500E	Hel	1987	1987	1	Helicopter trainer; to be followed by licensed production of 50
		2	HADR	Air defence radar	1985			Part of NADGE system
		. .	Helitow	Hel fire control	1987			Arming A-129 Mangusta helicopters; deal worth $100 m incl licence to produce in Italy
		20	Patriot btys	Mobile SAM system	1987			Deal worth $3 b; range of offsets yet to be negotiated
		6 629	BGM-71C I-TOW	ATM	1984	1986-87	(4 000)	Deal worth $67 m incl 1239 practice missiles

TRADE IN CONVENTIONAL WEAPONS 213

7	Japan	France	(3 900)	BGM-71D TOW-2	ATM	1987	(1 100)	Arming A-129 Mangusta helicopters
			450	FIM-92A Stinger	Port SAM	1984		Deal worth $51 m incl 150 launchers
			(512)	MIM-104 Patriot	Landmob SAM	1987	(400)	Arming 20 Patriot btys
		UK	3	AS-332	Hel	1987		
			2	Falcon-200	Mar patrol	1987		
			(400)	FH-70 155mm	TH	1984	1985-87	(129)	Ordered July 1984; 375 to be locally assembled
		USA	2	C-130H Hercules	Transport	1985	1987	2	Third order; total cost: $51 m
			3	C-130H Hercules	Transport	1987			Fourth order
			7	CH-47D Chinook	Hel	1984	1986-87	(7)	First 2 delivered directly; 5 assembled from kits; licensed production of at least 47 to follow
			(4)	KV-107/2A	Hel	(1987)			
			16	King Air C-90	Trainer	(1979)	1980-87	14	
			6	Learjet-35A	Mar patrol/trpt	1985	1985-87	(3)	1 for target towing; 5 configured for EW navigation and recce training
			1	Learjet-35A	Mar patrol/trpt	1986	1987	1	In addition to 1 delivered 1987; planned purchase of 2 in 1988
			(1)	Learjet-36A	Transport	(1987)			
			2	MH-53E	Hel	1986	1987	2	Replacing SH-3Bs; for ASW
			(2)	MH-53E	Hel	(1987)			
			2	SH-60B Seahawk	Hel	1983	1986-87	2	Arming 2 new 6000-ton destroyers
			(2)	AEGIS	Fire control radar	(1987)			On Hatakaze Class destroyers
			(2)	Phalanx	CIWS	(1985)	1986	(1)	US LoO July 1986; for Hatsuyuki Class destroyers; total cost: $70 m
			6	Phalanx	CIWS	1986			
			4	Phalanx	CIWS	1987			Arming new class of Japanese destroyer
			(84)	AGM-84A Harpoon	AShM	(1980)	1982-86	(84)	Arming P-3C Orions
			. .	FIM-92A Stinger	Port SAM	1982	1984-88	(555)	
			38	RGM-84A Harpoon	ShShM	1986			Incl some AGM/UGM-84 versions
			55	RGM-84A Harpoon	ShShM	(1987)			LoO to Congress; contract value for mix RGM- and AGM-84A Harpoons: $80 m
			(192)	RIM-67C/SM-2	ShAM/ShShM	1987			Part of AEGIS air defence system
4	Netherlands	Italy	20	A-129 Mangusta	Hel	1986			
		USA	21	MLRS 227mm	MRS	1986			
			46	MLRS 227mm	MRS	1987			Deal worth $192 m incl 2700 rocket pods; for delivery from 1989
			4	AN/TPQ-37	Tracking radar	1986			
			20	Patriot SAMS	Mobile SAM system	1984			Final decision Dec 1983; total cost: $300 m incl 160 missiles and 4 AN/MPQ-53 radar sets

Region code/ Recipient	Supplier	No. ordered	Weapon designation	Weapon description	Year of order	Year(s) of deliveries	No. delivered	Comments
		8	RGM-84A L	ShShM launcher	1986	1987	(1)	Arming 8 M Class frigates
		900	AIM-9L	AAM	1983	1985-87	(600)	Deal worth $78 m
		1 878	BGM-71D TOW-2	ATM	1986			Deal worth $22 m
		646	FIM-92A Stinger	Port SAM	1982	1985-87	(600)	
		160	MIM-104 Patriot	Landmob SAM	1983			Contract signed Dec 1983; total cost: $300 m incl 20 launchers and 4 AN/MPQ-53 radar sets in 4 units
		25	RGM-84A Harpoon	ShShM	1986	1987	(25)	Arming first M Class frigate; total cost: $37 m
7 New Zealand	Australia	24	Hamel 105mm	TG	1986	1987	8	Remaining 16 for delivery 1988-89; total cost: A$15 m
		..	ASI-315	PC	(1985)			For Cook Islands under Pacific Patrol Boat Programme
	Korea, South	1	Endeavour Class	Support ship/Tanker	(1985)	1987	1	Fleet oiler
4 Norway	Germany, FR	6	Type 210	Submarine	1983			Contract signed Sep 1983; for delivery 1989-92; offsets incl delivery of 12 fire control systems for West German submarines; designated Ula Class
	Sweden	4	MFI-15 Safari	Lightplane	1986	1987	(4)	Unspecified number; for coastal defence
		..	Ersta 120mm	CG	1986	1986-87	(5)	Unspecified number; for RBS-70 SAMs
		..	Giraffe	Fire control radar	1985	1986	(10)	Fifth order; cost: $90 m; some Norwegian production; for delivery 1987-90
		..	RBS-70	Port SAM	1985	1987	(50)	
	UK	1	SH-3D Sea King	Hel	(1987)			To replace 1 helicopter lost Nov 1986
	USA	(24)	F-16A	Fighter	1983			For delivery in early 1990s; mix of F-16 A and B versions; follows previous order of 72 ACs
		2	F-16A	Fighter	1986			Deal worth $30 m
		18	Model 412	Hel	1986	1987	(1)	Lead unit to be followed by licensed assembly of 17
		(6)	Model 412	Hel	(1987)			
		4	P-3C Orion	Mar patrol/ASW	1986			For delivery 1989
		16	M-113-A2	APC	(1986)			
		36	M-48-A5	MBT	1986	1987		In addition to 44 M-901 TOW TDs
		44	M-901 TOW	TD(M)	(1986)	1987	(15)	Refurbished; total cost: $26 m
		6	I-Hawk SAMS	Mobile SAM system	1983	1987	(6)	

TRADE IN CONVENTIONAL WEAPONS 215

		7 612	BGM-71D TOW-2	ATM	1985	(500)	Deal worth $126 m incl 300 launchers
		(162)	MIM-23B Hawk	Landmob SAM	1983	(162)	Purchase of 2 more btys (54 missiles) planned
5	Poland						
	USSR	5	SA-N-5 L	ShAM launcher	(1985)		Arming 5 Tarantul Class corvettes
		5	SSN-2 Styx L	ShShM launcher	(1985)		Arming 5 Tarantul Class corvettes; improved Styx variant with new guidance and longer range
		(60)	SA-N-5	ShAM	(1985)		Arming 5 Tarantul Class corvettes
		(60)	SSN-2 Styx	ShShM	(1985)		Arming 5 Tarantul Class corvettes
		(4)	Kilo Class	Submarine	(1984)	2	Replacing Whiskey Class submarines
		(5)	Tarantul Class	Corvette	(1985)		Order may be for 10 corvettes
4	Portugal						
	Germany, FR	3	Meko-200 Type	Frigate	1986		Deal worth $700 m
	Italy	4	A-109 Hirundo	Hel	1986		
		24	Aspide	AAM/SAM/ShAM	1986		Arming 3 Meko-200 frigates
		6	P-3B Orion	Mar patrol/ASW	1985	6	Ex-Australian; 1 refurbished in USA, 5 in Portugal
	USA	10	M-163 Vulcan	AAV	(1987)		LoO Feb 1987; total cost incl spares and support: $18 m
		5	M-730 Chaparral	AAV(M)	1986		Deal worth $45 m incl 66 missiles and 2 AN/MPQ-54 radars
		2	AN/MPQ-54	Guidance radar	1986		Part of low-level air defence system
		1	HADR	Air defence radar	1985		Part of NADGE air defence system
		3	Phalanx	CIWS	1986		Arming 3 Meko-200 Type frigates
		3	RGM-84A L	ShShM launcher	1986		Arming 3 Meko-200 Type frigates
		3	Seasparrow VLS	ShAM/PDM launcher	1986		Arming 3 Meko-200 Type frigates
		66	MIM-72F	SAM/ShAM	1986		
		24	RGM-84A Harpoon	ShShM	1986		Arming 3 Meko-200 Type frigates
4	Spain						
	Chile	40	T-35 Pillan	Trainer	1984	(40)	Offsetting Chilean purchase of C-101s; Spanish designation: E-26 Tamiz
	France	18	AS-332	Hel	1987		In exchange for French C-212 order; Spain will assemble up to 50 more for French clients and build parts
		18	AMX-30 Roland	AAV(M)	1984	(12)	Deal worth $182.4 m incl 414 Roland-2 mobile SAMs
		(2 000)	HOT	ATM	1984	(1 000)	Ordered Dec 1984; incl 150 launchers
		(3 500)	Milan	ATM	1984	(1 000)	Ordered Dec 1984; incl 250 launchers
		414	Roland-2	Landmob SAM	1984	(276)	Deal worth $182.4 m incl 18 AMX-30 Roland launch units; 50% of work to be done by Spain; offsets at 65% of order value

Region code/ Recipient	Supplier	No. ordered	Weapon designation	Weapon description	Year of order	Year(s) of deliveries	No. delivered	Comments
	Italy	28	Skyguard Unit	Mobile SAM system	1985	1987	(5)	For delivery over 5 years; 28 launch units in 6 byts
		(200)	Aspide	AAM/SAM/ShAM	1985	1987	(36)	Deal worth $129 m incl 13 Aspide/Spada launch systems; 40% of value assigned to Spanish industry in offsets
	USA	12	AV-8B Harrier	Fighter	1983	1987	(3)	For delivery 1987-88; cost: $378 m; off-set value: $130 m; to equip AC carrier
		2	B-707-320C	Transport	(1985)	1987	2	Civilian transport plane being converted by Boeing; including additional avionics
		1	C-130H Hercules	Transport	1987	1988	(1)	In addition to 1 delivered 1987
		1	C-130H-30	Transport	(1986)	1987	1	
		5	CH-47C Chinook	Hel	(1986)	1987	5	Originally for Nigeria
		6	CH-47D Chinook	Hel	1985	1986-87	(6)	For Army; in addition to 12 in service; total cost: $80 m; Model 414
		72	F/A-18 Hornet	Fighter	1983	1986-87	19	60 fighters and 12 trainers
		2	KC-135	Tanker/transport	(1985)	1987	(2)	
		6	SH-60B Seahawk	Hel	1984			For delivery 1988-89
		96	M54 Chaparral	Mobile SAM system	1981	1986-87	(18)	
		(3)	RGM-84A L	ShShM launcher	(1977)	1986-87	2	Arming 3 FFG-7 Class frigates
		1	RGM-84A L	ShShM launcher	(1986)	1986-87		Arming fourth FFG-7 Class frigate
		(3)	RIM-67A L	ShAM launcher	(1977)	1986-87		Arming 3 FFG-7 Class frigates
		1	RIM-67A L	ShAM launcher	(1986)		2	Arming fourth FFG-7 Class frigate; dual-purpose launcher for Harpoon ShShMs and Seasparrow SAMs
		20	AGM-84A Harpoon	AShM	(1987)			Arming F/A-18 fighters
		80	AGM-88 Harm	ARM	(1987)			Cost incl containers and spares; for F/A-18 fighters
		(400)	BGM-71D TOW-2	ATM	1987			Arming Piranha APCs; for co-production in addition to previous TOW orders
		50	MIM-23B Hawk	Landmob SAM	(1987)			Congress notified; total cost incl containers, spares and support: $22 m
		1 760	MIM-72C	Landmob SAM	1981	1986-87	(324)	Deal worth $272 m incl 96 M54 Chapparral launchers
		80	RGM-84A Harpoon	ShShM	1977	1986-87	(64)	Arming 3 FFG-7 Class frigates; partial batch of 25 Harpoons ordered 1985
		(16)	RGM-84A Harpoon	ShShM	(1986)			Arming fourth FFG-7 Class frigate
		20	RGM-84A Harpoon	ShShM	1987			
		(192)	RIM-67C/SM-2	ShAM/ShShM	(1977)	1985-87	(192)	Arming 3 FFG-7 Class destroyers

TRADE IN CONVENTIONAL WEAPONS 217

6	Sweden	France	10	AS-332	Hel	1987		(2)	For Navy; total cost: $106 m; first delivery due 1988
		Germany, FR	20	Bo-105CB	Hel	1984	1986-87	(20)	For Army; to carry 4 TOW ATMs
		UK	..	Sky Flash	AAM	1981	1983-87	(350)	Additional quantity for JA-37 Viggen; total cost: approx $26.5 m
		USA	1	Metro AWACS	AWACS	(1984)	1987	1	Prototype delivered; radar to be fitted by Ericsson of Sweden; flight test in USA
			16	Model 300C	Hel	1985			Total value; SEK 28 m
			2	Aardvark	Flail	(1986)	1987	(2)	1 for UNIFIL, 1 for trials
			700	AGM-114A	ASM/ATM	1987			Hellfire coastal defence version; cost incl launchers and spares: $65 m; local assembly and production of some parts
			(864)	AIM-9M	AAM	1984	1986-87	(864)	US DoD agreed to sell May 1982; delay due to funding problems; to arm JA-37 Viggen; total cost: approx $75 m
			(1 000)	BGM-71D TOW-2	ATM	1984			
6	Switzerland	France	3	AS-332	Hel	1987	1987	3	
		Germany, FR	35	Leopard-2	MBT	1983	1987	35	345 more to be built under licence; for delivery from 1987
		UK	1	Hawk	Jet trainer	1987			Delivery of 1 from UK prior to Swiss co-production of 19
		USA	30	Model 300C	Hel	(1985)			
			12 000	BGM-71D TOW-2	ATM	(1985)			12 000 missiles and 3000 inert practice rounds; total cost incl 400 night vision sights, 400 components for launcher assembly and support equipment: $209 m
4	Turkey	Canada	50	CF-104	Fighter	1985	1986-87	(50)	20 for active duty, 30 for spares
			12	T-33A	Jet trainer	1987			
		Egypt	33	F-4E Phantom	Fighter	(1987)			Negotiating; US approval granted for resale; Saudi funding expected
		France	5	Stentor	Battlefield radar	1987			Surveillance radars
			1	TRS-2230/15	Air defence radar	1987			Air defence package also incl surveillance radars and control centres; designations classified
			2	Tiger	Point defence radar	1987			Primary surveillance radars
		Germany, FR	40	Tornado IDS	Fighter/MRCA	(1987)			Negotiations deadlocked due to funding problems
			(200)	Leopard-1	MBT	1986	1987	(50)	Negotiations on Leopard-2 resulted in contract for Ex-West German Leopard-1s

218 MILITARY EXPENDITURE, ARMS TRADE, CONFLICTS

Region code/ Recipient	Supplier	No. ordered	Weapon designation	Weapon description	Year of order	Year(s) of deliveries	No. delivered	Comments
		75	Leopard-1-A4	MBT	(1987)			Delivery of first batch expected 1988; DM 600 m allocated in defence aid by FRG
		2	Meko-200 Type	Frigate	1983	1987	2	Prior to licensed production of 2
		52	CN-235	Transport	(1986)			For delivery from 1988; co-production expected; supplier unconfirmed, possibly Spain
	Indonesia							
	Italy	(96)	Aspide	AAM/SAM/ShAM	(1986)	1987	(24)	Arming 4 Meko-200 frigates
	Netherlands	24	F-5A	Fighter	1987	1988	(24)	
	Switzerland	4	Seaguard	CIWS	(1985)	1987	1	Arming 4 Meko-200 frigates
	USA	8	F-16C	Fighter	1984	1987-88	8	Licensed production to follow
		15	F-4E Phantom	Fighter	(1986)	1987	(15)	Deal worth $70 m; from surplus US stock; to be refurbished before delivery
		40	F-4E Phantom	Fighter	1987			Ex-USAF; stopgap until F-16 delivery starts
		1	Gulfstream-3	Transport	1987	1987	1	Local assembly; total cost: $33 m
		15	Model 205 UH-1H	Hel	1985			MAP; in addition to 18 in service
		18	S-2E Tracker	Fighter/ASW	(1985)	1986-87	(18)	To be produced over 8 years; deal to be signed Feb 1988, to replace M-113A AVs
		1 700	AIFV	MICV	1988			
		36	M-198 155mm	TH	(1986)			US LoO Sep 1986
		6	AN/TPQ-36	Tracking radar	(1986)			US LoO Sep 1986
		3	HADR	Air defence radar	1985			Part of NADGE air defence system
		8	Phalanx	CIWS	(1982)	1987	2	Arming 4 Meko-200 frigates
		4	RGM-84A L	ShShM launcher	1983	1987	(3)	Arming 4 Meko-200 frigates
		(4)	Seasparrow L	ShAM/PDM launcher	(1986)	1987	(3)	Arming 4 Meko-200 frigates
		30	AIM-7F Sparrow	AAM	(1986)	1987	30	Arming F-4Es from US stockpiles
		80	AIM-7F Sparrow	AAM	1987			Arming 40 F-4Es from US stockpiles
		(320)	AIM-7M Sparrow	AAM	(1983)	1986-87	(150)	
		30	AIM-9F	AAM	(1986)	1987	30	Arming F-4Es from US stockpiles
		80	AIM-9F	AAM	1987			Arming 40 F-4Es from US stockpiles
		(48)	RGM-84A Harpoon	ShShM	1983	1987	(36)	Arming 4 Meko-200 frigates
4 UK	France	(5)	Falcon-20G	Mar patrol	1985			Ordered number reportedly 5-10
		(600)	VBL-M11	AC	(1987)			Agreement in principle but no contract signed
	Netherlands	15	Goalkeeper	CIWS	1985	1987	1	6 systems for Type-22 frigates; 9 for Invincible Class AC carriers

TRADE IN CONVENTIONAL WEAPONS

Saudi Arabia	9	Goalkeeper	CIWS	1987	(42)	Returned as part of Tornado deal; may be sold to Nigeria
	(42)	Lightning F-53	Fighter/interceptor	(1985)		
Switzerland	11	AS-202 Bravo	Trainer	1986	(5)	For delivery to Saudi Arabia
	30	PC-9	Trainer	1985	(15)	Option on one more exercised Nov 1987; option on 8th remains; 130% offsets, 10% in aerospace
USA	6	E-3A Sentry	AEW	(1987)	(6)	
	1	E-3A Sentry	AEW	1987		In addition to 6 ordered earlier; deal worth $120 m with offsets of 130%
	19	PA-28 Warrior	Lightplane	1986	(10)	
	6	PA-34 Seneca-2	Lightplane	1986	(3)	
	4	Phalanx	CIWS	(1985)		For Type-23 frigates
	2	Phalanx	CIWS	(1986)		
	7	Phalanx	CIWS	1987		
	(8)	RGM-84A L	ShShM launcher	1984	(5)	Arming Type-22 and Type-23 frigates
	(192)	RGM-84A Harpoon	ShShM	1984	(120)	Arming Type-22 and Type-23 frigates; offsets worth 130% of order value
	(64)	Trident-2 D-5	SLBM	(1983)		Arming 4 Vanguard submarines; delivery mid-1990s; replacing Polaris force
	(210)	UGM-84A Harpoon	SuShM	1975	(210)	Arming Valiant, Swiftsure and Trafalgar submarines
Australia	7	N-24A Nomad	Transport	1987	7	'R&D barter' to offset Australian obligations to USA; for customs service
Canada	758	LAV-25	APC	1982	(436)	For US Marine Corps; developed from Swiss Piranha APC
	153	LAV-25	APC	(1987)		Request only for AF air base defence mobile armoured recce version
Chad	..	Mi-24 Hind-D	Hel	1987	(2)	Captured from Libya
	..	SA-13 TELAR	AAV(M)	1987	(2)	Captured from Libya with missiles
Finland	14	Magister	Jet trainer	(1987)	14	To private US buyers
Germany, FR	(27)	Roland L	Mobile SAM system	(1987)		For defence of USAF bases in FRG; terms of sale unclear
	72	Pershing-1a	IRBM	1987		To be returned to USA for destruction in support of INF Treaty; other missiles and warheads already under US control
Haiti	4	S-211	Trainer	1987		Haiti AF negotiating disposal of 4 S-211s to private US company; 2 aircraft still in crates
Israel	13	Kfir-C1	Fighter	1986	13	Rented for US Marine Corps adversary training

1 USA

220 MILITARY EXPENDITURE, ARMS TRADE, CONFLICTS

Region code/ Recipient	Supplier	No. ordered	Weapon designation	Weapon description	Year of order	Year(s) of deliveries	No. delivered	Comments
	Norway	12	Popeye	AGM	(1986)	1987	(6)	For evaluation by USAF
		10	F-5A	Fighter	1987	1987	10	Exchanged for full ownership of Kobben Class submarines; may be retransferred by USA under MAP
		212	Penguin-3	AShM	1986			Jeopardized by Toshiba/Kongsberg affair; offset for purchase of Hawk SAMs; for evaluation
	Saudi Arabia	4	B-707-320C	Transport	1987			Bought by Boeing for conversion to tanker/cargo configuration for Italian AF
	Spain	3	P-3A Orion	Mar patrol/ASW	(1988)			Returned to USA in exchange for ex-Norwegian P-3Bs
	Sweden	(32)	RBS-56 Bill	ATM	1986			For evaluation
	Switzerland	4	ADATS	SAM system	1987	1987	32	Initial order for evaluation; replaces cancelled Sgt. York Divad gun
	UK	1	Airship	AEW	1987			Prototype AEW/communications relay; option on 4 more at $294 m
		53	Light Gun 105mm	TG	1987			M-119 light gun for US Army light divisions
		(4)	Rapier SAMS	Mobile SAM system	1985	1987	(4)	For evaluation
		(100)	Rapier	Landmob SAM	1985	1987	(100)	To protect 2 USAF bases in Turkey
2 USSR	Afghanistan	..	Blowpipe	Port SAM	1987	1987	(10)	Captured from Mujahideen
		..	FIM-92A Stinger	Port SAM	1987	1987	(30)	Captured from Mujahideen
	Czechoslovakia	..	L-39 Albatross	Jet trainer	1972	1978-87	(200)	Replacing L-29 Delfin
		..	BMP-1	MICV	(1972)	1972-87	(4 800)	70 % of Czechoslovakian BMP production
	Romania	..	Yak-52	Trainer	(1980)	1981-88	(1 450)	About 200/year produced for USSR
6 Yugoslavia	Canada	1	CL-215	Amphibian	1986			Replacing 1 lost 1984
	USSR	..	SSC-3 L	SShM launcher	1983	1984-87	(8)	
		..	AT-3 Sagger	ATM	(1978)	1980-87	(480)	Arming Partizan helicopters
		..	SA-7 Grail	Port SAM	(1978)	1980-87	(480)	
		..	SSC-3	SShM	1983	1984-87	(40)	Coastal defence missile derived from Styx ShShM; replacing Samlet SShMs

II. Third World countries

| 9 Afghanistan | China | .. | Type-63 107mm | MRS | (1982) | 1982-87 | (252) | For Mujahideen; mortars, anti-aircraft artillery and heavy machine-guns also |

TRADE IN CONVENTIONAL WEAPONS 221

	Czechoslovakia	. .	Hong Ying-5	Port SAM	(1982)	1982-87	(650)	SA-7 copy; for Mujahideen
		. .	L-39 Albatross	Jet trainer	(1979)	1979-87	(16)	For Mujahideen; unconfirmed
	Egypt	. .	SA-7 Grail	Port SAM	(1984)	1985-87	(150)	Denied by Mujahideen and British; many
	Poland	. .	An-2	Lightplane	(1979)	1979-87	(19)	captured by USSR and Kabul forces
	UK	300	Blowpipe	Port SAM	1987	1987	(300)	
	USA	(600)	FIM-92A Stinger	Port SAM	(1986)	1987	(600)	For Mujahideen
	USSR	. .	AN-30 Clank	Survey aeroplane	(1985)	1985-87	(3)	
		. .	An-26 Curl	Transport	(1978)	1978-87	(48)	Replacing losses from fleet of approx
		. .	Mi-24 Hind-D	Hel	(1984)	1984-87	(27)	90 Hind-A/Bs
		. .	Mi-4 Hound	Hel	(1979)	1979-87	(13)	
		. .	Mi-8 Hip	Hel	(1979)	1979-87	(97)	
		. .	Su-22 Fitter-J	Fighter/grd attack	(1979)	1979-87	(32)	
		. .	BM-21 122mm	MRS	(1979)	1979-87	(130)	
		. .	BMP-1	MICV	(1979)	1979-87	(166)	May include Czechoslovakian-built BMPs
		. .	BTR-50P	APC	(1979)	1979-87	(500)	
		. .	BTR-70	APC	(1978)	1979-87	(500)	May include some BTR-60s and BTR-80s
		. .	D-1 152mm	TH	(1979)	1979-87	(108)	Designation unconfirmed
		. .	D-30 122mm	TH	(1978)	1978-87	(340)	
		. .	M-46 130mm	TG	(1979)	1979-87	(112)	
		. .	PT-76	LT	1979	1979	(85)	
		. .	T-55	MBT	(1978)	1978-87	(475)	
		. .	T-62	MBT	(1979)	1979-87	(125)	
12 Algeria	Brazil	2	EMB-111	Mar patrol	1987			Negotiating package incl Urutu APCs,
		. .	EE-9 Cascavel	AC	(1987)			lorries and technology transfers; total value: approx $400 m
	Czechoslovakia	16	L-39 Albatross	Jet trainer	1987	1984-87	(3 500)	
	France	(4 000)	VP-2000	APC	1983			
	Morocco	. .	AMX-155 Mk-F3	SPH	(1987)	1987	1	Captured by Polisario 25 Feb 1987
	Yugoslavia	. .	G-4 Super Galeb	Jet trainer	(1987)			Negotiating
13 Angola	Brazil	2	EMB-111	Mar patrol	1987	1986-87	(6)	Order incl 4 AS-365Ns; total cost: $47 m
	France	6	SA-342K Gazelle	Hel	1985	1986-87	(96)	Arming SA-365 and Gazelle helicopters
		(96)	HOT	ATM	1985	1986-87	(150)	For UNITA
		(150)	Milan	ATM	(1986)	1987	(100)	For UNITA
		(100)	Milan-2	ATM	(1986)	1986-87	(4)	
	Switzerland	4	PC-9	Trainer	(1985)	1987	(100)	Part of $15 m aid for UNITA; unconfirmed
	USA	(100)	BGM-71A TOW	ATM	(1986)	1987	(100)	For UNITA; unconfirmed
		. .	FIM-92A Stinger	Port SAM	(1986)	1984-87	(27)	
	USSR	. .	Mi-24 Hind-C	Hel	(1983)			

Region code/ Recipient	Supplier	No. ordered	Weapon designation	Weapon description	Year of order	Year(s) of deliveries	No. delivered	Comments
		. .	Mi-8 Hip	Hel	(1982)	1983-87	(52)	Follow-on order; flown by Cuban pilots
		. .	MiG-23	Fighter/interceptor	(1986)	1986-87	(36)	
		. .	BMP-2	MICV	(1987)	1987	(65)	
		. .	BRDM-2	SC	(1985)	1986-87	(40)	
		(20)	BRDM-2 Gaskin	AAV(M)	(1983)	1983-85	(17)	
		. .	BRDM-2 Gaskin	AAV(M)	(1986)	1987	(120)	Designation unconfirmed
		. .	BTR-60P	APC	1987	1987	(150)	Includes some BTR-70s
		. .	D-30 122mm	TH	(1985)	1986-87	(80)	D-44 85mm guns also delivered
		. .	D-30 122mm	TH	(1987)	1987	(36)	
		. .	M-46 130mm	TG	(1986)	1986-87	(36)	
		(150)	T-55	MBT	(1987)	1987	(150)	
		(35)	T-62	MBT	(1987)	1987	(35)	Designation uncertain
		(33)	SA-3 SAMS	Mobile SAM system	(1980)	1981-87	(33)	
		(300)	SA-3 Goa	Landmob SAM	(1980)	1981-87	(300)	Unconfirmed
		(240)	SA-9 Gaskin	Landmob SAM	(1983)	1983-86	(240)	
		(1 920)	SA-9 Gaskin	Landmob SAM	(1986)	1987	(1 920)	
15 Argentina	Brazil	30	EMB-312 Tucano	Trainer	1987	1987	30	Partly offset by Brazilian technology purchase; total cost: $50 m
	France	(12)	MM-40 L	ShShM launcher	1980	1985-87	(3)	Arming 6 Meko-140 frigates
		(144)	MM-40 Exocet	ShShM/SShM	1980	1985-87	(96)	Arming 6 Meko-140 frigates
	Israel	1	B-707-320C	Transport	(1985)	1987	(1)	For ELINT duties
	Italy	4	A-109 Hirundo	Hel	1987			For Navy; total cost incl spares: $7 m
		4	SH-3D Sea King	Hel	1987			
		(15)	Palmaria 155mm	SPH	(1983)	1987	(3)	Order may be for gun only; for adaptation on TAM chassis
	Korea, South	2	SHORAR	Tracking radar	(1986)			
		2	Hyundai Type	LS	(1982)	1986	1	
8 Bahrain	France	2	MM-40 L	ShShM launcher	1985	1986-87	2	Arming 2 TNC-45 FACs
		(24)	MM-40 Exocet	ShShM/SShM	1985	1986-87	(24)	Arming 2 TNC-45 FACs
	Germany, FR	2	TNC-45	FAC	1985	1986-87	2	In addition to 2 ordered 1979
	UK	(24)	Sea Skua	AShM	(1985)	1987	(24)	Arming helicopter deployed on Type-42 corvettes
	USA	12	F-16C	Fighter	(1987)			Partly financed by Saudi Arabia; with ALQ-131, ALR-69 and ALE-40 ECM and laser designator

TRADE IN CONVENTIONAL WEAPONS

		(2)	F-16D	Fighter/trainer	1987	8	Last Northrop F-5s built
		8	F-5E Tiger-2	Fighter	1985	(7)	Deal worth $90 m
		7	M-198 155mm	TH	(1985)	36	Arming 2 Type 62-001 corvettes
		50	M-60-A3	MBT	1986	(4)	For 12 F-16s
		4	RGM-84A L	ShShM launcher	1987		For 12 F-16s
		(24)	AGM-65D	ASM	1984		For 12 F-16s
		(48)	AIM-7M Sparrow	AAM	(1987)		For 12 F-16s
		(96)	AIM-9L	AAM	(1987)		For emergency stockpile as part of US Special Defense Acquisition Fund
		..	AIM-9P	AAM	(1987)	(250)	Terms include strict US safeguards; deal worth $7.1 m incl 14 launchers
					1986		Arming 2 Type 62-001 corvettes
		70	FIM-92A Stinger	Port SAM	1987		
		(48)	RGM-84A Harpoon	ShShM	1984	(48)	
					1987-88		
9	Bangladesh						
	Indonesia	1	AS-332	Hel	(1987)		Negotiating; for VIP use
13	Benin						
	France	2	ATR-42	Transport	(1987)		Negotiating
		1	Buffalo	APC	(1986)	1	Command vehicle
		(9)	VBL	Recce AC	(1986)		
15	Bolivia						
	Argentina	(12)	IA-63 Pampa	Jet trainer	(1987)		Negotiating
	Brazil	3	HB-315B Gavaio	Hel	1985		Deal worth $3.8 m
	USA	10	Model 205 UH-1H	Hel	(1987)	10	Surplus; against drug smugglers
13	Botswana						
	Indonesia	..	CN-235	Transport	(1987)		Unconfirmed
		6	Model 206B	Hel	(1986)		Unconfirmed
		(12)	V-150 Commando	APC	(1986)		Unconfirmed
	USA	1	AN/TPS-63	Surveillance radar	(1985)	1	
15	Brazil						
	Argentina	10	IA-63 Pampa	Jet trainer	(1987)		Negotiating
	China	(30)	F-7	Fighter	(1987)		Negotiating; linked to Chinese purchase of EMB-312
	France	6	AS-332	Hel	1985	6	For AF; reduced from 10
		10	AS-332	Hel	1986	10	For Navy; 6 used Brazilian Pumas will be part of payment
		15	AS-332	Hel	1987		For Navy
		30	AS-350 Ecureuil	Hel	1986	30	Co-produced by Helibras; for Navy
		11	Twin Ecureuil	Hel	1985	11	For Army; reduced from 15
		11	Twin Ecureuil	Hel	(1986)		For Navy
		2	MM-40 L	ShShM launcher	1984	(2)	Arming Inhauma Class frigates; future vessels will carry Brazilian Barracuda ShShMs

224 MILITARY EXPENDITURE, ARMS TRADE, CONFLICTS

Region code/ Recipient	Supplier	No. ordered	Weapon designation	Weapon description	Year of order	Year(s) of deliveries	No. delivered	Comments
		(24)	AM-39 Exocet	AShM	1985	1987	(12)	Arming 6 AS-332 helicopters on order
		(24)	MM-40 Exocet	ShShM/SShM	1984	1987	(24)	Arming Inhauma Class frigates; future vessels will carry Brazilian Barracuda ShShMs
	Germany, FR	1	Type 209/3	Submarine	1982	1987	1	Order incl 3 submarines for licensed production; also designated Type 1400
	Korea, South	25	F-5E Tiger-2	Fighter	(1986)			Negotiating
	Sweden	24	BOFI 40mm	Mobile AA system	1985	1986-87	(20)	For delivery 1986-87; total value: SEK 200 m
	UK	32	Sea Skua	AShM	1985	1986-87	(32)	Arming Lynx helicopters
	USA	4	B-707-320C	Transport	1985	1986-87	(4)	In tanker/transport configuration
		3	C-130C Hercules	Transport	(1987)			Attrition replacement
		3	Learjet-35A	Mar patrol/trpt	1987	1987	3	
		1	Model 208	Lightplane	(1987)	1987	1	For photographic survey
10 Brunei	France	30	VAB	APC	1987			
	USA	2	S-70C	Hel	1986	1987	(2)	
13 Burkina Faso	Italy	2	S-211	Trainer	(1986)			Unconfirmed
10 Burma	Viet Nam	(1)	BM-21 122mm	MRS	(1986)	1987	1	Transferred via Laos
13 Cameroon	France	4	Alouette-3	Hel	1987			
		7	Magister	Jet trainer	1987			
		2	SA-330 Puma	Hel	1987			
	Germany, FR	4	Do-228-200	Transport	(1985)			
	Israel	4	IAI-202 Arava	Transport	(1987)			Still in negotiation
		(10)	Kfir-C7	Fighter	(1987)	1987	2	In negotiation since 1985
	USA	(6)	UH-60 Blackhawk	Hel	(1986)			
		30	Swift 105 Type	PC	1986			Patrol craft
13 Chad	France	59	AML-90	AC	(1985)	1986-87	59	Many installed on Toyota lorries
	Libya	..	Milan	ATM	(1986)	1986-87	(400)	11 captured from Libya in 1987 fighting
		..	L-39Z Albatross	Jet trainer	1987	1987		3 captured from Libya; subsequently sold to France and USA
		..	Mi-24 Hind-D	Hel	1987	1987		
		..	SF-260 Warrior	Trainer/COIN	1987	1987		9 captured from Libya
		..	AML-90	AC	1987	1987		4 captured from Libya
		..	BM-21 122mm	MRS	1987	1987		Approx 20 captured from Libya

TRADE IN CONVENTIONAL WEAPONS 225

		BMP-1	MICV	..	1987	146 captured from Libya
		BRDM-2	SC	..	1987	10 captured from Libya
		BTR-60P	APC	..	1987	10 captured from Libya
		D-30 122mm	TH	..	1987	Approx40 captured from Libya
		EE-9 Cascavel	AC	..	1987	8 captured from Libya
		SA-13 TELAR	AAV(M)	..	1987	4 captured from Libya; subsequently sold to France and USA
		T-55	MBT	..	1987	113 captured from Libya; may include some T-54s
		T-62	MBT	..	1987	12 captured from Libya
		ZSU-23-4 Shilka	AAV	..	1987	4 captured from Libya
		Long Talk	Surveillance radar	..	1987	At least 1 captured from Libya
		P-12	Early warning radar	..	1987	At least 1 captured from Libya
		SA-3 SAMS	Mobile SAM system	..	1987	10 captured from Libya
		SA-6 SAMS	Mobile SAM system	..	1987	12 captured from Libya
		Thin Skin	Heightfinding radar	..	1987	At least 1 captured from Libya
		Two Spot	Fire control radar	..	1987	At least 1 captured from Libya
		AT-3 Sagger	ATM	..	1987	At least 100 captured from Libya
		SA-13 Gopher	Landmob SAM	..	1987	At least 16 captured from Libya; subsequently sold to France and USA
		SA-3 Goa	Landmob SAM	..	1987	At least 20 captured from Libya
		SA-6 Gainful	Landmob SAM	..	1987	At least 36 captured from Libya
		SA-7 Grail	Port SAM	..	1987	At least 100 captured from Libya
	USA	BGM-71C I-TOW	ATM	50	(1987) 1988	Incl 5 launchers
		FIM-92A Stinger	Port SAM	24	1987	Total may be 30 missiles and 10 launchers
15 Chile	France	Mirage-50	Fighter/MRCA	(3)	(1987)	Negotiating
		MM-38 Exocet	ShShM	(12)	1986	Arming ex-RN County Class destroyer HMS Glamorgan
		MM-38 Exocet	ShShM	(12)	1986	Arming Ex-RN County Class destroyer HMS Fife
	Germany, FR	MM-38L	ShShM launcher	(1)	1986	1 delivered complete; assembly of up to 30 planned
		Bo-105CB	Hel	(30)	1985	Armed with 105mm gun
	Israel	M-4 Sherman	MT	(30)	1987	
	Spain	C-101 Aviojet	Jet trainer	23	1984	
		C-212-200	Transport	(6)	(1986)	Unconfirmed
	UK	MM-38 L	ShShM launcher	1	1986	Arming Ex-RN County Class destroyer HMS Glamorgan
		Sea Slug L	SAM launcher	6	(1981) 1982-87	Equipping County Class destroyers
		Sea Slug	SAM	(72)	(1981) 1982-87	Arming County Class destroyers

226 MILITARY EXPENDITURE, ARMS TRADE, CONFLICTS

Region code/ Recipient	Supplier	No. ordered	Weapon designation	Weapon description	Year of order	Year(s) of deliveries	No. delivered	Comments
15 Colombia	Israel	1	County Class	Destroyer	1986	1987	1	Ex-Royal Navy HMS Glamorgan; hit by Exocet in 1982 and repaired
	Israel	1	County Class	Destroyer	1987	1987	1	Ex-Royal Navy HMS Fife
	Israel	14	Kfir-C2	Fighter	1981			Deal reactivated after US ban on sales lifted
	Spain	3	C-212-200	Transport	1986	1986-87	(3)	For AF airline SATENA
	USA	(6)	UH-60 Blackhawk	Hel	(1987)			Drug traffic control; cost incl training and support; $36 m; for Army
13 Cote d'Ivoire	USA	1	Metro-2	Transport	(1985)	1987	(1)	
14 Cuba	Peru	16	An-26 Curl	Transport	(1986)	1987	(16)	Number undisclosed; maximum of 16
	USSR	..	BMP-1	MICV	(1980)	1981-87	(70)	Unconfirmed
		(500)	SA-14 Gremlin	Port SAM	(1985)	1986-87	(500)	Unconfirmed
13 Djibouti	France	7	VBL	Recce AC	(1986)	1987	7	
15 Dominica	USA	(4)	A-37B Dragonfly	Fighter/COIN	(1986)	1987	(4)	Supplied for drug trade interception
15 Ecuador	Austria	(50)	Cuirassier	LT/TD	(1987)			Surplus vehicles; transfer being negotiated by a French broker
	Canada	3	DHC-6	Transport	1985	1986-87	(3)	
	Israel	12	Kfir-C7	Fighter	(1986)	1986-87	(12)	
		(2)	Barak Launcher	ShAM launcher	(1984)			Unconfirmed
		(16)	Barak	ShAM/SAM/PDM	(1984)			
		(96)	Shafrir-2	AAM	(1986)	1987	(96)	Arming Kfir-C7s
	Italy	(6)	A-109 Hirundo	Hel	(1986)			
	UK	6	BAC-167	Trainer/COIN	(1987)	1987-88	6	
	USA	5	Model 206B	Hel	(1986)			For Esmeralda Class corvettes
		1	Sabreliner	Transport	(1987)	1987	1	
		25	T-33A	Jet trainer	1985	1986-88	(25)	Ex-US reserves; refurbished to AT-33 standard before transfer
8 Egypt	France	20	Mirage-2000	Fighter	1981	1986-87	20	Ordered Dec 1981; total cost: $1000 m
		(20)	Mirage-2000	Fighter	(1986)			Option on 16-20 more taken up 1984 but still under discussion; assembly in Egypt possible

TRADE IN CONVENTIONAL WEAPONS 227

	(60)	ARMAT	ARM	1984	1986-87	(60)	Arming Mirage-2000s
	(60)	AS-30L	ASM	1983	1986-87	(60)	Arming Mirage-2000s
	(120)	R-550 Magic	AAM	1983	1986-87	(120)	Arming Mirage-2000s
	(80)	Super-530	AAM	1983	1986-87	(80)	Arming Mirage-2000s
Germany, FR	2	Jetstar-2	Transport	(1986)	1987	2	
Italy	(18)	Skyguard Unit	Mobile SAM system	1982	1985-87	(18)	18 btys comprising 2 twin 35mm AAGs and 2 quadruple Sparrow launchers
Libya	1	C-130C Hercules	Transport	1987	1987	1	Flown to Egypt by Libyan defectors on 2 Mar 1987
Netherlands	1	CH-47B Chinook	Hel	1987			Transferred by defectors 29 Mar 1987
	2	Alkmaar Class	Minehunter	(1986)			
Spain	600	BMR-600	ICV	1982	1985-87	(300)	Deal includes 3000 lorries; deliveries suspended in 1987 due to payment disputes
USA	6	Commuter-1900	Transport	1985	1988	(6)	2 for electronic surveillance and maritime patrol; delivery to start 1988
	4	E-2C Hawkeye	AEW	1983	1986-87	4	Deal worth $689 m
	1	E-2C Hawkeye	AEW	1985	1987	1	Deal worth $50 m
	34	F-16C	Fighter	1982	1986-87	(34)	Agreement in principle for a total of 150 aircraft; total cost incl 6 F-16D trainers: $1.2 b
	40	F-16C	Fighter	(1987)			Third order of 40; incl unspecified number of F-16Ds; for delivery 1989-90
	6	F-16D	Fighter/trainer	1982	1986-87	(6)	Unspecified number for delivery 1986-87; total cost: $22.8 m
	..	Commando Scout	Recce AC	(1986)	1986-87	(200)	
	48	M-109-A2 155mm	SPH	1985	1986-87	(48)	In addition to 100 supplied 1984
	472	M-113-A2	APC	(1984)	1985-87	(472)	US LoO Mar 1984; total cost incl M-125s, M-577s and M-548s: $157 m
	90	M-113-A2	APC	(1987)			
	42	M-198 155mm	TH	1983	1986-87	(42)	US LoO Oct 1983
	33	M-548	APC	1984	1986-87	(33)	US LoO Mar 1984
	56	M-88-A1	ARV	1984	1985-87	(56)	Deal worth $63 m
	2	AN/TPQ-37	Tracking radar	1986			
	..	AN/TPS-59	3-D radar	(1982)	1983-88	5	Total value: $190 m; assembly in Egypt of 34 more to follow
	8	AN/TPS-63	Surveillance radar	1984	1987	1	
	34	AN/TPS-63	Surveillance radar	(1985)	1987	(1)	To be completed by end 1992
	(10)	I-Hawk SAMS	Mobile SAM system	(1985)	1987	10	Third order
	26	M54 Chaparral	Mobile SAM system	1983	1986-87	(26)	Part of Skyguard air defence system
	424	AIM-7M Sparrow	AAM	(1984)	1985-87	(336)	Arming F-16s; incl training missiles
	282	AIM-7M Sparrow	AAM	(1987)			

228 MILITARY EXPENDITURE, ARMS TRADE, CONFLICTS

Region code/ Recipient	Supplier	No. ordered	Weapon designation	Weapon description	Year of order	Year(s) of deliveries	No. delivered	Comments
		560	AIM-9L	AAM	(1986)	1987	(189)	Arming F-16 fighters; total cost: $42 m
		(120)	MIM-23B Hawk	Landmob SAM	(1985)	1987	(120)	Third order
		483	MIM-72F	SAM/ShAM	1983	1986-87	(483)	Deal worth $160 m incl 26 towed launchers
		(800)	MIM-72F	SAM/ShAM	1983			Arming 25 Chaparral btys
		514	RIM-7M Sparrow	SAM	(1987)			For Skyguard/Sparrow air defence system; total cost incl 282 AIM-7M AAMs: $190 m
10 Fiji	Australia	(4)	ASI-315	PC	1985	1987	(2)	Status of programme unclear after military coup
	Israel	(3)	IAI-202 Arava	Transport	(1986)			
13 Gabon	France	3	AS-350 Ecureuil	Hel	(1984)	1984-87	(3)	
		5	SA-342L Gazelle	Hel	(1985)	1986-87	(5)	3 armed with HOT ATMs; part of package incl aircraft, missiles and ships
		(24)	AML-90	AC	(1985)	1986-87	(24)	Unconfirmed
		4	ERC-20 Kriss	Recce/AAV	1985	1987	(4)	
		6	ERC-90 Sagaie	AC	1985	1986-87	(6)	
		(9)	VBL	Recce AC	(1986)	1987	(6)	
		(72)	HOT	ATM	1985	1986-87	(72)	Arming 3 Gazelle helicopters
		(100)	Milan	ATM	(1985)	1986-87	(100)	
		2	P-400 Class	PC/FAC	1985	1987	(1)	For Presidential Guard
	Italy	1	ATR-42	Transport	(1985)	1987	(1)	Ordered Aug 1981
	Spain	2	Pelicano Class	LC	1981			
	USA	(15)	V-150 Commando	APC	(1985)	1987	(15)	
13 Ghana	Italy	2	MB-339A	Jet trainer	1987			
14 Honduras	UK	2	Jetstream-31	Transport	(1986)			
	USA	12	F-5E Tiger-2	Fighter	1987	1987	(2)	From USAF stocks; cost incl 2 F-5Fs: $75 m; deliveries due to be complete by Apr 1989
		2	F-5F Tiger-2	Jet trainer	1987	1987	1	From USAF stocks; part of 14 aircraft deal
9 India	France	9	Mirage-2000	Fighter	1986	1987	9	In addition to 40 ordered 1982; licensed production option dropped
		..	MM-38 L	ShShM launcher	(1983)			Arming Khukhri Class corvettes; unconfirmed

TRADE IN CONVENTIONAL WEAPONS

	(98)	ARMAT	ARM	1984		(98)	For Mirage-2000; unconfirmed
	(156)	AS-15	AShM	1987			Possibly arming Do-228 aircraft instead of BAe Sea Skua; unconfirmed
	(200)	AS-30L	ASM	(1984)	1987	(100)	For Mirage-2000; unconfirmed
	..	MM-38 Exocet	ShShM	(1983)			Arming new missile corvettes; unconfirmed
	(392)	Magic-2	AAM	(1984)	1986-87	(392)	Arming Mirage-2000s
	(558)	R-550 Magic	AAM	(1979)	1981-87	(558)	Arming 93 Jaguar fighters
	(186)	R-550 Magic	AAM	(1984)	1986-87	(124)	Arming 31 Jaguar fighters
	(296)	Super-530	AAM	1984	1986-87	(296)	Arming Mirage-2000s
Germany, FR	3	Do-228-100	Transport	1983	1987	3	Maritime patrol aircraft for Coast Guard delivered prior to licensed production
							Licensed production in progress
Netherlands	2	Type 1500	Submarine	1981	1987	2	To be followed by assembly; replaces Fledermaus in Indian Army
	8	Flycatcher	Mobile AA system	1987			
Poland	4	Polnocny Class	LS	(1985)			Possibly for licensed production; in addition to 8 in service
Singapore	(2)	Type 45	PC	1986	1987-88	(2)	For Coast Guard; additional 4 to be built in India
Sweden	410	FH-77 155mm	TH	1986	1986-87	(190)	Deal worth $1300 m incl ammunition, SAAB lorries and production technology; delivery over 5 years; co-production to follow
UK	3	Commando Mk-3	Hel	1986			
	10	Sea Harrier	Fighter	1985			Deal worth $230 m incl 1 trainer
	7	Sea Harrier	Fighter	1986			In addition to 19 ordered earlier
	1	Sea Harrier T-4	Fighter/trainer	1985			
	1	Sea Harrier T-4	Fighter/trainer	1986			
	25	Sea King HAS-5	Hel	1984	1986-87	(20)	In addition to 12 ordered 1983; to carry Sea Eagle AShMs; total cost: $80 m
	6	Sea King HAS-5	Hel	1986	1987	(2)	For delivery 1987-88; in addition to 37 ordered earlier
	(2)	Seacat L	ShAM launcher	(1986)	1987	(2)	Arming aircraft-carrier INS Viraat
	(1)	Watchman	Surveillance radar	(1987)	1987	(1)	For surveillance of missile test range
	(84)	Sea Eagle	AShM	1983			Arming Jaguar fighter bombers and Sea King helicopters
	(48)	Sea Eagle	AShM	1985	1987	(18)	Arming Sea Harriers
	(156)	Sea Skua	AShM	(1985)			Arming Navy and Coast Guard Do-228 aircraft; unconfirmed
	(24)	Seacat	ShAM/ShShM	(1986)	1987	(24)	Arming aircraft-carrier INS Viraat
USA	1	Hermes Class	AC carrier	1986	1987	1	Deal worth approx $74 m
	2	SRA-1	Recce	1987			

230 MILITARY EXPENDITURE, ARMS TRADE, CONFLICTS

Region code/ Recipient	Supplier	No. ordered	Weapon designation	Weapon description	Year of order	Year(s) of deliveries	No. delivered	Comments
	USSR	95	An-32 Cline	Transport	1980	1984-87	(95)	Delivery rate: 2/month; some Western avionics integrated
		23	An-32 Cline	Transport	1985	1987	23	Second order
		20	An-32 Cline	Transport	1987			Third order; built in USSR with Indian-made sub-systems
		20	Il-20	Transport	(1985)			Unconfirmed
		24	Il-76 Candid	Transport	1984	1985-87	(12)	Order increased from 20 to 24 in 1987
		(8)	Ka-27 Helix	Hel	(1985)	1985-87	(5)	8-18 ordered; on Kashin Class destroyers
		(100)	Mi-17 Hip-H	Hel	(1984)	1984-87	(70)	Replacing Mi-8s
		10	Mi-26 Halo	Hel	(1985)	1986-87	(10)	First 2 for evaluation
		(48)	MiG-29	Fighter	1984	1987	(48)	Assembled in India; initial delivery incl 4 2-seat trainers; eventual requirement may reach 150
		3	Tu-142 Bear	Recce/ASW	1984	1988	(3)	For Navy; deliveries in 1988 jeopardized by changes in Soviet production schedule
		..	SA-8 SAMS	Mobile SAM system	(1982)	1984-87	(32)	Reportedly operational early 1984
		6	SA-N-1 L	ShAM launcher	1982	1986-87	(4)	Arming 3 Kashin Class destroyers
		3	SA-N-4 L	ShAM launcher	(1978)	1983-87	(3)	Arming 3 Godavari Class frigates
		(5)	SA-N-4 L	ShAM launcher	1983			Arming 5 Nanuchka Class corvettes
		(6)	SSN-2 Styx L	ShShM launcher	(1978)	1983-87	(6)	Arming Godavari Class frigates
		3	SSN-2 Styx L	ShShM launcher	1982	1986-87	(2)	Arming 3 Kashin Class destroyers
		(5)	SSN-2 Styx L	ShShM launcher	1982	1986	(1)	Arming 5 Nanuchka Class corvettes
		(5)	SSN-2 Styx L	ShShM launcher	(1985)	1987	(1)	Arming Tarantul Class corvettes
		(576)	AA-7 Apex	AAM	(1984)	1987	(576)	Arming MiG-29s; designation unknown; may be AA-10 Alamos
		(386)	AA-8 Aphid	AAM	(1984)	1987	(386)	Arming MiG-29s
		..	SA-8 Gecko	Landmob SAM	(1982)	1984-87	(400)	Reportedly operational early 1984
		(72)	SA-N-1	ShAM	1982	1986-87	(48)	Arming 3 Kashin Class destroyers
		(60)	SA-N-4	ShAM	(1978)	1983-87	(60)	Arming 3 Godavari Class frigates
		(100)	SA-N-4	ShAM	1982			Arming 5 Nanuchka Class corvettes
		(36)	SSN-2 Styx	ShShM	(1978)	1983-87	(36)	Arming Godavari Class frigates
		(36)	SSN-2 Styx	ShShM	1982	1986-87	(24)	Arming 3 Kashin Class destroyers
		(60)	SSN-2 Styx	ShShM	1982	1986	(12)	Arming 5 Nanuchka Class corvettes
		(60)	SSN-2 Styx	ShShM	(1985)			Arming Tarantul Class corvettes
		1	Charlie-1 Class	NCMS	(1985)			Leased to Indian Navy; future delivery of up to 5 possible
		3	Kashin Class	Destroyer	1982	1986-87	(2)	In addition to 3 previously delivered
		8	Kilo Class	Submarine	(1984)	1986-87	2	Replacing Foxtrot Class
		(3)	Kresta-2 Class	Cruiser	(1983)			For delivery from 1988

TRADE IN CONVENTIONAL WEAPONS 231

	5	Nanuchka Class	Corvette	1982		In addition to 3 in service; for delivery from 1989
	12	Natya Class	MSO	1982	1984-87	
	(5)	Tarantul Class	Corvette	(1985)	1987	
	6	Yevgenia Class	MSC	(1985)	1987	In addition to 6 in service
10 Indonesia	2	Alkmaar Class	Minehunter	1985	1987	(1) First export order of Tripartite design; for delivery 1987-88
	4	V. Speijk Class	Frigate	1986	1986-87	(3) Request for further 2 depending on availability
Spain	6	CN-235	Transport	1987	1988	(3) For delivery by 1989
UK	(600)	FV-101 Scorpion	LT	(1987)		Negotiating
	(25)	Rapier SAMS	Mobile SAM system	1984	1986-87	(15) Total value: $128 m; offsets for Indonesian electronics industry
	(20)	Rapier SAMS	Mobile SAM system	1985		Repeat order; total value incl missiles: approx $100 m
	(10)	Rapier SAMS	Mobile SAM system	1986		Third order
	(8)	Seacat L	ShAM launcher	1986	1986-87	(6) Arming 4 Van Speijk Class frigates
	(300)	Improved Rapier	Landmob SAM	1984	1986-87	(170)
	(240)	Improved Rapier	Landmob SAM	1985		Repeat order; total value incl missiles: $100 m
	(120)	Improved Rapier	Landmob SAM	1986		Third order; total value: $60 m
	(96)	Seacat	ShAM/ShShM	1986	1986-87	(72) Arming 4 Van Speijk Class frigates
USA	8	F-16A	Fighter	1986		Delivery delayed until 1990 by financial difficulties; includes 4 F-16Bs; total cost $336 m; offsets worth $52 m
	4	F-16B	Fighter/trainer	1986		Together with 8 F-16A fighters
	8	RGM-84A L	ShShM launcher	1986	1986-87	(5) Arming 4 Van Speijk Class frigates
	(48)	AGM-65D	ASM	(1986)		Arming F-16s
	(48)	AGM-65D	ASM	1987		Arming F-16s
	(72)	AIM-9P	AAM	(1986)		Arming F-16s
	(96)	RGM-84A Harpoon	ShShM	1986	1986-87	(72) Arming 4 Van Speijk Class frigates
	8	RGM-84A Harpoon	ShShM	1987		
	4	Jetfoil	Hydrofoil FAC	1983	1984-87	4 In addition to 1 in service; total cost: $150 m; option on 6 more and licensed production of 36
8 Iran Afghanistan	..	FIM-92A Stinger	Port SAM	1987	1987	(9) Captured or bought from Afghan Mujahideen
China	24	F-6	Fighter	(1985)	1986-87	(24) Unconfirmed; reportedly part of $1.6 b deal allegedly signed Mar 1985
	..	F-7	Fighter	(1985)	1986-87	(24)
	..	T-59	MBT	(1986)	1987	(120)

232 MILITARY EXPENDITURE, ARMS TRADE, CONFLICTS

Region code/ Recipient	Supplier	No. ordered	Weapon designation	Weapon description	Year of order	Year(s) of deliveries	No. delivered	Comments
		(120)	Type 59/1 130mm	TG	(1986)	1987	(120)	
		:	Type-63 107mm	MRS	(1982)	1983-87	(700)	
		(8)	C-801 launcher	ShShM launcher	(1986)	1987	(8)	Unconfirmed
		:	Hai Ying-2 L	ShShM launcher	(1986)	1987-88	(8)	
		(100)	C-801	ShShM	(1986)	1987	(100)	May use HY-2 Silkworm fire control
		:	Hai Ying-2	ShShM/SShM	(1986)	1987-88	(96)	NATO designation: Silkworm
		:	Hong Jian-73	ATM	(1982)	1982-87	(5 000)	
		:	Hong Ying-5	Port SAM	(1986)	1987	(300)	
	Czechoslovakia	:	BMP-1	MICV	(1986)	1986-87	(200)	May be used Soviet BTR-60
		:	OT-64	APC	(1986)	1986-87	(200)	
	Germany, FR	6	Type 209/3	Submarine	1985			Originally ordered 1979; cancelled same year; order reopened for delivery after end of Iraq-Iran War
	Korea, North	:	Type 59/1 130mm	TG	(1983)	1983-87	(360)	Deliveries incl some Soviet M-46s
		:	Hai Ying-2 L	ShShM launcher	(1987)	1988	1	
		(6)	FROG-7	Landmob SSM	(1987)	1987	(6)	
		:	Hai Ying-2	ShShM/SShM	(1987)	1988	6	May be retransferred from China
	Libya	:	SCUD-B	Landmob SSM	1987	1987	(12)	
	Switzerland	(12)	PC-9	Trainer	(1985)			Unconfirmed
		(15)	AR-3D	3-D radar	1986			Denied by manufacturer
	UK	6	Watchman	Surveillance radar	(1987)			Negotiating
	Viet Nam	(5)	F-5E Tiger-2	Fighter	(1986)			Unconfirmed; reportedly part of $400 m arms package for old US equipment
		(12)	Model 205 UH-1H	Hel	(1986)			Unconfirmed
		:	M-107 175mm	SPG	(1986)			Unconfirmed
		(22)	M-113-A1	APC	(1986)			Unconfirmed; number may be as many as 200
		(80)	M-48 Patton	MBT	(1986)			Unconfirmed
		:	AIM-9E	AAM	(1986)			Unconfirmed
8 Iraq	Argentina	20	IA-58A Pucara	COIN	(1986)			Unconfirmed
	Brazil	(38)	Astros-II SS-30	MRS	(1985)	1986-87	(38)	Negotiating; in addition to 300 supplied 1984-85
		200	EE-3 Jararaca	SC	(1987)			
		250	EE-9 Cascavel	AC	1986	1987	(100)	Some with 25mm AA cannon
		:	Astros Guidance	Fire control radar	(1983)	1984-87	(10)	Fire control system for Astros MRS
	China	4	Tu-16	Bomber	(1985)			First export for Chinese Tu-16 copy; Chinese designation B-6
		:	T-59	MBT	(1981)	1982-87	(600)	

TRADE IN CONVENTIONAL WEAPONS 233

	30	Type 59/1 130mm	TG	(1981)	(576)	
		C-601	AShM	1987		Arming Tu-16 (B-6) bomber; deliveries may total 96
		Hai Ying-2	ShShM/SShM	(1986)	(72)	Arming Osa-2 Class FACs
Egypt	(80)	Hai Ying-2	ShShM/SShM	(1986)	(50)	From Brazil and from Egyptian licensed production; option on 30 more
		EMB-312 Tucano	Trainer	1983	1985-87	
	(70)	F-7	Fighter	1983	1983-87	(70)	Chinese version of MiG-21 assembled in Egypt
	10	SA-342L Gazelle	Hel	(1987)		Unconfirmed
	(100)	BM-21 122mm	MRS	(1985)	(150)	Numbers uncertain
	4	Sakr-30 122mm	MRS	(1987)	(100)	Egyptian version of BM-21 MRS
	40	SA-6 SAMS	Mobile SAM system	(1987)		Unconfirmed
		SA-6 Gainful	Landmob SAM	(1987)		Unconfirmed: 4 refurbished btys
		Sakr Eye	Port SAM	(1987)		Unconfirmed; unspecified number
		Mirage F-1C	Fighter/interceptor	1986	1986-87	(28)	Open-ended order for attrition replacements; delivery at 2/month 12 to 24 on order brings total since 1979 to 125-137
France	(12)	Mirage F-1C	Fighter/interceptor	(1987)		
	(150)	AMX-30 Roland	AAV(M)	1981	1982-87	(90)	At least 30 delivered by 1983
		AM-39 Exocet	AShM	1983	1983-87	(638)	Arming Mirage F-1s
		ARMAT	ARM	(1984)	1985-87	108	
		HOT	ATM	(1981)	1981-87	(1 400)	
		Milan	ATM	(1981)	1981-87	(4 200)	
		Roland-2	Landmob SAM	1981	1982-87	(900)	
Italy	2	A-109 Hirundo	Hel	1984		On 2 Wadi Class corvettes; total cost incl 5 AB-212ASW helicopters: $164 m; delivery halted due to war with Iran
	5	AB-212ASW	Hel	1984		On 4 Lupo Class frigates; delivery halted due to war with Iran
	(10)	Aspide/Albatros	ShAM/ShShM launcher	(1981)		Arming Lupo and Wadi Class; delivery prevented by war with Iran
	(14)	Otomat-2 L	ShShM launcher	(1981)		Arming Lupo and Wadi Class; delivery halted due to war with Iran
	(224)	Aspide	AAM/SAM/ShAM	(1981)		Arming 4 Lupo Class frigates and 6 Wadi Class corvettes; delivery prevented by war with Iran
	(60)	Otomat-2	ShShM	(1981)		Arming 4 Lupo Class frigates and 6 Wadi Class corvettes; delivery prevented by war with Iran
	4	Lupo Class	Frigate	1981		Order incl 6 Wadi Class corvettes and 1 Stromboli Class support ship; delivery prevented by war with Iran

234 MILITARY EXPENDITURE, ARMS TRADE, CONFLICTS

Region code/ Recipient	Supplier	No. ordered	Weapon designation	Weapon description	Year of order	Year(s) of deliveries	No. delivered	Comments
	South Africa	6	Wadi Class	Corvette	1981			Iraqi designation: Assad Class; delivery prevented by war with Iran
	Switzerland	(200)	G-5 155mm	TH	1984	1985-88	(200)	Total package worth $400 m
		(16)	PC-9	Trainer	(1985)	1987	(16)	Denied by manufacturer
		15	PC-9	Trainer	(1986)			Second order
	USA	45	Model 214ST	Hel	1985	1985-86	(25)	Commercial deal; may be for civil use
	USSR	. .	Mi-24 Hind-D	Hel	(1986)			Designation unconfirmed; reportedly part of $3 b deal
		(45)	MiG-27	Fighter/grd attack	(1986)			May include MiG-23s; withheld by USSR due to payment difficulties
		(24)	MiG-29	Fighter	(1986)	1987	(24)	Reported to contain degraded electronics
		. .	Su-25 Frogfoot	Fighter/grd attack	(1985)	1987	(40)	Designation unconfirmed; reportedly part of $3 b deal
		. .	BM-21 122mm	MRS	(1986)	1986-87	(240)	
		. .	BRDM-2 Gaskin	AAV(M)	1982	1982-87	(30)	Designation unconfirmed; reportedly part of $3 b deal
		. .	BTR-80	APC	(1986)			
		. .	D-30 122mm	TH	(1982)	1982-87	(504)	
		. .	M-1973 152mm	SPG	(1986)	1987	(40)	Mix of 152 and 122mm guns unknown
		. .	M-1974 122mm	SPH	(1986)	1987	(40)	Designation unconfirmed; reportedly part of $3 b deal
		. .	T-62	MBT	(1985)	1987	(150)	
		. .	T-72	MBT	(1985)	1987	(150)	
		. .	SA-6 SAMS	Mobile SAM system	1979	1980-87	(52)	
		. .	SA-8 SAMS	Mobile SAM system	(1982)	1982-87	(36)	
		. .	AA-7 Apex	AAM	(1986)	1987	(96)	
		(160)	AA-8 Aphid	AAM	(1985)	1987	(160)	Arming MiG-29s
		(144)	AA-8 Aphid	AAM	(1986)	1987	(144)	Arming MiG-29s
		. .	AT-4 Spigot	ATM	(1987)			Unconfirmed
		. .	SA-6 Gainful	Landmob SAM	1979	1980-87	(520)	
		. .	SA-8 Gecko	Landmob SAM	(1982)	1982-87	(432)	
		. .	SA-9 Gaskin	Landmob SAM	1982	1982-87	(240)	On BRDM-2 Gaskin vehicles
8 Israel	France	(6)	C-130B Hercules	Transport	(1987)			Negotiating
	USA	(20)	AS-365N	Hel	1987			To equip Saar FAC; US version of French design
		51	F-16C	Fighter	1983	1987	(40)	Deal worth $2200 m incl 24 F-16Ds; half grant, half credit

TRADE IN CONVENTIONAL WEAPONS 235

		(75)	F-16C	Fighter	1987		LoO only; alternative to cancelled Lavi fighter; may incorporate some Lavi avionics
		24	F-16D	Fighter/trainer	1983	1987	(24)
		25	Model 209 AH-1S	Hel	1986		
		150	AIM-7M Sparrow	AAM	1983	1986-87	(150) Arming F-15s; total cost: $52 m
8 Jordan	Austria	(200)	GHN-45 155mm	TH	(1984)		Unconfirmed
	Brazil	(180)	EE-11 Urutu	APC	1986	1987	(180) For special forces
	France	12	AS-332	Hel	(1987)	1987-88	(12) Agreement also covers modernization of Jordanian Mirage F-1s; order for 20 more planned 1990
		20	Mirage-2000	Fighter	1988		
	Spain	16	C-101 Aviojet	Jet trainer	1986	1987-88	(10) Deal worth $91 m; all to be delivered by May 1988
		1	C-212-200	Transport	1985	1987	(1) Option taken June 1985
		2	CN-235	Transport	1985	1987	(2) Negotiating
	UK	(248)	Khalid	MBT	(1987)		Marconi S-711 version
		(6)	S-700	Surveillance radar	1985		Deal signed during Thatcher visit 1985; designation unconfirmed
		..	S-723 Martello	3-D radar	1985		Negotiating
		(1 500)	Javelin	Port SAM	(1987)		
	USA	3	UH-60 Blackhawk	Hel	(1985)	1987	3 Instead of AS-332 helicopter
		3	UH-60 Blackhawk	Hel	(1986)	1987	3 Unconfirmed
	USSR	..	BRDM-2 Gaskin	AAV(M)	(1984)		Possibly financed by Iraq in return for Jordanian volunteer brigade
		(16)	BRDM-2 Gaskin	AAV(M)	1987		
		(12)	SA-13 TELAR	AAV(M)	(1987)		
		(192)	SA-13 Gopher	Landmob SAM	(1987)		
		(200)	SA-14 Gremlin	Port SAM	(1987)	1987	(200)
		..	SA-9 Gaskin	Landmob SAM	(1984)		Unconfirmed
		..	SA-9 Gaskin	Landmob SAM	(1987)		Unconfirmed
10 Kampuchea	Viet Nam	..	MiG-21F	Fighter	(1987)	1987	(12) Unconfirmed; designation uncertain; order may be for as many as 40
13 Kenya	Canada	4	DHC-5D Buffalo	Transport	1986	1986-87	(4)
	France	4	Otomat-2 L	ShShM launcher	1984	1987	(4) On 2 FACs ordered from UK
		(48)	Otomat-2	ShShM	1984	1987	(48) Arming 2 Type 56M FACs on order from UK
	UK	2	Type 56M	PC/FAC	1984	1987	(2) Similar to Omani Province Class
10 Korea, North	USSR	(45)	Mi-24 Hind-D	Hel	(1985)	1985-87	(45) Unconfirmed
		..	Su-25 Frogfoot	Fighter/grd attack	(1987)	1988	3 Reported to be in exchange for Soviet landing rights

Region code/ Recipient	Supplier	No. ordered	Weapon designation	Weapon description	Year of order	Year(s) of deliveries	No. delivered	Comments
10 Korea, South		(300)	AA-7 Apex	AAM	(1984)	1985-87	(300)	Reportedly arming MiG-23s
	France	..	MM-38 L	ShShM launcher	(1982)	1983-87	(4)	Arming HDC-1150 Class corvettes
		..	MM-38 Exocet	ShShM	(1982)	1983-87	(24)	Arming HDC-1150 Class corvettes
	Indonesia	10	CN-235	Transport	1986			For delivery from 1988 though S.Korea may buy C-130 Hercules instead
	UK	(600)	Javelin	Port SAM	(1986)			
	USA	(6)	C-130H-30	Transport	(1987)	1987	(50)	
		30	F-16C	Fighter	1981	1987-89	30	Cost incl 6 F-16Ds: $931 m; plans for total of 156
		6	F-16D	Fighter/trainer	1981	1986-87	6	LoO to Congress; from US stocks, total value of deal: $77 m
		24	F-4D Phantom	Fighter/interceptor	(1987)			US LoO (incl 60 engines) worth $115 m
		50	Model 205 UH-1H	Hel	1986			To be armed with TOW ATMs; total cost incl TOWs: $260 m
		42	Model 209 AH-1S	Hel	1986			
		(4)	RGM-84A L	ShShM launcher	(1985)	1985-86	(4)	Arming Ulsan Class frigates
		(144)	AIM-7M Sparrow	AAM	(1987)			Arming 24 F-4D Phantoms; unconfirmed
		504	BGM-71C I-TOW	ATM	(1985)			Arming 21 Model 209 Cobra helicopters
		(672)	BGM-71D TOW-2	ATM	1986			Arming AS-15 Cobra helicopters
		704	BGM-71D TOW-2	ATM	1987			
		(732)	FIM-92A Stinger	Port SAM	1986	1987	(150)	Deal worth $57 m incl 133 launch units
		..	RGM-84A Harpoon	ShShM	(1985)	1985-87	(144)	Arming Ulsan Class frigates
8 Kuwait	Egypt	..	Sakr Eye	Port SAM	1987			
	France	(78)	Magic-2	AAM	(1983)	1986-87	(78)	Arming Mirage F-1s
		(78)	Super-530	AAM	1983	1986-87	(78)	Arming Mirage F-1s
	Netherlands	(2)	Alkmaar Class	Minehunter	1987			Negotiating
	USA	(188)	M-113-A2	APC	1982	1984-87	(188)	
		4 840	BGM-71C I-TOW	ATM	1982	1984-87	(4 000)	Cost incl M-901s and M-113s: $97 m
10 Laos	USSR	(26)	MiG-21F	Fighter	(1987)	1987	(26)	
8 Lebanon	Israel	(36)	BTR-60P	APC	1987	1987	(18)	For Christian Militia
		(18)	M-1944 100mm	TG	1987	1987	(18)	For Christian Militia; designation uncertain
		(18)	T-54	MBT	1987	1987	(18)	For Christian Militia

TRADE IN CONVENTIONAL WEAPONS 237

13	Liberia	Romania	(6)	BM-21 122mm	MRS	(1986)	1987	(6)	Part of $4 m deal; also incl APCs, artillery, AA guns and anti-tank weapons
			(8)	BTR-50P	APC	(1986)	1987	(8)	Designation uncertain
			(8)	BTR-60P	APC	(1986)	1987	(8)	Designation uncertain
			(6)	M-1938 122mm	TG	(1986)	1987	(6)	Designation uncertain
			(8)	M-1944 100mm	TG	(1986)	1987	(8)	Designation uncertain
12	Libya	Austria	30	GHN-45 155mm	TH	(1987)	1987	30	Originally ordered by Brazil and redirected to Libya via Yugoslavia
		Brazil	(8)	EMB-111	Mar patrol	(1987)			Negotiating
			25	EMB-121 Xingu	Transport	(1987)			Negotiating
			(100)	EMB-312 Tucano	Trainer	(1987)			Negotiating for 100-150 aircraft
			(30)	Astros-II SS-40	MRS	(1985)	1986-87	(23)	
			(15)	Astros-II SS-60	MRS	(1987)	1987	(15)	
			..	EE-11 Urutu	APC	(1987)			Negotiating
			..	EE-3 Jararaca	SC	(1987)			Negotiating
			..	EE-9 Cascavel	AC	(1987)			Negotiating
			(100)	X-20 180mm	MRS	(1987)	1987	(50)	
			(3)	Astros Guidance	Fire control radar	(1985)	1987	(2)	Astros-II fire control system; denied by Brazilian Government
		Portugal	3	C-130B Hercules	Transport	(1987)	1987	3	Purchased through West German intermediaries; original owner uncertain
		USSR	...	SSN-2 Styx L	ShShM launcher	(1982)	1983-87	(20)	Land-based version
			(200)	AA-8 Aphid	AAM	(1986)	1987	(200)	Arming MiG-21,-23 and -25; replacing AA-2 Atoll; seen on Libyan MiG-23 only
			..	SSN-2 Styx	ShShM	(1982)	1983-87	(180)	Land-based version for protection of Gulf of Sirte
		Yugoslavia	2	Koni Class	Frigate	(1984)	1986	1	Based on Swedish Spica design; contract signed June 1985
			4	Koncar Class	FAC	1985			
13	Malawi	Germany, FR	3	Do-228-200	Transport	1985	1986	2	Third for delivery 1988
10	Malaysia	Indonesia	1	AS-332	Hel	(1987)			For trials
			4	CN-235	Transport	(1987)			Negotiating
		UK	6	Wasp	Hel	1987	1987	(6)	Ex-British Royal Navy
14	Mexico	France	40	ERC-90 Lynx	AC	1986	1987	(20)	For Navy
		Spain	10	C-212-200	Transport	1985	1986-87	(10)	
			20	PC-7	Trainer	1985	1986-87	(20)	
		Switzerland	1	B-727-200	Transport	(1987)			For VIP use; total cost: $40 m
		USA	2	Model 206L	Hel	(1985)	1987	2	Second order
			12	Model 206L	Hel	(1987)			For drug control

238 MILITARY EXPENDITURE, ARMS TRADE, CONFLICTS

Region code/ Recipient	Supplier	No. ordered	Weapon designation	Weapon description	Year of order	Year(s) of deliveries	No. delivered	Comments
12 Morocco	Brazil	8	Model 212	Hel	(1985)	1987	8	Surplus
		30	T-33A	Jet trainer	1987	1987	30	17 on loan from Libya for training prior to delivery from Brazil
	Denmark	60	EE-11 Urutu	APC	(1985)	1986-87	(60)	
	France	2	Osprey-55 Class	OPV	(1985)	1987	1	
		20	AML-90	AC	(1987)			
		108	AMX-10RC	Recce AC	1978	1982-87	(90)	
		32	AMX-155 Mk-F3	SPH	(1985)	1987	(32)	
		. .	HOT-2	ATM	1987			
	Libya	. .	AT-4 Spigot	ATM	(1987)			Unconfirmed; for Polisario insurgents
	Spain	3	Lazaga Class	PC/FAC	1985			In addition to 4 FACs delivered; option for 3 more
		6	Vigilance Class	PC	1985			Development of Lazaga Class; for fishery protection
	USA	1	KC-130H	Tanker/transport	(1985)	1987	(1)	In addition to 4 in service
		100	M-48-A5	MBT	1987			LoO to Congress July 1987; deal worth $68 incl ammunition and communication equipment
		. .	BGM-71C I-TOW	ATM	(1985)	1987	(200)	Undisclosed number ordered
14 Nicaragua	India	24	HTT-34	Trainer	(1987)			Negotiating; barter for oil; first export order
	Poland	(8)	An-2	Lightplane	(1987)			
	USA	(1)	DC-6	Transport	(1987)	1987	(1)	For Contras
		(150)	FIM-43A Redeye	Port SAM	(1987)	1987	(150)	Part of $100 m FY1987 Contra aid; also heavy machine-guns and 81mm mortars
	USSR	(12)	Mi-17 Hip-H	Hel	1987	1987	(12)	For fleet expansion and replacing losses
		(15)	Mi-24 Hind-D	Hel	(1985)	1985-87	(15)	Size of order confirmed only by Pentagon spokesman; 6 aircraft known to have been delivered
		(6)	Mi-24 Hind-E	Hel	(1986)	1987	(6)	
		(35)	Mi-8 Hip	Hel	(1981)	1981-87	(21)	Order confirmed by US DOD who claim all 35 have been delivered, which is now in doubt
		(20)	T-55	MBT	(1986)	1986	(20)	Unconfirmed
		(100)	SA-14 Gremlin	Port SAM	(1986)	1986-87	(100)	Unconfirmed
13 Nigeria	Czechoslovakia	(24)	L-39 Albatross	Jet trainer	(1984)	1986-87	(24)	Unconfirmed

TRADE IN CONVENTIONAL WEAPONS 239

	France	12	SA-330L Puma	Hel	1985	1986-87	(12)	Deal incl trade-in of 9 old Pumas
		40	ERC-90 Sagaie	AC	(1986)	1987-88	40	Ordered June 1983; deal worth $100 m
	Italy	2	Lerici Class	Minehunter	1983	1987	2	Negotiating; re-purchased by UK from Saudi Arabia
	UK	(18)	Lightning F-53	Fighter/interceptor	(1987)			Negotiating; re-purchased by UK from Saudi Arabia
		(4)	Lightning T-55	Fighter/trainer	(1987)			Negotiating; re-purchased by UK from Saudi Arabia
	USA	5	CH-47C Chinook	Hel	(1987)			Ordered Feb 1983; delivery halted due to funding problems; being re-negotiated
	USSR	12	MiG-21MF	Fighter	1984			Agreed late 1984
		6	MiG-21UTI	Jet trainer	1984			Agreed late 1984
8 Oman	Egypt	(6)	Fahd	APC	(1985)	1988	(6)	6 delivered before Feb 1988
	France	(24)	Vadar	AAV	(1980)	1985-87	(15)	
		(1)	MM-40 L	ShShM launcher	1986			Arming fourth Province Class FAC
		(24)	MM-40 Exocet	ShShM/SShM	1986			Arming fourth Province Class FAC
	UK	8	Tornado ADV	Fighter/MRCA	1987			Contract signed 1987 after years of financial problems; cost: $362.5 m Arming 8 Tornado ADV fighters; postponed until 1992
		48	Sky Flash	AAM	1985			
		1	Province Class	FAC	1986			In addition to 3 in service; for delivery 1988
9 Pakistan	Austria	(200)	GHN-45 155mm	TH	(1987)			Negotiating
	China	(100)	A-5 Fantan-A	Fighter/grd attack	1984	1986-87	(70)	For delivery 1986-88
		60	F-7	Fighter	(1983)	1986	(60)	Licensed production to follow
		(150)	F-7	Fighter	(1987)			Final requirement may be 300; to have US engine and fire control systems
	France	. .	T-59	MBT	(1975)	1978-87	(750)	
		(2)	Falcon-20G	Mar patrol	(1986)	1987	(2)	
	Sweden	. .	Giraffe	Fire control radar	(1986)	1987	(4)	Ordered with RBS-70 SAMs
		(800)	RBS-70	Port SAM	(1985)	1986-87	(800)	Version RBS-70+; deal includes Giraffe radars
	UK	(2)	EH-101	Hel	(1987)			Unconfirmed; to equip Type-23 frigate
		(24)	Seawolf-1	ShAM/PDM	(1987)			Unconfirmed; vertical launch system arming Type-23 frigates
		3	Type-23	Frigate	(1987)			Contract jeopardized by wrangle over price
	USA	. .	E-2C Hawkeye	AEW	(1987)			Negotiating; USA may offer ground radars instead to accommodate India
		3	Model 204 UH-1B	Hel	(1986)	1987	3	
		88	M-109-A2 155mm	SPH	(1985)	1986-87	(44)	US LoO Sep 1985; total value: $78 m
		110	M-113-A2	APC	(1985)	1986-87	(110)	US LoO Sep 1985; total value: $25 m

240 MILITARY EXPENDITURE, ARMS TRADE, CONFLICTS

Region code/ Recipient	Supplier	No. ordered	Weapon designation	Weapon description	Year of order	Year(s) of deliveries	No. delivered	Comments
		60	M-198 155mm	TH	(1987)			Price incl support equipment
		4	AN/TPQ-37	Tracking radar	(1985)	1987	(1)	Arming F-16 fighters; total cost: $50 m; quick delivery of first 100
		500	AIM-9M	AAM	1985	1985-87	(500)	
		2 030	BGM-71C I-TOW	ATM	1986	1987		Deal worth $20 m
		2 386	BGM-71D TOW-2	ATM	1987		(400)	First Pakistani TOW-2 order; with 144 launchers
		..	FIM-92A Stinger	Port SAM	(1987)	1987	(150)	Unconfirmed; diverted from Afghan Mujahideen
14 Panama	Spain	3	C-212-200	Transport	1987	1988	3	First deal in Latin America
		1	CN-235	Transport	1987			
	USA	1	AN/TPS-70	Air defence radar	1987	1988	1	First of 6 for Caribbean
10 Papua New Guinea	Australia	4	ASI-315	PC	1985	1987	2	For delivery 1987-89
15 Paraguay	Brazil	(10)	EMB-110	Transport	(1985)	1986-87	(10)	
		6	EMB-312 Tucano	Trainer	1987	1987	(6)	Ordered July 1987
	Israel	..	IAI-201 Arava	Transport	(1985)			
15 Peru	Brazil	3	EMB-111	Mar patrol	(1986)			Unconfirmed
		20	EMB-312 Tucano	Trainer	(1986)	1987	20	Deal worth $32 m incl spares and training
	Canada	8	DHC-6	Transport	1985	1986-87	(8)	Deal worth $21.1 m
	France	12	Mirage-2000	Fighter	1982	1986-87	12	Order reduced from 26 for financial reasons; option on 2 more; armed with AM-39 Exocets
		(24)	AM-39 Exocet	AShM	1982	1985-87	(24)	Ordered Dec 1982; arming Mirage-2000s
		(48)	R-530	AAM	(1982)	1986-87	(48)	Reduced for financial reasons; arming Mirage-2000s
		(96)	R-550 Magic	AAM	(1982)	1986-87	(96)	Reduced for financial reasons; arming Mirage-2000s
	Italy	1	Otomat-2 L	ShShM launcher	(1986)	1987	1	For modernization of De Ruiter Class cruiser
		(12)	Otomat-2	ShShM	(1986)	1987	(12)	Unconfirmed
	Spain	(24)	BMR-600	ICV	(1986)			
	UK	1	BN-2A Islander		(1987)	1987	1	For Coast Guard
	USA		Boeing 707	Transport	(1986)	1987	1	Converted for aerial refuelling

TRADE IN CONVENTIONAL WEAPONS 241

		1	C-123 Provider	Transport	(1987)	1987	1	For drug interdiction
		4	C-130B Hercules	Transport	(1986)	1986-87	4	Ex-USAF
		3	L-100-30	Transport	(1985)	1987	3	Delivery delayed for financial reasons
		5	UH-60 Blackhawk	Hel	(1984)			Status of deal uncertain
	USSR	(15)	An-32 Cline	Transport	(1986)	1987	10	Revealed by order for US Litton navigation systems
10 Philippines	Italy	24	S-211	Trainer	(1987)			LoI signed 1987
	Korea, South	3	PSMM-5 Type	FAC	1986			Old order possibly re-opened; arms: 2 MM-38 Exocet ShShMs and Bofors 57mm gun
	USA	10	Model 205 UH-1H	Hel	1987	1987	10	Part of $900 m US 5-year aid package
		7	T-33A	Jet trainer	1987	1988	7	Formerly USAF based at Clark AFB
		10	UH-60 Blackhawk	Hel	(1987)	1987		
		25	V-150 Commando	APC	1987		(10)	Ex-US Army
8 Qatar	France	16	Mirage F-1C	Fighter/interceptor	1987			
		6	AMX-10P	MICV	1987			Includes 1 AMX-10PC
		6	AMX-155 Mk-F3	SPH	1987			
		(128)	AS-30L	ASM	(1987)	1987	11	Arming Mirage F-1s
		(128)	Magic-2	AAM	(1987)			Arming Mirage F-1s
		(64)	R-530	AAM	(1987)			Arming Mirage F-1s
		..	Roland-1	Landmob SAM	(1987)			
13 Rwanda	France	(9)	VBL	Recce AC	(1986)			
10 Samoa	Australia	1	ASI-315	PC	1985	1988	(1)	
8 Saudi Arabia	Brazil	..	Astros-II SS-30	MRS	1987	1987		Deal worth $500 m
		..	Astros-II SS-40	MRS	1987	1987	(15)	Deal worth $500 m
		..	EE-9 Cascavel	AC	1987			Ordered during visit of Brazilian Army Minister according to Brazilian press
	France	..	FILA	Point defence radar	1987			Part of $500 m deal
		2	ATL-2	Mar patrol	(1987)			
		(80)	AMX-30 Shahine	AAV(M)	1984	1986-87	(19)	Improved version developed with Saudi financial assistance
		600	ERC-90 Sagaie	AC	(1987)			Negotiating; deal incl modernization of French vehicles in Saudi arsenal
		..	Otomat-2 L	ShShM launcher	1984	1986-87	(8)	Coastal defence btys; 'Al Thakeb' deal
		48	Shahine-2 L	Mobile SAM system	1984	1986-87	(18)	'Al Thakeb' deal; 16 mounted on AMX-30 chassis; 32 towed version
		..	Otomat-2/Teseo	SShM	1984	1986-87	(48)	'Al Thakeb' deal; for coastal defence
		(1 000)	Shahine-2	Landmob SAM	1984	1986-87	(250)	Total value of 'Al Thakeb' deal: $4.1 b
	Germany, FR	(60)	Wildcat	AAV	(1986)			Unconfirmed

242 MILITARY EXPENDITURE, ARMS TRADE, CONFLICTS

Region code/ Recipient	Supplier	No. ordered	Weapon designation	Weapon description	Year of order	Year(s) of deliveries	No. delivered	Comments
	Indonesia	40	CN-212	Transport	1979	1983-87	(35)	All delivered at end 1987
	Italy	5	MB-339A	Jet trainer	(1986)	1987	(5)	Deal worth approx $100 m; 2 for passenger use, 2 transports
	Spain	4	CN-235	Transport	1984	1987	4	Deal worth $62 m
	Switzerland	140	BMR-600	ICV	1984	1986-87	(60)	UK workshare: 10%; part of Tornado deal
	UK	30	PC-9	Trainer	1986	1986-87	24	Part of Tornado deal
		30	Hawk	Jet trainer	1986	1987	(5)	Part of Tornado deal
		2	Jetstream-31	Transport	1986	1987	2	Part of $5 b deal; deliveries to begin 1989
		24	Tornado ADV	Fighter/MRCA	1986			
		48	Tornado IDS	Fighter/MRCA	1986	1986-87	(28)	Total value incl 72 Tornados, 30 Hawks, 30 PC-9s and missiles: approx $5.5 b; first 8 from RAF inventory
		(96)	ALARM	ARM	(1986)			Arming Tornado IDS fighters
		(192)	Sea Eagle	AShM	1985	1987	(48)	Arming Tornado IDS fighters
		(192)	Sky Flash	AAM	(1986)			Arming Tornado ADV fighters
	USA	1	B-727	Transport	(1987)	1987	1	
		5	E-3A Sentry	AEW	1981	1986-87	5	Deal worth $2.4 b; includes 8 KC-135 tankers
		(12)	F-15C Eagle	Fighter	1987			Attrition replacements; approved after US Congress voted to deny F-15E Strike Eagle
		8	KC-135	Tanker/transport	1981	1986-87	8	Part of AWACS deal
		15	Model-406CS	Hel	1987			Part of $400 m deal
		1	Super King Air	Transport	1987			Part of $400 m deal
		(13)	UH-60 Blackhawk	Hel	(1987)			Part of $400 m deal; 1 for VIP use
		200	M-2 Bradley	MICV	1987			
		(214)	M-88-A1	ARV	(1985)			Unconfirmed
		(20)	AN/TPS-32	3-D radar	(1985)	1987	(2)	
		(6)	AN/TPS-43	3-D radar	1985	1987	(1)	
		100	AGM-84A Harpoon	AShM	1986			
		1 177	AIM-9L	AAM	1981	1982-87	(1 177)	Arming F-15s
		995	AIM-9L	AAM	1986			Arming F-15s
		671	AIM-9P	AAM	1986			Number ordered also reported to be 495 For delivery 1989-91
		(528)	AIM-9P	AAM	(1986)			Arming Tornado fighters
		2 538	BGM-71C I-TOW	ATM	1983	1986-87	(900)	Deal worth $26 m
		(120)	BGM-71D TOW-2	ATM	(1987)			For 10 Model-406 helicopter
13 Senegal	Denmark	1	Osprey-55 Class	OPV	1984	1987	1	Built without helicopter pad

TRADE IN CONVENTIONAL WEAPONS 243

10 Singapore	France	22	Model-50 155mm		(1986)	1987	(6) Number uncertain
	France	22	AS-332	Hel	1984	1985-87	(22) Prior to licensed production of 5
	Germany, FR	1	Type 62-001	Corvette	(1985)		
	USA	2	C-130C Hercules	Transport	1987	1988	2 Option on 2 more
		2	E-2C Hawkeye	AEW	1983	1987	2 For delivery 1988; in addition to 4 F-16Bs
		4	F-16A	Fighter	1985		
		4	F-16B	Fighter/trainer	1987		Arming 6 Type 62-001 corvettes
		6	Phalanx	CIWS	(1986)		Arming Type 62-001 corvettes; unconfirmed
		6	RGM-84A L	ShShM launcher	(1986)		
		(6)	RGM-84A L	ShShM launcher	(1987)	1988	(1) Arming TNC-45 FACs
		(32)	AGM-65D	ASM	1985		Arming F-16s
		31	AGM-84A Harpoon	AShM	1985	1987	(15) Arming AS-332s; chosen over AM-39 Exocets
		(64)	AIM-9P	AAM	1985		Arming F-16s
		(72)	RGM-84A Harpoon	ShShM	(1986)		Arming Type 62-001 corvettes
		(72)	RGM-84A Harpoon	ShShM	(1987)	1988	(12) Arming refitted TNC-45 FACs
10 Solomon Islands	Australia	1	ASI-315	PC	1985	1988	(1)
13 Somalia	Ethiopia	11	T-54	MBT	1987	1987	11 Captured 12 Feb 1987 with AA guns, small arms, ammunition, lorries and supplies
	Italy	(6)	S-211	Trainer	(1985)		Unconfirmed
16 South Africa	Israel	..	Gabriel L	ShShM launcher	1974	1978-86	9 Arming Reshef Class FACs; in 1987 Israel publicly accepted UN embargo on S.Africa
	Spain	(3)	C-212-200	Transport	(1986)		For Bophuthatswana AF
	USA	1	C-212-200	Transport	1986	1987	1 Second-hand, bought from civil US airline
9 Sri Lanka	China	(10)	Y-12	Transport	1986	1986-87	(10) Unspecified number ordered in addition to 10 delivered 1986-87
		..	Y-12	Transport	(1987)		
	Israel	8	Dvora Class	FAC	1986	1987-88	(6) In addition to 6 delivered earlier
		(6)	Dvora Class	FAC	1987		
	Italy	2	SF-260TP	Trainer	(1986)	1987	(2) Replacing losses
		(6)	SF-260TP	Trainer	(1986)	1987	(6) Second 1986 order
	UK	9	BAC-167	Trainer/COIN	1987		Refurbished by BAe; ex-Kuwaiti trainers; total cost: $11 m
	USA	3	Model 212	Hel	(1986)	1987	3 Armed in Singapore

Region code/ Recipient	Supplier	No. ordered	Weapon designation	Weapon description	Year of order	Year(s) of deliveries	No. delivered	Comments
13 Sudan	China	(4)	F-7	Fighter	(1986)			Unconfirmed
	Ethiopia	. .	Mi-24 Hind-D	Hel	1987	1987	1	Flown by defector 21 Aug 1987
		(10)	SA-7 Grail	Port SAM	(1986)	1987	(10)	Used by SPLA rebels to destroy government C-130 in May; supplier unconfirmed
	Italy	6	AB-212	Hel	1984			Designation unconfirmed
	Libya	(4)	MiG-23	Fighter/interceptor	(1987)	1987	(4)	
	UK	10	BAC-167	Trainer/COIN	(1983)	1984	3	Deliveries halted for financial reasons
	USA	24	V-150 Commando	APC	(1986)	1987	(12)	
15 Suriname	Venezuela	1	Model 206A	Hel	1986	1987	(1)	From AF inventory
8 Syria	USSR	. .	MiG-23M	Fighter/interceptor	1981	1982-86	(95)	Incl some MiG-23BNs (grd attack version)
		. .	MiG-27	Fighter/grd attack	(1980)	1980-87	(48)	
		(150)	MiG-29	Fighter	(1986)	1987	24	USSR appears hesitant to deliver more
		. .	BMP-1	MICV	1981	1982-87	(1 200)	
		. .	T-72	MBT	1980	1980-86	(1 050)	
		. .	T-74	MBT	(1985)	1986-87	(200)	Unconfirmed
		. .	T-80	MBT	(1986)	1987	(50)	Unconfirmed
		. .	ZSU-23-4 Shilka	AAV	1981	1982-87	(150)	
		. .	SA-8 SAMS	Mobile SAM system	(1982)	1982-87	(48)	
		. .	AA-7 Apex	AAM	(1984)	1984-87	(200)	Unconfirmed; arming MiG-21s and MiG-23s
		(276)	AA-7 Apex	AAM	(1986)	1987	(138)	Arming MIG-29 fighters; designation uncertain, may be AA-10 Alamo
		. .	AA-8 Aphid	AAM	(1984)	1984-87	(800)	Unconfirmed; arming MiG-21s andMiG-23s
		(276)	AA-8 Aphid	AAM	(1986)	1987	(138)	Unconfirmed; arming MiG-29 fighters
		. .	AT-4 Spigot	ATM	(1980)	1981-87	(600)	
		. .	AT-5 Spandrel	ATM	(1984)	1984-87	(400)	Unconfirmed
		. .	SA-14 Gremlin	Port SAM	(1985)	1987	(100)	Replaces SA-7 Grail
		. .	SA-8 Gecko	Landmob SAM	1982	1982-87	(384)	
		. .	SA-9 Gaskin	Landmob SAM	1978	1980-87	(384)	
		(60)	Sepal	GLCM	(1986)			Coastal defence missiles which also have surface-to-surface capabilities
		4	Nanuchka Class	Corvette	(1984)			Reportedly on order
10 Taiwan	Denmark	18	F-104G	Fighter	(1986)	1987	18	From Royal Danish AF stocks
	Indonesia	(15)	AS-332	Hel	(1986)			Negotiating
	Netherlands	2	Zwaardvis Class	Submarine	1981	1987	2	

TRADE IN CONVENTIONAL WEAPONS   245

	USA		(75)	M-60-A3	MBT	1984		For local assembly; hulls to be fitted with locally produced engines and equipment; some sources report 215 on order and 140 more on option
			(140)	M-60-A3	MBT	(1985)		Probably a second order in 1985 for a further 140 valued at $39.6 m
			(1)	AN/TPQ-37	Tracking radar	1986		For Army
			(12)	M54 Chaparral	Mobile SAM system	1983	1985-87	
			(8)	M54 Chaparral	Mobile SAM system	(1985)		
			(100)	AIM-7M Sparrow	AAM	1983	1986-87	
			384	MIM-72F	SAM/ShAM	1983	1985-87	
			(362)	MIM-72F	SAM/ShAM	(1985)	1986-87	
10	Thailand	Austria	6	GHN-45 155mm	TH	1987		
		China	30	T-69	MBT	(1987)	(30)	Option on 70 more; cost substantially below market value
			(200)	Type 531	APC	(1987)		
			..	Type-69 Spaag	SPAAG	1987	(200)	Unconfirmed
			(3)	Romeo Class	Submarine	(1986)		In addition to 2 ordered 1984-85; order may be extended to 6 minesweepers
		Germany, FR	2	M-40 Type	MSC/PC	1984	1986-87	
			(4)	M-40 Type	MSC/PC	1986		
		Indonesia	(25)	NBo-105	Hel	(1979)	1983-87	
		Italy	(2)	Aspide/Albatros	ShAM/ShShM launcher	1984	1987	Arming 2 Tattankesin Class corvettes ordered from USA
			24	Spada	Mobile SAM system	1986	(20)	To use Aspide missiles
			(48)	Aspide	AAM/SAM/ShAM	1984	(2)	Arming 2 Tattankesin Class corvettes
			(32)	Aspide	AAM/SAM/ShAM	1987	(48)	
		Netherlands	2	F-27 Mk-400M	Transport	1986		In addition to 4 supplied earlier
		Switzerland	(1)	Fieldguard	Mobile AA system	(1986)		Number unconfirmed
			2	Skyguard SAMS	Mobile SAM system	1986		Contract signed end-1986; delivery in 1988; for use with Sparrow or Aspide SAM
		UK	12	Sherpa	Transport	1987		
		USA	8	F-16A	Fighter	1985	8	Number reduced from 16 for cost reasons; for delivery 1988-89; total cost incl 4 F-16Bs: $378 m
			6	F-16A	Fighter	1987		Order of acceptance not yet signed for financial reasons
			4	F-16B	Fighter/trainer	1985	(4)	For delivery 1988
			3	Learjet-35A	Mar patrol/trpt	1987		
			10	Model 208	Lightplane	1985	(10)	For Army
			4	Model 209 AH-1S	Hel	1986		Armed with TOW ATMs; US LoO July 1986
			5	Model 214ST	Hel	(1987)	(5)	For Navy
			24	Model 300C	Hel	1987		Following previous delivery of 24 in 1986

Region code/ Recipient	Supplier	No. ordered	Weapon designation	Weapon description	Year of order	Year(s) of deliveries	No. delivered	Comments
		40	M-48-A5	MBT	1987			In addition to 65 in service; final Thai decision pending
		108	Stingray	LT	1987			First to be delivered in 1989; part of a $300 m deal incl 6 F-16s and 40 M-48-A5s
		..	AN/MPQ-4	Tracking radar	(1986)	1987	(1)	
		2	AN/TPQ-37	Tracking radar	1985	1986-87	(3)	
		..	AN/TPS-70	Air defence radar	1985	1987	1	
		(2)	Phalanx	CIWS	1987			For Tattankesin Class corvettes
		(2)	RGM-84A L	ShShM launcher	1983	1987	(2)	Arming 2 Tattankesin Class corvettes on order from USA
		(32)	AGM-65D	ASM	1985			Arming F-16s
		(32)	AGM-65D	ASM	(1987)			Arming F-16s
		(96)	AIM-9P	AAM	(1985)			Arming F-16s
		(48)	AIM-9P	AAM	(1987)			Arming F-16s
		48	RGM-84A Harpoon	ShShM	1983	1987	(48)	Arming 2 Tattankesin Class corvettes
		(3)	Tattankesin Class	Corvette	1983	1987	2	
13 Togo	France	1	Alpha Jet	Jet trainer	1987			
		1	TB-30 Epsilon	Trainer	1987			
	UK	(9)	VBL	Recce AC	(1986)	1987	(9)	Unspecified number received; 2 seen in military parade but designation uncertain
		(5)	FV-101 Scorpion	LT	(1986)	1987	(5)	
10 Tonga	Australia	2	ASI-315	PC	1985			Part of Pacific Patrol Boat Programme
12 Tunisia	USA	57	M-198 155mm	TH	1986			Deal worth $60 m incl 70 lorries, ammunition, spares and support equipment
13 Uganda	Italy	6	AB-412 Griffon	Hel	1982	1985	(2)	Held in storage due to funding problems; at least 2 delivered late 1985
		4	S-211	Trainer	1987			To re-establish Ugandan AF
		6	SF-260 Warrior	Trainer/COIN	1987			To re-establish Ugandan AF
	Korea, North	(14)	BA-64	AC	(1987)	1987	(14)	Designation uncertain
		10	BM-21 122mm	MRS	(1987)	1987	10	Part of a shipment incl 14 armoured cars; 60 AAGs and SA-7 SAMs
		..	SA-7 Grail	Port SAM	(1987)	1987	(10)	Quantity may be larger

TRADE IN CONVENTIONAL WEAPONS 247

8 United Arab Emirates	Libya	3	Mi-24 Hind-D	Hel	(1987)	1987	(3)	Unconfirmed
	France	18	Mirage-2000	Fighter	1983			For Abu Dhabi; modified for US AIM-9
		(18)	Mirage-2000	Fighter	1985			Second order; modified for US AIM-9 Sidewinder missiles
		(72)	Super-530	AAM	(1983)	1985-87	(72)	Arming Mirage-2000s
		(72)	Super-530	AAM	(1985)			Arming second batch of 18 Mirage-2000s
	Germany, FR	3	TNC-45	FAC	(1987)			Unconfirmed; to be armed with Goalkeeper; MM-40 Exocet; Crotale SAMs and 76mm gun; for Abu Dhabi
	Italy	5	MB-339A	Jet trainer	1987	1988	5	For Dubai
	Singapore	(1)	Al Fey Class	Tank landing craft	(1986)	1987	1	
		(1)	LC 40M	LC	(1986)			
	USA	3	AN/TPS-70	Air defence radar	1987	1987-88	(3)	One launched Mar 1987
		(25)	AGM-65C	ASM	(1987)			For Bahrain; probably version C
		(108)	AIM-9P	AAM	1983	1985-87	(108)	Arming Mirage-2000s
		(108)	AIM-9P	AAM	(1985)			Arming second batch of 18 Mirage-2000s
10 Vanuatu	Australia	1	ASI-315	PC	1985	1987	1	
15 Venezuela	Brazil	30	EMB-312 Tucano	Trainer	1986	1986-87	(30)	Deal worth $50 m; option on 14 more
	Spain	4	Cormoran Class	FAC	1987			
13 Zaire	Egypt	4	Fahd	APC	1985	1988	4	
	Italy	..	S-211	Trainer	(1985)			Unconfirmed
	USA	1	B-727	Transport	(1986)	1987	1	
13 Zimbabwe	China	15	F-6	Fighter	1984	1987	15	
		15	F-7	Fighter	1984	1985-87	(15)	F-7 fleet may number up to 48
	France	6	Alouette-3	Hel	1987	1988	6	
	Italy	10	AB-412 Griffon	Hel	1985	1986-87	(10)	
		10	AB-412 Griffon	Hel	(1986)	1987	10	
	Spain	6	C-212-200	Transport	1987	1987	(1)	Second order
	UK	4	Hunter FGA-9	Fighter/grd attack	(1987)	1987	4	

Appendix 7C. Register of licensed production of major conventional weapons in industrialized and Third World countries, 1987

This appendix lists licensed production of major weapons for which either the licence was bought, production was under way, or production was completed during 1987. This year the column 'Year(s) of deliveries' includes aggregates of all licensed production since the beginning of the contract. The sources and methods for the data collection, and the conventions, abbreviations and acronyms used, are explained in appendix 7D. The entries are made alphabetically, by recipient, licenser and weapon designation.

Region code/ Country	Licenser	No. ordered	Weapon designation	Weapon description	Year of license	Year(s) of deliveries	No. produced	Comments
I. Industrialized countries								
7 Australia	Sweden	6	Type-471	Submarine	1987			Combat systems from Rockwell (USA); work divided 25/25/50 between Sweden, the USA and Australia
	Switzerland	65	PC-9	Trainer	1986	1987	2	In addition to 2 delivered directly; 17 for local assembly; 48 for 100% indigenous production
	UK	59	Hamel 105mm	TG	(1982)	1985-87	(32)	First batch; for production 1985-89
	USA	73	F/A-18 Hornet	Fighter	1981	1985-87	56	In addition to 2 delivered directly; total cost incl 18 F/A-18B trainers: A $3396 m; for delivery 1985-90
		25	UH-60 Blackhawk	Hel	1986	1988	(16)	Co-production in addition to previous orders for 30 Blackhawk/Seahawks
		2	FFG-7 Class	Frigate	1983			For completion 1991-93
4 Belgium	USA	44	F-16A	Fighter	1983			In addition to 116 F-16A/Bs in service; offset share: 80%; for delivery 1988-91
		664	AIFV	MICV	1980	1982-88	(525)	Total number ordered: 1189 incl 525 M-113s; unit cost: $100 000; for production 1982-88
		525	M-113-A1	APC	1979	1982-86	(370)	For production 1982-88
5 Bulgaria	USSR	. .	MT-LB	APC	(1980)	1982-87	(110)	Unconfirmed; some produced with BMP-2 turret
4 Canada	Germany, FR	. .	BK-117	Hel	(1986)			
		. .	Bo-105LS	Hel	(1981)	1987	(5)	Civilian and military versions

TRADE IN CONVENTIONAL WEAPONS 249

3 China	France	50	AS-365N	Hel	1980	1984-87	35	Ordered July 1980; initial batch of 50, of which about half for military use; may carry HOT ATMs
		(10)	Super Frelon	Hel	(1981)	1986-87	(4)	Prototypes flew Dec 1985; possibly reverse-engineered
5 Czechoslovakia	USSR	..	BMP-1	MICV	1971	1971-87	(8 200)	70% exported back to USSR
		..	T-72	MBT	1978	1981-87	(560)	
4 France	USA	..	FTB-337	Trainer	1969	1975-87	(85)	Designation: FTB-337 Milirole; exported widely to Africa
4 Germany, FR	USA	..	AIM-120A AMRAAM	AAM	(1987)		(13 956)	For delivery 1981-89; NATO co-production programme; 7277 produced by end-1984
		..	AIM-9L	AAM	1977	1981-87		Dornier/Diehl (FRG) main contractor for FRG, Belgium, Greece, Italy, Netherlands and Turkey; production began 1987
		10 000	NATO Stinger	Port SAM	1983	1987	(100)	
								MoU signed between USA, FRG and Denmark
		(10 000)	RAM	ShAM/PDM	1985			
4 Greece	Austria	292	Steyr-4K 7FA	APC	1986	1987	(100)	Leonidas-2 APCs and MICVs; follows 300 ordered in 1981
		324	Steyr-4K 7FA	APC	1987			Third order signed Dec 1987
4 Italy	France	23 000	Milan	ATM	1980	1985-86	2 190	Contract signed 1984
	USA	..	AB-205	Hel	(1963)	1977-87	(780)	
		..	AB-206B	Hel	1972	1978-87	(500)	Jetranger-3 version available from 1984
		..	AB-212	Hel	1970	1979-87	(90)	In production since 1971
		..	AB-212ASW	Hel	1975	1978-87	(175)	
		..	AB-412 Griffon	Hel	1980	1983-87	(38)	Military version of Bell Model 412; Italy holds marketing rights
		..	CH-47C Chinook	Hel	1968	1972-87	(188)	Licensed production began 1970
		50	Model 500E	Hel	1987	1987	(1)	Helicopter trainers
		..	SH-3D Sea King	Hel	1965	1969-87	(90)	In production since 1969
		(15 000)	AGM-65D	ASM	(1983)	1987	(450)	Undecided whether joint NATO-European or only Italian production for NATO Europe
7 Japan	USA	21	CH-47D Chinook	Hel	(1984)	1988	(7)	For Army and AF; eventual requirement may reach 100
		14	F-15DJ	Fighter/trainer	1987			Deliveries scheduled to begin July 1988
		88	F-15J Eagle	Fighter/interceptor	1978	1981-87	(88)	In addition to 12 delivered directly from USA; total order of 100 incl 12 trainers

250 MILITARY EXPENDITURE, ARMS TRADE, CONFLICTS

Region code/ Country	Licenser	No. ordered	Weapon designation	Weapon description	Year of license	Year(s) of deliveries	No. produced	Comments
		55	F-15J Eagle	Fighter/interceptor	1985	1984-87	(15)	MoU signed Dec 1984; in addition to 100 on order; projected purchase of 15 for 1988
		(130)	F-16C	Fighter	1987			Selected as basis for SX-3 (FX-3) close support fighter; Mitsubishi will provide fire control and radar; requirement for 130
		..	KV-107/2A	Hel	(1982)	1984-87	(15)	In addition to 61 produced earlier; improved version
		.. (73)	Model 205 UH-1H Model 209 AH-1S	Hel Hel	1972 1982	1973-88 1984-88	(114) (38)	AH-1S Cobra; following direct delivery of 2 in 1977-78
		..	OH-6D	Hel	1977	1988	(14)	Identical to Hughes Model 500D; 82 ordered through 1986
		42 30	P-3C Orion P-3C Orion	Mar patrol/ASW Mar patrol/ASW	1978 1985	1982-87 1987	(42) 8	MoU signed Oct 1985; in addition to 45 previously ordered; projected purchase of 11 in 1988
		.. 60	SH-3B SH-60J Seahawk	Hel Hel	1979 (1986)	1981-87	(66)	Initial batch of 15 to be funded in FY 1988; delivery of 80-100 to begin 1990
		(195)	M-110-A2 203mm	SPH	(1981)	1983-88	(195)	Following direct delivery of 6; in production since 1983
		20	Patriot SAMS	Mobile SAM system	1984			Deal worth $730.7 m incl Patriot SAMs; licensed production to begin 1988
		1 350 .. .. 80	AIM-7F Sparrow AIM-9L BGM-71C I-TOW MIM-104 Patriot MIM-23B Hawk Seasparrow	AAM AAM ATM Landmob SAM Landmob SAM ShAM	(1979) (1982) (1983) 1984 1978 1980	1980-87 1983-87 1985-87 1978-87 1980-87	(1 300) (2 776) (716) (2 436) (145)	Arming F-15s Total requirement: up to 10 000 Licensed production to begin 1988
		2	..	Destroyer	(1987)			Arming various Japanese-built frigates and destroyers Modified US Burke Class design in development; employs US AEGIS air defence weapon system
4 Netherlands	Belgium	220	M-114/39 155mm	TH	1987	1985-87		For delivery 1988-89
	USA	18	F-16A	Fighter	1982		(18)	Third order

TRADE IN CONVENTIONAL WEAPONS 251

5 Poland		57 F-16A	Fighter	1983	1987	(9)	Fourth order; for delivery 1987-92
		14 F-16B	Fighter/trainer	1983			To follow production of 213 previously ordered; deliveries to begin in 1992
		840 AIFV	MICV	1981	1983-87	(840)	In addition to 880 in service; 119 are M-901 TOW missile version; Dutch designation: YPR-765
	USSR	.. An-2	Lightplane	1960	1960-87	(4 100)	In production since 1960; over 11 000 built; 7000 for civilian use
		.. An-28	Transport	1978	1984-87	(34)	Series production transferred from USSR to Poland 1978; first flight of Polish-built aircraft 1984
		.. Mi-2 Hoplite	Hel	(1956)	1979-87	(1 800)	In production since 1957
		(1 900) T-72	MBT	(1978)	1981-87	(560)	
4 Portugal	France	18 TB-30 Epsilon	Trainer	(1987)			Deal worth $17 m; assembly to be completed in Portugal by 1989
5 Romania	France	.. SA-316B	Hel	1971	1977-87	(245)	Initial order of 180; more than 185 produced by spring 1985
		.. SA-330 Puma	Hel	1977	1978-87	(150)	Initial order of 100; 112 delivered by spring 1985
	UK	20 BAC-111	Transport	1979	1982-87	(16)	Deal worth $615 m of which $205 m for licensed production of Rolls-Royce Spey engine; 20 aircraft for Romanian AF
	USSR	.. Yak-52	Trainer	(1979)	1980-87	(1 100)	Two-seat piston-engined primary trainer; 500th delivered 1983; production started 1979
		.. TAB-77	APC	(1975)	1976-87	(1 380)	Romanian version of Soviet BTR-70
4 Spain	France	18 AMX-30R	AAV(M)	1984	1986-87	(12)	
	USA	3 FFG-7 Class	Frigate	1977	1986-87	(2)	
		1 FFG-7 Class	Frigate	1986			In addition to 3 under construction
6 Switzerland	Germany, FR	345 Leopard-2	MBT	1983	1987	(2)	Deal worth $1400 m incl 35 delivered directly; final deliveries due 1993
	UK	19 Hawk	Jet trainer	1987			Deal worth $150 m incl training and logistics; deliveries expected from 1989
4 Turkey	Germany, FR	2 Meko-200 Type	Frigate	1983	1987	1	In addition to 2 built in FRG
		(9) Type 209/1	Submarine	1974	1981-85	2	Built under licence in addition to 3 delivered from FRG; planned production rate: 1 ship/year

Region code/ Country	Licenser	No. ordered	Weapon designation	Weapon description	Year of license	Year(s) of deliveries	No. produced	Comments
4 UK	USA	152	F-16	Fighter	1984	1987	2	Licensed assembly following direct delivery of 8 F-16C/Ds
	Brazil	130	EMB-312 Tucano	Trainer	1985	1987	(16)	Deal worth $145-50 m; option on 17 more
	France	..	Milan	ATM	1976	1977-87	(934)	UK requirement: 50 000; also produced for export as Euromissile production is phased out
	USA	..	AIM-120A AMRAAM	AAM	(1987)			Licensed production by Euraam (BAe, MBB, AEG and Marconi)
		..	BGM-71A TOW	ATM	1980	1982-87	(16 605)	
1 USA	Israel	..	EL/2106	Point defence radar	(1983)			For co-production with Martin Marietta
	Switzerland	..	Popeye	ASM	1987			Eventual requirement may reach 562; US version to be mounted on M2 Bradley chassis
		166	ADATS	SAM System	1987			
	UK	302	T-45 Hawk	Jet trainer	1981			First deliveries due 1989; total cost incl simulators and training: $3200 m
6 Yugoslavia	France	..	SA-342 Gazelle	Hel	1971	1973-87	(145)	SA-341/342 Gazelles produced since 1973
	USSR	..	T-74	MBT	(1977)	1984-87	(100)	Upgraded T-74 with Yugoslavian-designed laser aiming device

II. Third World countries

Region code/ Country	Licenser	No. ordered	Weapon designation	Weapon description	Year of license	Year(s) of deliveries	No. produced	Comments
12 Algeria	UK	3	Kebir Class	PC	1986			For delivery by 1988
15 Argentina	Germany, FR	(350)	TAM	MT	1976	1981-86	(350)	350 produced by 1987; some for Argentine armed forces; orders from Panama and Peru cancelled
		6	Meko-140 Type	Frigate	1980	1985-87	4	Armed with MM-40 Exocet ShShMs; last 2 will be available for export
	USA	4	Type TR-1700	Submarine	1977	1987	1	In addition to 2 delivered directly
		120	Model 500D	Hel	1972	1974-80	(120)	Assembly of knocked-down components; no production since 1980
15 Brazil	Austria	..	GHN-45 155mm	TH/TG	(1985)			Production expected from early 1990s
	France	6	HB-350M Esquilo	Hel	(1985)			Requirement for 40 more
	Germany, FR	(5)	Type 209/3	Submarine	1982			In addition to 1 delivered directly; 1 may be fitted with a nuclear propulsion system

TRADE IN CONVENTIONAL WEAPONS 253

15 Chile	Spain	(20)	T-36 Halcon	Jet trainer	1984	1986-87	(8) In addition to 16 delivered 1982-83; at least 1 armed with Sea Eagle AShMs
	Switzerland	(150)	Piranha	APC	1980	1981-86	(150) No production 1987; resumption expected 1988
	USA	(120)	T-35 Pillan	Trainer	1980	1985-87	(106) Developed from Piper PA-28 by US and Chilean engineers; 80 for Chile, 40 for Spain; being produced at 4/month
8 Egypt	Brazil	110	EMB-312 Tucano	Trainer	1983	1985-87	(110) 30 for Egypt, 80 for Iraq; last of 110 knockdown kits delivered by Dec 1987; option on 60 more
	France	..	AS-332	Hel	1983		Dec 1983 licence to assemble components possibly leading to full assembly
		15	Alpha Jet	Jet trainer	1985		Negotiating continued production
		..	SA-342L Gazelle	Hel	(1986)		3320 produced by end-1985
	UK	..	Swingfire	ATM	1977	1979-87	(5 513)
	USA	555	M-1 Abrams	MBT	1987		Licensed assembly could start mid-1990s, but unclear
9 India	France	..	SA-316B Chetak	Hel	(1962)	1964-87	(267) Also for civilian use; some production of parts for French AS-316s; programme winding down
	Germany, FR	(42 000)	Milan	ATM	1982	1985-87	(11 832) First missile completed 1985
		50	Do-228	Transport	1983	1987	(3) For civil and military use; initial deliveries to civil airline began 1986
		2	Type 1500	Submarine	1981		In addition to 2 directly delivered; first delivery due 1990
		2	Type 1500	Submarine	(1987)		Exercise of option from 1981 jeopardized after allegations that Indian officials were bribed by HDW
	UK	45	Jaguar	Fighter	1978	1982-87	(45) Local production of components; in addition to 40 purchased directly
		31	Jaguar	Fighter	1982		Local production of components; plans for complete local manufacture abandoned
	USSR	(220)	MiG-21bis	Fighter	1976	1979-87	(220) Indian production phased out 1987 in favour of MiG-27
		(165)	MiG-27	Fighter/grd attack	1983	1987	(20) First flight 1987 after lengthy delays
		..	BMP-1	APC/ICV	1983	1987	(8) Production under way 1987
		(1 000)	T-72	MBT	(1980)	1987	(4) Production under way 1987; initially 10% Indian content
		(2 200)	AA-2 Atoll	AAM	(1963)	1968-87	(2 200) Arming MiG fighters

254 MILITARY EXPENDITURE, ARMS TRADE, CONFLICTS

Region code/ Country	Licenser	No. ordered	Weapon designation	Weapon description	Year of license	Year(s) of deliveries	No. produced	Comments
10 Indonesia	France	. .	AA-8 Aphid	AAM	(1986)			Unconfirmed
		(56)	AS-332	Hel	(1982)	1985-87	8	Production switched from Puma to Super Puma 1983; total orders by end-1984: 69; military orders: 56
	Germany, FR	(100)	BK-117	Hel	1982	1984	2	Total production schedule: 100; 2 pre-production aircraft delivered 1984
		(50)	NBo-105	Hel	1976	1976-87	(50)	Military order for approx 50 helicopters
		(80)	NBo-105	Hel	1987			Follow-on licensed production of 80-100 to include export orders
	Spain	6	PB-57 Type	PC	1982	1985-87	(6)	Probably 4 for Coast Guard
		(80)	CN-212	Transport	1976	1978-86	(20)	80 produced by end 1986 for military and civil customers; 18 delivered to military customers by early 1986
	USA	(100)	Model 412	Hel	1982	1986-87	8	For military and civil users; 28 delivered to military customers by 1986
8 Israel	USA	. .	Westwind 1124	Transport	1968	1976-87	(24)	Wide range of versions for military and civil users produced since 1968
10 Korea, South	USA	. .	Model 205 UH-1H	Hel	(1987)			Negotiating
		(139)	Model 500MD	Hel	1976	1978-86	(125)	Production of components incl engine parts
		. .	M-101-A1 105mm	TH	(1971)	1977-86	(100)	Possibly without US consent
		242	M-109-A2 155mm	SPH	1983	1984-87	(48)	Co-production; 23 to be delivered in 1988; 26 in 1989; 70 in 1990
		. .	M-114-A1	TH	(1971)	1978-86	(90)	Production of components to modernize US APCs in service in S. Korea
		. .	PSMM-5 Type	FAC	(1974)	1977-80	8	4 for S. Korea; 4 for Indonesia
14 Mexico	UK	5	Azteca Class	PC	1983	1987	4	In addition to 31 in service
13 Nigeria	Austria	(200)	Steyr-4K 7FA	APC	(1981)			Various versions to be built; possibly also Cuirassier LT/TD; status uncertain due to financial problems
9 Pakistan	Sweden	(180)	Supporter	Trainer	1974	1977-87	(155)	Assembly from imported kits began 1976; from 1982 local raw materials; production transferred to Kamra 1981

TRADE IN CONVENTIONAL WEAPONS   255

10 Philippines	Germany, FR	..	Bo-105C	Hel	1974	1976-86	(14)	Approx 15 in service incl 5 from FRG
	UK	(100)	BN-2A Islander	Lightplane	1974	1974-85	(60)	
10 Singapore	Germany, FR	5	Type 62-001	Corvette	1985			Mini-corvettes of Luerssen design
	Italy	30	S-211	Trainer	1983	1984-87	(30)	4 to be imported directly; 26 assembled locally; deal worth approx $60 m
16 South Africa	Israel	(96)	Gabriel-2	ShShM	(1984)	1986-87	(24)	Unclear whether licensed production, reverse-engineered or imported directly
		..	Reshef Class	FAC	1974	1978-86	6	In addition to 3 previously acquired; armed with 6 Scorpion ShShMs derived from Israeli Gabriel ShShM
10 Taiwan	Israel	..	Gabriel L	ShShM/SShM launcher	(1978)	1980-85	(48)	Taiwanese designation Hsiung Feng; no production in 1986-87 but expected to resume in 1988
		..	Gabriel-2	ShShM	(1978)	1980-85	(375)	
	Singapore	(22)	Suikiang Class	FAC	(1983)	1986-87	(8)	Armed with Hsiung Feng ShShMs;
	USA	30	F-5E Tiger-2	Fighter	1982	1983-86	(30)	Deal worth $620 m incl 30 F-5Fs; last delivery made Dec 1986
		30	F-5F Tiger-2	Jet trainer	1982	1983-86	(30)	Option on 6 more; armed with Hsiung Feng ShShMs
		6	FFG-7 Class	Frigate	1987			
10 Thailand	France	1	PS-700 Class	LS	1984	1987	(1)	To be built by Ital Thai Ltd; due for delivery 1987
		1	PS-700 Class	LS	(1985)			In addition to 1 ordered 1984; further orders probable
	Germany, FR	45	Fantrainer	Trainer	1983	1985-86	(4)	2 imported directly from FRG; followed by local assembly and some component manufacture; first delivery mid-1985
		1	Hysucat-18	PC	(1982)	1987	1	West German catamaran/hydrofoil design; orders for up to 11 more probable
	UK	(3)	Province Class	Corvette	1987			

Appendix 7D. Sources and methods

I. The SIPRI sources

The sources of the data presented in the SIPRI arms trade registers are of six general types. Five of these are published sources, available to the general public: newspapers; periodicals and journals; books, monographs and annual reference works; official national documents; and documents issued by international and intergovernmental organizations. The total number of sources regularly searched for arms trade data is about 200. It is from these that the overwhelming bulk of the arms trade registers is compiled. The sources listed below represent a selection of the first-priority sources of arms trade and arms production data. Reliance on publicly available information provides superior accuracy, independence and accountability. However, total dependence on published sources makes it difficult to record significant transactions concealed deliberately or by inadequate reporting. A formal estimating procedure has been introduced for this *SIPRI Yearbook* to overcome such oversights. It has been applied initially to Afghanistan (see below). The establishment of this sixth procedure is an effort to rectify an obvious deficiency in the comprehensiveness of the data.

The problems of official and commercial secrecy referred to in chapter 7 mean that the arms trade is not fully reported in the open literature. Published reports often omit essential facts. There can also be substantial disagreement among reports. Therefore estimation and the exercise of judgement have always been important elements in compiling the SIPRI arms trade data base. Both the order dates and the delivery dates for arms transactions are continuously revised in the light of new information, but where they are not disclosed the dates are estimated. The exact number of weapons ordered as well as the number of weapons delivered may not always be known and are sometimes estimated, particularly with respect to missiles. It is common for reports of arms deals involving large platforms—whether ships, aircraft or armoured vehicles—to ignore missile armaments classified as major weapons by SIPRI. Unless there is explicit evidence that platforms were disarmed or altered before delivery, it is assumed that they carry the armaments specified in one of the major reference works such as the *Jane's* or *Interavia* series.

II. Selection criteria

The SIPRI arms trade data cover five categories of major weapons: aircraft, armour and artillery, guidance and radar systems, missiles and warships. The statistics presented refer to the value of the trade in these five categories only. The registers and statistics do not include the trade in small arms, artillery under 100-mm calibre, ammunition, support items, services and components or component technology. In general, publicly available information is not sufficient to track these other categories satisfactorily.

There are two criteria for the selection of major weapon transfers for the registers. The first is that of military application. The aircraft category excludes aerobatic aeroplanes, remotely piloted vehicles, drones and gliders. Transport aircraft and VIP transports are included only if they bear military insignia or are otherwise confirmed as military registered.

The armour and artillery category includes all types of tanks, tank destroyers, armoured cars, armoured personnel carriers, armoured support vehicles, infantry combat vehicles as well as multiple rocket launchers, self-propelled and towed guns and howitzers with a calibre equal to or above 100 mm. Military lorries, jeeps and other unarmoured support vehicles are not included.

The category of guidance and radar systems is a residual category for electronic tracking, fire control, launch and guidance systems that are either (*a*) deployed independently of a weapon system listed under another weapon category (e.g., certain ground-based SAM launch systems) or (*b*) shipborne missile launch or point defence (CIWS) systems. The values of acquisition, fire control, launch and guidance systems on aircraft and armoured vehicles are included in the value of the respective aircraft or armoured vehicle. The reason for treating shipborne systems separately is that a given type of ship is often equipped with numerous combinations of different acquisition, launch and guidance systems.

The missile category includes only guided missiles. Unguided rockets such as light anti-armour weapons are excluded. Free-fall aerial munitions (such as 'iron bombs') are also excluded.

The ship category excludes some types of ship, such as small patrol craft (with a displacement of less than 100 t, unless they carry cannon, missiles or torpedoes), research vessels, tugs and ice-breakers. Naval combat support vessels such as fleet replenishment ships are included.

The second criterion for selection of items is the identity of the buyer. The items must be destined for export to the armed forces of another country. Transfers to paramilitary forces or police are included if they involve major weapons. Major weapons received by intelligence agencies are also included. Arms supplied to guerrilla forces pose a problem. For example, if weapons are delivered to the Contra rebels they are listed as imports to Nicaragua with a comment in the arms trade register indicating the local recipient. The entry of any arms transfer is made corresponding to the five weapon categories listed above. This means that missiles and their guidance/launch vehicles are often entered separately under their respective category in the arms trade register.

III. New estimating procedure

The traditional SIPRI method of relying on published sources breaks down when arms deals are poorly publicized or concealed. This can lead to omissions in the registers. Such lapses are undesirable but statistically tolerable if they only involve isolated cases. They become a serious problem when large transfers continue to be unpublicized for years. To correct for such omissions, SIPRI now employs a new standardized estimating procedure. This combines information about a recipient's arsenal, aggregate trade statistics, data on specific arms deals and estimating rules to arrive at a conservative estimate of the covert trade with particular recipients.

For arms transfers to Afghanistan, on which no sufficiently accurate or detailed records have been published, this method was applied. Several sources provided a general picture. They include annual volumes of: *World Military Expenditures and Arms Transfers, Military Balance, Jane's Armour and Artillery*, selected monographs and articles, the SIPRI arms trade data base and literature on military operations in Afghanistan.

Most transfers to the Kabul Government are assumed to be replacements for war losses. The battle on the ground has been taken as constant because the tactics and anti-armour equipment available to the Afghan resistance have not altered dramatically. The air battle, on the other hand, has increased in intensity as the Mujahideen have become better armed. Attrition replacements have varied accordingly.

The designations and quantities of aircraft transfers were better documented than other categories of weapon. The designations and numbers of aircraft operated by the

Afghan Republican Air Force are also published in various sources. SIPRI's estimates of the actual numbers of aircraft delivered each year were based on the probable losses, given the reported intensity of the air battle. From the reported aggregate deliveries from the Soviet Union and other East European countries to the South Asian region, the Afghan imports were confirmed.

With regard to ground forces weapons, the same estimating rules were applied. For this category, the contribution of judgement in the estimating procedure was more important since sources were less accurate. While open sources contain accurate information on the volume of deliveries, they say little about the designation or structure of the Afghan armed forces. Here the point of reference was the structure of Soviet divisions, although account was taken of the specific problems of the Afghan Army.

In all cases, the preference is to rely on detailed published sources. Estimating procedures are used only in lieu of published data. The estimating procedures are designed to be conservative, providing the lowest credible figures. These will be revised as better data become available.

The use of an estimating procedure is not without analytical consequences. Analysts requiring uniformly generated data may find SIPRI arms trade statistics harder to use owing to the combination of methodologies. It also creates additional possibilities for error in the registers. The role of judgement in producing the registers becomes greater and more explicit. The SIPRI arms trade staff believes that these disadvantages are offset by the advantage of greater comprehensiveness, accuracy and comparability.

IV. The value of the arms trade

The SIPRI system for evaluating the arms trade was designed as a *trend-measuring device*, to enable the measurement of changes in the total flow of major weapons and its geographic pattern to be made. Expressing the evaluation in monetary terms reflects both the quantity and the quality of the weapons transferred. Aggregate values and shares are based only on *actual deliveries* during the year or years covered in the relevant tables and figures.

The SIPRI valuation system is not comparable to official economic statistics such as gross domestic product, public expenditure and export/import figures. The monetary values chosen do not correspond to the actual prices paid, which vary considerably depending on different pricing methods, the length of production runs and the terms involved in individual transactions. For instance, a deal may or may not cover spare parts, training, support equipment, compensation, offset arrangements for the local industries in the buying country, and so on. Furthermore, if only actual sales prices were used—even assuming that the information were available for all deals, which it is not—military aid and grants would be excluded, and the total flow of arms would therefore not be measured.

Production under licence is included in the arms trade statistics in such a way that it should reflect the import share embodied in the weapon. In reality, this share is normally high in the beginning, and then it gradually decreases over time. SIPRI has attempted to estimate an average import share for each weapon produced under licence.

V. Priority sources

Journals and periodicals

Afrique Défense (Paris)
Air et Cosmos (Paris)
Air Force Magazine (Washington)
Antimilitarismus Information (Frankfurt/M)
Armed Forces Journal (Washington)
Asian Defence Journal (Kuala Lumpur)
Aviation Week & Space Technology (New York)
Campaign against Arms Trade (London)
Current News (US Department of Defense: Washington)
Defence Journal (Karachi)
Defence Today (Rome)
Defensa (Madrid)
Defense & Economy World Report and Survey (Washington)
Defense & Foreign Affairs Daily (Washington)
Defense & Foreign Affairs Digest (Washington)
Defense Daily (Washington)
Defense Electronics (Palo Alto)
Defense & Armament (Paris)
DMS Intelligence (Greenwich, Connecticut)
Far Eastern Economic Review (Hong Kong)
Flight International (Sutton, UK)
IDF Journal (Jerusalem)
Interavia (Geneva)
Interavia Airletter (Geneva)
International Defense Review (Geneva)
Jane's Defence Weekly (London)
Latin America Weekly Report (London)
Marine-Rundschau (Stuttgart)
Middle East Review (New York)
Milavnews (Romford, UK)
Military Electronics & Countermeasures (Santa Clara, California)
Military Technology (Cologne)
NACLA Report on the Americas (New York)
NATO's Sixteen Nations (Brussels)
Naval Forces (Aldershot, UK)
Navy International (Dorking, UK)
News Review (Institute for Defence Studies & Analyses, New Delhi)
Osterreichische Militärische Zeitung (Vienna)
Pacific Defence Reporter (Melbourne, Australia)
Soldat und Technik (Frankfurt/M)
Der Spiegel (Hamburg)
Technología Militar (Bonn)
Wehrtechnik (Bonn)
World Fighting Vehicle and Ordnance Forecast (Newtown, Connecticut)

Newspapers

Dagens Nyheter (Stockholm)
Daily Telegraph (London)
El País (Madrid)
Financial Times (London)
Frankfurter Allgemeine Zeitung (Frankfurt/M)
Frankfurter Rundschau (Frankfurt/M)
International Herald Tribune (Paris)
The Independent (London)
Jerusalem Post (Jerusalem)
Le Monde (Paris)
Le Monde Diplomatique (Paris)
Neue Zürcher Zeitung (Zürich)
Svenska Dagbladet (Stockholm)
The Guardian (London)
The Times (London)

Annual reference publications

'Aerospace Forecast and Inventory', annually in *Aviation Week & Space Technology* (McGraw-Hill: New York)
Combat Fleets of the World (Naval Institute Press: Annapolis, Maryland)
Defense and Foreign Affairs Handbook (Copley & Associates: Washington, DC)
Interavia Data: Air Forces of the World (Interavia: Geneva)
Interavia Data: Aircraft Armament (Interavia: Geneva)
Interavia Data: World Aircraft Production (Interavia: Geneva)
Interavia Data: World Helicopter Systems (Interavia: Geneva)
International Air Forces and Military Aircraft Directory (Aviation Advisory Services: Stapleford, UK)
Jane's All the World's Aircraft (Jane's: London)
Jane's Fighting Ships (Jane's: London)
Jane's Weapon Systems (Jane's: London)
Jane's Armour and Artillery (Jane's: London)
Keesing's Contemporary Archives (Keesings: Bristol)
Labayle Couhat, J. (ed.), *Flottes de Combat* (Editions Maritimes et d'Outre Mer: Paris)
The Middle East Military Balance (Jaffee Center for Strategic Studies: Tel Aviv)
'Military Aircraft of the World' and 'Missile Forces of the World', annually in *Flight International* (IPC Transport Press: Sutton, UK)
The Military Balance (International Institute for Strategic Studies: London)
World Military Expenditure and Arms Transfers (US Arms Control and Disarmament Agency: Washington, DC)

Other reference books

Conway's All the World's Fighting Ships 1922–1946 (Conway Maritime Press: London, 1980)
Conway's All the World's Fighting Ships 1947–1982 (Conway Maritime Press: London, 1983)
Hewish, M. *et al.*, *Air Forces of the World* (Salamander Books: London, 1979)
Keegan, J. (ed.), *World Armies*, second edition (Macmillan: London, 1983).

VI. Conventions

The following conventions are used in appendices 7B and 7C and in table 8.1:

..	Data not available or not applicable
—	Negligible figure (<0.5) or none
( )	Uncertain data or SIPRI estimate

Abbreviations and acronyms

AA	Anti-aircraft
AAG	Anti-aircraft gun
AAM	Air-to-air missile
AAV	Anti-aircraft vehicle (gun-armed)
AAV(M)	Anti-aircraft vehicle (missile-armed)
AC	Aircraft/armoured car
AC carrier	Aircraft carrier
Acc to	According to
ADV	Air defence version
Adv	Advanced
AEV	Armoured engineering vehicle
AEW	Airborne early-warning system
AEW&C	Airborne early warning and control
AF	Air Force
AFSV	Armoured fire support vehicle
Amph	Amphibious/amphibian
APC	Armoured personnel carrier
Approx	Approximately
ARM	Anti-radar missile
ARV	Armoured recovery vehicle
AShM	Air-to-ship missile
ASM	Air-to-surface missile
ASV	Anti-surface vessel
ASW	Anti-submarine warfare
ATGM	Anti-tank guided missile
ATM	Anti-tank missile
AV	Armoured vehicle
AWACS	Airborne early warning and control system
BL	Bridge-layer
Bty	Battery
CIWS	Close-in weapon system
CG	Coastal gun
COIN	Counter-insurgency
CP	Coastal patrol
CPC	Command post carrier
CS	Coastal surveillance
DoD	Department of Defense (USA)
ECM	Electronic countermeasure
Elint	Electronic intelligence
EW	Early warning
Excl	Excluding/excludes

FAC	Fast attack craft (missile/torpedo-armed)
FMS	Foreign Military Sales (USA)
FY	Fiscal year
Grd	Ground
Hel	Helicopter
ICV	Infantry combat vehicle
IDS	Interdictor/strike version
Incl	Including/includes
IRBM	Intermediate-range ballistic missile
Landmob	Land-mobile (missile)
LC	Landing craft (<600t displacement)
LS	Landing ship (>600t displacement)
LT	Light tank
LOA	Letter of Offer and Acceptance (USA)
LoO	Letter of Offer (USA)
MAP	Military Assistance Program
Mar patrol	Maritime patrol aircraft
MBT	Main battle tank
MCM	Mine countermeasure (ship)
MICV	Mechanized infantry combat vehicle
Mk	Mark
MoU	Memorandum of Understanding
MR	Maritime reconnaissance
MRCA	Multi-role combat aircraft
MRL	Multiple rocket launcher
MRS	Multiple rocket system
MSC	Minesweeper, coastal
MSO	Minesweeper, ocean
MT	Medium tank
OPV	Offshore patrol vessel
PAR	Precision approach radar
PC	Patrol craft (gun-armed/unarmed)
PDM	Point defence missile
Port	Portable
RAAF	Royal Australian Air Force
Recce	Reconnaissance (aircraft/vehicle)
RN	Royal Navy (UK)
SAM	Surface-to-air missile
SAR	Search and rescue
SC	Scout car
SEK	Swedish crowns
ShAM	Ship-to-air missile
ShShM	Ship-to-ship missile
ShSuM	Ship-to-submarine missile
SLBM	Submarine-launched ballistic missile
SPAAG	Self-propelled anti-aircraft gun
SPG	Self-propelled gun
SPH	Self-propelled howitzer
SShM	Surface-to-ship missile
SSM	Surface-to-surface missile
SuShM	Submarine-to-ship missile

SY	Shipyard
TD	Tank destroyer (gun-armed)
TD(M)	Tank destroyer (missile-armed)
TG	Towed gun
TH	Towed howitzer
Trpt	Transport
UNITA	National Union for the Total Independence of Angola
VIP	Very important person

Region codes

1. USA
2. USSR
3. China
4. NATO, excluding USA
5. WTO, excluding USSR
6. Other Europe, neutral
7. Industrialized, Pacific
8. Middle East
9. South Asia
10. Far East & Oceania
12. North Africa
13. Sub-Saharan Africa (excluding South Africa)
14. Central America
15. South America
16. South Africa

8. The naval arms trade and implications of changes in maritime law

IAN ANTHONY

I. Introduction

The concept of 'maritime security' has in the 1980s come to include more dimensions than only the naval activities of major powers as a result of changes in the relationship between the sea and the international system of the 1970s. However, many of the maritime functions discussed in this chapter are not new. Writing in the nineteenth century, a British Admiral stated: 'I don't think we thought very much about war with a big W. We looked on the Navy more as a World Police Force than as a warlike institution. We considered that our job was to safeguard law and order throughout the world . . . and act as a guide, philosopher and friend to the merchant ships of all nations'.[1]

An increasing number of young states began in the 1980s to exercise their maritime responsibilities. In addition, there have been changes in the jurisdictional rights at sea, notably as a result of the signature of the United Nations Convention on the Law of the Sea in Jamaica in December 1982.[2] Whether the negotiations under the auspices of the United Nations which culminated in the Convention were a catalyst for or a reflection of a new approach is not an issue here, but the investment of so much time and effort by so many governments was itself evidence of changing attitudes towards the sea.[3]

A growing body of literature interprets the completion of three United Nations Conferences on the Law of the Sea and the Convention which emerged as an effort to manage the implications of two developments which challenge traditional attitudes among at least the major naval powers. The high seas beyond narrow coastal strips have traditionally been seen as open for commercial and military use. However, new territorial sea claims and the prospect that these would be backed by increased naval power threatened the extension of a 'creeping jurisdiction' over the high seas and international straits.[4]

This chapter focuses on the implications of these recent changes in maritime law for the trade in certain naval systems and defines some of the new dimensions of the maritime environment. In particular, it deals with what Geoffrey Till calls the management of the 'offshore estate',[5] in itself a challenging notion for maritime strategists who have traditionally been hostile to the idea of tying military assets to the defence of a fixed sea area.

These fundamental changes have been linked to the trade in naval weapons and equipment by several authors.[6] In their 1986 study of the naval arms race the United Nations Group of Governmental Experts stated: 'As with other conventional weapons, there has been a noticeable increase in the demand for

SIPRI Yearbook 1988: World Armaments and Disarmament

the most modern weapons, including anti-ship guided missiles, the delivery of which has provided relatively small coastal navies with a significant increase in war fighting capabilities'.[7]

Studies of the naval arms trade, cast in terms of the process of maritime enclosure and changes in the legal/political environment, cannot fully explain the demand for new vessels because they ignore the need for navies to modernize. Many hulls currently serving around the world were laid down in the 1950s and, as a result, some important naval powers are currently facing a problem of block obsolescence.[8] The relationship between modernization and the arms trade is beyond the scope of this chapter, which is solely concerned with the implications of legal and political changes. However, if Third World governments with widely differing economic and military potential invest in increased naval forces, this suggests important qualitative differences between naval arms transfers and the wider arms trade. There is a broad consensus that the total level of arms transfers to developing countries has been static for almost a decade.[9] The area of missile-armed attack craft has been identified as the exception to this general rule.[10] Discussion of a proliferation in missile-armed fast attack craft (FACs) flows from events that have focused media attention on the vulnerability of surface vessels in hostile Third World environments.[11] However, the focus on the trade in offensive weaponry has obscured a process whose implications are as important for the security of regional countries, namely the spread of systems dedicated to maritime surveillance and patrol.

For the majority of countries national resources are scarce, and the way in which they are allocated is a strong indicator of what concerns their governments the most. This chapter demonstrates that small countries, even some micro-states, invest large amounts of time and money in the acquisition of maritime surveillance and patrol capabilities, suggesting that for them security has a far more complex definition than issues of inter-state war and peace. It suggests that the Law of the Sea (LOS) Convention and the process which accompanied it reflect many though not all of the dimensions of these security considerations in the maritime sphere. This will demonstrate that developing countries match procurement policy to their security environment. On that basis, governments pursue what they consider to be appropriate technologies. In this area, as in others, the arms trade is not an uncontrolled process responding to market forces, but a function of security requirements.

Combined operations by maritime aircraft and patrol vessels illustrate this organic link between arms procurement and local security. The possibility of a major conflict is a contingency of which planners have to be aware, especially where there is a dispute over maritime jurisdiction. However, more routine but equally important functions have to be performed.

II. Implications of Part V of the LOS Convention

The LOS Convention is an immense, complex document. That a convention emerged at all from eight years of negotiation was in part a consequence of the attitude towards security and arms control adopted by the participants. Certain countries—such as Indonesia—whose geography makes them acutely aware of their maritime security periodically tried to discuss the military uses of the oceans and bring naval arms control issues to the table. However, given the problems of producing a document that stood a realistic chance of acceptance and ratification by the major naval powers, the prevalent feeling was that a limited agenda would be more profitable.[12] Part V of the United Nations Convention on the Law of the Sea gave coastal countries rights to exploit an exclusive economic zone (EEZ) to a limit of 200 nautical miles (370 km) measured from the baseline of their coastal sea, and placed on them a responsibility for the management of this sea space.[13] The LOS Convention has not entered into force because the depositary (the United Nations Secretary-General) has not received the 60 signatures needed for ratification. However, this has not prevented a large number of countries from claiming an EEZ as defined in the LOS Convention. These claims have no status in international law, but have acquired a form of legitimacy through usage and statements by major power non-signatories—especially the USA—that they will observe and respect portions of the document. This ambiguity has been a major contributory factor in the spread of surveillance and patrol systems. Signatories do not have sovereignty over their EEZ, but they have been awarded jurisdiction over certain specific activities. Other parties have rights of transit and overflight, and the LOS Convention does not countermand or override other international laws. The language of the LOS Convention is intentionally ambiguous in delimiting the rights and obligations of coastal states, but it is clear that they have a responsibility for overseeing activities in the EEZ. However, fishing vessels as much as any other have rights of transit through the EEZ. If a coastal state cannot legally prevent the passage of a fishing vessel or fleet, clearly they have an interest in monitoring the activities of boats in the waters of their EEZ. Because of the lack of clarity over the legal status of the LOS Convention, whether a coastal state has the right to do more than monitor the activities of such vessels is open to question. This issue will not be dealt with here since, whatever the law says about their actions, certain countries have decided that they will take action against foreign fishing vessels within their EEZ, and have invested in the systems that will allow them to do so more effectively.

Naval forces have a clear role in the process of 'national enclosure' within national waters, but these responsibilities do not extend into the EEZ according to the LOS Convention. The LOS Convention lacks any specific procedure for resolution where the delineation of the EEZ is in dispute. Overlapping EEZs should be delineated 'by agreement on the basis of international law . . . in order to achieve an equitable resolution'.[14]

In safeguarding maritime economic assets and ensuring against encroachment on exclusive rights, the lack of clarity regarding both the legal status of the EEZ and what is permissible in meeting even limited interpretations of the LOS Convention and in delineation of the EEZ may lead to actions interpreted as interference in areas claimed by a neighbour.

Demarcating national boundaries has traditionally been a function for land forces. However, the introduction of the EEZ has made marking a new form of maritime boundary an important issue. Once made, 200-nautical mile claims have to be underlined and enforced, but this function of demarcation and enforcement of the offshore estate has to be discharged differently around the world. In places where states share congested coastlines or border on semi-enclosed stretches of sea there is a problem of allocating sea area. Here questions of surveillance and patrol quickly become meshed with the possibility of naval conflict. Countries in this situation—littoral countries in the South China Seas, the Persian Gulf and the Arabian Sea, for example—are those with the greatest demand for vessels of the FAC/corvette type. This does not necessarily mean that the demand for patrol vessels will be less in these countries, but it does mean that the process of routine maritime reconnaissance and patrol will be subsumed beneath other elements of maritime security. However, this describes a relative handful of countries.

In countries where economic development is slow and uneven, the possibility of exclusive access to the fruits of an EEZ has obvious attractions. However, where there is a lack of any form of maritime security force, there is a parallel problem of exploiting resources efficiently. Countries where the sea provides a significant revenue are vulnerable to extortion or the illegal use of national assets. This is particularly true in abuses of fishing rights by foreign fishing fleets, an issue that has become contentious in several parts of the world.

In 1981 Ecuadorian naval forces seized US tuna boats, in retaliation for which the USA cancelled the transfer of the *USS Southerland* to Ecuador, the culmination of a series of incidents in what was referred to as the 'tuna war'.[15] In June 1984 the Solomon Islands seized US tuna boats, precipitating a US ban on imports of Solomon Island fish lifted at the end of that year.[16] In 1987, private sector representatives of the fishing industries of Thailand and Malaysia concluded a fishery co-operation pact which, it is hoped, will end an acrimonious dispute over the activities of Thai fishermen.[17] However, estimates that two-thirds of the catch landed in Thai hulls is taken illegally from non-national waters illustrate the danger that there will always be a disparity between national stocks and the capacity of the fishing fleet. The economic imperative for Thai fleets to roam in search of fish means that agreement with one country may simply displace the problem of illegal activities by Thai boats to other waters. In 1987 the USA and the Forum Fishing Association (FFA, formed under the auspices of the Pacific Forum regional association) concluded a five-year fishing agreement under which the US Tuna Association would not only pay an increased sum for fishing in the waters of the Pacific Islands, but would also accept FFA officials on board to monitor compliance with regulations concerning such things as the size of the catch.[18] However, the Pacific Island states still have outstanding disputes with Japan over fishing regulations. Japan has preferred country-to-country agreements to multilateral talks, and none of those agreements signed so far allows for disclosure of the size or value of the catch.[19] A series of disputes over fishing rights stretches from Pakistan into the Gulf, and naval forces in Bahrain, India, Kuwait and Pakistan have been active in impounding one another's fishing boats.

A number of countries have significant maritime economic assets of different sorts, notably oil rigs. Not only do rigs exploit minerals lying in waters over which there is a dispute regarding ownership, but once expensive assets have been established offshore their security from terrorist or other threats needs to be guaranteed.[20]

III. The need for sea surveillance

Navies have a role in the process of 'national enclosure', in counter-insurgency and protection from subversion, in maintaining maritime law and order and in safeguarding access to maritime economic assets. However, the first step in looking after any maritime interests has to be visible and demonstrable surveillance and patrol of existing national sea space. For a majority of countries, therefore, the starting-point in addressing maritime security needs is an improvement in surveillance, data processing and communications, without which it is impossible to know what is happening in a large ocean area. Moreover, this information has to be supported by national means for practical as well as political reasons. In extreme circumstances such as a crisis or war, intelligence may be available from a major power as a function of alliance membership or because it suits the purpose of that power to disseminate the information. This is not likely to be the case where contingencies are of a lower order of magnitude, occur as a matter of routine or are purely domestic in their implications.

As is clear from table 8.1, a wide range of countries have invested in capabilities to undertake some form of maritime surveillance from the air. Comparison of the figures presented in column 5 with those for the total sea area within the national maritime jurisdictional claim suggests that for most countries a comprehensive knowledge of all activities within the offshore estate is impossible. There is simply too much sea to survey. Nevertheless, it is clear that fixed-wing aircraft designed for maritime patrol can cover considerable areas. Offshore assets are in specific locations, and other legal responsibilities such as the maintenance of law and order are also to some extent confined by geography. Piracy must follow shipping trade routes, coastal geography may limit the places where insurgents or smugglers can put ashore, and so on. Consequently it may be that even small countries can make a considerable national effort at effective surveillance if the missions planned are specific, rather than if they engage in speculative patrolling.

Airborne surveillance allows a large sea area to be covered in a relatively short period, particularly if there is a network of coastal air bases that allows more flexible patrol routes to be followed. Few developing countries have the trained air crews, air base infrastructure or electronic equipment needed for comprehensive coverage, and furthermore it is too costly to sustain constant patrols. As an indication of the cost (although clearly in the case of a developing country the scale of operations would be different) the United States Navy and Air Force flew over 6000 hours of patrols in the first six months of 1986, as part of the effort to support drug law enforcement in the Caribbean, at a cost of some $7000 per hour.[21] Even after such a colossal investment, one estimate

Table 8.1. An inventory of maritime patrol aircraft and their surveillance capabilities

Country/System	Seller	No./ordered	Role	Search capability (thousand km² per h/day)	Radar type
Argentina: marine jurisdictional claim 339 500 km²; 200-naut. mile fishing zone					
SA 319B Alouette III	France	7	ASW	7.6/38	Omera ORB-31S1SA 330
Puma	France	3	SAR	16/66	RDR 1400/RCA Primus 500
Bell 212 ASW	USA	10	ASW	10/51	Ferranti Seaspray
ASH-3D/H Sea King	Italy	11	ASW	49/172	SMA/APS-707
CH-47C Chinook	USA	2	SAR	Human eye	..
S-2E Tracker	USA	10	MR/ASW	126/440	Retractable search radar
L-188E Electra	USA	7	MR/ASW	167/668	..
SP-2H Neptune	USA	6	MR/ASW	178/712	..
Lynx Mk 23	UK	1/..	ASW	24/83	Ferranti Seaspray
Hughes MD500	USA	6	SAR	..	..
Australia: marine jurisdictional claim 1 854 000 km²; 12-naut. mile fishing zone					
Bae HS 748	L: UK	2	Elint	..	..
Searchmaster B		..	MR	41/162	Bendix RDR 1400
Searchmaster L		..	MR	81/284	Litton APS-504(v)2
P-3C/Orion update	USA	20	MR	77/383	AN/APS-94F SLR AN/APS-115
SH-60B-2 Seahawk	USA	16/16	ASW	39/136	MEL 'Supersearcher'
Sea King HAS 50/50A	USA	7/1	ASW	47/172	AW 391
Wessex HAS 31B	UK	10	SAR	..	Special search equipment
Brazil: marine jurisdictional claim 924 000 km²; 200-naut. mile fishing zone					
AS-332F Super Puma	France	6	ASW	..	Thomson CSF
ASH-3H Sea King	USA	8/4	ASW	47/163	SMA/APS-707
EMB-110 Bandeirante		14	MR/SAR	..	..
EMB-111		12	MR	177/618	AIL AN/APS-128 SPAR-1
S-2A Tracker	USA	7	ASW	126/440	Retractable search radar
S-2E Tracker	USA	8	ASW	126/440	Retractable search radar
RC-130E Hercules	USA	5	MR/SAR	315/1.1	AN/APQ-122(V) on A
Lynx Mk 21	UK	9	ASW	24/83	Ferranti Seaspray
Westland Wasp	UK	7	SAR	..	..
Canada: marine jurisdictional claim 1 370 000 km²; 200-naut. mile fishing zone					
Labrador/Voyageur		6/8	SAR	..	..
CS2F-3 Tracker	L: USA	15	CS	126/440	Retractable search radar
Aurora	USA	18	MR	231/963	AN/APS-116
CHSS-2 Sea King	USA	32	ASW	..	AN/APS-503
Chile: marine jurisdictional claim 667 300 km²; 200-naut. mile fishing zone					
SA 319B Alouette III	France	10	ASW/SAR	7.6/38	Omera ORB-31S1
206A Jetranger	USA	3	ASW/SAR	17/85	..
Embraer EMB-111	Brazil	6	MR	177/618	AIL AN/APS-128 SPAR-1
China, People's Republic of: marine jurisdictional claim 281 000 km²					
SA 321G Super Frelon	France	12	ASW	33/131	Omera ORB-31D/32
Be-6 Madge	USSR	8	MR	196/686	..
Y-8 (An-12BP)		1	MR	168/672	Litton search radar
H-5 (Il-28 Beagle)		150	Recce	65/262	..
Z-5 (Mi-4 Hound)		40/50	ASW/SAR	8/40	..
Z-9 SA 365N Dauphin 2	L: France	3/22	ASW	9/54	Agrion 15
H-6 (Tu-16 Badger)		50	MR	192/672	..

THE NAVAL ARMS TRADE

Country/System	Seller	No./ ordered	Role	Search capability (thousand km² per h/day)	Radar type
Egypt: marine jurisdictional claim 50 600 km²					
E-2C Hawkeye	USA	4	AEW&C	77/310	AN/APS-138/125
Il-28 Beagle	USSR	13	MR	65/262	..
Sea King Mk 47	UK	5/12	ASW	49/172	MEL AW391
India: marine jurisdictional claim 587 500 km²; 200-naut. mile fishing zone, 200-naut. mile EEZ					
SA 319B Alouette III/ Chetak	L: France	21	ASW/SAR	7.6/38	Omera ORB-31S1
Br 1050 Alize	France	8	ASW	25/150	Thomson-CSF Iguane
Sea Harrier FRS Mk 51	UK	6	Recce	..	Ferranti Blue Fox
Do-228	L: FRG	60	MR	121/424	MEL Marec 2
Il-38 May	USSR	3	MR	215/859	..
Ka-25 Hormone	USSR	5	ASW	13/65	..
Ka-27 Helix	USSR	18	ASW	16/80	..
L-1049 Super Constellation	USA	4	MR	296/1.04	..
BN-2 Maritime Defender	UK	17	MR	83/333	Bendix RDR 1400
Tu-142 Bear-F[a]	USSR	3	MR	502/1.76	..
Sea King Mk 42/42A/ 42B	UK	35	ASW	49/172	MEL AW 391
Indonesia: marine jurisdictional claim 1 577 000 km²; 200-naut. mile fishing zone, 200-naut. mile EEZ					
B-737-200 Surveiller	USA	3	MR	188/656	SLAMMRGAF
Searchmaster B	Australia	12	MR	41/162	Bendix RDR 1400
Searchmaster L	Australia	6	MR	81/284	Litton APS-504(V)2
HU-16B Albatross	USA	5	SAR	..	Nose radome
C-130H-MP Hercules	USA	1	MR	315/1.1	SSR, SLAR AN/ APQ-122
NAS-332 Super Puma	France	26	ASW	38/133	Omera ORB 3214
Wasp (HAS Mk 1)	UK	10	ASW	..	..
Iran[b]: marine jurisdictional claim 45 400 km²; 50-naut. mile fishing zone					
Bell 212 ASW	Italy	7	ASW	10/51	Ferranti Seaspray
ASH-3D Sea King	Italy	12	ASW	19/105	SMA/APS-707
P-3F Orion	USA	2	MR/ASW	77/383	AN/APS-94F SLR AN/APS-115
Iraq: marine jurisdictional claim 200 km²					
SA 321 H Super Frelon	France	8	SAR	33/131	Omera ORB-31D/32
AB-212 ASW	Italy	8	ASW	10/51	Ferranti Seaspray
Israel: marine jurisdictional claim 6800 km²					
206A Jetranger	USA	2	SAR	..	..
Bell 212	USA	25	SAR/ECM	10/51	..
E-2C Hawkeye	USA	4	AEW	77/310	AN/APS-138/125
1124 Sea Scan	7		CP	278/973	Litton APS-504(V)2
SA 364F Dolphin	USA/Fr.	2	MR	..	Israeli-designed radar
Japan: marine jurisdictional claim 112 600 km²; 200-naut. mile fishing zone					
Super King Air 200T	USA	15	MR	..	2 alt. search radars DITACS
Bell-212	USA	29	CP	10/51	..
Kawasaki P-2J	L: USA	58	ASW/MR	267/980	AN/APS-80J
P-3C Update II	L: USA	24	ASW/MR	77/383	AN/APS-94F SLR AN/APS-115

Country/System	Seller	No./ ordered	Role	Search capability (thousand km² per h/day)	Radar type
P-3C Update III	L: USA	30/20	MR	300/997	Japanese avionics suite
Mitsubishi SH-3A	L: USA	64	ASW	47/163	SMA/APS-707
S-61/S-62	L: USA	12	SAR	26/91	SMA/APS-707
PS-1/US-1A		22	ASW/SAR	..	Litton AN/APS-504

Korea, South: marine jurisdictional claim 101 600 km²; 200-naut. mile fishing zone

S-2A/F Tracker	USA	20	ASW	126/440	Retractable search radar
500MD/ASW Defender	USA	10	ASW	..	Search radar

Kuwait: marine jurisdictional claim 4100 km²

AS 332F Super Puma	France	12	ASV	38/133	Omera ORB 3214
SA 365F Dauphin 2	France	4	SAR	9/54	Agrion 15

Libya: marine jurisdictional claim 98 600 km²

SA 321 M Super Frelon	France	8	SAR	33/131	Omera ORB-31D/32
Mi-14 Haze	USSR	12	ASW	16/80	..
SA 319B Alouette III	France	12	SAR/ASW	7.6/38	Omera ORB-31

Malaysia: marine jurisdictional claim 138 700 km²; 200-naut. mile fishing zone, 200-naut. mile EEZ

C-130H-MP Hercules	USA	3	MR/SAR	315/1.1	AN/APQ-122

Mexico: maritime jurisdictional claim 831 500 km²; 200-naut. mile fishing zone, 200-naut. mile EEZ

BO 105C	FRG	12	SAR	26/92	Bendix search radar
HU-16A Albatross	USA	8	MR/SAR	..	..
Arava-201	Israel	8	SAR	..	..

Morocco: marine jurisdictional claim 81 000 km²; 200-naut. mile fishing zone, 200-naut. mile EEZ

HH-43B Huskie	USA	4	SAR	..	..

New Zealand: marine jurisdictional claim 1 058 000 km²; 200-naut. mile fishing zone, 200-naut. mile EEZ

P-3B Orion	USA	6	MR	245/997	AN/APS-94F SLR AN/APS-115 [AN/APS-134(V)]
Westland Wasp HAS Mk1	UK	7	ASW	..	..
F-27 Maritime	Netherl.	3	SAR	300/1.05	Litton AN/APS-504(V)2

Pakistan: marine jurisdictional claim 92 900 km²; 200-naut. mile fishing zone, 200-naut. mile EEZ

SA 319B Alouette III	France	4	SAR	7.6/38	Omera ORB-31S1
Br 1150 Atlantic 1	France	3	ASW/MR	90/540	Thomson CSF
E-2C Hawkeye[c]			AEW&C	77/310	AN/APS-138
HH-43B Huskie	USA	4	SAR	..	..
Sea King Mk 45	UK	6	ASW	49/172	AW 391
F-27 Maritime	Netherl.	1	MR	300/1.05	Litton AN/APS-504

Papua New Guinea: marine jurisdictional claim 684 200 km²

N22B Missionmaster	Australia	6	MR	Human eye	–

Philippines[d]: marine jurisdictional claim 551 400 km²; 200-naut. mile fishing zone, 200-naut. mile EEZ

F-27 Maritime	Netherl.	3	MR	300/1.05	Litton AN/APS-504(V)2
BO 105	FRG	5	ASW/SAR	26/92	Search radar
BN-2A Islander	L: UK	19	MR/SAR	83/333	Bendix

Country/System	Seller	No./ordered	Role	Search capability (thousand km² per h/day)	Radar type
Saudi Arabia: marine jurisdictional claim 54 900 km²					
SA 365F Dauphin 2	France	24	ASV/SAR	9/54	Omera ORB-32
E-3A Sentry	USA	5	AWACS	..	AN/APY-1
Seychelles: marine jurisdictional claim: continental shelf; 200-naut. mile fishing zone, 200-naut. mile EEZ					
Merlin IIIB	Belgium	1	MR	Human eye	–
BN-2 Maritime Defender	UK	1	MR	83/333	Bendix RDR 1400
SA 319B Alouette III/ Chetak	India	2	SAR	7.6/38	Omera ORB-31
Singapore: marine jurisdictional claim 100 km²					
E-2C Hawkeye	USA	2	AEW/MR	77/310	AN/APS-138/125
South Africa: Marine jurisdictional claim 295 000 km²; 200-naut. mile fishing zone					
P.166S Albatross	Italy	18	CP	..	Nose radar
Westland Wasp HAS Mk 1	UK	9	ASW	Human eye	–
Douglas Dakelton	USA	20	MR	..	Search radar
Taiwan: marine jurisdictional claim 114 400 km²					
UH-1H Iroquois	USA	10	SAR	10/51	AN/APS-94F
HU-16B Albatross	USA	8	SAR		Nose radar
S-2 Tracker version A	USA	9	ASW	126/440	Retractable search radar
version E	USA	20	MR	126/440	
version F	USA	9	ASW/MR	126/440	
500MD/ASW	USA	12	ASW	..	Search radar
Thailand: marine jurisdictional claim 94 700 km²; 12-naut. mile fishing zone					
Canadair CL-215	Canada	2	SAR	126/440	Search radar
F-27 Maritime	Netherl.	6	MR	300/1.05	Litton AN/APS-504(V)2
Searchmaster B	Australia	5	MR	41/162	Bendix RDR 1400
HU-16B Albatross	USA	2	SAR	..	Nose radome
S-2F Tracker	USA	10	ASW/MR	126/440	Retractable search radar
United Arab Emirates: marine jurisdictional claim 17.3 km²					
AS 332F Super Puma	France	4	ASW	38/133	Omera ORB 3214
BN-2A Islander	UK	2	MR	83/333	Bendix RDR 1400

Acronyms and abbreviations in the Role column are defined in appendix 7D.

For conventions used in the table, see appendix 7D.

[a] Delivery delayed by changes in production schedule in the Soviet Union.

[b] Iran also uses Swiss-supplied Pilatus PC-7 aircraft for spotting and target acquisition. It is questionable how many of these aircraft remain in service in Iran because of Iran's demands on maintenance and repair.

[c] In spite of much discussion, the prospect of Pakistan getting access to early-warning aircraft of this level of sophistication remained distant at the time of writing (Dec. 1987). However, Pakistan may be the first country to use airships for this role. They are cheaper, easier to maintain and can carry a large payload of electronic equipment.

[d] Owing to chronic problems with repair and maintenance, few of these aircraft may be operational.

Sources:
Jane's Fighting Ships, 1986–87 (Jane's: London, 1986); *Jane's Fighting Ships, 1987–88* (Jane's: London, 1987); *Combat Fleets of the World, 1986/87* (Arms and Armour Press: US Naval Institute,

Sources to table 8.1 *cont.*
Annapolis, Md., 1986); *Jane's Weapon Systems, 1986–87* (Jane's: London, 1986); *Jane's Weapon Systems, 1987–88* (Jane's: London, 1987); *Air Forces of the World, 1986* (Interavia: Geneva, 1986); *Aviation Week & Space Technology*, 28 Sep. 1987; *Flight International*, 26 Sept. 1987; and *Defense and Foreign Affairs Handbook, 1987–88* (Perth Corporation: Washington, DC, 1987).

Methods:
This is an inventory of all aircraft in service in the listed countries dedicated to the task of maritime reconnaissance or which one would normally expect to find at sea—although clearly in cases of necessity any aircraft could assist in providing information. The countries listed exclude members of the major alliances because these countries have forces dedicated to the function of maritime patrol which, while nominally under the command of the armed forces and certainly a factor in contingency planning, maintain a distinct profile in day-to-day operations. Moreover, many of these countries have national production capabilities for these systems and so are not participants in the trade.

The data on maritime geography list first, the sea space over which the country concerned claims some jurisdiction; and second, the specific nature of claims that have been made—whether the country has claimed an EEZ or an exclusive fishing zone.

The columns are self-explanatory except for columns two, five and six—the seller, search capability and radar type.

An *L:* in the seller column indicates that a system is produced under licence in the country in whose inventory it is listed. No entry in the column indicates that a system is produced indigenously.

The search capability is a product of the following process: (*a*) identification of the aircraft in service dedicated to the task of maritime reconnaissance or which one would normally expect to find at sea—ASW helicopters on board ships, for example; (*b*) matching radars to the aircraft since the same airframe can mount different radars (the same aircraft in the inventories of different countries have different capabilities); and (*c*) calculation of the search capability per hour by dividing the maximum range for one flight (in km) by the maximum speed of which the aircraft is capable (in km per hour) and adding a fraction to allow for the fact that none of these missions is likely to be undertaken at full speed or to the outer limits of the range. This gives an estimate of the aircraft's hourly progress, which is multiplied by the range of the radar on the aircraft. The daily figure is based on this but is multiplied by the number of sorties an aircraft might reasonably be expected to make per day. In countries with limited ground support facilities and aircrew it would not be possible to turn around aircraft continuously. Italic figures in the search capability column indicate that the area is given in *millions of square miles* per day.

In column six, more than one radar entry for the same system indicates that both or all radars are installed on this platform.

suggests that only 10 per cent of the surface traffic was identified and intercepted.[22]

For reasons other than the cost of comprehensive air patrols, maritime surveillance and patrol has to include surface vessels as a component. A table documenting the trade in such vessels cannot practically be presented here because of the problem of defining 'patrol craft' as a category, a problem discussed below. There are obvious limits to the effectiveness of aircraft in lower-level security operations, in particular the problem of interdiction. From the air there is a stark choice once a suspicious vessel has been detected below. Either the vessel can be tailed in the hope of pursuing enquiries once it puts ashore, or it can be attacked without further investigation. It is easy to think of situations in which aircraft would be completely incapable of carrying out missions without the support of surface vessels—for example, wherever the purpose of a ship under surveillance is unknown. Surface vessels offer many more possibilities, ranging from shadowing the vessel at a distance to engagement and boarding.

The implications of management of the offshore estate therefore extend beyond the trade in reconnaissance aircraft to the sale of offshore patrol vessels capable of meeting this specific maritime role. There is no absolute demarcation between the various levels of maritime security policy, and clearly on occasion larger naval forces can be called on to fulfil this role. In some cases countries have established special forces to meet specific needs, although these forces normally sustain institutional links to the defence establishment so as to be available in a crisis.

Egypt, Indonesia, Morocco, Peru, the Philippines, Saudi Arabia, South Korea and Taiwan have in the past five years all bought ships for coast guard-type forces that are armed and over 100 tons in weight. Peru and the Philippines are countries that have embarked on coast guard programmes at a time when their navies are finding it difficult to obtain funding for equipment of any type.[23] In 1978 Indonesia established a Maritime Security Agency specifically to monitor and police the EEZ. The Federal Republic of Germany is to supply Indonesia with up to five PB-57 patrol craft of 350 tons with a small helicopter pad and armed with 76-mm and 40-mm guns in kit form as part of the programme for this force. The first two kits were delivered in 1984, with work to be completed by the P.T.PAL Shipyard.[24]

Forces of this type have been identified by Western industry as a potentially lucrative market, and designers have produced a variety of highly adaptable ships able to perform a wide range of missions and modified subsequently to carry a variety of weapon systems if so desired. Shipbuilders in Denmark, the Netherlands, the UK and FR Germany are likely to compete most fiercely in this market. Classifying patrol vessels is difficult because, as noted above, they have to cope with a variety of sea conditions and accomplish a range of missions. Many of these craft share the following characteristics: twin propulsion systems for economical patrol with greater speed as and when required; sizeable and separated storage areas located where they can become magazines if required; helicopter facilities; communications systems; extensive crew quarters to allow increases in the ship's company if helicopter, anti-submarine warfare (ASW) or electronic warfare (EW) operations should ever be undertaken and hard points for the attachment of equipment such as sonars or missile systems. (According to one estimate, by these criteria over 140 patrol vessels of this type have been sold to other countries since 1977.[25]) However, the above characteristics alone are inadequate as a definition. It is necessary to look at classification in terms other than technology alone in order to include vessels that perform the same function without meeting these criteria. To begin with, different sea conditions and coastal geography mean that vessels with identical missions can be of widely different tonnages, sea-keeping capacity, crew complements and on-board equipment. Finally, classification of equipment will break down unless technological characteristics are related to function and geography. To illustrate this, in achieving the British goal of safely evacuating civilians during a brief cease-fire in the civil war in South Yemen in January 1986, the *Royal Yacht Britannia* was more effective than an aircraft-carrier could have been in the same situation. Yet one still would not define it as a warship—although it is under the command of the Royal Navy. The definition of a patrol vessel must incorporate not only what it can do, but also what mission it is intended to perform.

Patrol vessels are required to conduct visible operations in contingencies short of war. This criteria of visibility means that the boats need to remain on station for extended periods, and there will need to be several of them. The consequent need for a rugged, cheap vessel excludes more heavily armed craft. The addition of advanced cruise missiles with associated target acquisition/fire control systems raises the capital costs of ships dramatically. It also raises running costs. Not only are repair and maintenance more complicated, but the effective use of these weapons also requires specialist crewmen who may be poorly trained for other duties. Apart from the financial implications of mounting advanced weapon systems, together with their related ordnance, they take up space, necessarily reducing the carrying capacity for other equipment. Effective day-to-day management of the offshore estate and an investment in missile-armed FACs and light corvettes may be alternatives. This is supported by a closer analysis of the recipients of FACs and corvettes, which, as noted in section II, turn out to be a very specific group of countries facing identifiable maritime threats.

IV. The LOS Convention and other maritime law

The full implications of the LOS Convention have been the subject of much debate, principally surrounding whether the existence of sovereign rights beyond territorial waters is a symptom of a process of 'creeping jurisdiction'. One author wonders if 'states might choose a maximalist response whereby the state would broadly construe the language of the LOS Convention, undertake to fulfil the legal obligations to the maximum, and also undertake to fulfil the nonlegal intentions and expectations created by the treaty'.[26] As noted above, the LOS Convention is additional to and does not undermine or countermand existing international law. Coastal states therefore remain accountable for any act that they perpetrate beyond their national waters in the same way as before. However, table 8.1 suggests that investment in maritime surveillance capabilities is one indicator of a country's attitude to the interpretation of the LOS Convention in this regard. Countries such as Indonesia, India, Malaysia and the Philippines, which took a central role in the LOS process, were not only among the first to declare 200-nautical mile fishing and exclusive economic zones, but also made the requisite investment in surveillance capabilities.

As noted above, patrol vessels cannot meet the needs of states located in areas where ocean boundaries are in dispute because they run the risk of being trumped by superior forces. However, this situation describes relatively few countries and a very particular problem. There remains another body of security interests to which maritime surveillance is also closely related. Forces constructed to meet the needs of EEZ management may contribute to generally sanctioned actions such as the enforcement of national and international laws relating to issues such as controlling immigration or the eradication of smuggling and piracy.

In some countries maritime operations have been conducted against domestic insurgents or foreign subversives who use the sea as a supply route but have no significant naval forces of their own. The clearest recent example has been the inability of the Sri Lankan Government prior to July 1987 to prevent supplies from reaching Tamil guerrillas who were dependent on the sea for supplies of weapons and explosives. In the Philippines, there have been unconfirmed reports that equipment of Chinese and Vietnamese origin for Moro National Liberation Front (MNLF) guerrillas enters the country by sea. More certain is that the MNLF has a rudimentary navy, the Bangsa Moro, based on a few motor boats fitted with heavy-calibre machine-guns.[27] In Israel the integration of the surveillance function with the defence force involves maritime aircraft in 24-hour patrols. Israeli patrol boats, responsible for 240 km of coastline from the border with Lebanon in the north to Egypt in the south, conduct 11-hour patrols on constant alert because of the danger of seaborne terrorist attack. Beyond this, Israeli warships patrol as far north as Beirut, and Israeli law allows the checking of any vessel outside territorial waters if it is believed to be a threat.

Maritime terrorism in the Middle East became an issue of wider public concern in 1985 as a result of a series of events. In April 1985 a cargo ship from Algiers was intercepted with 28 Palestinian guerrillas on board, 20 of whom were killed in a firefight when the ship was stopped. Later the same month a dinghy with five guerrillas on board was intercepted off the coast of northern Israel, although boats of this size often escape radar detection.[28] In October terrorists took control of the passenger liner *Achille Lauro*, murdering one passenger and wounding two others. The Israeli Government dates an increase in the threat of maritime terrorism to 1985 and cites explicit linkages between Lebanese Shi'ite groups, notably Hizbollah, and Iranian revolutionary guards. The tactics adopted by the two groups are similar, with fast raids employing light weapons against undefended craft.[29]

In Israel, the scale of the threat is seen to justify a major and continuous surveillance and patrol effort. However, elsewhere counter-insurgency and combatting terrorists are more dependent on the quality of intelligence. Assuming that terrorists are detected *en route* to a target, it is unlikely that information from airborne surveillance can be processed and relayed to surface forces in time to prevent an attack.

To some degree, the same argument applies to the problem of piracy. However, since the early 1980s 'known pirate zones' have been outlined by organizations such as the International Maritime Bureau in London, which collects information on attacks of all kinds on shipping. In the past, coastal states have been reluctant to assume the entire burden of efforts to police areas beyond their national waters, arguing that, since international shipping is the target, the costs of any operations should be shared. This argument may become increasingly difficult to sustain alongside the concept of exclusive jurisdiction over other activities in a defined area of sea, especially if the assets required for some form of police action are in being for other purposes.

Piracy remains a major threat to commerce and in particular to shipborne refugees in the Association of South East-Asian Nations (ASEAN) area. According to the International Maritime Organization there was an escalation of attacks on shipping in South-East Asia in the early 1980s, and in October 1985, after Filipino pirates raided ashore in the Malaysian territory of Sabah,

Malaysian gunboats and helicopter gunships made retaliatory strikes against pirate bases in the Philippines. Fifty people were either killed or arrested by Malaysian forces on the island of Maddanas. On receiving a formal protest from Manila, the Malaysian Government denied that the raid ever took place.[30] In February 1986, pirates seized the Japanese cargo ship *Monte Ruby* in the Gulf of Thailand, one of three such attacks in the first quarter of that year. The Thai Government is trying to develop an intelligence network among local fishermen to combat the pirates as well as stepping up maritime patrols with Nomad surveillance aircraft presented by the Australian Government specifically for the purpose.[31] A part of the world with an escalating problem of piracy is West Africa, where the Nigerian response has been to establish a force of around 30 light patrol vessels armed with 20-mm guns bought from France, the Netherlands, the USA and the UK before the British company concerned went into liquidation.

V. Prospects for regional co-operation in maritime surveillance and patrol

Multinational naval activity of any kind, including arms procurement, presupposes a degree of political cohesion between the states concerned. However, with this major caveat, in the realm of naval programmes as they relate to the LOS Convention the best opportunity for confidence building may be through co-operation over procurement.

In West Africa, the tasks of surveillance and patrol are being tackled through a US-sponsored programme initiated in 1985 under the title West African Coastal Surveillance (WACS), amended to the African Coastal Security (ACS) programme in 1986, reflecting increases in its geographical scope. The programme aims at increasing the number of small local bases with facilities for ship repair and maintenance. The programme illustrates a wider trend within the trade in smaller naval craft. The naval inventories of many countries in Africa and elsewhere retain quantities of Soviet and Chinese craft in the 200-ton range with which they experience enormous difficulties of repair and maintenance. The modernization and maintenance of these craft have been identified by Western companies as a potentially lucrative enterprise.[32]

In the Caribbean, South West Pacific and (to a lesser extent) Latin America, naval procurement has already become a tool used in addressing common security concerns and in offsetting shortages in national resources.[33] However, countries in these regions find it easier to address common security concerns than those where inter-state disputes threaten naval conflict. This may not always be the case. In spite of traditional disputes over activities in the Palk Straits, India and Sri Lanka have moved towards naval co-operation. For Sri Lanka this reflects the urgency created by the civil war. Tamil separatists have depended on supplies from Madras, and prior to the Indo-Sri Lankan Peace Accord signed on 29 July 1987 the Indian Navy on occasion prevented the harassment of Tamil boats *en route* to Sri Lanka. The Accord included provision for patrols of the Palk Straits aimed at sealing off new supplies to

Tamil guerrillas. While the parts of the Accord relating to the role of the Tamil Tigers (the Liberation Tigers of Tamil Eelam, LTTE) in Sri Lankan politics were in effect torn up on 31 October 1987 by President Jayewardene, sections pertaining to Indian access to Sir Lankan ports will remain in force. It is clear that since the signature of the Accord, the Indian and Sri Lankan navies have made concerted efforts to monitor and intercept shipping around the coast of Sri Lanka.[34]

The successful supply operations by Tamils before the Accord was signed are likely to stimulate demand in Sri Lanka for independent surveillance and interception capabilities. However, this may not result in joint Indo-Sri Lankan procurement since Indian dockyards will be filling orders for the Navy and Coast Guard over the next 10 years. However, some form of Indian assistance—either unilateral or in the context of the South Asian Association for Regional Cooperation (SAARC)—for Sri Lanka is possible. Not only is the scale of economic reconstruction needed on the island immense, but India has a clear interest in avoiding a lengthy deployment of land forces subject to sporadic attack by extremist groups from either the Sinhalese or Tamil communities.

It is difficult to imagine joint or co-ordinated military operations in the ASEAN region, given the antagonism between China and Viet Nam (indirectly between China and the Soviet Union) and between China and Taiwan (indirectly between China and the USA). The Five Power Defence Arrangement includes the deployment of Australian maritime patrol aircraft and surveillance planes in Malaysia, from where they make regular patrols of the South China Sea and pay particularly close attention to the Soviet facilities at Cam Ranh Bay in Viet Nam. Geographically slightly removed, and currently less tense, China and Japan also dispute sovereignty over offshore islands.

Nevertheless, the nature of the maritime tasks demanded by the LOS Convention may force a co-operative framework if they are to be performed successfully. The problem of fishery management was touched on above. Since fish may not respect national boundaries, a failure to reach some agreement about the exploitation of stocks may lead to the pursuit of national policies which result in a rapid depletion of resources, which in the medium term can serve the purpose of no country. Equally, mineral deposits on or under the sea-bed do not always lie within the EEZ of one country, and the alternative to multinational control of their exploitation may be competitive extraction without consideration for the impact on market prices or for future economic development.

If the possibility of more efficient management of the offshore estate is one factor which may promote co-operative ventures, the problem of finding the resources to undertake patrols is another. In section II it is noted that those countries with a substantial investment in surveillance and patrol equipment have also made an overt claim for 200-nautical mile fishing and economic exclusion zones, and it was suggested that these countries are the ones that could be expected to adopt a 'maximalist' interpretation of the LOS Convention. However, some states have claimed 200-nautical mile zones without making an investment in patrol and surveillance equipment of similar proportions. In many cases these are countries which have both limited resources and economies in which the exploitation of the sea is a key component. Islands and ocean archipelagoes such as Grenada, the Maldives, Mauritius, the Seychelles and Sri Lanka have all made claims beyond their 12-nautical mile territorial waters.

Moreover, there is wide scope for actions in tackling low-level threats and co-operating in areas that do not threaten the sovereignty or security of neighbours. Co-operation may be possible in areas such as disaster relief, policing against smuggling of goods or people, search and rescue, immigration control, collection of customs duties, aid to navigation, pollution control and protection of the marine environment. In South Asia, the regional association SAARC has discussed the prospect for movement in all of these spheres, and in the areas of immigration control and disaster relief SAARC has provided the institutional setting for formal agreement.[35]

All of these functions require at the least an awareness of what is happening in the EEZ, and consequently effective surveillance and the subsequent exchange of information. The successful practice of such an arrangement may ease actions at a higher level, encompassing activities which are difficult to imagine at present, such as joint surveillance of EEZs and fishery protection.

VI. A co-operative programme in action

As noted above, regions where co-operative projects in naval procurement have the clearest chance are the Caribbean and the South-West Pacific. Two recent articles have discussed developments in the Caribbean.[36] In the South-West Pacific, maritime co-operation has found a focus in the Pacific Forum and has received added impetus from changes in foreign policy in the largest regional states, Australia and New Zealand.

The Pacific Forum, of which Australia and New Zealand are members, began life as an economic association with a remit similar to ASEAN.[37] However, the Pacific Patrol Boat programme is evidence of the evolution of a more broadly based regional security network with a variety of channels through which local states can communicate. This development has already manifested itself in the area of joint procurement.

The Pacific Patrol Boat programme was launched in 1983 to provide a total of twelve 31.5-m patrol boats to Papua New Guinea (4), Fiji (4), Solomon Islands, Cook Islands, Western Samoa and Vanuatu (1 each). Tuvalu is considering participation in the project. Paid for by Australia, the programme also includes training and advice and has been complemented by Australian naval visits and bilateral efforts to improve communications facilities, hydrographic skills and the accurate delineation of 200-nautical mile zones. Australian P-3C Orion maritime patrol aircraft have been deployed at air bases in the South-West Pacific on a regular basis since 1983. The most recent official statements by the Australian Government envisage increasing the number of such deployments and the participation of New Zealand patrol aircraft in a co-ordinated deployment schedule.[38] The programme has been disrupted by the second coup staged by Colonel Rabuka in Fiji on 25 September 1987, following which

Australia suspended all deliveries to Fiji, recalled defence co-operation advisers and suspended all aid with the exception of grants paid to Fijian students already in Australia.[39] However, the rift between Fiji on the one hand and Australia and New Zealand on the other may prove to be temporary, given the efforts to strengthen existing regional security linkages. Australia and New Zealand will engage in the joint purchase and production of major naval vessels, while Australia and Papua New Guinea have reinforced their 1977 Joint Statement on defence by concluding an agreement similar in wording to Canberra's defence arrangements with Malaysia and Singapore.[40]

VII. Conclusions

The concern among traditional maritime powers over the prospect of creeping jurisdiction is understandable. One way to test the probability of it being a serious proposition is to look at the behaviour of countries which may try to extend their maritime jurisdiction. There is little change in prospect in the international maritime order. Most states are occupied with problems far removed from challenging freedom of navigation, which implies a confrontation with major naval powers. Freedom of navigation is not the issue for most states. Invited to participate in joint naval operations aimed at safeguarding freedom of navigation through the Gulf, the Indian Government declined to become involved, preferring to see the USA and European countries absorb the political and economic costs of this questionable enterprise. Other countries are preoccupied with managing a complex web of political, economic and security problems from an inadequate resource base. Countries undertaking more expansive naval programmes tend to be those which have had the technical capacity to challenge the users of regional waters for the past 15 years. In these countries the implications of any form of challenge have long been held to be counter-productive. Publications which speculate on the extension of 'creeping jurisdiction' do not make clear why these countries would suddenly make a different judgement about the relative costs and benefits of efforts at maritime policing in international waters.

Changes in the naval equipment market consequent of changes in maritime law have occurred at a different level. The creation of the 200-nautical mile EEZ offers opportunities only to those coastal states that can devise an effective method of exploiting offshore resources. Claims to these resources need to be reinforced by forces under national control, and compliance with the management scheme established by coastal states can be ensured only through policing.

The creation of the EEZ also places on coastal states an obligation to regulate and manage offshore economic activities in an orderly fashion. Countries which argue that their needs receive too little international consideration can demonstrate that they are able as well as willing to play a wider role in the international system by discharging the responsibilities implied by the LOS Convention effectively.

Notes and references

[1] Quoted in Marder, A. J., *British Naval Policy 1880–1905: The Anatomy of British Sea Power* (New York, 1940).

[2] The text of the Law of the Sea Convention is reproduced in *International Legal Materials*, no. 21 (Nov. 1982), pp. 1261–354.

[3] *The Law of the Sea* (United Nations: New York, 1983).

[4] Darman, R. G., 'The law of the sea: rethinking U.S. interests', *Foreign Affairs*, vol. 56 (Jan. 1978); Larson, D. L., 'Naval weaponry and the law of the sea', *Ocean Development and International Law*, vol. 18, no. 2 (1987); United Nations, *A Quiet Revolution: The United Nations Convention on the Law of the Sea* (United Nations: New York, 1984); US House of Representatives, Committee on Foreign Affairs, *Hearings*, 17 June, 17 Aug., 16 Sep. 1982; and Boothby, D., 'Maritime change in developing countries', paper for Conference on Naval Forces and Arms Control, SIPRI, 1–3 Oct. 1987.

[5] Till, G., *Maritime Strategy in the Nuclear Age* (Macmillan: London, 1984).

[6] Larson and Boothby (note 4). See also Morris, M., *Expansion of Third World Navies* (Macmillan: London, 1987); and United Nations, *The Naval Arms Race*, the United Nations Study Series on Disarmament no. 16 (United Nations: New York, 1986), sections 74/80.

[7] *The Naval Arms Race* (note 6), section 79, p. 21. Another commentator identifies a 'burgeoning' of countries with maritime forces and the prospect that 'where there's one flower now soon there may be a garden': Moore, J. E., *Jane's Fighting Ships, 1987–88* (Jane's: London, 1987), p. 125.

[8] Navies facing the most severe problems of obsolescence are those of Bangladesh, Brazil, Chile, Mexico, Pakistan, Peru, the Philippines, South Korea, Taiwan and Uruguay.

[9] With the exception of the Iraq–Iran War which has consumed enormous amounts of *matériel*; see Ohlson, T. and Skons, E., in SIPRI, *SIPRI Yearbook 1987: World Armaments and Disarmament* (Oxford University Press: Oxford, 1987), pp. 181–3. The implied contrast is not intuitively unlikely, given the characteristics of naval equipment. Ships are expensive, a relatively small number are traded and those have a service life in excess of 25 years. The extended procurement cycle offers scope for life extension programmes and 'slippage' in new orders. Naval programmes therefore require long and hard thought before initiation but are very difficult to stop once in progress.

[10] See note 4.

[11] For example, the loss of six British ships, including four major surface combatants, during the Falklands/Malvinas War of 1982 and the attack on the frigate *USS Stark* in the Persian Gulf on 17 May 1987.

[12] The most comprehensive overview of the law of the sea remains O'Connell, D. P., *The International Law of the Sea*, 2 vols (Clarendon Press: Oxford, 1982).

[13] Part V of the Law of the Sea Convention is reproduced in Westing, A. H. (ed.), SIPRI, *Global Resources and International Conflict* (Oxford University Press: Oxford, 1986), pp. 233–60.

[14] *Keesing's Contemporary Archives* (Longman: Milton Keynes, 1983), reference 31929.

[15] *Keesing's Contemporary Archives* (Longman: Milton Keynes, 1981), reference 30772.

[16] *Asian Defence Journal*, Aug. 1987. The USA has limited discretion because of the Magnuson Act, which makes the imposition of a trade embargo under these circumstances mandatory and automatic. For a discussion of the political impact of these decisions in recipient countries, see Hegarty, D., *Small State Security in the South Pacific*, Strategic and Defence Studies Working Paper 126 (Australian National University: Canberra, 1987), mimeo.

[17] *Far Eastern Economic Review*, 24 July 1987. Malayan authorities, increasingly frustrated at the inability to stem illegal Thai fishing, had begun to harrass innocent Thai boats *en route* to international waters.

[18] *Far Eastern Economic Review*, 23 Aug. 1987.

[19] See note 18.

[20] Establishing offshore oil and gas extraction involves the construction of a complex infrastructure vulnerable to many different threats. Moreover, many of the extraction programmes draw on personnel and capital from industrialized countries, giving them a stake in the success and safety of the projects. *Far Eastern Economic Review*, 26 Nov. 1987, pp. 84–6.

[21] *The Role of the US Military in Narcotics Control Overseas*, Hearings before the Committee on Foreign Affairs, 5 Aug. 1986, especially the testimony of Col. Harvey Pothier, USAF, Acting Director Task Force on Drug Enforcement.

[22] Barnes, R. K., *The Threat to Society Posed by the International Narcotics Trade*, Seaford House Papers 1986, p. 117. Barnes is a colonel in the Jamaican Defence Force.

[23] In the Philippines the Coast Guard received two patrol vessels built by Japan as war reparation. The newest and probably most capable vessels in the country, their induction into the Coast Guard and not the navy reflects the fact that Japanese export policy forbids sales of military equipment rather than a choice by Manila.

[24] Labayle Couhat, J. (ed.), *Combat Fleets of the World, 1986–87* (Arms and Armour Press: US Naval Institute, Annapolis, Md., 1986).

[25] Tarpgaard, P., Principal Security Analyst in the Congressional Budget Office, quoted in Larson (note 4).

[26] McDorman, T. L., 'The LOS Convention and the ASEAN states', *Ocean Development and International Law*, vol. 18: H, no. 3 (1987).

[27] *Pacific Defence Reporter* (Canberra), May 1987, pp. 14–15.

[28] *The Times*, 8 July 1985.

[29] *Jerusalem Post*, International Edition, 19 Dec. 1987.

[30] *Keesing's Contemporary Archives*, vol. 32 (Longman: Milton Keynes, Apr. 1986), reference 34295.

[31] *Navy International* (London), May 1986.

[32] *World Weapons Review*, 23 Dec. 1987, pp. 9–12.

[33] The growth of joint procurement and patrol in the Caribbean has been discussed at length in Morris, M., 'The politics of Caribbean straits', *Ocean Development and International Law*, vol. 18, no. 4 (1987); and Fenton, R. E., 'Caribbean coast guard: a regional approach', *Naval War College Review*, vol. 37 H, no. 2 (Mar.–Apr. 1984).

[34] At least five boats allegedly re-supplying Tamil guerrillas were sunk in late 1987–early 1988. However, there are reports that supplies are now offloaded at sea to smaller fishing boats which land along the east coast of Sri Lanka. In response, Indian naval vessels previously confined to the north and north-west have extended their areas of operation. *Times of India*, 13 Jan. 1988.

[35] A regional foodstuff stock in the case of natural disaster was agreed at the meeting of SAARC heads of state in November 1987, although whether its collection and distribution are successful remains to be seen.

[36] See note 33.

[37] *Asian Defence Journal*, Aug. 1987.

[38] *The Defence of Australia*, Australian Department of Defence White Paper (Government Publishing Service: Canberra, 1987), p. 18.

[39] Statement by Foreign Minister Hayden, 29 Sep. 1987.

[40] *Jane's Defence Weekly*, 19 Dec. 1987; Hegarty (note 16).

9. Major armed conflicts in 1987

G. KENNETH WILSON and PETER WALLENSTEEN*

I. Introduction

At the end of 1987 there were 36 major armed conflicts being waged in the world according to the following criteria: prolonged combat between the military forces of two or more governments or of one government and organized armed opposition forces, involving the use of manufactured weapons and incurring battle-related deaths of at least 1000 persons.[1]

Table 9.1 identifies the location, starting dates, contending parties, number of combatants, deaths and intensity for each of the conflicts. Obviously, the criteria used to identify major armed conflicts will significantly affect the number of conflicts included in any such list. At the level of magnitude set by the present criteria the number of conflicts included has tended to grow at a relatively constant rate. From 1945 to 1987 the number of wars of a magnitude comparable to those recorded in this survey increased from around three per year to 36.[2]

A closer look reveals that each of these major conflicts is composed of a number of different disputes. They are labelled together here as they involve the same territorial entity. When approaching these conflicts from a perspective of conflict resolution, they have to be broken down into smaller units. Thus, while the conflict in Lebanon is listed in table 9.1 as one conflict, there are a number of competing interests clashing in this territory. If the conflicts are to be solved, these various interests have to be analysed.

The basic issues involved in the major armed conflicts of 1987 were largely related to internal matters. A seemingly 'typical' inter-state war, such as the Iraq–Iran War, had important internal components. A considerable number of conflicts dealt with who should exercise political power. In some places the principal focus was ideology (e.g., Nicaragua, Guatemala and El Salvador). A great number of conflicts concerned ethnic minorities trying to hold on to power (e.g., South Africa) or demanding autonomy in one form or another (e.g., Sudan, the Horn of Africa and Sri Lanka). Elsewhere ethnic issues mingle with questions of religion, most noticeably in conflicts involving Sikhs in India and Muslims in the southern Philippines. All of the conflicts combine several root causes.

The *SIPRI Yearbook 1987* listed 36 armed conflicts in 1986. The conflict between India and Pakistan, which is recorded here, was not included in the 1986 list because it was regarded as a 'sporadic border conflict'. The heightened border tension and loss of life on the Siachin Glacier in 1987 have led to its inclusion this year. The conflict in Ecuador, which was recorded for 1986, is not included for 1987 because the guerrilla war reported in 1986 ended following the death of the leader of the guerrilla group. According to available information fatalities do not seem to have reached 1000.

SIPRI Yearbook 1988: World Armaments and Disarmament

II. Conflict characteristics

Most of these armed conflicts are taking place in Third World countries and only one is recorded for Europe: the Northern Ireland (Ulster) conflict.[3]

There were six major armed conflicts in the Middle East. In the war between Iran and Iraq significant developments were reported during the year. Attacks on merchant shipping continued, shipping lanes were mined, major powers increased the number of naval vessels deployed in and around the Gulf, and some of these vessels escorted tankers in convoy. The UN Security Council passed Resolution 598 on 20 July 1987, demanding a cease-fire and a withdrawal of forces to internationally recognized borders. During the autumn negotiations took place to find a formula for meeting the remaining Iranian demand that Iraq be held responsible for the war.

Five major armed conflicts took place in South Asia, the most devastating continuing to be the war in Afghanistan, where tactical changes on both sides seem to have intensified the war in the southern and south-eastern parts of the country. The world's largest flow of refugees (five million) is from Afghanistan, most of them remaining in Pakistan and Iran. Indirect talks continued in Geneva through UN auspices on issues of Soviet troop withdrawals and the formation of a coalition government in Afghanistan. Regional conflicts were among the issues discussed at the fourth Reagan–Gorbachev summit meeting in Washington in December 1987, following which Soviet Foreign Minister Shevardnadze, visiting Kabul, said: 'We would like 1988 to be the last year of the stay of Soviet troops in your country. . . . Virtually the entire package of the necessary arrangements has been agreed upon at the Afghan-Pakistan talks conducted through the United Nations secretary-general. There is an opportunity to conclude these talks at the next round in February (1988).'[4]

The conflict in Sri Lanka escalated dramatically. In the first half of 1987, fighting between the Government and Tamil groups, in particular the Liberation Tigers of Tamil Eelam, intensified. As part of a peace process codified in a peace accord signed on 29 July 1987 an Indian Peacekeeping Force was sent to the island. From October this force fought pitched battles with Tamil forces in the north of the island. In August 1987 a new party, the Janatha Vimukhti Peramuna (JVP), entered the conflict with an assassination attempt on a Sri Lankan parliamentary committee meeting at which President Jayewardene was present.

In the eight major armed conflicts in the Far East cease-fire agreements and amnesty contributed to a reduction in fatalities during the year in at least two cases (the Philippines and Malaysia). In the Philippines, the Aquino regime remained exposed to pressures from the left and from the military.

In Africa, several of the 11 conflicts showed increased fatalities. The war in Chad escalated dramatically, only to subside following a cease-fire agreement in September 1987. Other wars that intensified were the struggles between front-line governments and South African-sponsored insurgencies especially in Angola (UNITA) and Mozambique (MNR), as well as the armed conflict over Namibia.

Finally, several of the five conflicts in Latin America showed an intensification of armed actions towards the end of 1987. For Central America, this was an unintended consequence of the plan for the suspension of hostilities concluded among five Central American Presidents in Esquipulas, Guatemala, on 7 August 1987: the parties seem to have intensified their struggle to improve their position before any cease-fire agreement was concluded.

III. Armed conflicts and the international community

In addition to the direct participants identified in table 9.1 many of the conflicts have an international dimension which is central to the prospects for their resolution. One of the manifestations of this is the supply of arms and military equipment to combatants. Arms shipments have been a factor shaping the Iraq–Iran War. Not only have all five permanent members of the UN Security Council been involved, but actors from the developing world, notably Brazil, Egypt and North Korea, have played an increasingly important role as arms suppliers.

The United States and the Soviet Union were also actively involved in military support to opposite sides in the conflicts over Angola, Nicaragua and Kampuchea. The provision of portable surface-to-air missiles to the armed opposition in Afghanistan by China, Egypt, the UK and the USA increased Soviet aircraft losses. Superpower involvement in regional conflicts can complicate conflict resolution, as it may threaten an escalation in warfare locally and introduce linkages between conflicts that would otherwise be geographically distinct. During the year, hearings in the US Senate revealed the links between hostage crises in Lebanon, secret US arms deliveries to Iran in part via Israel, and financial support for the Contras in Nicaragua.

Of the several attempts to find solutions, actions outside the UN framework, and thus outside direct superpower influence, seem to have been the most productive (Central America and Chad). In other cases, the actions of the Secretary-General, rather than the Security Council, have been of some importance (the Iraq–Iran War).

Although there was limited progress in 1987 towards the solution of some of the major armed conflicts, no formal peace treaty was signed. In Sri Lanka, a peace accord was signed, but it did not provide for a full solution to the dispute. In Central America, a preliminary peace agreement (the 'Arias Plan') was signed on 7 August. Although the document did not acquire the status of a treaty, it did lead to a number of temporary cease-fire agreements and kept open a possible negotiated solution to several conflicts in the region. Some smaller disputes were solved during the year, notably the Naga conflict in India and the Mesquito conflict in Nicaragua. It appears that some of the agreements reached have reduced the number of fatalities in several conflicts (the Philippines and Chad) and thus have a value in their own right in reducing the burden on the civilian population. In general, civilian and military casualties seem to be about equal in most conflicts. In cases where the civilian deaths significantly outnumber the military ones, there is reason to believe that this is the result of deliberate massacres or indiscriminate military strategies on either side. Modern warfare takes an additional heavy toll in triggering famines, in the breakdown of medical and social services, in creating refugees and in its wider economic impact. The refugee situation in the world showed no improvement during the year.

Notes and references

* Department of Peace and Conflict Research, Uppsala University, Uppsala, Sweden.

[1] The data in table 9.1 exclude, as far as sources of information allow, deaths owing to famine and disease. Other conflict lists, using fatality criteria of fewer or more deaths or such criteria as numbers of fighting troops, show a greater or smaller number of conflicts at any given point in time. The criteria employed by the present authors for the Conflict Data project at the Department of Peace and Conflict Research, for example, produce a list of over three times as many conflicts as are registered here. The 1000-fatality threshold, however, produces a list of conflicts which most people regard as 'wars'. It is also used, for example, by the Correlates of War project at the University of Michigan for delineating 'wars' from 'serious disputes'.

[2] Armed conflicts of yet lower magnitudes increased at an even higher rate. With the exception of some periods (1870–90, 1920–39 and 1965–75), the frequency of major armed conflicts has steadily increased by a factor of six since 1816. See Gantzel, K. J. and Meyer-Stamer, J. (eds), *Die Kriege nach dem Zweiten Weltkrieg bis 1984* (Weltforum: Munich, 1986); and Kaye, G. D., Grant, D. A. and Emond, E. J., *Major Armed Conflict, A Compendium of Interstate and Intrastate Conflict 1729 to 1985* (Operational Research and Analysis Establishment, Canadian Department of National Defence: Ottawa, 1985).

[3] In addition there are a number of events of lower magnitude in Europe, notably regional conflicts in Corsica (France), and Kosovo (Yugoslavia) as well as armed action of groups on the left or right in France, Italy, FR Germany and Greece. The Basque conflict has resulted in at least 600 deaths. A particular phenomenon has been attacks in European capitals on foreign embassies or on foreign dissidents, a pattern where conflicts are transferred to Europe from other areas.

[4] *Baltimore Sun*, 7 Jan. 1988.

Table 9.1. Major armed conflicts in the world, 1987

Location/ conflict	Year formed/ year joined[a]	Warring parties	No. of troops in 1986[b] (thou.)	Deaths[c] (thou.)	Change from 1986[d]
Europe					
Northern Ireland (Ulster)	1922/1969	Protestant Irish paramilitary, British Govt. vs. IRA	(10) 9 0.2–0.5	1969–87: 2.5 <0.1 yearly	+

Comments: The present conflict was formed in 1922 following the agreement to divide Ireland and create the Republic of Ireland in the south of the island. The conflict was rejoined in 1969. Since then, British troops and Protestant paramilitary forces in Northern Ireland battle against Catholic Irish nationalists—primarily the Irish Republican Army (Provisional IRA), which seeks reunification of Northern Ireland with the Republic of Ireland. The Protestant majority wants to remain part of the UK. An Anglo–Irish agreement of Nov. 1985 granting increased rights to Ulster Catholics did not diminish the violence. In 1987 anti-agreement demonstrations diminished but paramilitary violence increased slightly on both sides. The IRA bombing of the annual Armistice Day remembrance in Enniskillen produced shock-waves of anti-terrorist feeling and may have paved the way for greater Anglo–Irish co-operation in searching border areas for IRA suspects and arms caches.

ARMED CONFLICTS IN 1987   289

Location/ conflict	Year formed/ year joined[a]	Warring parties	No. of troops in 1986[b] (thou.)	Deaths[c] (thou.)	Change from 1986[d]
Middle East					
Iran	1972/1979	Iranian Govt. vs. Kurds, People's Mujahideen and other opposition	100 (10–15)	1979–84: 10–20 yearly low: <0.1	0

Comments: Kurds seeking greater autonomy or independence in the mountainous north-west became very active militarily following the overthrow of the Shah in 1979. The establishment of 'liberated zones' led to the 1983–84 campaign by Iranian forces to regain control. Kurds in Iran have received support from Iraq since the beginning of the war. While opposition inside Iran has largely been suppressed, other ethnic minorities have at times been in armed revolt against the Khomeini Govt., including Baluchis, Azerbaijanis and Khuzistani Arabs. In addition, the People's Mujahideen wants to topple the Khomeini Govt. It receives aid from Iraq, where its leadership is now based. Iran is accused of executing 6000–20 000 political opponents since 1979.

| Iraq | 1961/1962 /1972 /1980 | Iraqi Govt. vs. Kurds and Communists (ICP) | 100 12 1 | 1961–70: 5 (mil.) 100 (civ.) 1987: internal low front-line >0.1 | 0 |

Comments: Kurds have received aid from Iran since the outbreak of the Iraq–Iran War. Leading parties have been the Democratic Party of Kurdistan (DPK) and Patriotic Union of Kurdistan (PUK). In 1987 a new alliance reportedly formed with the Syrian-based Kurdish Workers Party (PKK). Armed opposition from the Iraqi Communist Party (ICP) was reported.

| Iraq–Iran | 1979/1980 | Iraqi Govt. vs. Iranian Govt. | 845 700 | 1980–82: 27 (mil.) 1982–86: 600 1987: >5 (mil.) | + |

Comments: See also *SIPRI Yearbook 1987*, chapter 9, and this *Yearbook*, chapter 15. During 1987 the war continued on a high level, increasingly involving attacks on third-nation shipping in the Gulf. The perceived threat to shipping led to the increased deployment of naval vessels and minesweepers from the USA, the USSR, the UK, France, Belgium, Italy, the Netherlands and other Gulf countries. UN Security Council Resolution 598 of July 1987 called upon the parties to observe an immediate ceasefire and to withdraw all forces to the internationally recognized boundaries. The central question for resolution became the determination of who was responsible for initiating the war. The UN Secretary-General explored ways of setting up an impartial body.

| Israel–Palestinians | 1948/1948 | Israeli Govt. vs. PLO | 149[e] 8 | 1948–87: >10 yearly low: 0.1 | 0 |

Comments: Israel and Palestinians (mainly the Palestine Liberation Organization) have been fighting in various locations, including Israel and Lebanon. Israel's invasion of Lebanon in 1982 and occupation until 1985 did not slow down the pace of warfare. Armed Palestinians returned to Lebanon. Some 25 000 Syrian troops are stationed in Lebanon. 1000 Israeli troops remain in southern Lebanon. The UN UNIFIL peacekeeping operation patrols the area. Attacks continued in 1987 against Israeli soldiers in Lebanon and against Israel proper. Israel carried out raids, usually air strikes against bases, in Lebanon. In Dec. 1987 violence was centred in Israeli-occupied territory, notably the Gaza Strip but also the West Bank, where a significant uprising occurred.

Location/ conflict	Year formed/ year joined[a]	Warring parties	No. of troops in 1986[b] (thou.)	Deaths[c] (thou.)	Change from 1986[d]
Lebanon	1975/1975	Lebanese Govt. vs. Christians, Druse, Muslim Militia, Syria, Israel, PLO	15 (40) (40) 25 1 8	1975–87: >130 (2/3 mil.) 1987: relatively low, 0.3	0

Comments: Civil war among Christians, Muslims, Druse and Palestinians in 1975. Muslims probably form the majority of the population. Christians dominate political and economic life. Different Christian armed units are in conflict with each other. Sunni Muslim armed units are in conflict with Christian troops. During the 1980s Amal (Shi'ite Muslim) fought with the Sunnis as well as with the Palestinians. Syria repeatedly sent 'peacekeeping' troops into Beirut. Syrian intervention in Beirut in Feb. 1987 broke the Amal siege of Palestinian refugee camps. The Israeli-supported South Lebanese Army controls the southernmost part of Lebanon. Israeli attacks continued. UN peacekeeping troops are in place. Attempts at political solution centred on Syria.

Syria	1970/1976	Syrian Govt. vs. Sunni, other opposition	392–395[e] 42 ..	1976–87: >15 1987: very low, <0.1	--

Comments: The main armed opposition to the Assad Government, formed in 1970, is the Sunni Muslim Brotherhood. Sunnis make up the majority. Alawite Muslims control politics and the economy. Disaffection with the Assad regime erupted in 1976 and fighting climaxed with the destruction in Feb. 1982 of Hamah, a town suspected of being a Muslim Brotherhood stronghold, resulting in 5000–25 000 deaths. A new wave of bombings and assassinations occurred in 1986. Armed opposition also from pro-Iraqi Ba'athists and Palestinians. After a relatively high death toll (400) in 1986, armed opposition was mainly extra-territorial in 1987, aimed at individual diplomats and Syrian property abroad.

South Asia

Afghanistan	1978/1978	Afghan Govt. and USSR vs. Afghan Mujahideen	40–45 115 50	1978–87: 100–150 (mil.) (>350) (civ.)	0

Comments: The conflict began as an insurrection against the new Marxist Govt., itself a product of internal rivalries within the Afghan Communist parties. The Soviet intervention of Dec. 1979 was claimed to be in support of the Govt. Soviet troops do most of the fighting, as the Afghan Army has disintegrated to half its former size. The military situation remains a stand-off, with neither side able to make significant or lasting gains. Soviet deaths are estimated at 10 000–15 000. The USA and others provide aid to the Afghan opposition. The war increasingly spills into Pakistan. Pakistan claimed over 650 airspace violations in 1986 and lodged 20 formal protests. From mid-1986 the military initiative has been held mainly by the Govt. and Soviet forces, especially in the north. The 6-month ceasefire announced by the Kabul regime on 15 Jan. 1987 was rejected. The Govt. offensive in the east and south in Dec. 1987 produced the heaviest fighting of the war. UN mediation continued in Geneva. Estimates of civilian deaths are highly uncertain and could be much higher than reported here.

Location/ conflict	Year formed/ year joined[a]	Warring parties	No. of troops in 1986[b] (thou.)	Deaths[c] (thou.)	Change from 1986[d]
India	1947/1947 /1981	Indian Govt. vs. Sikh separatists, ethnic and religious opposition	1260[e] 9	1983–87: <10 1987: 0.6	0

Comments: In 1987 ethnic and religious violence was at the highest level since independence in 1947. The sharpest conflict is in Punjab Province with the Sikhs (13 m. total), who desire greater autonomy or independence. Attacks by Sikh organizations (the Khalistan Liberation Army and the Khalistan Commando Force) led to the Govt.'s military assault in June 1984 on the Golden Temple (the holiest Sikh shrine), resulting in 1000 deaths. Sikhs assassinated Prime Minister Indira Gandhi in Oct. 1984. Close to 6000 died from Sikh violence in 1984–87. Armed opposition in Assam quieted after massive violence in 1983. Separatist struggles continue in the north-eastern region (Manipur, Mizoram and Tripura). Agreement between the central Govt. and Naga groups led to elections which may have ended the continuous guerrilla campaign by tribal groups wanting autonomy/independence for Nagaland.

India–Pakistan	1947/1965 /1971 /1984	Indian Govt. vs. Pakistani Govt.	1260[e] 481[e]	1971: 11 (mil.) 1987: 0.1	+

Comments: Since independence in 1947 there have been several wars, first over partition, then over Kashmir and East Pakistan. Long-standing mistrust between the two countries has been increased by trouble in Punjab Province. India claims Pakistan supports Sikh militants in India. Tension rose as a result of large-scale military exercises close to the border in the early part of 1987. In Sep. and Oct. 1987 virtually continuous sniping by Indian and Pakistani troops on the Siachin Glacier in Kashmir led to an estimated 150 deaths.

Pakistan	1972/1972	Pakistani Govt. vs. Pathan/Baluchi separatists	481[e] (5)	1973–77: 3 (mil.) 6 (civ.)	0

Comments: Low-level separatist guerrilla campaigns since the early 1970s in the three provinces dominated by an ethnic minority. Baluchi, Pathan and Sindhi constitute about 40% of the population (the majority are Punjabi). Armed clashes in Baluchistan left thousands dead in the 1970s and continue today, as do terrorist bombings by Pathans in the North-West Frontier Province. Unrest in the Sind Province. Sindhis resent domination of the central Govt. by Punjabis. Fighting between ethnic groups in Sind in Nov. and Dec. 1986 left about 200 dead. In 1987 there was a decrease in separatist violence but a rise in violence against Afghan refugee villages alleged to be the work of Afghan agents. Some opposition groups use terrorist methods.

Sri Lanka	1976/1983	Sri Lankan Govt. and India vs. Tamil opposition	38 35 5–7	1983–86: 4.5–5 1987: >2	++

Comments: The conflict between the Buddhist Sinhalese (74% of the population) and Hindu Tamils (18%) erupted into sustained civil war in 1983. Certain Tamil groups want a separate nation. The Liberation Tigers of Tamil Eelam (LTTE) is the largest of six Tamil armed groups. Opposition controls the countryside in the north. The Tamil Nadu state in southern India was used as a sanctuary and the base of operations before the agreement of July 1987 between India and Sri Lanka placed Indian peacekeeping troops on the island. In Oct. 1987 Indian troops fought against forces from the Tamil Tigers. The Sinhalese People's Liberation Front (JVP), opposed to the agreement, became a new party to the conflict in Nov. 1987.

Location/ conflict	Year formed/ year joined[a]	Warring parties	No. of troops in 1986[b] (thou.)	Deaths[c] (thou.)	Change from 1986[d]
Far East					
Burma	1948/1948	Burmese Govt. vs. Communists, KNLA and other ethnic opposition	186[e] 10–15 4–10 12–20	1948–51: 8 1980: 5 >1 yearly	+

Comments: At least 14 separatist and revolutionary armed groups have been fighting against the central Govt. since Burma gained independence in 1948. Govt. control in many areas is weak. The Burma Communist Party (BCP) is regarded as the largest opposition force; its activities have lessened in recent years as support from China has decreased. The heaviest fighting is now with the Karen National Liberation Army (KNLA), which seeks an autonomous state for 2–3 m. ethnic Karens. Other significant rebellions in Kachin and Shan states, plus many smaller ethnic minority armed opposition groups. In Mar. 1986 a military-political alliance was formed between the Karens and the Communists. A Govt. offensive in 1987 pushed Karen forces over the border into Thailand, though they later re-grouped in Burma.

| China–Viet Nam | 1979/1979 | Chinese Govt. vs.
Vietnamese
Govt. | 250
250 | 1979: 21 (mil.)
9 (civ.)
1980–87: 1 | 0 |

Comments: Border skirmishes have continued since the Sino–Vietnamese War in 1979. There have been mostly artillery exchanges, cross-border raids and limited ground attacks. China claims that Viet Nam has made 10 000 incursions and fired over half a million artillery shells since 1980. Viet Nam claims that China has fired over 20 000 shells a day during offensives. Attacks appear tied to Vietnamese actions in Kampuchea. Armed activity in 1987 was a continuation of the previous pattern.

| Indonesia (East
Timor) | 1975/1975 | Indonesian Govt.
vs. Fretilin,
separatist groups | 218[e]
0.2
8 | 1975–80: 10 (mil.)
90 (civ.)
1980–87: 0.1 yearly | 0 |

Comments: Indonesia's invasion in 1975 of East Timor, a former Portuguese colony seeking independence through the political organization Fretilin, resulted in over 100 000 deaths by 1979. Indonesian troops still occupy East Timor (since annexed by Indonesia). Other armed separatist movements include those in West Irian (the Free Papua Movement) and Northern Sumatra (the Free Aceh Movement).

| Kampuchea | 1970/1970
/1975 | Heng Samrin
Govt., Viet Nam
vs. Khmer
Rouge, KPNLF,
ANS,
Thailand | 30
140
30
11
5
256[e] | (1970–78: 2500)
1979–87: 10 (mil.)
14 (civ.)
1987: <1 | – |

Comments: A series of conflicts has hit Kampuchea since 1970. Wars, invasion and war-related famines have resulted in 2–3 m. deaths since 1970, most during the brutal reign of Pol Pot's Khmer Rouge (1975–78). The Vietnamese invasion forced Pol Pot to leave the capital in 1978. 140 000 Vietnamese troops remain in Kampuchea and conduct most of the fighting. Armed opposition is made up of a coalition of Khmer Rouge, Khmer People's National Liberation Front (KPNLF) and Armée Nationale Sihanoukist (ANS). The coalition is recognized by the UN as the legitimate Govt. of Kampuchea. The war has affected Thailand, which houses refugee camps. The USSR supports the Heng Samrin Govt., China supports the Khmer Rouge, and the USA and ASEAN support the non-Communist guerrillas. The 2 Dec. 1987 meeting in Paris between Sihanouk, who temporarily gave up his leadership role, and the Viet Nam-supported Kampuchean Prime Minister Hun Sen gave rise to temporary speculation about a possible peace agreement.

ARMED CONFLICTS IN 1987   293

Location/ conflict	Year formed/ year joined[a]	Warring parties	No. of troops in 1986[b] (thou.)	Deaths[c] (thou.)	Change from 1986[d]
Laos	1975/1975	Pathet Lao Govt., Viet Nam vs. NLF, Thailand	54[e] 40–45[e] 2–3 256[e]	1975–87: 10 (mil.) 30 (civ.) 1987: <0.1	+

Comments: Widespread warfare in 1975–79 following the Pathet Lao's assumption of power has dwindled to low-level insurgency. Four opposition groups formed a coalition (the National Liberation Front, NLF) in 1981 aimed at the ouster of the Pathet Lao Govt. and Vietnamese troops, but co-operation is sporadic. The largest opposition group is the Hmong tribesmen, led by Gen. Van Pao (remnants of the CIA's 'secret army'). The opposition is largely based in Thailand. Clashes between Thai troops and Lao Govt. troops over the disputed frontier increased at the end of 1987.

Malaysia	1945/1945	Malaysian Govt., Thailand vs. CPM	110 256[e] 1–2	<0.1 yearly	–

Comments: The Govt. has been fighting the forces of the Communist Party of Malaysia (CPM) since World War II. CPM guerrillas are based mostly in Thailand. Thai and Malaysian armed forces conduct joint operations against the CPM. An agreement in Apr. 1987 between the Thai Govt. and the CPM offered amnesty, and some members of the CPM faction surrendered. Some terrorist attacks against minority ethnic Chinese occurred in 1986–87.

Philippines	1968/1970 /1986	Philippine Govt. vs. NPA, MNLF, MILF, military opposition	113[e] 16–22 10 ..	1972–87: 20 (mil.) 15 (civ.) 1987: <1	–

Comments: President Aquino took over Govt. in Feb. 1986. It faces continued military opposition favouring the return of the deposed President Marcos. During 1987 a series of military coups were attempted against the Aquino Govt. The left-wing armed opposition, the New People's Army (NPA), doubled in size in 1983–85. The 60-day ceasefire of 10 Dec. 1986 did not end warfare between the Govt. and NPA. Armed conflict between the central Govt. and the MNLF (Moro National Liberation Front) since the 1970s has resulted in more than 50 000 dead. The MNLF, which desires independence for the island of Mindanao, has declined in strength. An agreement was concluded in Jan. 1987 between the Aquino Govt. and the MNLF on full autonomy, but talks on the autonomous area broke down in July. The MILF (Muslim Islamic Liberation Front) criticized the agreement and fought against both the MNLF and the Philippine Army, beginning in Jan. 1987.

Thailand	1965/1965	Thai Govt. vs. CPT, CPM, PULO, Viet Nam	256[e] 0.8–1 2 140[e]	<0.1 yearly	0

Comments: Communist and separatist armed opposition reached a peak in the 1970s. The Communist Party of Thailand (CPT) armed forces are estimated to have decreased to fewer than 1000. Four leaders of the CPT were arrested in Apr. 1987. The Thai Govt. forces also combat Muslim separatists in the south (the Patani United Liberation Organization (PULO) and others). In early 1987 there were frequent border clashes between Vietnamese and Thai forces on the Kampuchean border, and talks were held between Thailand and Viet Nam.

Location/ conflict	Year formed/ year joined[a]	Warring parties	No. of troops in 1986[b] (thou.)	Deaths[c] (thou.)	Change from 1986[d]
Africa					
Angola	1975/1975	Angolan Govt., Cuba vs. UNITA and S. Africa	50 40 40 6[f]	1975–85: >11 1985–87: 4 (mil.)	+

Comments: The Govt. faces armed opposition by UNITA (Union for the Total Independence of Angola), claiming control of one-third of the country. UNITA's main supporter is S. Africa. S. African troops have attacked inside Angola and held the southern province of Cunene since 1980. The USA has an open 'covert' aid programme for UNITA. The Govt. is supported by Cuban troops and the USSR (arms and advisers). There has been an intensification of the fighting in recent years. A S. African offensive into Angola, ostensibly against SWAPO (South West African People's Organization, Namibia), was launched in Jan. 1987. Govt. forces suffered heavy losses. In a counter-offensive in Oct. against UNITA, S. African troops intervened.

Chad	1965/1975 /1979	Habré Govt., France vs. Oueddai forces, other opposition vs. Libya	142 2.4 3 0.3 5	1965–86: >22 1987: 1.5–2	++

Comments: There have been decades of war between different factions. Libyan troops have occupied the Aouzou strip in the north since 1973. 1200 French forces have been in Chad since 1980; they doubled in size during 1987. Conflicts in the 1980s have mainly pitted Habré Govt. forces against the Libyan-backed forces of Goukouni Oueddai. The multinational OAU peacekeeping force was deployed in Nov. 1981. French troops intervened on behalf of Habré in July 1983–Nov. 1984 and Feb. 1986; troops from Zaire in 1983. In Oct. 1986 Oueddai switched sides and joined Habré in fighting Libyan troops in Chad. In 1987 the war turned into a struggle between the combined forces of the Habré Govt. and Oueddai against Libya, with France giving active support to the Chad Govt. After Libyan forces were defeated a ceasefire was agreed between Chad and Libya on 11 Sep. 1987. Libyan forces remain in the Aouzou area, and forces from Chad crossed the border into Libya, destroying considerable quantities of Libyan armour.

Ethiopia	1961/1962	Ethiopian Govt. vs. EPLF, TPLF and other opposition	227[e] 50–60	1962–87: 45 (mil.) >50 (civ.)	0

Comments: The largest armed opposition group is the EPLF (Eritrean People's Liberation Front), about 30 000 strong, fighting for independence since the annexation of Eritrea in 1962. Other major opposition is the TPLF (Tigre People's Liberation Front), about 10 000 strong. Smaller opposition groups are in the Oromo, Wollo and Gondar regions. Cuban troops supporting the Govt. number fewer than 5000, down from a peak of 20 000 in 1977, mostly stationed to face military attack from Somalia. Peace talks were held between the Govt. and EPLF in 1987, but fighting continued. There have been repeated famines, and relief operations are hampered by military activity.

Location/ conflict	Year formed/ year joined[a]	Warring parties	No. of troops in 1986[b] (thou.)	Deaths[c] (thou.)	Change from 1986[d]
Ethiopia–Somalia	1964/1969	Ethiopia, Somali opposition vs. Somali Govt., Ethiopian anti-regime forces	227[e] 3.5 42.7 1	1964–86: 38 1980–87: 2	0

Comments: This conflict combines a border war and several guerrilla conflicts. Ethiopia and Somalia dispute their border in the Ogaden region. Somali opposition in Ogaden desires alignment with Somalia and has fought the Ethiopian Govt. since 1964. The conflict was most intense during the Somali invasion of Ogaden in 1977. The Ethiopian Govt. supports the Democratic Front for the Salvation of Somalia (DFSS) and the Somali National Movement (SNM) which are based in Ethiopia. The Somali Govt. supports the Western Somali Liberation Front (WSLF) and the Somali Abu Liberation Front (SALF) which are based in Somalia. Skirmishes and Ethiopian air strikes continued over the Somali border in 1987.

Mozambique	1978/1981	Mozambican Govt., Zimbabwe, Tanzania vs. MNR (S. Africa)	25 11 .. (20)	1985–87: 4–6 (mil.)	+

Comments: The National Resistance Movement (MNR or RENAMO) grew rapidly from 3000–5000 rebels in 1983 to about 20 000 in 1986. MNR receives weapons, training, logistic and other support from S. Africa. Apparent MNR goal is to disrupt and destroy Govt. infrastructure. The Mozambican Govt. has received military aid from the USSR and some assistance from the UK. Combat support from troops of Zimbabwe and Tanzania. Several MNR massacres of civilians occurred during 1987, the most severe involving the death of nearly 400 civilians. In 1987 the conflict also tended to spill over into Zimbabwe. Land-locked neighbours were seriously affected by the disruption of transport.

Namibia	1966/1967	S. African Govt. vs. SWAPO	21 6–9	1967–84: >10 1985–87: 1.5	+

Comments: In 1966 the UN renunciated S. Africa's mandate over South West Africa (and renamed it Namibia), but S. Africa has ignored the UN. SWAPO (South West African People's Organization), the national anti-colonial movement leading the war for independence, has widespread support among Namibia's population. SWAPO's military arm, the People's Liberation Army of Namibia (PLAN), is based in Angola. S. African troops regularly attack SWAPO inside Angola. In 1986–87 S. Africa claimed a significant depletion of the resistance forces. Promising negotiations with the UN 'contact group' on a solution were brought to a standstill in 1981, following the US linking of the issue to Cuban troops in Angola.

South Africa	1950/1979	S. African Govt. vs. ANC	106.4[e] 10	1984–87: >3	–

Comments: A core problem is the policy of apartheid in S. Africa, which deprives the majority of the population of equal political, human and economic rights to the benefit of the white minority. There has been a new phase of increased violence since 1984. Increasing use of S. African military in the townships. The African National Congress (ANC) has emerged as the main armed anti-apartheid organization; its military wing, the Spear of the Nation, has grown to about 10 000 armed forces. The main warfare is economic sabotage and hit-and-run attacks on police and military facilities. 1987 saw a reduction in violence, which the Govt. attributed to martial law restrictions. S. Africa strikes at armed opposition based in neighbouring countries. A UN mandatory arms embargo on S. Africa has been in place since 1977. Economic sanctions are now also imposed by the USA and the EC. 1987 saw open contacts between white leaders and the leadership of the ANC in a common search for a solution.

Location/ conflict	Year formed/ year joined[a]	Warring parties	No. of troops in 1986[b] (thou.)	Deaths[c] (thou.)	Change from 1986[d]
Sudan	1980/1983	Sudanese Govt. vs. SPLA	57 20	1983–86: >3 1987: low	0

Comments: In 1983 civil war resumed, which had killed hundreds of thousands in 1955–72 in south Sudan. The non-Muslim south desires greater autonomy and better distribution of national income. The SPLA (Sudan People's Liberation Army) is the main armed opposition. A second group, Anyana II, broke from SPLA and is now fighting with Govt. forces against SPLA. During 1987 SPLA made gains in the province of Equatoria.

| Uganda | 1979/1981 | NRA Govt. vs. opposition | (6) (6) | 1981–87: 5–6 (mil.) 100 (civ.) 1987: 2 | + |

Comments: Uganda has been plagued for decades with fighting among ethnic, tribal and private armies. The guerrilla National Resistance Army (NRA), which took up arms in 1981, seized power in Jan. 1986 and is now fighting forces led by three previous leaders of Uganda: Okello, Obote and Amin. Widespread massacres and attacks on the civilian population resulted in massive deaths in 1983–85. During 1987 a new group emerged in the south under the leadership of Alice Lakwena ('Messiah of the poor'), who was eliminated as a serious force after most of her followers were annihilated in sacrificial battles.

| Western Sahara | 1975/1975 | Moroccan Govt. vs. Polisario | 100–120 4–15 | 1975–78: >7 (mil.) 1987: 0.5 (mil.) | + |

Comments: The former Spanish colony of Western Sahara was divided between Morocco and Mauritania in 1975. Morocco annexed Mauritania's half in 1979, following Mauritania's withdrawal from the war and an agreement with Polisario. The Polisario Liberation Front is fighting for independence, based mainly in Algeria. Morocco has built a 2500-km wall, enclosing 75% of Western Sahara, to force Polisario out. Feb. 1987 saw the heaviest fighting in two and a half years. Nightly attacks were carried out by Polisario over the wall. In late 1987 a UN group visited Western Sahara as part of a referendum plan.

| Zimbabwe | 1979/1980 | Mugabe Govt. vs. ZAPU, MNR | 42[e] .. | 1979–87: >1.5 0.1 yearly | – |

Comments: The agreement of Dec. 1979 transferred power from the white minority Govt. to the black majority and ended the civil war. Subsequent fighting between forces loyal to leaders of the two main black guerrilla groups (Robert Mugabe, elected Prime Minister in Mar. 1980, leader of ZANU (Zimbabwe African National Union) and Joshua Nkomo, leader of ZAPU (Zimbabwe African People's Union)) effectively ended in 1986 with the attempted unity of the two groups. Warfare continues against 'dissidents', a collection of disaffected guerrilla fighters. S. African proxies and criminals conducting a campaign of terrorism and economic sabotage in the Matabele Province, with the aim of destabilizing the Govt. ZANU and ZAPU agreed in Dec. 1987 to create a joint party. The fighting in Mozambique between the Govt. and the South African-supported MNR spills over into Zimbabwe.

ARMED CONFLICTS IN 1987   297

Location/ conflict	Year formed/ year joined[a]	Warring parties	No. of troops in 1986[b] (thou.)	Deaths[c] (thou.)	Change from 1986[d]
Latin America					
Colombia	1978/1979	Colombian Govt. vs. M-19, FARC and other groups	66.2[e] 0.1–1.5 10–12 1–1.5	1980–85: 1 yearly 1987: 0.2	0

Comments: Several armed revolutionary groups engage in bombings, kidnappings and armed attacks. Govt. forces mount offensives and counter-offensives but are unable to defeat the armed opponents. The May 1984 peace accord with four main groups did not end the violence. The biggest group—the Colombian Revolutionary Armed Forces (FARC)—abided by it at least until 1987. In 1987 either FARC or a splinter group of the main organization resumed attacks on police stations (Mar. 1987, 100 dead) and security forces (June 1987, 30 dead). The most active and most heavily armed group has been the M-19 (April 19 Movement).

| El Salvador | 1976/1977 /1979 | Salvadorean Govt. vs. FMLN | 43 4.5–6 | 1979–85: 15 (mil.) 40 (civ.) 1986: 1.5 (mil.) 1987: >1 (mil.) | – |

Comments: FMLN (Farabundo Marti Front for National Liberation) is a coalition of groups fighting rightist Salvadorean armed forces and the Govt. The present conflict dates from 1979. Opposition controls portions of the countryside. Extensive arms deliveries, military training and other combat support for Govt. forces are provided by the USA. A large number of massacres of civilians by the Govt. and paramilitary forces. Exiled members of the political opposition and refugees returned as part of the Arias (Esquipulas II) Peace Plan of 7 Aug. 1987. A national reconciliation commission was established but no ceasefire concluded.

| Guatemala | 1967/1968 | Guatemalan Govt. vs. URNG | 32[e] 2–2.5 | 1967–87: 2 (mil.) 43 (civ.) 1987: low | – |

Comments: Armed opposition dates to the early 1960s against right-wing, military govts. Four guerrilla groups formed the Guatemalan National Revolutionary Unity (URNG) in 1982. The massive counter-insurgency campaign of 1982–83 cut the guerrilla strength by more than half; extensive civilian casualties with entire villages destroyed. Counter-insurgency measures restrain guerrilla activity. The Arias (Esquipulas II) Peace Plan of 7 Aug. 1987 applies also to Guatemala. No ceasefire has been concluded.

| Nicaragua | 1979/1980 | Nicaraguan Govt. vs. opposition (Contras), Mesquito Indians | 72 12–17 .. | 1981–87: 9 (mil.) 3 (civ.) | – |

Comments: The right-wing Contras (counter-revolutionaries) are attempting to overthrow the Sandinista Govt., which came into power in 1979 following the national uprising against the Somoza regime. The Contras are largely based in Honduras. The largest Contra group is the Democratic Forces of Nicaragua (FDN). The Contras continued to receive arms, training and other support from citizens of the USA in spite of the suspension of funds for military aid by Congress. The provision of this assistance was supported by a group within the Administration which included National Security Advisor Poindexter and Colonel Oliver North. The scale of Soviet military deliveries to the Sandinista Govt. and the presence of Cuban military advisers have been subject to widely differing estimates. The Arias (Esquipulas II) Peace Plan of 7 Aug. 1987 applies also to Nicaragua. Domestic efforts at conflict resolution have included a Govt. offer of amnesty, a national reconciliation commission and the negotiation of a short ceasefire. The Mesquito Indians, who previously fought alongside the Contras, entered into an agreement with the Sandinista Govt. in autumn 1987 which gave them some regional autonomy.

Location/ conflict	Year formed/ year joined[a]	Warring parties	No. of troops in 1986[b] (thou.)	Deaths[c] (thou.)	Change from 1986[d]
Peru	1980/1980	Peruvian Govt. vs. Sendero Luminoso	127[e] 2–3	1980–87: 2 (mil.) 1987: 0.1	0

Comments: The Sendero Luminoso (Shining Path) describes itself as 'Maoist', with the goal of putting workers and peasants in power. The conflict has expanded since late 1982 when Sendero moved from the main base in the Ayacucho region to become active in several provinces and Lima. The Govt. deployed ever larger numbers of Army troops. Widespread abuse of civilians by both the Army and the Sendero. The involvement of armed opposition in drug traffic was reported in 1987. Confrontations were mainly over Sendero attempts to release prisoners and from security force raids on drug-traffic associates of Sendero.

[a] 'Year formed' is the year in which the two (or more) parties last formed their conflicting policies or the year in which a new party, state or alliance involved in the conflict came into being. 'Year joined' is the year in which the armed fighting last began or the year(s) in which armed fighting recommenced after a period for which no armed combat was recorded. For conflicts with very sporadic armed combat over a long period, the 'year joined' may also refer to the beginning of a period of sustained and/or exceptionally heavy combat.

[b] The number of troops is given for 1986 since reliable figures for 1987 were not available; most are as in the *SIPRI Yearbook 1987*, table 8.1, pp. 310–17. The figures in this column refer to the troops of the respective warring parties in the previous column, and correspond to the order in which they are named in that column.

[c] The figures for deaths refer to total battle-related deaths for the duration of the conflict. The figures exclude, as far as data allow, deaths owing to famine and disease. 'Mil.' and 'civ.' refer to estimates, where available, of military and civilian deaths; where there is no such indication, the figure refers to total battle-related deaths in the entire period of conflict or in the period given.

[d] The change from 1986 is measured as the increase or decrease in battle-related deaths in 1987 compared to those in 1986. Although based on data that cannot be considered totally reliable, the symbols represent the following changes:
++   increase in battle deaths of more than 100%
+   increase in battle deaths of less than 100%
0   stable rate of battle deaths (+ or −10%)
−   decrease in battle deaths of less than 50%
− −   decrease in battle deaths of more than 50%.
Where there is a figure for the number of battle-related deaths or an indication of 'high' or 'low' numbers of deaths in 1987, these are given in the preceding column.

[e] Not all these troops are engaged in actual combat.

[f] Estimated number of South African forces involved in the Dec. 1987 offensive.

Sources: Goose, S., 'Armed conflicts in 1986, and the Iraq–Iran War', SIPRI, *SIPRI Yearbook 1987: World Armaments and Disarmament* (Oxford University Press: Oxford, 1987); SIPRI Arms Trade Project data base; BBC World Service News (London); *Washington Post*; *World Reporter* (Datasolve: London); *Keesing's Contemporary Archives*; Sivard, R., *World Military and Social Expenditures* (World Priorities Inc.: Washington, DC, annual); *The Statesman's Yearbook* (Macmillan: London, annual); *Defense and Foreign Affairs* (USA); *Defense and Foreign Affairs Handbook* (Copley: Washington, DC, 1976); *Far Eastern Economic Review* (Hong Kong); *The Times* (London); *International Herald Tribune* (The Hague); *Dagens Nyheter* (Stockholm); *Svenska Dagbladet* (Stockholm); Jongman, B., *War, Armed Conflict and Political Violence* (Polemological Institute, National University: Groningen, the Netherlands, 1982); Kaye, G. D. Grant, D. A. and Emond, E. J., *Major Armed Conflict, A Compendium of Interstate and Intrastate Conflict 1720 to 1985* (Operational Research and Analysis Establishment (ORAE), Canadian Department of National Defence: Ottawa, 1985); Small, M. and Singer, J. D., *Resort to Arms, International and Civil Wars 1816–1980* (Sage: Beverley Hills, Calif., 1982); Gantzel, K.-J. and Meyer-Stamer, J. (eds), *Die Kriege nach dem Zweiten Weltkrieg bis 1984* (Weltforum: Munich, 1986); research reports on particular conflicts; and information available at the Department of Peace and Conflict Research, Uppsala University, in the continuing research project on armed conflicts.

Part III. Developments in arms control

Chapter 10. US–Soviet nuclear arms control

Chapter 11. Conventional arms control in Europe: problems and prospects

Chapter 12. Multilateral arms control efforts

10. US–Soviet nuclear arms control

CHRISTOPH BERTRAM*

I. Introduction

1987 was the year in which, on the surface at least, the Reagan approach to arms control came close to being vindicated. The US President had set out in 1980 to ridicule and repudiate the traditional, gradualist arms control method and had replaced it with a new, apparently more ambitious brand: instead of merely regulating the East–West military competition, the goal was now to achieve deep cuts in nuclear arsenals that could be comprehensively verified.

The INF Treaty of December 1987 (see chapter 13) was the first agreement to meet these requirements. Yet the real test for Reagan-type arms control was still to be met: whether the superpowers could reach an agreement on drastically cutting their strategic nuclear arsenals before the end of Mr Reagan's term of office. As 1987 progressed, such an agreement, while still unlikely to be completed in time, came closer. Yet the old doubts over the wisdom of the Reagan approach persisted. Would the new regime, even if accomplished, successfully restrain Soviet–US nuclear competition in the 1990s? And would it achieve what arms control had always aspired to, namely, a more stable, strategic balance between the major powers?

II. START: narrowing the gap

At their first summit meeting in November 1985, President Reagan and General Secretary Gorbachev had formulated their ambitious goal: to cut the strategic nuclear forces by 50 per cent. At first, there had been little progress as both sides stuck to incompatible positions.[1] But then the Soviet Union, in the summer of 1986, showed signs of increasing flexibility which gave new impetus to the negotiations, although much of it remained obscured by other developments: the failure of the Reykjavik summit meeting in October 1986 and the rapid progress after March 1987 in the negotiations on intermediate-range nuclear forces (INF). Yet even before the December 1987 Washington summit meeting both the Soviet Union and the United States had indicated that the Strategic Arms Reduction Talks (START), not INF, were for both of them the more ambitious goal: the total ban of all their ground-based medium-range missiles was to be a 'fine prelude',[2] as Mr Gorbachev called it, to the real thing, an agreement on halving their respective strategic forces.

Since the Reykjavik meeting there had been agreement on the overall limit that a START accord would impose on the strategic nuclear arsenals of the USA and the USSR: neither would keep more than 1600 delivery vehicles and more than 6000 nuclear warheads deployed. This would not be quite the 'fifty per cent cut' of official communiqués but, at least in the numbers of deliverable warheads, a sizeable reduction (see table 10.1).

SIPRI Yearbook 1988: World Armaments and Disarmament

Table 10.1. Soviet and US strategic forces under START

		USA	USSR
I. Pre-START			
Launchers			
ICBMs		1 000	1 390
SLBMs		640	948
Bombers		324	160
Total launchers		**1 964**	**2 498**
Warheads			
On ICBMs		2 268	6 388
On SLBMs		5 632	3 668
On bombers[a]		2 100	840
Total warheads		**10 000**	**10 896**
II. Post-START[b]	*Limits*	*Percentage cuts*	
Launchers	1 600	18.6	36.9
(excluding SLCMs)			
Warheads	6 000	40.0	44.9
On ballistic missiles	4 900	38.0	51.2
On bombers[c]	1 100	47.7	0.0

[a] Assuming agreed counting rules which envisage that each bomber would be counted as one warhead unless equipped with ALCM, and assuming further that US bomber loadings will be 12 ALCMs per dedicated aircraft.
[b] Assuming currently envisaged sub-ceilings.
[c] Minimum for USA, maximum for USSR.

Source: Figures based on compilation in *Arms Control Today*, Oct. 1987, pp. 10–11. However, actual percentage cuts are likely to be significantly less—more of the order of 30% than 59%—as a result of (*a*) the exclusion of all strategic SLCMs from the launcher and warhead total (the permitted number and range remain to be settled); (*b*) the exclusion of all bomber loadings of free-fall bombs and short-range stand-off weapons which will be counted as 1 warhead, regardless of actual loadings; and (*c*) the possible exclusion of capacity counting for ALCM carriers, permitting both sides to maintain larger arsenals than are held accountable.

Yet, there remained important hurdles on the road to agreement. The most significant of these was the now familiar problem of whether and how to restrict limitations on strategic defences (see section III). But even within the context of reducing strategic offensive forces, disagreement persisted, particularly on three aspects of the proposed Treaty: (*a*) which strategic forces would be counted within the overall ceiling—the problem of definition and of counting rules; (*b*) how these forces would be structured—the problem of sub-limits; and (*c*) how an agreement would be verified.

Defining and counting the arsenals

There had never been any disagreement about whether a START accord would include intercontinental ballistic missiles (ICBMs), submarine-launched ballistic missiles (SLBMs) and strategic bombers—the traditional 'triad'. But, thanks to the relentless march of technology, new weapon systems had become increasingly part of the strategic forces of each side. And while detailed understanding of how to cope with the traditional triad of weapons was to emerge fairly swiftly, the 'new' weapon systems—mobile ICBMs, and air-launched and sea-launched cruise missiles—posed serious problems for the negotiators.

For the traditional systems, counting rules were soon established. Fixed ICBMs would be counted as carrying the number of warheads which had been tested for each type; the communiqué of the 1987 Washington summit meeting listed these numbers.[3] As regarded SLBMs, the Soviet Union made a potentially significant concession to the United States; although the Trident II D-5 missile was to be tested with up to 12 warheads, the Soviet Union agreed to count only 8 warheads per missile, thus making it easier for the Reagan Administration to repudiate somewhat the critics who had claimed that the START agreement would force the USA to hold too many warheads on too few submarines.[4] As to strategic bombers, here, too, the Soviet Union had agreed in Reykjavik to a counting rule which, because of the much larger US strategic bomber force, would favour the United States: each bomber would be counted as carrying one warhead (and one delivery vehicle), regardless of how many free-fall nuclear explosives or how many nuclear-tipped stand-off weapons it carried on board.

Yet both sides remained significantly apart on the question of how to treat the 'new' types of strategic forces. And while the possibilities for compromise on some of these systems seemed not too distant, the sheer complexity implied by others would make the rapid achievement of an accord difficult even if the will to compromise were there.

Mobile ICBMs

In November 1985, just prior to the first Reagan–Gorbachev summit meeting, the US position on START had changed abruptly; now the USA demanded that all mobile land-based missiles be banned. Clearly, one concern driving this demand was that of the new land-mobile Soviet SS-25 and the rail-mobile version of the SS-24 missile; the corresponding US systems were still far from deployment. In addition, there was the worry that mobile missiles would be much more difficult to detect.

Yet the US antipathy towards mobile missiles was unlikely to block an agreement in the end, if only because it would be difficult to maintain this position not only at the negotiating table in Geneva but with the Congress in Washington as well. After all, the United States had responded to Soviet attempts to constrain sea-mobile missiles with the well-founded argument that mobility at sea reduces the vulnerability of strategic forces and is thus a contribution to stability; why then should land mobility contribute to instability? And in Washington, interest in also obtaining mobile missiles for the United States was not limited to the Congress which had long pushed a reticent Pentagon to study the possibility of a small, mobile ICBM, the so-called Midgetman. Frank Carlucci who succeeded Caspar Weinberger as US Secretary of Defense in November 1987, publicly advocated a mobile version of the MX ICBM shortly after assuming office.[5] Although in early 1988 US negotiatiors still insisted on a ban on mobile missiles, it seemed to be only a matter of time and context before the USA would be prepared to trade that issue for other advantages in Geneva.

Air-launched cruise missiles

While both sides agreed to include air-launched cruise missiles (ALCMs) in the overall warhead ceiling, counting each missile as one warhead, two items remained to be resolved in early 1988; how many of these missiles to attribute, for the purpose of verification, to each ALCM configured bomber (USA: six per bomber; USSR: number to be dependent on each type of aircraft), and how to define the—limited—ALCMs from the—unlimited—stand-off missiles on aircraft.

Of the two, the latter problem would be more difficult to sort out, for it concerned the thorny question of when an ALCM is a tactical and when a strategic weapon, a question which also posed itself for the sea-based cruise missile. The Soviet Union insisted on the range limit that had been used in the SALT II Treaty: every cruise missile with a range above 600 km should be counted as 'strategic'. The United States, on the other hand, sought the much higher range ceiling of 1500 km. Not only were they clearly concerned to exclude nuclear ALCMs for theatre use from the START restrictions; but perhaps even more significant, setting the ceiling on range rather high would allow the bomber forces of both sides to carry considerable nuclear firepower on stand-off missiles, which were defined, in the US position, as all aircraft-delivered missiles below the ALCM range.[6] The probable compromise might be a range definition somewhere between the Soviet and the US positions.

Sea-launched cruise missiles

It was this category of weapons which was likely to pose the most serious challenge to the negotiators. The United States had only reluctantly accepted that there should be a ceiling on these systems at all, not least because of its intention to build a total of approximately 4000 such weapons, of which about 800 would be nuclear tipped, with a range of 2500 km each. But for that same reason, the Soviet Union had always been keen on including them in any future strategic agreement.

At the Washington summit an uneasy compromise had been struck: the sides committed themselves to finding a mutually acceptable solution to limiting the longer-range nuclear SLCMs, but in a separate ceiling, that is, in addition to the limit of 6000 warheads, and only on condition that such limitation could be verified.

Yet this was only half of a breakthrough. For example, the Soviet Union tabled proposals which, for the USA, were plainly one-sided; all cruise missiles under 600-km range should be excluded, leaving practically all existing Soviet SLCM systems out of the equation. Moreover, the Soviet Union suggested that neither side should have more than a total of 1000 longer-range SLCMs, of which only 400, roughly half the programmed US force, would be nuclear. The matter was complicated by the fact that much of the attention of the US strategic community had been increasingly attracted by non-ballistic systems for strategic and theatre tasks,[7] as was evidenced by the proposals made at the

Reykjavik summit to forgo all ballistic nuclear delivery vehicles within a 10-year period.

Finally, from the US perspective, the SLCMs envisaged in current programmes would serve a regional rather than a strategic role, just as would their conventional counterparts; limitations on the nuclear variety would, therefore, both be outside the focus of START and restrict US naval flexibility considerably. Related to this was the issue of to what extent nuclear SLCMs in the European theatre might compensate for the removal of all land-based INF.

In short, restricting SLCM warheads would be distinctly unwelcome for the United States, even if Washington recognized the logic of the Soviet demand.

The fall-back line for the United States was that of non-verifiability. Indeed, it would prove highly difficult to devise an adequate verification regime which would be able to distinguish between both conventional and nuclear-tipped SLCMs and between shorter- and longer-range ones. Soviet statements in December 1987 indicating that Soviet scientists had developed a method for distinguishing conventional from nuclear warheads without actually looking inside the munition cannisters received short shrift from US experts.

Yet it seemed difficult to expect the Soviet Union to accept deep cuts in its strategic nuclear arsenal without some restraint on US longer-range SLCMs. Two possible methods of dealing with the issue presented themselves in early 1988.

The first, originally devised by non-governmental US experts, envisaged a ceiling not on nuclear but on conventional SLCMs: these would be counted as they left the factories, their munition cannisters inspected by Soviet or US monitoring teams; all other cruise missiles leaving the factory compound would then be regarded as nuclear. This suggestion was clearly more attractive to the Soviet side than to the USA. The other approach would be to ban nuclear SLCMs only for ranges that neither side desired—a limitation without bite which would have more appeal to the US than to the Soviet side. While there were weighty arguments against either of these compromises, it nevertheless seemed likely that some restrictions would be imposed on SLCMs in connection with a START treaty.

Thus the negotiations during 1987 and even the Washington summit had not fully clarified what weapons would be included under the agreed ceiling of 6000 warheads. The separate ceiling for SLCMs as well as the permissive counting rules for bomber loads suggested, however, that far from halving the total size of strategic nuclear arsenals, the future treaty would impose rather more modest cuts which, moreover, would not only leave the basic mission of the strategic forces of both sides unimpaired but also allow them to pursue these tasks with modern weapons.

Structuring for deterrence: the problem of sub-limits

Originally, in proposing its own approach to strategic arms limitations, the Reagan Administration had been guided by an objective which had been dear to US arms controllers for some years, namely, to reduce the threat of a disarming first strike by Soviet land-based missiles against US ICBMs. The greater the US concern over this assumed 'window of vulnerability', based on the MIRVed and increasingly accurate Soviet ICBM forces, the more intense the US insistence on sub-ceilings within START which would curb those forces. Hence, the original US plans for strategic arms reductions had envisaged a reduction of land- and sea-based ballistic missiles to 850 on each side, with no more than 2500 warheads of these two categories:[8] the effect would have been a reduction of over 50 per cent in Soviet ICBM warheads.[9]

In early 1987, it still seemed that the issue of sub-ceilings would represent a major stumbling-block on the road to agreement. The US proposal now envisaged four sub-ceilings under the overall one of 6000 warheads on 1600 strategic delivery systems: there should be no more than 4800 warheads on ballistic missiles (ICBMs and SLBMs combined), no more than 3300 warheads on ICBMs forces, no more than 1540 warheads on heavy ICBMs (the Soviet SS-18), and no more than 1650 warheads 'on permitted ICBMs except those on silo-based light and medium ICBMs with 6 or fewer warheads', a formula designed to restrict not only all heavy ICBMs but also all ICBMs with more than 6 warheads as well as all mobile ICBMs. If accepted by the Soviet Union, these proposals would pose very hard choices for Moscow, forcing Soviet planners to consider a painful trade-off between the heavy SS-18 ICBM, the new 10-warhead mobile SS-24 missile and the equally mobile one-warhead SS-25.

Yet, perhaps as a result of the emergence of greater pragmatism in the last years of the Reagan Administration, a new flexibility on sub-limits was to emerge. Although still part of the official US proposal, the 1650-warhead ceiling for specific ICBMs gradually drifted under the negotiating table. The United States now seemed more interested in maintaining its own force-planning flexibility than in cutting that of its opponent. Yet it was now the Soviet Union's turn to try to see if START might not be used to restructure US strategic forces to Soviet liking. Given the imminent hard-target kill capability of the US Trident II missile, Soviet negotiatiors sought to constrain the development of US sea-launched forces. In September 1987, the Soviet side suggested the following sub-ceilings:[10] 3000–3300 warheads on land-based missiles; 1800–2000 warheads on submarine-launched ballistic missiles and 800–900 warheads on air-launched cruise missiles. However, there would be no 'freedom to mix', each category of weapons being contained under an agreed limit.

Here again, however, it was difficult to imagine that compromise would evade the negotiators in the end. After all, the Soviet demand seemed to be partly influenced by no more than considerations of equality: if the United States wanted rigid limitations on ICBMs (on which, under the proposed counting rules, the United States would have no more than 23 per cent of its total warheads, but the Soviet Union 60 per cent), then, it was argued in Moscow, there should also be strict limits on SLBMs (57 per cent of US but only 34 per cent of Soviet strategic warheads), and the United States should not have the right to shift from the ICBM systems into bomber-carried or sea-based ones. Yet that was in essence more of a prestige than a strictly strategic argument and one which, for this reason, was likely to be traded in at some stage. Moreover, both sides indicated that there could well be fewer than the originally envisaged 3300 ICBM warheads; if this were to be the case, then the overall ceiling for warheads on ballistic delivery vehicles of 4900 which was agreed at the Washington summit would offer a margin of flexibility.

In addition to demanding sub-ceilings on specific delivery systems, the United States had insisted that the throw-weight of ballistic missiles should be halved, a category in which the Soviet Union enjoyed, owing to its heavy land-based missiles and the large component of ICBM forces in its arsenal, an advantage of some 5.7 million kg to the USA's 2 million kg. While initially the Soviet response had been cool, significant movement was subsequently made to meet the US demand. By the end of 1987, the Soviet Union had agreed in principle to reduce ballistic missile throw-weight to 50 per cent below existing levels, although there was still uncertainty over how this would be finalized and verified.

Thus the issue of sub-ceilings and counting rules which, for most of the START negotiations, had appeared as a major hurdle, were increasingly put in perspective. As in previous negotiations on strategic arms limitations, here, too, the law of declining ambitions imposed itself. No longer was START an attempt to fundamentally restructure the nuclear arsenals. The aim was now to achieve limitations which would be acceptable to both sides precisely because they would not curtail those options which each respectively regarded as essential for its deterrent. Once that became accepted, if tacitly, the task of the negotiations was no longer to bridge incompatible principles but to spell out, on the basis of agreed principles, the limitations they regarded as acceptable.

Verifying START

This change from competing philosophies to an agreed road-map was even more obvious in an area which, in the past, had been among the most controversial: verification. But since the Soviet Union had agreed in principle on intrusive controls, including on-site inspections, much of that controversy melted away. It was now no longer a dispute over principle but one over the best way to make sure that the stipulations of the new treaty could be verified adequately.

That breakthrough came in the wake of the INF Treaty. Significantly, the rules of how to ensure that the ban on all land-based medium-range systems would be observed were negotiated by both sides in the knowledge that they were creating a precedent for a START treaty. Consequently, the Washington communiqué listed the same inspection methods for the START treaty as were contained in the INF Treaty: the establishment of a baseline inventory on deployments, production and assembly plants, storage and testing sites; initial inspections to verify this data; on-site inspection of the destruction of systems; permanent perimeter portal monitoring of production sites and supply depots; on-site inspection of declared sites, including those no longer in use; suspect-site inspections at short notice; the prohibition of concealment measures, including telemetric information transmitted during flight-tests; and co-operative measures to improve the effectiveness of national technical means, including 'open displays of treaty-limited items at missile bases, bomber bases, and submarine ports at locations and times chosen by the inspecting party'.[11]

Yet there were two important and potentially complicating differences with the INF rule. For one, in a START treaty, not only delivery systems but also warheads and throw-weight would be the units of account; for another, the INF Treaty aimed not at the total but only at the partial removal of weapon systems. Both complications made for either more intrusive or less reliable verification: warheads are easier to hide than missiles, and the distinction between permitted and prohibited quantities of weapon systems is much more difficult to monitor than if all systems are banned, as in the INF Treaty.

It was clear, therefore, that if both sides were to stick to their earlier positions—the Soviet side objecting to on-site inspections, the US side insisting on comprehensive verification—no agreement would be possible. But both sides had moved towards a common ground on which a deal seemed possible: the Soviet side, at least in principle, declared its willingness to accept whatever controls were required to verify the agreement; the USA recognized that adequate verification—which provides for a sufficient barrier against unnoticed, militarily relevant break-outs—rather than perfect verifiability would be the objective. This change of mind in Washington had been brought about not least because the Defense Department, the former champion of comprehensive monitoring, had concluded during the INF negotiations that the ability of Soviet inspectors to observe all relevant US military activities might be less conducive to US security interests than the US ability to do the same on Soviet territory.[12]

Thus while it would remain a major technical task to draw up an agreement on verification, this no longer seemed a politically impossible task. Indeed, it might even be easier for US and Soviet negotiators to agree than for the Administration in Washington, which had set out under the banner of comprehensive verification, to convince its conservative supporters in the Senate.

In sum, the START negotiations made considerable progress in 1987. On issues where both sides were still wide apart, such as how to deal with SLCMs and how to define critical sub-ceilings, compromise seemed possible. On issues which presented primarily practical obstacles, such as verification, the INF Treaty provided an encouraging precedent.

The central question, at the beginning of 1988, was not, therefore, whether the negotiations would succeed in isolation. Rather it was whether Moscow and Washington could find a solution for the problem which had overshadowed the START negotiations since 1985: how to deal with strategic defences in space.

III. Strategic defence: a bridge over troubled waters?

In March 1983 President Reagan announced his plans for a major programme designed to make nuclear missiles 'impotent and obsolete': the Strategic

Defense Initiative (SDI), as it was later to be called, was born. Most arms control experts claimed at the outset that these plans would prove incompatible with objectives of limiting offensive strategic arms—for the obvious reason that, unless strategic defences are clearly constrained, limits on offensive forces cannot endure. It was only with the renewal of serious negotiations between the Soviet Union and the United States, in January 1985, that this issue had been put to the test. But then it seemed that these warnings were justified. Indeed, the 1986 Reykjavik summit, the most ambitious and potentially far-reaching meeting on arms control between President Reagan and General Secretary Gorbachev, had failed precisely because Mr Gorbachev had asked for constraints on the SDI programme which the President refused to accept.

During 1987, however, both sides tried to learn the lessons from Reykjavik. Both knew that—given the 'extraordinary' cancellation clause in the Anti-Ballistic Missile Treaty which allows either side to give six months' notice of withdrawal for reasons vital to national security—it could not hold the other indefinitely to the existing constraints on ballistic missile defences. Hence the Soviet Union had suggested, even prior to the Reykjavik meeting, a limited period of mandatory compliance with the ABM Treaty which, after all, had been entered into indefinitely: deployment should be permitted after a number of years which, since Reykjavik, the Soviet side had fixed at 10. In return, of course, the Soviets wanted both sides to comply fully with the ABM Treaty during that period.

Originally, the Soviet Union set out to scuttle the SDI programme by imposing rigid restrictions on permitted research and development. At Reykjavik, it demanded that all tests should be limited to laboratories. But shortly afterwards, Soviet spokesmen indicated that tests within the atmosphere might be permitted and even suggested, in April 1987, quantitative limits for permitted tests in space: by restricting velocity, brightness of lasers, and the like.

Significantly, during 1987 Soviet emphasis on the centrality of the ABM Treaty became increasingly marked. In September 1987, Foreign Minister Shevardnadze presented an alternative proposal to his US counterpart, the first suggesting a readiness to amend the Treaty by agreeing on a list of devices which would not be allowed to be put into space if they exceeded certain performance parameters; the second insisting instead on strict compliance with the ABM Treaty 'as signed and ratified in 1972'.[13] (See also chapter 14.) In December 1987, just prior to the Washington summit, General Secretary Gorbachev, in a televised interview with the US television company NBC, confirmed the growing Soviet preference for this second approach. Admitting for the first time that the Soviet Union, too, was involved in the research and development of space defences, Gorbachev declared that the Soviet Union no longer wished to prohibit the US SDI programme but instead set store on full respect for the ABM Treaty.[14] In order to underline that point and as if to remove all stains from the Soviet image as the arch-defender of the ABM Treaty, the Soviet Union decided to stop all further work on the giant Krasnoyarsk radar which had been viewed by many as a violation of the Treaty provisions. The United States, however, called upon the Soviet Union to tear down the radar facility or encase it behind a huge wall.[15]

The Washington communiqué reflected this change of approach, in a somewhat roundabout manner. Both Mr Reagan and Mr Gorbachev instructed their respective delegates in Geneva to work out an:

> agreement [that] would commit the sides to observe the Anti-Ballistic Missile (ABM) treaty, as signed in 1972, while conducting their research, development, and testing as required, which are permitted by the ABM treaty, and not to withdraw from the ABM treaty, for a specified period of time. Intensive discussions of strategic stability shall begin not later than three years before the end of the specified period after which, in the event the sides have not agreed otherwise, each side would be free to decide its course of action.[16]

Initially this looked to some like a major Soviet concession. Did the new formula not constitute an agreement to disagree, leaving the United States free to pursue whatever tests it wished as long as it could be even remotely argued that they complied with the ABM Treaty? As President Reagan's new National Security Advisor, General Colin Powell, explained on 10 December: 'Nothing that was done today restricts this administration or any future administration to the narrow interpretation . . . of the ABM-Treaty'.[17] President Reagan, it seemed, was on his way to obtaining what he had wanted all along: an agreement on deep cuts in strategic forces, unencumbered by any restrictions on his SDI programme.

This might have been true if the Administration alone had been able to decide the range of permitted activities under the ABM Treaty. But this it clearly could not, given the power and mood of the Congress. The Washington communiqué thus boiled down, in practice, to a confirmation of the restrictive rules of the ABM Treaty. Any attempt by the Administration to undertake tests which went beyond the Treaty limits as presented in 1972 would be a violation of the Treaty. And as such it would allow the Soviet Union in turn to forgo whatever commitments it had made under a START treaty, provided that link would be firmly established. The Soviet Union had, through its insistence on the ABM Treaty, assured that US compliance on SDI would affect the treaty implementation of START.

Indeed, Soviet negotiators lost no time in making quite clear that cuts in offensive forces and restraint in strategic defences were interconnected. A month after the Washington summit, the Soviet delegation in Geneva tabled a protocol, to be attached to the START treaty, which, in the words of the new chief Soviet negotiator, Ambassador Obukhov, would make 'legally binding an understanding reached on the issue of compliance with, and withdrawal from, the ABM Treaty within an agreed period of time'.[18]

In early 1988 it was still not clear how the gap would be bridged between the confirmation of the ABM Treaty, as demanded by the Soviet Union, and moving away from it, as proposed by the United States. During the remainder of President Reagan's tenure it seemed doubtful if the gap could be bridged. All that President Reagan seemed likely to secure before his term expired was a START treaty with which Soviet compliance would be conditional on US compliance with the ABM Treaty—scarcely a bargain which this President would want to put before the Senate. The incompatibility of imposing constraints on offensive strategic forces while refusing constraints on strategic defences was likely to reassert itself in the end—and thus block or, more likely, delay anything the two sides would be able to agree on in START.

IV. A step towards stability?

There was little doubt, however, that an agreement on deep cuts in offensive strategic forces would ultimately emerge, if not during Mr Reagan's presidency, then in that of his successor. The considerable progress made in the START negotiations was, therefore, unlikely to be lost entirely. Mr Reagan's specific approach to arms control—cutting deeply into the arsenals rather than regulating the competition within agreed limits—would thus still have to show whether it could meet the decisive test: whether the result would promote strategic stability, both in inducing caution in crises and in reducing the incentive to compete in an unpredictable manner.

On the plus side for stability was the encouragement, through the counting rules of the emerging agreement, of less vulnerable SLBMs and bombers rather than fixed ICBMs, and of minimum-MIRVed rather than maximum-MIRVed delivery vehicles. Concerns such as those over the 'window of vulnerability' could now be put at rest even more convincingly than before. The number of first-strike targets for strategic forces would be reduced significantly once a START treaty is ratified. On the other side of the ledger, a number of elements were likely to run against the traditional notions of strategic stability. The hard-target kill capability that was emerging for modern SLBMs would not be constrained but positively encouraged. The more flexible use of nuclear weapons would also be enhanced, as ALCMs and SLCMs and stand-off weapons on aircraft are increasingly included in operational plans for strategic purposes. The traditional type of strategic stability which seeks to minimize the incentive for a first disarming strike will be enhanced. But, since the ability to use nuclear weapons well short of a disarming strike will be improved, the problem of stability would pose itself in a different way. And there was nothing in the emerging START agreement short of unrealistically drastic limits on cruise missiles which would prevent that.

In fact, the most obvious impact of the START treaty would be to signal the end of the fixed land-based ICBM as the main element of nuclear deterrence. It had long ceased to play that role for the United States, and it was now rapidly relinquishing it for the Soviet Union as well. The agreement was thus one which was designed to cope with the instabilities of the past; it was much less equipped to deal with the instabilities of the future.

What these might consist of was highlighted by the 1988 report *Discriminate Deterrence*, prepared by a high-level Commission on Integrated Long-Term Strategy, set up by the US Defense Department in 1986.[19] It included among its members many of those who, over the past decades, had been closley involved with the evolution of US strategic thought: Albert Wohlstetter and Fred Iklé, Henry Kissinger and Zbigniew Brzezinski, Samuel Huntington and John

Vessey. On strategic arms, the report called for 'promoting military programs in which the United States have a special advantage vis-à-vis the Soviets', and on strategic arms control it advised: 'A good arms control agreement will be consistent with a long-term military strategy. This means that we want agreements that (a) do not assume nuclear vulnerability as a desirable condition for the American people; (b) do not assume that accuracy is an undesirable attribute of US weapons; and (c) do not assume that defense against nuclear attacks is more threatening than offense'.[20] The United States, according to the commission, needed capabilities for discriminate nuclear strikes to deter limited nuclear attacks on allied or US forces.

While the report was by no means an expression of official policy of the present or any future Administration, it made clear, nevertheless, that the cuts envisaged in the expected START treaty would not make much difference to the future state of US strategic forces. Indeed, one of the striking aspects of the prospective treaty would be that it would have remarkably little impact on US (and probably Soviet) force planning. In essence the new limitations would bring Soviet and US forces back to the level of the mid-1970s albeit with much less reliance on vulnerable fixed land-based missiles. START was likely in the end to have cut drastically only into what neither side regarded as essential for deterrence in the future.

Thus the central task of arms control remained to be accomplished: how to regulate the military competition in times of technological, doctrinal and political change. At best, a successful completion of the START accord, coupled with great restraint on strategic defences, would provide a basis from which to proceed towards that task with greater trust and confidence. At worst, it would provide a licence to do what each side wanted without much regard to the interdependence of strategic stability.

Notes and references

* Diplomatic correspondent, *Die Zeit*, FR Germany.

[1] SIPRI, *SIPRI Yearbook 1987: World Armaments and Disarmament* (Oxford University Press: Oxford, 1987), pp. 326–7.

[2] Flournoy, M. A., 'A rocky START: optimism and obstacles on the road to reductions', *Arms Control Today*, Oct. 1987, p. 71.

[3] Communiqué of the Washington summit, 'Excerpts from joint statement on summit', *Arms Control Reporter*, Dec. 1987, p. 611.D.71.

[4] Scowcroft, B., Deutch, J. and Woolsey, R. J., 'The real danger is in the next arms treaty', *International Herald Tribune*, 5 Dec. 1987.

[5] 'Carlucci favors shift in MX basing', *New York Times*, 2 Feb. 1988.

[6] For most of these details, see 'Nuclear and Space Talks: US and Soviet proposals,' United States Information Agency Fact Sheet, Feb. 1988.

[7] *Discriminate Deterrence: Report of the Commission on Integrated Long-Term Strategy* (US Government Printing Office: Washington, DC, Jan. 1988), pp. 49–51.

[8] International Institute for Strategic Studies, *Strategic Survey 1982/83* (IISS: London, 1983), pp. 24–7.

[9] Given a total of roughly 2400 Soviet ICBMs and SLBMs with about 10 000 warheads. (See table 10.1.)

[10] 'Missile snag curbs summit hopes', *Sunday Times* (London), 15 Nov. 1987.

[11] See note 3, p. 611.D.72.

[12] Mendelsohn, J., 'INF verification: a guide for the perplexed', *Arms Control Today*, Sep. 1987, pp. 25, 28 and 29.

[13] 'Nuclear and Space Talks: US and Soviet proposals', United States Information Agency, 6 Oct. 1987.
[14] The text of the interview is reprinted in *Neues Deutschland* (East Berlin), 2 Dec. 1987.
[15] *Arms Control Reporter*, Dec. 1987, p. 603.B.147.
[16] See note 6.
[17] Quoted in *Arms Control Today*, Jan.–Feb. 1988, p. 22.
[18] *International Herald Tribune*, 16–17 Jan. 1988.
[19] See note 7.
[20] See note 7.

11. Conventional arms control in Europe: problems and prospects

JANE SHARP

I. The negotiation forums

The first step to understanding European arms control is to put the different negotiation forums in perspective and to know who negotiates about what with whom. Table 11.1 lists the 35 countries participating in negotiations on European security. Figure 11.1 depicts the different forums as concentric circles spreading out from the heaviest concentrations of military power in the centre of Europe.

At the core are bilateral talks between the United States and the Soviet Union. On 8 December 1987 President Ronald Reagan and General Secretary Mikhail Gorbachev signed an agreement banning US and Soviet ground-launched intermediate- and shorter-range missiles, not only in Europe but world-wide. Assuming that both parties ratify this agreement, a treaty should be concluded in 1988.

In the second layer are the 11 direct participants in the talks on mutual and balanced force reductions (MBFR). These comprise the Warsaw Treaty Organization (WTO) and North Atlantic Treaty Organization (NATO) states with forces deployed in the central region: the Soviet Union, Poland, the German Democratic Republic (GDR) and Czechoslovakia in the East, and the USA, Canada, Britain, the Federal Republic of Germany (FRG) and the three Benelux countries in the West. France has troops in NATO's MBFR guidelines area but has always objected to the limited geographical scope and bloc-to-bloc nature of the talks.

The third layer comprises the larger, 19-state MBFR circle which includes the eight flank states that are indirect participants in the talks: five NATO states—Norway, Denmark, Italy, Greece and Turkey—and three WTO states—Hungary, Romania and Bulgaria. They do not have voting rights, but sit in on the discussions on a rotating basis.

The fourth layer includes France, Iceland, Spain and Portugal, the four Western states that do not participate in either MBFR group but that will be full members (with all the other NATO and WTO states) in new 23-state talks scheduled for 1988 and aimed at achieving 'stability at lower levels'.[1]

In the outermost layer are the four neutral (Austria, Finland, Sweden and Switzerland) and the eight non-aligned states (Cyprus, Holy See, Ireland, Liechtenstein, Malta, Monaco, San Marino and Yugoslavia) that, together with the 16 NATO and 7 WTO states, participate in the continuing 35-state Conference on Security and Co-operation in Europe (CSCE), and are signatories to the 1975 Helsinki Final Act and the 1986 Stockholm Document on Confidence- and Security-Building Measures and Disarmament in Europe.

SIPRI Yearbook 1988: World Armaments and Disarmament

Table 11.1. European negotiation forums

Country	INF (2) Talks	MBFR (11) Talks	MBFR (19) Talks	Stability (23) Talks	CSCE (35)[a]
7 Eastern countries:					
USSR	×	×	×	×	×
GDR		×	×	×	×
Poland		×	×	×	×
Czechoslovakia		×	×	×	×
Hungary			×	×	×
Romania			×	×	×
Bulgaria			×	×	×
16 Western countries:					
USA	×	×	×	×	×
Canada		×	×	×	×
UK		×	×	×	×
FR Germany		×	×	×	×
Belgium		×	×	×	×
Netherlands		×	×	×	×
Luxembourg		×	×	×	×
Norway			×	×	×
Denmark			×	×	×
Italy			×	×	×
Greece			×	×	×
Turkey			×	×	×
Iceland				×	×
France				×	×
Spain				×	×
Portugal				×	×
12 neutral and non-aligned countries:					
Finland					×
Sweden					×
Ireland					×
Switzerland					×
Liechtenstein					×
Austria					×
Holy See					×
Malta					×
Cyprus					×
Monaco					×
San Marino					×
Yugoslavia					×

[a] Albania is the only European country that does not participate in the CSCE.

A third follow-up review meeting of the CSCE, which began in Vienna on 4 November 1986, will determine the next phase of this forum, to which the group of 23 states will report.

This chapter focuses on developments in 1987 at the MBFR and CSCE forums, as well as on the prospects for the new 23-state stability talks.[2]

II. Recurrent problems

In 1987, General Secretary Gorbachev's dynamic diplomacy, a new disarmament initiative from Poland, an apparent increase in French interest in negotiations about force reductions, and West European anxieties about Soviet conventional superiority in the wake of an intermediate-range nuclear force (INF) agreement, all suggested that a serious effort might be under way to

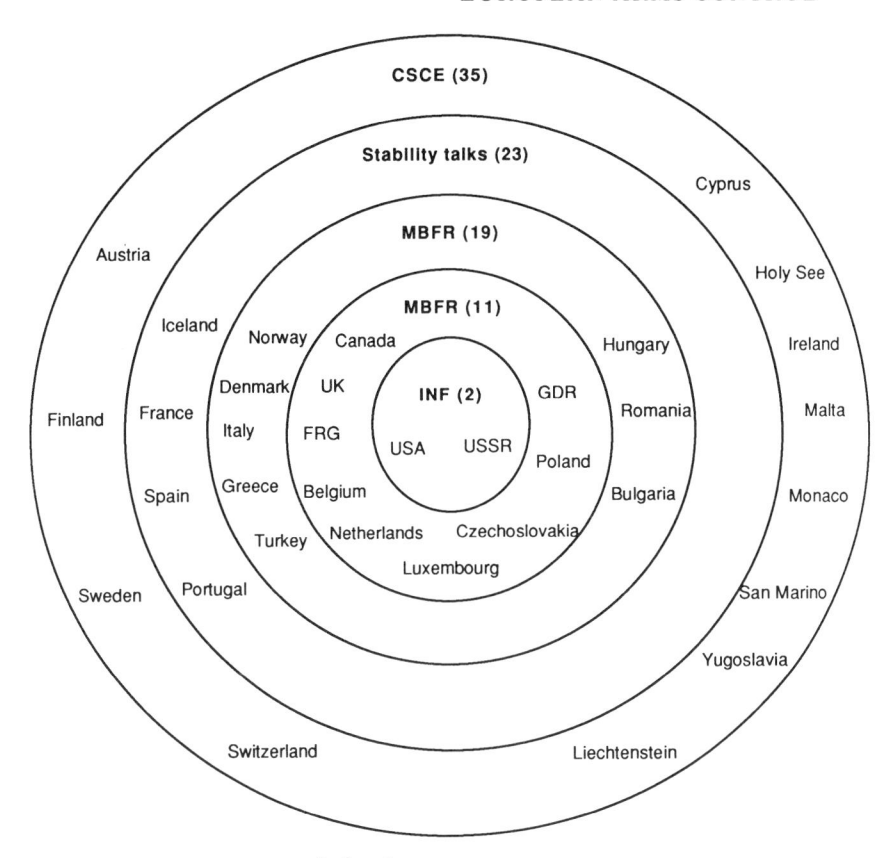

Figure 11.1. European negotiation forums

reduce the extraordinarily high levels of military forces in Europe. Nevertheless, exploratory talks on the mandate for the new stability talks showed that the perceived security interests of many European states could limit the possibilities for negotiated agreement there as they have at the MBFR Talks these past 15 years.

Moreover, in some NATO circles, anxiety that an INF agreement would decouple the United States from Europe generated pressure to improve both nuclear and conventional forces. British Prime Minister Margaret Thatcher, and others, called for a NATO summit meeting early in 1988 to present co-ordinated West European views to President Reagan before his next meeting with General Secretary Gorbachev. At its December 1987 meeting NATO's Defence Planning Committee urged Allied governments to reinvigorate both the 1983 Montebello decision on nuclear modernization and the 1985 Conventional Defence Improvement (CDI) programme, although Lord Carrington noted that modernization must not be confused with buildup.[3]

For NATO the most positive aspect of the INF Treaty was that the Soviet Union was willing to make asymmetrical reductions. In Europe, balanced agreements would be particularly difficult to negotiate given the many asymmetries between NATO and the WTO. Different geographical conditions, historical experiences and political systems have shaped different security needs and military force postures in both alliances which complicate the arms control process even when all parties negotiate in good faith.

Geographical asymmetries

As an alliance of maritime nations heavily dependent on sea-links, NATO seeks to avoid limits on its naval capability. By contrast, with a vast land mass to defend, Russian leaders have traditionally relied on large standing armies, and (despite 'new thinking' about the virtues of a defensive doctrine) it is hard to imagine the Soviet military readily accepting deep cuts in their ground forces.

Geography permits the Soviet Union to introduce reinforcements into Eastern Europe over land, while the United States must reinforce Western Europe by air and sea lift. This suggests a strategic advantage to the USSR, but permanently deployed US forces in Western Europe give the United States an option to invade Soviet territory, while the Soviet Union has no similar option vis-à-vis the United States.[4] This asymmetry poses problems for dealing with any troops and equipment to be withdrawn. At the MBFR Talks, for example, the WTO states want treaty provisions that require arms and equipment to be withdrawn with manpower, whereas NATO states want US ammunition and equipment in POMCUS (the European Prepositioning of Materiel Configured to Unit Sets) stocks to remain in Europe.

Geography gives the Soviet Union the luxury of a protective buffer zone in Eastern Europe, whereas NATO cannot defend in depth. This asymmetry also generates intra-NATO differences since in particular West German leaders are unwilling to relax NATO's doctrine of forward defence at the inter-German border, while most military experts in the rest of NATO would trade space for time to enhance the defence of NATO territory overall. West Germans do not want to erect physical barriers on their territory, because these would emphasize the division of Germany, whereas other NATO Allies believe barriers would be relatively non-provocative and cost-effective means to slow any WTO advance.[5] Geography also makes West Germans sensitive to the problem of singularity, particularly to proposals for weapon-free corridors between the blocs since these would distinguish FR Germany from the rest of NATO in terms of inspection regimes. There are, however, signs of growing impatience within the Alliance on this issue.[6]

Economic asymmetries

Assessments of the NATO–WTO balance vary as to the number of combat forces available on short notice, but all agree that the wartime production and manpower potential of the NATO countries are much higher than that of the Eastern bloc.[7] This is particularly relevant for mobilization rates. A net assessment prepared by the Staff of the US Joint Chiefs of Staff in late 1987 noted that the quality and readiness of NATO reserves is far superior to that of the WTO.[8] This gives some European countries confidence that they could meet any likely challenge from the Soviet Union, but others worry that the

Soviet Union must prepare for a short-warning attack because it cannot afford to allow NATO time to gear up to a war footing.

The greater economic potential of the NATO countries gives them an edge in most of the technologies relevant to weaponry.[9] In the past, the Soviet Union has tried to curb Western innovation through arms control, and in some areas to compensate for technological inferiority with quantitative superiority, but they are clearly concerned that new Western systems could make their forces inoperable; for example, that sophisticated US anti-tank weapons could render Soviet armoured forces obsolete.

Political asymmetries

In both Eastern and Western Europe, allied governments are more enthusiastic about retaining stationed superpower forces than are the general publics. Nevertheless, Soviet troops are in Eastern Europe in the nature of occupying forces propping up client governments, whereas in most NATO countries US troops are accepted as welcome symbols of the US security guarantee to NATO. In Greece and Spain, however, US bases are unpopular because they are identified with the former military dictatorships in those countries.[10]

Asymmetries in NATO and WTO political systems sometimes suggest that the WTO is more cohesive. West European countries guard their sovereignty more jealously than those in the East, making political cohesion in NATO difficult to demonstrate in peacetime. In an East–West conflict, however, West European troops are likely to be more politically reliable than East European troops fighting under Soviet orders.[11]

Political asymmetries also affect intelligence gathering, since the Western states are more open than those in the WTO. This makes NATO more conservative in its estimates of WTO capabilities and more demanding in terms of on-site inspections than might be the case if WTO data were openly available. Prior to General Secretary Gorbachev's leadership, Soviet unwillingness to provide military data or to open up WTO territory for inspection presented serious stumbling-blocks to negotiated arms control. Even under Gorbachev, the Soviet Union resisted NATO's December 1985 suggestions for on-site inspections at the MBFR Talks. On the other hand, in both the 1986 Stockholm Document and the 1987 INF Treaty the Soviet Union accepted on-site inspection, and the INF Treaty requires periodic exchanges of data. This gives some ground for optimism about better data exchanges at the new round of conventional arms talks, and for an effective monitoring regime should a treaty be concluded.

III. WTO arms control goals

Since World War II, Soviet leaders have used arms control diplomacy as an integral part of their security policy to limit the nuclear threat to the Soviet homeland, to maintain control over their East European buffer zone and to curb the political and military potential of NATO, in particular the Bonn–Washington axis. Since achieving strategic parity in the late 1960s, an important Soviet political objective of arms control has been to codify and re-affirm equal status with the United States. Finally, there has been the persistent hope that arms control agreements might permit a re-allocation of scarce economic resources from the military to the civilian sector of the Soviet economy.

Thus, Soviet proposals have consistently sought to impose limits on nuclear forces around the periphery of the Soviet Union, especially those based in FR Germany, to impose national sub-limits on the Bundeswehr, and to preserve the territorial and political *status quo* in Europe. A new Soviet concern is to counter the growing pressure for a more coherent West European pillar within NATO, especially in so far as this might imply arrangements for sharing control of nuclear weapons between Britain, France and FR Germany.[12]

The most important new element in Soviet policy under Gorbachev, however, appears to be the greater priority given to arms control as a means of re-allocating resources from the military to the civilian sector of the Soviet economy. His comprehensive programme for nuclear disarmament (outlined on 14 January 1986) and for conventional disarmament in Europe (in the Budapest Appeal of June 1986) both appear to be closely co-ordinated with his rolling five-year programmes for radical economic reform.[13] Moreover, the Soviet leadership is showing increasing interest in the conversion of Chinese military plants to civilian production.[14]

Though often dismissed in the West as propaganda moves, the Soviet Union has usually responded to each new NATO force modernization with an arms control initiative before undertaking military countermeasures. Thus, NATO decisions in the 1950s and 1970s, to deploy new generations of nuclear weapons in Western Europe, generated a variety of WTO proposals for nuclear weapon-free zones; NATO proposals for limited nuclear war-fighting options intensified Soviet pressure for a no-first-use agreement in the late 1970s and early 1980s; and new US initiatives in space prompted Soviet initiatives to limit the testing and deployment of weapons in space. One motivation for the current Soviet interest in conventional force reductions is to curb the development, and pre-empt the deployment, of a new generation of non-nuclear weapon systems by the NATO countries, especially those that exploit sophisticated electronics and can strike deep into WTO territory.[15]

The security interests of East European states are not always consistent either with each other or with those of the Soviet Union. East German and Polish leaders, for example, are particularly anxious to preserve post-1945 borders intact. Having lost a slice of its eastern territory to the Soviet Union, Poland is anxious not to lose the slice of German territory accorded to it at the end of World War II, while the GDR wants to preserve its political and territorial independence from the FRG.

East European governments face at least three kinds of threat, and these sometimes dictate different arms control priorities: domestic, intra-alliance and inter-alliance. Internal political threats to the ruling Communist parties justify (at least for some regimes) stationed Soviet forces, and argue against radical force reduction agreements that might remove all foreign troops. By contrast, the threat of intra-bloc police action (such as occurred in the GDR in

1953, in Hungary in 1956 and in Czechoslovakia in 1968) could be ameliorated by agreements that limited Soviet forces in Eastern Europe.

External threats to Eastern Europe stem from the risk of being caught in the cross-fire of an East–West conflict. In so far as Soviet arms control policy seeks to avoid war of any kind, and to limit NATO nuclear forces, it also curbs these external threats to East European security, but Soviet leaders have not always been as energetic in their efforts to limit NATO's short-range nuclear weapons (that have threatened the territory of their East European allies since the late 1950s) as they have to limit intermediate-range systems that threatened Soviet territory. East European governments did not complain as loudly about this as some West Europeans did about what they saw as a lack of US concern about Soviet SS-20 missiles in the late 1970s. But the GDR and Czechoslovakia objected to the deployment of Soviet nuclear forces in response to Pershing II and cruise missile deployments in Western Europe in the early 1980s and, together with all WTO countries, supported the INF Treaty signed in December 1987. These two East European governments, however, may be much less certain about the virtue of Soviet troop withdrawals; and some of the more conservative Czechoslovakian leaders even complained that Gorbachev moved too far too fast on the INF agreement.[16]

IV. NATO arms control goals

In NATO also, the security needs of the United States are not always consistent with those of their West European Allies, nor do all West Europeans face similar security dilemmas.[17] It is in the US interest, for example, to reduce the risks inherent in its nuclear guarantee to the Allies by developing a NATO capability to delay as long as possible the nuclear phase of any conflict that might occur. Hence the move from a policy of massive nuclear retaliation to one of flexible response in the late 1960s, the pressure (from former Defense Secretary Robert McNamara and others) to move to a policy of no-first-use of nuclear weapons, and the persistent effort to persuade West Europeans to spend more money on conventional forces.

Such measures are welcomed by many nuclear arms control proponents in Europe, but can be unsettling for those NATO leaders who believe that a policy of flexible response, and especially the US threat to initiate the use of nuclear weapons, are vital elements of NATO's deterrent posture.

West German leaders, having renounced independent nuclear weapons and being situated on the forward edge of a potential battle area with the Eastern bloc, face a particularly acute security dilemma and, of all the NATO Allies, appear to feel the most dependent on the United States. Britain and France, by contrast, have their own nuclear weapons and their own geographical buffers: the Channel for Britain and the territory of the Federal Republic of Germany for France.

Geography and history thus produce a variety of NATO responses to any given arms control proposal. In debating the mandate for the new stability talks, for example, France and Britain consistently opposed WTO proposals to include nuclear or dual-capable systems, whereas the Government of the FRG and the other smaller Allies were more sympathetic, especially to efforts to limit short-range battlefield weapons.[18] In late 1987, West German officials increasingly complained that both German states were unduly threatened by short-range battlefield nuclear weapons in the wake of the INF agreement.[19]

V. MBFR[20]

The current conventional wisdom is that MBFR is a failed effort: 15 years wasted and no agreement in sight. Public expectations of force 'reductions' have certainly been disappointed, but given NATO's initial objectives of preventing unilateral Western reductions, the talks have been successful, with troop levels on both sides remaining remarkably stable.

Initially both sides agreed to negotiate limits on armaments as well as manpower in the MBFR guidelines area. A NATO proposal in December 1975, for example, proposed an asymmetrical trade of US nuclear weapons against a Soviet tank army.[21] Later, in 1978, both sides agreed to focus on manpower limits; specifically, common alliance ceilings of 900 000 for ground plus air forces, and 700 000 for ground forces alone. By June 1983, when the Soviet Union agreed to some form of on-site inspection, a first-phase agreement to make token reductions in the levels of stationed US and Soviet forces looked close to completion.

Four areas of disagreement remained: (*a*) troop data—NATO claimed that the WTO had some 150 000–200 000 more troops in the guidelines area than they admitted; (*b*) frequency of inspection in a verification regime—NATO sought an agreed annual quota and the WTO only accepted inspection by challenge; (*c*) NATO's wish to permit temporary fluctuations in permitted ceilings to accommodate the NATO practice of bringing in troops from the United States for regular Alliance manoeuvres; and (*d*) the issue of whether departing troops should take their equipment with them—NATO has consistently argued for a manpower-only agreement, whereas the WTO argued that withdrawing troops should take their arms and equipment too.

In December 1985, NATO called for more modest reductions than had previously been agreed (5000 US troops out of Western Europe and 11 500 Soviet troops out of Eastern Europe), but stopped insisting on an agreed data base prior to reductions.[22] Many observers of MBFR thought this was an important breakthrough that would soon produce an agreement, but the three remaining areas of dispute proved intractable, especially the frequency of inspection, with NATO now asking for 30 annual inspections over a three-year period and the WTO only willing to agree to a handful.

Prospects for an MBFR agreement

During the 40th round of MBFR negotiations (September–December 1986) the Soviet delegation several times proposed a modest first-phase reduction of Soviet and US troops, combined with a two- to three-year commitment to freeze alliance force levels in the MBFR reduction zone, during which time fresh discussions could begin in a broader forum.[23] This suggests that in the wake of General Secretary Gorbachev's more ambitious arms reduction plans in other forums, the Soviet Union is looking for a graceful exit from the MBFR forum.

Many in the West also predict that MBFR will fold if and when the new 23-state stability talks get under way.[24] The question is whether an agreement, however modest, might be signed in the interim.

On the issue of verification requirements the Soviet position appears to be in flux. In the 20 February 1986 Soviet draft treaty, for example, the Soviet Union accepts on-site inspections in principle but only in response to 'justifiable requests'.[25] Soviet spokesmen claim that 30 inspections annually are too many given the modest troop withdrawals that NATO proposed.[26] Since then, however, a precedent has been set in the September 1986 Stockholm Document for up to three annual challenge inspections, and the INF Treaty (if ratified) will subject Soviet territory to several hundred inspections over a period of 13 years.[27] Moreover, the Soviet Union has co-operated with several challenge inspections of WTO forces under the 1986 Stockholm provisions.

Even though an agreement has not yet been signed, the MBFR forum succeeds in less tangible ways. It is here, for example, that most of the confidence- and security-building measures (CSBMs) negotiated in the Stockholm Document were first proposed and refined as 'associated measures'. The NATO draft MBFR agreement currently on the table provides for a consultative commission to resolve any compliance ambiguities,[28] but it can be argued that the negotiations themselves serve as a *de facto* European security commission, in which East and West Europeans increase their understanding of each other's security needs and anxieties. Many MBFR delegates, past and present, both NATO and WTO, testify to the fact that communication channels are well established here, and worry that comparable East–West links may be difficult to recreate in a larger forum.

Virtues of an MBFR agreement

General Secretary Gorbachev appears impatient with the kind of plodding incrementalism that has characterized the MBFR negotiations to date, and Soviet spokesmen at the MBFR Talks complain that the most recent reductions proposed by NATO are too small to codify in a formal treaty. But an MBFR agreement, however modest, could serve several useful political and military functions:

1. It would cap 15 years of effort with a measure of success that would enhance East–West *détente*.

2. An MBFR consultative commission, designed to resolve compliance ambiguities, would be a valuable confidence-building measure as a useful East–West forum in which to discuss wider security issues in the region.

3. Security could be enhanced by the increased transparency that would result from a regime of regular on-site inspections.

4. Even if it did little more than freeze current manpower levels, an agreement could dampen down pressure to compensate for an INF agreement with increased conventional forces.

VI. The CSCE–CDE

A characteristic feature of the early CSCE process was a careful balancing of three 'baskets' of issues: Basket I dealing with military security; Basket II with East–West technological and economic co-operation; and Basket III with humanitarian and cultural contacts.[29] At the Second Follow-up Meeting in Madrid in 1983, the mandate for the next phase of the CSCE separated these baskets into different negotiating forums.[30] Three new conferences began in 1984: one in Stockholm to discuss military security issues, another in Athens to settle international disputes, and a third in Venice to discuss economic co-operation. A fourth conference was held in Ottawa in 1985 to discuss human rights, and a fifth in Berne in 1986 to discuss individual and family contacts. Apart from the Stockholm Conference on Confidence- and Security-Building Measures and Disarmament in Europe (CDE), none of these CSCE Follow-up Meetings amounted to anything.

Separating the CSCE baskets is resisted by many in the West, who argue that the military security aspects of the CSCE ought to be suspended until more progress has been achieved in the human rights area.[31] Keeping the baskets separate meets the interests of Soviet and East European leaders, however, since they were subject to severe criticism of their human rights policies by Western and neutral and non-aligned (NNA) delegates at the first and second CSCE Follow-up Meetings in Belgrade and Madrid. A separate pan-European forum on military security also suits the French who object to discussing force reductions in a geographically limited bloc-to-bloc forum like the MBFR.[32] In addition the smaller European states strongly supported the Madrid mandate to negotiate politically binding CSBMs that would expand both the geographical scope and military significance of the 1975 Helsinki confidence-building measures (CBMs). On all three criteria the Stockholm Document can claim a measure of success.[33]

The Stockholm CSBMs

On the prior notification and observation of military activities, the Stockholm provisions require much more reporting than the Soviet Union wanted initially even though it is still less than NATO countries asked for.

On actual constraints, the Stockholm Document prohibits activities involving more than 75 000 troops unless announced two years in advance, as well as activities involving more than 40 000 troops if they are not included in the annual calendar. (The calendar of planned notifiable military activities in 1988 and forecast for 1989, as required by the Stockholm Document, is reproduced here as appendix 11A.) This represents a compromise between the WTO desire to impose more constraints, such as restricting the absolute size of exercises, and NATO's reluctance to accept constraints of any kind.

Inspections may be requested, by ground or air, of a state whose compliance is in doubt. A state need accept no more than three inspections annually, nor more than one inspection by the same state. Members of the same alliance may not inspect each other. These provisions marked the first time the Soviet Union has signed an international agreement that provides for on-site challenge inspections of military activity.

The Stockholm CSBMs went into effect on 1 January 1987 and worked well throughout the year. Western observers saw room for improvement at exercises in Czechoslovakia in February, but reported meticulous observation of the CDE rules at exercises in the GDR in March and April. In August the USA made a challenge inspection of Soviet forces near Minsk, and in September the UK made an inspection of a joint Soviet–East German exercise in the GDR. Eastern observers complained about late Western reporting of exercises in April but reported excellent conditions at Franco–German exercises in September and at British exercises in Stranraer in Scotland in early November.[34] These experiences are in marked contrast to the period between 1975 and 1985 when compliance with the CBMs of the Helsinki Final Act was a bone of contention between East and West.

Prospects for improving European CSBMs

All 35 states at the Third CSCE Follow-up Meeting in Vienna saw room for further improvement in the Stockholm CSBMs. The next phase of CSCE will therefore involve another 35-state forum dealing with the notification, regulation and constraint of military activity in the area from the Atlantic to the Ural Mountains.

The WTO states are anxious for new CSBMs that would mandate notification and constraints on independent air and naval activities since the Stockholm provisions only cover air and naval activity that is integral to activity on the ground. The Soviet Union also wants to broaden the geographical scope of the next phase of the CSCE to monitor military activity in North America.[35]

The NATO countries will continue to press for 'arrangements for exchanges of information and on-site inspection that go beyond Stockholm' with the intention of catching more of the smaller WTO exercises.[36]

The NNA states will want to constrain the size and frequency of both NATO and WTO manoeuvres on the continent, while at the same time avoiding any limitation on their own mobilization plans.[37]

The Stockholm CSBMs are important primarily because they reflect and reinforce the degree to which a co-operative East–West security regime already exists in Europe. Until now they have been essentially 'fair weather' measures which impose tolerable constraints on military systems not planning aggression. To the extent that more constraining measures are proposed, however, resistance can be expected among defence establishments even in the NNA states—and there are signs of it already in Sweden and Switzerland—since force planners see a dichotomy between the military goal of readiness and the political goal of confidence-building.

The Stockholm CSBMs and, more important, recent advances in space-based observation and information processing have already created a transparency of military establishments in both East and West such that surreptitious preparations for attack are now virtually impossible. But this new transparency also raises the value of military deception and leads to an increase in the technology available to deceive an adversary's intelligence-gathering systems. An important criterion for future constraints will therefore be the extent to which measures, such as on-site inspections, serve not merely to prevent but also to disrupt a short-warning attack after it has been launched.[38]

Prospects for the stability talks

At the Third CSCE Follow-up Meeting in Vienna, delegates from the 23 member states of the North Atlantic Treaty Organization and the Warsaw Treaty Organization began a series of informal meetings in February 1987 to decide on the participation, geographical scope, negotiation mandate and venue for a new set of European force reduction talks. Table 11.2 summarizes the NATO–WTO differences on these issues.

Participation

At issue here was whether and how to separate confidence- and security-building measures (that deal primarily with notification and regulation and only to a lesser degree with constraining military activity) from measures that seek to reduce or restructure armed forces. The 12 NNA states, as well as France, wanted to negotiate force reductions in the full 35-state forum. After several months of discussion, however, two separate forums emerged: the 23 member states of NATO and the WTO will discuss force reductions to seek stability at lower levels, and the full 35-state CSCE will meet to improve the confidence- and security-building measures negotiated in the 1986 Stockholm Document. France insists that the stability talks will not be an inter-alliance negotiation but a forum of 23 independent states. For all practical purposes, however, these negotiations promise to be an expanded, more unwieldy, version of MBFR—plagued by the problems inherent in the asymmetries between the two alliances outlined above.

Table 11.2. NATO–WTO differences on the mandate for the stability talks

Issue	NATO stance	WTO stance
Participation	23 allied states	23 allied states
Link to CSCE	Regular reports	Possible indirect NNA participation or observer status
Zone of application	Atlantic to Urals excl. SE Turkey	All Turkey plus Soviet Transcaucasus
Reduction categories:		
Ground forces	Include	Include
Air forces	Exclude	Include
Nuclear weapons	Exclude all	Include both nuclear and dual-capable missiles and aircraft
Chemical weapons	Exclude	Include
Goals:		
General	Damage-limiting exercise	Reduce NATO deep-strike potential
Specific	Parity in tanks and artillery[a]	Offset WTO tanks against NATO combat aircraft
Long-term	WTO reduce to NATO levels	Reduce current NATO and WTO levels by 25% by the 1990s
Venue	France rejects Vienna	WTO accepts Vienna

[a] Except that France rejects common alliance ceilings.

Geographical scope

'From the Atlantic to the Urals' is usually taken to include the territories of all the European member states of NATO and the WTO plus the Soviet military districts west of the Caspian Sea and the Ural River. In the Stockholm Document the geographical zone of application for CSBMs excludes the south-eastern regions of Turkey adjacent to Iran, Iraq and Syria. Turkey is asking that its forces in this area also be exempt from any controls imposed by the new talks. The WTO proposes, however, to extend the zone to include all of Turkey and is offering to include the Transcaucasus region of the USSR to compensate.[39] Still to be resolved is whether there will be an inner circle for first-phase reductions, probably the current MBFR guidelines area plus Denmark and Hungary, although most NATO countries want to include the western military districts of the Soviet Union as early as possible.

Negotiation mandate

NATO wants to limit the initial discussion to non-nuclear land armaments such as tanks, heavy artillery and attack helicopters. The Allies differ among themselves on whether to include nuclear, dual-capable and chemical weapons later, but France adamantly refuses to consider nuclear weapon systems and even threatens to walk out of the talks if they are introduced. The WTO would be prepared to consider limits on all arms and equipment within the zone, and would especially like to include nuclear, chemical and multi-capable weapon systems. As the talks recessed in December 1987 the common denominator appeared to have sunk to the French position as both sides agreed to seek 'a stable and secure balance of conventional armed forces which includes conventional arms and equipment'.[40] WTO spokesmen emphasized that this did not preclude nuclear and chemical weapon systems, but the language appears to have been chosen to allow the talks to begin with France fully on board. Soviet Foreign Minister Eduard Shevardnadze, on a visit to Bonn in January 1988, reiterated the Soviet preference for moving quickly to negotiate limits on European-based nuclear weapons but acknowledged that the new forum would focus initially on conventional systems.[41]

Venue

The Austrian Government offered to host the new forum in Vienna, but France argued that another city would be preferable, given the association of Vienna with the MBFR negotiations.[42]

Thus, while the new forum still required a formal mandate from the full 35-state CSCE Vienna meeting, the group of 23 states ended 1987 with informal agreement on the number of participants and the initial focus of the stability talks, but with the venue and the precise geographical zone still to be settled in 1988.

VII. WTO goals at the stability talks

If one of General Secretary Gorbachev's primary motives for radical cuts in conventional forces is a reordering of resources to the civilian economy, another is to curb NATO's capability to strike targets deep in WTO territory as outlined in the doctrine of Follow-on Forces Attack (FOFA) adopted by the Alliance in 1984.[43] A critical question for these talks is whether, as he did in the INF agreement, Gorbachev is willing to make asymmetrical concessions to curb Western developments, for example, whether to give up the WTO superiority in tanks in order to impose limits on NATO combat aircraft.

Encouraging signs of flexibility emerged in October 1985, when General Secretary Gorbachev, in Paris, and Soviet Chief of Staff Akhromeyev, in Moscow, began to talk of asymmetries in the conventional balance and to admit that in some areas the WTO was ahead of NATO. Both Akhromeyev and Gorbachev, over the next year and a half, reiterated on several occasions that these asymmetries should be resolved by the side that is ahead levelling down, rather than the side that is behind levelling up. This proposal also appears in the communiqué following the WTO Political Consultative Committee on 29 May 1987. This marks a change from the pre-Gorbachev days when, for example at the MBFR Talks, Soviet spokesmen maintained that NATO and WTO forces were evenly balanced and insisted that any force reductions must be by equal percentages to maintain the balance at the same ratio.

Gorbachev's comprehensive package for European force reductions was first presented in a speech to the East German Socialist Unity Party (SED) Congress in East Berlin on 18 April 1986, repeated on 22 April 1986 in a statement from the Foreign Ministry and presented as WTO policy at the Consultative Commission meeting in Budapest on 11 June 1986. The basic package includes:[44]

1. Staged reductions of NATO and WTO forces—manpower and equipment, nuclear and non-nuclear—from the Atlantic to the Urals: (*a*) stage I: reductions of US and Soviet forces by 150 000 to 200 000 men over 1–2 years, including the reduction of tactical air forces and short-range nuclear forces; (*b*) stage II: 25 per cent reductions of NATO and WTO force levels by the early 1990s; and (*c*) stage III: NNA participation in the reductions;

2. A ban on chemical weapons;

3. On-site inspections and detailed exchanges of data;

4. A negotiating forum—perhaps an expanded MBFR forum or the next phase of the CSCE; and

5. The adoption of manifestly defensive military doctrines and force postures by both alliances, to cut down mutual fear of surprise attack.

From the Western perspective the most disturbing aspect of this proposal, emerging so soon after NATO had made an effort to set aside the data dispute at the MBFR negotiations, was that it could be interpreted as an attempt to undermine the smaller bloc-to-bloc talks just as an agreement was in sight.[45] A more optimistic assessment is that Gorbachev wanted to break away from the cautious and conservative positions adopted by the Soviet Union at the MBFR

Talks since 1973, and judged that it would be easier to be innovative in a new forum. As already noted, the Soviet preference at the MBFR Talks is for token Soviet and US withdrawals, followed by a freeze on the manpower and equipment of both NATO and the WTO, after which the participants would quietly move to an expanded forum.

On 22 June 1987, at one of the informal meetings of the group of 23 states in Vienna, Soviet Ambassador Yuri Kashlev tabled a draft mandate for European force reductions. In accordance with the 1986 Budapest Appeal this included limits on all weapons integral to NATO and WTO air and ground forces deployed between the Atlantic and the Urals, thus including chemical and nuclear systems.[46]

On 19 October 1987, at one of the biweekly meetings of the 23 states, the Soviet delegate defined the forces to be included in the mandate for the stability talks as 'conventional land-based armaments'. While it was made clear that this language did not exclude either nuclear or dual-capable systems, it nevertheless suggested movement towards the Western preference for limiting the initial discussion to heavy conventional armaments like tanks, artillery and attack helicopters.

Proposals to defuse the offensive aspects of military doctrines

In speeches in East Berlin and Prague in the spring of 1987 General Secretary Gorbachev pressed NATO to enter talks—at the experts' level—on military doctrine, so that each side could explain what they found offensive and provocative about the other. The effort to define defensive and non-provocative military postures and doctrines has long been advocated by Western security analysts and thoroughly debated over many years at Pugwash conferences and symposia. In addition, proposals for meetings between senior Soviet and US military officers have been made on several occasions in the West. In the United States, Senators Carl Levin and Sam Nunn proposed an exchange of senior military officers in March 1983, for example. Until recently, the reaction to these proposals from the East was cool and cautious. Ironically, once these ideas were warmly embraced by Gorbachev and other WTO leaders, the official Western response was lukewarm. This reflects Western differences not only about the value of an inter-alliance discussion on doctrine, but also on NATO doctrine itself. France, for example, has never accepted the concept of limited nuclear strikes implied by NATO's flexible response doctrine. A new bipartisan study submitted to President Reagan in January 1988, that calls for even more discriminate nuclear strikes, further complicated the intra-NATO debate.[47]

The Jaruzelski proposal

In early May 1987, General Jaruzelski presented a new initiative for European disarmament that updated earlier Polish proposals for a nuclear weapon-free corridor and embraced the basic Gorbachev package. The Jaruzelski Plan endorsed a forum of the 35 CSCE nations for certain arms control tasks, but at the same time proposed, in effect, a new forum of 13 states—the 11 direct MBFR participants plus Denmark and Hungary—to negotiate special limitations in the central European zone. The plan is flexible as to participation and scope but recognizes that the problems of the central zone are different from those of the periphery, and emphasizes limits on armaments and equipment rather than manpower.[48]

The Jaruzelski Plan appears to have been motivated in part by a desire to recapture Polish activism in formulating WTO arms control policy. In recent years, while the Polish Government was preoccupied with domestic problems, Czechoslovakia and the GDR were more prominent in the arms control field with proposals for nuclear and chemical weapon-free zones and actual talks on these proposals with the Social Democratic Party (SPD) in FR Germany. In addition, in the East–West dimension, the Polish proposal reflects a desire to pre-empt Western moves to compensate for an agreement limiting INF with an increase in either the quality or the quantity of NATO's conventional forces.

While generally complementary to the Gorbachev proposals and the Budapest Appeal of June 1986, the Jaruzelski Plan differs in two important respects from the comprehensive WTO package:

1. Its geographical scope is central Europe, rather than from the Atlantic to the Urals, embracing the MBFR guidelines area plus Denmark and Hungary. This would subject more Soviet forces to potential limits than would an MBFR agreement, and recognizes Hungarian dismay at being excluded from the MBFR forum.

2. The focus is on limiting weapons and equipment, not manpower, in an effort to remove heavy equipment and offensive weaponry from forward areas.

A refinement was announced on 11 November when General Jaruzelski returned from a visit to Moscow and proposed a specific trade in which reductions in Soviet tanks would be offset by reductions in NATO's combat aircraft.[49]

VIII. NATO goals at the stability talks

In response to General Secretary Gorbachev's force reduction proposals in the spring of 1986, NATO formed a High Level Task Force (HLTF) to formulate a comprehensive Alliance strategy for European arms control. The group's main task was to reconcile French views with those of the rest of the Alliance. Three issues dominated the discussions. First, France was adamantly against an inter-alliance forum (even to the point of denying that the HLTF was a NATO group) but wanted to include the full 35 CSCE states. This is a fundamental disagreement, and one that is likely to frustrate most of the practical arms control proposals at the talks. France refuses, for example, to accept the principle of common alliance ceilings, but insists that each of the 23 participants in the stability talks accept only national rights and obligations under any treaty negotiated.[50] Second, France refused to include nuclear weapons in the mandate for the new talks and threatened to walk out if any participant raised the issue once talks were under way. Third, France did not want the new forum in Vienna.

On the issue of participation, as the NNA states are unwilling to reduce their own forces, most NATO states feel they should not have a say in imposing force limits on others. One US official even suggested that the NNA states at CSCE have no more right to dictate alliance force levels than do states like Australia, Japan or China.[51]

In its report to NATO in December 1986, the HLTF recommended two separate sets of negotiations:[52]

1. The 35 CSCE states would build upon and expand the results of the Stockholm Conference;
2. 'The countries whose forces bear most immediately upon the essential security relationship in Europe' (namely, the 23 states belonging to NATO and the WTO) would seek to eliminate existing disparities, from the Atlantic to the Urals, and establish conventional stability at lower levels.

France and several NNA countries objected to another set of bloc-to-bloc reduction talks and insisted that force reduction talks be held under the auspices of the CSCE. Despite the fact that the French representative agreed to the December 1986 HLTF document on 30 January 1987, France issued a statement qualifying its understanding of NATO's Brussels Declaration as a two-tier approach under the CSCE umbrella.[53] In February 1987 informal meetings of the 23 nations began at the French embassy in Vienna with the French delegate continuing to underscore the connection to the CSCE. Meanwhile, the debate continued within the HLTF and on 10 July, in a formal presentation to the Vienna Follow-up Meeting, NATO repeated its earlier proposal for two sets of talks—but this time explicitly admitted that the 23 nations would regularly brief the CSCE.

On whether to include nuclear weapons, although President Reagan and General Secretary Gorbachev agreed in Reykjavik in October 1986 to discuss limits on short-range nuclear weapons, like France neither the United States nor Britain wanted to include them in multilateral European talks. Some West Europeans argued that the United States would be more likely to withdraw its ground forces if there were no nuclear 'protection'.[54] Others, especially in FR Germany, were more enthusiastic about an early discussion of short-range battlefield nuclear weapons. But NATO Foreign Ministers meeting in Reykjavik in July, as well as the 12 December communiqué from the North Atlantic Council meeting, listed NATO arms control priorities as[55]: (*a*) a 50 per cent cut in Soviet and US strategic systems; (*b*) a global ban on chemical weapons; (*c*) stable and secure conventional forces; and (*d*) an agreement on equal ceilings of short-range battlefield nuclear weapons only in conjunction with a ban on chemical weapons and an agreement on conventional forces.

The 16 Western nations presented their draft mandate for the stability talks to the Vienna Follow-up Meeting on 27 July. This includes:[56] (*a*) provisions to regularly inform the NNA states in the CSCE of progress by the 23 states; (*b*) a prime objective of eliminating the capacities for launching a surprise attack; (*c*) an initial focus on classic land forces, thus on tanks, helicopters and artillery rather than air forces (the WTO by contrast, wants to include air forces in which the NATO training and offensive capability is superior); (*d*) exclusion of naval, chemical and nuclear forces from the first phase of the talks (the WTO would include all three, and especially nuclear weapons of less than 500-km range); (*e*) a possible NATO willingness to discuss limits on dual-capable artillery—suggesting a willingness to make these systems unambiguously conventional or unambiguously nuclear; (*f*) asymmetrical rather than equal cuts to a common ceiling; and (*g*) 'step by step' reductions with on-site inspection to verify each stage.

NATO spokesmen emphasize that the main differences between this mandate and the Western position at MBFR are, first, that France is fully on board and, second, that not only manpower but also armaments are now on the negotiating agenda.

While the specifics of the opening Western negotiating position were still under discussion in late 1987, proposals circulating in Washington suggest the asymmetries being addressed. James A. Thompson (Rand Corporation) and Robert Blackwill (a former US Ambassador to MBFR), for example, suggested equal NATO and WTO tank holdings in the area from the Atlantic to the Urals of 20 000 and in the area of the old MBFR guidelines of 10 000. This, they claim, would require the Soviet Union to withdraw 30 000 tanks, and the NATO states about 4000. A similar proposal for equal artillery holdings of 15 000 in the larger area would require that the WTO get rid of 25 000 artillery pieces, while NATO would only have to withdraw some 2000.[57]

Philip Karber (BDM Corporation) proposed a more modest first-phase reduction of 2500 of the 7500 most modern Soviet tanks from the GDR and 500 of the 1900 most modern US tanks from FR Germany.[58]

Both these proposals require highly asymmetrical cuts and do not address attack aircraft or other weapon categories in which NATO enjoys an advantage. Prior to the INF agreement, such proposals would have seemed too inequitable for the Soviet Union to take seriously. But given the precedence of asymmetrical cuts in the INF agreement, and General Secretary Gorbachev's manifest interest in reducing superfluous military capability, these and similar proposals cannot be dismissed out of hand.

Jonathan Dean (also a former US Ambassador to the MBFR negotiations) recommends a goal of parity in tanks, but suggests that reductions should be limited to active-duty units in central Europe—defined as the older MBFR reduction zone plus Denmark, Hungary and the western military districts of the Soviet Union. This would ensure, *inter alia*, that significant cuts were made in the most modern Soviet tanks, not in the far more numerous holdings of 1960s and 1950s vintage tanks in Category III and reserve units.[59] Dean estimates the WTO has 65 000 tanks in the area from the Atlantic to the Urals, but only 15 000 in Category I and II active units in the central zone.[60] NATO has approximately 11 000 in the central zone so a first-phase reduction agreement that set alliance ceilings of 10 000 tanks in the zone described above would require NATO to withdraw 1000 tanks from active service and the WTO 5000.

Dean suggests, in addition, that if the Soviet Union makes these asymmetrical cuts in tanks, NATO should offer a 25 per cent reduction in fighter bombers, and parity in attack helicopters at lower-than-current levels. Dean also recommends alliance ceilings of 200–300 tactical missiles (under 500-km range) to meet the West German interest in achieving major reductions in short-range Soviet missiles deployed in Eastern Europe. Following the precedent established by the INF Treaty, of focusing on the missile range rather than the kind of warhead, these ceilings could accommodate planned production of NATO's Army Tactical Missile System (ATACM) conventional missiles, and modernization of the Lance nuclear missile: practical considerations with an eye to political support for ratification.[61]

Analysts at the Congressional Research Service (CRS) in Washington offered a similar set of proposals designed to ease both sides' fears of a short-warning attack, while retaining robust defences.[62] Like Dean, the CRS team suggests that initial reductions should concentrate on a zone smaller than that from the Atlantic to the Urals. They would *inter alia*: withdraw all short-range missiles (whether nuclear, chemical or conventional high-explosive) but retain anti-tank missiles; withdraw ground-attack fixed-wing aircraft but retain fighter interceptor aircraft and helicopters; place in storage tanks self-propelled artillery, mobile air defence systems and bridging equipment; establish extensive on-site inspection provisions and appoint permanent international inspection teams, as well as a joint NATO–WTO crisis centre to monitor compliance.

IX. Conclusion

If MBFR were the guide to future East–West negotiating behaviour, there would be little reason to expect early results from the new conventional stability talks. Expanding the negotiating mandate to include armaments as well as manpower, increasing the number of participants, and expanding the geographical scope of the proposed reductions would only suggest a more unwieldy process and less likelihood of success than before. Given the new Soviet emphasis on radical domestic economic reforms, however, and the precedent of the INF agreement, there are grounds for optimism: specifically, that increased interest in reductions will make the Soviet Union more flexible at the negotiating table, more open with data, and willing to open up WTO territory for inspection.

On balance, there seems more opportunity than danger in NATO making radical arms control proposals, as long as these are not accompanied by the acquisition of extra capability as bargaining currency. Here the precedent of the INF agreement could prove counter-productive. Some Western officials assert that it was NATO solidarity in deploying Pershing II and cruise missiles that made General Secretary Gorbachev flexible at the INF Talks, but this oversimplifies the determinants of Soviet policy.[63] A vigorous programme of conventional force modernization at this stage, by either side, could jeopardize progress in the new talks.

Arms control diplomacy ought to build confidence and create a political climate conducive to unilateral restraints. Negotiated 'balanced' force reductions are, after all, not the key to enhanced security in Europe, as much as force restructuring designed to reduce the offensive elements in each side's military doctrine and posture. If backed by concrete measures, Gorbachev's promise that the WTO doctrine is unambiguously defensive could be the most far-reaching of his new initiatives.

At the end of 1987 it was not clear whether Gorbachev was asserting that WTO doctrine and posture had always been defensive, or was seeking to restructure WTO forces to emphasize defence over offence. Visitors to Moscow reported that party leaders (especially in the new International Department headed by Anatoly Dobrynin) and analysts (at the IMEMO—Institute of World Economy and International Relations—and the USA and Canada Studies institutes) emphasized the new military thinking, in particular that 'reasonable sufficiency' (rather than superiority or even parity) was now the criterion for force planning and that this would require restructuring military forces and should allow reduced defence spending.[64] But career military officers were still having difficulty coming to terms with concepts like defensive defence and other new thinking in the military field.[65] Previous Soviet military writings asserted the need for both counter-offensive and short-warning attack capabilities, so sceptics in the West will need some reassurances that go beyond the rhetoric of the 1986 Budapest Appeal.

Inter-alliance talks on doctrine may not yet be on NATO's agenda, but discussions on doctrine are sorely needed both within and between alliances, not least because this kind of dialogue would help to prevent early problems in the new negotiations.

Potential for unilateral initiatives

There is some evidence to suggest that Gorbachev's recent initiatives reflect important changes already under way in the Soviet armed forces and that his purpose is to gain reciprocal NATO reductions and restructuring to complement what the Soviet Union intends to do anyway.[66] Many in the West, including senior military officers, believe that this presents important opportunities to stabilize both East–West political relations and military force postures on the continent.[67] Without a positive response from the West, however, and in the wake of the negative response to the recent Soviet moratorium on nuclear testing, it may be politically difficult for Gorbachev to take unilaterally the steps that would be necessary to demonstrate a new defensive posture; for example, to pull back bridging equipment, attack helicopters and armoured divisions.

Gorbachev issued several invitations to NATO to debate these issues in 1987, in particular to discuss which forces on each side are most offensive to the other. NATO's official responses were uniformly negative. On the other hand, NATO has recently engaged in some unilateral measures of its own: 2400 US nuclear warheads were recently withdrawn from Europe, the US Army is being restructured from heavy to light brigades, and economic pressures may force several West European countries to reassess their commitments to the central front—all of which might have some East–West tension-reducing effects in Europe. Thus, unilateral restructuring already under way in both alliances, even if primarily dictated by demographic and budgetary constraints, might provide the rationale for useful changes that could further reduce the confrontation in Europe.

Notes and references

[1] Ambassador Warren Zimmerman, speaking to reporters in Brussels on 23 Jan. 1987, cited in *NATO Report*, 26 Jan. 1987.

[2] For an analysis of the INF Treaty, see chapter 13.

[3] *NATO Defence Planning Committee Communiqué*, 3 Dec. 1987. See also *Atlantic News*, no. 1972 (3 Dec. 1987), p. 1.

[4] Skaggs, D. C., 'Update: MBFR', *Military Review*, vol. 67, no. 2 (Feb. 1987), pp. 85–94.

[5] On the advantages of physical barriers see, *inter alia*, Beach, (Gen.) H., 'On improving NATO strategy', in ed. A. Pierre, *The Conventional Defense of Europe* (Council on Foreign Relations: New York, 1986), pp. 177–8; Killebrew, R. B., *Conventional Defense and Total Deterrence* (Scholarly Resources: Wilmington, Del., 1986), pp. 128–9; Dean, J., *Watershed in Europe: Dismantling the East–West Military Confrontation* (Lexington Books: Lexington, 1987), pp. 77–8.

[6] David Mellor, British Minister of State, at the WEU Conference, 9 Dec. 1987, claimed that all NATO states with forces deployed in FR Germany were equally vulnerable to the Soviet threat. *Atlantic News*, no. 1973 (9 Dec. 1987), p. 3.

[7] Renewed interest in conventional arms control generated a new crop of NATO–WTO balance assessments in 1987: WEU Committee on Defence Questions and Armaments, *Threat Assessment*, WEU Document 1115 (Assembly of the Western European Union: Paris, 2 Nov. 1987); Voigt, K., Rapporteur, *Draft General Report on Alliance Security: NATO–Warsaw Pact Military Balance*, and *Nuclear Arms Control After Reykjavik* (North Atlantic Assembly: Brussels, Sep. 1987); Kelly, A., *The Myth of Soviet Superiority: A Critical Analysis of the Current Balance of Conventional Forces on the Central Front in Europe*, Peace Research Report no. 14, School of Peace Studies, Bradford University, Mar. 1987; Unterseher, L., *Conventional Land Forces for Central Europe: a Military Threat Assessment*, Peace Research Report no. 15, School of Peace Studies, Bradford University, Mar. 1987; Biddle, S., 'The European conventional balance debate: a reinterpretation', in ed. T. Wander, *Nuclear and Conventional Forces in Europe* (American Association for the Advancement of Science: Washington, DC, 1987), pp. 25–57; Posen, B., 'Is NATO decisively outnumbered?' *International Security*, vol. 12, no. 4 (spring 1988), pp. 186–202; Epstein, J., 'Dynamic analysis and the conventional balance', ibid., pp. 154–73; Mearsheimer, J., 'Numbers, strategy and the European balance', ibid., pp. 174–85; Sullivan, L., Jr and Etzold, T. H., *Differing Perceptions of the Conventional Force Balance* (Atlantic Council of the United States: Washington, DC, 3 Dec. 1987); Dean, J., 'The military balance in Europe: what do the figures mean?' in Dean (note 5), pp. 38–59. For Soviet views on the balance, see: Arbatov, A., *et al.*, *Disarmament and Security 1986 Yearbook, Volume I* (Institute of World Economy and International Relations and Soviet Academy of Sciences: Moscow, 1987), pp. 206–10; Almquist, P., 'Moscow's conventional wisdom: Soviet views of the European balance', *Arms Control Today*, vol. 17, no. 10 (Dec. 1987), pp. 16–21.

[8] Trainor, B., 'US concludes NATO can deter Soviet attack', *International Herald Tribune*, 1 Dec. 1987.

[9] United States Secretary of Defense, 'Relative US/USSR standing in the 20 most important basic technology areas,' *Annual Report to Congress FY 1988* (Department of Defense: Washington, DC, 12 Jan. 1987), p. 245.

[10] Duke, S., SIPRI, *United States Military Forces and Installations in Europe* (Oxford University Press: Oxford, forthcoming).

[11] On the reliability of East European troops, see Herspring, D. A. and Volgyes, I., 'Political reliability in the Eastern European Warsaw Pact armies', *Armed Forces and Society*, vol. 6, no. 3 (winter 1980).

[12] For Soviet concerns about the Franco–West German brigade, see *Pravda*, 23 June 1987, p. 5; *Foreign Broadcast and Information Service–Soviet Union (FBIS-SU)*, 29 June 1987, pp. H2.

[13] Bialer, S., 'Change in Russia: Gorbachev's move', *Foreign Policy*, no. 68 (fall 1987), pp. 59–87; Frank, P., 'The new leadership and foreign policy', lecture to the British International Studies Association, Aberystwyth, 18 Dec. 1987.

[14] BBC World Service, 10 Jan. 1988.

[15] Many of these technologies are still in the development stage; see Office of Technology

Assessment (OTA), *New Technology for NATO Implementing Following-On Forces Attack* (US Government Printing Office: Washington, DC, June 1987).

[16] Diehl, J., 'In Prague, dissent on US pact: hard-liners offer first Soviet bloc resistance to treaty', *International Herald Tribune*, 17 Nov. 1987.

[17] On Alliance arms control dilemmas, see Sharp, J., 'After Reykjavik: arms control and the allies', *International Affairs*, vol. 63, no. 2 (spring 1987).

[18] West German Foreign Minister Genscher has been particularly vocal in urging efforts to negotiate limits on short-range nuclear systems. See, *inter alia*, *Atlantic News*, no. 1956 (14 Oct. 1987); *Financial Times*, 19, 20 Nov. 1987.

[19] Bonnart, F., 'NATO needs a leader as it enters a year of challenge,' *International Herald Tribune*, 28 Dec. 1987.

[20] On the early negotiating history of MBFR, see Dean, J., 'MBFR: from apathy to accord', *International Security*, vol. 7, no. 4 (spring 1983); Keliher, J. G., *The Negotiations on Mutual and Balanced Force Reductions: The Search for Arms Control in Central Europe* (Pergamon Press: New York, 1980).

[21] Keliher (note 20), pp. 97–110.

[22] 'Press conference statement by Michael Alexander, head of the United Kingdom delegation, on behalf of Western participants in the M(B)FR negotiations, 413th Plenary Session, 5 Dec. 1985,' reprinted in *The Arms Control Reporter (ACR)* (Institute for Defense and Disarmament, IDDS: Brookline, Mass., 1986), pp. 401.D.7–13.

[23] Stanislav Babaevsky on 23 Oct., as reported by Blum, P., *Financial Times*, 24 Oct. 1986; Ambassador Mikhailov at the plenary meeting concluding the 40th round of M(B)FR, 4 Dec. 1986, see *ACR*, 1986, p. 401.B.127.

[24] See for example the statement by Ambassador Warren Zimmerman in Jan. 1987, cited by Blum, P., 'NATO stresses commitment to MBFR', *Financial Times*, 30 Jan. 1987.

[25] Text of the draft treaty reprinted in *FBIS-SU*, 21 Feb. 1986, pp. AA1–AA2.

[26] Ambassador Mikhailov at a briefing for foreign reporters in Moscow as reported on TASS transcript in *FBIS-SU*, 8 Apr. 1986, pp. AA6–AA7.

[27] See INF Treaty text, reproduced in appendix 13A.

[28] *ACR*, 1986, p. 401.D.10.

[29] On the early history of the CSCE, see ed. V. Mastny, *The CSCE and Expansion of European Security* (Duke University Press: Durham, N.C., 1987).

[30] For the Madrid Mandate, see SIPRI, *World Armaments and Disarmament: SIPRI Yearbook 1984* (Taylor & Francis: London, 1984), pp. 570–1.

[31] See for example the statements by William Bauer, Canadian Ambassador to the CSCE, on 31 July and 9 Oct. 1987, reported in *ACR*, 1987, p. 402.B.164.

[32] On French attitudes to arms control, see *inter alia*: Klein, J., 'The allies and arms control: the French position', in F. Hampson and J. Roper (eds), *The Allies and Arms Control* (Johns Hopkins University Press: Baltimore, Md., 1988, forthcoming); Schutze, W., 'France and Germany: co-operation and conflict in defence and security', *PSIS Occasional Paper No. 2*, Graduate Institute of International Studies, Geneva, Sep. 1987; Yost, D., *France and Conventional Defense in Central Europe* (Westview Press: Boulder, Colo., 1985); Barre, R., 'Foundations for European security and co-operation', *Survival*, vol. 29, no. 4, pp. 291–300; Howorth, J., 'Consensus of silence: the French Socialist Party and defence policy under François Mitterrand', *International Affairs*, vol. 60, no. 4 (autumn 1984), pp. 579–600.

[33] The Stockholm Document is reprinted in SIPRI, *SIPRI Yearbook 1987: World Armaments and Disarmament* (Oxford University Press: Oxford, 1987), appendix 10A, pp. 355–69.

[34] *ACR*, 1987, pp. 402.B.141 and 402.B.146; 'Warsaw Pact views British forces,' *Financial Times*, 10 Nov. 1987; Walker, C., 'NATO benefits from military Glasnost', *Times*, 11 Sep. 1987.

[35] East German Ambassador Peter Steglich cited in *ACR*, 1987, p. 402.B.151; and Soviet Ambassador Yuri Kashlev, cited in *ACR*, 1987, p. 402.B.162.

[36] *Atlantic News*, 15 July 1987, on the 10 July NATO submission to the Vienna Follow-up Meeting of the CSCE.

[37] Blaise Schenk, Swiss delegate to the CSCE cited in the *ACR*, 1986, p. 402.B.124.

[38] For more on this point, see Blaker, J., 'Transparency, inspections, and surprise attack,' in S. Windass and E. Grove (eds), *Cooperative Security* (Foundation for International Security: Adderbury, 1987), pp. 1–25.

[39] *ACR*, 1987, p. 401.B.179.

[40] Dempsey, J., 'Warsaw Pact makes concession on troop cut talks', *Financial Times*, 15 Dec. 1987.

[41] The Shevardnadze speech is published in full in *Pravda*, 20 Jan. 1988. For the English text see *Daily Review* (Novosti Press Agency, Moscow), vol. 34, no. 13 (20 Jan. 1988), pp. 4–10.

[42] Ambassador Gilles Curien's statement of 31 July 1987 reprinted in *ACR*, 1987, pp. 402.B.152–3.
[43] General Yuri Lebedev, in an interview with *Corriera della Sera*, 2 Mar. 1987, cited in *ACR*, 1987, p. 401.B.136.
[44] The 'Appeal by the Warsaw Treaty Member States to the Member States of NATO and to all European countries for the reduction of armed forces and conventional armaments in Europe' (The Budapest Appeal), 11 June 1986 is reprinted in *ACR*, 1986, pp. 401.D.14–17.
[45] Ambassador Robert Blackwill cited in *ACR*, 1986, p. 401.B.110.
[46] WTO draft mandate of 22 June 1987, cited in *ACR*, 1987, p. 401.B.163.
[47] Iklé, F., et al., *Discriminate Deterrence: Report of the Commission on Integrated Long-Term Strategy* (Washington, DC, 11 Jan. 1988); for European reactions, see *inter alia*, Howard, M., Kaiser, K. and de Rose, F., 'Deterrence policy: a European response,' *International Herald Tribune*, 4 Feb. 1988.
[48] *Memorandum of the Government of the People's Republic on Decreasing Armaments and Increasing Confidence in Central Europe*, Warsaw, 7 July 1987.
[49] Hoagland, J. and Diehl, J., 'Warsaw Pact makes a new arms offer', *International Herald Tribune*, 12 Nov. 1987.
[50] *Atlantic News*, no. 1972, 3 Dec. 1987, p. 1.
[51] Ledogar briefing, 22 Apr. 1987 in *ACR*, 1987, pp. 401.B.145 and 401.D.21–2.
[52] HLTF–NATO, *Brussels Declaration on Conventional Arms Control*, 11 Dec. 1986, in *ACR*, 1986, pp. 401.D.19–20.
[53] *ACR*, 1987, pp. 402.B.139–40 and 401.B.133.
[54] Heisbourg, F., *The Times*, 11 Dec. 1987.
[55] North Atlantic Council communiqué, 12 Dec. 1987, paragraph 4.
[56] *Atlantic News*, no. 1941 (29 July 1987).
[57] Blackwill, R. D. and Thompson, J. A., 'Negotiating force reductions in Europe', *Los Angeles Times*, 25 Oct. 1987; see also, Thompson, J. A. and Gantz, N. C., 'Conventional arms control revisited: objectives in the new phase', *Atlantik-Brucke Conference Paper* (Berlin), 16–18 Sep. 1987.
[58] *NATO Report* (Brussels), 12 Oct. 1987.
[59] For details of the tank balance in Europe, see Chalmers, M. and Unterseher, L., 'Is there a tank gap? A comparative assessment of the tank fleets of NATO and the Warsaw Pact', Peace Research Report no. 19, School of Peace Studies, University of Bradford; WEU Document 1115 (note 6); Karber, P., 'Conventional instabilities in the NATO/Warsaw Pact Balance,' paper presented at the Aspen Berlin meeting, 14–16 June 1987.
[60] Categories I, II and III are NATO designations for WTO divisions. Category I can attain full strength on 24 hours' notice, Category II are manned and equipped at 50–75 per cent strength and Category III at 20 per cent strength. See IISS, *Military Balance 1986–1987* (IISS: London, 1987), p. 37.
[61] Dean, J., 'Will negotiated force reductions build down the NATO–Warsaw Pact confrontation?', *Washington Quarterly*, summer 1988.
[62] Sloan, C. R., Bowman, S. R., Gallis, P. E. and Goldman, S., *Conventional Arms Control and Military Stability in Europe* (Congressional Research Service: Washington, DC, 16 Oct. 1987).
[63] See for example US Secretary of State George Shultz, speech to NATO Ministers in Brussels, 11 Dec. 1987; Shultz, G., 'Meeting our foreign policy goals,' *Current Policy* (US State Department), no. 1054 (10 Mar. 1988), p. 1; Shultz, G., 'The INF Treaty: advancing US security interest,' *Current Policy*, no. 1057 (14 Mar. 1988), p. 1.
[64] Dobrynin, A., in *Kommunist*, no. 9 (June 1986), pp. 18–31.
[65] Chervov, General N., press conference, 23 June 1987 reported in *FBIS-SU*, 23 June 1987, p. AA3.
[66] Donnelly, C., 'Allies and alliances', in *The Soviet Science of War* (Jane's: London, 1988), chapter 12.
[67] Pond, E., 'Soviets seen as reshaping basic arms philosophy', *Christian Science Monitor*, 14 Jan. 1987.

Appendix 11A. Calendar of planned notifiable military activities in 1988 and forecast for 1989, as required by the Stockholm Document

Prepared by RICHARD W. FIELDHOUSE

One requirement of the Document of the Stockholm Conference (see *SIPRI Yearbook 1987*, appendix 10A) is that each of the participating states must prepare and exchange with all the other CSCE states, by 15 November each year, an annual calendar of notifiable military activities planned for the following year (paragraph 55). Each state is also required to provide information on activities involving more than 40 000 troops that are planned for the second subsequent year (paragraph 59). The results of these requirements this year—the annual calendar for 1988 and the advance forecast for 1989—are presented in the table.

The Stockholm Document specifies the information to be included in each calendar (paragraph 56): type of military activity and its designation; general characteristics and purpose of the activity; states involved; area, indicated by appropriate geographic features and/or defined by geographic co-ordinates; planned duration and the 14-day period ('start window'), indicated by dates, within which the military activity is envisaged to start; the envisaged total number of troops engaged; the types of armed forces involved; the envisaged level of command under which it will take place; the number and type of divisions whose participation is envisaged; and any additional information concerning, *inter alia*, components of armed forces, which the participating state planning the military activity considers relevant. Participating states are also required to make a formal notification of each military activity at least 42 days before it begins (paragraph 29). The information in the notifications is more detailed than in the calendars.

The table is a compilation (based on official information submitted to SIPRI) of the information from 35 states' calendars, and thus gives the overall picture of all their notifiable military activities. States are required to report all such activities occurring on their territory or in which their participation reaches the notifiable level (paragraph 31). Nineteen states reported that they plan no notifiable activities for 1988 (see notes to the table), although some participate in such activities. The table presents activities in chronological order rather than by participating state. Each activity is listed as one event, regardless of the number of states notifying or participating, or the number of exercises occurring simultaneously. In the table, some of the dates are more precise and some less so than prescribed. In the column for the number and type of divisions, the table maintains the names of units given by participating states. For all activities at or above the threshold for observation, observers must be invited from all other participating states (paragraph 38).

Since the exchanged calendars represent *planned* activities, some changes are inevitable. For example, concerning 1987 (see *SIPRI Yearbook 1987*, appendix 10A), Romania did not participate in the planned activity (No. 13), and all three of Switzerland's activities (Nos. 38, 43 and 45) were conducted with numbers of troops below the threshold of notification—as was the case with several activities of other

EUROPEAN ARMS CONTROL 339

Calendar of planned notifiable military activities in 1988 and forecast for 1989, as required by the Stockholm Document

State(s)/ Location	Dates/ Start window	Type/Name of activity[a]	Area	Level of command	No. of troops	Type of forces or equipment	No. and type of divisions[a]	Comments
1. Hungary, USSR and Czechoslovakia in Hungary	1–10 Feb.	FTX 'Baratsag 88'	Csor-Iszkaszent-Gyoergy-Nyirad-Tapolca	Defence Ministry	15 000	Ground and air forces	1 mech. corps (−)	
2. USSR	6–7 days, 1–14 Feb.	FTX	Ushachi, Begoml'–Aleksandrovo–Onkora–Bezenkovichi	Army	14 000	Ground and air forces	1 mot. rifle div. 1 tank div. (−)	
3. USA and Canada in FRG	13 days, 9–22 Feb.	FTX 'Caravan Guard 88'	Neuwied–Wildeck–Mellrichstadt–Wertheim–Wörms	Corps (US-5th)	66 200 (61 000 USA) (5 200 Can.)	Ground and air forces	1 arm. div. 1 mech. inf. div. 1 mech. brig. (−)	Observers to be invited
4. USSR	5–6 days, 24 Feb.–8 Mar.	FTX	Dnieprovskoye–Vis gorad–Koselyi–Kosevogy	Kiev Military District	13 000	Ground and air forces	1 mot. rifle div. (+)	
5. Norway, Canada, FRG, Italy, Netherlands, UK and USA in Norway	6 days, 1–14 Mar.	FTX 'Arrowhead Express'	Malangen–Balsfjord–Bardufoss	Division	14 000	Ground and air forces	1 lgt. inf. div.	
6. Czechoslovakia and USSR in Czechoslovakia	6–7 days, 15–28 Mar.	FTX	Jachymov–Decin–Liberec–Benatky–Becov	Central Group of Forces	17 300 (17 000 USSR) (300 Czech.)	Ground and air forces	1 mech. inf. div. 1 tank div. (−) (USSR) 1 mech. inf bn. (Czech.)	Observers to be invited

State(s)/ Location	Dates/ Start window	Type/Name of activity[a]	Area	Level of command	No. of troops	Type of forces or equipment	No. and type of divisions[a]	Comments
7. GDR, USSR and Poland in GDR	6–7 days, 1–14 Apr.	FTX	Havelberg–Potsdam–Golssen–Magdeburg–Gardelegen	Defence Ministry	22 000 (11 000 GDR) (7 000 USSR) (4 000 Pol.)	Ground and air forces	3 mot. rifle divs. (−)	Observers to be invited
8. USSR	5–6 days, 1–14 Apr.	FTX	Kaushany–Tarutino–Sarata–Starokazach'ye	Commander, Airborne Troops	3 000 (airborne)	Airborne and air forces	1 abn. regt. (+)	
9. USSR	5–6 days, 1–14 Apr.	FTX	Kostopol–Ravno–Dovbych–Yemil'chino	Army	13 000	Ground and air forces	1 mot. rifle div. (+)	
10. Finland	5 days, 7–20 Apr.	FTX 'Tuisku'	Rovaniemi–Kittilä–Sodankylä–Kemijärvi	Corps	13 000	Ground forces	3 brigs. (−)	
11. USSR	5–6 days, 15–28 Apr.	FTX	Podgornoye–Sarata–Varvarovka–Veselinovo	Odessa Military District	13 000	Ground and air forces	1 mot. rifle div. (+)	
12. Czechoslovakia	4–6 days, 1–15 June	FTX 'Sumava 88'	Strakonice–Ceske Budejovice–Vyssi Brod–Zelezna Ruda	Army	17 350	Ground and air forces, 269 main battle tanks	2 mech. inf. divs. (−)	Observers to be invited
13. Czechoslovakia	4–6 days, 15–30 June	FTX	Pisek–Tabor–Jindrichuv Hradec–Vyssi Brod–Volary	Army	13 000	Ground and air forces	1 tank div. 1 mech. inf. bn.	
14. Poland, USSR, GDR and Czechoslovakia in Poland	5–6 days, 16–30 June	FTX 'Tarcza 88'	Goleniow–Wegliniec–Rawicz–Chojnice	General staff	14 000	Ground forces	1 regt. (Pol.) 1 regt. (USSR)	Air and naval staff elements included

EUROPEAN ARMS CONTROL 341

15. USSR and GDR in GDR	7–8 days, 15–28 July	FTX	Brandenburg–Luckenwalde–Eisenhüttenstadt–Peitz–Jessen–Altengrabow	Group of Soviet Forces in Germany	18 000 (17 500 USSR) (500 GDR)	Ground and air forces	1 mot. rifle div. 1 tank div. (–)	Observers to be invited
16. USSR and Poland in Poland	5–6 days, 15–28 July	FTX	Borne-Sulinowo–Zlocieniec–Dobrzany–Walcz–Sypniewo	Northern Group of Forces	13 500	Ground and air forces	1 mech. div. 1 inf. bn. (USSR) 1 tank co.	
17. USSR and GDR in GDR	6–7 days, 1–14 Aug.	FTX	Burg–Luckenwalde–Teupitz–Lübbenau–Jessen	Group of Soviet Forces in Germany	15 000 (14 500 USSR) (500 GDR)	Ground and air forces	1 mot. rifle div. (–) 1 tank div. (–)	
18. Bulgaria	5–6 days, 15–29 Aug.	CPX 'Maritsa 88'	Velingrad–Kardjali–Rakovski–Panagyurishte–Ihtiman	Defence Ministry	13 000	Ground and air forces	1 mot. inf. div. 1 tank brig. (–)	
19. USSR	5–6 days, 15–28 Aug.	FTX	Sagaredsko–Gardabani–Salogly–Gettebe	Transcaucasus Military District	13 000	Ground and air forces	2 mot. rifle divs. (–)	
20. Denmark, UK and FRG in Denmark	33 days (22 Aug.)	FTX 'Bold Grouse'	Island group around Seeland	Corps	20 000 (12 500 UK)	Ground and air forces	2 arm. inf. divs. (Den.) 1 inf. brig. (UK)	Observers to be invited
21. USA, Canada and FRG in FRG	14 days, 29 Aug.– 11 Sep.	'Reforger'-related FTX 'Certain Challenge'	Aschaffenburg–Bad Neustadt–Nürnberg–München–Kempten-Stuttgart–Heidelberg–Aschaffenburg	Army	97 000 (75 000 USA) (17 500 FRG) (5 200 Can.)	Ground and air forces	3 mech. inf. divs. (–) 3 arm. divs. (–) 1 mech. brig.	Observers to be invited

State(s)/ Location	Dates/ Start window	Type/Name of activity[a]	Area	Level of command	No. of troops	Type of forces or equipment	No. and type of divisions[a]	Comments
22. FRG, USA, France and Canada in FRG	6 days, 2–16 Sep.	FTX 'Landesverteidigung 88'	Siegen–Limburg–Aschaffenburg–Karlsruhe–(border with France, Belgium, Luxembourg	Territorial Command	30 100 (27 000 FRG) (1 500 USA) (1 500 France) (100 Can.)	Ground and air forces	. .	Observers to be invited
23. Belgium, UK and FRG in FRG	20 days, 3–15 Sep.	FTX 'Golden Crown'	Soest–Göttingen–Bad Hersfeld–Giessen–Siegen–Hagen	Corps	30 000 (22 000 Bel.) (7 000 FRG) (1 000 UK)	Ground and air forces	2 mech. inf. divs. 1 arm. inf. div. (–)	Observers to be invited
24. Netherlands, USA, UK and FRG in FRG	8 days, 9–23 Sep.	FTX 'Free Lion'	Borgholzhausen–Brome–Schladen–Duderstadt–Lippstadt	Corps (1st Neth.)	44 500 (33 500 Neth.) (5 700 FRG) (4 400 USA) (900 UK)	Ground and air forces	2 mech. inf. divs. (–)	Observers to be invited
25. Norway, USA, UK and Netherlands in Norway	1–2 days, 9–23 Sep.	Amphibious exercise 'Teamwork 88'	Harstad–Bjerkvik–Evenes–Salangen	Norwegian Regional Command and US Brigade	8 000 (4 500 USA) (2 800 UK) (700 Neth.)	Amphibious forces, landing craft and helicopters	2 brigs.	Observers to be invited; in conjunction with exercise 'Barfrost' (No. 26)
26. Norway, USA, Netherlands and UK in Norway	6 days, 11–25 Sep.	FTX 'Barfrost'	Harstad–Bjerkvik–Evenes–Salangen–Bardufoss	Norwegian Regional Command	14 100	Ground, amphibious and air forces	1 inf. brig. (Nor.) 1 amph. brig.	In conjunction with exercise 'Teamwork 88' (No. 25)
27. USSR	7–8 days, 15–28 Sep.	FTX	Slonim–Ivanyevichi–Beryosino–Ulda	Belorussian Military District	>45 000	Ground and air forces	4 tank divs. (–)	Observers to be invited

EUROPEAN ARMS CONTROL 343

28. USSR	5–6 days, 16–29 Sep.	FTX	Rava Russkaya–Mostiska–Gorodok–Sholbunnov–Berdischev–Brusilov–Beryosno	Carpathian Military District	16 000	Ground and air forces	2 mot. rifle divs. (–)
29. USSR	6–7 days, 17–30 Sep.	FTX	Tiraspol–Chadyr-Lunga–Satoka–Snigirievka–Veselinovo	Odessa Military District	14 000	Ground and air forces	1 mot. rifle div. 1 tank div. (–)
30. Italy, USA, Turkey, France and Portugal in Italy	18–30 Sep.	FTX 'Display Determination'	Northern Italy and Sardinia	Corps	9 500 (2 500 amphib.)	Ground, naval and air forces	. . Below notification threshold
31. Switzerland	9 days, 21–29 Sep.	FTX 'Rotondo'	East and Central Alps	Mountain Army Corps	23 200	Ground and air forces	1 mountain div. 1 brig. Elements of 2 territorial zones Observers to be invited
32. USSR	6–7 days, 1–14 Oct.	FTX	Dubravka–Vishtitis–Kibartay–Gelgaudishkis–Ershvilkas–Viyeshvide	Baltic Military District	15 000	Ground and air forces	2 mot. rifle divs. (–)
33. France	7 days, 1–15 Oct.	FTX 'Extel 1'	Sainte-Menehold–Vouziers–Longuyon–Etain	Corps	13 000	Ground forces, 170 main battle tanks	1 div.

344 DEVELOPMENTS IN ARMS CONTROL

State(s)/ Location	Dates/ Start window	Type/Name of activity[a]	Area	Level of command	No. of troops	Type of forces or equipment	No. and type of divisions[a]	Comments
34. USSR and GDR in GDR	5–6 days, 15–28 Oct.	FTX	Wittstock–Feldberg–Zehdenick–Magdeburg–Gardelegen	Group of Soviet Forces in Germany	18 000 (17 500 USSR) (500 GDR)	Ground and air forces	2 tank divs. (–)	Observers to be invited
35. USSR and Hungary in Hungary	5–7 days, 15–28 Oct.	FTX	Celldömölk–Keszthely–Szekesfeherrar–Bodayk	Southern Group of Forces	17 000 (16 500 USSR) (500 Hung.)	Ground and air forces	1 mot. rifle div. 1 tank div.	Observers to be invited
36. UK, FRG and Belgium in FRG	21 days, 28 Oct.–9 Nov.	FTX 'Iron Hammer'	Saltzgitter–Göttingen–Bad Pyrmont–Beckum–Saltzgitter	Division	30 000 (25 000 UK) (3 500 FRG) (1 500 Bel.)	Ground and air forces	1 tank div. (UK) 1 tank brig. (FRG) 1 mech. regt. (Bel.)	Observers to be invited
37. FRG	12 days, 14–28 Nov.	Logistical and medical units field exercise 'Sachsentross 88'	Osnabrück–Delmenhorst–Velzen–Peine–Osnabrück	Corps	15 500	Ground and air forces	1 tank div. (–)	
38. Switzerland	4 days, 21–24 Nov.	FTX 'Feuerdorn'	Central midland	Field Army Corps	25 000	. .	1 field div. Elements of 1 territorial zone	Observers to be invited
Advance forecast for 1989								
1. USA in FRG	15 days, 7–20 Feb.	FTX 'Caravan Guard 89'	Central FRG	Corps, Central Army Group, Central Europe (CENTAG)	45 000–60 000	Ground and air forces	. .	Observers to be invited

2. USA and others in FRG	14 days, 2–15 Sep.	'Reforger'-related FTX	Central FRG	Army, Central Army Group, Central Europe (CENTAG)	50 000–75 000	Ground and air forces	..	Observers to be invited
3. FRG, Netherlands and others in FRG	12 days, 4–17 Sep.	FTX 'Herresübung 89'	Osnabrück–Bremerhaven–Lüneburg-Velzen-Peine	Corps, Northern Army Group, Central Europe (NORTHAG)	55 000	Ground and air forces	..	Observers to be invited
4. Turkey	7 days, Sep.	FTX 'Mehmetcik-89'	Thrace	Army	>40 000	Ground and air forces	..	Observers to be invited
5. France	..	FTX	..	..	40 000	Ground and air forces	..	Observers to be invited

[a] See the list of abbreviations below. (−) means that the division is below full strength or not comprised of all its component units; (+) means that the division is at full strength or with reinforcement units assigned to it.

Abbreviations used in the table:

abn.	airborne	co.	company	lgt.	light
arm.	armoured	CPX	command post exercise	mech.	mechanized
bn.	battalion	div(s).	division(s)	mot.	motorized
brig(s).	brigade(s)	FTX	field training exercise	regt.	regiment
		inf.	infantry		

States participating in notifiable military activities in 1988, by activity number:

Belgium: 23, 36
Bulgaria: 18
Canada: 3, 5, 21, 22
Czechoslovakia: 1, 6, 12, 13, 14
Denmark: 20
Finland: 10
France: 22, 30, 33

GDR: 7, 14, 15, 17, 34
FRG: 3, 5, 20, 21, 22, 23, 24, 36, 37
Hungary: 1, 35
Italy: 5, 30
Netherlands: 5, 24, 25, 26
Norway: 5, 25, 26
Poland: 7, 14, 16

Portugal: 30
Switzerland: 31, 38
Turkey: 30
UK: 5, 20, 23, 24, 25, 26, 36
USA: 3, 5, 21, 22, 24, 25, 26, 30
USSR: 1, 2, 4, 6, 7, 8, 9, 11, 14, 15, 16, 17, 19, 27, 28, 29, 32, 34, 35

States planning no notifiable military activities in 1988: Austria, *Canada*, Cyprus, Greece, the Holy See, Iceland, Ireland, *Italy*, Liechtenstein, Luxembourg, Malta, Monaco, *Portugal*, Romania, San Marino, Spain, Sweden, *Turkey* and Yugoslavia.

(States participating in notifiable activities but not responsible for notification are given in italics.)

countries. These routine changes are communicated to the other participating states in the formal notifications required at least 42 days before the activity begins.

The one exception to this requirement concerns notifiable activities 'carried out without advance notice to the troops involved', for which notification is to be given when the troops begin such activities (paragraph 32). There were three such cases in 1987, all by NATO countries. Italy conducted a short-notice activity, 'Active Edge', on 28–30 April, involving 24 200 troops. The USA held a similar exercise in the FRG on 21–24 May, involving 21 400 troops. NATO held a large exercise in the FRG, also named 'Active Edge', involving some 200 000 troops from Belgium, Canada, the FRG, the Netherlands, the UK and the USA.

After the first year, the record of implementation with the Stockholm Document has been remarkably good. All of the provisions were exercised and complied with: the exchange of calendars, prior notification of activities, observation of activities above the stated threshold, and inspection of activities without the right of refusal. Although some questions and difficulties arose concerning compliance, these were generally of a routine or technical nature, given the lack of prior experience with the Document's implementation. Observers were invited to and were present at all activities that were notified at the threshold for observation. There were a number of voluntary notifications of activities below the threshold level and other cases where the spirit, in addition to the letter, of the Document was met.

Among the provisions of the Stockholm Document exercised for the first time in 1987, the most significant were the five inspections conducted. On 28–30 August the USA conducted its first-ever inspection of a Soviet exercise, near Minsk, USSR. On 10–12 September Britain inspected a joint USSR-GDR exercise near Cottbuss, GDR. On 5–7 October the USSR inspected a Turkish exercise near Istanbul, and on 28–30 October it inspected an activity in the FRG. The GDR held its first inspection on 11–13 November in and around Göttingen, FRG. From the little public information available, these inspections appear to have gone well. The USA expressed its satisfaction with 'the positive approach demonstrated by the Soviet Union' during the first US inspection.[1]

In answer to a SIPRI request sent to all 35 CSCE participating states, none of the 19 states responding indicated dissatisfaction with the process of implementation during 1987. However, since just over half of the states responded—and very few provided information on implementation—this is not a full sample.[2] Many states are not yet willing to extend the CDE objective of openness or transparency to the public domain. It is hoped that in the future all CSCE states will see the confidence- and security-building value of making public the information they already share with each other.

[1] 'US inspects Soviet military exercise', *Department of State Bulletin*, Nov. 1987, p. 46.
[2] States that did not respond to the SIPRI request: Austria, Belgium, Canada, Denmark, Finland, Greece, Hungary, Luxembourg, Malta, Monaco, Portugal, Romania, San Marino, the USSR, the UK and Yugoslavia.

12. Multilateral arms control efforts

JOZEF GOLDBLAT

I. Introduction

US–Soviet talks on intermediate-range nuclear forces (INF), which culminated in 1987 in the signing of a bilateral treaty for the elimination of these forces, have overshadowed all other arms control negotiations. The positive development of relations between the United States and the Soviet Union, whose important role in bringing about arms control is univerally recognized, has warmed up the international political climate and improved prospects for multilateral agreements. This is particularly true for chemical disarmament.

There is, however, a growing concern, especially among the neutral and non-aligned countries, that arms control issues of universal importance may in the future be resolved exclusively within the bilateral US–Soviet or NATO–Warsaw Treaty Organization framework. The willingness of the superpowers to integrate their bilateral dealings with multilateral efforts is increasingly in doubt. The refusal of at least one of them at the Geneva-based 40-nation Conference on Disarmament (CD) to engage in substantive considerations of matters related to nuclear testing or to the prevention of an arms race in outer space has reinforced this concern. The expectation of many countries was that the 1988 third UN General Assembly special session devoted to disarmament would reaffirm the role of the United Nations in disarmament and halt the disquieting trend away from multilateralism.

II. Chemical disarmament

In 1987, a series of important obstacles which had stood in the way of a comprehensive ban on chemical weapons were removed. In particular, the Soviet Union has accepted the principle of mandatory, that is, non-refusable, on-site inspection on challenge, which can be set in motion, on very short notice, upon request by any state party suspecting a violation.[1] It has thus acceded to the view held by the United States since 1984.[2] As a result, the positions of the principal negotiating parties in the politically sensitive field of verification of compliance are now closer than ever before. Moreover, the Soviet Union, which earlier had not even admitted to possessing chemical weapons, indicated the amount of toxic substances it had stockpiled and followed the US example set 18 years before by announcing that it had ceased the production of chemical weapons. It also declared that it did not have chemical weapons outside its borders and that it had begun the construction of a special facility for the destruction of chemical weapon stocks.[3] These statements, coupled with international visits to US and Soviet chemical weapon storage facilities,[4] have helped to build a significant measure of confidence in the seriousness of the superpowers' intent to be rid of chemical weapons.

SIPRI Yearbook 1988: World Armaments and Disarmament

There are still many problems that remain to be solved before a convention effectively prohibiting the possession of chemical weapons can be signed. However, the number of controversial political issues relating to the convention has diminished. Chemical disarmament is now the most promising item on the agenda of the multilateral arms control negotiations; the treaty is no longer a distant goal but a real possibility.[5] The CD faces the task of transforming this possibility into reality. The task is urgent, because at least two great powers, the USA and France, have started or are about to start the production of new systems of chemical weapons, and because the continued use of chemical weapons by Iraq against Iranian combatants and civilians,[6] as well as the recently revealed manufacture of such weapons by Iran,[7] have demonstrated the danger of proliferation of these weapons in the Third World.

Areas of agreement

Scope of the obligations

The aim of the envisaged convention is to bring about general and complete chemical disarmament and thereby to complement the 1925 Geneva Protocol. Consequently, the parties should undertake not to develop, produce, otherwise acquire, stockpile or retain chemical weapons, or transfer them to anyone, as well as not to assist, encourage or induce others to engage in these activities.

In order to ensure the implementation of these undertakings, all chemical weapons and chemical weapon production facilities would be declared to an international authority and placed under international control. On-site inspections conducted by international inspectors, both systematic and *ad hoc*, as well as continuous monitoring with the use of specialized on-site instruments, would be provided for, with a view to preventing the clandestine removal of chemical weapons from the declared stocks and to precluding further chemical weapon production. It is noteworthy that, after years of hesitation, the Soviet Union has finally expressed its readiness to describe the precise locations and to declare the detailed inventory of its chemical weapons upon entry into force of the convention.[8] Only France is still opposed to an early and complete disclosure of stocks. France claims, on security grounds, the need for each state to preserve for a number of years a certain amount of chemical weapons at undeclared locations (see below).

Elimination of chemical weapon stocks and production facilities would be carried out under international supervision and within a 10-year period, beginning not later than 12 months after the convention became effective. Some countries would prefer that this period be shorter,[9] but it is widely acknowledged that for technical and practical reasons (such as the need to install specially designed equipment and to take precautionary measures for the protection of the environment) it might be difficult to complete sooner the elimination of the existing, presumably large, chemical weapon arsenals. Since the Soviet Union has withdrawn its proposal that some chemical warfare agents should be permitted to be diverted to peaceful uses, the consensus is that the stocks are to be eliminated only by destruction. This means that the chemicals in question would be converted in an irreversible way to a form unsuitable for the production of chemical weapons, while the munitions would be rendered unusable. The chemical weapon production facilities would be either destroyed, dismantled or converted into facilities for destruction of chemical weapons.

The parties would have the right to produce, or otherwise acquire, and use toxic chemicals for purposes not prohibited by the convention, but these chemicals, as well as the facilities producing them, would be subject to international verification. Czechoslovakia argued that laboratories where supertoxic lethal chemicals can be synthesized should be subject to inspection on challenge.[10] However, research in the field of chemical weapons is deemed to be non-verifiable and would not be covered by the convention's prohibitions.

Verification of compliance

Since different categories of chemical would require verification regimes with different degrees of stringency, depending on the risk they entail, control lists or 'schedules' have been drawn up for each category to facilitate the tasks of the inspectorate. The reporting of data, using monitoring equipment and carrying out systematic on-site inspections, would be the common verification measure. Their function would be to confirm that prohibited activities were not taking place and that parties were fulfilling their obligations. Bilateral and multilateral consultation would be envisaged on any matter which might be raised relating to the objectives or the implementation of the convention.

Inspections on challenge would be resorted to only exceptionally: in those cases when allegations had been made that chemical weapons were being clandestinely stored, produced or otherwise acquired, transferred or used, and when these concerns could not be resolved by routine measures. The procedure would have to be rapid to allay suspicions; 48 hours has often been mentioned as the desirable time span from the request to the arrival of inspectors at the site. It is understood that the burden of proof of innocence would then be on the accused party. In any case, the on-challenge inspection regime is meant to serve as a deterrent against violations rather than as a method of disclosing them.

Areas of major disagreement

Order of destruction

While it is accepted that the destruction of chemical weapon stocks should start simultaneously for all states possessing such stocks, and that the principle of undiminished national security should be observed throughout the destruction process, there are sharp differences of opinion regarding the actual order of destruction. In 1985, China worked out a special formula for a balanced order of destruction of chemical weapon stockpiles to prevent any of the parties possessing chemical weapons from gaining a military advantage,[11] but the formula was found by many to be too complicated and was never thoroughly discussed. The Soviet Union proposed that, in view of possible differences in the composition of chemical weapon stockpiles, and because of technical difficulties in working out a means of comparing various categories of chemical, the entire elimination period should be divided into nine one-year sub-periods. Within each sub-period the parties concerned would have to eliminate no less than one-ninth of their chemical weapon stockpiles in each of the existing categories.[12] Mexico and Argentina would prefer that the most dangerous chemical weapons be destroyed first and that the least lethal ones be left until the end of the destruction process. Such an order would, in the view of these two countries, help build confidence from the early stages of the convention's implementation.[13]

According to a suggestion made by the chairman of the CD *Ad Hoc* Committee on Chemical Weapons, the order of destruction should be based on the principle of levelling out the stockpiles of chemical weapons possessed by the parties. To this end, chemical weapons declared by each party might be divided into three categories. Those included in the schedule of the most toxic warfare agents would constitute the first category; their destruction would have to be completed within 10 years of the entry into force of the convention. Other chemical warfare agents would constitute the second category, the destruction of which would be completed not later than five years after the convention had become effective, whereas for the third category—that of unfilled munitions and devices, and equipment specifically designed for use directly in connection with employment of chemical weapons—the period of destruction would remain to be negotiated. The idea is that within each category the destruction of chemical weapons should be carried out in such a way that no more than the quantities agreed in advance and specified in the convention would remain at the end of each annual period.[14]

France has put forward a concept of 'security balance', which would allow each country—during the first eight years after entry into force of the convention—to keep and maintain a stock of chemical weapons. This so-called security stock, composed of munitions (shells, rockets, bombs, etc.), could contain up to 1000–2000 tons of toxic chemicals, including nerve agents, which is the amount regarded by France as militarily significant. The stock would be declared at the end of the eighth year and be subject to destruction only during the ninth and tenth years—or even later if the agreed 10-year period of stock destruction were to be extended and the timetable called into question. To ensure the maintenance of the security stock, as well as its renewal and modernization, the parties would also be allowed to possess technical means for the production of toxic chemicals and chemical munitions. The relevant production facility would be destroyed or withdrawn from service before the end of the ninth year after entry into force of the convention.[15] The French proposal has met with criticism. It was interpreted by many as an encouragement to those countries which do not possess chemical weapons to acquire them, contrary to the objective of the planned convention. Pakistan stated that secret stockpiling of chemical weapons by the parties, even in limited quantities, would deepen suspicion among states and undermine confidence in the convention.[16] The Soviet Union considered that the French proposal would lead to a legalized proliferation of chemical weapons and thereby to 'increased insecurity'.[17]

'Balanced' security on a world-wide scale could be achieved either by building up chemical arsenals in non-chemical weapon countries or by eliminating all existing chemical weapons. The first solution amounts to rearmament. It is the second solution that constitutes the essence of the convention under consideration. French comparisons between a chemical weapons convention and the 1968 Non-Proliferation Treaty (NPT), made with the purpose of demonstrating the alleged unequal treatment of the parties, seem out of place.[18] The NPT contains only a pledge to pursue negotiations on measures of disarmament, whereas a chemical treaty would provide for actual disarmament to be completed within a specified period of time. Moreover, the principle of undiminished security in the process of eliminating the chemical weapon potential is applicable exclusively to chemical weapon countries. Those which do not possess chemical weapons cannot claim that they would feel less secure at a time when other states were destroying stocks of these weapons. According to statements by high French officials, France belongs to the category of non-chemical weapon states,[19] as it is only now planning to acquire a deterrent capability in this area.[20]

Institutional arrangements

Since the principal organ of the convention, a 'consultative committee' or a 'general conference', is to be composed of all states parties, it may not be able to intervene rapidly and effectively in case of a crisis. It has therefore been agreed that there should be a subsidiary body of limited membership—an executive council—having the day-to-day responsibility for ensuring compliance. In the performance of its functions it would be assisted by a technical secretariat which would include an international inspectorate. As a central management authority, the executive council would, in political terms, be the most 'powerful' body set up by the convention. Its composition, however, has not yet been agreed upon. Quite naturally, each country defends those formulas which could make its own participation possible. Sharing the view of several non-aligned countries, Mexico has expressed preference for an equitable political and geographical distribution of seats and is opposed to creating two classes of membership—permanent and non-permanent (following the example of the UN Security Council)—as was suggested by some.[21]

Even more controversial is the decision-making procedure. The choice is between majority (simple or qualified) decisions and unanimous (or consensus) decisions. The latter would be tantamount to introducing the right of veto, which could paralyse the operation of the convention. A view was expressed that reports of fact-finding inquiries should not be put to a vote at all.[22]

Other outstanding issues

Definitions

The term 'chemical weapons' applies both to toxic chemicals and to munitions or other devices designed to cause harm by the release of toxic chemicals, as well as to any equipment designed for use directly in connection with the employment of such munitions or devices. But it is still not clear whether this formula would be taken as a final definition of the object of the intended ban.

The task of agreeing on a definition is all the more complicated because toxicity alone is not enough to classify a chemical substance as a chemical warfare agent; it is the purpose for which it has been acquired that is decisive. Thus, there is the problem of irritants (such as tear gas) that may be used in warfare but are also often employed for domestic law enforcement and riot control; therefore, many countries would not like to see them covered by the definition of chemical weapons. Similarly, the dual-purpose status of herbicides raises a problem for the planned chemical weapons convention. Apart from their peaceful applications in forestry, agriculture, and so on, herbicides were extensively used during the Second Indo-China War after having been first employed in Malaya during the 1950s. One formula proposed is that the parties should undertake not to use herbicides 'as a method of warfare', which would not preclude other uses. However, such a non-use obligation may have implications for the scope of the 1925 Geneva Protocol, which is also controversial. Indeed, in 1969 the UN General Assembly adopted a resolution declaring as contrary to the generally recognized rules of international law the use in international armed conflicts of chemical agents of warfare, having a direct toxic effect not only on humans and animals but also on plants, but the resolution was not unanimous. Many states abstained, and a few voted against such an extensive definition of chemical weapons.[23] Appropriate wording will also have to be found to deal with overlap between a chemical weapons convention and the 1972 BW Convention. The latter treaty forbids the development, production and stockpiling not only of biological agents and natural toxins but also of synthesized toxins which are regarded as chemical weapons.

The need for a precise definition of chemical weapons may become less acute with the establishment of agreed schedules specifying chemicals subject to different verification regimes. However, such schedules cannot be definitive. They would have to be reviewed and, if necessary, amended. The first review could take place when states had declared their arsenals to the international authority, since it may then become apparent that certain toxic chemicals possessed by chemical weapon countries had not been taken into account in the course of negotiations. Subsequently, there might be a need for periodic updating. To this end, France has suggested that an authority be created to draw attention to new products and technologies that warrant monitoring and to propose suitable verification measures and procedures. This authority, the scientific council, would comprise independent persons chosen for their competence. In fulfilling its consultative role, the scientific council would meet regularly or upon request.[24] 'Chemical weapon production facility' has not as yet been fully defined either. It is understood only that both the means of production of toxic chemicals, as well as the equipment for filling munitions with such chemicals, should be covered by the definition. The United States proposed that reference be made specifically to facilities or establishments that 'specialize' in chemical weapon development, so as to cover the locations of direct interest and to avoid including those that may have only an indirect or one-time involvement.[25]

Another important term calling for elaboration is 'under jurisdiction and control of a state party'. It is used in connection with the undertaking to eliminate all chemical weapon stockpiles and production facilities, whatever their location. The Soviet Union asked for clarification of the status of the subsidiaries of transnational chemical corporations: which state would be responsible for ensuring that these corporations were observing the provisions of the convention, especially if the manufacturing operations were conducted in a country which was not party to it.[26] In partial response to these apprehensions, the United States stated that any corporation incorporated under US law, wherever its activities took place, would be prohibited from aiding a non-party in chemical weapon production.[27] None the less, an agreed interpretation of the term in question would be in order. The parties must be assured that no physical or legal person, including any operating outside the territory of the home country, would be in a position to circumvent the obligations undertaken by states.

Systematic inspection

International verification through systematic on-site inspection would apply to the declared stocks of chemical weapons and to the process of their destruction. It would also apply to the closure and elimination of chemical weapon production facilities, as well as to certain facilities of the civilian chemical industry to ensure that chemical weapons were not being produced there. Regarding the civilian industry, China proposed that a chemical production 'threshold value' be set, below which on-site inspection would not be required, as there would be no particular threat to the objective of the convention; data reporting might then be sufficient.[28] In the opinion of the United States, production of lower-risk chemicals of up to 30 tons per year would not need even to be declared. Only above this threshold would an annual declaration be required.[29] The number, intensity and duration of routine on-site inspections and detailed inspection procedures, as well as operation and maintenance of the monitoring devices, remain to be established. They would be specified in agreements on subsidiary arrangements (taking account of the characteristics of each facility) to be concluded by states parties with the international authority on the basis of a generally applicable model agreement. Whereas controls on the civil chemical industry are necessary in order to maintain confidence in the treaty regime, a postulate of generally recognized importance is that of ensuring that technical and commercial secrets of the industry not be revealed through inspection. Appropriate procedures, capable of satisfying this postulate without defeating the purpose of inspection, would have to be developed, drawing perhaps upon the experience of the International Atomic Energy Agency (IAEA) which meets such requirements in the application of nuclear safeguards. An outline of a step-by-step approach to verifying the elimination of production facilities has been submitted by the United States.[30] International verification of temporary conversion of a chemical weapon production facility into a chemical weapon destruction facility has not yet been elaborated.

On-site inspection on challenge

As a rule, unimpeded access to suspected sites should be given to inspectors in order to enable them to clarify doubts about compliance. However, it is deemed permissible for the requested state to demonstrate compliance through alternative arrangements, as has been proposed by the United Kingdom.[31] The need to resort to such arrangements might arise when, by disclosing sensitive data not connected with chemical weapons, the intrusiveness of on-site inspection could affect legitimate national interests.

The following examples of alternative arrangements were given by the Soviet Union: provision of pertinent information by the challenged party; visual inspection of the suspected facility without entering it, in so far as the installations used for the maintenance of chemical weapon stocks (such as ventilation systems) may be observable from the outside; partial access to the facility in question; and collection and analysis of air and water samples around the facility for traces of relevant chemicals. The Soviet Union expressed the view that, if it proved impossible for the challenging and the challenged parties to agree on alternative measures, all facts should be submitted to an international authority which would evaluate the case and decide by a two-thirds majority whether a breach had occurred.[32] The USA, however, voiced doubts as to whether the measures suggested by the USSR could be sufficient to determine the contents of a suspect munition bunker.[33] It insisted that if an alternative to on-site inspection could not be agreed upon, the mandatory right of access to any location, within the shortest possible time, should remain. Denial of entry to a given facility would—in the US opinion—result in an assumption that that facility contained forbidden material.[34] The Netherlands proposed that in such a situation the challenged state might be declared as violating the convention.[35] Thus, the positions are still apart on what would happen if alternative measures proposed by the challenged state did not satisfy the challenger.

Another unresolved problem is how to prevent the abuse of the right to on-site inspection through frivolous challenges. Each request would have to specify the site to be inspected and the matters on which reassurance was sought, including the nature of the suspected activity, as well as indicate the relevant provision of the convention about which doubts of compliance had arisen. But no screening or 'filtering' mechanism is to be set up to decide whether a particular challenge is justified and thus whether the inspection should be allowed to be carried out. One way of dealing with the danger of abuse could be, as proposed by the Soviet Union, to provide for states' liability for losses suffered by the challenged state as a result of an unjustified on-challenge inspection.[36] Similarly, Egypt suggested that compensation be envisaged for damages resulting from an abuse of inspection.[37] It is worth noting, by way of analogy, that according to the 1967 Treaty of Tlatelolco prohibiting nuclear weapons in Latin America the costs of a special inspection must, as a rule, be borne by the requesting state (Article 16.2).

Non-use of chemical weapons

Since the 1925 Geneva Protocol banning the use of chemical weapons does not provide for verification of compliance, the chemical weapons convention, which is to re-affirm the ban on use, may embody procedures for checking possible allegations. Specific proposals to this end have been made by Norway and Canada.[38] The working papers submitted to the CD by these two countries in 1987 deal with the identification and survey of the allegedly contaminated area, the collection of samples of soil, sand, water, vegetation and snow, as well as the preparation and transportation of the samples to specially designated laboratories for analysis. These papers supplement the *Handbook for the Investigation of Allegations of the Use of Chemical and Biological Weapons*, presented in the CD by Canada a year earlier.[39]

It will be recalled that the UN Secretary-General is empowered by the General Assembly to investigate, with the assistance of experts, information brought to his attention concerning activities that may constitute a violation of the Geneva Protocol, including on-site collecting of evidence, and to report the results to all UN member states.[40] Procedures for such investigation have been elaborated by a group of consultant experts. Its report, submitted in 1983 and supplemented in 1984, spells out the criteria to guide the Secretary-General in deciding whether or not to initiate an investigation, specifies actions related to the initiation of an investigation and provides guidance for its organization and implementation.[41] The modalities now available to the Secretary-General for the investigation of reports on the alleged use of chemical weapons may have to be reviewed upon entry into force of the chemical weapons convention.

Agreement on the techniques of investigation is, of course, essential, but there are also other important problems to be tackled in the case of a suspected use of chemical weapons. They include ways to ensure access to the place of alleged use, especially if it is located on the territory controlled by the perpetrator and not on the territory of the victim; determination of the degree of reliability of eyewitnesses; and the reaching of an unambiguous conclusion regarding the identity of the culprit. Furthermore, one must bear in mind that several dozen parties to the Geneva Protocol have reserved the right to a 'second' (or retaliatory) use of chemical weapons. Such a reservation is, of course, incompatible with a convention intended to completely exclude the possibility of chemical warfare. The reservation could either be allowed to lapse upon completion of the process of elimination of chemical weapon stocks, which may take up to 10 years, or be withdrawn sooner, for example, upon entry into force of the convention. The latter procedure would reinforce the confidence necessary for the implementation of the convention, and would help attract a wider range of adherents. It is significant that, in order to avoid incompatibility with the obligations under the BW Convention, several countries have found it opportune formally to withdraw a similar reservation attached to the Geneva Protocol ban on the use of biological means of warfare.

Peaceful uses

The usual proviso, patterned after other arms control treaties (such as the BW Convention or the NPT), that a ban on military uses of the pertinent items should not hinder civilian production, will most certainly be part of the chemical weapons convention. There will, no doubt, be a pledge to promote international co-operation and assistance in the peaceful application of chemical science and technology which, as underlined by Brazil, is of special importance to the developing countries.[42]

It is difficult, however, to predict the extent to which such a pledge of co-operation and assistance would be considered binding for the parties: commercial deals, in whatever commodity, are subject more to economic rules than to political considerations. Nevertheless, the chances to intensify the development of chemical research and industrial production world-wide are likely to increase upon the conclusion of a chemical weapons convention because the existing restrictions on trade in chemical compounds and on transfer of technology, which had been introduced for security reasons, would be removed for the parties to the convention. States remaining outside the convention might encounter added difficulties in the development of their chemical industry because of the inevitable suspicion that they either possessed chemical weapons or were planning to manufacture them.

Entry into force

The United Kingdom has proposed that the chemical weapons convention should require at least 60 ratifications, including those by states that had declared that they possessed chemical weapons.[43] The Soviet Union would be satisfied with some 30–40 ratifications.[44] This would be comparable to the NPT, which entered into force after the deposit of 40 instruments of ratification plus those of the three depositaries—the UK, the USA and the USSR—whereas the BW Convention required only 22 ratifications, including those of the three depositaries. The United States sees the need for a 'global' ban but has not indicated the number of ratifications that would satisfy this requirement.[45] In any event, both superpowers consider that the convention must encompass all 'chemical weapon-capable' states.[46]

To be truly effective, arms control agreements must have the widest possible adherence. However, if the requirement for the entry into force of the chemical weapons convention were placed too high, many years might pass before it could start operating. One cannot expect that a treaty abolishing an entire category of weapon and the industrial base for its production, which has been worked out by a group of 40 CD members, would be automatically accepted by all or most of the remaining nations, as has been the case with several other agreements. In the meantime, the danger of further chemical weapon proliferation might increase. According to US estimates, about 15 countries already possess or are seeking to acquire chemical weapons.[47] British estimates are even higher.[48] Egypt remarked that, as far as the developing countries are concerned, their joining the treaty would depend to a large extent on the provisions for international co-operation in the peaceful uses of chemical industry.[49]

Withdrawal from the convention

The major arms control agreements contain a clause that allows withdrawal from the treaty whenever extraordinary events related to its subject-matter have jeopardized the supreme interests of the country concerned. If the chemical weapons convention follows this precedent—which is likely— withdrawal could be justified by the retention or acquisition of a chemical weapon capability by a state remaining outside the convention, or by a violation committed by a party.

In order to deter the parties from acting in breach of the obligations they have assumed, and also to deter other states from engaging in activities inconsistent with the objectives of the convention, Pakistan proposed the following undertakings: (*a*) provision of assistance to the state party which feels endangered by a violation of the convention by another party or by the activities of other states posing a threat to the objectives of the convention; and (*b*) applying collective sanctions against the states guilty of such transgressions.[50] The envisaged assistance would include measures for the protection against chemical weapons of military forces and the civilian population of the requesting state, and the training of its personnel in the use of protective equipment. These measures could be taken by the executive council as well as by individual parties to the convention. The actions suggested to be taken in case of violation include measures of trade embargo,[51] in addition to possible political pressure put on the violator and the diplomatic support provided to the country affected.

Conclusion

Success of the present multilateral negotiations regarding chemical weapons depends in the first place on the determination of the superpowers definitively to renounce chemical warfare and to dispose of their chemical arsenals, the largest in the world. Verification is no longer an insurmountable obstacle. But even with good will on the part of the main protagonists, as well as of the other negotiators, a long time may be needed to settle the controversies still outstanding and to work out the missing provisions of the chemical weapons convention. Moreover, the 'rolling text' now before the CD must be transposed into proper treaty language; the redundancies must be removed and the terminology streamlined.[52] The inevitably lengthy drafting process could be shortened if the elaboration of certain technical details were left to the organs to be created by the convention rather than attempting to make them final in the body of the convention itself. It is impossible to foresee all eventualities before the convention starts operating. In any event, a periodic review of the operation of the convention will certainly be provided for, as it has been in several other arms control agreements.

The cause of chemical disarmament would be considerably enhanced if all states clearly stated, even before the convention is concluded, whether or not they possess chemical weapon stockpiles and chemical weapon production facilities, and if those which do possess chemical weapons provided information regarding the amount as well as the assortment and possibly ceased their production.[53] Strict export controls, introduced as quickly as possible, on those chemical substances which could be used in making chemical weapons would also be very helpful. Above all, states must become convinced that a world free of chemical weapons will be a safer one. Consequently, a resolute response from the international community is called for to the established facts of use of chemical weapons in violation of the Geneva Protocol, whatever the identity of the violator.

III. Nuclear non-proliferation

Since the 1985 NPT Review Conference, the nuclear non-proliferation regime has experienced fluctuating trends. The positive trends are attributable to new accessions to the NPT—the centrepiece of the regime—and to the tightening of nuclear-related export requirements, as well as to progress in nuclear arms control and regional denuclearization. No violations of the NPT have been reported, and no withdrawals from the Treaty have been notified. The negative trends are due to the incipient trade in nuclear-powered submarines, which may heavily tax the nuclear safeguards rules, and to the disclosed or suspected smuggling of nuclear material and sensitive equipment to certain non-nuclear weapon countries known to have nuclear weapon aspirations.

Indeed, the main problems are those regarding non-nuclear weapon states which refuse to join the NPT but conduct significant nuclear activities and operate unsafeguarded plants capable of making weapon-usable material. These so-called nuclear threshold countries are Argentina, Brazil, India, Israel, Pakistan and South Africa. There is an overhanging danger that some might cross the threshold to become fully-fledged nuclear weapon states. This would be a serious blow to the non-proliferation regime, which has been laboriously developed over several decades, and a set-back for the cause of regional and international stability and security.

Strengthening the non-proliferation regime

New participants in the regime

The NPT has attracted more adherents than any other arms control treaty: by 1 January 1988, the number of parties had reached 137. Among the recent accessions, that of Spain is especially remarkable because Spain belongs to the group of countries conducting significant peaceful nuclear activities. With this addition, all the industrially developed non-nuclear weapon states are fully covered by the non-proliferation regime.

After years of refusal to conclude a safeguards agreement with the IAEA, as provided for in the NPT, Nigeria—party to the NPT since 1968—stated that it was ready to negotiate and sign such an agreement.[54] Moreover, for the first time a non-party to the NPT (and to the Treaty of Tlatelolco) had agreed to accept full-scope safeguards, identical to those required for the parties to the

NPT. The agreement was concluded between Albania and the IAEA in accordance with the provisions of the IAEA Statute which authorizes the Agency to apply safeguards at the request of a state to any of that state's activities in the field of atomic energy.[55]

Protection of nuclear material

An important step towards reducing the risks of the diversion of nuclear material to non-peaceful purposes was made on 8 February 1987, with the entry into force of the 1980 Convention on the Physical Protection of Nuclear Material. The provisions of the Convention oblige the parties to ensure that, during international transport across their territory or on ships or aircraft under their jurisdiction, nuclear material for peaceful purposes as categorized in a special annex (plutonium, uranium-235, uranium-233 and irradiated fuel) is protected at the agreed level. Furthermore, the parties undertake not to export or import nuclear material or allow its transit through their territory unless they have received assurances that this material will be protected during international transport in accordance with the levels of protection determined by the Convention, and to apply these levels of protection also to material which, during transit from one part of their territory to another, will pass through international waters or airspace. The parties to the Convention agree to share information on missing nuclear material to facilitate recovery operations. Robbery, embezzlement or extortion in relation to nuclear material, and acts without lawful authority involving nuclear material which cause or are likely to cause 'death or serious injury to any person or substantial damage to property', are to be treated as punishable offences. Unfortunately, the members of the European Community have not yet ratified the Physical Protection Convention, even though shipments of nuclear material in the territories of the Community are very intensive.

Towards the end of 1987, an alarm was raised in FR Germany and Belgium because of alleged illegal cross-border transportation of canisters with nuclear wastes. It was asserted that at least some canisters were falsely labelled and actually contained fissionable material destined for Pakistan and Libya. At the time of writing (February 1988), no concrete evidence was available to support the above allegation. The IAEA stated that 'there is no reason to believe that any diversion of material under the IAEA safeguards has taken place'. Similarly, a high official of Euratom said that 'inspections do not allow the conclusion that nuclear material has gone astray'.[56] Indeed, the IAEA report regarding the results of the safeguards implementation stated that 'it was considered reasonable to conclude that nuclear material under Agency safeguards remained in peaceful nuclear activities and was properly accounted for'.[57] Moreover, a joint IAEA–Euratom inventory of fissionable material, conducted at the request of the governments concerned, did not reveal any deficiencies. It seems, none the less, that some serious irregularities in the transportation of radioactive substances did take place.

In the interest of nuclear non-proliferation, strict adherence to agreed rules of physical protection of nuclear material is essential, both in international transport and in domestic use, storage and transport.

Missile export controls

One recommendation, frequently made for the strengthening of the non-proliferation regime, has been to complement the existing restraints on supplies of nuclear material and equipment by restraints on supplies of dual-capable weapon systems, that is, systems capable of delivering both a conventional and a nuclear weapon. This recommendation was partly put into practice on 16 April 1987 when, after more than four years of diplomatic transactions, seven governments (those of Britain, Canada, France, the FRG, Italy, Japan and the USA) adopted identical guidelines to control the transfer of equipment and technology which 'could make a contribution' to missile systems capable of delivering a nuclear weapon. The established export regime does not constitute an international agreement in the usual sense of the term; it is rather a set of identical national policies announced at the same time. Consequently, the implementation of the agreed rules is left to individual states. (Actually, even before the guidelines had been formally established, the seven nations were informally applying corresponding restraints in their supply policies.)

The guidelines are accompanied by an identical annex of items to be controlled, so as to prevent commercial advantage or disadvantage to any of the governments in question. The items fall into two categories. Item 1 of category I covers complete rocket systems (including ballistic missile systems, space-launched vehicles and sounding rockets) and unmanned air vehicle systems (including cruise missile systems, target drones and reconnaissance drones) capable of delivering at least a 500-kg payload within a range of at least 300 km, as well as the specially designed production facilities for these systems. Item 2 of the same category covers complete sub-systems usable in item 1 systems, as well as the specially designed production facilities and production equipment therefor. If a category I item is included in a system, that system will also be considered as category I, except when the incorporated item cannot be separated, removed or duplicated. All other items (3–18) in the annex are category II items. Particular restraint will be exercised in the consideration of category I item transfers because of their great sensitivity, and there is a presumption of denial with respect to such transfers. Until further notice, transfer of category I production facilities will not be authorized. Category II items are not on a 'denial' list. Almost all items in this category have uses other than for projects of proliferation concern, and their transfers will be considered on a case-by-case basis. Understandably, nuclear proliferation occupies a prominent place among the factors which must be taken into account in the evaluation of export applications.

The missile export control guidelines constitute an important international initiative. Unfortunately, the regime is focused on large missiles and rockets; it is not designed to constrain more sophisticated forces. It ignores such an important and relatively easily available nuclear delivery vehicle as aircraft. Moreover, the restrictions have come somewhat late. Both the USA and the USSR have already provided different types of missile to several countries. In particular, Iraq, Iran and Syria are now in possession of Soviet-made missiles, some of which have been modified to reach a range of several hundred kilometres.[58] India put a satellite into orbit with its own rocket and has started testing a 250-km range missile.[59] Argentina is developing—in co-operation with Egypt—a medium-range (800 km) rocket.[60] Brazil manufactures and exports a wide variety of rockets, and there have been allegations that Israel has deployed intermediate-range ballistic missiles in the Negev Desert.[61] A major deal, made known only recently, was the purchase by Saudi Arabia (another non-party to the NPT) of Chinese surface-to-surface ballistic missiles having a range of about 3000 km, and designed to deliver nuclear warheads.[62]

Nevertheless, the missile technology control regime can make it more difficult, and perhaps more expensive, for countries to acquire a nuclear weapon delivery capability. This circumstance may further reduce the risk of nuclear weapon proliferation, but it is essential, in the interest of international security, that the established suppliers, such as the Soviet Union and China, as well as the potential suppliers also join the regime.[63]

Regional denuclearization

On 11 December 1986 the Treaty of Rarotonga, which has set up a nuclear-free zone in the South Pacific, entered into force. So far, the parties include Australia, the Cook Islands, Fiji, Kiribati, Nauru, New Zealand, Niue, Tuvalu and Western Samoa. The adherents have undertaken not to manufacture or otherwise acquire or have control over nuclear weapons, and to prevent the stationing of such weapons in their territories as well as nuclear testing in the zone. Each party may decide whether to make an exception for nuclear weapons that may be aboard ships visiting its ports or navigating its territorial seas or archipelagic waters, and for weapons that may be aboard aircraft visiting its airfields or transiting its airspace. Of the three protocols annexed to the Treaty, two have been signed by the Soviet Union and China: Protocol 2, which contains an obligation not to contribute to a violation of the Treaty and not to use or threaten to use a nuclear explosive against the parties; and Protocol 3, which prohibits tests of such an explosive. Protocol 1 is meant to be adhered to only by France, the United Kingdom and the United States, if these powers undertake to apply the Treaty prohibitions to the territories in the zone for which they are internationally responsible. The Western powers have so far declined to sign any of these protocols.[64]

As an underpinning of the Treaty of Rarotonga, the Parliament of New Zealand adopted in 1987 an act establishing the New Zealand Nuclear Free Zone which comprises all of the land, territory and inland waters within the territorial limits of New Zealand; the internal waters and the territorial sea of New Zealand; as well as the airspace above all these areas. Amplifying the provisions of the Treaty of Rarotonga, the Act states that the Prime Minister may grant approval for the entry of foreign warships into the internal waters of New Zealand only if he is satisfied that the warships will not be carrying any nuclear explosive device upon their entry into these waters. Similarly, approval for the landing in New Zealand by foreign military aircraft may be granted only by the Prime Minister if he is satisfied that the aircraft will not be carrying any nuclear explosive device when it lands. Entry into the internal waters of New

Zealand by any ship whose propulsion is wholly or partly dependent on nuclear power is prohibited. The right of innocent passage through the territorial sea of New Zealand, and the right of transit passage by any ship or aircraft through or over any strait used for international navigation, are not to be limited. 'Passage' is defined as continuous and expeditious navigation without stopping or anchoring except in as much as these are incidental to ordinary navigation or are rendered necessary by distress or for the purpose of rendering assistance to persons, ships or aircraft in distress.[65]

Australia has adopted a policy of totally rejecting nuclear power. Recently, this policy has found expression in a change of name and direction of the Australian Atomic Energy Authority. The new Australian Nuclear Science and Technology Organization will no longer carry out research into uranium mining and enrichment or other aspects of the fuel cycle and power generation, which were the basis of the Authority's charter. The only exception is the project for nuclear waste disposal. The Organization will concentrate on the application of nuclear science to industry, medicine and the environment.[66] On 14 April 1988, at the initiative of the opposition Social Democratic Party, the Parliament of Denmark passed a resolution requesting the Government to notify all visiting warships that they must not carry nuclear arms into Danish ports. From the purely formal point of view, the resolution merely reiterated the official Danish policy, which had been proclaimed more than three decades earlier, namely, that in time of peace introduction of nuclear weapons to the country is prohibited. In practice, however, such a 'reminder' implies that the visiting party is requested to reveal, though only indirectly, which of its vessels are *not* nuclear-armed, it being assumed that the commanders of the vessels having nuclear weapons on board would not purposefully disregard the law of the land. Thereby, the Danish resolution signified a rejection of the policy of 'neither confirming nor denying' the presence of nuclear weapons, which has been so far strictly adhered to, on security grounds, by the navies of all the nuclear weapon powers. (Norway has also unilaterally declared its territory to be free of nuclear weapons in peacetime, but it proceeds on the assumption that this declaration is respected by the visiting foreign ships or aircraft, and it does not see the need to seek specific assurances.)

The Danish decision was criticized within NATO, in particular by the United States and Great Britain, as an act undermining co-operation among the allies. It was also qualified by some as a move endangering the so-called Nordic strategic balance. As a result, the visit of British vessels to Denmark in the spring of 1988, as well as their joint manoeuvres with the Danish Navy, did not take place as planned. The minority Government of Denmark, which was opposed to the parliamentary resolution, called a general election for 10 May 1988.[67]

In Sweden, the ruling Social Democratic Party decided, at its latest congress, held in 1987, that efforts should be made to make the nuclear powers forgo the practice of not giving information regarding the presence of nuclear weapons on their warships. It was further resolved that, should the nuclear powers decline to give up this practice, the rules for military visits would be tightened: the powers in question would be requested to make an explicit statement that nuclear weapons were not entering Swedish territory, including the airspace. The visits would be refused if no such information were provided.[68]

Non-explosive uses of nuclear energy

Naval propulsion

The decision of the Canadian Government to acquire a fleet of nuclear-powered submarines, as announced in the summer of 1987, has given rise to doubts in some people's minds about the compatibility of such an acquisition with Canada's obligations under the NPT. Indeed, nuclear naval propulsion uses highly enriched uranium which can also be used to produce nuclear weapons. However, under the NPT, non-nuclear weapon states, such as Canada, are prohibited only from using nuclear materials for explosive purposes; the use of such materials for naval propulsion is not prohibited. Paragraph 14 of the Structure and Content of Agreements between the Agency and States, required in connection with the NPT, provides for a special arrangement for withdrawing nuclear material from IAEA safeguards, so that it can be used in non-proscribed military activities.[69] The arrangement between the state in question and the IAEA should identify the circumstances or the period during which safeguards would not be applied. The state would have to make it clear that the unsafeguarded material (the quantity and composition of which must be known to the Agency) would not be used for the production of nuclear weapons or other nuclear explosive devices. According to the authoritative interpretation, based on the negotiating history, the exemption from safeguards is to be strictly limited to the material in the propulsion reactors and should not include other stages of the nuclear fuel cycle; safeguards must again apply as soon as the nuclear material is re-introduced into a peaceful nuclear activity for reprocessing or for other, inherently non-military, industrial treatment.[70]

If Canada actually comes into possession of nuclear-powered submarines, it will be the first non-nuclear weapon state to avail itself of the exemption provision referred to above. Canada may have difficulties in obtaining the necessary nuclear material from abroad, because of the legislation in force in a number of countries that restricts or prohibits exports of such material for any military purpose. Even Canada's bilateral nuclear co-operation agreements, including the agreement with Euratom, contain a prohibition on the military use of nuclear items exported by Canada. The Canadian Government will probably try to buy complete nuclear-powered submarines from one of the Western powers.[71] If these happen to be British submarines, the US Government would have to be asked to approve the transfer, as the submarines use US technology in their reactors.[72] All this may not affect Canada's commitment to the cause of non-proliferation of nuclear weapons but would be very unfortunate, because it would set a significant precedent for the non-application of nuclear safeguards by the parties to the NPT.

Among other states known to plan the acquisition of nuclear-powered submarines are Argentina, Brazil and India. As non-parties to the NPT, these countries are not subject to full-scope NPT safeguards. On the other hand, they have all agreed to accept non-NPT safeguards on the material and equipment supplied to them so far. These safeguards are designed to ensure that imported nuclear material is not used in such a way as to further any military purpose.[73] If, therefore, all NPT states, which include the most important nuclear suppliers, were consistent in requiring the application of such safeguards to all their future nuclear exports to non-NPT states, without exception, the acquisition of nuclear-powered submarines by the latter would be greatly complicated: they would have to use their own resources. Building a nuclear-powered submarine is not an easy undertaking. India has long tried to develop an indigenously designed nuclear-propulsion system but has failed to make headway.[74] In this situation, the unprecedented lease to India of a Soviet nuclear-powered submarine,[75] reportedly equipped with cruise missiles capable of delivering nuclear charges,[76] came as a surprise. The conditions of the transaction have not been publicized, but it appears that the lease is intended to lead to the sale of several submarines.[77]

Considering the nuclear weapon powers' obligations under the NPT, the legality of the Soviet–Indian deal could be contested if it implied relinquishing control over weapon-grade nuclear material to a non-nuclear weapon state which refuses to forsake the nuclear weapon option. Bilateral Soviet–Indian safeguards over the submarine reactor fuel, whatever their stringency, would not suffice. They cannot replace international IAEA safeguards required by the NPT. Such activities contradict the sense of the guidelines for nuclear transfers agreed in 1977 by the nuclear supplier nations and may undermine the NPT.

Conclusion

In spite of some reverses, the nuclear non-proliferation regime has proved to be fairly robust. There is a good chance that, barring unforeseen circumstances before or during the 1995 NPT conference, which is to decide the Treaty's future, the duration of the NPT will be extended for another lengthy period.

None the less, the problem of nuclear threshold countries will not be quickly resolved. Particularly troublesome is the Indian–Pakistani nuclear relationship. Consequently, international non-proliferation efforts, especially those of the superpowers, should in the first place be directed towards bringing these two nations to the negotiating table with a view to halting the militarization of their nuclear capabilities. A nuclear arms race in South Asia would not only undermine the security, economy and the unstable political structures of the countries in the region but could also have adverse global consequences, including break-outs or withdrawals from the NPT or the other constituent parts of the non-proliferation regime.

Moreover, the NPT parties have failed to take effective steps, as recommended by the third NPT Review Conference, to achieve acceptance of full-scope safeguards as a 'necessary basis' for the transfer of relevant supplies to non-nuclear weapon states not party to the NPT. Some of the threshold countries have entered the world nuclear market as sellers of hardware and services of proliferation concern. These new suppliers are not bound by the obligations undertaken by the traditional suppliers regarding restraints on transfer of sensitive items. An uncontrolled trade in such items, including nuclear reprocessing and enrichment technologies, would undercut the existing guidelines for nuclear exports, thus weakening the non-proliferation regime. A dialogue would therefore be desirable between the emerging and established suppliers with a view to working out generally acceptable rules.[78]

Non-proliferation has become a norm of international behaviour which cannot be easily reversed. However, the ultimate solution to the problem of nuclear proliferation would be possible only in a world in which the possession of nuclear weapons were recognized as both unnecessary and unacceptable. This goal is still very remote. To bring it nearer, the process of nuclear arms reduction and elimination should continue uninterruptedly.

IV. Nuclear test ban

Among the measures often indicated as necessary to reinforce the NPT is the cessation of nuclear weapon test explosions.

Arms control impact of a test ban

There is a widespread belief that without a test ban the risks are great that additional countries will enter the nuclear arms race. In fact, testing would not be indispensable for newcomers to the nuclear club. First-generation fission devices could be produced without testing, and the producer might be confident that the device would actually explode. But the weapon would be highly unsophisticated, of uncertain yield and perhaps also difficult to deliver. It is unlikely that countries would be willing to create a large arsenal of such untested devices. This circumstance would slow down nuclear weapon proliferation among states. Thermonuclear weapons involve a quantum jump in physical processes over first-generation atomic devices; their development without tests would therefore be out of the question, and their horizontal spread would be precluded.

As regards the so-called vertical proliferation of nuclear weapons, it is clear that under a test ban the offensive capabilities of the nuclear weapon states would not decline since one need not perform tests to manufacture additional weapons using old designs and since delivery systems would not be affected. But further nuclear weapon development would be rendered largely impossible. Designing and deploying new nuclear weapons without testing would involve too many uncertainties to be resorted to.

In so far as concern about 'technological surprise' drives the arms race, the cessation of tests may remove at least one of the causes of this apprehension by making it unlikely that something completely new, unpredictable and exotic would suddenly emerge in the nuclear field. Thereby, the race for qualitative improvement of nuclear weapons—an important channel of the potentially destabilizing superpower arms competition—would be considerably narrowed. A step would be taken towards fulfilling the great powers' obligation under the NPT to pursue measures relating to the cessation of the nuclear arms race.

The question of a test ban has been on the agenda of the UN General Assembly ever since the late 1950s; it also figures high in the order of business of the CD. Many proposals for an agreement have been put forward, by Western, socialist and non-aligned states. Among them, the most noteworthy are the 1980 British–US–Soviet Tripartite Report on the test ban negotiations[79] and the 1983 draft treaty (with protocols) 'banning any nuclear weapon test explosion in any environment', presented by Sweden.[80]

New proposals

In June 1987, a group of socialist countries in the CD submitted a document entitled 'Basic provisions of a treaty on the complete and general prohibition of nuclear weapon tests'.[81] The document is more explicit, especially on the issue of verification, than previous Soviet proposals. In particular, it provides that the location of all nuclear test ranges would have to be declared and that international inspectors would have to verify that no tests were conducted there. In addition to an international seismic monitoring network, international exchanges of data on atmospheric radioactivity would be carried out. On-site inspections would be mandatory: a state receiving a request for such an inspection would be obliged to allow 'unconditional access' to the location indicated in the request; a special international inspectorate would be established.[82] An important requirement was that measures should be envisaged to prevent the ban on nuclear weapon test explosions from being circumvented by means of peaceful nuclear explosions. Indeed, it is not possible to develop nuclear explosive devices which would be capable only of peaceful applications. The German Democratic Republic suggested, in a separate working paper, that peaceful explosions should be prohibited from the outset, or be carried out 'under certain conditions', but it did not specify these conditions.[83] Furthermore, the Soviet Union proposed the establishment of a special group of scientific experts to prepare recommendations regarding the structure and functions of the entire verification system needed for an agreement banning nuclear weapon tests.[84]

Australia reiterated its proposal for the establishment of a global seismic network even before the conclusion of a comprehensive test ban treaty.[85]

The submitted proposals were not even discussed because of the unresolved dispute about the mandate of the CD working body which should deal with testing. The non-aligned members of the CD, supported by the socialist delegations, insisted that the objective of such a body (to be called the *ad hoc* committee) should be to conduct multilateral 'negotiations' of a comprehensive nuclear test ban treaty,[86] as recommended by the 1986 UN General Assembly,[87] whereas the United States could accept only a non-negotiating mandate. Explaining its position, the United States reiterated its view that a comprehensive ban on nuclear testing is a long-term objective which must be seen 'in the context of a time when it and its allies did not need to depend on nuclear deterrence to ensure international security and stability'.[88] France also maintained that cessation of tests could become significant only at the end of a long-term process resulting in real and effective nuclear disarmament.[89]

It will be noted that the preamble to the 1963 Partial Test Ban Treaty (PTBT) states that the parties are 'seeking to achieve the discontinuance of all test explosions of nuclear weapons for all time' and are determined to continue 'negotiations' to this end; the preamble to the NPT reaffirms this determination. The United States is party to both treaties, as is the Soviet Union; France is not.

Verification

The only substantive discussions related to a comprehensive nuclear test ban took place in the *Ad Hoc* Group of Scientific Experts, established by the CD to consider international co-operative measures to detect and identify seismic events. The Group discussed the concept of a modern international seismic data exchange system based on the expeditious exchange of level I and level II data. Level I data are basic parameters derived by the operators of each seismic station from the recordings of the detected events. Level II data (more voluminous) are waveform data, that is, the original recordings.

It was agreed that, in order to assist states in their national verification of a comprehensive ban, the data exchange system should consist of the following major components: a global network of modern seismograph stations; modern telecommunications channels; and international data centres to collect and analyse the data and to distribute the results of the analyses. The network would include at least 50 stations located in such a way as to ensure adequate global coverage, and preferably at sites where the background noise level is low. Technical specifications would have to be worked out for a prototype station able to collect high quality waveform data from seismic events at all distances. Array stations, consisting of a number of sensors placed in a defined configuration, would improve the detection capability and provide preliminary location data for detected events. National data centres (NDCs) would be responsible for providing seismic data from the participating stations within the countries to international data centres (IDCs). Various technical options for establishing high-speed communication links were considered.

An experiment was planned to test the methods and procedures developed by the *Ad Hoc* Group to extract and transmit data from stations to experimental IDCs, to process them there, and to transmit the results back to the participants. Four experimental IDCs are envisaged: in Canberra, Moscow, Stockholm and Washington, DC.[90]

Partial limitation of tests

In the latter part of 1987, the United States and the Soviet Union decided jointly to elaborate improved verification measures for the 1974 Threshold Test Ban Treaty (TTBT) and the 1976 Peaceful Nuclear Explosions Treaty (PNET), with a view to ratifying these treaties, and to proceed subsequently to negotiate further limitations on nuclear testing.[91] The TTBT and the PNET have imposed a limit of 150 kt on the yield of all underground explosions conducted by the two powers. The treaties have not yet formally entered into force, but the parties said that they would observe the yield limit during the pre-ratification period.

Despite its unratified status, the TTBT has to some extent constrained the development of new high-yield warheads. The yield limitation has also made it difficult for the parties to carry out certain stockpile sampling, because existing large thermonuclear weapons may not be tested at their full yield. Moreover, cessation of explosions in the high-megaton range has had a positive environmental effect: it has further reduced the risks of radioactive venting and of ground disturbance. None of this alters the fact that the TTBT has hardly contributed to the cessation of the nuclear arms race. The 150-kt yield threshold is too high to be really meaningful: the parties do not experience onerous restraints in continuing their nuclear weapon programmes. Nor does the agreed threshold reflect present verification capabilities: the detection and identification of nuclear explosions of far lower size are possible. Unlike the PTBT or other nuclear arms control agreements, the TTBT was not welcomed by the UN General Assembly; nor has any international appeal been made for its ratification.

The PNET, also still unratified, was an indispensable complement to the TTBT: the latter treaty would be deprived of meaning if peaceful explosions were allowed without restrictions. However, the PNET has not increased the very limited arms control value of the TTBT. By unduly emphasizing the importance of civil applications of nuclear explosives, it may even have had a negative impact on the policy of preventing nuclear weapon proliferation by providing respectability to the arguments of those states that seek to develop a nuclear weapon capability under the guise of an interest in peaceful explosions. Nor has the PNET solved the intractable problem of accommodating peaceful nuclear explosions under a test ban. It is true that some constraints have been provided for in the Treaty to limit the possibility of gaining weapon-related information from the peaceful application of nuclear explosions. This, however, would not prevent testing the performance of a stockpiled warhead or, perhaps more important, some limited testing of a new weapon design.

Possible transitional measures

Restraints on nuclear tests are no doubt better than unrestrained testing. However, to have arms control significance, a treaty limiting nuclear weapon testing would have: (*a*) to make a direct mitigating impact on the arms race; (*b*) to reinforce the nuclear non-proliferation regime by rendering it more difficult for non-nuclear weapon states to develop a nuclear weapon capability; (*c*) to provide a reasonable assurance of compliance through verification measures adapted to the scope of the undertakings; (*d*) to contain no loopholes facilitating circumvention of the basic obligations; and (*e*) to constitute a concrete step towards a complete prohibition of nuclear explosions.

The requirements enumerated above could be met, if the limitations, both on the explosive yield of tests and on the rate of testing were meaningful. An effective yield limitation would have to set the threshold low enough to preclude the development of new weapon designs; a threshold not higher than 1 kt would be suitable for this purpose. One or two tests with a yield of up to 5 kt, per nuclear country and per year, could be permitted; they might enable the scaling up of results from such explosions to estimate the effectiveness of certain important components of stockpiled weapons, but they would not support a nuclear weapon development programme.

While not allowing significant qualitative improvement of nuclear weapons, the freedom to conduct a very limited number of tests with a yield higher than 1 kt but not exceeding 5 kt would meet one of the main objections to a comprehensive ban put forward by some US scientists, namely, that the nuclear stockpile would deteriorate and become unreliable, or that the repairs of weapons could not be trusted, without the benefit of testing. Furthermore, the freedom to conduct an unlimited number of tests with a yield of up to 1 kt would preclude a controversy over the military value of sub-kiloton-yield explosions and their verifiability. It might also satisfy the interest in learning more about the physics and the effects of nuclear weapons, and thereby dispose of the apprehensions voiced by the weapon laboratories that their technical teams would disperse.

Verification procedures for such a very-low-threshold test ban (VLTTB) could build upon those already accepted under the TTBT and the PNET. In addition to an extensive exchange of data and a few calibration shots to aid in yield estimation, there would be a need for suitably located in-country seismic monitoring stations to reduce the possibility of evasion. All tests would be notified in advance and conducted only at agreed designated sites. Those tests subject to an annual quota would be monitored by foreign observers. On-site inspections could be envisaged for suspicious events. Moreover, obligatory international observation of chemical explosions for mining or other engineering purposes, exceeding a specified size, might be provided for at sites capable of accommodating a 'decoupled' nuclear explosion producing muffled seismic signals. However, since some tests would be permitted, the incentive to cheat could not be high.

A VLTTB would, of course, apply only to the present nuclear weapon powers. It could not be a universal commitment, because most non-nuclear weapon countries have already renounced the very possession of nuclear weapons and consequently also the testing of nuclear explosives. These countries could, however, contribute to the verification procedures. In fact, the greatest possible participation in a world-wide system of seismic monitoring would be indispensable for the viability of a VLTTB.

Any partial arrangement should be seen as transitional and contain an unequivocal, internationally binding commitment to achieving a complete prohibition of tests by all states.[92]

Notes and references

[1] Conference on Disarmament document CD/PV.429.
[2] Conference on Disarmament document CD/500.
[3] Conference on Disarmament document CD/PV.428.
[4] Conference on Disarmament document CD/789 and *Krasnaya Zvezda* (Moscow), 21 Nov. 1987.
[5] Statement of 27 Aug. 1987 by the chairman of the *Ad Hoc* Committee on chemical weapons at the Conference on Disarmament.
[6] Conference on Disarmament documents CD/740 and CD/PV.404.

[7] *Svenska Dagbladet* (Stockholm), 28 Dec. 1987. Nevertheless, on 31 March 1988, the Iranian Foreign Minister stated that Iran would 'never' use chemical weapons (as quoted in *Journal de Genève*, 2 Apr. 1988).
[8] Conference on Disarmament document CD/PV.389.
[9] Conference on Disarmament documents CD/PV.421 and CD/PV.425.
[10] Conference on Disarmament document CD/PV.390.
[11] Conference on Disarmament document CD/613.
[12] Conference on Disarmament document CD/PV.394.
[13] Conference on Disarmament documents CD/PV.421 and CD/PV.428.
[14] Conference on Disarmament document CD/CW/WP.185.
[15] Conference on Disarmament documents CD/757 and CD/PV.413.
[16] Conference on Disarmament document CD/PV.413.
[17] Conference on Disarmament document CD/PV.418.
[18] Exposé by Jean Desazars de Montgailhard, counsellor for political and military affairs at the Embassy of France in Washington, made at an international conference organized by the Canadian Centre for Arms Control and Disarmament, Ottawa, 8 Oct. 1987.
[19] *Le Monde*, 22–23 Feb. 1987.
[20] Conference on Disarmament document CD/PV.390.
[21] Conference on Disarmament document CD/PV.421.
[22] Conference on Disarmament document CD/795.
[23] UN documents A/PV.1928 and A/8187.
[24] Conference on Disarmament documents CD/747 and CD/PV.400.
[25] Conference on Disarmament document CD/403.
[26] Conference on Disarmament document CD/PV.418.
[27] Conference on Disarmament document CD/PV.424.
[28] Conference on Disarmament document CD/PV.406.
[29] Conference on Disarmament documents CD/802 and CD/CW/WP.186.
[30] Conference on Disarmament document CD/749.
[31] Conference on Disarmament document CD/715.
[32] Conference on Disarmament document CD/PV.406.
[33] Conference on Disarmament document CD/PV.408.
[34] Conference on Disarmament document CD/PV.403.
[35] Conference on Disarmament document CD/PV.396.
[36] Conference on Disarmament document CD/PV.429.
[37] Conference on Disarmament document CD/PV.432.
[38] Conference on Disarmament documents CD/761, CD/762 and CD/766.
[39] Conference on Disarmament document CD/677.
[40] UN General Assembly Resolution 37/98 D.
[41] UN document A/39/488.
[42] Conference on Disarmament document CD/PV.432.
[43] Conference on Disarmament document CD/769.
[44] Conference on Disarmament document CD/PV.429.
[45] Conference on Disarmament document CD/PV.424.
[46] US–Soviet statement on the Dec. 1987 summit talks, *New York Times*, 12 Dec. 1987.
[47] Statement by Sherry Stetson Mannix, US Arms Control and Disarmament Agency, made at an international conference organized by the Canadian Centre for Arms Control and Disarmament, Ottawa, 8 Oct. 1987.
[48] Conference on Disarmament document CD/PV.370.
[49] Conference on Disarmament document CD/PV.389.
[50] Conference on Disarmament documents CD/752 and CD/CW/WP.165.
[51] *Holmenkollen Report on the Chemical Weapons Convention* (Royal Norwegian Ministry of Foreign Affairs: Oslo, May 1987).
[52] Conference on Disarmament document CD/787.
[53] A proposal along similar lines was made by the Soviet Union in 1987, in the course of its bilateral talks with the United States, as reported in *Krasnaya Zvezda*, 11 Nov. 1987. In addition, on 18 Feb. 1988 the Soviet Deputy Foreign Minister suggested at the CD that, as a 'step towards establishing an international inspectorate', the negotiating parties designate a facility where an international group of experts could test procedures for systematic verification of the non-production of chemical weapons in commercial industries.
[54] Statement by the Representative of Nigeria in 1967, at the 31st Regular Session of the IAEA General Conference.
[55] IAEA Press Release PR 86/15.

[56] *International Herald Tribune*, 16–17 Jan. 1988.
[57] IAEA Press Release PR 88/3; *Süddeutsche Zeitung*, 26 Feb. 1988.
[58] *Le Monde*, 8 Apr. 1988.
[59] *International Herald Tribune*, 26 Feb. 1988.
[60] Frankfurter Allgemeine Zeitung, 22 Dec. 1987.
[61] Spector, L. S., *Going Nuclear* (Ballinger: Cambridge, Mass., 1987).
[62] *International Herald Tribune*, 19–20 Mar. and 30 Mar. 1988; *Le Monde*, 7 Apr. 1988.
[63] UK Foreign & Commonwealth Office; US Information Service, EUR–404, Stockholm, 16 Apr. 1987; *Le Monde*, 17 Apr. 1987; *International Herald Tribune*, 21 Apr. 1987; *US Department of State Bulletin*, July 1987.
[64] For an analysis of the Treaty of Rarotonga, see Goldblat, J., 'The Treaty of Rarotonga: A modest but significant contribution to the cause of nuclear non-proliferation' in *Transnational Perspectives* (Geneva), vol. 13, no. 2 (1987).
[65] New Zealand Nuclear Free Zone, Disarmament, and Arms Control Act 1987.
[66] *Nature*, vol. 327 (14 May 1987).
[67] *Berlingske Tidende* (Copenhagen), 15 Apr. 1988; *Svenska Dagbladet* (Stockholm), 20, 22, 23 and 24 Apr. 1988.
[68] Swedish Social Democratic Party Congress Protocol MO–103–gh–0010, Sep. 1987.
[69] IAEA document INFCIRC/153.
[70] Fischer, D. and Szasz, P., ed. J. Goldblat, SIPRI, *Safeguarding the Atom: A Critical Appraisal* (Taylor & Francis: London, 1985); Blix, H., 'Aspects juridiques des garanties de l'Agence internationale de l'énergie atomique', *Annuaire français du droit international*, vol. 29 (1983).
[71] *Le Monde*, 7 Jan. 1988.
[72] *Christian Science Monitor*, 22 Feb. 1988.
[73] IAEA document INFCIRC/66/Rev.2.
[74] *Far Eastern Economic Review*, 24 Dec. 1987.
[75] *Pravda*, 6 Jan. 1988.
[76] *Le Monde*, 11 Feb. 1988.
[77] *Times of India*, 7 Jan. 1988.
[78] For detailed proposals to this effect, see Dunn, L. A., 'Nonproliferation: The next steps', *Arms Control Today* (Washington), Nov. 1987.
[79] Committee on Disarmament document CD/130.
[80] Committee on Disarmament document CD/381.
[81] Conference on Disarmament document CD/756.
[82] Conference on Disarmament documents CD/PV.411, DC/PV.413, CD/PV.416 and CD/PV.418.
[83] Conference on Disarmament document CD/746.
[84] Conference on Disarmament document CD/PV.430.
[85] Conference on Disarmament document CD/PV.423.
[86] Conference on Disarmament document CD/772.
[87] UN document 41/46 A.
[88] Conference on Disarmament document CD/PV.391; *Department of State Bulletin*, June 1987.
[89] Conference on Disarmament document CD/PV.390.
[90] Conference on Disarmament documents CD/745 and CD/778.
[91] Federal News Service and TASS.
[92] For an elaboration of this proposal, see Goldblat, J. and Cox, D. (eds), SIPRI, *Nuclear Weapon Tests: Prohibition or Limitation?* (Oxford University Press: Oxford, 1988).

Part IV. Special features

Chapter 13. The INF Treaty negotiations

Chapter 14. The ABM Treaty and the strategic relationship: an uncertain future

Chapter 15. The United Nations and the Iraq–Iran War

Chapter 16. The United Nations International Conference on the Relationship between Disarmament and Development

Chapter 17. The SIPRI 1987 Olof Palme Memorial Lecture—'Security and disarmament: change and vision'

13. The INF Treaty negotiations

JONATHAN DEAN*

I. Introduction

On 8 December 1987, the most turbulent chapter in the history of East–West arms control culminated with the televised signature at the Washington summit meeting of the treaty on intermediate-range nuclear forces (INF Treaty)—its proper designation is 'Treaty between the United States of America and the Union of Soviet Socialist Republics on the elimination of their intermediate-range and shorter-range missiles' (see appendices 13A–13D).

The INF Treaty will result in destruction of all US and Soviet ground-based missiles of 500–5500 km range and prohibition of their future production. For many in the West, signature of the Treaty vindicated the much criticized two-track strategy of deploy-and-negotiate which NATO member states had adopted as their guide-line for the INF negotiations precisely eight years earlier. For a worried minority of NATO defence experts and conservative political leaders, the conclusion of the Treaty meant serious weakening of US nuclear protection for the defence of Europe and a resultant increase in the risk of conventional attack by the Warsaw Treaty Organization (WTO) or of successful Soviet intimidation of Western Europe.

For the Soviet Union, the agreement marked the success of a long effort, begun in the late 1950s, to prevent deployment in Europe of land-based medium-range US nuclear missiles capable of a rapid, destructive strike against vital targets in the western USSR, ultimately including Moscow itself, while keeping US strategic nuclear forces in reserve. This was a disadvantage which the USSR could not make good through weapon deployments of its own, although the further development of sea-launched cruise missiles brings a countermove closer.

The ultimately successful outcome of the INF talks after long, often dramatic negotiation probably resulted more from the emergence of a conciliation-minded Soviet leadership than from a particular Western negotiating approach. Whether the conclusion of the INF Treaty also marks the beginning of a decisive turning-point in East–West relations or was merely an episode in a continuing East–West confrontation is largely dependent on the continuation of this conciliatory Soviet course. A definitive answer to that question may not be available for some years. Yet one outcome of INF seems already clearly established: the entire INF episode did more than nearly any other single development of the past 40 years to change the nature of the defence relationship between the United States and the European members of the NATO Alliance.

SIPRI Yearbook 1988: World Armaments and Disarmament

II. Genesis of the INF issue

Conclusion of the SALT I Agreement provided the impetus for development of new medium-range missiles in both the USA and the USSR, although in different ways. With regard to the Soviet Union, SALT I restricted as strategic the variable-range Soviet SS-11 missile, which the USSR may have intended to replace the ageing single-warhead SS-4s and SS-5s. In the early 1970s, possibly before the actual conclusion of the SALT I Agreement, the decision was reached to proceed with the development of the new SS-20 missile.

In doing so, the Soviet leadership left two things out of account. The first was the extent of the improvements incorporated in the new SS-20: longer range, triple, MIRV warheads, greater accuracy, mobility and the solid fuel which gave the new missile quick launch capacity, as distinguished from the liquid-fuelled SS-4s and SS-5s.[1] Even if the Soviet leadership had in mind only a replacement for SS-4s or SS-5s, it had produced a weapon of much greater capacity. As SS-20 deployment began in 1977, NATO governments concluded that the deployment would change the nuclear balance in Europe with a counterforce weapon which could be used for pre-emptive strikes on NATO command posts, ports and nuclear weapon sites.

The second element which Soviet leaders overlooked was the capacity of the NATO governments, especially against the background of the Christmas 1979 Soviet invasion of Afghanistan, to convince Western public opinion that deployment of the SS-20 was a quantum jump in Soviet nuclear armaments which signified a Soviet effort to achieve regional nuclear superiority; despite important improvements in the SS-20, many US experts doubted that the deployment had decisive military significance for the overall nuclear balance in Europe.[2] In a dispute accompanied by extensive propaganda and public diplomacy on both sides, the capacity of Western governments to put across this point effectively must be considered a major achievement.

In retrospect, some Soviet officials and academicians seem to consider the decision to deploy the SS-20 a mistake because potential military advantages of the deployment were outweighed by the strong impression of Soviet aggressiveness which it created in the West, countering Soviet efforts to improve relations with Western Europe and also providing the main impetus behind the ultimate Western decision to reintroduce in Europe much improved US medium-range missiles capable of striking Soviet territory.[3] In an interview in November 1987, Deputy Foreign Minister Aleksander Bessmertnykh said that the decision to deploy SS-20s in 1977 was not 'optimal. . . . We had quite enough SS-4 and SS-5 missiles in Europe. Then we began to deploy SS-20s. Technically, they are more perfect. But the question is how they fitted into our military-strategic concept of the European theatre'.[4]

In the United States, the modification of the Pershing 1 missile to give it increased range and accuracy had also been under way since the early 1970s. (The Pershing 1 had been deployed in the FRG since the 1960s.) Full field development was decided on in 1977 under the Carter Administration, a product of three military considerations. The first of these was the growing effectiveness of WTO air defences, which undermined longstanding qualitative advantages of NATO attack aircraft—forward-based systems (FBS), in Soviet terminology—and their capacity to penetrate WTO airspace. Most Western military experts believed that missiles were the best answer to the penetration problem. A second aspect of the US decision to develop the Pershing follow-on missile and its companion ground-launched cruise missile (GLCM), as with the Soviet decision to deploy the SS-20, was simply the availability of the new technology. The third and probably decisive factor lay in the SALT I Agreement—not the numerical limitations on ICBM launchers which provided one motive for Soviet development of the SS-20, but rather the Agreement's recognition that the Soviet Union, after 25 years of assiduous effort, had achieved parity with the United States in strategic nuclear weapons.

In the minds of European NATO experts (who none the less showed a strong tendency to consider parity as preferable to the superiority of either superpower), this most momentous military development of the Cold War had created new doubts as to the credibility of US nuclear protection embodied in the NATO strategy of flexible response, doubts not shared by the general public in Western Europe. Senior NATO officers and defence officials decided that deployment in Europe of US ground-based missiles capable of hitting targets in the Soviet Union would create the means for the US President to deliver a serious message of determination to continue fighting in the event of an overwhelming Soviet conventional attack on Western Europe. These weapons were more likely to be used in such circumstances than strategic weapons—and could inflict serious damage on targets in the Soviet homeland—in the hope of eliciting a negotiated end to hostilities rather than escalation to strategic war.

But the success of Western governments in convincing Western public opinion that deployment of the Soviet SS-20s represented a dangerous new threat had unintended consequences for NATO. It revived and intensified public worries about the possibility and consequences of limited nuclear war in Europe. At the same time, it obscured the actual rationale for deployment of the US INF, leaving the European NATO governments without convincing grounds to support their strong preference to retain some US INF when, in the course of the negotiations, the Soviet Union accepted elimination of all INF missiles.

The Carter Administration made a serious miscalculation of the state of public opinion in NATO states in deciding that new US nuclear missiles should be ground-based for visual assurance rather than sea-based. At this stage, the European public needed no additional assurance that the USA would use nuclear weapons in defence of Europe. Rather, it needed assurance that, in the event of war, the superpowers would not use their newly deployed intermediate-range nuclear missiles against targets in Europe while refraining from strategic attack on their respective homelands. These fears, heightened but not originated by astute Soviet propaganda, subsequently resolved in public demonstrations directed against deployment both of the new US 'Euromissiles' and of the Soviet SS-20s.

But these developments lay in the future as NATO neared its decision to deploy the new US missiles. In 1978, a year after the initial deployment of SS-20s in the Soviet Union, the Carter Administration tentatively decided to deploy newly developed US 'neutron' warheads in Europe. Whatever the merits of this issue, it resulted in an important Soviet propaganda success. Against this background of friction in US–NATO relations, the Carter Administration, which had earlier questioned the military need to deploy new US intermediate-range ballistic missiles (IRBMs) in Europe, sent emissaries to Europe to ascertain whether European leaders were really determined on deployment. The decision in principle to do so was reached in January 1979 at an economic summit meeting of Western leaders at Guadalupe. Smarting from the neutron warhead issue, the Carter Administration insisted, with fateful consequences, that deployment should have explicit public approval by European NATO governments; this insistence made change in US nuclear dispositions in Europe, previously handled by defence officials, a political issue in each NATO country.

For their part, Soviet leaders showed belated awareness that deployment of the SS-20s could elicit a serious counter-reaction from NATO. In an October 1979 speech in East Berlin clearly aimed at heading off the NATO missile deployment decision, General Secretary Brezhnev announced the unilateral withdrawal of a Soviet division from the GDR and offered a freeze on SS-20 deployments if NATO would forgo deployment.

Like many great powers, the Soviet Union has often been impervious to the effects of its actions on its less powerful neighbours. Thus it is unclear whether, in deploying the SS-20, it had objectives beyond replacing the seriously ageing SS-4s and SS-5s and creating a substitute weapon for the SS-11. But Soviet statements and actions made clear that they did consider that the deployment of the new US INF missiles would significantly increase NATO theatre nuclear capability. In emotional public presentations, Soviet experts stressed that the range, short flight-time and accuracy of the new US INF missiles, especially of Pershing II, made them capable of a decapitating first strike against command and control installations in the western USSR. They claimed that the Pershing II had a range (or improved versions could be given a range) of 2400 kilometres, as compared to the 1800 kilometres claimed for it by Western experts, so that it could reach Moscow and suddenly destroy the vital decision-making centre of the USSR without a similar risk to Washington; and they also claimed that the slower GLCM already had a range of 2400 kilometres and could be made much faster in future versions.

III. NATO's two-track decision

At a special meeting of NATO foreign and defence ministers in Brussels on 12 December 1979, the Alliance took the best-known decision in its 30-year history, the 'two-track' decision. In the projected SALT III talks, NATO would negotiate for limits on future deployments of US INF missiles still in the development stage, in return for reductions in the level of Soviet INF missiles already deployed at that time; it would proceed with deployment of 572 US INF (108 Pershing IIs and 464 GLCMs), if those negotiations did not succeed. In the communiqué of their meeting, the NATO ministers gave as justification for their decision the expansion of Soviet long-range nuclear capability, in particular, deployment of the SS-20 missiles and of Backfire bombers; the ageing of NATO long-range theatre nuclear capabilities and the absence from the NATO arsenal of land-based long-range theatre nuclear delivery systems; and Soviet achievement of intercontinental parity with the United States, emphasizing a gap in NATO's theatre-range deterrent capacity and affecting the credibility of NATO's strategy of flexible response.

NATO ministers also decided that, for each new single-warhead US missile deployed, the United States would withdraw a further nuclear warhead from its European stockpile. To make their decision to deploy new missiles more palatable to the European public, the NATO ministers announced unilateral withdrawal of 1000 US nuclear warheads.

As they had in the Mutual and Balanced Force Reduction (MBFR) talks, NATO ministers in their INF decision proposed an equal ceiling for both the USA and the USSR, this time in deployed missiles. They indicated that their objective was 'a more stable overall nuclear balance at lower levels of nuclear weapons on both sides. . . . The success of arms control in constraining the Soviet build-up can enhance alliance security' and 'modify the scale of NATO's INF requirements'.

Rather than total elimination of Soviet and US INF missiles, NATO ministers believed that some US deployment, and reduction of Soviet missiles to that level, would be the only realistic solution. Indeed, the unpublicized NATO decision document which underlay the published communiqué describing the ministers' decision determined that INF deployment should start at the end of 1983 without specifically relating this deadline to the status of East–West negotiation at that time. The ministers set no specific level of deployment as a desired negotiation outcome, either in their communiqué or in their unpublicized decision document. There had been no time to fully mesh the work of the two separate committees of Western officials which had considered deployment options and arms control positions. Moreover, closing the perceived gap in NATO's deterrent capability had priority. None the less, the idea of negotiating an intended Western deployment against an already existing Soviet deployment was, already at that time, criticized by some in the West as making the final decision to deploy a hostage to the negotiation process.

IV. A slow beginning for the INF talks

When, in mid-December 1979, the NATO ministers endorsed bilateral US–Soviet negotiations on INF, they assumed that this negotiation would take place in the framework of the SALT III talks foreseen in the SALT II Treaty. But only days after NATO's dual-track decision, the Soviet Union invaded Afghanistan. In consequence, President Carter requested the US Senate to suspend consideration of the SALT II Treaty. With the SALT II Treaty unratified and hopes for SALT III extinguished, the INF negotiations were left in limbo. Yet Chancellor Schmidt, on a visit to the Soviet Union in June 1980, succeeded in obtaining the agreement of General Secretary Brezhnev to separate US–Soviet talks on INF.

Preliminary exchanges began in October 1980 in the last months of the Carter Administration, at the height of the Carter–Reagan presidential election campaign, and ended after a few weeks. (The talks were then called negotiations on 'Theatre Nuclear Forces'; this designation was changed in the Reagan Administration to reflect European uneasiness over terminology which implied that Western Europe might be an area of long-range military operations from a distant and secure United States.) The United States presented basic crieteria for an INF agreement drawn from the principles which had been approved by NATO in connection with its 1979 decision.

Even this brief encounter raised the main issues of the subsequent negotiations. These were:

1. Which Soviet and US nuclear delivery systems should be included? From the outset, the US position, previously approved by the NATO allies in all aspects, was to limit the scope of the negotiations to land-based INF missile systems of both countries. The United States wanted to postpone (actually, to avoid) consideration of sea-based missiles and of aircraft, considered a complicating factor because of the numerous different types deployed by the two countries but also an area of technological advantage for the United States. In conformity with their traditional effort to cover the US forward-based systems, the USSR wanted to include both. They insisted on coverage of all US fighter-bombers, including not only intermediate-range F-111s, but also the short-range F-4s and carrier-based A-6s and A-7s.

2. Geographic coverage. To prevent circumvention and to meet the interests of Asian countries, the United States wanted an agreement to cover the highly mobile INF missiles in the whole of the Soviet Union, both Europe and Asia, including Soviet nuclear weapons directed at Japan and China. The Soviet Union wished to include only armaments deployed in Europe west of the Urals.

3. Third-country forces. The Soviet Union insisted on taking account of British and French nuclear forces through additional US reductions. Reviving a classic Soviet position for which they had failed to gain acceptance in the SALT I or SALT II agreements, Soviet negotiators insisted on 'equal security' for the USSR—in this case, equality between total Soviet INF and the total number of INF weapons of all countries that could be used against the Soviet Union in Europe. The consequence would be to permit the United States fewer weapons than the Soviet Union. US negotiators refused to codify such inequality and insisted that Britain and France were sovereign countries for which the United States could not speak.

4. From the outset, the United States stressed the need for full verification, given the mobility and reload capability of SS-20s, although US negotiators advanced a specific verification approach only in the spring of 1986 and a detailed text only in the spring of 1987. The Soviets were reticent on the subject; they customarily argued either that national technical means (satellite photography and sensors) would be sufficient for verification or (as in other negotiations) that it was premature to deal with verification measures until the

outlines of a specific agreement had emerged and participants knew precisely what they had to verify.

After President Ronald Reagan assumed office in January 1981, European NATO governments, worried by his militantly anti-Soviet election campaign and by the emerging sentiment in their publics against INF deployment, brought great pressure on the new Administration to resume the INF negotiations. The talks resumed at the end of November 1981; two years had elapsed of the four years provided for negotiation results in NATO's 1979 decision to deploy by the end of 1983.

In mid-November 1981, just before the INF negotiations resumed, President Reagan intensified the public diplomacy character of the renewed INF talks by inaugurating the practice, subsequently actively followed by both governments, of publicly announcing a new negotiating position—the zero option—prior to its presentation at the negotiating table. Under the zero-option approach, NATO would relinquish its decision to deploy new US INF missiles, deploying none, if the Soviet Union would eliminate all its existing INF missiles (SS-4s, SS-5s and SS-20s) in both European and Asian portions of the Soviet Union. In a draft treaty presented in Geneva in February 1982, the United States proposed in addition a freeze on the shorter-range Soviet SS-21, SS-22 and SS-23 missiles. Aircraft were left to later negotiation, and British and French forces were not taken into account. Informal statements of Administration officials, among them Secretary of State Alexander Haig after he left office, indicate that the proposal for reduction to zero of both US and Soviet INF missiles was made for public diplomacy purposes, to take the 'high ground' in propaganda, without real expectation that the Soviet Union would ever accept this outcome.[5]

Only a week after President Reagan's announcement in November 1981, General Secretary Brezhnev also went public with a Soviet proposal for a bilateral freeze on INF missiles in Europe.[6] He offered unilateral reduction of a 'certain portion' of Soviet INF in European USSR west of the Urals and presented his own zero option. The ultimate negotiating goal after interim reductions, he said, should be elimination of all nuclear weapons, both INF and tactical, from Europe. Deployment in Asia was not covered. In its treaty draft presented in Geneva in February 1982, the Soviet Union proposed a staged reduction of INF, including some aircraft of both countries, to 600 delivery systems on each side in a first phase and 300 in a second phase; no new US INF were to be deployed.

Taken together, the US and Soviet positions excluded the most logical potential compromises on the INF issue. The Western call for elimination of INF in the entire Soviet Union made it difficult to compromise on eliminating Soviet INF deployed in the western USSR in return for relinquishing US INF deployment, while freezing Soviet INF in the Far East. Soviet proposals were equally non-negotiable, making it impossible to compromise on NATO's preferred outcome of some US INF deployment and some Soviet INF reductions. Indeed, the whole thrust of the Soviet negotiating and public diplomacy effort was aimed at preventing any INF deployment by the United

States—and Soviet leaders persisted in this position all the way to their withdrawal from the talks in 1983, showing the significance they attached to the possible deployment of the new US missiles.

In a series of informal discussions in June and July 1982, US INF negotiator Paul Nitze and Soviet negotiator Yuli Kvitsinsky worked out what became known as the 'walk-in-the-woods' compromise. The compromise would have permitted the United States to deploy 75 cruise-missile launchers, each with four single-warhead missiles, while the Soviets would reduce their INF forces deployed in sites capable of reaching Europe to 75 SS-20s with three warheads each. Soviet INF forces in Asia would be frozen. The United States would not deploy any Pershing IIs; no account would be taken of French or British forces in this interim agreement. There is disagreement as to which of the two governments first indicated a negative reaction to this proposal. In any event, both rejected it, although it probably would have been acceptable to the European NATO governments had the United States backed it and made this known to them; it was certainly acceptable to Chancellor Schmidt.[7] But the Reagan Administration was not willing to relinquish all Pershing deployment, and the Soviet authorities, although they clearly feared the Pershing IIs more than the GLCMs, were still not prepared to accept any deployment of US INF missiles in Europe.

In the period remaining before the collapse of the INF talks in November 1983, the Soviet Union made one concession after another in the effort to block any US deployment of INF missiles.

The governments of European NATO countries—where the public, under the impact of Soviet criticism, had come to consider the original US zero-option position inequitable and non-negotiable—now pressed the Reagan Administration to adopt a less extreme negotiating position. In March 1983, President Reagan publicly offered the Soviets a second possible outcome in addition to the zero option, which remained valid. Under the new proposal, the United States would limit its Pershing and GLCM deployments in Europe—both types of missile would be deployed, although the relative number of both was later made negotiable—to a specific number of warheads between 50 and 450, provided that the Soviet Union reduced the total of all its INF warheads on a global basis to the same level. As before, British and French nuclear forces were excluded.

In May 1983, General Secretary Andropov publicly announced Soviet willingness to limit Soviet INF warheads in Europe to the level of British and French warheads. Again no mention was made of destroying withdrawn Soviet missiles; Soviet INF in Asia would not be included; and no new US INF missiles would be permitted. Seeking to counter negative trends in European public opinion, NATO defence ministers, meeting at Montebello, Canada, in October 1983, announced the unilateral withdrawal of a further 1400 US tactical nuclear warheads from Europe.[8]

As NATO's 1983 deadline for beginning deployment of US INF missiles neared, the Soviet Union appeared ready to offer still more to prevent this outcome. In Geneva, Soviet negotiator Kvitsinsky offered to go down to about 120 SS-20s in Europe in return for zero US deployment, roughly equivalent to making equal warhead reductions from existing Soviet levels and from planned US levels. British and French forces would not be limited in INF. Instead, they would be credited to the US total of strategic weapons in the US–Soviet talks on reducing strategic systems. Also in the fall of 1983, Andropov offered for the first time to freeze Soviet SS-20 deployments in Asia.

Given its position at the outset, the USSR had shown considerable flexibility: an agreement on this basis would have meant more than a 50 per cent cut in Soviet INF warheads aimed at Europe from their level when the INF talks began in 1980, a result far beyond Western expectations at that time, and one that would probably have met the original West European desire to include reduction of Soviet INF in US–Soviet negotiations on nuclear arms control.

The last day of the negotiations was 23 November 1983, the day after the West German Bundestag confirmed the Pershing II deployment and the same day the first nine Pershing IIs reached a US unit in the southern FRG. Soviet negotiators walked out of the INF negotiations and subsequently out of the Strategic Arms Reduction Talks (START) and, in less categorical terms, out of the MBFR talks.

The reason for the breakdown was quite clear: most US officials were unwilling to accept any outcome that did not entail some deployment of US INF, given that the zero solution was not under serious discussion at the time. For its part, the Soviet Union took the categorical position of rejecting even a minimal US deployment with only limited military significance. But by the time the INF talks broke down, the issue had ceased to be one of East–West force balance, intra-alliance coupling or negotiation. It had become a question of whether the European NATO governments, primarily the United Kingdom and the FRG, where the first deployments were to take place, had sufficient political strength and determination to carry out the initial deployments against powerful opposition from their own public opinion and from the Soviet Union. Western governments felt that, whether the original NATO decision to deploy had been right or wrong and whether the projected deployment of US INF would bring additional security, giving in to Soviet pressure against deployment would be a serious political defeat for NATO, one that would leave it in dangerous disarray. In response to the beginning of NATO deployment, the Soviet Union announced 'countermeasures', including deployment of SS-12 missiles forward from the USSR into the GDR and Czechoslovakia. For the peoples of Europe in particular, it appeared that the only result of the INF negotiations had been to increase nuclear deployments on both sides.

V. Rapid movement at the new negotiations

Soon after the breakdown at Geneva, the Soviet Union indicated interest in returning to the negotiating table. But it was not until after the re-election of President Reagan in November 1984 that agreement was reached to resume the negotiations on INF and strategic weapons in a format expanded to include the issue of weapons in space. Soviet leaders insisted that all three subjects be addressed as a single package; no final agreement on any one subject could be concluded until all were resolved. Mikhail Gorbachev was designated General

Secretary of the CPSU in March 1985 just as the Geneva talks resumed. Shortly thereafter, and in direct connection with the emergence of Gorbachev as the Soviet leader, there began a series of important Soviet moves towards the US position on INF:

1. Soviet leaders agreed to a separate agreement on INF missiles. Although the January 1985 Gromyko-Shultz communiqué established that the INF issue was to be dealt with as a single package with strategic and space weapons—this reflected Soviet views on the strategic significance of US INF missiles—Soviet officials informally hinted early in the resumed talks that a separate INF agreement might be possible. The ups and downs of this issue of a separate agreement are complex: General Secretary Gorbachev agreed to it at the 1985 Geneva summit, only to revoke it in the aftermath of the breakdown of the Reykjavik summit, and then to revalidate it at the end of February 1987.

2. The USSR accepted that the agreement should be confined to US and Soviet armaments only. In General Secretary Gorbachev's proposal for elimination of all nuclear weapons, announced in January 1986, he dropped the Soviet insistence that British and French nuclear weapons be taken account of in an INF agreement and confirmed this position at the October 1986 Reykjavik summit meeting.

3. At the November 1985 Geneva summit and in his January 1986 proposal for elimination of all INF and other nuclear armaments, General Secretary Gorbachev agreed to focus on reduction of land-based missiles; Soviet negotiators subsequently dropped demands for inclusion of US nuclear-capable aircraft in the INF Treaty, the most recent relinquishment of the longstanding Soviet objective to restrict US FBS.

4. The Soviets moved from proposing that the United States have zero INF in Europe and the USSR about 120 warheads—their last offer before breaking off the negotiations in 1983—to a zero-zero outcome for Europe. They agreed to eliminate US and Soviet INF to zero and agreed to do so within the three-year period proposed by the United States.

5. Although the Soviets insisted at the outset that the scope of the INF talks be confined to Soviet SS-20 missiles deployed in Europe to the Urals, they subsequently agreed to freeze their SS-20s in Asia. Then, at the October 1986 Reykjavik summit, they agreed to reduce Soviet INF in the Asian USSR to 100 warheads. In July 1987, they agreed to reduce warheads in Asia to zero, making elimination of INF complete.

6. Reflecting a particular interest of European NATO countries, the United States had proposed in 1981 that, in order to avoid circumvention of an agreement to eliminate missiles in the 1000- to 5500-km range, an INF agreement must also include a no-increase agreement on missiles of 500- to 1000-km range, that is, Soviet SS-23 and SS-12 missiles. At the Reykjavik summit, the USSR offered a freeze on missiles of this range. In late February 1987, they offered to take up the whole issue in separate negotiations. But in the April 1987 Moscow visit of Secretary of State Shultz they offered to eliminate these missiles in Europe. In July 1987 General Secretary Gorbachev broadened this proposal to include elimination of these shorter-range missiles

in Asia, but Soviet negotiators then made this offer dependent on elimination of 72 Pershing 1a missiles owned and operated by West German forces, with their warheads in US custody. In August 1987, this issue was resolved by a pledge by Chancellor Kohl, who was under considerable pressure, to destroy the ageing German Pershing 1a missiles after destruction of Soviet and US INF missiles was completed.

7. After maintaining for years the position that verification of an INF agreement should rely primarily on national technical means and that it was premature to deal with verification until agreement had been reached on details of a specific reduction accord, the USSR agreed in principle at the 1986 Reykjavik summit to US concepts for verifying an INF accord, including an exchange of data, on-site monitoring of destruction of missiles and monitoring of production facilities. Detailed US proposals on these subjects were presented at Geneva in March 1987 and the Soviets agreed to most of these in conceptual terms; the two sides began work on the detailed procedures to implement these concepts only in September 1987. (The United States dropped a proposal for 'suspect site' challenge inspection anywhere in the United States or Soviet Union after objections from some US security agencies and after the need for such inspection had been reduced by Soviet agreement to eliminate all INF missiles.)

VI. Terms of the Treaty

The INF Treaty (see appendices 13A–13D) contains 17 articles and 2 protocols. The first, the protocol on elimination, specifies the way in which INF missiles will be destroyed. The second, the protocol on inspection, contains agreed procedures for verifying the Treaty. A Memorandum of Understanding contains the data base for the Treaty; it lists the total numbers of missiles and launchers covered by the Treaty and the geographic location of each.

The Treaty documents distributed to the United States Senate for information as part of the ratification process include the text of an agreement between the United States and the five European NATO member states which deployed INF missiles (Belgium, the Federal Republic of Germany, Italy, the Netherlands and the United Kingdom) to permit inspection by the USSR of US missile sites located on their territory. The Treaty documents also include a note from the Soviet Union to the United States that parallel agreements have been reached between it and the German Democratic Republic and Czechoslovakia to permit the conduct of inspections by the United States of Soviet missile sites in the GDR and Czechoslovakia, as well as exchanges of notes between the United States and the governments of the German Democratic Republic and Czechoslovakia confirming inspection procedures for Soviet missile sites on East German and Czechoslovakian territory. Soviet authorities submitted counterpart documents to the Supreme Soviet as part of their ratification process.

The Treaty proper provides for the elimination of all US and Soviet ground-launched ballistic and cruise missiles with a range of over 500 km but not over 5500 km. 'Elimination' means destruction of existing missiles including their front sections, but minus their nuclear warheads and guidance systems (which are retained by the deploying countries), prohibition of production or flight-testing of any INF missiles and prohibition of production of either the stages or launchers of these missiles for third parties. Destruction of missiles, launchers and associated equipment for missiles of ranges between 1000 and 5500 km must take place within three years, and that of missiles in the 500- to 1000-km range, within 18 months.

Within the first six months, each party may destroy up to 100 missiles in the 1000- to 5500-km range by means of launching, a provision initiated by the USSR on the grounds that elimination sites were too distant for rapid, safe destruction of some SS-20 missiles. The Treaty applies on a world-wide basis and has unlimited duration. It contains agreed procedures for destruction of missile launchers, launch canisters, erectors, transporter vehicles, propellant tanks and launch pad shelters, whether the equipment is deployed, stored or under repair. Some transporter equipment and storage shelters may be salvaged and used for other purposes.

Eight different types of existing missiles will be destroyed under the Treaty. For the United States, these are the Pershing II, the BGM-109G ground-launched cruise missile and the Pershing 1a. (Following elimination of all missiles deployed by the United States and the Soviet Union, the re-entry vehicles now associated with the Federal Republic of Germany's Pershing 1a missiles will be returned to the United States for separation of their nuclear warheads and guidance systems and for destruction of their front sections or nose cones.) For the Soviet Union, the missiles are the SS-20, SS-4, SS-5, SS-12 and SS-23. Further, two missiles which were tested but not deployed are to be eliminated: the United States' Pershing 1B, of which none now exist, and the Soviet SSC-X-4, a ground-launched cruise missile of which 84 undeployed missiles will be destroyed. Counting the SSC-X-4s, the USSR will destroy 1836 missiles and the United States 867, a ratio of more than two to one. (The Memorandum of Understanding lists only 859 US missiles, but 8 defective Pershing 1a missiles were located and reported to the USSR after its signature.)

It is important to note that the INF Treaty provides for the elimination of all ground-based missiles of the specified range. No exception is made permitting deployment of missiles equipped with conventional rather than nuclear warheads. An agreement providing for elimination of only those missiles equipped with nuclear warheads while permitting deployment of the same missiles if armed with conventional warheads would have been unworkable because of the ease with which illicit nuclear warheads could be mounted on deployed missiles. In the US Senate ratification process, further clarification was demanded in view of the Anti-Ballistic Missile Treaty interpretation dispute. Consequently, in a last-minute exchange of notes, the two governments confirmed that the elimination and prohibition of INF missiles would also preclude development of missiles equipped with 'futuristic' weapons like microwave, radiation and laser weapons.

To further communication, article XIII(2) provides for the use of the Nuclear Risk Reduction Centers (established according to a US–Soviet agreement on 15 September 1987) to enable a continuous exchange of data and to provide and receive required notifications. These centres would also communicate requests for co-operative measures (see appendix 13E).

VII. Verification

The unprecedented verification provisions of the INF Treaty will allow for the monitoring of mutual compliance with considerable confidence. Supplementing verification by satellite imagery and other national technical means, the Treaty establishes totally new procedures for on-site inspections of missile production plants, operating bases and support facilities. Some details of the verification procedures were still being resolved during Senate ratification, but the main aspects are clear: 84 locations are designated for inspection on the Soviet side, including seven in Eastern Europe; for the United States, there are 34 locations, including 12 in Western Europe.

Each country will carry out several different types of inspection during the three-year elimination period, some for 10 years thereafter:

1. Baseline inspections, within 90 days of the Treaty's entry into force, to verify the starting counts for missile and launcher destruction;

2. Elimation inspections to supervise the destruction of the missiles and launchers by burning, cutting, crushing, exploding or firing;

3. Close-out inspections to confirm elimination of the missiles and launchers;

4. Periodic inspections of missile bases and support facilities to verify their elimination. Operating in teams of 10 to 30, the inspectors may carry out—on 16 hours' notice—up to 20 inspections per year in the first three years of the agreement, 15 per year during the next five years, and 10 per year in the remaining five years;

5. Continuous perimeter monitoring over a 13-year period of one production plant in each country, to be carried out by teams in residence near the site. The US plant is the Hercules Aerospace Company's facility in Magna, Utah, which manufactured stages for the Pershing II. The Soviet plant is the Votkinsk Machine Building Plant, a facility which has produced both SS-20 and SS-25 missiles and which will continue to produce the latter.

6. An additional verification measure requires the USSR to facilitate surveillance of the long-range SS-25 mobile missile, which is not covered by the Treaty and is similar to the SS-20. Until a strategic reduction agreement goes into effect or for a period of not more than three years, the USSR will be required at US request to open the roofs of shelters covering SS-25 missile launchers up to six times a year and to keep them open for a 12-hour period. This will allow US satellites to confirm that no banned SS-20s are being concealed at SS-25 sites.

7. An exchange of letters between the Soviet and US negotiators permits the United States to conduct a total of up to six on-site inspections of former silo launchers of SS-4 missiles dismantled by the USSR prior to signature of the Treaty.

VIII. What the INF Treaty does not do

The INF Treaty eliminates only ground-launched ballistic and cruise missiles having ranges between 500 and 5500 km. It leaves untouched US and Soviet ground-launched ballistic and cruise missiles of over 5500-km or under 500-km range, all air- and sea-launched ballistic and cruise missiles, as well as nuclear-capable artillery and rockets with ranges of under 500 km. It does not affect the nuclear delivery systems of third countries, like those of the UK and France. Nor does it prohibit US or Soviet surface-to-air missiles against objects in the atmosphere or space, including those for anti-satellite, anti-ballistic missile and anti-tactical ballistic missile purposes, or unarmed remotely piloted vehicles (RPVs)—drones. Land-based testing of permitted missiles can be carried out at designated test sites, including testing under controlled conditions of booster stages not used for INF missiles but having ranges between 500 and 1000 km (*inter alia*, for strategic re-entry vehicles and SDI [Strategic Defense Initiative]-type defence systems). And, as noted, the Treaty does not provide for destruction of the nuclear warheads and guidance systems of missiles which are destroyed.

In the ratification hearings held by the US Senate beginning in February 1988, critics of the INF Treaty pointed out that the Treaty would not prevent the secret conversion of SS-25 mobile ICBMs (which have a first stage outwardly similar to the SS-20 but are, according to Soviet statements, not interchangeable with it) to a variable-range capability, equipping the SS-25s with the guidance systems and warheads of destroyed SS-20s. This is a theoretical possibility, although these covert actions could not create a capability which could be publicly used to induce restraint and caution in the NATO Alliance, as was clearly the aim of Soviet IRBM deployment from its beginnings in the late 1950s. Moreover, a strategic reduction agreement, if achieved, would also bring strong motivation in the USSR not to further subtract from an already reduced quota of ICBMs.

Treaty critics also claim that the USSR, assisted by the absence of a provision for short-notice suspect-site inspection anywhere, could hide existing SS-20 missiles without deploying them or even produce further SS-20 missiles covertly and then suddenly field these concealed missiles in a break-out at a time of crisis or conflict.

However, while it is possible that some SS-20s could be concealed and even that clandestine manufacture could continue in undeclared sites, actual use of such missiles would require personnel recently trained in their deployment, and an array of ground-based guidance and control systems. The latter cannot be set up without considerable risk of observation; and, if rapidly deployed, without prior, combined testing of all items of equipment, they cannot actually be used with real confidence. The still more intrusive inspection requirements of the prospective strategic nuclear reduction agreement would make clandestine storage or production still more difficult. Moreover, as a result of the INF Treaty, the USA and the USSR are likely to increase their coverage of the other countries' territory by national technical means, especially satellite photography, further reducing the possibility of militarily significant evasion.

Treaty critics also claim that its definitions do not capture a 'hyper-velocity glide vehicle' which is propelled by a ballistic missile on a high arc, then glides to a low altitude when it is propelled by a cruise missile mechanism. Treaty proponents point out that no such delivery system now exists and that it might well be covered by Treaty definitions if it did. The INF Treaty also establishes a Special Verification Commission that will meet at either side's request to resolve questions or complaints regarding compliance with the Treaty.

IX. Significance of the agreement

How did this outcome, remarkable by any previous standard of US–Soviet arms control negotiation, come about? What changed the position of the USSR between 1983—when it broke off the talks—and 1985, when it began a steady move towards the NATO position as represented by the United States?

Several factors played a role in the outcome; absence of any one of them might have brought a different result. On the Western side, the evident concerns of the West European public brought about separate INF negotiations in 1980 after the collapse of SALT II Treaty ratification, and brought about resumption of these negotiations in 1981 by the newly elected Reagan Administration. These concerns may also have played some role in the Administration's adoption of the proposal for reducing INF missiles to zero on both sides. The vehement opposition of large segments of West European opinion to missile deployment also created the erroneous expectation in the Soviet leadership that deployment of US INF could be blocked and surely played some role in the 1983 Soviet withdrawal from the Geneva negotiations. At the same time, this clear evidence of a desire for positive change in East–West relations on the part of so many West Europeans seems to have weakened deep-seated Soviet worries about irredentist German militarism and probably played a material role in the general shift of the Soviet position on arms control that began in 1985.

One key factor in the outcome was NATO's capacity to move to deployment of the new US missiles in the face of this strong resistance from the West European public and of massive Soviet political opposition, including forward deployment of Soviet missiles in the GDR and Czechoslovakia as well as threats of an 'ice age' in inner German relations. The actual deployment of the US missiles, especially the Pershing IIs, whose threat to the USSR was so often emphasized by Soviet negotiators, may have influenced a Soviet decision to pay still more for the elimination of these US delivery systems, to the extent of wholly eliminating the SS-20s. Yet the sweeping scope of Soviet moves both in arms control generally and in INF itself—agreement to destroy not only the SS-20s, SS-4s and SS-5s in Europe, but also those in Asia and the SS-23 and SS-12, plus agreement to stringent verification—argue for additional, broader motives on their part. Some Western officials believe that the Reagan defence buildup was the decisive factor, but the Soviet Union had no apparent difficulty in adding additional warheads and strategic delivery systems to keep up with increases in US strategic forces.

Broad changes in the Soviet position on arms control, which, in addition to moves on INF, brought major Soviet moves with regard to reduction of strategic nuclear arms, prohibition of chemical weapons and nuclear testing, and the Stockholm Conference on Disarmament in Europe, was the major factor in the successful outcome of the INF negotiations. The main motivation for this broad range of moves appears to be a Soviet desire to improve relations with Western governments during an important effort to reform the Soviet economic system—in other words, a mainly domestic motivation. From this viewpoint, concluding an INF Treaty—technically the most separable aspect of the current or prospective East–West arms control agenda, less complex than US–Soviet strategic reductions or reducing conventional forces in Europe—was a logical first step, even at high cost in Soviet moves toward the Western position. Certainly, the Soviet leadership was willing to pay a high price to eliminate US INF missiles. Some Western observers consider that the present Soviet political and military leadership has a serious desire to keep conflict non-nuclear if war should break out, and that elimination of INF was a first step in this direction.[9]

Other Western observers see the main Soviet objective as a deliberate effort to render unworkable the NATO strategy of flexible response through negotiated elimination of all nuclear weapons from Europe, in order to improve prospects for eventual WTO conventional attack on Western Europe or for political intimidation based on superior conventional forces.[10] Continued caution in interpreting Soviet actions is highly advisable, but this negative assessment of Soviet objectives seems a narrow, Eurocentric view, given the above-mentioned Soviet arms control moves outside the European context, which argue more convincingly for a general Soviet effort, of whatever duration, to improve relations with the West.

What are the effects of the INF Treaty on the security situation in Europe? Destruction of the INF missiles will eliminate a category of weapons which might have been used early in a conflict in Europe. Although both alliances have many other systems of adequate range which could deliver nuclear weapons on targets in the NATO or WTO areas, these systems are either more dispersed, more distant or less vulnerable than INF systems. Consequently, there is less incentive to use them pre-emptively at the outset of conflict to prevent the use of similar weapons by the opposing alliance. The Treaty thus brings a gain in crisis stability. Moreover, other existing delivery systems are either less accurate, less capable of assured penetration of defences or less capable of precision strikes with limited yield on specific targets at these ranges.

Destruction of the Soviet SS-23 eliminates the only weapon of this range which presently has the accuracy to deliver conventional or chemical warheads against NATO airfields, command posts and anti-aircraft installations; NATO commanders had taken this threat so seriously that they were considering developing special defences against it. Now, both the threat and the need for additional defences have been sharply reduced, if not eliminated. The WTO also gains from eliminating the possibility of deployment by NATO governments of missiles of this range armed with conventional or chemical warheads. Given the incentives to use missiles of this type early in a conflict, without the inhibitions attached to the use of nuclear weapons, there is also an appreciable gain in crisis stability from this aspect of the Treaty.

Although a good deal has been said about the possible effects of the INF Treaty in weakening NATO's strategy of flexible response and possible first use of nuclear weapons, the Treaty does not materially affect the probability that any East–West military conflict in Europe would ultimately escalate to the use of strategic nuclear weapons by both the USA and the USSR and recognition of this fact by the leadership on both sides. Although in eliminating a Soviet numerical superiority, that in medium-range nuclear missiles, the INF Treaty draws attention to continuing WTO numerical superiority in armaments, the Treaty does not increase NATO's vulnerability to conventional attack.

The INF Treaty has considerable significance for other aspects of East–West arms control. Movement towards conclusion of the INF Treaty has already drawn with it very considerable progress towards a US–Soviet agreement on strategic reductions; such an agreement appears quite possible within the next years, if not in the present Administration, then in its successor. Already, verification procedures agreed for INF have been taken over by agreement for use in a strategic reduction agreement, where they will be supplemented by other measures.

The INF agreement is also a substantial first move towards lowering the level of the East–West military confrontation in Europe. The conclusion of the INF Treaty has increased Western hopes for similar Soviet flexibility in the Atlantic-to-the-Urals force negotiations which will probably get under way in 1988. Moreover, expressions of concern by NATO officials[11] and defence experts over the possible effects of an INF agreement on the East–West conventional balance in Europe have elicited statements from General Secretary Gorbachev[12] and other WTO officials of willingness to reduce asymmetries in holdings of major weapons where they exist on both sides. It is possible that, in these new talks, the initial negotiating approaches of both alliances will require major modification before they can serve as a basis for a mutually acceptable agreement. But the outlook for some progress in the next three to five years is favourable.

Confirmation of these further positive effects of INF lies in the future; it will depend, as indicated above, on the continuation of the reform course inside the USSR and of the foreign policy flexibility associated with it. But the entire course of the INF episode from 1979 to 1987 has already had highly important and probably enduring effects on the relationship between the United States and the European NATO members in the defence field. First, the dispute in Western Europe over the US INF missiles ruptured, probably permanently, the existing consensus among major West European political parties over the role of nuclear weapons in NATO strategy. Opposition to INF deployment was strongest in Social Democratic opposition parties which have as a result since the early 1980s questioned NATO strategy, US nuclear protection for Europe, the US leadership role in decision-making in the NATO Alliance, and the gravity of the military threat from the WTO. Outside the political parties, important segments of the European public continue to concern themselves with issues of this kind.

Second, while the INF debate was going on, France became worried about what it considered a drift to neutralism in FR Germany and demonstratively showed greater interest in defence co-operation with the FRG.

Third, all of the NATO governments have strongly and repeatedly endorsed the INF Treaty, as does a large majority of Western public opinion. At the same time, the INF Treaty—or, rather, the way it was achieved—has shaken the confidence of some senior political officials of NATO governments. These officials would have preferred to retain some US INF missiles even at the cost of some continued Soviet deployment. They were shaken by the willingness of President Reagan at the Reykjavik summit not only to agree to zero INF, but also to propose mutual elimination of strategic ballistic missiles, the back-up force for the US nuclear guarantee for Europe.[13]

The negative reaction was strongest in France, where Defence Minister André Giraud called the INF Treaty 'a nuclear Munich', and in the FRG.[14] In a wrenching struggle within Chancellor Kohl's Christian Democratic Union, a substantial group of Christian Democrats indicated dissatisfaction with the total elimination of US INF, with the elimination of the 500- to 1000-km category of missiles including the German Pershing 1a, and with being left facing a large WTO preponderance in tactical-range nuclear weapons, which, if used, would have their main effect on German soil.[15] These West German conservatives joined the West German Left in demanding early reduction or elimination of tactical-range nuclear weapons from central Europe. This nearly unanimous position placed the FRG at odds with most of its NATO allies, who insisted that NATP must modernize its remaining nuclear weapons and that the USSR and its WTO allies must first make deep cuts in their numerically superior conventional forces before NATO could consider further negotiated reductions in its nuclear weapons.

Therefore, the first paradoxical fruit of the INF Treaty was a falling out between the Federal Republic of Germany and its NATO allies, which might be temporarily bridged over but would leave unresolved differences.[16] More generally, it was a falling out between the United States and the most direct supporters in Europe of US military involvement there. This segment of European opinion comprises those most concerned by the military threat from the Warsaw Treaty Organization, and many of the original proponents of INF deployment and of the US nuclear deterrent. They also formed the group most committed to the NATO Alliance with the United States and in the past most inclined to resist efforts to intensify intra-European defence co-operation, which they saw as weakening the defence relationship with the United States. Many adherents of this view came to the conclusion, earlier reached by France through different reasoning, that intensified Franco-German and intra-European co-operation in defence was necessary as a long-term alternative to excessive dependence on the United States for the defence of Europe.[17]

Thus, one aspect or another of the INF issue—deployment of the US missiles or the agreement to eliminate them—elicited grave doubts from the entire spectrum of European political opinion about the defence alliance with the United States; this related especially to the nuclear connection, which for many has been the heart of this relationship.

Although deployment of new US medium-range missiles was originally designed to bolster West European confidence in the US–European defence relationship, in historical retrospect, the entire 10-year long INF episode may have done more than almost any other single development of the past 40 years to bring about a re-evaluation of that relationship, to promote an enduring conviction that West European defence interests differ from those of the United States, to create a serious long-term determination to intensify intra-European defence co-operation in Western Europe, and to end the era of relatively unquestioning European acceptance of US primacy in defining Western strategy for the defence of Europe. Only the achievement by the USSR of nuclear parity with the United States has clearly had equal or greater impact. The NATO Alliance, as such, is likely to continue indefinitely, in one form or another, together with its WTO counterpart, and to evolve towards greater equality between its US and European components, but it is improbable that anything other than an East–West crisis of extreme nature could restore the earlier primacy of the United States over its European allies.

Thus, in an interim balance of gains and losses in the entire intermediate-range nuclear forces experience, the United States sacrificed more in the political sense, the Soviet Union more in the military sense. Both made a gain in security, as did all the peoples of Europe. The future will determine whether that gain can be consolidated and become enduring.[18]

Notes and references

* Union of Concerned Scientists, Cambridge, Mass., USA.

[1] These took from 8 to 24 hours to fuel, and their highly volatile fuel had to be topped up every five hours to keep them in ready status.

[2] Howard, M., *The Times*, 3 Nov. 1981; Garthoff, R. L., 'The NATO decision on theater nuclear forces', *Political Science Quarterly*, vol. 98 (summer 1983), pp. 197–214; Garthoff, R. L., 'European theater nuclear forces 1977–80', *Detente and Confrontation: American–Soviet Relations from Nixon to Reagan* (Brookings Institution: Washington, DC, 1986), pp. 849–86; Gordon, M., 'INF: A hollow victory', *Foreign Policy*, vol. 68 (fall 1987), pp. 162–3; International Institute for Strategic Studies, 'The balance of theatre nuclear forces in Europe', *The Military Balance 1979–1980* (IISS: London, 1980), pp. 114–9; Metzger, R. and Doty, P., 'Arms control enters the gray area', *International Security*, vol. 3, no. 3 (winter 1978–1979), pp. 17–52.

[3] Bovin, A., 'Breakthrough', *Moscow News*, no. 10 (1987), p. 3.

[4] Interview with the weekly Soviet magazine *New Times*, 20 Nov. 1987.

[5] See, for example, Haig, A., *Caveat: Realism, Reagan and Foreign Policy* (Macmillan: New York, 1984), p. 229.

[6] International Institute for Strategic Studies, *Strategic Survey 1981–82* (IISS: London, 1982), p. 140.

[7] See Schmidt, H., *A Grand Strategy for the West* (Yale University Press: New Haven, Conn., 1985), p. 6.

[8] Montebello Communiqué, NATO Nuclear Planning Group, 28 Oct. 1983.

[9] McGwire, M., *Military Objectives in Soviet Foreign Policy* (Brookings Institution: Washington, DC, 1987); Shenfield, S., *The Nuclear Predicament: Explorations in Soviet Ideology*, RIIA (Routledge & Kegan Paul: London, 1987).

[10] Lellouche, P., 'Architect Gorbachev has designs on Europe', *International Herald Tribune*, 12 Feb. 1988; Platt, A., *Soviet–West European Relations: Recent Trends and Near-Term Prospects*, Santa Monica: RAND R–3316–AF, Mar. 1986; Laird, R. F., 'The Soviet Union and the Western alliance: elements of an anti-coalition strategy', *The Soviet Union, The West and the Nuclear Arms Race* (Wheatsheaf Books: Brighton, 1986), pp. 210–34.

[11] Bernard Rogers and John Galvin have both expressed concern about INF; see, for example, Buchan, D., 'NATO Commander warns of risks in missile deal', *Financial Times*, 16 Sep. 1987;

Evans, M., 'NATO chief warns of INF missile risk', *The Times*, 16 Sep. 1987; Evans, M., 'Outgoing NATO chief warns of arms deal risks', *The Times*, 19 June 1987.

[12] See chapter 11.

[13] Markham, J. M., 'Western allies grumble about Reykjavik plans', *New York Times*, 22 Oct. 1986; Dobbs, M., 'France prods US to consult on arms', *Washington Post*, 22 Nov. 1986; Markham, J. M., 'A Europe of two minds', *New York Times*, 9 Mar. 1987; Hoagland, J., 'Allies show growing unease over US stance on missiles', *Washington Post*, 8 Mar. 1987.

[14] Housego, D., 'Soviet arms proposal splits French Cabinet', *Financial Times*, 6 Mar. 1987; Amalric, J., 'L'affaire des euromissiles divise la majorité', *Le Monde*, 6 Mar. 1987; see also Marshall, D. B., 'France and the INF negotiations: an "American Munich"', *Strategic Review*, vol. 15, no. 3 (summer 1987), pp. 20–30.

[15] Markham, J. M., 'Bonn coalition openly split on short-range arms', *New York Times*, 8 May 1987; McCartney, R. J., 'Soviet offer poses dilemma for Bonn', *Washington Post*, 6 May 1987; McCartney, R. J., 'Rejection of Soviet offer on missiles signaled by Bonn', *Washington Post*, 8 May 1987; Tagliabue, J., 'Kohl in reversal, rejects plan to abolish only some missiles', *New York Times*, 16 May 1987.

[16] Shipler, D. K., 'Kohl, in Washington, meets with Reagan to discuss Iceland talks', *New York Times*, 22 Oct. 1986; McCartney, R. J., 'Kohl wants wider accord on missiles', *Washington Post*, 16 May 1987; McCartney, R. J., 'West Germany may renege on battlefield missile plan', *Washington Post*, 12 July 1987; DeYoung, K., 'Nuclear issues linger for NATO', *Washington Post*, 23 Dec. 1987.

[17] Speech by Dr A. Dregger, Member of the Bundestag, at the American Institute for Contemporary German Studies at the John Hopkins University, Washington, DC, 5 May 1988.

[18] Much of this chapter rests on the author's own direct knowledge from involvement with political-military issues as a government official. Much comes from informal discussion with negotiators on both sides. The best published sources remain: Freedman, L., *The Evolution of Nuclear Strategy* (St. Martin's Press: New York, 1983); Garthoff, R. L., *Detente and Confrontation* (Brookings Institution: Washington, DC, 1985); Schwartz, D. N., *NATO's Nuclear Dilemmas* (Brookings Institution: Washington, DC, 1983); Smith, G., *Double Talk* (University Press of America: Lanham, 1985) (paperback edn); and Talbot, S., *Deadly Gambits* (Knopf: New York, 1984). Dean, J., *Watershed in Europe* (Lexington Books: Lexington, Mass., 1987) contains a detailed description of the development of the INF talks up to the spring of 1986.

Appendix 13A. Treaty between the United States of America and the Union of Soviet Socialist Republics on the elimination of their intermediate-range and shorter-range missiles[1]

The United States of America and the Union of Soviet Socialist Republics, hereinafter referred to as the Parties,

Conscious that nuclear war would have devastating consequences for all mankind,

Guided by the objective of strengthening strategic stability,

Convinced that the measures set forth in this Treaty will help to reduce the risk of outbreak of war and strengthen international peace and security, and

Mindful of their obligations under Article VI of the Treaty on the Non-Proliferation of Nuclear Weapons,

Have agreed as follows:

Article I

In accordance with the provisions of this Treaty which includes the Memorandum of Understanding and Protocols which form an integral part thereof, each Party shall eliminate its intermediate-range and shorter-range missiles, not have such systems thereafter, and carry out the other obligations set forth in this Treaty.

Article II

For the purposes of this Treaty:

1. The term "ballistic missile" means a missile that has a ballistic trajectory over most of its flight path. The term "ground-launched ballistic missile (GLBM)" means a ground-launched ballistic missile that is a weapon-delivery vehicle.

2. The term "cruise missile" means an unmanned, self-propelled vehicle that sustains flight through the use of aerodynamic lift over most of its flight path. The term "ground-launched cruise missile (GLCM)" means a ground-launched cruise missile that is a weapon-delivery vehicle.

3. The term "GLBM launcher" means a fixed launcher or a mobile land-based transporter-erector-launcher mechanism for launching a GLBM.

4. The term "GLCM launcher" means a fixed launcher or a mobile land-based transporter-erector-launcher mechanism for launching a GLCM.

5. The term "intermediate-range missile" means a GLBM or a GLCM having a range capability in excess of 1000 kilometers but not in excess of 5500 kilometers.

6. The term "shorter-range missile" means a GLBM or a GLCM having a range capability equal to or in excess of 500 kilometers but not in excess of 1000 kilometers.

---

[1] The Treaty reproduced in this Yearbook appears as it was signed on 8 December 1987 and printed in *Selected Documents no. 25*, Department of State Publication 9555 (US Department of State, Bureau of Public Affairs, Office of Public Communication Editorial Division: Washington, DC, Dec. 1987). The Corrigendum appended to it lists five technical errors identified by the US Government, which were to be corrected through an exchange of diplomatic notes with the Soviet Union. In the Treaty text reproduced in this appendix, these corrections are inserted in bold print, within square brackets, immediately after the relevant items.

7. The term "deployment area" means a designated area within which intermediate-range missiles and launchers of such missiles may operate and within which one or more missile operating bases are located.

8. The term "missile operating base" means:

(a) in the case of intermediate-range missiles, a complex of facilities located within a deployment area at which intermediate-range missiles and launchers of such missiles normally operate, in which support structures associated with such missiles and launchers are also located and in which support equipment associated with such missiles and launchers is normally located; and

(b) in the case of shorter-range missiles, a complex of facilities located any place at which shorter-range missiles and launchers of such missiles normally operate and in which support equipment associated with such missiles and launchers is normally located.

9. The term "missile support facility," as regards intermediate-range or shorter-range missiles and launchers of such missiles, means a missile production facility or a launcher production facility, a missile repair facility or a launcher repair facility, a training facility, a missile storage facility or a launcher storage facility, a test range, or an elimination facility as those terms are defined in the Memorandum of Understanding.

10. The term "transit" means movement, notified in accordance with paragraph 5(f) of Article IX of this Treaty, of an intermediate-range missile or a launcher of such a missile between missile support facilities, between such a facility and a deployment area or between deployment areas, or of a shorter-range missile or a launcher of such a missile from a missile support facility or missile operating base to an elimination facility.

11. The term "deployed missile" means an intermediate-range missile located within a deployment area or a shorter-range missile located at a missile operating base.

12. The term "non-deployed missile" means an intermediate-range missile located outside a deployment area or a shorter-range missile located outside a missile operating base.

13. The term "deployed launcher" means a launcher of an intermediate-range missile located within a deployment area or a launcher of a shorter-range missile located at a missile operating base.

14. The term "non-deployed launcher" means a launcher of an intermediate-range missile located outside a deployment area or a launcher of a shorter-range missile located outside a missile operating base.

15. The term "basing country" means a country other than the United States of America or the Union of Soviet Socialist Republics on whose territory intermediate-range or shorter-range missiles of the Parties, launchers of such missiles or support structures associated with such missiles and launchers were located at any time after November 1, 1987. Missiles or launchers in transit are not considered to be "located."

Article III

1. For the purposes of this Treaty, existing types of intermediate-range missiles are:

(a) for the United States of America, missiles of the types designated by the United States of America as the Pershing II and the BGM-109G, which are known to the Union of Soviet Socialist Republics by the same designations; and

(b) for the Union of Soviet Socialist Republics, missiles of the types designated by the Union of Soviet Socialist Republics as the RSD-10, the R-12 and the R-14, which are known to the United States of America as the SS-20, the SS-4 and the SS-5, respectively.

2. For the purposes of this Treaty, existing types of shorter-range missiles are:

(a) for the United States of America, missiles of the type designated by the United States of America as the Pershing IA, which is known to the Union of Soviet Socialist Republics by the same designation; and

(b) for the Union of Soviet Socialist Republics, missiles of the types designated by the Union of Soviet Socialist Republics as the OTR-22 and the OTR-23, which are known to the United States of America as the SS-12 and the SS-23, respectively.

Article IV

1. Each Party shall eliminate all its intermediate-range missiles and launchers of such missiles, and all support structures and support equipment of the categories listed in the Memorandum of Understanding associated with such missiles and launchers, so that no later than three years after entry into force of this Treaty and thereafter no such missiles, launchers, support structures or support equipment shall be possessed by either Party.

2. To implement paragraph 1 of this Article, upon entry into force of this Treaty, both Parties shall begin and continue throughout the duration of each phase, the reduction of all types of their deployed and non-deployed intermediate-range missiles and deployed and non-deployed launchers of such missiles and support structures and support equipment associated with such missiles and launchers in accordance with the provisions of this Treaty. These reductions shall be implemented in two phases so that:

(a) by the end of the first phase, that is, no later than 29 months after entry into force of this Treaty:

(i) the number of deployed launchers of intermediate-range missiles for each Party shall not exceed the number of launchers that are capable of carrying or containing at one time missiles considered by the Parties to carry 171 warheads;

(ii) the number of deployed intermediate-range missiles for each Party shall not exceed the number of such missiles considered by the Parties to carry 180 warheads;

(iii) the aggregate number of deployed and non-deployed launchers of intermediate-range missiles for each Party shall not exceed the number of launchers that are capable of carrying or containing at one time missiles considered by the Parties to carry 200 warheads;

(iv) the aggregate number of deployed and non-deployed intermediate-range missiles for each Party shall not exceed the number of such missiles considered by the Parties to carry 200 warheads; and

(v) the ratio of the aggregate number of deployed and non-deployed intermediate-range GLBMs of existing types for each Party to the aggregate number of deployed and non-deployed intermediate-range missiles of existing types possessed by that Party shall not exceed the ratio of such intermediate-range GLBMs to such intermediate-range missiles for that Party as of November 1, 1987, as set forth in the Memorandum of Understanding; and

(b) by the end of the second phase, that is, no later than three years after entry into force of this Treaty, all intermediate-range missiles of each Party, launchers of such missiles and all support structures and support equipment of the categories listed in the Memorandum of Understanding associated with such missiles and launchers, shall be eliminated.

Article V

1. Each Party shall eliminate all its shorter-range missiles and launchers of such missiles, and all support equipment of the categories listed in the Memorandum of Understanding associated with such missiles and launchers, so that no later than 18 months after entry into force of this Treaty and thereafter no such missiles,

launchers or support equipment shall be possessed by either Party.

2. No later than 90 days after entry into force of this Treaty, each Party shall complete the removal of all its deployed shorter-range missiles and deployed and non-deployed launchers of such missiles to elimination facilities and shall retain them at those locations until they are eliminated in accordance with the procedures set forth in the Protocol on Elimination. No later than 12 months after entry into force of this Treaty, each Party shall complete the removal of all its non-deployed shorter-range missiles to elimination facilities and shall retain them at those locations until they are eliminated in accordance with the procedures set forth in the Protocol on Elimination.

3. Shorter-range missiles and launchers of such missiles shall not be located at the same elimination facility. Such facilities shall be separated by no less than 1000 kilometers.

Article VI

1. Upon entry into force of this Treaty and thereafter, neither Party shall:

(a) produce or flight-test any intermediate-range missiles or produce any stages of such missiles or any launchers of such missiles; or

(b) produce, flight-test or launch any shorter-range missiles or produce any stages of such missiles or any launchers of such missiles.

2. Notwithstanding paragraph 1 of this Article, each Party shall have the right to produce a type of GLBM not limited by this Treaty which uses a stage which is outwardly similar to, but not interchangeable with, a stage of an existing type of intermediate-range GLBM having more than one stage, providing that that Party shall not produce any other stage which is outwardly similar to, but not interchangeable with, any other stage of an existing type of intermediate-range GLBM.

Article VII

For the purposes of this Treaty:

1. If a ballistic missile or a cruise missile has been flight-tested or deployed for weapon delivery, all missiles of that type shall be considered to be weapon-delivery vehicles.

2. If a GLBM or GLCM is an intermediate-range missile, all GLBMs or GLCMs of that type shall be considered to be intermediate-range missiles. If a GLBM or GLCM is a shorter-range missile, all GLBMs or GLCMs of that type shall be considered to be shorter-range missiles.

3. If a GLBM is of a type developed and tested solely to intercept and counter objects not located on the surface of the earth, it shall not be considered to be a missile to which the limitations of this Treaty apply.

4. The range capability of a GLBM not listed in Article III of this Treaty shall be considered to be the maximum range to which it has been tested. The range capability of a GLCM not listed in Article III of this Treaty shall be considered to be the maximum distance which can be covered by the missile in its standard design mode flying until fuel exhaustion, determined by projecting its flight path onto the earth's sphere from the point of launch to the point of impact. GLBMs or GLCMs that have a range capability equal to or in excess of 500 kilometers but not in excess of 1000 kilometers shall be considered to be shorter-range missiles. GLBMs or GLCMs that have a range capability in excess of 1000 kilometers but not in excess of 5500 kilometers shall be considered to be intermediate-range missiles.

5. The maximum number of warheads an existing type of intermediate-range missile or shorter-range missile carries shall be considered to be the number listed for missiles of that type in the Memorandum of Understanding.

6. Each GLBM or GLCM shall be considered to carry the maximum number of warheads listed for a GLBM

or GLCM of that type in the Memorandum of Understanding.

7. If a launcher has been tested for launching a GLBM or a GLCM, all launchers of that type shall be considered to have been tested for launching GLBMs or GLCMs.

8. If a launcher has contained or launched a particular type of GLBM or GLCM, all launchers of that type shall be considered to be launchers of that type of GLBM or GLCM.

9. The number of missiles each launcher of an existing type of intermediate-range missile or shorter-range missile shall be considered to be capable of carrying or containing at one time is the number listed for launchers of missiles of that type in the Memorandum of Understanding.

10. Except in the case of elimination in accordance with the procedures set forth in the Protocol on Elimination, the following shall apply:

(a) for GLBMs which are stored or moved in separate stages, the longest stage of an intermediate-range or shorter-range GLBM shall be counted as a complete missile;

(b) for GLBMs which are not stored or moved in separate stages, a canister of the type used in the launch of an intermediate-range GLBM, unless a Party proves to the satisfaction of the other Party that it does not contain such a missile, or an assembled intermediate-range or shorter-range GLBM, shall be counted as a complete missile; and

(c) for GLCMs, the airframe of an intermediate-range or shorter-range GLCM shall be counted as a complete missile.

11. A ballistic missile which is not a missile to be used in a ground-based mode shall not be considered to be a GLBM if it is test-launched at a test site from a fixed land-based launcher which is used solely for test purposes and which is distinguishable from GLBM launchers. A cruise missile which is not a missile to be used in a ground-based mode shall not be considered to be a GLCM if it is test-launched at a test site from a fixed land-based launcher which is used solely for test purposes and which is distinguishable from GLCM launchers.

12. Each Party shall have the right to produce and use for booster systems, which might otherwise be considered to be intermediate-range or shorter-range missiles, only existing types of booster stages for such booster systems. Launches of such booster systems shall not be considered to be flight-testing of intermediate-range or shorter-range missiles provided that:

(a) stages used in such booster systems are different from stages used in those missiles listed as existing types of intermediate-range or shorter-range missiles in Article III of this Treaty;

(b) such booster systems are used only for research and development purposes to test objects other than the booster systems themselves;

(c) the aggregate number of launchers for such booster systems shall not exceed 35 for each Party at any one time; and

(d) the launchers for such booster systems are fixed, emplaced above ground and located only at research and development launch sites which are specified in the Memorandum of Understanding.

Research and development launch sites shall not be subject to inspection pursuant to Article XI of this Treaty.

Article VIII

1. All intermediate-range missiles and launchers of such missiles shall be located in deployment areas, at missile support facilities or shall be in transit. Intermediate-range missiles or launchers of such missiles shall not be located elsewhere.

2. Stages of intermediate-range missiles shall be located in deployment areas, at missile support facilities or moving between deployment areas, between missile support facilities or between missile support facilities and deployment areas.

3. Until their removal to elimination facilities as required by paragraph 2 of Article V of this Treaty, all shorter-range missiles and launchers of such missiles shall be located at missile operating bases, at missile support facilities or shall be in transit. Shorter-range missiles or launchers of such missiles shall not be located elsewhere.

4. Transit of a missile or launcher subject to the provisions of this Treaty shall be completed within 25 days.

5. All deployment areas, missile operating bases and missile support facilities are specified in the Memorandum of Understanding or in subsequent updates of data pursuant to paragraphs 3, 5(a) or 5(b) of Article IX of this Treaty. Neither Party shall increase the number of, or change the location or boundaries of, deployment areas, missile operating bases or missile support facilities, except for elimination facilities, from those set forth in the Memorandum of Understanding. A missile support facility shall not be considered to be part of a deployment area even though it may be located within the geographic boundaries of a deployment area.

6. Beginning 30 days after entry into force of this Treaty, neither Party shall locate intermediate-range or shorter-range missiles, including stages of such missiles, or launchers of such missiles at missile production facilities, launcher production facilities or test ranges listed in the Memorandum of Understanding.

7. Neither Party shall locate any intermediate-range or shorter-range missiles at training facilities.

8. A non-deployed intermediate-range or shorter-range missile shall not be carried on or contained within a launcher of such a type of missile, except as required for maintenance conducted at repair facilities or for elimination by means of launching conducted at elimination facilities.

9. Training missiles and training launchers for intermediate-range or shorter-range missiles shall be subject to the same locational restrictions as are set forth for intermediate-range and shorter-range missiles and launchers of such missiles in paragraphs 1 and 3 of this Article.

Article IX

1. The Memorandum of Understanding contains categories of data relevant to obligations undertaken with regard to this Treaty and lists all intermediate-range and shorter-range missiles, launchers of such missiles, and support structures and support equipment associated with such missiles and launchers, possessed by the Parties as of November 1, 1987. Updates of that data and notifications required by this Article shall be provided according to the categories of data contained in the Memorandum of Understanding.

2. The Parties shall update that data and provide the notifications required by this Treaty through the Nuclear Risk Reduction Centers, established pursuant to the Agreement Between the United States of America and the Union of Soviet Socialist Republics on the Establishment of Nuclear Risk Reduction Centers of September 15, 1987.

3. No later than 30 days after entry into force of this Treaty, each Party shall provide the other Party with updated data, as of the date of entry into force of this Treaty, for all categories of data contained in the Memorandum of Understanding.

4. No later than 30 days after the end of each six-month interval following the entry into force of this Treaty, each Party shall provide updated data for all categories of data contained in the Memorandum of Understanding by informing the other Party of all changes, completed and in process, in that data, which have occurred during the six-month interval since the preceding data exchange, and the net effect of those changes.

5. Upon entry into force of this Treaty and thereafter, each Party shall provide the following notifications to the other Party:

(a) notification, no less than 30

days in advance, of the scheduled date of the elimination of a specific deployment area, missile operating base or missile support facility;

(b) notification, no less than 30 days in advance, of changes in the number or location of elimination facilities, including the location and scheduled date of a change;

(c) notification, except with respect to launches of intermediate-range missiles for the purpose of their elimination, no less than 30 days in advance, of the scheduled date of the initiation of the elimination of intermediate-range and shorter-range missiles, and stages of such missiles, and launchers of such missiles and support structures and support equipment associated with such missiles and launchers, including:

(i) the number and type of items of missile systems to be eliminated;

(ii) the elimination site;

(iii) for intermediate-range missiles, the location from which such missiles, launchers of such missiles and support equipment associated with such missiles and launchers are moved to the elimination facility; and

(iv) except in the case of support structures, the point of entry to be used by an inspection team conducting an inspection pursuant to paragraph 7 of Article XI of this Treaty and the estimated time of departure of an inspection team from the point of entry to the elimination facility;

(d) notification, no less than ten days in advance, of the scheduled date of the launch, or the scheduled date of the initiation of a series of launches, of intermediate-range missiles for the purpose of their elimination, including:

(i) the type of missiles to be eliminated;

(ii) location of the launch, or, if elimination is by a series of launches, the location of such launches and number of launches in the series;

(iii) the point of entry to be used by an inspection team conducting an inspection pursuant to paragraph 7 of Article XI of this Treaty; and

(iv) the estimated time of departure of an inspection team from the point of entry to the elimination facility;

(e) notification, no later than 48 hours after they occur, of changes in the number of intermediate-range and shorter-range missiles, launchers of such missiles and support structures and support equipment associated with such missiles and launchers resulting from elimination as described in the Protocol on Elimination, including:

(i) the number and type of items of a missile system which were eliminated; and

(ii) the date and location of such elimination; and

(f) notification of transit of intermediate-range or shorter-range missiles or launchers of such missiles, or the movement of training missiles or training launchers for such intermediate-range and shorter-range missiles, no later than 48 hours after it has been completed, including:

(i) the number of missiles or launchers;

(ii) the points, dates and times of departure and arrival;

(iii) the mode of transport; and

(iv) the location and time at that location at least once every four days during the period of transit.

6. Upon entry into force of this Treaty and thereafter, each Party shall notify the other Party, no less than ten days in advance, of the scheduled date and location of the launch of a research and development booster system as described in paragraph 12 of Article VII of this Treaty.

Article X

1. Each Party shall eliminate its intermediate-range and shorter-range missiles and launchers of such missiles and support structures and support equipment associated with such missiles and launchers in accordance

with the procedures set forth in the Protocol on Elimination.

2. Verification by on-site inspection of the elimination of items of missile systems specified in the Protocol on Elimination shall be carried out in accordance with Article XI of this Treaty, the Protocol on Elimination and the Protocol on Inspection.

3. When a Party removes its intermediate-range missiles, launchers of such missiles and support equipment associated with such missiles and launchers from deployment areas to elimination facilities for the purpose of their elimination, it shall do so in complete deployed organizational units. For the United States of America, these units shall be Pershing II batteries and BGM-109G flights. For the Union of Soviet Socialist Republics, these units shall be SS-20 regiments composed of two or three battalions.

4. Elimination of intermediate-range and shorter-range missiles and launchers of such missiles and support equipment associated with such missiles and launchers shall be carried out at the facilities that are specified in the Memorandum of Understanding or notified in accordance with paragraph 5(b) of Article IX of this Treaty, unless eliminated in accordance with Sections IV or V of the Protocol on Elimination. Support structures, associated with the missiles and launchers subject to this Treaty, that are subject to elimination shall be eliminated *in situ*.

5. Each Party shall have the right, during the first six months after entry into force of this Treaty, to eliminate by means of launching no more than 100 of its intermediate-range missiles.

6. Intermediate-range and shorter-range missiles which have been tested prior to entry into force of this Treaty, but never deployed, and which are not existing types of intermediate-range or shorter-range missiles listed in Article III of this Treaty, and launchers of such missiles, shall be eliminated within six months after entry into force of this Treaty in accordance with the procedures set forth in the Protocol on Elimination. Such missiles are:

(a) for the United States of America, missiles of the type designated by the United States of America as the Pershing IB, which is known to the Union of Soviet Socialist Republics by the same designation; and

(b) for the Union of Soviet Socialist Republics, missiles of the type designated by the Union of Soviet Socialist Republics as the RK-55, which is known to the United States of America as the SSC-X-4.

7. Intermediate-range and shorter-range missiles and launchers of such missiles and support structures and support equipment associated with such missiles and launchers shall be considered to be eliminated after completion of the procedures set forth in the Protocol on Elimination and upon the notification provided for in paragraph 5(e) of Article IX of this Treaty.

8. Each Party shall eliminate its deployment areas, missile operating bases and missile support facilities. A Party shall notify the other Party pursuant to paragraph 5(a) of Article IX of this Treaty once the conditions set forth below are fulfilled:

(a) all intermediate-range and shorter-range missiles, launchers of such missiles and support equipment associated with such missiles and launchers located there have been removed;

(b) all support structures associated with such missiles and launchers located there have been eliminated; and

(c) all activity related to production, flight-testing, training, repair, storage or deployment of such missiles and launchers has ceased there.

Such deployment areas, missile operating bases and missile support facilities shall be considered to be eliminated either when they have been inspected pursuant to paragraph 4 of Article XI of this Treaty or when 60 days have elapsed since the date of the scheduled elimination which was notified pursuant to paragraph 5(a) of

Article IX of this Treaty. A deployment area, missile operating base or missile support facility listed in the Memorandum of Understanding that met the above conditions prior to entry into force of this Treaty, and is not included in the initial data exchange pursuant to paragraph 3 of Article IX of this Treaty, shall be considered to be eliminated.

9. If a Party intends to convert a missile operating base listed in the Memorandum of Understanding for use as a base associated with GLBM or GLCM systems not subject to this Treaty, then that Party shall notify the other Party, no less than 30 days in advance of the scheduled date of the initiation of the conversion, of the scheduled date and the purpose for which the base will be converted.

Article XI

1. For the purpose of ensuring verification of compliance with the provisions of this Treaty, each Party shall have the right to conduct on-site inspections. The Parties shall implement on-site inspections in accordance with this Article, the Protocol on Inspection and the Protocol on Elimination.

2. Each Party shall have the right to conduct inspections provided for by this Article both within the territory of the other Party and within the territories of basing countries.

3. Beginning 30 days after entry into force of this Treaty, each Party shall have the right to conduct inspections at all missile operating bases and missile support facilities specified in the Memorandum of Understanding other than missile production facilities, and at all elimination facilities included in the initial data update required by paragraph 3 of Article IX of this Treaty. These inspections shall be completed no later than 90 days after entry into force of this Treaty. The purpose of these inspections shall be to verify the number of missiles, launchers, support structures and support equipment and other data, as of the date of entry into force of this Treaty, provided pursuant to paragraph 3 of Article IX of this Treaty.

4. Each Party shall have the right to conduct inspections to verify the elimination, notified pursuant to paragraph 5(a) of Article IX of this Treaty, of missile operating bases and missile support facilities other than missile production facilities, which are thus no longer subject to inspections pursuant to paragraph 5(a) of this Article. Such an inspection shall be carried out within 60 days after the scheduled date of the elimination of that facility. If a Party conducts an inspection at a particular facility pursuant to paragraph 3 of this Article after the scheduled date of the elimination of that facility, then no additional inspection of that facility pursuant to this paragraph shall be permitted.

5. Each Party shall have the right to conduct inspections pursuant to this paragraph for 13 years after entry into force of this Treaty. Each Party shall have the right to conduct 20 such inspections per calendar year during the first three years after entry into force of this Treaty, 15 such inspections per calendar year during the subsequent five years, and ten such inspections per calendar year during the last five years. Neither Party shall use more than half of its total number of these inspections per calendar year within the territory of any one basing country. Each Party shall have the right to conduct:

(a) inspections, beginning 90 days after entry into force of this Treaty, of missile operating bases, and missile support facilities other than elimination facilities and missile production facilities, to ascertain, according to the categories of data specified in the Memorandum of Understanding, the numbers of missiles, launchers, support structures and support equipment located at each missile operating base or missile support facility at the time of the inspection; and

(b) inspections of former missile operating bases and former missile support facilities eliminated pursuant to paragraph 8 of Article X of this Treaty other than former missile production facilities.

6. Beginning 30 days after entry into force of this Treaty, each Party shall have the right, for 13 years after entry into force of this Treaty, to inspect by means of continuous monitoring:

(a) the portals of any facility of the other Party at which the final assembly of a GLBM using stages, any of which is outwardly similar to a stage of a solid-propellant GLBM listed in Article III of this Treaty, is accomplished; or

(b) if a Party has no such facility, the portals of an agreed former missile production facility at which existing types of intermediate-range or shorter-range GLBMs were produced.

The Party whose facility is to be inspected pursuant to this paragraph shall ensure that the other Party is able to establish a permanent continuous monitoring system at that facility within six months after entry into force of this Treaty or within six months of initiation of the process of final assembly described in subparagraph (a). If, after the end of the second year after entry into force of this Treaty, neither Party conducts the process of final assembly described in subparagraph (a) for a period of 12 consecutive months, then neither Party shall have the right to inspect by means of continuous monitoring any missile production facility of the other Party unless the process of final assembly as described in subparagraph (a) is initiated again. Upon entry into force of this Treaty, the facilities to be inspected by continuous monitoring shall be: in accordance with subparagraph (b), for the United States of America, Hercules Plant Number 1, at Magna, Utah; in accordance with subparagraph (a), for the Union of Soviet Socialist Republics, the Votkinsk Machine Building Plant, Udmurt Autonomous Soviet Socialist Republic, Russian Soviet Federative Socialist Republic.

7. Each Party shall conduct inspections of the process of elimination, including elimination of intermediate-range missiles by means of launching, of intermediate-range and shorter-range missiles and launchers of such missiles and support equipment associated with such missiles and launchers carried out at elimination facilities in accordance with Article X of this Treaty and the Protocol on Elimination. Inspectors conducting inspections provided for in this paragraph shall determine that the processes specified for the elimination of the missiles, launchers and support equipment have been completed.

8. Each Party shall have the right to conduct inspections to confirm the completion of the process of elimination of intermediate-range and shorter-range missiles and launchers of such missiles and support equipment associated with such missiles and launchers eliminated pursuant to Section V of the Protocol on Elimination, and of training missiles, training missile stages, training launch canisters and training launchers eliminated pursuant to Sections II, IV and V of the Protocol on Elimination.

Article XII

1. For the purpose of ensuring verification of compliance with the provisions of this Treaty, each Party shall use national technical means of verification at its disposal in a manner consistent with generally recognized principles of international law.

2. Neither Party shall:

(a) interfere with national technical means of verification of the other Party operating in accordance with paragraph 1 of this Article; or

(b) use concealment measures which impede verification of compliance with the provisions of this Treaty by national technical means of verification carried out in accordance with paragraph 1 of this Article. This obligation does not apply to cover or concealment practices, within a deployment area, associated with normal training, maintenance and operations, including the use of environmental shelters to protect missiles and launchers.

3. To enhance observation by national technical means of verification, each Party shall have the right until a treaty between the Parties reducing and limiting strategic offensive arms enters into force, but in any event for no more than three years after entry into force of this Treaty, to request the implementation of cooperative measures at deployment bases for road-mobile GLBMs with a range capability in excess of 5500 kilometers, which are not former missile operating bases eliminated pursuant to paragraph 8 of Article X of this Treaty. The Party making such a request shall inform the other Party of the deployment base at which cooperative measures shall be implemented. The Party whose base is to be observed shall carry out the following cooperative measures:

(a) No later than six hours after such a request, the Party shall have opened the roofs of all fixed structures for launchers located at the base, removed completely all missiles on launchers from such fixed structures for launchers and displayed such missiles on launchers in the open without using concealment measures; and

(b) The Party shall leave the roofs open and the missiles on launchers in place until twelve hours have elapsed from the time of the receipt of a request for such an observation.

Each Party shall have the right to make six such requests per calendar year. Only one deployment base shall be subject to these cooperative measures at any one time.

Article XIII

1. To promote the objectives and implementation of the provisions of this Treaty, the Parties hereby establish the Special Verification Commission. The Parties agree that, if either Party so requests, they shall meet within the framework of the Special Verification Commission to:

(a) resolve questions relating to compliance with the obligations assumed; and

(b) agree upon such measures as may be necessary to improve the viability and effectiveness of this Treaty.

2. The Parties shall use the Nuclear Risk Reduction Centers, which provide for continuous communication between the Parties, to:

(a) exchange data and provide notifications as required by paragraphs 3, 4, 5 and 6 of Article IX of this Treaty and the Protocol on Elimination;

(b) provide and receive the information required by paragraph 9 of Article X of this Treaty;

(c) provide and receive notifications of inspections as required by Article XI of this Treaty and the Protocol on Inspection; and

(d) provide and receive requests for cooperative measures as provided for in paragraph 3 of Article XII of this Treaty.

Article XIV

The Parties shall comply with this Treaty and shall not assume any international obligations or undertakings which would conflict with its provisions.

Article XV

1. This Treaty shall be of unlimited duration.

2. Each Party shall, in exercising its national sovereignty, have the right to withdraw from this Treaty if it decides that extraordinary events

related to the subject matter of this Treaty have jeopardized its supreme interests. It shall give notice of its decision to withdraw to the other Party six months prior to withdrawal from this Treaty. Such notice shall include a statement of the extraordinary events the notifying Party regards as having jeopardized its supreme interests.

Article XVI

Each Party may propose amendments to this Treaty. Agreed amendments shall enter into force in accordance with the procedures set forth in Article XVII governing the entry into force of this Treaty.

Article XVII

1. This Treaty, including the Memorandum of Understanding and Protocols, which form an integral part thereof, shall be subject to ratification in accordance with the constitutional procedures of each Party. This Treaty shall enter into force on the date of the exchange of instruments of ratification.

2. This Treaty shall be registered pursuant to Article 102 of the Chapter of the United Nations.

DONE at Washington on December 8, 1987, in two copies, each in the English and Russian languages, both texts being equally authentic.

FOR THE UNITED STATES OF AMERICA

RONALD REAGAN

President of the United States of America

FOR THE UNION OF SOVIET SOCIALIST REPUBLICS

M. GORBACHEV

General Secretary of the Central Committee of the CPSU

Appendix 13B. Memorandum of Understanding regarding the establishment of the data base for the Treaty

Pursuant to and in implementation of the Treaty Between the Union of Soviet Socialist Republics and the United States of America on the Elimination of Their Intermediate-Range and Shorter-Range Missiles of December 8, 1987, hereinafter referred to as the Treaty, the Parties have exchanged data current as of November 1, 1987, on intermediate-range and shorter-range missiles and launchers of such missiles and support structures and support equipment associated with such missiles and launchers.

I. Definitions

For the purposes of this Memorandum of Understanding, the Treaty, the Protocol on Elimination and the Protocol on Inspection:

1. The term "missile production facility" means a facility for the assembly or production of solid-propellant intermediate-range or shorter-range GLBMs, or existing types of GLCMs.

2. The term "missile repair facility" means a facility at which repair or maintenance of intermediate-range or shorter-range missiles takes place other than inspection and maintenance conducted at a missile operating base.

3. The term "launcher production facility" means a facility for final assembly of launchers of intermediate-range or shorter-range missiles.

4. The term "launcher repair facility" means a facility at which repair or maintenance of launchers of intermediate-range or shorter-range missiles takes place other than inspection and maintenance conducted at a missile operating base.

5. The term "test range" means an area at which flight-testing of intermediate-range or shorter-range missiles takes place.

6. The term "training facility" means a facility, not at a missile operating base, at which personnel are trained in the use of intermediate-range or shorter-range missiles or launchers of such missiles and at which launchers of such missiles are located.

7. The term "missile storage facility" means a facility, not at a missile operating base, at which intermediate-range or shorter-range missiles or stages of such missiles are stored.

8. The term "launcher storage facility" means a facility, not at a missile operating base, at which launchers of intermediate-range or shorter-range missiles are stored.

9. The term "elimination facility" means a facility at which intermediate-range or shorter-range missiles, missile stages and launchers of such missiles or support equipment associated with such missiles or launchers are eliminated.

10. The term "support equipment" means unique vehicles and mobile or transportable equipment that support a deployed intermediate-range or shorter-range missile or a launcher of such a missile. Support equipment shall include full-scale inert training missiles, full-scale inert training missile stages, full-scale inert training launch canisters, and training launchers not capable of launching a

missile. A listing of such support equipment associated with each existing type of missile, and launchers of such missiles, except for training equipment, is contained in Section VI of this Memorandum of Understanding.

11. The term "support structure" means a unique fixed structure used to support deployed intermediate-range missiles or launchers of such missiles. A listing of such support structures associated with each existing type of missile, and launchers of such missiles, except for training equipment, is contained in Section VI of this Memorandum of Understanding.

12. The term "research and development launch site" means a facility at which research and development booster systems are launched.

II. Total Numbers of Intermediate-Range and Shorter-Range Missiles and Launchers of Such Missiles Subject to the Treaty

1. The numbers of intermediate-range missiles and launchers of such missiles for each Party are as follow:

	USA	USSR
Deployed missiles	429	470
Non-deployed missiles	260	356
Aggregate number of deployed and non-deployed missiles	689	826
Aggregate number of second stages	236	650
Deployed launchers	214	484
Non-deployed launchers	68	124
Aggregate number of deployed and non-deployed launchers	282	608

2. The numbers of shorter-range missiles and launchers of such missiles for each Party are as follow:

	USA	USSR
Deployed missiles	0	387
Non-deployed missiles	170[178]	539
Aggregate number of deployed and non-deployed missiles	170[178]	926
Aggregate number of second stages	175[182]	726
Deployed launchers	0	197
Non-deployed launchers	1	40
Aggregate number of deployed and non-deployed launchers	1	237

III. Intermediate-Range Missiles, Launchers of Such Missiles and Support Structures and Support Equipment Associated With Such Missiles and Launchers

1. Deployed

The following are the deployment areas, missile operating bases, their locations and the numbers, for each Party of all deployed intermediate-range missiles listed as existing types in Article III of the Treaty, launchers of such missiles and the support structures and support equipment associated with such missiles and launchers. Site diagrams, to include boundaries and center coordinates, of each listed missile operating base are appended to this Memorandum of Understanding.[1] The boundaries of deployment areas are indicated by specifying geographic coordinates, connected by straight lines or linear landmarks, to include national boundaries, rivers, railroads or highways.

---

[1] See the sample of site diagrams at the end of appendix 13B.

410 SPECIAL FEATURES

(a) UNITED STATES OF AMERICA

(i) Pershing II

Deployment Area One
The Federal Republic of Germany
Boundaries:
The territory of The Federal Republic of Germany bounded on the north by 51 degrees 00 minutes 00 seconds north latitude; on the east by 012 degrees 00 minutes 00 seconds east longitude; on the south by 48 degrees 00 minutes 00 seconds north latitude; and within the national boundaries of The Federal Republic of Germany.

	Missiles	Launchers	Support Structures and Equipment	
Missile Operating Bases				
Schwaebisch-Gmuend 48 48 54 N 009 48 29 E	40 (includes 4 spares)	36	Launch Pad Shelter Training Missile Stage	0 24
Neu Ulm 48 22 40 N 010 00 45 E	40 (includes 4 spares)	43 (includes 7 spares)	Launch Pad Shelter Training Missile Stage	0 24
Waldheide-Neckarsulm 49 07 45 N 009 16 31 E	40 (includes 4 spares)	36	Launch Pad Shelter Training Missile Stage	0 24

(ii) BGM-109G

Deployment Area One
The United Kingdom of Great Britain and Northern Ireland

THE INF TREATY   411

Boundaries:
The territory of The United Kingdom bounded on the north by 52 degrees 40 minutes 00 seconds north latitude; on the west by 003 degrees 30 minutes 00 seconds west longitude; on the south by the English Channel; and on the east by the English Channel and the North Sea.

Missile Operating Base
Greenham Common
51 22 35 N   001 18 12 W

101 with launch canister (includes 5 spares)	29 (includes 5 spares)
Training Missile	0
Training Launch Canister	7

Deployment Area Two
The United Kingdom of Great Britain and Northern Ireland
Boundaries:
The territory of The United Kingdom bounded on the north by 53 degrees 45 minutes 00 seconds north latitude; on the west by 002 degrees 45 minutes 00 seconds west longitude; on the south by 51 degrees 05 minutes 00 seconds north latitude; and on the east by the English Channel and the North Sea.

Missile Operating Base
Molesworth
52 23 00 N   000 25 35 W

18* with launch canister	6*
Training Missile	0
Training Launch Canister	7

*In preparation for operational status.

412 SPECIAL FEATURES

	Missiles	Launchers	Support Structures and Equipment		

Deployment Area
The Republic of Italy
Boundaries:
 The territory of The Republic of Italy within the boundaries of the Island of Sicily.

Missile Operating Base
Comiso
36 59 44 N   014 36 34 E

| | 108 with launch canister (includes 12 spares) | 31 (includes 7 spares) | Training Missile Training Launch Canister | 0 7 |

Deployment Area
The Kingdom of Belgium
Boundaries:
 The territory of The Kingdom of Belgium.

Missile Operating Base
Florennes
50 13 35 N   004 39 00 E

| | 20 with launch canister (includes 4 spares) | 12 (includes 8 spares) | Training Missile Training Launch Canister | 0 7 |

Deployment Area Two
The Federal Republic of Germany
Boundaries:
 The territory of The Federal Republic of Germany bounded on the north by 51 degrees 25 minutes 00 seconds north latitude; on the east by 009 degrees 30 minutes 00 seconds east longitude; on the south by 48 degrees 43 minutes 00 seconds north latitude; and on the

west by the national boundaries of The Federal Republic of Germany.

Missile Operating Base
Wueschheim
50 02 33 N   007 25 06 E **[007 25 40 E]**   62 with launch canister (includes 14 spares)   ,31**[21]** (includes 9 spares)   Training Missile   1
Training Launch Canister   10

Deployment Area
The Kingdom of the Netherlands
Boundaries:
The territory of The Kingdom of the Netherlands bounded on the north by 52 degrees 30 minutes 00 seconds north latitude and within the national boundaries of The Kingdom of the Netherlands.

Missile Operating Base
Woensdrecht
51 26 12 N   004 21 15 E   0 with launch canister   0   Training Missile   0
Training Launch Canister   0

(b) UNION OF SOVIET SOCIALIST REPUBLICS

(i) SS-20

Deployment Area
Postavy
55 12 13 N   027 00 00 E
54 52 47   026 41 18
54 43 58   026 04 07
55 01 13   026 03 43

414 SPECIAL FEATURES

	Missiles	Launchers	Support Structures and Equipment	
Missile Operating Base				
Postavy				
55 09 47 N 026 54 21 E	9	9	Launch Canister	9
			Missile Transporter Vehicle	0
			Fixed Structure for Launcher	9
			Training Missile	0
Deployment Area				
Vetrino				
55 28 44 N 028 42 29 E				
55 01 03 028 15 03				
55 01 16 027 48 46				
55 16 22 027 49 05				
Missile Operating Base				
Vetrino				
55 24 19 N 028 33 29 E	9	9	Launch Canister	9
			Missile Transporter Vehicle	0
			Fixed Structure for Launcher	9
			Training Missile	0
Deployment Area				
Polotsk				
55 37 36 N 028 23 49 E				
55 28 07 029 20 25				
54 32 15 029 09 47				
54 39 32 028 10 40				
Missile Operating Base				
Polotsk				
55 22 34 N 028 44 17 E	9	9	Launch Canister	9
			Missile Transporter Vehicle	0
			Fixed Structure for Launcher	9
			Training Missile	0

THE INF TREATY

Deployment Area
Smorgon'
54 37 43 N   026 52 34 E
54 22 37   026 52 37
54 37 18   025 41 58
54 45 21   026 15 13

Missile Operating Base
Smorgon'
54 36 16 N   026 23 05 E

Launch Canister	9
Missile Transporter Vehicle	0
Fixed Structure for Launcher	9
Training Missile	0

Deployment Area
Smorgon'
54 29 01 N   026 26 40 E
54 05 04   025 53 59
54 24 14   025 31 18
54 35 27   026 19 10

Missile Operating Base
Smorgon'
54 31 36 N   026 17 20 E

Launch Canister	9
Missile Transporter Vehicle	0
Fixed Structure for Launcher	9
Training Missile	0

Deployment Area
Lida
53 45 24 N   025 29 02 E
53 34 00   024 49 35
53 42 25   024 38 15
53 58 05   025 10 17

Missile Operating Base
Lida
53 47 39 N   025 20 27 E

Launch Canister	9
Missile Transporter Vehicle	0
Fixed Structure for Launcher	9
Training Missile	0

416 SPECIAL FEATURES

	Missiles	Launchers	Support Structures and Equipment	
Deployment Area				
Gezgaly				
53 38 53 N 025 25 38 E				
53 23 48 025 26 12				
53 12 46 025 08 38				
53 22 57 024 35 43				
Missile Operating Base				
Gezgaly	6	6	Launch Canister	6
53 32 50 N 025 16 48 E			Missile Transporter Vehicle	0
			Fixed Structure for Launcher	6
			Training Missile	0
Deployment Area				
Slonim				
52 58 15 N 025 55 42 E				
52 45 02 025 31 08				
53 04 08 025 09 00				
53 08 45 025 30 20				
Missile Operating Base				
Slonim	9	9	Launch Canister	9
52 55 54 N 025 21 59 E			Missile Transporter Vehicle	0
			Fixed Structure for Launcher	9
			Training Missile	0
Deployment Area				
Ruzhany				
52 55 21 N 024 58 40 E				
52 46 32 024 48 25				
52 45 52 024 16 26				
53 07 34 024 22 14				
Missile Operating Base				
Ruzhany	6	6	Launch Canister	6
52 49 29 N 024 45 45 E			Missile Transporter Vehicle	0
			Fixed Structure for Launcher	6
			Training Missile	0

THE INF TREATY 417

Deployment Area
Zasimovichi
52 37 55 N   024 48 50 E
52 22 00   024 10 52
52 32 36   023 56 54
52 45 52   024 16 26

Missile Operating Base
Zasimovichi
52 30 38 N   024 08 43 E

Launch Canister	6	6
Missile Transporter Vehicle	0	
Fixed Structure for Launcher	6	
Training Missile	0	

Deployment Area
Mozyr'
52 05 31 N   029 13 04 E
51 39 05   029 39 31
51 42 00   029 01 30
51 52 57   028 51 32

Missile Operating Base
Mozyr'
52 02 27 N   029 11 15 E

Launch Canister	9	9
Missile Transporter Vehicle	0	
Fixed Structure for Launcher	9	
Training Missile	0	

Deployment Area
Petrikov
52 16 29 N   029 03 04 E
52 08 06   028 48 40
52 08 33   028 13 37
52 27 47   028 28 17

Missile Operating Base
Petrikov
52 10 29 N   028 34 52 E

Launch Canister	6	6
Missile Transporter Vehicle	0	
Fixed Structure for Launcher	6	
Training Missile	0	

SPECIAL FEATURES

	Missiles	Launchers	Support Structures and Equipment	
Deployment Area Zhitkovichi				
52 23 40 N 028 10 31 E				
52 08 35 028 10 07				
52 08 55 027 14 01				
52 24 01 027 14 06				
Missile Operating Base Zhitkovichi			Launch Canister	6
52 11 36 N 027 48 07 E	6	6	Missile Transporter Vehicle	0
			Fixed Structure for Launcher	6
			Training Missile	0
Deployment Area Rechitsa				
52 26 34 N 030 21 10 E				
52 05 27 030 43 26				
51 47 47 030 23 27				
52 13 08 030 00 53				
Missile Operating Base Rechitsa			Launch Canister	6
52 11 58 N 030 07 11 E	6	6	Missile Transporter Vehicle	0
			Fixed Structure for Launcher	6
			Training Missile	0
Deployment Area Slutsk				
53 28 29 N 027 57 50 E				
53 02 31 028 07 59				
53 13 35 027 25 09				
53 28 40 027 28 55				
Missile Operating Base Slutsk			Launch Canister	9
53 14 20 N 027 42 15 E	9	9	Missile Transporter Vehicle	0
			Fixed Structure for Launcher	9
			Training Missile	0

THE INF TREATY 419

Deployment Area
Lutsk
51 08 14 N   025 54 51 E
50 50 45   025 34 49
51 16 24   025 16 49
51 20 51   025 26 59

Missile Operating Base
Lutsk
50 56 07 N   025 36 26 E

Launch Canister	9	9
Missile Transporter Vehicle		0
Fixed Structure for Launcher		9
Training Missile		0

Deployment Area
Lutsk
51 10 05 N   025 27 21 E
50 43 54   025 07 49
50 47 35   024 33 38
51 11 22   024 35 49

Missile Operating Base
Lutsk
50 50 06 N   025 04 02 E

Launch Canister	9	9
Missile Transporter Vehicle		0
Fixed Structure for Launcher		9
Training Missile		0

Deployment Area
Brody
50 14 00 N   025 29 11 E
50 00 46   025 09 30
50 17 32   024 41 55
50 22 10   024 58 33

Missile Operating Base
Brody
50 06 09 N   025 12 14 E

Launch Canister	9	9
Missile Transporter Vehicle		0
Fixed Structure for Launcher		9
Training Missile		0

420 SPECIAL FEATURES

	Missiles	Launchers	Support Structures and Equipment	
Deployment Area Chervonograd 50 41 07 N 024 33 58 E 50 13 10 024 38 45 50 19 02 024 11 30 50 36 26 024 17 15				
Missile Operating Base Chervonograd 50 22 45 N 024 18 16 E	9	9	Launch Canister Missile Transporter Vehicle Fixed Structure for Launcher Training Missile	9 0 9 0
Deployment Area Slavuta 50 18 55 N 027 03 22 E 50 08 07 027 03 21 50 07 59 026 16 22 50 29 38 026 29 34				
Missile Operating Base Slavuta 50 17 05 N 026 41 31 E	9	9	Launch Canister Missile Transporter Vehicle Fixed Structure for Launcher Training Missile	9 0 9 0
Deployment Area Belokorovichi 51 10 19 N 028 12 04 E 50 51 05 027 51 07 51 21 28 027 01 43 51 21 22 027 37 54				
Missile Operating Base Belokorovichi 51 10 45 N 028 03 20 E	9	9	Launch Canister Missile Transporter Vehicle Fixed Structure for Launcher Training Missile	9 0 9 0

THE INF TREATY

Deployment Area
Lipniki
51 11 38 N   029 10 28 E
50 52 28   028 55 56
51 05 53   028 22 14
51 20 57   028 26 07

Missile Operating Base
Lipniki
51 12 22 N   028 26 37 E   9   9   Launch Canister   9
                                              Missile Transporter Vehicle 0
                                              Fixed Structure for Launcher 9
                                              Training Missile   0

Deployment Area
Vysokaya Pech'
50 29 13 N   028 21 10 E
50 09 49   028 20 37
50 10 10   027 40 19
50 29 33   027 43 58

Missile Operating Base
Vysokaya Pech'
50 10 11 N   028 16 22 E   6   6   Launch Canister   6
                                              Missile Transporter Vehicle 0
                                              Fixed Structure for Launcher 6
                                              Training Missile   0

Deployment Area
Vysokaya Pech'
50 13 33 N   029 01 05 E
49 56 07   029 10 23
49 52 42   028 06 47
50 07 39   028 20 33

Missile Operating Base
Vysokaya Pech'
50 05 43 N   028 22 09 E   6   6   Launch Canister   6
                                              Missile Transporter Vehicle 0
                                              Fixed Structure for Launcher 6
                                              Training Missile   0

	Missiles	Launchers	Support Structures and Equipment	
Deployment Area Korosten' 50 54 31 N 029 02 51 E 50 41 34 029 02 16 50 42 05 028 28 20 50 55 01 028 28 44				
Missile Operating Base Korosten' 50 52 22 N 028 31 17 E	6	6	Launch Canister Missile Transporter Vehicle Fixed Structure for Launcher Training Missile	6 0 6 0
Deployment Area Lebedin 50 35 26 N 034 41 41 E 50 12 10 034 00 31 50 14 25 033 50 28 50 35 42 034 21 21				
Missile Operating Base Lebedin 50 33 06 N 034 26 02 E	9	9	Launch Canister Missile Transporter Vehicle Fixed Structure for Launcher Training Missile	9 0 9 0
Deployment Area Glukhov 52 02 16 N 033 52 28 E 51 36 21 033 55 26 51 34 22 033 27 42 52 02 21 033 38 28				
Missile Operating Base Glukhov 51 41 00 N 033 30 56 E	9	9	Launch Canister Missile Transporter Vehicle Fixed Structure for Launcher Training Missile	9 0 9 0

Deployment Area
Glukhov
 51 42 59 N   033 27 47 E
 51 23 31   033 37 56
 51 23 37   032 56 33
 51 43 02   033 10 25

Missile Operating Base
Glukhov
 51 36 44 N   033 29 17 E   Launch Canister   9
                                Missile Transporter Vehicle   0
                                Fixed Structure for Launcher   9
                                Training Missile   0

Deployment Area
Akhtyrka
 50 17 58 N   034 54 32 E
 49 49 59   034 50 05
 50 10 03   033 57 06
 50 18 24   034 24 13

Missile Operating Base
Akhtyrka
 50 16 01 N   034 49 53 E   Launch Canister   9
                                Missile Transporter Vehicle   0
                                Fixed Structure for Launcher   9
                                Training Missile   0

Deployment Area
Akhtyrka
 50 10 43 N   035 34 34 E
 49 54 08   035 00 16
 50 18 24   034 24 13
 50 26 42   034 48 07

Missile Operating Base
Akhtyrka
 50 21 59 N   034 57 03 E   Launch Canister   9
                                Missile Transporter Vehicle   0
                                Fixed Structure for Launcher   9
                                Training Missile   0

424   SPECIAL FEATURES

	Missiles	Launchers	Support Structures and Equipment	
Deployment Area				
Novosibirsk				
55 51 09 N 083 52 28 E				
55 14 33 083 49 49				
55 21 52 083 08 41				
55 30 29 083 09 09				
Missile Operating Base				
Novosibirsk	9	9	Launch Canister	9
55 22 05 N 083 13 52 E			Missile Transporter Vehicle	0
			Fixed Structure for Launcher	9
			Training Missile	0
Deployment Area				
Novosibirsk				
55 06 17 N 083 34 11 E				
54 57 40 083 33 38				
55 04 53 082 52 45				
55 24 16 082 53 40				
Missile Operating Base				
Novosibirsk	9	9	Launch Canister	9
55 22 57 N 082 55 16 E			Missile Transporter Vehicle	0
			Fixed Structure for Launcher	9
			Training Missile	0
Deployment Area				
Novosibirsk				
55 31 47 N 084 08 57 E				
55 13 26 082 56 55				
55 20 01 082 49 41				
55 40 13 084 00 42				
Missile Operating Base				
Novosibirsk	9	9	Launch Canister	9
55 19 32 N 082 56 18 E			Missile Transporter Vehicle	0
			Fixed Structure for Launcher	9
			Training Missile	0

THE INF TREATY 425

Deployment Area
Novosibirsk
55 08 01 N   083 53 07 E
54 52 56   083 52 02
55 11 17   082 56 49
55 22 00   083 01 07

Missile Operating Base
Novosibirsk
55 18 44 N   083 01 38 E

Launch Canister	9
Missile Transporter Vehicle	0
Fixed Structure for Launcher	9
Training Missile	0

Deployment Area
Novosibirsk
55 03 58 N   084 18 27 E
54 53 12   084 19 10
55 04 49   082 56 30
55 22 00   083 01 07

Missile Operating Base
Novosibirsk
55 19 07 N   083 09 59 E

Launch Canister	9
Missile Transporter Vehicle	0
Fixed Structure for Launcher	9
Training Missile	0

Deployment Area
Drovyanaya
51 44 02 N   113 08 33 E
51 22 28   113 07 32
51 22 49   112 46 52
51 44 16   112 54 39

Missile Operating Base
Drovyanaya
51 27 20 N   113 03 42 E

Launch Canister	9
Missile Transporter Vehicle	0
Fixed Structure for Launcher	9
Training Missile	0

	Missiles	Launchers	Support Structures and Equipment	
Deployment Area Drovyanaya 51 37 34 N 113 08 14 E 51 22 28 113 07 32 51 18 39 112 36 23 51 27 14 112 40 08				
Missile Operating Base Drovyanaya 51 26 10 N 113 02 43 E	9	9	Launch Canister Missile Transporter Vehicle Fixed Structure for Launcher Training Missile	9 0 9 0
Deployment Area Drovyanaya 51 24 52 N 112 53 51 E 51 20 36 112 50 13 51 18 54 112 15 44 51 23 13 112 15 51				
Missile Operating Base Drovyanaya 51 22 59 N 112 49 55 E	9	9	Launch Canister Missile Transporter Vehicle Fixed Structure for Launcher Training Missile	9 0 9 0
Deployment Area Drovyanaya 51 26 54 N 113 00 50 E 51 18 13 113 03 54 51 18 47 112 26 03 51 29 39 112 19 29				
Missile Operating Base Drovyanaya 51 20 18 N 113 00 54 E	9	9	Launch Canister Missile Transporter Vehicle Fixed Structure for Launcher Training Missile	9 0 9 0

THE INF TREATY

Deployment Area
Drovyanaya
51 33 19 N   113 04 35 E
51 22 32   113 04 05
51 22 49   112 46 52
51 33 36   112 47 17

Missile Operating Base
Drovyanaya
51 23 49 N   112 52 13 E   9   Launch Canister   9
                                 Missile Transporter Vehicle 0
                                 Fixed Structure for Launcher 9
                                 Training Missile   0

Deployment Area
Barnaul
53 54 32 N   084 01 02 E
53 43 46   084 01 48
53 35 30   083 43 07
53 44 16   083 36 24

Missile Operating Base
Barnaul
53 46 08 N   083 57 11 E   9   Launch Canister   9
                                 Missile Transporter Vehicle 0
                                 Fixed Structure for Launcher 9
                                 Training Missile   0

Deployment Area
Barnaul
53 29 21 N   084 31 45 E
52 58 43   083 47 57
53 13 47   083 48 56
53 29 02   084 17 18

Missile Operating Base
Barnaul
53 18 21 N   084 08 47 E   9   Launch Canister   9
                                 Missile Transporter Vehicle 0
                                 Fixed Structure for Launcher 9
                                 Training Missile   0

		Missiles	Launchers	Support Structures and Equipment	
Deployment Area					
Barnaul					
53 16 38 N	084 43 16 E				
52 59 32	084 51 20				
52 55 09	084 47 58				
53 16 02	084 14 31				
Missile Operating Base					
Barnaul		9	9	Launch Canister	9
53 13 29 N	084 40 10 E			Missile Transporter Vehicle	0
				Fixed Structure for Launcher	9
				Training Missile	0
Deployment Area					
Barnaul					
53 27 33 N	084 49 55 E				
53 16 42	084 46 52				
53 16 02	084 14 31				
53 26 58	084 21 02				
Missile Operating Base					
Barnaul		9	9	Launch Canister	9
53 18 47 N	084 30 27 E			Missile Transporter Vehicle	0
				Fixed Structure for Launcher	9
				Training Missile	0
Deployment Area					
Kansk					
56 32 14 N	096 12 14 E				
56 15 16	095 34 54				
56 28 30	095 20 13				
56 34 39	095 36 13				
Missile Operating Base					
Kansk		9	9	Launch Canister	9
56 22 31 N	095 28 35 E			Missile Transporter Vehicle	0
				Fixed Structure for Launcher	9
				Training Missile	0

Deployment Area
Kansk
   56 30 47 N   095 12 33 E
   56 19 53   095 19 41
   56 13 45   094 59 58
   56 31 03   094 56 58

Missile Operating Base
Kansk
   56 20 09 N   095 16 34 E   9   Launch Canister   9
                                                       Missile Transporter Vehicle   0
                                                       Fixed Structure for Launcher   9
                                                       Training Missile   0

Deployment Area
Kansk
   56 19 29 N   096 20 56 E
   56 08 43   096 21 41
   56 08 17   096 02 24
   56 19 14   095 50 42

Missile Operating Base
Kansk
   56 11 19 N   096 03 13 E   9   Launch Canister   9
                                                       Missile Transporter Vehicle   0
                                                       Fixed Structure for Launcher   9
                                                       Training Missile   0

Deployment Area
Kansk
   56 14 50 N   096 05 46 E
   55 59 57   096 14 35
   55 59 41   096 03 03
   56 15 00   095 46 30

Missile Operating Base
Kansk
   56 02 19 N   096 04 58 E   9   Launch Canister   9
                                                       Missile Transporter Vehicle   0
                                                       Fixed Structure for Launcher   9
                                                       Training Missile   0

430 SPECIAL FEATURES

(ii) SS-4

	Missiles	Launchers	Support Structures and Equipment	
Deployment Area				
Sovetsk				
55 05 33 N 021 52 38 E				
55 03 22 021 56 20				
54 57 04 021 29 58				
55 01 23 021 26 16				
Missile Operating Base				
Sovetsk	5	6 (Launch Stand)	Missile Transporter Vehicle	11
54 59 07 N 021 36 36 E			Missile Erector	7
			Propellant Tank	52
			Training Missile	6
Deployment Area				
Gusev				
54 46 02 N 022 07 07 E				
54 24 14 022 28 42				
54 20 01 022 21 10				
54 43 58 021 55 53				
Missile Operating Base				
Gusev	5	7 (Launch Stand)	Missile Transporter Vehicle	12
54 43 59 N 022 03 27 E			Missile Erector	7
			Propellant Tank	52
			Training Missile	7

THE INF TREATY

Deployment Area
Malorita
51 53 50 N 024 05 39 E
51 43 09   024 09 49
51 42 59   023 57 07
51 53 45   023 57 50

Missile Operating Base
Malorita
51 51 47 N 024 01 55 E   6 (Launch Stand)   Missile Transporter Vehicle   14
                                              Missile Erector   7
                                              Propellant Tank   48
                                              Training Missile   5

Deployment Area
Pinsk
52 15 03 N 025 49 43 E
52 04 09   025 39 30
52 03 56   025 22 00
52 14 54   025 35 40

Missile Operating Base
Pinsk
52 10 56 N 025 41 27 E   5 (Launch Stand)   Missile Transporter Vehicle   13
                                              Missile Erector   6
                                              Propellant Tank   47
                                              Training Missile   6

Deployment Area
Vyru
57 49 33 N 027 00 00 E
57 43 05   027 00 00
57 43 04   026 43 54
57 49 32   026 43 51

Missile Operating Base
Vyru
57 45 47 N 026 47 13 E   6 (Launch Stand)   Missile Transporter Vehicle   11
                                              Missile Erector   5
                                              Propellant Tank   51
                                              Training Missile   6

	Missiles	Launchers	Support Structures and Equipment	
Deployment Area Aluksne				
57 25 51 N 026 56 00 E				
57 21 32 026 56 01				
57 17 12 026 40 06				
57 25 49 026 40 01				
Missile Operating Base Aluksne				
57 25 04 N 026 49 46 E	5	6 (Launch Stand)	Missile Transporter Vehicle	12
			Missile Erector	6
			Propellant Tank	45
			Training Missile	6
Deployment Area Ostrov				
57 38 21 N 028 20 22 E				
57 21 04 028 23 43				
57 21 14 028 07 47				
57 38 28 028 08 19				
Missile Operating Base Ostrov				
57 31 53 N 028 12 19 E	5	8 (Launch Stand)	Missile Transporter Vehicle	12
			Missile Erector	7
			Propellant Tank	48
			Training Missile	6
Deployment Area Karmelava				
55 06 12 N 024 22 04 E				
54 57 49 024 33 51				
54 55 00 024 04 05				
55 01 28 024 03 36				
Missile Operating Base Karmelava				
55 00 51 N 024 14 16 E	5	5 (Launch Stand)	Missile Transporter Vehicle	13
			Missile Erector	6
			Propellant Tank	47
			Training Missile	6

THE INF TREATY

Deployment Area
Ukmerge
55 17 41 N   024 59 06 E
55 04 25   024 40 58
55 08 35   024 33 12
55 19 43   024 51 26

Missile Operating Base
Ukmerge
55 07 51 N   024 38 36 E

5

6 (Launch Stand)

Missile Transporter Vehicle 14
Missile Erector   7
Propellant Tank   50
Training Missile   6

Deployment Area
Taurage
55 18 07 N   022 30 42 E
55 09 30   022 30 22
55 03 10   022 18 52
55 13 35   022 21 01

Missile Operating Base
Taurage
55 04 58 N   022 19 38 E

5

6 (Launch Stand)

Missile Transporter Vehicle 12
Missile Erector   6
Propellant Tank   47
Training Missile   6

Deployment Area
Kolomyya
48 45 01 N   024 55 59 E
48 36 23   024 56 20
48 36 04   024 40 04
48 44 42   024 39 40

Missile Operating Base
Kolomyya
48 39 32 N   024 48 04 E

5

6 (Launch Stand)

Missile Transporter Vehicle 12
Missile Erector   6
Propellant Tank   46
Training Missile   7

	Missiles	Launchers	Support Structures and Equipment	
Deployment Area Stryy 49 19 59 N 023 58 46 E 49 11 22 023 58 29 49 21 09 023 31 57 49 29 46 023 32 24				
Missile Operating Base Stryy 49 25 23 N 023 34 56 E	5	7 (Launch Stand)	Missile Transporter Vehicle Missile Erector Propellant Tank Training Missile	12 7 49 7
Deployment Area Skala–Podol'skaya 48 54 37 N 026 17 26 E 48 48 09 026 17 32 48 48 02 026 01 12 48 54 30 026 01 04				
Missile Operating Base Skala–Podol'skaya 48 51 02 N 026 08 36 E	5	6 (Launch Stand)	Missile Transporter Vehicle Missile Erector Propellant Tank Training Missile	12 6 46 5

2. Non-Deployed

The following are missile support facilities, their locations and the numbers, for each Party of all non-deployed intermediate-range missiles listed as existing types in Article III of the Treaty, launchers of such missiles and support structures and support equipment associated with such missiles and launchers. Site diagrams for agreed missile support facilities, to include boundaries and center coordinates, are appended to this Memorandum of Understanding.

THE INF TREATY

	Missiles	Launchers	Support Structures and Equipment	

(a) UNITED STATES OF AMERICA

(i) Pershing II

Missile Production Facilities:

Hercules Plant #1 Magna, Utah 40 39 40 N 112 03 14 W	0	0	Launch Pad Shelter Training Missile Stage	0 0

Launcher Production Facilities:

Martin Marietta Middle River, Maryland 39 35 N 076 24 W	0	0	Launch Pad Shelter Training Missile Stage	0 0

Missile Storage Facilities:

Pueblo Depot Activity Pueblo, Colorado 38 19 N 104 20 W	111	0	Launch Pad Shelter Training Missile Stage	0 4
Redstone Arsenal Huntsville, Alabama 34 36 N 086 38 W	1	0	Launch Pad Shelter Training Missile Stage	0 20
Weilerbach Federal Republic of Germany 49 27 N 007 38 E	12	0	Launch Pad Shelter Training Missile Stage	0 0

Launcher Storage Facilities:

Redstone Arsenal Huntsville, Alabama 34 35 N 086 37 W	0	1	Launch Pad Shelter Training Missile Stage	0 0

436 SPECIAL FEATURES

	Missiles	Launchers	Support Structures and Equipment

Missile/Launcher Storage Facilities:
NONE

Missile Repair Facilities:
Pueblo Depot Activity
Pueblo, Colorado
38 18 N   104 19 W
| | 0 | 0 | Launch Pad Shelter 0 |
| | | | Training Missile Stage 0 |

Launcher Repair Facilities:
EMC Hausen, Frankfurt
Federal Republic of Germany
50 08 N   008 38 E
| | 0 | 0 | Launch Pad Shelter 0 |
| | | | Training Missile Stage 0 |

Redstone Arsenal
Huntsville, Alabama
34 37 N   086 38 W
| | 0 | 10 | Launch Pad Shelter 0 |
| | | | Training Missile Stage 0 |

Ft. Sill
Ft. Sill, Oklahoma
34 40 N   098 24 W
| | 0 | 2[38] | Launch Pad Shelter 0 |
| | | | Training Missile Stage 0 |

Pueblo Depot Activity
Pueblo, Colorado
38 19 N   104 20 W
| | 0 | 0 | Launch Pad Shelter 0 |
| | | | Training Missile Stage 0 |

Missile/Launcher Repair Facilities:
NONE

Test Ranges:
Complex 16
Cape Canaveral, Florida
28 29 N   080 34 W
| | 3 | 0 | Launch Pad Shelter 0 |
| | | | Training Missile Stage 0 |

Training Facilities:
Ft. Sill
  Ft. Sill, Oklahoma
  34 41 N   098 34 W   0   Launch Pad Shelter   0
                              Training Missile Stage   78

Elimination Facilities:
(Not determined)

Missiles, Launchers, and Support Equipment in Transit: 0   Training Missile Stage   4

(ii) **BGM-109G**

Missile Production Facilities:
McDonnell-Douglas
  Titusville, Florida
  28 32 N   080 40 W   52
                         with launch
                         canister   0   Training Missile   0
                                          Training Launch Canister   0

General Dynamics
  Kearney Mesa, California
  32 50 N   117 08 W   48
                         with launch
                         canister   0   Training Missile   0
                                          Training Launch Canister   0

Launcher Production Facilities:
Air Force Plant 19
  San Diego, California
  32 45 N   117 12 W   2
                         with launch
                         canister   4   Training Missile   0
                                          Training Launch Canister   0

Missile Storage Facilities:
NONE

438 SPECIAL FEATURES

	Missiles	Launchers	Support Structures and Equipment

Launcher Storage Facilities:
NONE

Missile/Launcher Storage Facilities:
NONE

Missile Repair Facilities:
SABCA
  Gosselies, Belgium
  50 27 N   004 27 E | 16 with launch canister | 0 | Training Missile   0
Training Launch Canister   0

Launcher Repair Facilities:
NONE

Missile/Launcher Repair Facilities:
NONE

Test Ranges:
Dugway Proving Grounds
  Utah
  40 22 N   113 04 W | 0 with launch canister | 0 | Training Missile   0
Training Launch Canister   0

Training Facilities:
Davis-Monthan AFB
  Tucson, Arizona
  32 11 N   110 53 W | 0 with launch canister | 7 | Training Missile   2
Training Launch Canister 27

Ft. Huachuca
  Ft. Huachuca, Arizona
  31 29 N   110 19 W | 0 with launch canister | 6 | Training Missile   0
Training Launch Canister   8

Elimination Facilities:
(Not determined)

| Missiles, Launchers, and Support Equipment in Transit | 15 with launch canister | | Training Missile
Training Launch Canister | 0
2 |

(b) UNION OF SOVIET SOCIALIST REPUBLICS

(i) SS-20

Missile Production Facilities:

| Votkinsk Machine Building Plant
Udmurt ASSR, RSFSR
57 01 30 N   054 08 00 E | 36* | | Launch Canister
Missile Transporter Vehicle
Fixed Structure for Launcher
Training Missile | 36
0
0
0 |

Launcher Production Facilities:

| Barrikady Plant
Volgograd
48 44 N   044 32 E | 0 | 1 | Launch Canister
Missile Transporter Vehicle
Fixed Structure for Launcher
Training Missile | 0
0
0
0 |

Missile Storage Facilities:
NONE

Launcher Storage Facilities:
NONE

Missile/Launcher Storage Facilities:

| Postavy
55 10 N   026 55 E | 2 | 3 | Launch Canister
Missile Transporter Vehicle
Fixed Structure for Launcher
Training Missile | 3
10
0
1 |

---

*In various stages of manufacture.

	Missiles	Launchers	Support Structures and Equipment	
Gezgaly 53 36 N 025 28 E	2	2	Launch Canister Missile Transporter Vehicle Fixed Structure for Launcher Training Missile	6 10 0 4
Mozyr' 52 03 N 029 11 E	2	2	Launch Canister Missile Transporter Vehicle Fixed Structure for Launcher Training Missile	4 10 0 2
Lutsk 50 53 N 025 30 E	1	1	Launch Canister Missile Transporter Vehicle Fixed Structure for Launcher Training Missile	3 10 0 2
Belokorovichi 51 09 N 028 00 E	2	2	Launch Canister Missile Transporter Vehicle Fixed Structure for Launcher Training Missile	3 10 0 1
Lebedin 50 36 N 034 25 E	2	1	Launch Canister Missile Transporter Vehicle Fixed Structure for Launcher Training Missile	5 10 0 3
Novosibirsk 55 16 N 083 02 E	1	1	Launch Canister Missile Transporter Vehicle Fixed Structure for Launcher Training Missile	3 10 0 2
Drovyanaya 51 30 N 113 03 E	2	2	Launch Canister Missile Transporter Vehicle Fixed Structure for Launcher Training Missile	4 10 0 2

THE INF TREATY 441

Kansk			
56 16 N	095 39 E	1	Launch Canister 2
			Missile Transporter Vehicle 1
			Fixed Structure for Launcher 0
			Training Missile 1
Barnaul			
53 34 N	083 48 E	1	Launch Canister 1
			Missile Transporter Vehicle 3
			Fixed Structure for Launcher 0
			Training Missile 0
Kolosovo			
53 31 N	026 55 E	144	Launch Canister 144
			Missile Transporter Vehicle 0
			Fixed Structure for Launcher 0
			Training Missile 0
Zherebkovo			
47 51 N	029 54 E	20	Launch Canister 21
			Missile Transporter Vehicle 2
			Fixed Structure for Launcher 0
			Training Missile 1

Missile Repair Facilities:
NONE

Launcher Repair Facilities:
NONE

Missile/Launcher Repair Facilities:

Bataysk			
47 08 N	039 47 E	0	Launch Canister 2
			Missile Transporter Vehicle 4
			Fixed Structure for Launcher 0
			Training Missile 2

Test Ranges:

Kapustin Yar			
48 37 N	046 18 E	0	Launch Canister 0
			Missile Transporter Vehicle 3
			Fixed Structure for Launcher 1
			Training Missile 0

	Missiles	Launchers	Support Structures and Equipment	
Training Facilities:				
Serpukhov 54 54 N 037 28 E	0	6	Launch Canister Missile Transporter Vehicle Fixed Structure for Launcher Training Missile	4 1 0 4
Krasnodar 45 03 N 038 58 E	0	1	Launch Canister Missile Transporter Vehicle Fixed Structure for Launcher Training Missile	2 1 0 2
Training Center at Test Range Kapustin Yar 48 38 N 046 10 E	0	7	Launch Canister Missile Transporter Vehicle Fixed Structure for Launcher Training Missile	12 1 3 12
Elimination Facilities:				
Sarny 51 21 N 026 35 E	29	68	Launch Canister Missile Transporter Vehicle Fixed Structure for Launcher Training Missile	32 35 0 3
Aral'sk 46 50 N 61 18 E	0	0	Launch Canister Missile Transporter Vehicle Fixed Structure for Launcher Training Missile	0 0 0 0
Chita 52 22 N 113 17 E	0	0	Launch Canister Missile Transporter Vehicle Fixed Structure for Launcher Training Missile	0 0 0 0
Kansk 56 20 N 095 06 E	0	0	Launch Canister Missile Transporter Vehicle Fixed Structure for Launcher Training Missile	0 0 0 0

THE INF TREATY 443

Missiles, Launchers, and Support Equipment in Transit:
NONE

(ii) SS-4

Missile Production Facilities:
NONE

Launcher Production Facilities:
NONE

Missile Storage Facilities:
NONE

Launcher Storage Facilities:
NONE

Missile/Launcher Storage Facilities:

Kolosovo 53 31 N 026 55 E	35	1 (Launch Stand)	Missile Transporter Vehicle Missile Erector Propellant Tank Training Missile	9 10 59 31
Zherebkovo 47 51 N 029 54 E	56	3 (Launch Stand)	Missile Transporter Vehicle Missile Erector Propellant Tank Training Missile	5 4 11 30

Missile Repair Facilities:

Bataysk 47 08 N 039 47 E	0	0 (Launch Stand)	Missile Transporter Vehicle Missile Erector Propellant Tank Training Missile	0 0 0 6

Launcher Repair Facilities:
NONE

SPECIAL FEATURES

	Missiles	Launchers	Support Structures and Equipment	
Missile/Launcher Repair Facilities: NONE				
Test Ranges: Kapustin Yar 48 35 N 046 18 E	14	2 (Launch Stand)	Missile Transporter Vehicle Missile Erector Propellant Tank Training Missile	4 2 4 1
Training Facilities: NONE				
Elimination Facilities: Lesnaya 52 59 N 025 46 E	0	0 (Launch Stand)	Missile Transporter Vehicle Missile Erector Propellant Tank Training Missile	0 0 0 0

Missiles, Launchers, and Support Equipment in Transit:
NONE

(iii) SS-5

Missile Production Facilities:
NONE

Launcher Production Facilities:
NONE

Missile Storage Facilities:
Kolosovo
53 31 N 026 55 E   6   0

Launcher Storage Facilities:
NONE

Missile/Launcher Storage Facilities:
NONE

Missile Repair Facilities:
NONE

Launcher Repair Facilities:
NONE

Missile/Launcher Repair Facilities:
NONE

Test Ranges:
NONE

Training Facilities:
NONE

Elimination Facilities:
Lesnaya   0   0
52 59 N   025 46 E

Missiles, Launchers, and Support Equipment in Transit:
NONE

3. Training Launchers

In addition to the support equipment listed in paragraphs 1 and 2 of this Section, the Parties possess vehicles, used to train drivers of launchers of intermediate-range missiles, which shall be considered for purposes of this Treaty to be training launchers. The number of such vehicles for each Party is:

(a) for the United States of America—29; and
(b) for the Union of Soviet Socialist Republics—65.

Elimination of such vehicles shall be carried out in accordance with procedures set forth in the Protocol on Elimination.

IV. Shorter-Range Missiles, Launchers of Such Missiles and Support Equipment Associated With Such Missiles and Launchers

1. Deployed

The following are the missile operating bases, their locations and the numbers, for each Party, of all deployed shorter-range missiles listed as existing types in Article III of the Treaty, and launchers of such missiles, and the support equipment associated with such missiles and launchers. Site diagrams, to include boundaries and center coordinates, of each listed missile operating base are appended to this Memorandum of Understanding.

	Missiles	Launchers	Support Equipment	

(a) UNITED STATES OF AMERICA

(i) Pershing IA

Missile Operating Base:
NONE

(b) UNION OF SOVIET SOCIALIST REPUBLICS

(i) SS-12

Missile Operating Bases:

	Missiles	Launchers	Support Equipment	
Koenigsbrueck German Democratic Republic 51 16 40 N 013 53 20 E	19	11	Missile Transporter Vehicle Training Missile	9 10
Bischofswerda German Democratic Republic 51 08 33 N 014 12 18 E	8	5	Missile Transporter Vehicle Training Missile	0 4

THE INF TREATY 447

Waren German Democratic Republic 53 32 40 N 012 37 30 E	22	12	Missile Transporter Vehicle Training Missile	9 7
Wokuhl German Democratic Republic 53 16 20 N 013 15 50 E	5	6	Missile Transporter Vehicle Training Missile	0 7
Hranice Czechoslovak Socialist Republic 49 33 00 N 017 45 00 E	39	24	Missile Transporter Vehicle Training Missile	15 13
Pashino 55 16 37 N 082 59 42 E	0	4	Missile Transporter Vehicle Training Missile	1 5
Gornyy 51 33 10 N 113 01 30 E	36	14	Missile Transporter Vehicle Training Missile	4 10
Lapichi 53 25 30 N 028 30 00 E	9	5	Missile Transporter Vehicle Training Missile	1 10
Kattakurgan 39 38 18 N 065 58 40 E	9	5	Missile Transporter Vehicle Training Missile	1 6
Saryozek 44 31 58 N 077 46 20 E	36	15	Missile Transporter Vehicle Training Missile	3 16
Novosysoyevka 44 11 58 N 133 26 05 E	37	14	Missile Transporter Vehicle Training Missile	5 17

(ii) **SS-23**

Missile Operating Bases:

Weissenfels German Democratic Republic 51 11 50 N 011 59 50 E	6	4	Missile Transporter Vehicle Training Missile	3 18
Jena–Forst German Democratic Republic 50 54 55 N 011 32 40 E	47	12	Missile Transporter Vehicle Training Missile	8 3

	Missiles	Launchers	Support Structures and Equipment	
Stan'kovo 53 38 30 N 027 13 20 E	40	18	Missile Transporter Vehicle Training Missile	18 10
Tsel' 53 23 38 N 028 28 06 E	26	12	Missile Transporter Vehicle Training Missile	11 9
Slobudka 52 30 30 N 024 31 30 E	26	12	Missile Transporter Vehicle Training Missile	12 10
Bayram-Ali 37 36 18 N 062 10 40 E	0	12	Missile Transporter Vehicle Training Missile	12 0
Semipalatinsk 50 23 00 N 080 09 30 E	22	12	Missile Transporter Vehicle Training Missile	12 4

2. Non-Deployed

The following are missile support facilities, their locations and the numbers, for each Party of all non-deployed shorter-range missiles listed as existing types in Article III of the Treaty, and launchers of such missiles and support equipment associated with such missiles and launchers. Site diagrams for agreed missile support facilities, to include boundaries and center coordinates, are appended to this Memorandum of Understanding.

	Missiles	Launchers	Support Equipment	

(a) UNITED STATES OF AMERICA

(i) Pershing IA

Missile Production Facilities:

| Longhorn Army Ammunition Plant
Marshall, Texas
32 39 N 094 08 W | 0[8] | 0[1] | Training Missile Stage | 0[1] |

Launcher Production Facilities:
Martin Marietta
Middle River, Maryland
39 35 N   076 24 W   0   0   Training Missile Stage   0

Missile Storage Facilities:
Pueblo Depot Activity
Pueblo, Colorado
38 19 N   104 20 W   169   0   Training Missile Stage   53

Launcher Storage Facilities:
NONE

Missile/Launcher Storage Facilities:
NONE

Missile Repair Facilities:
NONE

Launcher Repair Facilities:
Pueblo Depot Activity
Pueblo, Colorado
38 19 N   104 20 W   0   1   Training Missile Stage   0

Missile/Launcher Repair Facilities:
NONE

Test Ranges:
NONE

Training Facilities:
NONE

Elimination Facilities:
(Not determined)

450 SPECIAL FEATURES

		Missiles	Launchers	Support Equipment	
Missiles, Launchers, and Support Equipment in Transit:		1	0	Training Missile Stage	0

(b) **UNION OF SOVIET SOCIALIST REPUBLICS**

(i) SS-12

Missile Production Facilities:

Votkinsk Machine Building Plant Udmurt ASSR, RSFSR 57 01 30 N 054 08 00 E		0	0	Missile Transporter Vehicle Training Missile	0 0

Launcher Production Facilities:

Barrikady Plant Volgograd 48 44 N 044 32 E		0	0	Missile Transporter Vehicle Training Missile	0 0

Missile Storage Facilities:

Lozovaya 48 55 N 036 22 E		126	0	Missile Transporter Vehicle Training Missile	0 12
Ladushkin 54 35 N 020 12 E		72	0	Missile Transporter Vehicle Training Missile	0 18
Bronnaya Gora 52 37 N 025 04 E		170	0	Missile Transporter Vehicle Training Missile	0 3
Balkhash 46 50 N 075 36 E		138	0	Missile Transporter Vehicle Training Missile	0 47

Launcher Storage Facilities:

Berezovka 50 20 N 028 26 E		0	15	Missile Transporter Vehicle Training Missile	10 0

Missile/Launcher Storage Facilities:
NONE

Missile Repair Facilities:
NONE

Launcher Repair Facilities:
NONE

Missile/Launcher Repair Facilities:
NONE

Test Ranges:
NONE

Training Facilities:

Saratov 51 34 N 046 01 E	0	3	Missile Transporter Vehicle / Training Missile	2 / 0
Kazan' 55 58 N 049 11 E	0	2	Missile Transporter Vehicle / Training Missile	2 / 0
Kamenka 53 11 N 044 04 E	0	0	Missile Transporter Vehicle / Training Missile	0 / 0

Elimination Facilities:

Saryozek (Missiles) 44 32 N 077 46 E	0	0	Missile Transporter Vehicle / Training Missile	0 / 0
Stan'kovo (Launchers and Missile Transporter Vehicles) 53 38 N 027 13 E	0	0	Missile Transporter Vehicle / Training Missile	0 / 0

Missiles, Launchers, and Support Equipment in Transit:
NONE

(ii) SS-23

	Missiles	Launchers	Support Equipment	
Missile Production Facilities:				
Votkinsk Machine Building Plant Udmurt ASSR, RSFSR 57 01 30 N 054 08 00 E	0	0	Missile Transporter Vehicle Training Missile	0 0
Launcher Production Facilities:				
V.I. Lenin Petropavlovsk Heavy Machine Building Plant Petropavlovsk 54 51 N 069 09 E	0	0	Missile Transporter Vehicle Training Missile	0 0
Missile Storage Facilities:				
Ladushkin 54 35 N 020 12 E	33	0	Missile Transporter Vehicle Training Missile	0 42
Launcher Storage Facilities:				
Berezovka 50 20 N 028 26 E	0	13	Missile Transporter Vehicle Training Missile	5 0

Missile/Launcher Storage Facilities:
NONE

Missile Repair Facilities:
NONE

Launcher Repair Facilities:
NONE

Missile/Launcher Repair Facilities:
NONE

Test Ranges:
NONE

Training Facilities:

Saratov			
51 34 N	046 01 E	0	3	Missile Transporter Vehicle	2
				Training Missile	0
Kazan'			
55 58 N	049 11 E	0	3	Missile Transporter Vehicle	2
				Training Missile	0
Kamenka			
53 11 N	044 04 E	0	1	Missile Transporter Vehicle	1
				Training Missile	0

Elimination Facilities:

Saryozek (Missiles)			
44 32 N	077 46 E	0	0	Missile Transporter Vehicle	0
				Training Missile	0
Stan'kovo (Launchers and Missile Transporter Vehicles)			
53 38 N	027 13 E	0	0	Missile Transporter Vehicle	0
				Training Missile	0

Missiles, Launchers, and Support Equipment in Transit:
NONE

V. Missile Systems Tested, But Not Deployed, Prior to Entry into Force of the Treaty

The following are the missile support facilities, their locations and the numbers, for each Party of all intermediate-range and shorter-range missiles, and launchers of such missiles, which were tested prior to entry into force of the Treaty, but were never deployed, and which are not existing types of intermediate-range or shorter-range missiles listed in Article III of the Treaty. Site diagrams for agreed missile support facilities, to include boundaries and center coordinates, are appended to this Memorandum of Understanding.

454   SPECIAL FEATURES

	Missiles	Launchers	Support Equipment

(a) UNITED STATES OF AMERICA

(i) Pershing IB

Missile Production Facilities:
NONE

Launcher Production Facilities:
NONE

Missile Storage Facilities:
NONE

Launcher Storage Facilities:
NONE

Missile/Launcher Storage Facilities:
NONE

Missile Repair Facilities:
NONE

Launcher Repair Facilities:
NONE

Missile/Launcher Repair Facilities:
NONE

Test Ranges:
NONE

Training Facilities:
NONE

Elimination Facilities:
NONE

Missiles, Launchers, and Support Equipment in Transit:
NONE

(b) UNION OF SOVIET SOCIALIST REPUBLICS

(i) SSC-X-4

Missile Production Facilities:
NONE

Launcher Production Facilities:
Experimental Plant of the Amalgamated Production Works "M. I. Kalinin Machine Building Plant"
Sverdlovsk
56 47 24 N   060 47 03 E

0
with launch canister

Missile Storage Facilities:
NONE

Launcher Storage Facilities:
NONE

Missile/Launcher Storage Facilities:
Jelgava
56 40 N   024 06 E

6

84
with launch canister

Missile Repair Facilities:
NONE

	Missiles	Launchers	Support Equipment

Launcher Repair Facilities:
NONE

Missile/Launcher Repair Facilities:
NONE

Test Ranges:
NONE

Training Facilities:
NONE

Elimination Facilities:
Jelgava
  56 40 N   024 06 E   0   0
                                      with
                                      launch
                                      canister

Missiles, Launchers, and Support Equipment in Transit:
NONE

VI. Technical Data

Following are agreed categories of technical data for missiles and launchers subject to the Treaty, support structures and support equipment associated with such missiles and launchers and the relevant data for each of these categories. Photographs of missiles, launchers, support structures and support equipment listed below are appended to this Memorandum of Understanding.

1. Intermediate-Range Missiles
(a) Missile Characteristics:

	P-II	BGM-109G	SS-20	SS-4	SS-5	SSC-X-4
(i) Maximum number of warheads per missile	1	1	3	1	1	1
(ii) Length of missile, with front section (meters)	10.61	6.40	16.49	22.77	24.30	8.09
(iii) Length of						
1st stage (meters)	3.68	—	8.58	18.60	21.62	—
2nd stage (meters)	2.47	—	4.60	—	—	—
(iv) Maximum diameter of						
1st stage (meters)	1.02	0.53	—	1.65	2.40	0.51
2nd stage (meters)	1.02	—	1.79	—	—	—
			1.47			
(v) Weight of GLBM, in metric tons (without front section; for liquid-fueled missiles, empty weight)						
1st stage	6.78	—	—	3.35	4.99	—
2nd stage	4.15	—	26.63	—	—	—
Missile in canister	2.63	—	8.63	—	—	—
	—	—	42.70	—	—	—
(vi) Weight of assembled GLCM, in metric tons (with fuel)						
In canister	—	1.71	—	—	—	2.44
Without canister	—	1.47	—	—	—	1.70

(b) Launcher Characteristics:

	P-II	BGM-109G	SS-20	SS-4	SS-5	SSC-X-4
(i) Dimensions (maximum length, width, height in meters)	9.60	10.64	16.81	3.02	—	12.80
	2.49	2.44	3.20	3.02	—	3.05
	2.86	2.64	2.94	3.27	—	3.80
(ii) Maximum number of missiles each launcher is capable of carrying or containing at one time	1	4	1	1	—	6
(iii) Weight (in metric tons)	12.04	14.30	40.25	6.90	—	29.10

	P-II	BGM-109G	SS-20	SS-4	SS-5	SSC-X-4
(c) *Characteristics of Support Structures Associated With Such Missiles and Launchers*						
Dimensions of support structures are as follows (maximum length, width, height in meters):						
(i) Fixed structure for a launcher	—	—	27.70 9.07 6.82	—	—	—
(ii) Launch pad shelter	74.00 14.60 10.00	—	—	—	—	—
(d) *Characteristics of Support Equipment Associated With Such Missiles and Launchers*						
Dimensions of support equipment are as follows (maximum length, width, height in meters):						
(i) Launch canister (Diameter)	— —	6.94 0.53	19.32 2.14	— —	— —	8.39 0.65
(ii) Missile transporter vehicle (number of missiles per vehicle)	—	—	17.33 3.20 2.90 (1)	22.85 2.72 2.50 (1)	—	—
(iii) Missile erector	—	—	—	15.62 3.15 3.76	—	—
(iv) Propellant tank (Transportable) Fuel Oxidizer	— — —	— — —	— — —	11.38 2.63 2.96 10.70 2.63 3.35	— — —	— — —

2. Shorter-Range Missiles

	Pershing IA	Pershing IB	SS-12	SS-23
(a) *Missile Characteristics:*				
(i) Maximum number of warheads per missile	1	1	1	1
(ii) Length of missile, with front section (meters)	10.55	8.13	12.38	7.52
(iii) Length of				
1st stage (meters)	2.83	3.68	4.38	5.17
2nd stage (meters)	2.67	—	5.37	—
(iv) Maximum diameter of				
1st stage (meters)	1.02	1.02	1.01	0.97
2nd stage (meters)	1.02	—	1.01	—
(v) Weight of GLBM, in metric tons (without front section)	4.09	4.15	8.80	3.99
1st stage	2.45	—	4.16	—
2nd stage	1.64	—	4.64	—
(b) *Launcher Characteristics:*				
(i) Dimensions (maximum length, width, height in meters)	9.98	9.60	13.26	11.76
	2.44	2.49	3.10	3.13
	3.35	2.86	3.45	3.00
(ii) Maximum number of missiles each launcher is capable of carrying or containing at one time	1	1	1	1
(iii) Weight (in metric tons)	8.53	12.04	30.80	24.07
(c) *Characteristics of Support Equipment Associated With Such Missiles and Launchers:*				
Dimensions of support equipment are as follows (maximum length, width, height in meters):				
Missile transporter vehicle (number of missiles per vehicle)	—	—	13.15	11.80
			3.10	3.13
			3.50	3.00
			(1)	(1)

VII. Research and Development Booster Systems

Following are the numbers and locations for each Party of launchers of research and development booster systems.

1. Research and Development Launch Sites

(a) UNITED STATES OF AMERICA

	Number of Launchers
Eastern Test Range, Florida 28 27 N 080 42 W	1
Eglin AFB, Florida 30 36 N 086 48 W	5
White Sands Missile Range, New Mexico 32 30 N 106 30 W	4
Green River, Utah 38 00 N 109 30 W	2
Poker Flats Research Range, Alaska 65 07 N 147 29 W	6
Roi Namur, Kwajalein 09 25 N 167 28 E	3
Barking Sands, Kauai, Hawaii 22 06 N 159 47 W	4
Western Test Range, California 34 37 N 120 37 W	1
Cape Cod, Massachusetts 42 01 N 070 07 W	1

Wake Island
19 18 N   166 37 E   2

Wallops Island, Virginia
37 51 N   075 28 W   1

(b) UNION OF SOVIET SOCIALIST REPUBLICS

Plesetskaya
62 53 N   040 52 E   3

Kapustin Yar
48 32 N   046 18 E   2

Each Party, in signing this Memorandum of Understanding, acknowledges it is responsible for the accuracy of only its own data. Signature of this Memorandum of Understanding constitutes acceptance of the categories of data and inclusion of the data contained herein.

This Memorandum of Understanding is an integral part of the Treaty. It shall enter into force on the date of entry into force of the Treaty and shall remain in force so long as the Treaty remains in force.

DONE at Washington on December 8, 1987, in two copies, each in the English and Russian languages, both texts being equally authentic.

FOR THE UNITED STATES OF AMERICA

RONALD REAGAN

President of the United States of America

FOR THE UNION OF SOVIET SOCIALIST REPUBLICS

M.S. GORBACHEV

General Secretary of the Central Committee of the CPSU

SPECIAL FEATURES

**Missile Operating Base
Schwaebisch-Gmuend
48 48 54 N   009 48 29 E**

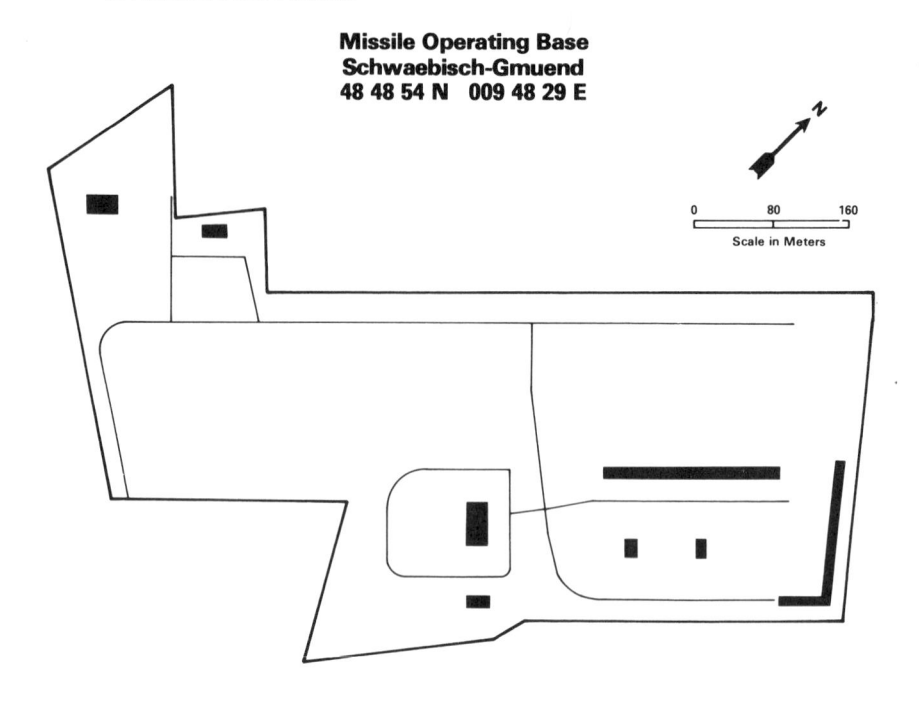

Scale in Meters

ПЛАН РАКЕТНОЙ ОПЕРАЦИОННОЙ БАЗЫ
ПОСТАВЫ
(55 09 47 с.ш.   026 54 21 в.д.)

MISSILE OPERATING BASE
POSTAVY
55 09 47 N   026 54 21 E

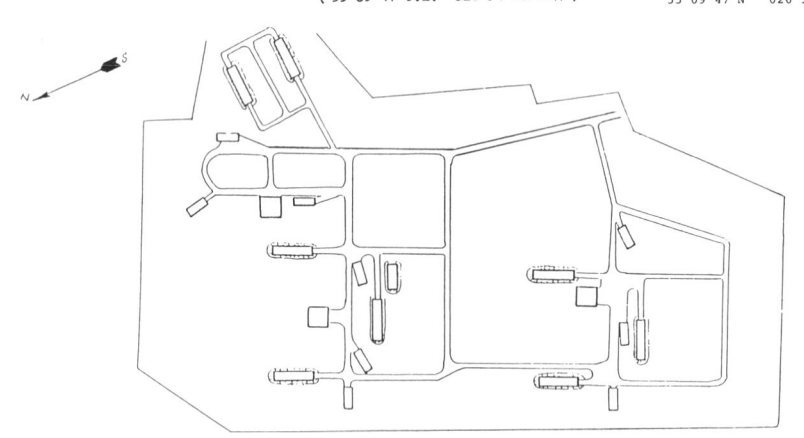

1:5000

Sample of site diagrams appended to the Memorandum of Understanding

Appendix 13C. Protocol on procedures governing the elimination of the missile systems subject to the Treaty

Pursuant to and in implementation of the Treaty Between the United States of America and the Union of Soviet Socialist Republics on the Elimination of Their Intermediate-Range and Shorter-Range Missiles of December 8, 1987, hereinafter referred to as the Treaty, the Parties hereby agree upon procedures governing the elimination of the missile systems subject to the Treaty.

I. Items of Missile Systems Subject to Elimination

The specific items for each type of missile system to be eliminated are:

1. For the United States of America:

   Pershing II: missile, launcher and launch pad shelter;
   BGM-109G: missile, launch canister and launcher;
   Pershing IA: missile and launcher; and
   Pershing IB: missile.

2. For the Union of Soviet Socialist Republics:

   SS-20: missile, launch canister, launcher, missile transporter vehicle and fixed structure for a launcher;
   SS-4: missile, missile transporter vehicle, missile erector, launch stand and propellant tanks;
   SS-5: missile;
   SSC-X-4: missile, launch canister and launcher;
   SS-12: missile, launcher and missile transporter vehicle; and
   SS-23: missile, launcher and missile transporter vehicle.

3. For both Parties, all training missiles, training missile stages, training launch canisters and training launchers shall be subject to elimination.

4. For both Parties, all stages of intermediate-range and shorter-range GLBMs shall be subject to elimination.

5. For both Parties, all front sections of deployed intermediate-range and shorter-range missiles shall be subject to elimination.

II. Procedures for Elimination at Elimination Facilities

1. In order to ensure the reliable determination of the type and number of missiles, missile stages, front sections, launch canisters, launchers, missile transporter vehicles, missile erectors and launch stands, as well as training missiles, training missile stages, training launch canisters and training launchers, indicated in Section I of this Protocol, being eliminated at elimination facilities, and to preclude the possibility of restoration of such items for purposes inconsistent with the provisions of the Treaty, the Parties shall fulfill the requirements below.

2. The conduct of the elimination procedures for the items of missile systems listed in paragraph 1 of this Section, except for training missiles, training missile stages, training launch canisters and training launchers, shall be subject to on-site inspection in accordance with Article XI of the Treaty and the Protocol on Inspection. The Parties shall have the right to conduct on-site inspections to confirm the completion of the elimination

procedures set forth in paragraph 11 of this Section for training missiles, training missile stages, training launch canisters and training launchers. The Party possessing such a training missile, training missile stage, training launch canister or training launcher shall inform the other Party of the name and coordinates of the elimination facility at which the on-site inspection may be conducted as well as the date on which it may be conducted. Such information shall be provided no less than 30 days in advance of that date.

3. Prior to a missile's arrival at the elimination facility, its nuclear warhead device and guidance elements may be removed.

4. Each Party shall select the particular technological means necessary to implement the procedures required in paragraphs 10 and 11 of this Section and to allow for on-site inspection of the conduct of the elimination procedures required in paragraph 10 of this Section in accordance with Article XI of the Treaty, this Protocol and the Protocol on Inspection.

5. The initiation of the elimination of the items of missile systems subject to this Section shall be considered to be the commencement of the procedures set forth in paragraph 10 or 11 of this Section.

6. Immediately prior to the initiation of the elimination procedures set forth in paragraph 10 of this Section, an inspector from the Party receiving the pertinent notification required by paragraph 5(c) of Article IX of the Treaty shall confirm and record the type and number of items of missile systems, listed in paragraph 1 of this Section, which are to be eliminated. If the inspecting Party deems it necessary, this shall include a visual inspection of the contents of launch canisters.

7. A missile stage being eliminated by burning in accordance with the procedures set forth in paragraph 10 of this Section shall not be instrumented for data collection. Prior to the initiation of the elimination procedures set forth in paragraph 10 of this Section, an inspector from the inspecting Party shall confirm that such missile stages are not instrumented for data collection. Those missile stages shall be subject to continuous observation by such an inspector from the time of that inspection until the burning is completed.

8. The completion of the elimination procedures set forth in this Section, except those for training missiles, training missile stages, training launch canisters and training launchers, along with the type and number of items of missile systems for which those procedures have been completed, shall be confirmed in writing by the representative of the Party carrying out the elimination and by the inspection team leader of the other Party. The elimination of a training missile, training missile stage, training launch canister or training launcher shall be considered to have been completed upon completion of the procedures set forth in paragraph 11 of this Section and notification as required by paragraph 5(e) of Article IX of the Treaty following the date specified pursuant to paragraph 2 of this Section.

9. The Parties agree that all United States and Soviet intermediate-range and shorter-range missiles and their associated reentry vehicles shall be eliminated within an agreed overall period of elimination. It is further agreed that all such missiles shall, in fact, be eliminated fifteen days prior to the end of the overall period of elimination. During the last fifteen days, a Party shall withdraw to its national territory reentry vehicles which, by unilateral decision, have been released from existing programs of cooperation and eliminate them during the same timeframe in accordance with the procedures set forth in this Section.

10. The specific procedures for the elimination of the items of missile systems listed in paragraph 1 of this

Section shall be as follows, unless the Parties agree upon different procedures to achieve the same result as the procedures identified in this paragraph:

For the Pershing II:

Missile:

(a) missile stages shall be eliminated by explosive demolition or burning;

(b) solid fuel, rocket nozzles and motor cases not destroyed in this process shall be burned, crushed, flattened or destroyed by explosion; and

(c) front section, minus nuclear warhead device and guidance elements, shall be crushed or flattened.

Launcher:

(a) erector-launcher mechanism shall be removed from launcher chassis;

(b) all components of erector-launcher mechanism shall be cut at locations that are not assembly joints into two pieces of approximately equal size;

(c) missile launch support equipment, including external instrumentation compartments, shall be removed from launcher chassis; and

(d) launcher chassis shall be cut at a location that is not an assembly joint into two pieces of approximately equal size.

For the BGM-109G:

Missile:

(a) missile airframe shall be cut longitudinally into two pieces;

(b) wings and tail section shall be severed from missile airframe at locations that are not assembly joints; and

(c) front section, minus nuclear warhead device and guidance elements, shall be crushed or flattened.

Launch Canister: launch canister shall be crushed, flattened, cut into two pieces of approximately equal size or destroyed by explosion.

Launcher:

(a) erector-launcher mechanism shall be removed from launcher chassis;

(b) all components of erector-launcher mechanism shall be cut at locations that are not assembly joints into two pieces of approximately equal size;

(c) missile launch support equipment, including external instrumentation compartments, shall be removed from launcher chassis; and

(d) launcher chassis shall be cut at a location that is not an assembly joint into two pieces of approximately equal size.

For the Pershing IA:

Missile:

(a) missile stages shall be eliminated by explosive demolition or burning;

(b) solid fuel, rocket nozzles and motor cases not destroyed in this process shall be burned, crushed, flattened or destroyed by explosion; and

(c) front section, minus nuclear warhead device and guidance elements, shall be crushed or flattened.

Launcher:

(a) erector-launcher mechanism shall be removed from launcher chassis;

(b) all components of erector-launcher mechanism shall be cut at locations that are not assembly joints into two pieces of approximately equal size;

(c) missile launch support equipment, including external instrumentation compartments, shall be removed from launcher chassis; and

(d) launcher chassis shall be cut at a location that is not an assembly joint into two pieces of approximately equal size.

For the Pershing IB:

Missile:

(a) missile stage shall be

eliminated by explosive demolition or burning;

(b) solid fuel, rocket nozzle and motor case not destroyed in this process shall be burned, crushed, flattened or destroyed by explosion; and

(c) front section, minus nuclear warhead device and guidance elements, shall be crushed or flattened.

For the SS-20:

Missile:

(a) missile shall be eliminated by explosive demolition of the missile in its launch canister or by burning missile stages;

(b) solid fuel, rocket nozzles and motor cases not destroyed in this process shall be burned, crushed, flattened or destroyed by explosion; and

(c) front section, including reentry vehicles, minus nuclear warhead devices, and instrumentation compartment, minus guidance elements, shall be crushed or flattened.

Launch Canister: launch canister shall be destroyed by explosive demolition together with a missile, or shall be destroyed separately by explosion, cut into two pieces of approximately equal size, crushed or flattened.

Launcher:

(a) erector-launcher mechanism shall be removed from launcher chassis;

(b) all components of erector-launcher mechanism shall be cut at locations that are not assembly joints into two pieces of approximately equal size;

(c) missile launch support equipment, including external instrumentation compartments, shall be removed from launcher chassis;

(d) mountings of erector-launcher mechanism and launcher leveling supports shall be cut off launcher chassis;

(e) launcher leveling supports shall be cut at locations that are not assembly joints into two pieces of approximately equal size; and

(f) a portion of the launcher chassis, at least 0.78 meters in length, shall be cut off aft of the rear axle.

Missile Transporter Vehicle:

(a) all mechanisms associated with missile loading and mounting shall be removed from transporter vehicle chassis;

(b) all mountings of such mechanisms shall be cut off transporter vehicle chassis;

(c) all components of the mechanisms associated with missile loading and mounting shall be cut at locations that are not assembly joints into two pieces of approximately equal size;

(d) external instrumentation compartments shall be removed from transporter vehicle chassis;

(e) transporter vehicle leveling supports shall be cut off transporter vehicle chassis and cut at locations that are not assembly joints into two pieces of approximately equal size; and

(f) a portion of the transporter vehicle chassis, at least 0.78 meters in length, shall be cut off aft of the rear axle.

For the SS-4:

Missile:

(a) nozzles of propulsion system shall be cut off at locations that are not assembly joints;

(b) all propellant tanks shall be cut into two pieces of approximately equal size;

(c) instrumentation compartment, minus guidance elements, shall be cut into two pieces of approximately equal size; and

(d) front section, minus nuclear warhead device, shall be crushed or flattened.

Launch Stand: launch stand components shall be cut at locations that are not assembly joints into two pieces of approximately equal size.

Missile Erector:

(a) jib, missile erector leveling supports and missile erector mechanism shall be cut off missile erector at locations that are not assembly joints; and

(b) jib and missile erector leveling supports shall be cut into two pieces of approximately equal size.

Missile Transporter Vehicle: mounting components for a missile and for a missile erector mechanism as well as supports for erecting a missile onto a launcher shall be cut off transporter vehicle at locations that are not assembly joints.

For the SS-5:

Missile:

(a) nozzles of propulsion system shall be cut off at locations that are not assembly joints;

(b) all propellant tanks shall be cut into two pieces of approximately equal size; and

(c) instrumentation compartment, minus guidance elements, shall be cut into two pieces of approximately equal size.

For the SSC-X-4:

Missile:

(a) missile airframe shall be cut longitudinally into two pieces;

(b) wings and tail section shall be severed from missile airframe at locations that are not assembly joints; and

(c) front section, minus nuclear warhead device and guidance elements, shall be crushed or flattened.

Launch Canister: launch canister shall be crushed, flattened, cut into two pieces of approximately equal size or destroyed by explosion.

Launcher:

(a) erector-launcher mechanism shall be removed from launcher chassis;

(b) all components of erector-launcher mechanism shall be cut at locations that are not assembly joints into two pieces of approximately equal size;

(c) missile launch support equipment, including external instrumentation compartments, shall be removed from launcher chassis;

(d) mountings of erector-launcher mechanism and launcher leveling supports shall be cut off launcher chassis;

(e) launcher leveling supports shall be cut at locations that are not assembly joints into two pieces of approximately equal size; and

(f) the launcher chassis shall be severed at a location determined by measuring no more than 0.70 meters rearward from the rear axle.

For the SS-12:

Missile:

(a) missile shall be eliminated by explosive demolition or by burning missile stages;

(b) solid fuel, rocket nozzles and motor cases not destroyed in this process shall be burned, crushed, flattened or destroyed by explosion; and

(c) front section, minus nuclear warhead device, and instrumentation compartment, minus guidance elements, shall be crushed, flattened or destroyed by explosive demolition together with a missile.

Launcher:

(a) erector-launcher mechanism shall be removed from launcher chassis;

(b) all components of erector-launcher mechanism shall be cut at locations that are not assembly joints into two pieces of approximately equal size;

(c) missile launch support equipment, including external instrumentation compartments, shall be removed from launcher chassis;

(d) mountings of erector-launcher mechanism and launcher leveling supports shall be cut off launcher chassis;

468   SPECIAL FEATURES

(e) launcher leveling supports shall be cut at locations that are not assembly joints into two pieces of approximately equal size; and

(f) a portion of the launcher chassis, at least 1.10 meters in length, shall be cut off aft of the rear axle.

Missile Transporter Vehicle:

(a) all mechanisms associated with missile loading and mounting shall be removed from transporter vehicle chassis;

(b) all mountings of such mechanisms shall be cut off transporter vehicle chassis;

(c) all components of the mechanisms associated with missile loading and mounting shall be cut at locations that are not assembly joints into two pieces of approximately equal size;

(d) external instrumentation compartments shall be removed from transporter vehicle chassis;

(e) transporter vehicle leveling supports shall be cut off transporter vehicle chassis and cut at locations that are not assembly joints into two pieces of approximately equal size; and

(f) a portion of the transporter vehicle chassis, at least 1.10 meters in length, shall be cut off aft of the rear axle.

For the SS-23:

Missile:

(a) missile shall be eliminated by explosive demolition or by burning the missile stage;

(b) solid fuel, rocket nozzle and motor case not destroyed in this process shall be burned, crushed, flattened or destroyed by explosion; and

(c) front section, minus nuclear warhead device, and instrumentation compartment, minus guidance elements, shall be crushed, flattened, or destroyed by explosive demolition together with a missile.

Launcher:

(a) erector-launcher mechanism shall be removed from launcher body;

(b) all components of erector-launcher mechanism shall be cut at locations that are not assembly joints into two pieces of approximately equal size;

(c) missile launch support equipment shall be removed from launcher body;

(d) mountings of erector-launcher mechanism and launcher leveling supports shall be cut off launcher body;

(e) launcher leveling supports shall be cut at locations that are not assembly joints into two pieces of approximately equal size;

(f) each environmental cover of the launcher body shall be removed and cut into two pieces of approximately equal size; and

(g) a portion of the launcher body, at least 0.85 meters in length, shall be cut off aft of the rear axle.

Missile Transporter Vehicle:

(a) all mechanisms associated with missile loading and mounting shall be removed from transporter vehicle body;

(b) all mountings of such mechanisms shall be cut off transporter vehicle body;

(c) all components of mechanisms associated with missile loading and mounting shall be cut at locations that are not assembly joints into two pieces of approximately equal size;

(d) control equipment of the mechanism associated with missile loading shall be removed from transporter vehicle body;

(e) transporter vehicle leveling supports shall be cut off transporter vehicle body and cut at locations that are not assembly joints into two pieces of approximately equal size; and

(f) a portion of the transporter vehicle body, at least 0.85 meters in length, shall be cut off aft of the rear axle.

11. The specific procedures for the elimination of the training missiles,

training missile stages, training launch canisters and training launchers indicated in paragraph 1 of this Section shall be as follows:

Training Missile and Training Missile Stage: training missile and training missile stage shall be crushed, flattened, cut into two pieces of approximately equal size or destroyed by explosion.

Training Launch Canister: training launch canister shall be crushed, flattened, cut into two pieces of approximately equal size or destroyed by explosion.

Training Launcher: training launcher chassis shall be cut at the same location designated in paragraph 10 of this Section for launcher of the same type of missile.

III. Elimination of Missiles by Means of Launching

1. Elimination of missiles by means of launching pursuant to paragraph 5 of Article X of the Treaty shall be subject to on-site inspection in accordance with paragraph 7 of Article XI of the Treaty and the Protocol on Inspection. Immediately prior to each launch conducted for the purpose of elimination, an inspector from the inspecting Party shall confirm by visual observation the type of the missile to be launched.

2. All missiles being eliminated by means of launching shall be launched from designated elimination facilities to existing impact areas for such missiles. No such missile shall be used as a target vehicle for a ballistic missile interceptor.

3. Missiles being eliminated by means of launching shall be launched one at a time, and no less than six hours shall elapse between such launches.

4. Such launches shall involve ignition of all missile stages. Neither Party shall transmit or recover data from missiles being eliminated by means of launching except for unencrypted data used for range safety purposes.

5. The completion of the elimination procedures set forth in this Section, and the type and number of missiles for which those procedures have been completed, shall be confirmed in writing by the representative of the Party carrying out the elimination and by the inspection team leader of the other Party.

6. A missile shall be considered to be eliminated by means of launching after completion of the procedures set forth in this Section and upon notification required by paragraph 5(e) of Article IX of the Treaty.

IV. Procedures for Elimination *In Situ*

1. Support Structures

(a) Support structures listed in Section I of this Protocol shall be eliminated *in situ.*

(b) The initiation of the elimination of support structures shall be considered to be the commencement of the elimination procedures required in paragraph 1(d) of this Section.

(c) The elimination of support structures shall be subject to verification by on-site inspection in accordance with paragraph 4 of Article XI of the Treaty.

(d) The specific elimination procedures for support structures shall be as follows:

(i) the superstructure of the fixed structure or shelter shall be dismantled or demolished, and removed from its base or foundation;

(ii) the base or foundation of the fixed structure or shelter shall be destroyed by excavation or explosion;

(iii) the destroyed base or foundation of a fixed structure or shelter shall remain visible to national technical means of verification for six months or until completion of an on-site inspection conducted in accordance with Article XI of the Treaty; and

(iv) upon completion of the above requirements, the elimination procedures shall be considered to have been completed.

2. Propellant Tanks for SS-4 Missiles

Fixed and transportable propellant tanks for SS-4 missiles shall be removed from launch sites.

3. Training Missiles, Training Missile Stages, Training Launch Canisters and Training Launchers

(a) Training missiles, training missile stages, training launch canisters and training launchers not eliminated at elimination facilities shall be eliminated *in situ*.

(b) Training missiles, training missile stages, training launch canisters and training launchers being eliminated *in situ* shall be eliminated in accordance with the specific procedures set forth in paragraph 11 of Section II of this Protocol.

(c) Each Party shall have the right to conduct an on-site inspection to confirm the completion of the elimination procedures for training missiles, training missile stages, training launch canisters and training launchers.

(d) The Party possessing such a training missile, training missile stage, training launch canister or training launcher shall inform the other Party of the place-name and coordinates of the location at which the on-site inspection provided for in paragraph 3(c) of this Section may be conducted as well as the date on which it may be conducted. Such information shall be provided no less than 30 days in advance of that date.

(e) Elimination of a training missile, training missile stage, training launch canister or training launcher shall be considered to have been completed upon the completion of the procedures required by this paragraph and upon notification as required by paragraph 5(e) of Article IX of the Treaty following the date specified pursuant to paragraph 3(d) of this Section.

V. Other Types of Elimination

1. Loss or Accidental Destruction

(a) If an item listed in Section I of this Protocol is lost or destroyed as a result of an accident, the possessing Party shall notify the other Party within 48 hours, as required in paragraph 5(e) of Article IX of the Treaty, that the item has been eliminated.

(b) Such notification shall include the type of the eliminated item, its approximate or assumed location and the circumstances related to the loss or accidental destruction.

(c) In such a case, the other Party shall have the right to conduct an inspection of the specific point at which the accident occurred to provide confidence that the item has been eliminated.

2. Static Display

(a) The Parties shall have the right to eliminate missiles, launch canisters and launchers, as well as training missiles, training launch canisters and training launchers, listed in Section I of this Protocol by placing them on static display. Each Party shall be limited to a total of 15 missiles, 15 launch canisters and 15 launchers on such static display.

(b) Prior to being placed on static display, a missile, launch canister or launcher shall be rendered unusable for purposes inconsistent with the Treaty. Missile propellant shall be removed and erector-launcher mechanisms shall be rendered inoperative.

(c) The Party possessing a missile, launch canister or launcher, as well as a training missile, training launch canister or training launcher that is to be eliminated by placing it on static display shall provide the other Party with the place-name and coordinates of the location at which such a missile, launch canister or launcher is to be on static display, as well as the location at which the on-site inspection provided for in paragraph 2(d) of this Section, may take place.

(d) Each Party shall have the right to conduct an on-site inspection of such a missile, launch canister or launcher within 60 days of receipt of the notification required in paragraph 2(c) of this Section.

(e) Elimination of a missile, launch canister or launcher, as well as a training missile, training launch canister or training launcher, by placing it on static display shall be considered to have been completed upon completion of the procedures required by this paragraph and notification as required by paragraph 5(e) of Article IX of the Treaty.

This Protocol is an integral part of the Treaty. It shall enter into force on the date of the entry into force of the Treaty and shall remain in force so long as the Treaty remains in force. As provided for in paragraph 1(b) of Article XIII of the Treaty, the Parties may agree upon such measures as may be necessary to improve the viability and effectiveness of this Protocol. Such measures shall not be deemed amendments to the Treaty.

DONE at Washington on December 8, 1987, in two copies, each in the English and Russian languages, both texts being equally authentic.

FOR THE UNITED STATES OF AMERICA

RONALD REAGAN

President of the United States of America

FOR THE UNION OF SOVIET SOCIALIST REPUBLICS

M. GORBACHEV

General Secretary of the Central Committee of the CPSU

Appendix 13D. Protocol regarding inspections relating to the Treaty

Pursuant to and in implementation of the Treaty Between the United States of America and the Union of Soviet Socialist Republics on the Elimination of Their Intermediate-Range and Shorter-Range Missiles of December 8, 1987, hereinafter referred to as the Treaty, the Parties hereby agree upon procedures governing the conduct of inspections provided for in Article XI of the Treaty.

I. Definitions

For the purposes of this Protocol, the Treaty, the Memorandum of Understanding and the Protocol on Elimination:

1. The term "inspected Party" means the Party to the Treaty whose sites are subject to inspection as provided for by Article XI of the Treaty.

2. The term "inspecting Party" means the Party to the Treaty carrying out an inspection.

3. The term "inspector" means an individual designated by one of the Parties to carry out inspections and included on that Party's list of inspectors in accordance with the provisions of Section III of this Protocol.

4. The term "inspection team" means the group of inspectors assigned by the inspecting Party to conduct a particular inspection.

5. The term "inspection site" means an area, location or facility at which an inspection is carried out.

6. The term "period of inspection" means the period of time from arrival of the inspection team at the inspection site until its departure from the inspection site, exclusive of time spent on any pre- and post-inspection procedures.

7. The term "point of entry" means: Washington, D.C., or San Francisco, California, the United States of America; Brussels (National Airport), The Kingdom of Belgium; Frankfurt (Rhein Main Airbase), The Federal Republic of Germany; Rome (Ciampino), The Republic of Italy; Schiphol, The Kingdom of the Netherlands; RAF Greenham Common, The United Kingdom of Great Britain and Northern Ireland; Moscow, or Irkutsk, the Union of Soviet Socialist Republics; Schkeuditz Airport, the German Democratic Republic; and International Airport Ruzyne, the Czechoslovak Socialist Republic.

8. The term "in-country period" means the period from the arrival of the inspection team at the point of entry until its departure from the country through the point of entry.

9. The term "in-country escort" means individuals specified by the inspected Party to accompany and assist inspectors and aircrew members as necessary throughout the in-country period.

10. The term "aircrew member" means an individual who performs duties related to the operation of an airplane and who is included on a Party's list of aircrew members in accordance with the provisions of Section III of this Protocol.

II. General Obligations

1. For the purpose of ensuring verification of compliance with the provisions of the Treaty, each Party shall facilitate inspection by the other Party pursuant to this Protocol.

2. Each Party takes note of the

assurances received from the other Party regarding understandings reached between the other Party and the basing countries to the effect that the basing countries have agreed to the conduct of inspections, in accordance with the provisions of this Protocol, on their territories.

III. Pre-Inspection Requirements

1. Inspections to ensure verification of compliance by the Parties with the obligations assumed under the Treaty shall be carried out by inspectors designated in accordance with paragraphs 3 and 4 of this Section.

2. No later than one day after entry into force of the Treaty, each Party shall provide to the other Party: a list of its proposed aircrew members; a list of its proposed inspectors who will carry out inspections pursuant to paragraphs 3, 4, 5, 7 and 8 of Article XI of the Treaty; and a list of its proposed inspectors who will carry out inspection activities pursuant to paragraph 6 of Article XI of the Treaty. None of these lists shall contain at any time more than 200 individuals.

3. Each Party shall review the lists of inspectors and aircrew members proposed by the other Party. With respect to an individual included on the list of proposed inspectors who will carry out inspection activities pursuant to paragraph 6 of Article XI of the Treaty, if such an individual is unacceptable to the Party reviewing the list, that Party shall, within 20 days, so inform the Party providing the list, and the individual shall be deemed not accepted and shall be deleted from the list. With respect to an individual on the list of proposed aircrew members or the list of proposed inspectors who will carry out inspections pursuant to paragraphs 3, 4, 5, 7 and 8 of Article XI of the Treaty, each Party, within 20 days after the receipt of such lists, shall inform the other Party of its agreement to the designation of each inspector and aircrew member proposed. Inspectors shall be citizens of the inspecting Party.

4. Each Party shall have the right to amend its lists of inspectors and aircrew members. New inspectors and aircrew members shall be designated in the same manner as set forth in paragraph 3 of this Section with respect to initial lists.

5. Within 30 days of receipt of the initial lists of inspectors and aircrew members, or of subsequent changes thereto, the Party receiving such information shall provide, or shall ensure the provision of, such visas and other documents to each individual to whom it has agreed as may be required to ensure that each inspector or aircrew member may enter and remain in the territory of the Party or basing country in which an inspection site is located throughout the in-country period for the purpose of carrying out inspection activities in accordance with the provisions of this Protocol. Such visas and documents shall be valid for a period of at least 24 months.

6. To exercise their functions effectively, inspectors and aircrew members shall be accorded, throughout the in-country period, privileges and immunities in the country of the inspection site as set forth in the Annex to this Protocol.

7. Without prejudice to their privileges and immunities, inspectors and aircrew members shall be obliged to respect the laws and regulations of the State on whose territory an inspection is carried out and shall be obliged not to interfere in the internal affairs of that State. In the event the inspected Party determines that an inspector or aircrew member of the other Party has violated the conditions governing inspection activities set forth in this Protocol, or has ever committed a criminal offense on the territory of the inspected Party or a basing country, or has ever been sentenced for committing a criminal offense or expelled by the inspected Party or a basing country, the inspected Party making such a determination shall so notify the inspecting Party, which shall immediately strike the individual from the lists of inspectors or the list of aircrew members. If, at that time, the

individual is on the territory of the inspected Party or a basing country, the inspecting Party shall immediately remove that individual from the country.

8. Within 30 days after entry into force of the Treaty, each Party shall inform the other Party of the standing diplomatic clearance number for airplanes of the Party transporting inspectors and equipment necessary for inspection into and out of the territory of the Party or basing country in which an inspection site is located. Aircraft routings to and from the designated point of entry shall be along established international airways that are agreed upon by the Parties as the basis for such diplomatic clearance.

IV. Notifications

1. Notification of an intention to conduct an inspection shall be made through the Nuclear Risk Reduction Centers. The receipt of this notification shall be acknowledged through the Nuclear Risk Reduction Centers by the inspected Party within one hour of its receipt:

(a) For inspections conducted pursuant to paragraphs 3, 4 or 5 of Article XI of the Treaty, such notifications shall be made no less than 16 hours in advance of the estimated time of arrival of the inspection team at the point of entry and shall include:

(i) the point of entry;

(ii) the date and estimated time of arrival at the point of entry;

(iii) the date and time when the specification of the inspection site will be provided; and

(iv) the names of inspectors and aircrew members.

(b) For inspections conducted pursuant to paragraphs 7 or 8 of Article XI of the Treaty, such notifications shall be made no less than 72 hours in advance of the estimated time of arrival of the inspection team at the point of entry and shall include:

(i) the point of entry;

(ii) the date and estimated time of arrival at the point of entry;

(iii) the site to be inspected and the type of inspection; and

(iv) the names of inspectors and aircrew members.

2. The date and time of the specification of the inspection site as notified pursuant to paragraph 1(a) of this Section shall fall within the following time intervals:

(a) for inspections conducted pursuant to paragraphs 4 or 5 of Article XI of the Treaty, neither less than four hours nor more than 24 hours after the estimated date and time of arrival at the point of entry; and

(b) for inspections conducted pursuant to paragraph 3 of Article XI of the Treaty, neither less than four hours nor more than 48 hours after the estimated date and time of arrival at the point of entry.

3. The inspecting Party shall provide the inspected Party with a flight plan, through the Nuclear Risk Reduction Centers, for its flight from the last airfield prior to entering the air space of the country in which the inspection site is located to the point of entry, no less than six hours before the scheduled departure time from that airfield. Such a plan shall be filed in accordance with the procedures of the International Civil Aviation Organization applicable to civil aircraft. The inspecting Party shall include in the remarks section of each flight plan the standing diplomatic clearance number and the notation: "Inspection aircraft. Priority clearance processing required."

4. No less than three hours prior to the scheduled departure of the inspection team from the last airfield prior to entering the airspace of the country in which the inspection is to take place, the inspected Party shall ensure that the flight plan filed in accordance with paragraph 3 of this Section is approved so that the inspection team may arrive at the point of entry by the estimated arrival time.

5. Either Party may change the point or points of entry to the territories of the countries within which its deployment areas, missile operating bases or missile support facilities are located, by giving notice of such change to the other Party. A change in a point of entry shall become effective five months after receipt of such notification by the other Party.

V. Activities Beginning Upon Arrival at the Point of Entry

1. The in-country escort and a diplomatic aircrew escort accredited to the Government of either the inspected Party or the basing country in which the inspection site is located shall meet the inspection team and aircrew members at the point of entry as soon as the airplane of the inspecting Party lands. The number of aircrew members for each airplane shall not exceed ten.

The in-country escort shall expedite the entry of the inspection team and aircrew, their baggage, and equipment and supplies necessary for inspection, into the country in which the inspection site is located. A diplomatic aircrew escort shall have the right to accompany and assist aircrew members throughout the in-country period. In the case of an inspection taking place on the territory of a basing country, the in-country escort may include representatives of that basing country.

2. An inspector shall be considered to have assumed his duties upon arrival at the point of entry on the territory of the inspected Party or a basing country, and shall be considered to have ceased performing those duties when he has left the territory of the inspected Party or basing country.

3. Each Party shall ensure that equipment and supplies are exempt from all customs duties.

4. Equipment and supplies which the inspecting Party brings into the country in which an inspection site is located shall be subject to examination at the point of entry each time they are brought into that country. This examination shall be completed prior to the departure of the inspection team from the point of entry to conduct an inspection. Such equipment and supplies shall be examined by the in-country escort in the presence of the inspection team members to ascertain to the satisfaction of each Party that the equipment and supplies cannot perform functions unconnected with the inspection requirements of the Treaty. If it is established upon examination that the equipment or supplies are unconnected with these inspection requirements, then they shall not be cleared for use and shall be impounded at the point of entry until the departure of the inspection team from the country where the inspection is conducted. Storage of the inspecting Party's equipment and supplies at each point of entry shall be within tamper-proof containers within a secure facility. Access to each secure facility shall be controlled by a "dual key" system requiring the presence of both Parties to gain access to the equipment and supplies.

5. Throughout the in-country period, the inspected Party shall provide, or arrange for the provision of, meals, lodging, work space, transportation and, as necessary, medical care for the inspection team and aircrew of the inspecting Party. All the costs in connection with the stay of inspectors carrying out inspection activities pursuant to paragraph 6 of Article XI of the Treaty, on the territory of the inspected Party, including meals, services, lodging, work space, transportation and medical care shall be borne by the inspecting Party.

6. The inspected Party shall provide parking, security protection, servicing and fuel for the airplane of the inspecting Party at the point of entry. The inspecting Party shall bear the cost of such fuel and servicing.

7. For inspections conducted on the territory of the Parties, the inspection team shall enter at the point of entry on the territory of the inspected Party that is closest to the inspection site. In the case of inspections carried out in accordance with paragraphs 3, 4 or 5 of

Article XI of the Treaty, the inspection team leader shall, at or before the time notified pursuant to paragraph 1(a)(iii) of Section IV of this Protocol, inform the inspected Party at the point of entry through the in-country escort of the type of inspection and the inspection site, by place-name and geographic coordinates.

VI. General Rules for Conducting Inspections

1. Inspectors shall discharge their functions in accordance with this Protocol.

2. Inspectors shall not disclose information received during inspections except with the express permission of the inspecting Party. They shall remain bound by this obligation after their assignment as inspectors has ended.

3. In discharging their functions, inspectors shall not interfere directly with on-going activities at the inspection site and shall avoid unnecessarily hampering or delaying the operation of a facility or taking actions affecting its safe operation.

4. Inspections shall be conducted in accordance with the objectives set forth in Article XI of the Treaty as applicable for the type of inspection specified by the inspecting Party under paragraph 1(b) of Section IV or paragraph 7 of Section V of this Protocol.

5. The in-country escort shall have the right to accompany and assist inspectors and aircrew members as considered necessary by the inspected Party throughout the in-country period. Except as otherwise provided in this Protocol, the movement and travel of inspectors and aircrew members shall be at the discretion of the in-country escort.

6. Inspectors carrying out inspection activities pursuant to paragraph 6 of Article XI of the Treaty shall be allowed to travel within 50 kilometers from the inspection site with the permission of the in-country escort, and as considered necessary by the inspected Party, shall be accompanied by the in-country escort. Such travel shall be taken solely as a leisure activity.

7. Inspectors shall have the right throughout the period of inspection to be in communication with the embassy of the inspecting Party located within the territory of the country where the inspection is taking place using the telephone communications provided by the inspected Party.

8. At the inspection site, representatives of the inspected facility shall be included among the in-country escort.

9. The inspection team may bring onto the inspection site such documents as needed to conduct the inspection, as well as linear measurement devices; cameras; portable weighing devices; radiation detection devices; and other equipment, as agreed by the Parties. The characteristics and method of use of the equipment listed above, shall also be agreed upon within 30 days after entry into force of the Treaty. During inspections conducted pursuant to paragraphs 3, 4, 5(a), 7 or 8 of Article XI of the Treaty, the inspection team may use any of the equipment listed above, except for cameras, which shall be for use only by the inspected Party at the request of the inspecting Party. During inspections conducted pursuant to paragraph 5(b) of Article XI of the Treaty, all measurements shall be made by the inspected Party at the request of the inspecting Party. At the request of inspectors, the in-country escort shall take photographs of the inspected facilities using the inspecting Party's camera systems which are capable of producing duplicate, instant development photographic prints. Each Party shall receive one copy of every photograph.

10. For inspections conducted pursuant to paragraphs 3, 4, 5, 7 or 8 of Article XI of the Treaty, inspectors shall permit the in-country escort to observe the equipment used during the inspection by the inspection team.

11. Measurements recorded during inspections shall be certified by the signature of a member of the

inspection team and a member of the in-country escort when they are taken. Such certified data shall be included in the inspection report.

12. Inspectors shall have the right to request clarifications in connection with ambiguities that arise during an inspection. Such requests shall be made promptly through the in-country escort. The in-country escort shall provide the inspection team, during the inspection, with such clarifications as may be necessary to remove the ambiguity. In the event questions relating to an object or building located within the inspection site are not resolved, the inspected Party shall photograph the object or building as requested by the inspecting Party for the purpose of clarifying its nature and function. If the ambiguity cannot be removed during the inspection, then the question, relevant clarifications and a copy of any photographs taken shall be included in the inspection report.

13. In carrying out their activities, inspectors shall observe safety regulations established at the inspection site, including those for the protection of controlled environments within a facility and for personal safety. Individual protective clothing and equipment shall be provided by the inspected Party, as necessary.

14. For inspections pursuant to paragraphs 3, 4, 5, 7 or 8 of Article XI of the Treaty, pre-inspection procedures, including briefings and safety-related activities, shall begin upon arrival of the inspection team at the inspection site and shall be completed within one hour. The inspection team shall begin the inspection immediately upon completion of the pre-inspection procedures. The period of inspection shall not exceed 24 hours, except for inspections pursuant to paragraphs 6, 7 or 8 of Article XI of the Treaty. The period of inspection may be extended, by agreement with the in-country escort, by no more than eight hours. Post-inspection procedures, which include completing the inspection report in accordance with the provisions of Section XI of this Protocol, shall begin immediately upon completion of the inspection and shall be completed at the inspection site within four hours.

15. An inspection team conducting an inspection pursuant to Article XI of the Treaty shall include no more than ten inspectors, except for an inspection team conducting an inspection pursuant to paragraphs 7 or 8 of that Article, which shall include no more than 20 inspectors and an inspection team conducting an inspection activities pursuant to paragraph 6 of that Article, which shall include no more than 30 inspectors. At least two inspectors on each team must speak the language of the inspected Party. An inspection team shall operate under the direction of the team leader and deputy team leader. Upon arrival at the inspection site, the inspection team may divide itself into subgroups consisting of no fewer than two inspectors each. There shall be no more than one inspection team at an inspection site at any one time.

16. Except in the case of inspections conducted pursuant to paragraphs 3, 4, 7 or 8 of Article XI of the Treaty, upon completion of the post-inspection procedures, the inspection team shall return promptly to the point of entry from which it commenced inspection activities and shall then leave, within 24 hours, the territory of the country in which the inspection site is located, using its own airplane. In the case of inspections conducted pursuant to paragraphs 3, 4, 7 or 8 of Article XI of the Treaty, if the inspection team intends to conduct another inspection it shall either:

(a) notify the inspected Party of its intent upon return to the point of entry; or

(b) notify the inspected Party of the type of inspection and the inspection site upon completion of the post-inspection procedures. In this case it shall be the responsibility of the inspected Party to ensure that the inspection team reaches the next inspection site without unjustified delay. The inspected Party shall determine the means of transportation and route involved in such travel. With respect to subparagraph (a), the procedures set forth in paragraph 7 of Section V of this Protocol and paragraphs 1 and 2 of Section VII of this Protocol shall apply.

VII. Inspections Conducted Pursuant to Paragraphs 3, 4 or 5 of Article XI of the Treaty

1. Within one hour after the time for the specification of the inspection site notified pursuant to paragraph 1(a) of Section IV of this Protocol, the inspected Party shall implement pre-inspection movement restrictions at the inspection site, which shall remain in effect until the inspection team arrives at the inspection site. During the period that pre-inspection movement restrictions are in effect, missiles, stages of such missiles, launchers or support equipment subject to the Treaty shall not be removed from the inspection site.

2. The inspected Party shall transport the inspection team from the point of entry to the inspection site so that the inspection team arrives at the inspection site no later than nine hours after the time for the specification of the inspection site notified pursuant to paragraph 1(a) of Section IV of this Protocol.

3. In the event that an inspection is conducted in a basing country, the aircrew of the inspected Party may include representatives of the basing country.

4. Neither Party shall conduct more than one inspection pursuant to paragraph 5(a) of Article XI of the Treaty at any one time, more than one inspection pursuant to paragraph 5(b) of Article XI of the Treaty at any one time, or more than 10 inspections pursuant to paragraph 3 of Article XI of the Treaty at any one time.

5. The boundaries of the inspection site at the facility to be inspected shall be the boundaries of that facility set forth in the Memorandum of Understanding.

6. Except in the case of an inspection conducted pursuant to paragraphs 4 or 5(b) of Article XI of the Treaty, upon arrival of the inspection team at the inspection site, the in-country escort shall inform the inspection team leader of the number of missiles, stages of missiles, launchers, support structures and support equipment at the site that are subject to the Treaty and provide the inspection team leader with a diagram of the inspection site indicating the location of these missiles, stages of missiles, launchers, support structures and support equipment at the inspection site.

7. Subject to the procedures of paragraphs 8 through 14 of this Section, inspectors shall have the right to inspect the entire inspection site, including the interior of structures, containers or vehicles, or including covered objects, whose dimensions are equal to or greater than the dimensions specified in Section VI of the Memorandum of Understanding for the missiles, stages of such missiles, launchers or support equipment of the inspected Party.

8. A missile, a stage of such a missile or a launcher subject to the Treaty shall be subject to inspection only by external visual observation, including measuring, as necessary, the dimensions of such a missile, stage of such a missile or launcher. A container that the inspected Party declares to contain a missile or stage of a missile subject to the Treaty, and which is not sufficiently large to be capable of containing more than one missile or stage of such a missile of the inspected Party subject to the Treaty, shall be subject to inspection only by external visual observation, including measuring, as necessary, the dimensions of such a container to confirm that it cannot contain more than one missile or stage of such a missile of the inspected Party subject to the Treaty. Except as provided for in paragraph 14 of this Section, a container that is sufficiently large to contain a missile or stage of such a missile of the inspected Party subject

to the Treaty that the inspected Party declares not to contain a missile or stage of such a missile subject to the Treaty shall be subject to inspection only by means of weighing or visual observation of the interior of the container, as necessary, to confirm that it does not, in fact, contain a missile or stage of such a missile of the inspected Party subject to the Treaty. If such a container is a launch canister associated with a type of missile not subject to the Treaty, and declared by the inspected Party to contain such a missile, it shall be subject to external inspection only, including use of radiation detection devices, visual observation and linear measurement, as necessary, of the dimensions of such a canister.

9. A structure or container that is not sufficiently large to contain a missile, stage of such a missile or launcher of the inspected Party subject to the Treaty shall be subject to inspection only by external visual observation including measuring, as necessary, the dimensions of such a structure or container to confirm that it is not sufficiently large to be capable of containing a missile, stage of such a missile or launcher of the inspected Party subject to the Treaty.

10. Within a structure, a space which is sufficiently large to contain a missile, stage of such a missile or launcher of the inspected Party subject to the Treaty, but which is demonstrated to the satisfaction of the inspection team not to be accessible by the smallest missile, stage of a missile or launcher of the inspected Party subject to the Treaty shall not be subject to further inspection. If the inspected Party demonstrates to the satisfaction of the inspection team by means of a visual inspection of the interior of an enclosed space from its entrance that the enclosed space does not contain any missile, stage of such a missile or launcher of the inspected Party subject to the Treaty, such an enclosed space shall not be subject to further inspection.

11. The inspection team shall be permitted to patrol the perimeter of the inspection site and station inspectors at the exits of the site for the duration of the inspection.

12. The inspection team shall be permitted to inspect any vehicle capable of carrying missiles, stages of such missiles, launchers or support equipment of the inspected Party subject to the Treaty at any time during the course of an inspection and no such vehicle shall leave the inspection site during the course of the inspection until inspected at site exits by the inspection team.

13. Prior to inspection of a building within the inspection site, the inspection team may station subgroups at the exits of the building that are large enough to permit passage of any missile, stage of such a missile, launcher or support equipment of the inspected Party subject to the Treaty. During the time that the building is being inspected, no vehicle or object capable of containing any missile, stage of such a missile, launcher or support equipment of the inspected Party subject to the Treaty shall be permitted to leave the building until inspected.

14. During an inspection conducted pursuant to paragraph 5(b) of Article XI of the Treaty, it shall be the responsibility of the inspected Party to demonstrate that a shrouded or environmentally protected object which is equal to or larger than the smallest missile, stage of a missile or launcher of the inspected Party subject to the Treaty is not, in fact, a missile, stage of such a missile or launcher of the inspected Party subject to the Treaty. This may be accomplished by partial removal of the shroud or environmental protection cover, measuring, or weighing the covered object or by other methods. If the inspected Party satisfies the inspection team by its demonstration that the object is not a missile, stage of such a missile or launcher of the inspected Party subject to the Treaty, then there shall be no further inspection of that object. If the container is a launch canister associated with a type of missile not subject to the Treaty, and declared by the inspected Party to

contain such a missile, then it shall be subject to external inspection only, including use of radiation detection devices, visual observation and linear measurement, as necessary, of the dimensions of such a canister.

VIII. Inspections Conducted Pursuant to Paragraphs 7 or 8 of Article XI of the Treaty

1. Inspections of the process of elimination of items of missile systems specified in the Protocol on Elimination carried out pursuant to paragraph 7 of Article XI of the Treaty shall be conducted in accordance with the procedures set forth in this paragraph and the Protocol on Elimination:

  (a) Upon arrival at the elimination facility, inspectors shall be provided with a schedule of elimination activities.

  (b) Inspectors shall check the data which are specified in the notification provided by the inspected Party regarding the number and type of items of missile systems to be eliminated against the number and type of such items which are at the elimination facility prior to the initiation of the elimination procedures.

  (c) Subject to paragraphs 3 and 11 of Section VI of this Protocol, inspectors shall observe the execution of the specific procedures for the elimination of the items of missile systems as provided for in the Protocol on Elimination. If any deviations from the agreed elimination procedures are found, the inspectors shall have the right to call the attention of the in-country escort to the need for strict compliance with the above-mentioned procedures. The completion of such procedures shall be confirmed in accordance with the procedures specified in the Protocol on Elimination.

  (d) During the elimination of missiles by means of launching, the inspectors shall have the right to ascertain by visual observation that a missile prepared for launch is a missile of the type subject to elimination. The inspectors shall also be allowed to observe such a missile from a safe location specified by the inspected Party until the completion of its launch. During the inspection of a series of launches for the elimination of missiles by means of launching, the inspected Party shall determine the means of transport and route for the transportation of inspectors between inspection sites.

2. Inspections of the elimination of items of missile systems specified in the Protocol on Elimination carried out pursuant to paragraph 8 of Article XI of the Treaty shall be conducted in accordance with the procedures set forth in Sections II, IV or V of the Protocol on Elimination or as otherwise agreed by the Parties.

IX. Inspection Activities Conducted Pursuant to Paragraph 6 of Article XI of the Treaty

1. The inspected Party shall maintain an agreed perimeter around the periphery of the inspection site and shall designate a portal with not more than one rail line and one road which shall be within 50 meters of each other. All vehicles which can contain an intermediate-range GLBM or longest stage of such a GLBM of the inspected Party shall exit only through this portal.

2. For the purposes of this Section, the provisions of paragraph 10 of Article VII of the Treaty shall be applied to intermediate-range GLBMs of the inspected Party and the longest stage of such GLBMs.

3. There shall not be more than two other exits from the inspection site. Such exits shall be monitored by appropriate sensors. The perimeter of and exits from the inspection site may be monitored as provided for by paragraph 11 of Section VII of this Protocol.

4. The inspecting Party shall have the right to establish continuous monitoring systems at the portal specified in paragraph 1 of this Section

and appropriate sensors at the exits specified in paragraph 3 of this Section and carry out necessary engineering surveys, construction, repair and replacement of monitoring systems.

5. The inspected Party shall, at the request of and at the expense of the inspecting Party, provide the following:

(a) all necessary utilities for the construction and operation of the monitoring systems, including electrical power, water, fuel, heating and sewage;

(b) basic construction materials including concrete and lumber;

(c) the site preparation necessary to accommodate the installation of continuously operating systems for monitoring the portal specified in paragraph 1 of this Section, appropriate sensors for other exits specified in paragraph 3 of this Section and the center for collecting data obtained during inspections. Such preparation may include ground excavation, laying of concrete foundations, trenching between equipment locations and utility connections;

(d) transportation for necessary installation tools, materials and equipment from the point of entry to the inspection site; and

(e) a minimum of two telephone lines and, as necessary, high frequency radio equipment capable of allowing direct communication with the embassy of the inspecting Party in the country in which the site is located.

6. Outside the perimeter of the inspection site, the inspecting Party shall have the right to:

(a) build no more than three buildings with a total floor space of not more than 150 square meters for a data center and inspection team headquarters, and one additional building with floor space not to exceed 500 square meters for the storage of supplies and equipment;

(b) install systems to monitor the exits to include weight sensors, vehicle sensors, surveillance systems and vehicle dimensional measuring equipment;

(c) install at the portal specified in paragraph 1 of this Section equipment for measuring the length and diameter of missile stages contained inside of launch canisters or shipping containers;

(d) install at the portal specified in paragraph 1 of this Section non-damaging image producing equipment for imaging the contents of launch canisters or shipping containers declared to contain missiles or missile stages as provided for in paragraph 11 of this Section;

(e) install a primary and back-up power source; and

(f) use, as necessary, data authentication devices.

7. During the installation or operation of the monitoring systems, the inspecting Party shall not deny the inspected Party access to any existing structures or security systems. The inspecting Party shall not take any actions with respect to such structures without consent of the inspected Party. If the Parties agree that such structures are to be rebuilt or demolished, either partially or completely, the inspecting Party shall provide the necessary compensation.

8. The inspected Party shall not interfere with the installed equipment or restrict the access of the inspection team to such equipment.

9. The inspecting Party shall have the right to use its own two-way systems of radio communication between inspectors patrolling the perimeter and the data collection center. Such systems shall conform to power and frequency restrictions established on the territory of the inspected Party.

10. Aircraft shall not be permitted to land within the perimeter of the monitored site except for emergencies at the site and with prior notification to the inspection team.

11. Any shipment exiting through the portal specified in paragraph 1 of this Section which is large enough and

heavy enough to contain an intermediate-range GLBM or longest stage of such a GLBM of the inspected Party shall be declared by the inspected Party to the inspection team before the shipment arrives at the portal. The declaration shall state whether such a shipment contains a missile or missile stage as large or larger than and as heavy or heavier than an intermediate-range GLBM or longest stage of such a GLBM of the inspected Party.

12. The inspection team shall have the right to weigh and measure the dimensions of any vehicle, including railcars, exiting the site to ascertain whether it is large enough and heavy enough to contain an intermediate-range GLBM or longest stage of such a GLBM of the inspected Party. These measurements shall be performed so as to minimize the delay of vehicles exiting the site. Vehicles that are either not large enough or not heavy enough to contain an intermediate-range GLBM or longest stage of such a GLBM of the inspected Party shall not be subject to further inspection.

13. Vehicles exiting through the portal specified in paragraph 1 of this Section that are large enough and heavy enough to contain an intermediate-range GLBM or longest stage of such a GLBM of the inspected Party but that are declared not to contain a missile or missile stage as large or larger than and as heavy or heavier than an intermediate-range GLBM or longest stage of such a GLBM of the inspected Party shall be subject to the following procedures.

(a) The inspecting Party shall have the right to inspect the interior of all such vehicles.

(b) If the inspecting Party can determine by visual observation or dimensional measurement that, inside a particular vehicle, there are no containers or shrouded objects large enough to be or to contain an intermediate-range GLBM or longest stage of such a GLBM of the inspected Party, then that vehicle shall not be subject to further inspection.

(c) If inside a vehicle there are one or more containers or shrouded objects large enough to be or to contain an intermediate-range GLBM or longest stage of such a GLBM of the inspected Party, it shall be the responsibility of the inspected Party to demonstrate that such containers or shrouded objects are not and do not contain intermediate-range GLBMs or the longest stages of such GLBMs of the inspected Party.

14. Vehicles exiting through the portal specified in paragraph 1 of this Section that are declared to contain a missile or missile stage as large or larger than and as heavy or heavier than an intermediate-range GLBM or longest stage of such a GLBM of the inspected Party shall be subject to the following procedures.

(a) The inspecting Party shall preserve the integrity of the inspected missile or stage of a missile.

(b) Measuring equipment shall be placed only outside of the launch canister or shipping container; all measurements shall be made by the inspecting Party using the equipment provided for in paragraph 6 of this Section. Such measurements shall be observed and certified by the in-country escort.

(c) The inspecting Party shall have the right to weigh and measure the dimensions of any launch canister or of any shipping container declared to contain such a missile or missile stage and to image the contents of any launch canister or of any shipping container declared to contain such a missile or missile stage; it shall have the right to view such missiles or missile stages contained in launch canisters or shipping containers eight times per calendar year. The in-country escort shall be present during all phases of such viewing. During such interior viewing:

(i) the front end of the launch canister or the cover of the shipping container shall be opened;

(ii) the missile or missile stage shall not be removed from its launch canister or shipping container; and

(iii) the length and diameter of the stages of the missile shall be measured in accordance with the methods agreed by the Parties so as to ascertain that the missile or missile stage is not an intermediate-range GLBM of the inspected Party, or the longest stage of such a GLBM, and that the missile has no more than one stage which is outwardly similar to a stage of an existing type of intermediate-range GLBM.

(d) The inspecting Party shall also have the right to inspect any other containers or shrouded objects inside the vehicle containing such a missile or missile stage in accordance with the procedures in paragraph 13 of this Section.

X. Cancellation of Inspection

An inspection shall be cancelled if, due to circumstances brought about by *force majeure,* it cannot be carried out. In the case of a delay that prevents an inspection team performing an inspection pursuant to paragraphs 3, 4 or 5 of Article XI of the Treaty, from arriving at the inspection site during the time specified in paragraph 2 of Section VII of this Protocol, the inspecting Party may either cancel or carry out the inspection. If an inspection is cancelled due to circumstances brought about by *force majeure* or delay, then the number of inspections to which the inspecting Party is entitled shall not be reduced.

XI. Inspection Report

1. For inspections conducted pursuant to paragraphs 3, 4, 5, 7 or 8 of Article XI of the Treaty, during post-inspection procedures, and no later than two hours after the inspection has been completed, the inspection team leader shall provide the in-country escort with a written inspection report in both the English and Russian languages. The report shall be factual. It shall include the type of inspection carried out, the inspection site, the number of missiles, stages of missiles, launchers and items of support equipment subject to the Treaty observed during the period of inspection and any measurements recorded pursuant to paragraph 10[11] of Section VI of this Protocol. Photographs taken during the inspection in accordance with agreed procedures, as well as the inspection site diagram provided for by paragraph 6 of Section VII of this Protocol, shall be attached to this report.

2. For inspection activities conducted pursuant to paragraph 6 of Article XI of the Treaty, within 3 days after the end of each month, the inspection team leader shall provide the in-country escort with a written inspection report both in the English and Russian languages. The report shall be factual. It shall include the number of vehicles declared to contain a missile or stage of a missile as large or larger than and as heavy or heavier than an intermediate-range GLBM or longest stage of such a GLBM of the inspected Party that left the inspection site through the portal specified in paragraph 1 of Section IX of this Protocol during that month. The report shall also include any measurements of launch canisters or shipping containers contained in these vehicles recorded pursuant to paragraph 11 of Section VI of this Protocol. In the event the inspecting Party, under the provisions of paragraph 14(c) of Section IX of this Protocol, has viewed the interior of a launch canister or shipping container declared to contain a missile or stage of a missile as large or larger than and as heavy or heavier than an intermediate-range GLBM or longest stage of such a GLBM of the inspected Party, the report shall also include the measurements of the length and diameter of missile stages obtained during the inspection and recorded pursuant to paragraph 11 of Section VI of this Protocol. Photographs taken during the inspection in accordance with agreed procedures shall be attached to this report.

3. The inspected Party shall have the right to include written comments in the report.

4. The Parties shall, when possible,

resolve ambiguities regarding factual information contained in the inspection report. Relevant clarifications shall be recorded in the report. The report shall be signed by the inspection team leader and by one of the members of the in-country escort. Each Party shall retain one copy of the report.

This Protocol is an integral part of the Treaty. It shall enter into force on the date of entry into force of the Treaty and shall remain in force as long as the Treaty remains in force. As provided for in paragraph 1(b) of Article XIII of the Treaty, the Parties may agree upon such measures as may be necessary to improve the viability and effectiveness of this Protocol. Such measures shall not be deemed amendments to the Treaty.

DONE at Washington on December 8, 1987, in two copies, each in the English and Russian languages, both texts being equally authentic.

FOR THE UNITED STATES OF AMERICA

RONALD REAGAN

President of the United States of America

FOR THE UNION OF SOVIET SOCIALIST REPUBLICS

M. GORBACHEV

General Secretary of the Central Committee of the CPSU

ANNEX

Provisions on Privileges and Immunities of Inspectors and Aircrew Members

In order to exercise their functions effectively, for the purpose of implementing the Treaty and not for their personal benefit, the inspectors and aircrew members referred to in Section III of this Protocol shall be accorded the privileges and immunities contained in this Annex. Privileges and immunities shall be accorded for the entire in-country period in the country in which an inspection site is located, and thereafter with respect to acts previously performed in the exercise of official functions as an inspector or aircrew member.

1. Inspectors and aircrew members shall be accorded the inviolability enjoyed by diplomatic agents pursuant to Article 29 of the Vienna Convention on Diplomatic Relations of April 18, 1961.

2. The living quarters and office premises occupied by an inspector carrying out inspection activities pursuant to paragraph 6 of Article XI of the Treaty shall be accorded the inviolability and protection accorded the premises of diplomatic agents pursuant to Article 30 of the Vienna Convention on Diplomatic Relations.

3. The papers and correspondence of inspectors and aircrew members shall enjoy the inviolability accorded to the papers and correspondence of diplomatic agents pursuant to Article 30 of the Vienna Convention on Diplomatic Relations. In addition, the aircraft of the inspection team shall be inviolable.

4. Inspectors and aircrew members shall be accorded the immunities accorded diplomatic agents pursuant to paragraphs 1, 2 and 3 of Article 31 of the Vienna Convention on Diplomatic Relations. The immunity from jurisdiction of an inspector or an aircrew member may be waived by the inspecting Party in those cases when it is of the opinion that immunity would impede the course of justice and that it

can be waived without prejudice to the implementation of the provisions of the Treaty. Waiver must always be express.

5. Inspectors carrying out inspection activities pursuant to paragraph 6 of Article XI of the Treaty shall be accorded the exemption from dues and taxes accorded to diplomatic agents pursuant to Article 34 of the Vienna Convention on Diplomatic Relations.

6. Inspectors and aircrew members of a Party shall be permitted to bring into the territory of the other Party or a basing country in which an inspection site is located, without payment of any customs duties or related charges, articles for their personal use, with the exception of articles the import or export of which is prohibited by law or controlled by quarantine regulations.

7. An inspector or aircrew member shall not engage in any professional or commercial activity for personal profit on the territory of the inspected Party or that of the basing countries.

8. If the inspected Party considers that there has been an abuse of privileges and immunities specified in this Annex, consultations shall be held between the Parties to determine whether such an abuse has occurred and, if so determined, to prevent a repetition of such an abuse.

Appendix 13E. Agreement between the United States of America and the Union of Soviet Socialist Republics on the establishment of nuclear risk reduction centers

The United States of America and the Union of Soviet Socialist Republics, hereinafter referred to as the Parties,

Affirming their desire to reduce and ultimately eliminate the risk of outbreak of nuclear war, in particular, as a result of misinterpretation, miscalculation, or accident,

Believing that a nuclear war cannot be won and must never be fought,

Believing that agreement on measures for reducing the risk of outbreak of nuclear war serves the interests of strengthening international peace and security,

Reaffirming their obligations under the Agreement on Measures to Reduce the Risk of Outbreak of Nuclear War between the United States of America and the Union of Soviet Socialist Republics of September 30, 1971, and the Agreement between the Government of the United States of America and the Government of the Union of Soviet Socialist Republics on the Prevention of Incidents on and over the High Seas of May 25, 1972,

Have agreed as follows:

Article 1
Each Party shall establish, in its capital, a national Nuclear Risk Reduction Center that shall operate on behalf of and under the control of its respective Government.

Article 2
The Parties shall use the Nuclear Risk Reduction Centers to transmit notifications identified in Protocol I which constitutes an integral part of this Agreement.

In the future, the list of notifications transmitted through the Centers may be altered by agreement between the Parties, as relevant new agreements are reached.

Article 3
The Parties shall establish a special facsimile communications link between their national Nuclear Risk Reduction Centers in accordance with Protocol II which constitutes an integral part of this Agreement.

Article 4
The Parties shall staff their national Nuclear Risk Reduction Centers as they deem appropriate, so as to ensure their normal functioning.

Article 5
The Parties shall hold regular meetings between representatives of the Nuclear Risk Reduction Centers at least once each year to consider matters related to the functioning of such Centers.

Article 6
This Agreement shall not affect the obligations of either Party under other agreements.

Article 7
This Agreement shall enter into force on the date of its signature.

The duration of this Agreement shall not be limited.

This Agreement may be terminated by either Party upon 12 months written notice to the other Party.

Done at Washington on September 15, 1987, in two copies, each in the English and Russian languages, both texts being equally authentic.

FOR THE UNITED STATES OF AMERICA

FOR THE UNION OF SOVIET SOCIALIST REPUBLICS

Protocol I

Pursuant to the provisions and in implementation of the Agreement between the United States of America and the Union of Soviet Socialist Republics on the Establishment of Nuclear Risk Reduction Centers, the Parties have agreed as follows:

Article 1

The Parties shall transmit the following types of notifications through the Nuclear Risk Reduction Centers:

(a) notifications of ballistic missile launches under Article 4 of the Agreement on Measures to Reduce the Risk of Outbreak of Nuclear War between the United States of America and the Union of Soviet Socialist Republics of September 30, 1971;

(b) notifications of ballistic missile launches under paragraph 1 of Article VI of the Agreement between the Government of the United States of America and the Government of the Union of Soviet Socialist Republics on the Prevention of Incidents on and over the High Seas of May 25, 1972.

Article 2

The scope and format of the information to be transmitted through the Nuclear Risk Reduction Centers shall be agreed upon.

Article 3

Each Party also may, at its own discretion as a display of goodwill and with a view to building confidence, transmit through the Nuclear Risk Reduction Centers communications other than those provided for under Article 1 of this Protocol.

Article 4

Unless the Parties agree otherwise, all communications transmitted through and communications procedures of the Nuclear Risk Reduction Centers' communication link will be confidential.

Article 5

This Protocol shall enter into force on the date of its signature and shall remain in force as long as the Agreement between the United States of America and the Union of Soviet Socialist Republics on the Establishment of Nuclear Risk Reduction Centers of September 15, 1987, remains in force.

Done at Washington on September 15, 1987, in two copies, each in the English and Russian languages, both texts being equally authentic.

FOR THE UNITED STATES OF AMERICA

FOR THE UNION OF SOVIET SOCIALIST REPUBLICS

Protocol II

Pursuant to the provisions and in implementation of the Agreement between the United States of America and the Union of Soviet Socialist Republics on the Establishment of Nuclear Risk Reduction Centers, the Parties have agreed as follows:

Article 1

To establish and maintain for the purpose of providing direct facsimile communications between their national Nuclear Risk Reduction Centers, established in accordance with Article 1 of this Agreement, hereinafter referred to as the national Centers, an INTELSAT satellite circuit and a STATSIONAR satellite circuit, each with a secure orderwire communications capability for operational monitoring. In this regard:

(a) There shall be terminals equipped for communication between the national Centers;

(b) Each Party shall provide communications circuits capable of simultaneously transmitting and receiving 4800 bits per second;

(c) Communication shall begin with test operation of the INTELSAT satellite circuit, as soon as purchase, delivery and installation of the necessary equipment by the Parties are completed. Thereafter, taking into account the results of test operations, the Parties shall agree on the transition to a fully operational status;

(d) To the extent practicable, test operation of the STATSIONAR satellite circuit shall begin simultaneously with test operation of the INTELSAT satellite circuit. Taking into account the results of test operations, the Parties shall agree on the transition to a fully operational status.

Article 2

To employ agreed-upon information security devices to assure secure transmission of facsimile messages. In this regard:

(a) The information security devices shall consist of microprocessors that will combine the digital message output with buffered random data read from standard $5\frac{1}{4}$ inch floppy disks;

(b) Each Party shall provide, through its Embassy, necessary keying material to the other.

Article 3

To establish and maintain at each operating end of the two circuits, facsimile terminals of the same make and model. In this regard:

(a) Each Party shall be responsible for the purchase, installation, operation and maintenance of its own terminals, the related information security devices, and local transmission circuits appropriate to the implementation of this Protocol;

(b) A Group III facsimile unit which meets CCITT Recommendations T.4 and T.30 and operates at 4800 bits per second shall be used;

(c) Direct facsimile messages from the USSR national Center to the U.S. national Center shall be transmitted and received in the Russian language, and from the U.S. national Center to the USSR national Center in the English language;

(d) Transmission and operating procedures shall be in conformity with procedures employed on the Direct Communications Link and adapted as necessary for the purpose of communications between the national Centers.

Article 4

To establish and maintain a secure orderwire communications capability necessary to coordinate facsimile operation. In this regard:

(a) The orderwire terminals used with the information security devices described in paragraph (a) of Article 2 shall incorporate standard USSR Cyrillic and United States Latin keyboards and cathode ray tube displays to permit the exchange of messages between operators. The specific layout of the Cyrillic keyboard shall be as specified by the Soviet side;

(b) To coordinate the work of operators, the orderwire shall be configured so as to permit, prior to the transmission and reception of messages, the exchange of all information pertinent to the coordination of such messages;

(c) Orderwire messages concerning transmissions shall be encoded using the same information security devices specified in paragraph (a) of Article 2;

(d) The orderwire shall use the same modem and communications link as used for facsimile message transmission;

(e) A printer shall be included to provide a record copy of all information exchanged on the orderwire.

Article 5
To use the same type of equipment and the same maintenance procedures as currently in use for the Direct Communications Link for the establishment of direct facsimile communications between the national Centers. The equipment, security devices, and spare parts necessary for telecommunications links and the orderwire shall be provided by the United States side to the Soviet side in return for payment of costs thereof by the Soviet side.

Article 6
To ensure the exchange of information necessary for the operation and maintenance of the telecommunication system and equipment configuration.

Article 7
To take all possible measures to assure the continuous, secure and reliable operation of the equipment and communications link, including the orderwire, for which each Party is responsible in accordance with the Protocol.

Article 8
To determine, by mutual agreement between technical experts of the Parties, the distribution and calculation of expenses for putting into operation the communication link, its maintenance and further development.

Article 9
To convene meetings of technical experts of the Parties in order to consider initially questions pertaining to the practical implementation of the activities provided for in this Protocol and, thereafter, by mutual agreement and as necessary for the purpose of improving telecommunications and information technology in order to achieve the mutually agreed functions of the national Centers.

Article 10
This Protocol shall enter into force on the date of its signature and shall remain in force as long as the Agreement between the United States of America and the Union of Soviet Socialist Republics on the Establishment of Nuclear Risk Reduction Centers of September 15, 1987, remains in force.

Done at Washington on September 15, 1987, in two copies, each in the English and Russian languages, both texts being equally authentic.

FOR THE UNITED STATES OF AMERICA

FOR THE UNION OF SOVIET SOCIALIST REPUBLICS

14. The ABM Treaty and the strategic relationship: an uncertain future

REGINA COWEN

I. Introduction

When the Anti-Ballistic Missile (ABM) Treaty was signed and ratified in 1972, the essence of the nuclear age was well understood and the Treaty as a whole stands as a recognition of this understanding. The negotiators and their respective governments shared the view that defences against ballistic missiles would in themselves undermine strategic stability and most likely trigger an offence–defence arms race that could create grave political and military uncertainties. It was the professed intent of the Treaty to forestall these developments and exclude strategic defences from the principal features of the US–Soviet security relationship. Their newly claimed importance is largely politically informed and does not reflect an actual change in the strategic environment. Despite periodic anxieties about the vulnerability of fixed land-based strategic missiles, the force configurations on both sides are such that a successful first strike against silo-based systems would still leave sufficient sea- and air-based forces to execute a devastating retaliatory strike.[1]

What can be observed is a change in the US political consensus that took policy-making guidance from an endorsement of deterrence based on offensive nuclear weapons. Much of this consensus eroded during the latter part of the 1970s: different US and Soviet objectives in the pursuit of *détente* had become visible and proved irreconcilable; Soviet and Cuban involvement in Third World conflicts, culminating in the Soviet invasion of Afghanistan in 1979, aborted Senate ratification of the SALT II Treaty and fuelled demands in the United States for more assertive leadership. What the first Reagan Administration did was to institutionalize the rapid erosion of this consensus on national security. But the second Reagan Administration has not managed to translate the search for a new domestic security consensus into policy objectives that enjoy bipartisan support.

In early 1988, at the beginning of Ronald Reagan's last year in office, there was still a noticeably greater agreement on the value and meaning of the ABM Treaty between the US Congress and the Soviet leadership than between Congress and the White House. Although arms control as a major tool of communication with the Soviet Union was rehabilitated with the conclusion of the INF Treaty in December 1987 and considerable progress in the Strategic Arms Reduction Talks (START), there is no agreement between the two countries on the purpose and role of ballistic missile defences and the future of the ABM Treaty.

The ABM Treaty entered into force on 3 October 1972. Article XIV(2) prescribes a joint review of the Treaty at five-year intervals. The previous two reviews in 1977 and 1982 were handled by the Standing Consultative Commission and each party expressed its commitment to the Treaty.[2]

At the December 1987 summit meeting in Washington, both sides agreed on a formula that allows them to interpret the ABM Treaty 'as signed', to conduct BMD (ballistic missile defence) research, development and testing 'as required' and to observe the Treaty for a period of time to be specified.[3] While this accord suggests that a Treaty review of sorts took place during the summit meeting, it papers over persistently crucial differences and endorses unilateral interpretations of what the Treaty allows. The accord saved the summit and gave it relevance beyond the signing of the INF Treaty, yet it resolved none of the BMD and ABM Treaty issues that have haunted the strategic defence debate since the US Government unilaterally reinterpreted the Treaty in the autumn of 1985.

II. Ballistic missile defence and the Treaty reinterpretation issue

In October 1985, the US Administration announced a revised interpretation of some of the ABM Treaty's most important provisions.[4] The reinterpretation challenges the basic intent of the Treaty which is 'to limit anti-ballistic missile systems', article 1(1), and to commit each party 'not to deploy ABM systems for a defense of the territory of its country and not to provide a base for such a defense', article 1(2). The vehicle for the new interpretation was the Treaty's handling of defensive systems based on new physical principles. The Treaty traditionally permits research of any kind, but the Administration also claims that the Treaty permits development and testing of anti-ballistic missile systems and components that are sea-based, air-based, space-based and mobile land-based as long as they are founded on new physical principles or post-1972 technology.[5] The reinterpretation was a unilateral undertaking on the part of the US Government based on a selective reading of Treaty articles and an incomplete review of the negotiating record, and was specifically tailored to facilitate the scope of the Strategic Defense Initiative (SDI).[6] Indeed, there is a striking parallel between the leeway gained from a broader reading of the ABM Treaty and the leeway necessary to conduct development and testing of SDI technology.

Five years have passed since President Reagan announced his plan for a defence initiative aiming to render 'nuclear weapons impotent and obsolete'.[7] Initially conceived as a technological inquiry into the possibilities of defending against a ballistic missile attack, definition of the SDI research programme and its ultimate purpose quickly turned into an acrimonious scientific and political debate with the debate itself reflecting the evolving nature of SDI.[8]

Soon after SDI was launched it became clear to both its supporters and critics that the technological means for neutralizing the effect of ballistic missiles lay, if anywhere at all, in the very distant future and that the cost of such an endeavour would be exorbitant.[9] It was this recognition that changed the near-term goals of SDI from a research effort geared solely towards the stated ultimate objective of perfect strategic defences to the much more modest goal of enhancing strategic deterrence through the introduction of partial defences into US force structure.[10] Politically, the change in SDI programme focus from perfect defences to near-term enhancement of deterrence did not involve sacrificing the long-term aims of SDI. Indeed, its proponents have claimed that a strengthening of deterrence through strategic defences is a mere stepping-stone towards fulfilment of the President's vision.[11] What the change in focus has brought about, however, is a time-urgent political effort to put the meat of technological achievements in defence research on the skeleton of the research programme and the space-based defence architecture. The Administration has made numerous claims of technological breakthroughs but many scientists are noticeably cautious about the achievable performance levels in an adverse environment.[12] Technological breakthroughs aside, the crucial questions to answer are these: Does a technological capability merit the case for strategic defences? What role could strategic defences play given the realities of the nuclear age? Could strategic stability be more effectively maintained with a ballistic missile defence than without it? These questions are not new, yet they are back on the political agenda—the Strategic Defense Initiative and the accompanying debate about BMD reflect a much broader dispute about the basis upon which the security relationship between the United States and the Soviet Union is predicated and the policy implications it postulates.

The security relationship between the United States and the Soviet Union is based on a range of invulnerable strategic nuclear forces and both sides deter one another from striking first because such a strike would invite a devastating retaliatory blow. The stability of the relationship depends on how effectively it allows both sides to maintain the invulnerability of retaliatory forces and control over crises. It also requires an assured effectiveness of retaliatory forces. If one side cannot be certain that its forces are able to reach their targets in retaliation, that side loses confidence in its ability to deter a first strike upon its territory. Retaliatory capacity may be lost through the vulnerability of strategic forces, that is, forces that are relatively easily targetable by the other side. Not only would such vulnerability reduce the deterrent effect of these forces but, perhaps even more important, it would persuade decision makers to use them in a crisis situation before they could be destroyed by the adversary. However, at present both the United States and the Soviet Union have the ability to deter and retaliate; they can inflict unacceptable damage upon each other and mutual assured destruction exists. It is a characteristic of the strategic relationship, an indisputable fact of the nuclear era. An equally basic fact is that deterrence of nuclear attack through nuclear retaliation makes the survival of one side dependent upon the rational co-operation of the other. As those conditions are indisputable, they are also indispensable security policy determinants. What President Reagan's Strategic Defense Initiative has done is to make nuclear reality appear adaptable to changes in policy, when, in fact, it is not.

SDI presents a policy choice where there are no options. It promises a technological solution for the constraints imposed on unilateral action by the existence of mutually deterrent nuclear forces. Nuclear weapons have made strategic security a bilateral affair; no amount of political imagination and technological inventiveness (short of the most dramatic science-fiction-type defensive dome) is likely to change this situation. Moreover, in the nuclear age, where the stakes are high, it makes neither political nor military sense to redirect policy today to fulfil tomorrow's future. Enhancing strategic deterrence with strategic defences on the road to a perfect defensive shield harbours the potential for an offence–defence arms race, reduces crisis stability and makes reductions in strategic nuclear forces less likely.[13]

During the past four years the US Government has vigorously defended the case for ballistic missile defences. Although frequently not speaking with one voice, the Administration has clung to the concept of deterrence through denial which aims to both complicate a Soviet first strike and, should that fail, to render a first strike increasingly ineffective, thus hoping to dissuade the USSR from striking at all. The problem with the Administration's case is that it is based on entirely political motives. It ridicules the essence of the nuclear age and the strategic relationship: war must in the first instance be avoided through bilateral efforts; stopping missiles from arriving on their targets is not quite the same thing. It presupposes the outbreak of war and a breakdown of the bilateral security relationship.

III. Treaty reinterpretation, grey areas and loopholes

The Administration's push for strategic defences and the reinterpretation of the ABM Treaty involve not merely the question of the correct legal position but also the question of an appropriate policy response to what have been identified as legal uncertainties. To address the legal situation first, what does the Treaty say about testing and development of exotic technology, such as lasers and particle beam weapons?

The reinterpretation takes issue with the traditional reading of articles II, III and V and Agreed Statement D. Article II defines what an ABM system is, namely, 'a system to counter strategic ballistic missiles or their elements in flight trajectory, currently consisting of . . .' and then proceeds to identify what an ABM system consists of: ABM interceptor missiles, ABM launchers and ABM radars. Traditionally, the term 'currently' has been interpreted as illustrative, that is, covering a wider range of ABM system elements than specifically stated in the Treaty, irrespective of their technological basis. The reinterpretation claims that the term 'currently' has the function of restricting the application of article II to technologies known in 1972. Article III reaffirms that 'each Party undertakes not to deploy ABM systems or their components' but allows each side to deploy 100 ABM interceptor missiles at one specified deployment site. This exception has traditionally been interpreted as definitively banning all deployments other than those explicitly specified. Article V, and in particular article V(1), issues a comprehensive ban on development, testing and deployment of ABM systems or components that are sea-based, air-based, space-based or mobile land-based. Again, the traditional reading has been that article V(1) prohibits other than the specifically exempted (land-based) ABM basing modes, irrespective of technology. Agreed Statement D is the only place in the Treaty that refers to 'ABM systems based on other physical principles'. It states that:

In order to ensure fulfilment of the obligation not to deploy ABM systems and their components except as provided in Article III of the Treaty, the Parties agree that in the event ABM systems based on other physical principles and including components capable of substituting for ABM interceptor missiles, ABM launchers, or ABM radars are created in the future, specific limitations on such systems and their components would be subject to discussion in accordance with Article XIII and in agreement with Article XIV of the Treaty.

The reinterpretation dispute is this: Do articles II, III and V cover all types of technology or do they not? If they do, Agreed Statement D should be read as reinforcing article III; if they do not, then ABM systems and components based on other physical principles can be tested and developed, and only their deployment is subject to discussion with the Soviet Union.[14] Article V, with its ban on testing and development of ABM systems and components other than fixed land-based, is of crucial importance in determining the extent to which the ABM Treaty can be used to facilitate SDI—precisely the kind of undertaking it was meant to impede under the traditional interpretation.

The US Administration has supported the case for the reinterpretation on several grounds.

1. It has pointed to Soviet ABM Treaty violations and the Soviet Union's own BMD efforts.[15]

2. It holds that the Soviet Union has an understanding of Treaty provisions on exotic technology that differs from the traditional Treaty interpretation and that for this reason the USSR could not be held to a narrow reading of the Treaty.[16]

3. The Reagan Administration claims that a broader reading of the Treaty is necessary in order to establish the feasibility of SDI.[17] Most important, however, the Administration claims the legal correctness of the new interpretation.[18]

Following the reinterpretation Senator Sam Nunn, Chairman of the Senate Armed Services Committee and a strong supporter of the ABM Treaty, demanded Senate access to the classified negotiating record in order to examine the claims made by the Administration. Confidential access was granted in August 1986, and on 19 May 1987 Senator Nunn issued a critique of the Administration's position that individually and comprehensively rejected that position on points of legality, established procedure and common sense. He concluded that there was no question about the congruence between what the US ABM Treaty negotiators were asked to negotiate, what they negotiated and what the US Senate ratified in 1972.[19]

Among the evidence presented by Senator Nunn to the US Senate is a written reply by Secretary of Defense Laird to a question put to him by Senator Goldwater during the 1972 ratification hearings. The question concerned the development of space-based lasers for boost-phase interception of Soviet strategic missiles. Laird's reply supplies two crucial pieces of evidence in support of the traditional Treaty interpretation.

1. It shows that the US Senate in 1972 was aware of the Treaty's regulations

on exotic technology and that these regulations were fully discussed by Senators.

2. Secretary Laird made an unequivocal link between the development of space-based lasers and the ban on space-based ABM systems contained in article V(1) of the Treaty.

Laird's written reply, available to the Reagan Administration as part of the negotiating record it based its reinterpretation on, clearly refutes the Administration's assertion that the prohibitions in article V(1) apply to non-exotic ABM systems alone. Such evidence refutes the legality of the Administration's case against a narrow Treaty interpretation.[20]

If the case for the reinterpretation cannot be made on legal grounds, the Treaty most certainly provides the USA with the opportunity to introduce emerging defensive technologies, because of grey areas and loopholes in Treaty language, applicability and definitional scope. In 1972, components of an ABM system were identified as interceptor missiles, launchers and radars. Substitution of components and upgrading of non-ABM components to counter strategic ballistic missiles are prohibited; neither can these be tested in an ABM mode. However, the Treaty does not define the term 'component'. The question is, when is a component a component and not a sub-component or an adjunct? Interceptor missiles with built-in guidance systems, for example, do not need radar guidance. If the built-in guidance system substitutes for the radar, it must, according to the Treaty, be defined as a component. Defining it as an adjunct circumvents the Treaty's substitution clause—article VI(a). A similar problem arises with space-based mirrors that could be used to bounce off laser beams from a ground-based laser station and direct them towards ballistic missiles. Are the mirrors components? Their role is essential to the performance of the ground-based laser station. They should therefore be regarded as components although they do not substitute for existing components, and they would therefore contravene the ban on space basing.[21] There is also the issue of air-defence surface-to-air missiles to be considered. Their capabilities have increased and they could have a latent ABM potential. If they are tested against non-strategic ballistic missiles, the Treaty permits it because they would not have been tested in an ABM mode. Another opportunity to circumvent Treaty BMD constraints stems from the absence of an anti-satellite (ASAT) treaty. Much of the technology necessary to destroy a satellite is also useful for prohibited BMD. Finally, there is the ambiguity about the cut-off point for research permitted under the ABM Treaty. Should research tests outside the laboratory be allowed? How could research tests and field tests be distinguished? Taken together, these ambiguities and loopholes give rise to one-sided interpretations as to what is and is not permitted by the Treaty. They also, however, give opportunity for exploitation to those wishing to subvert the spirit if not the letter of the Treaty.

IV. The Soviet position

The Soviet Union's reaction to the US interpretation of the ABM Treaty must be distinguished from Soviet views on the US Strategic Defense Initiative. The evidence available points to a Soviet view on the Treaty that supports the traditional narrow interpretation well before the Reagan Administration launched SDI and reinterpreted the Treaty in October 1985.[22] Prior to 1983 and the President's SDI speech, there was no reason for the USSR to call for a continued restrictive interpretation because there was only one accepted version of the Treaty. It cannot therefore be credibly argued, as some US Administration officials do, that Soviet views on the ABM Treaty should not be taken seriously since they are solely made in opposition to SDI.[23] There is no evidence suggesting a Soviet distinction between traditional ABM systems and those based on new physical principles. The links made by the USSR since 1983 between SDI and the challenges to the ABM Treaty are, of course, not incidental. The Soviet position on SDI is not only determined by a sole desire to maintain the ABM Treaty. A broader interpretation of the ABM Treaty that would allow the United States to forge ahead with testing and development of sophisticated space-based defences would require a Soviet response not only in the security field but also in the economic field. The economic and technological challenge that SDI poses to the Soviet economy is formidable because it aims at its most vulnerable sectors: information technology and industrial innovation. At a time of economic redirecting and restructuring, an SDI-type concerted short-term effort could make it impossible to achieve difficult economic reform programmes within the set time-frame.

Most of all, however, the Soviet Union considers SDI as a challenge to the nuclear *status quo* between the two powers. To the USSR, strategic nuclear parity reflects as much a political as a military equilibrium. Thus, the US unilateral interpretation is not only viewed as a security risk to the Soviet Union but as an unequivocal cancellation of the Soviet Union's equal status *vis-à-vis* the United States. Moreover, SDI has come at a time when the Soviet Union is in great need of a favourably structured environment: a challenge to the Soviet Union's international position may well endanger the prospect for successful reform internally.[24]

It is therefore not surprising for the USSR to have employed a variety of tactics to stop SDI in its tracks. Its most successful one has been to hold arms reduction at the strategic level hostage to SDI limits.[25] Another tactic was the timely playing of the arms control card. In the spring of 1987, the USSR delinked intermediate-range nuclear force elimination from SDI in order to make the December 1987 Washington summit meeting possible. At the summit, General Secretary Gorbachev agreed to differ with President Reagan on SDI and a joint commitment to maintain the ABM Treaty.[26] This should not be seen as the impending end to Soviet opposition to SDI. Rather, it should be remembered that arms control has many audiences. In the case of the INF summit, the audiences on both sides were domestic or in allied countries, not among military analysts and strategists. What is important to note is the interplay between Soviet arms control objectives, Soviet attempts to slow down and shape the US Strategic Defense Initiative and Soviet aims to maintain the ABM Treaty in its original form. The USSR has forged a link between progress in arms control and the maintenance of an existing treaty, but it has also demonstrated willingness to delink the two if and when it suited other political objectives.

Yet, it is correct to say that the Soviet position on SDI has evolved since 1983 and particularly during the course of 1987. The USSR has increasingly adopted a position that would allow for a negotiated settlement with the United States. In April, the USSR offered to discuss a list of SDI tests permitted by the Treaty; in July it submitted such a list at the Geneva negotiations; in September, Soviet Foreign Minister Eduard Shevardnadze further discussed SDI test limits with Secretary of State George Shultz.[27] In exchange for relinquishing total opposition to SDI, the USSR wants a US commitment not to withdraw from the ABM Treaty for 10 years. Thus far (March 1988), the US Government has refused to discuss limits on SDI testing with the USSR. It appears that the US unwillingness to explore Soviet suggestions rests primarily upon the fear that any US–Soviet bargaining over what is and is not allowed under the ABM Treaty would force the US Government to accommodate Soviet concerns and give the USSR the opportunity to influence and perhaps even restructure the SDI programme.[28]

The evolution of the Soviet position from comprehensive rejection of SDI research to negotiated SDI test limits does suggest a certain reassessment of the US SDI programme, its progress and the US capability to put a space-based BMD system in place. However, a Soviet relaxation of SDI prohibitions has not altered Soviet views on the maintenance of the ABM Treaty as, at least, a medium-term regulator of the US–Soviet security relationship.[29] There can hardly be any doubt that Soviet flexibility regarding SDI has been encouraged by congressional measures to keep the Administration to a narrow Treaty interpretation and probable further financial cuts of SDI. On 17 November 1987 the US Administration entered a compromise with Congress that confines SDI tests planned for 1988 to the traditional interpretation of the ABM Treaty for one year. This compromise made the passage of the congressional defence bill possible and constitutes an effective congressional disavowal of the 1985 reinterpretation of the Treaty.[30] Growing concerns about the federal deficit are likely to delay the SDI programme deployment decision too. Initially expected to be taken in 1992, 1993 appears to be the earliest date when such a decision might be taken. Defense Secretary Frank C. Carlucci's request for SDI funding of $4.5 billion for fiscal year 1989 is $1.7 billion less than the Administration intended to ask for.[31] Thus, for the first time, SDI budget requests are less than those of the previous year.

With a congressional mandate to keep within the bounds of the traditional ABM Treaty interpretation and a substantially reduced budget request forced upon the Administration in order to decrease the national deficit, the Administration finds itself politically isolated on the broad interpretation of the Treaty and under pressure from the Soviet Union to negotiate limits on space testing. (Given the persistence of the national debt, the Administration will be forced to continually scale down its annual SDI budget requests, which will, in all likelihood, be further cut by Congress.)

It would, however, be premature to suggest that the USSR is planning to cash in its position on the strict observance of the ABM Treaty for a reduction of strategic offensive forces at the START negotiations. The Washington summit communiqué made it clear that agreement to disagree on SDI was only temporary and made so as not to sacrifice the summit meeting; the USSR still does not share the US view that space-based defences contribute positively to deterrence and strategic stability. Yet despite Soviet urgings to keep to the narrow Treaty interpretation, serious question marks about Soviet BMD programmes and offensive nuclear force modernization remain, and Soviet efforts in these areas must be weighed carefully against Soviet claims to champion the cause of arms control.

The ABM Treaty allows the parties to deploy 100 ABM interceptors each, either around their capital city or around a strategic missile field. In 1976, the United States closed its ABM facility at Grand Forks, North Dakota, judging it ineffective and costly. The Soviet Union has maintained its ABM interceptor ring around Moscow and is engaged in upgrading it from 64 Galosh interceptors to 100 SH-04 and SH-08 nuclear-tipped missiles. The SA-12 surface-to-air missile which the USSR is deploying could have a limited ABM capacity especially against submarine-launched ballistic missiles.[32] If this is the case, it will violate article VI(a), which prohibits the upgrading of missiles other than ABM interceptor missiles. Since the early 1960s, the Soviet Union has also been engaged in research into directed-energy weapon technology and, while Soviet activities in this field do not appear to be the subject of the same policy imperatives as SDI, little is known about Soviet BMD research motives.[33] It is, of course, entirely possible that Soviet defence research has similar objectives to US BMD research prior to 1983, which would identify it as research undertaken in order to hedge against a break-out from the ABM Treaty by the other side.

One of the most controversial issues in the Western debate on Soviet ABM Treaty violations is the location and purpose of the large phased-array radar at Krasnoyarsk. According to article VI(b), the Parties are prohibited from deploying radars for early warning of a strategic missile attack except at locations along the periphery of their national territory and oriented outward. The contention about the Soviet radar rests on the fact that it is located some 600 km within Soviet borders, facing some 5000 km of Soviet territory—a clear violation of article VI(b) if it is an ABM radar. The USSR has consistently maintained that the radar is for space-tracking only, a purpose not prohibited by the Treaty.[34] The problem is that a radar for space-tracking could also carry out the task of BMD battle management and that this dual capability is not recognized in the Treaty. As long as radar purpose is defined as space-tracking, any number can be deployed without geographic restrictions.

In early September 1987, upon an invitation by the Soviet Union, a US congressional delegation visited the radar site at Krasnoyarsk. Its findings were largely inconclusive. The radar facility is years from completion and the delegation felt that, while the visit in itself had been an interesting one, they were unable to judge the radar's eventual capability as either an early-warning or a space-tracking radar.[35] The US Administration has maintained its claim that the Treaty is being violated precisely because the visit did not clarify the ambiguity of the radar's eventual purpose.[36] Other US concerns about Soviet motivations and intentions are fuelled by the massive Soviet modernization effort in offensive nuclear forces. Even if the Soviet Union remains within the quantitative sub-limits of the SALT II Treaty, it could increase the number of strategic nuclear warheads from the current 9000 to 12 000 by 1990. Without SALT-type constraints, warhead numbers could reach levels of 16 000–21 000 by the mid-1990s.[37] While reductions of strategic forces remain dependent upon resolution of the SDI issue, there are no agreed constraints upon offensive force modernizations. Should these be realized, the tasks defensive systems would have to perform would be vastly greater than those envisaged under current offensive force levels. Controlling the expansion of offensive forces could, in theory, ease the burden on defensive systems and make it easier for SDI proponents to argue the effectiveness of defensive systems. Yet, it should also be remembered that deep reductions in offensive strategic systems would deprive strategic defences of their rationale. If arms control negotiations can reverse the process of warhead proliferation, impose total warhead limits and agree on sub-limits and basing modes, the often exaggerated but none the less real fears of a disarming first-strike attack could be offset. Once the right kind of deep reductions in offensive forces are achieved, there would be no need for defensive deployments; first-strike targets would be less attractive and their destruction would consume such a great number of missiles and warheads that the attacking side would deprive itself of its retaliatory forces in a first strike. Under such conditions, offensive reductions could fulfil the function the Reagan Administration is pushing for with SDI and an offence–defence forces mix, namely, to complicate and therefore deter a Soviet first strike.

The larger and in the long term more important puzzle is whether SDI is really necessary to bring about strategic reductions, even at the price of the ABM Treaty. This puzzle would not exist if there was a shared US–Soviet understanding of the basis of the strategic relationship, the dynamics that can threaten the relationship and the powerful forces of the technical *status quo* that make militarily meaningful levels of nuclear superiority so elusive. This shared understanding could be lost entirely if the stabilizing influence of the ABM Treaty is allowed to dissipate, with attendant losses of security by both sides. East–West relations are still suffering from the breakdown of the *détente* of the 1970s; there is a still persistent inability to tackle security problems at the policy-making level rather than at the level of highly publicized visions of security and disarmament.

V. The Treaty's uncertain future

Arms control reflects the competitive nature of the strategic relationship. Agreements between the United States and the Soviet Union are as much concluded to safeguard national interests as they are to preserve the security of both. In 1972, when the ABM Treaty was signed, the security of both was a major national interest of each power. This shared perception is being eroded, and the strategic concept that informed the Treaty and its specific recommendations is being questioned.

It is not unusual for treaties between states to become irrelevant. The interests of one or both parties may change or political, technological and economic opportunities arise that are perceived to serve the interests of the parties more adequately if they act on their own rather than within the confines of an existing treaty. When treaties are perceived to constrain rather than promote the interests of the parties, they appear as cumbersome obstacles to a more promising alternative.

The ABM Treaty codifies the strategic relationship between the United States and the Soviet Union as one of mutual vulnerability based on offensive nuclear forces. The Treaty has helped stabilize strategic relations, permitted the arms control process to play a moderating role in the nuclear arms race and maintained the confidence each side needs in the effectiveness of its retaliatory nuclear systems.

However, in the light of competing objectives regarding the future role of BMD technology, it will not be a simple task for the United States and the Soviet Union to reach agreement during the remaining months of the 1987/88 ABM Treaty review period.

Soviet flexibility during 1987 on what tests of sophisticated BMD technology the Soviet Union might consider permissible could break the arms control deadlocks at the START and space negotiations in Geneva, but does not settle the question as to the ultimate purpose of going beyond the 1972 constraints. Any discussions on relaxation of Treaty provisions should therefore be preceded by an agreed understanding of long-term objectives.

It is precisely an agreement on long-term BMD objectives that continues to elude the negotiations at Geneva. With the passing, on 23 March 1988, of the fifth anniversary of President Reagan's SDI speech, the US SDI effort has not yielded tangible technological results or persuaded the USSR of the logic of deterrence through denial.

At the negotiating table, the two teams are facing each other with proposals that are as far apart as proposals can be, although compromise makes political and military sense. The US proposal reiterates the joint statement issued at the Washington summit. Since that statement allows for the broad Treaty interpretation, there was and is no need for the USA to modify the wording of the communiqué. The USSR, on the other hand, has added some clarifying language to its proposal, making clear what it believes the Washington statement means: a protocol on the conditions of adherence to the ABM Treaty would 'come into force simultaneously with a START treaty for a duration of 10 years. [A] START treaty ceases to be in force if either party violates the ABM treaty or protocol regarding that treaty'.[38] In other words, the USSR is ready to sign a START treaty contingent upon a 10-year US compliance with the ABM Treaty as defined by the Soviet Union, since the USSR reserves the right to abrogate START in case of US non-compliance with the ABM Treaty. It is highly unlikely that a US Senate will ratify a START agreement that gives the Soviet Union veto powers with respect to ABM Treaty compliance questions. Likewise, the USSR will not ratify a START agreement whose implementation could one day put Soviet security at risk. Is there a way out of this deadlock, and what options are there?

One option would be to maintain the Treaty as it was interpreted prior to the change in the US position in 1985. This would severely curtail the SDI test programme and make it virtually impossible to demonstrate the technical feasibility of SDI projects. In order to maintain the effectiveness of the traditional Treaty, this option would also have to deal with existing Treaty ambiguities relating to definitions of 'research tests', 'component' and the similarities between BMD and ASAT technologies. These clarifications can only be undertaken if and when the Soviet Union is ready to reveal a great deal more about its BMD research than it has done thus far.

The second option would be to tighten traditional ABM restrictions. No testing, development and deployment of ABM systems would be allowed. The USSR would have to give up its existing system around Moscow and SDI would stay permanently inside the laboratory. Under this option it would be essential to close the ASAT loophole in order to prevent circumvention of new and tighter restrictions. Existing Treaty ambiguities would resolve themselves since no activity apart from research would be permitted.

The third option would be to ease the constraints of the Treaty on testing and development of systems and components based on new physical principles but create a regime for tightly controlling newly permitted BMD activities. Unambiguous definitions and strict verification procedures would be essential. Notification of planned tests would probably also be necessary. Each side would have to behave so that it was beyond charges of non-compliance. They would also have to recognize the evolving nature of BMD tests and developments and therefore face the problems of progressive permissiveness. While particular capability thresholds such as laser brightness and space-based mirror apertures could be agreed upon, thresholds can be crossed, inviting suspicion from the other side, cause problems of interpretation and decrease confidence in the regime altogether.

The fourth option would be to abrogate the Treaty. Article XV(2) provides for withdrawal from the Treaty after six months' notification. SDI could proceed uninhibited, although it would be years before space-based lasers or particle beam weapons could be put into orbit; more likely in the short term would be ground-based lasers and space-based kinetic-kill vehicles.[39] The Soviet Union could be expected to respond with ASAT weapons and accelerated strategic offensive missile procurement. The much dreaded offence–defence arms race would have been initiated.

From the point of view of the international community, the second option, permitting research into BMD technologies only, would be the most desirable of the four. It is, however, also the least likely. The measure of consensus achieved in the early 1970s that made the ABM Treaty possible was as great a consensus as is attainable in relations between adversaries; to aim beyond that would be unrealistic.

The first option is favoured by the arms control community for it would recommit the Parties to and strengthen the central provisions of the Treaty. By clarifying Treaty ambiguities it would put aside many of the existing compliance and interpretation issues. SDI could be kept in check and strategic stability maintained; reductions in offensive strategic forces could be undertaken. Since this option would drastically curb SDI, its proponents would most likely oppose it on grounds of increasing US retaliatory force and command and control vulnerabilities.

Option four is not one contemplated by either the US Government or the Soviet Union: neither wants a destabilizing offence–defence arms race, although proponents of SDI and the broad ABM Treaty interpretation suffer from a lamentable under-appreciation of the risks to strategic stability which their advocacy of BMD entails.

The political, strategic and technological uncertainties that have bedevilled US–Soviet relations for the best part of the past 10 years point to option three as the most probable course for the future. It is also the one that would most tax the managerial skills of both powers. It requires a commitment to sustained co-operation in what will in all likelihood be a period of transition from deterrence with only offensive forces to deterrence by denial and retaliation. The risks along the way will be grave, and as yet unforeseen instabilities and crises may arise—a future that does not inspire confidence.

However, there is also a fifth option which might be called the 'muddling through' option.[40] Principally, it would entail a postponement of everything: a treaty on deep cuts in strategic offensive forces, an agreement on adherence to the ABM Treaty, a resolution on the purposes of BMD in the age of strategic parity, and a joint definition of the future role of outer space in international security. In sum, 'muddling through' would result in a continuation of strategic uncertainty. The record of the past five years does not inspire confidence and it is urgent that both sides find the wisdom to reaffirm the *co-operative imperatives* of their security relationship; if that happens, the biggest lesson of the nuclear age will have been learnt.

Notes and references

[1] For a discussion of survivable force structures pre- and post-START, see chapter 10; for an assessment that coincides with the President's SDI speech, see *Report of the President's Commission on Strategic Forces*, Washington, DC, Apr. 1983, especially pp. 7–10.

[2] Durch, W. J., *The Future of the ABM Treaty*, Adelphi Papers, no. 223 (IISS: London, 1987), p. 62.

[3] 'How the US and Soviet officials agreed to disagree', *New York Times*, 12 Dec. 1987, p. 1.

[4] 'White House revises interpretation of ABM Treaty', *Washington Post*, 9 Oct. 1985.

[5] *ABM Treaty Interpretation Dispute*, Hearing before the Subcommittee on Arms Control, International Security and Science of the Committee on Foreign Affairs, House of Representatives, Ninety-Ninth Congress, 1st Session, 22 Oct. 1985 (US Government Printing Office: Washington, DC, 1986), pp. 9–18.

[6] Garthoff, R., *Politics versus the Law* (Brookings Institution: Washington, DC, 1987), pp. 100–5.

[7] *Weekly Compilation of Presidential Documents*, vol. 19, no. 12 (28 Mar. 1983), pp. 423–66, in D. Drell, J. Farley and D. Holloway, *The Reagan Strategic Defense Initiative* (Stanford University: Stanford, 1984), pp. 101–3.

[8] As particular examples of this debate, see *Report to the American Physical Society of the Study Group on Science and Technology of Directed Energy Weapons* (The American Physical Society: New York, 1987). Longstreth, T. K., Pike, J. E. and Rhinelander, J. B., *The Impact of US and*

Soviet Ballistic Missile Defense Programs on the ABM Treaty, A Report for the National Campaign To Save The ABM Treaty, Washington, DC, Mar. 1985.

[9] Degrasse, R. W. and Daggett, S., *An Economic Analysis of the President's Strategic Defense Initiative: Costs and Cost Exchange Ratios* (Council on Economic Priorities: New York, 1984); '"Star Wars" would absorb new research funds, provide few benefits, study says', *Los Angeles Times*, 27 Oct. 1984; Waller, D., Bruce, J. and Cook, D., Staff Report submitted to Senator William Proxmire, Senator J. Bennet Johnston and Senator Lawton Chiles, *SDI: Progress and Challenges*, 17 Mar. 1986.

[10] Caspar W. Weinberger, *Secretary of Defense, Annual Report to Congress* (US Government Printing Office: Washington DC), Fiscal year 1985, p. 58; Fiscal Year 1986, p. 54; Fiscal Year 1987, p. 74; Fiscal Year 1988, p. 52.

[11] Weinberger (note 10), Fiscal Year 1988, pp. 51–4, 281–7.

[12] Waller, Bruce and Cook (note 9).

[13] For a discussion of these issues, see Stützle, W., Jasani, B. and Cowen, R. (eds), SIPRI, *The ABM Treaty, To Defend or Not To Defend?* (Oxford University Press: Oxford, 1987); Jasani, B. (ed.), SIPRI, *Space Weapons and International Security* (Oxford University Press: Oxford, 1987), especially Part III; Cowen, R., 'SDI and the Atlantic alliance: doctrine versus security', in R. Cowen, P. Rajcsanyi and V. Bilandzic, *SDI and European Security* (Westview Press: Boulder, Colo., 1987), pp. 13–57.

[14] *ABM Treaty Interpretation Dispute* (note 5), p. 40; on the history of the reinterpretation, see Garthoff, R., *Politics Versus the Law* (Brookings Institution: Washington, DC, 1987), pp. 2–9: Garthoff claims that another version of the Oct. 1985 reinterpretation even considered deployment of systems based on new physical principles a legitimate option under the Treaty.

[15] 'Soviet radar a "militarily significant" violation', in *Wireless File*, US Information Agency, EUR–405, 10 Sep. 1987, pp. 11–12; 'Krasnoyarsk radar site in violation of ABM Treaty', in *Wireless File*, US Information Agency, EUR–303, 9 Sep. 1987, p. 3; United States Department of State, *Soviet Noncompliance with Arms Control Agreements*, Special Report no. 175, Washington, DC, 2 Dec. 1987.

[16] *ABM Treaty Interpretation Dispute* (note 5), pp. 7, 33–5; Nitze, P. H., 'Interpreting the ABM Treaty', in *Department of State Bulletin*, vol. 87, no. 2123 (June 1987), pp. 31–3.

[17] *ABM Treaty Interpretation Dispute* (note 5), pp. 2–18; Caspar Weinberger: 'It's time to get SDI off the ground', in *Wireless File*, US Information Agency, EUR–504, 21 Aug. 1987, pp. 1–3; Longstreth, T., *Space-Based Interceptors for Star Wars: Untestable Under Any Interpretation of the ABM Treaty*, A Staff Study, Federation of American Scientists, Washington, DC, 22 Oct. 1987.

[18] Evidence given by Sofaer, A. D., legal adviser, Department of State before Subcommittee on Arms Control, International Security and Science of the Committee on Foreign Affairs, House of Representatives, Ninety-Ninth Congress, 1st Session, 22 Oct. 1985, pp. 4–21.

[19] *Congressional Record*, Proceedings and Debates of the 100th Congress, First Session, vol. 133, no. 38, Washington, 11–13 Mar. 1987; Part One: The Senate Ratification Hearings, Part Two: Subsequent Practice under the ABM Treaty, Part Three: The ABM Negotiating Record. On what the ABM Treaty negotiators thought they had negotiated in 1972, see the contributions by Smith, G. C. and Semenov, V., in Stützle, Jasani and Cowen (note 13); and *ABM Treaty Interpretation Dispute* (note 5), pp. 2–96.

[20] *Congressional Record* (note 19). See also Garthoff (note 6), pp. 100, 101: the attempt by the US Administration to reinterpret the Treaty resulted, according to Garthoff, in a 'distortion of the facts, a fatally flawed interpretation of the Treaty, and travesty of the law' (p. 100).

[21] Owing to the curvature of the earth, a laser beam has to bounce off a space-based mirror in order to hit enemy missiles rising out of the earth's atmosphere.

[22] Garthoff (note 6), pp. 80–8.

[23] US Department of State, Special Report no. 175, Washington, DC, 2 Dec. 1987; 'Disinformation bid aimed at SDI', *Defence Week*, 21 Dec. 1987, p. 6; 'Star Wars is still very much on the table', *Philadelphia Inquirer*, 16 Dec. 1987; Garthoff (note 6), pp. 80–1.

[24] Conversation with high-ranking Soviet official, Mar. 1988.

[25] This has been the Soviet position throughout 1987. For a chronicle of Soviet statements on the linkage between offensive reductions, SDI limits and a strengthening of the ABM regime, see *Arms Control Reporter*, Section 611: START (Institute for Defense and Disarmament Studies: Brookline, Mass.).

[26] 'Soviet Union and US still split on SDI', *Financial Times*, 14 Dec. 1987, p. 1; 'As required, Reagan and Gorbachev made summit a success', *International Herald Tribune*, 14 Dec. 1987, pp. 1, 5; 'By sidestepping SDI, summit ended as a success', *International Herald Tribune*, 12–13 Dec. 1987, pp. 1, 2.

[27] 'Would negotiated limits help, rather than hurt, "Star Wars"', *Christian Science Monitor*, 23 Oct. 1987, p. 8.

[28] 'US demands Moscow agree to "broad" view of ABM Treaty', *International Herald Tribune*, 23/24 Jan. 1988, pp. 1, 5; *Wireless File*, US Information Agency, EUR–206, 24 Nov. 1987, p. 33; *Wireless File*, US Information Agency, EUR–205, 24 Nov. 1987, p. 25.

[29] 'Reagan's dream of SDI is sharply scaled back', *International Herald Tribune*, 28 Mar. 1988, p. 1; 'SDI accord raises more questions', *Washington Post* (final edn), 11 Dec. 1987, p. 29; 'In the end Gorbachev yielded on Star Wars', *Philadelphia Inquirer*, 11 Dec. 1987, p. 1; 'How the US and Soviet officials agreed to disagree on Star Wars', *New York Times*, 13 Dec. 1987, p. 1; 'US, Soviets still apart on SDI, adviser says', *Washington Post*, 30 Dec. 1987, p. 5; 'Soviet pressing limits on "Star Wars" testing', *New York Times*, 16 Jan. 1988, p. 3.

[30] 'Congressional defense leaders, White House agree on SDI tests', *Aviation Week & Space Technology*, 16 Nov. 1987, p. 24; 'Reagan agrees to narrow reading of ABM Treaty—for now', *Christian Science Monitor*, 19 Nov. 1987, p. 6; 'Star Wars facing cuts and delays; '92 goal in doubt', *New York Times*, 22 Nov. 1987, p. 1.

[31] 'Star Wars defense plan loses steam', *Washington Post*, 20 Feb. 1988, p. 4; 'Reductions to delay SDI defense decision', *Washington Times*, 19 Feb. 1988, p. B7.

[32] US Department of Defense, *Soviet Military Power 1987*, chapter III: 'Strategic defense and space operations' (US Government Printing Office: Washington, DC, 1987), pp. 45–61.

[33] Kassel, S., 'Soviet research and development of directed energy weapons', in Stützle, Jasani and Cowen (note 13); 'Gorbachev admits "star wars" research', *Washington Times*, 1 Dec. 1987, p. 1.

[34] For a discussion of the Krasnoyarsk issue, see *ACCESS—Security Spectrum: On Treaties and Cheating (and Cheating on Treaties)*, vol. 1, no. 3 (Oct. 1987); see also, Haas, R. N., 'The ABM Treaty: verification and compliance issues' in Stützle, Jasani and Cowen (note 13), pp. 121–35.

[35] 'Moscow's decision on radar site: opening the door for political gains', *International Herald Tribune*, 10 Sep. 1987, p. 5; 'Administration disputes findings of U.S. visit to Soviet radar', *Aviation Week & Space Technology*, 14 Sep. 1987, pp. 26–8.

[36] 'US asks Moscow to alter radar', *International Herald Tribune*, 15 Dec. 1987, pp. 1, 6: this article also offers an explanation of the history of the Krasnoyarsk radar as given by unnamed Soviet sources; *Arms Control Reporter 1987*, no. 12, 1987, Section 603.B.147 (Institute for Defense and Disarmament Studies: Brookline, Mass.).

[37] 'Forgoing SALT: potential costs and effects on strategic capabilities', *Congress of the United States, Congressional Budget Office*, staff working paper, Aug. 1986, pp. 14–15.

[38] *Wireless File*, US Information Agency, EUR–208, 16 Feb. 1988, p. 15.

[39] 'Moderne Raketenabwehr nach dem Kamikaze Prinzip', *Frankfurter Allgemeine Zeitung*, 16 Apr. 1987, p. 7; 'Loblied auf neuen SDI-test', *Frankfurter Rundschau*, 25 May 1987; 'Pentagon being forced to show its hand on SDI', *International Combat Arms*, July 1987, p. 31; 'Weinberger sees Star Wars deployment starting by 1994', *The Times*, 22 Aug. 1987; 'Wandlungen des SDI Programs', *Frankfurter Allgemeine*, 5 Sep. 1987; interview with Secretary of Defense Caspar W. Weinberger, British Broadcasting Company, 8 Feb. 1987.

[40] For a discussion of possible options, see *Spacewatch Fortnightly*, vol. II, no. 4 (24 Feb. 1988); Garthoff, R. L., 'Refocusing the SDI debate', *Bulletin of the Atomic Scientists*, Sep. 1987, pp. 44–50.

15. The United Nations and the Iraq–Iran War

Co-ordinated by BRIAN URQUHART*

I. Introduction

The war between Iraq and Iran, now in its eighth year, is a matter of grave international concern at several levels. The war has appalling human consequences in terms of casualties, physical destruction and social disruption; it puts a continuous and dangerous strain on neighbouring countries, particularly in the Gulf area. Taking place in a highly sensitive strategic and economic area of the world, the war poses a continuous threat to world peace in a wider sense, including the balance of the superpower relationship. Not least, the Iraq–Iran War has been an important test of the capacity of the United Nations, and especially of the Security Council, to maintain international peace and security. This chapter focuses on the role of the Security Council, since the contrasts between its mandate, public statements by its five permanent members and the course of events have been a striking feature of the conflict. The conflict has demonstrated that the activities of the Security Council cannot be insulated from relations between its permanent members or from the competing foreign policy objectives of any one of them, and has underlined the fact that the usefulness of the United Nations in stabilizing situations of conflict is contingent on the attitudes of the parties to the dispute as well as the members of the Security Council.

II. The mandate of the Security Council**

The Security Council's performance at the outset of the Iraq–Iran War was a pale shadow of the possibilities that the United Nations Charter gives the Council for dealing with precisely this kind of situation. Although the member states, as US Ambassador Donald McHenry reminded the Security Council on 28 September 1980, have, under Article 24 of the Charter, entrusted the United Nations with 'the primary responsibility for the maintenance of international peace and order', the Charter also requires that member states themselves 'settle their international disputes by peaceful means' [Article 2(3)] and that they refrain from the threat or use of force. Article 33(1) states that 'the parties to any dispute shall, first of all, seek a solution by negotiation, inquiry, mediation . . . or other peaceful means of their own choice'. Should the parties fail to resolve the dispute peacefully, 'they shall refer it to the Security Council' [Article 37(1)].[1]

If the parties are unwilling to follow this procedure for various reasons of their own, one of which may well be a desire to take an opportunity to settle a

---

** The following account has drawn extensively on the study by Ralph P. H. King, *The United Nations and the Iran–Iraq War, 1980–1986* (Ford Foundation: New York, 1987).

SIPRI Yearbook 1988: World Armaments and Disarmament

grievance by force, the responsibility reverts to the Security Council, which has the primary responsibility for the maintenance of international peace and order. The Council, in any case, under Article 34, has the power to 'investigate any dispute, or any situation which might lead to international friction or give rise to a dispute, in order to determine whether the continuance of the dispute or situation is likely to endanger the maintenance of international peace and security'.

If the parties to a dispute cannot settle it by negotiation, the Council may intervene or recommend appropriate methods or terms of settlement. Finally, the Council may have recourse to the provisions of Chapter VII of the Charter, which include economic and other sanctions [Article 41] and even the necessary military action [Article 42].

Over the years a prevailing view has emerged that the Security Council can act in a dispute only if it has been brought to its attention by a member state as provided for in Article 35, or by the Secretary-General under Article 99. Thus the normal course is for the Council to act at the instigation of a member state or, on rare occasions, on the proposal of the Secretary-General. The Council's hypothetical powers have rarely been invoked to the full, and this applies in particular to the provisions of Chapter VII, which have been used on rare occasions, and then sparingly.[2]

III. UN peace initiatives in the Iraq–Iran War

On 22 September 1980 the Secretary-General of the United Nations, Kurt Waldheim, appealed to both sides to seek a peaceful solution to the Iraq–Iran dispute and offered his personal good offices.[3] He also requested an urgent Security Council meeting, and the President of the Security Council issued a statement supporting the Secretary-General's offer and calling upon the parties to settle their dispute peacefully.[4]

In spite of these statements, the Security Council did not hurry to meet to discuss this new threat to international peace and security. They met formally for the first time only on 26 September. At a meeting on 28 September 1980, the Council adopted Resolution 479 which called for an immediate end to the use of force and peaceful settlement of the dispute and urged both sides to accept any appropriate offer of mediation.[5]

Resolution 479 contained no reference to the Iraqi invasion, nor did it call for the withdrawal of forces to internationally recognized frontiers. This omission, which was to have important consequences later on, caused President Bani-Sadr to inform the Secretary-General on 1 October that Iran saw 'no use in any discussions, directly or indirectly' while Iraqi forces remained on Iranian soil. By the time of the Council's sixth meeting on 24 October 1980, it was clear that neither belligerent would heed the Council's urgings or declarations.

After its initial cursory deliberations, the Security Council did not meet again to discuss the war formally until July 1982, nearly two years later. The negotiating effort in the United Nations devolved almost entirely upon the Secretary-General and his representative, Olof Palme of Sweden, while initiatives were also undertaken by the Islamic Conference Organization, the Government of Algeria, and other groups and individuals.

While other initiatives had come to nothing, the actions of the Secretary-General and his representative became the only effective international effort to put an end to the war. Palme's early efforts to bring about a comprehensive settlement foundered on the rigid positions taken by both sides regarding the Shatt-el-Arab waterway. In retrospect it appears that there may have been a point in early 1982 when there was a possibility of reaching a settlement in the war—a point when Iraq was being forced out of Iran and Iran had not yet made the resignation of President Saddam Hussein and the designation of Iraq as the aggressor the basic conditions for formally agreeing to a cease-fire. A determined attempt by the Foreign Minister of Algeria to reach a settlement at that time was tragically brought to an end by the shooting down of his aircraft on a journey between Baghdad and Tehran. Little is known of the exact nature or state of development of this aborted negotiation.

Since July 1982, the Security Council has passed seven resolutions and issued many presidential statements. Not all of these were calls to end hostilities. Some referred to specific issues, and in particular the right of free navigation in the Gulf and attacks on merchant shipping. Until the summer of 1987, these resolutions were largely welcomed by Iraq and rejected or ignored by Iran, which boycotted Security Council discussions almost from the outset.

Intensive efforts in 1980–81 to secure the release of the ships trapped in the Shatt-el-Arab finally came to nothing, mainly due to the insistence of Iraq that the context of the release should plainly demonstrate Iraq's full sovereignty over the waterway. As regards attacks on civilian targets, a UN team was dispatched to both countries in May and early June 1983, and its findings were presented to the Security Council in June 1983. After a lull, attacks on civilian targets began again in early 1984 with each side claiming that its actions were retaliatory.

By mid-1984 the attacks—mainly Iraqi—on cities and on tankers in the Gulf were escalating, and the Secretary-General addressed the Presidents of Iran and Iraq urging them to cease all deliberate attacks on purely civilian centres and targets. This time both sides accepted. A moratorium on civilian attacks was instituted on 12 June 1984, and observer teams were sent to Baghdad and Tehran to monitor compliance with the agreement. This truce effectively ended in March 1985 when Iran retaliated against Iraqi raids on Busheir and Ahvaz by shelling Basra. In spite of further appeals by the Secretary-General, attacks by both sides on civilian targets have steadily increased.

Iranian allegations about the use of chemical weapons first surfaced on 18 August 1983. In spite of Iraqi denials, Iran reported a large-scale chemical attack on 29 February 1984, and in March 1984 the Secretary-General decided to send a mission on his own authority to investigate the charges. The report of his experts, which he submitted to the Security Council on 26 March 1984, concluded that chemical weapons had indeed been employed on Iranian territory, although neither of the belligerents was specifically named. The President of the Security Council issued a statement which condemned the use of chemical weapons. None the less in March 1985, when more Iranian victims of poison gas had arrived in European hospitals, a further specialist report concluded that they had been affected by Yperite, and that hydrocyanic gas and Tabun might also have been used. The Security Council issued a stronger statement on this occasion and condemned the use of all weapons banned by the 1925 Geneva Protocol. Further UN missions in 1986 and 1987 concluded that on numerous occasions Iraqi forces had used chemical weapons against Iranian forces. In response the President of the Council for the first time made a statement openly condemning Iraq for this practice.

In the absence of progress on settlement, the Secretary-General, by 1983, turned his attention to particular issues. In April 1985 the Secretary-General visited Baghdad and Tehran and put before the governments an eight-point plan based on the idea of a step-by-step agreement in which both sides accepted a negotiated settlement as the ultimate aim. The elements of this phased plan included an end to attack on population centres, on civil aviation, on merchant shipping and on ports and oil facilities; a ban on the use of chemical weapons; and the exchange of prisoners of war, leading to a cease-fire and a withdrawal of forces to international boundaries and the initiation of peace negotiations.

The Secretary-General reported that both parties had agreed to these eight points as a basis for further discussions. In fact, however, Iraq maintained that the goal should be an immediate cease-fire as called for in Resolution 582 (1986) of the Security Council, while Iran had considered the Secretary-General's plan only as a basis for future talks. In addition, Iran categorically rejected the possibility of negotiations with the existing regime in Iraq, and the military situation had become more complicated. Attacks on population centres had become a common tactic on both sides, while Iraqi use of chemical weapons demonstrated a certain desperation. Attacks on oil facilities, which were vital to both war economies, and on tankers in the Gulf broadened the scope of the war. By the end of 1986, when a massive Iranian assault was threatening the Iraqi city of Basra, about the only positive aspect of the situation appeared to be that the Secretary-General had been accepted as a go-between by both governments with a potential for playing a direct role in negotiations in the future.

In January 1987 the Secretary-General, in talks with the permanent members of the Security Council, called on them to undertake a new initiative through the Council to bring an end to the war, making specific suggestions as to measures to be taken. A particularly important proposal was for an impartial body to identify the responsibility for the conflict. This initiative coincided with Iran's launching of Operation Karbala V, which failed, after bitter fighting, to capture Basra. By mid-1987 a new international dimension was added with the further involvement of outside powers, including the United States and the Soviet Union, in efforts to protect shipping in the Gulf. This new dimension, with all its implicit risks, gave momentum to the new effort to find an end to the war.

After intensive consultations among themselves, with the Secretary-General and with the other members of the Security Council, the permanent members finally presented to the Council the text of Resolution 598 (1987), which was adopted unanimously on 20 July 1987. The resolution, which cited Articles 39 and 40 of the Charter of the United Nations as the relevant articles under which the Council was acting, demanded as a first step towards a negotiated settlement that the parties observe an immediate cease-fire and withdraw all forces to the internationally recognized boundaries without delay. (The designation of these articles gave notice that the Council would be following up the matter under Chapter VII, 'Action with Respect to Threats to the Peace . . .'.) It went on to request the Secretary-General to send a team of UN observers to verify, confirm and supervise the cease-fire and withdrawal and urged that prisoners of war be released and repatriated without delay after the cease-fire had come into effect. It further called on Iraq and Iran to co-operate with the Secretary-General in mediation efforts to achieve a comprehensive, just and honourable settlement acceptable to both sides, and on all other states to exercise the utmost restraint and to refrain from any act which might lead to a further escalation of the conflict. In deference to the longstanding Iranian grievance about the origins of the war, the resolution made specific suggestions as to measures to be taken. A particularly important proposal was for an impartial body to identify the responsibility for the conflict. This resolution was hailed as a considerable achievement by the Security Council as well as a harbinger of more effective and co-operative action in the Council by the permanent members. Once again, however, the main responsibility for implementing the Security Council's belated decision devolved on the Secretary-General.

Neither Iraq nor Iran rejected Resolution 598. Iraq specifically accepted it and emphasized that it expected the resolution to be implemented paragraph by paragraph, in the order of its component parts. Iran initially denounced the resolution as 'a vicious American diplomatic manoeuvre', but later said that it contained certain good points and that it could be a basis for discussion. Iran demanded, however, that the Security Council should first condemn Iraq for starting the war before it could formally accept a cease-fire.

Iraq indicated that it would continue to observe an informal truce in the tanker war, at least for a few weeks, while Iran, for its part, said that it would carry out new shipping attacks only in retaliation for any Iraqi attacks.

The general expectation was that the Secretary-General would now negotiate with both sides about the implementation of the resolution, it being understood that if nothing happened there would soon be pressure for a new step to enact an arms embargo against violators of the resolution. During July and August 1987, the Secretary-General engaged in contacts with both sides and in consultations with the Security Council with little signs of progress. On 4 September the Secretary-General informed the Security Council of Iran's written invitation to visit Tehran and its position as to the basis for the discussion, and the Council authorized the Secretary-General to visit the area. On 12–15 September the Secretary-General held talks in Tehran and in Baghdad to discuss his outline plan for the implementation of Resolution 598.

The Secretary-General's plan provided for a specific date, to be agreed upon and referred to as D-Day, on which the cease-fire would be observed. On a specific date after D-Day, the withdrawal of all forces to the internationally recognized boundaries would start. On D-Day a team of UN observers would be dispatched to verify, confirm and supervise the cease-fire and withdrawal, and prisoners of war would begin to be released and repatriated. On D-Day also the Secretary-General would start negotiations with Iraq and Iran with a view to achieving a comprehensive, just and honourable settlement of all outstanding issues, and the impartial body would start its inquiry into the responsibility for the conflict.

Iran insisted that this inquiry must be given the highest priority and that, therefore, there must be a link between the cease-fire and the impartial inquiry: thus the observance of a formal cease-fire must be preceded by the process of the identification of the party responsible for starting the conflict. Meanwhile an undeclared cessation of hostilities could come into effect during this process.

Iraq's reaction was a repetition of its readiness to implement Resolution 598 as an integrated whole, but in the order of its various provisions. Iraq would by no means accept the Iranian idea that the establishment of responsibility for the conflict should precede the declaration of a formal cease-fire, nor was it prepared to accept an undeclared, informal cease-fire. Iraq also emphasized that the cease-fire must be followed immediately by the withdrawal of all forces to the international borders.

As a result of these exchanges a stalemate developed over the implementation of Resolution 598, while the war continued its desultory course. At the United Nations the United States' effort to get the Security Council to discuss and adopt an arms embargo encountered delaying tactics from China and the USSR, which maintained that the Secretary-General should be given time for further efforts. No great Iranian offensive was declared in 1987, as had been the case in previous years, but there was a general harassment in the tanker war in the Gulf from both sides. It became clear, as the Secretary-General informed the Security Council, that the world faced a fundamental problem of interpretation and timetable as regards Resolution 598. The Security Council continued to support the Secretary-General's efforts, and he, for his part, continued his contacts with the governments of Iraq and Iran. In November the Secretary-General called for special emissaries to be sent by the two governments to New York to continue the negotiations. These consultations took place in the first days of December 1987, but with no specific result.

III. Iraqi and Iranian relations with the United Nations

In 1980, neither Iraq nor Iran had any reason to believe that recourse to the United Nations would further their interests, while the approach of the Security Council was hamstrung by conflicts of interest between permanent members on the one hand, and the complexity of relations with Iran and Iraq on the other.

It is possible to speculate that, apart from desired territorial corrections, the Iraqi Government was alarmed at the real or apparent political threat posed by the appeal of Ayatollah Khomeini. This had already been the source of complaints to the United Nations by the Iraqi Government in June in a protest against Khomeini's presumption to speak for the Shi'ite majority in Iraq. (It was Saddam Hussein who had expelled Ayatollah Khomeini from Iraq at the Shah's request in 1978.) At a time when the Iranian regime was perceived to be in a weak international and military position, Iraq could pursue a series of goals. A desire to regain territory and to change the regime in the Shatt-el-Arab[6] blended with a series of vaguer fears and preoccupations, all of which could be served by the neutralization or weakening of a revolutionary regime that posed an ideological threat to many others besides Iraq. Such a complex of motives would not be likely to incline the Government of Iraq to approach the Security Council about its differences with Iran.[7]

Iran also had few reasons, and little inclination, to approach the Security Council to intervene over its differences with Iraq. The Council's unfavourable reaction to the seizure of the US hostages had caused the Iranian Government to regard the United Nations as closely linked to the US State Department. Secretary-General Waldheim had also participated in efforts to release the hostages and had originally brought the question to the Security Council under Article 99.

Iran made no secret of its dislike for, and mistrust of, the Security Council—an attitude which derived essentially from the failure of the Council's first resolution (Resolution 479) to call for the withdrawal of all forces to recognized international boundaries, and also from the Council's failure to denounce Iraqi aggression. The first call for a withdrawal to recognized boundaries was in Resolution 514 of 12 July 1982, when Iranian forces had already entered Iraqi territory.

Iran's basic objection to the Council's resolutions, which it saw as unbalanced, meant that UN negotiation on the war could only be carried out by the office of the Secretary-General. Among all the efforts at negotiating a settlement, the Secretary-General has had the most, albeit limited, success.

If there was no disposition on the side of either party concerned to come to the Security Council, what was the feeling among the members of the Council? Generally it can be said that the position in the Security Council militated against taking an active concern in the political situation in the Gulf or in the relations between Iraq and Iran. The poor state of Soviet–US relations had been further exacerbated by the Soviet invasion of Afghanistan in December 1979. It was unlikely that the Soviet Union and the United States would easily join in any collective action in the Security Council at this time.

The relations of the nuclear superpowers with the two parties were equally complex. While the Soviet Union evidently looked forward to the prospect of improving its relations with Iran, which was now in the grip of a violently anti-US movement, the Soviet Union also had a Treaty of Friendship with Iraq and evidently hoped to maintain normal relations with Baghdad. The Soviet Union would, therefore, be reluctant to take a public position on any territorial or political dispute between the two states.

The United States did not have diplomatic relations with either Iran or Iraq[8] and had correspondingly little influence over either party. In addition, the United States was preoccupied with the plight of the hostages in Tehran, as well as being apprehensive of any Soviet moves in the region following the invasion of Afghanistan. The United States, although it took only a small fraction of its oil supplies from the Gulf, was also preoccupied with any move which might jeopardize the Gulf oil supply on which its major allies were dependent.

The other members of the Security Council as a whole had a negative view of the Iranian regime and, given their own special interests, would be unlikely to wish to have the Council actively involved in the Iraq–Iran dispute. France, in particular, had a close military and economic relationship with Iraq, to which the Soviet Union was also a major arms supplier. With their nervousness about each other's motives and intentions and their lack of interest in taking a firm position on the Iraq–Iran dispute, it was unlikely that the Council would develop the consensus necessary to make a decisive move in the opening stages of the war.

The Security Council's slowness to react in spite of the Secretary-General's initiative was a result of all of these factors as well as a considerable complaisance over the probable outcome of the war. Iraq itself evidently believed in an early victory and was successful in pressuring the non-aligned members of the Council to prevent them from agreeing to the convening of a formal meeting during the days when it believed that its offensive would be decisive. The permanent members were certainly aware of the doubtful nature of Iraq's arguments but were not sufficiently concerned about Iran's fate to come to its aid. In any case they did not expect a prolonged conflict, and by the time this expectation was shown to have been mistaken it was too late to take effective action. This expediency, and a studied inattention to the principles of the Charter about acts of aggression and the use of force in international disputes, proved a heavy burden later on when, after more than seven years of war, the Council did finally manage to produce a unanimous decision designed to put an end to the war.

IV. Prospects for an arms embargo

As noted in section I, the activities of the Security Council must be seen in the context of the wider relations between its permanent members and their competing foreign policy objectives. In 1987, the discussions about an arms embargo on one or both of the Gulf combatants highlighted these difficulties in particularly sharp relief.

Initiated by the United States and co-ordinated by the UK, discussions in the Security Council continued through the second half of 1987 and into 1988 on the possibility of an arms embargo on any party refusing to implement Resolution 598. However, the future for an arms embargo has been blurred by messages from Iran stating that Iran did not reject Security Council Resolution 598. In a letter of 28 February 1988 from the Foreign Minister of Iran, Iran maintained that it had accepted in principle the Secretary-General's outlined plan and that this was tantamount to the acceptance of Resolution 598. Moreover, Iran has pressed the United Nations for a definition of 'non-compliance' with Resolution 598. Also in February 1988, a document claimed to be a draft resolution for an arms embargo, naming Iran as the non-complying party and reportedly agreed by all five Security Council members, was leaked to the official newspaper of the United Arab Emirates, *Al Ittihad*, but at the time of writing (March 1988) it has not been formally submitted.[9]

At the same time, the bombardment of civilian targets reached a new stage with the heavy exchange of ground-to-ground missiles directed at Baghdad and Tehran and other civilian targets. The origin of the missiles exchanged is unclear. While Iraq and Iran have both developed a capacity for the production of military equipment, there is good reason for scepticism about whether they could manufacture missile systems with a range in excess of 270 km that remained accurate enough to be usable.[10] This development has been denounced by the Security Council in a presidential statement.

At the time of writing, the situation remains uncertain, both as to the development of the war and as to future international efforts.

V. Conclusions

The Iraq–Iran War has provided many insights into the problem of dealing with regional conflicts, as well as with the present limitations to the capacity of the world community, as represented in the United Nations, to deal with dangerous international conflicts in the way the UN Charter intended that it should.

The war was the culmination of a long and awkward historical relationship between Iraq and Iran. The Iranian revolution and the shock waves which it sent out, the personal antipathy of the two leaders, and gross misperceptions of the nature of the opportunity offered by Iran's apparent disarray and international unpopularity all contributed to the initial hostilities.

The complex relationship of the superpowers to each other, to Iraq and Iran as well as to other developments in the region and elsewhere certainly discouraged any joint exercise of their authority as permanent members of the Security Council, and, as often before, the Council happily delegated any responsibility for an active effort to end the war to the Secretary-General. Nor was the Secretary-General on this occasion dealing with any ordinary dispute between conventional members of the international community. The country which had, ostensibly at any rate, initiated the active hostilities soon had a tiger by the tail, and it was a tiger of unusual habits and strange preoccupations. Moreover, it was a tiger with a grievance, not wholly unjustified, not only against its adversary but also against the entire international community.

When, seven years into the war, the Security Council finally and unanimously adopted Resolution 598, it was hailed as an encouraging sign of a new vitality, consensus and responsibility. This was to some extent true, but the authority in following up the resolution which might have come from true consensus and unanimity was not yet present. Mutual suspicions about motivations and activities persisted, and the argument about further measures to end the war continued. The responsibility for active negotiation remained with the Secretary-General.

It is clear that respect for the UN Charter and the Security Council, and the international authority which would be derived from that respect, had been seriously eroded for over 40 years by the perennial differences of the Council's permanent members. The efforts of 1987, which produced unanimity on Resolution 598, represented a first step in reversing this trend and restoring the respect and authority of the Security Council. There is still a very long way to go.

Notes and references

* The Ford Foundation, Program Division, International Affairs Programs, New York.

[1] See *Charter of the United Nations, Statute and Rules of Court and other Documents* (International Court of Justice: The Hague, 1978).

[2] A good example of this hesitancy is the current difficulty in agreeing on an arms embargo to support Security Council Resolution 598 on the Iraq–Iran War. See section IV.

[3] The full correspondence of the United Nations with the governments of Iraq and Iran is reproduced in the quarterly publication *Supplements of the Official Records of the Security Council* (United Nations: New York).

[4] In the minds of the international community, the war formally commenced on 22 Sep. 1980, when Iraqi aircraft struck at targets deep inside Iran, although Iraq later claimed that the war had begun with heavy Iranian cross-border shelling on 14 Sep. On 23 Sep. Iraqi ground forces invaded Iran in strength. For an overview of the course of the war, see King, R. P. H., *The United Nations and the Iran–Iraq War, 1980–1986* (Ford Foundation: New York, 1987); and Cordesman, A. H., *The Iran–Iraq War and Western Security 1984–87* (RUSI/Brassey's: London, 1987).

[5] UN resolutions pertaining to the Iraq–Iran War are contained in *Resolutions and Decisions of the Security Council* (United Nations: New York), published annually since 1965.

[6] At a meeting of the OPEC heads of state in Algiers on 4–6 Mar. 1975, Iran and Iraq issued a joint communiqué in which they agreed *inter alia* to delimit the river frontier. On 13 June 1975, in Baghdad, the two governments signed the Treaty Relating to the State Boundary and Good Neighbourliness. Saddam Hussein unilaterally abrogated the Treaty on 17 Sep. 1980, claiming Iraqi sovereignty over the Shatt-el-Arab, and Iraq invaded Iran on 23 Sep.

[7] Iraq laid out its limited objectives in a letter of 26 Sep. to the Secretary-General. President Saddam Hussein stated that 'Iraq's objective [was] only to gain Iran's irrevocable recognition of Iraq's rights over its land and sovereignty over its territorial waters'. For a not entirely convincing argument that Iraqi attacks on Iran were in fact pre-emptive, see Karsh, E., 'The Iran–Iraq War' *International Affairs* (RIIA: London, 1988).

[8] The USA restored relations with Iraq in Nov. 1984.

[9] Houk, M., 'The Gulf conflict's other battleground', *The Middle East* (London), Mar. 1988, pp. 28–9.

[10] This is the range of SS-1 Scud B missiles known to have been supplied to both sides either in their original form or as copies. Although the origin of Iranian missiles is much disputed, they are believed to have come from Libya and/or North Korea; see, for example, *World Weapons Review* (USA), 9 Dec. 1987. The Soviet Union has acknowledged transfers to Iraq; see 'Russia admits supplying missiles to Iraq', *The Guardian*, 10 Mar. 1988. The distance to Baghdad would allow Iran to use these or comparable missiles with some modification; for Iraq to strike at Tehran requires the range of a Scud B to be *doubled*. While either side may have extended the range of these weapons by reducing the weight of the warhead, there would be a corresponding price to pay in accuracy unless the technicians of either side have developed the capacity to produce missile guidance systems.

16. The United Nations International Conference on the Relationship between Disarmament and Development

SAADET DEGER

1. Introduction

The United Nations International Conference on the Relationship between Disarmament and Development (ICRDD) was held at the UN Headquarters in New York between 24 August and 11 September 1987. It was a major initiative since it focused exclusively on the interrelationships between two crucial issues—disarmament and development. In addition to being the first UN conference to be held on the subject, it was attended by an overwhelmingly large number of member states (150 in total). The Final Document, adopted by *consensus*, is an important landmark; it establishes a firm framework within which the twin processes, pertaining to international peace and prosperity, can be interlinked.

The United States was absent from the ICRDD deliberations. Given the crucial importance of the USA in this field, the possible reasons for US non-attendance are analysed below. Despite the US absence, however, the very fact that a special conference took place and the high position which the notions of disarmament and development occupy on the UN political agenda are heartening signs of the increasing awareness by the international community of the importance and closely interrelated nature of the subjects.

The Conference took place against a rather sombre background of world-wide long-term politico–military and economic realities. Over the past one and a half decades, the international economy has passed through a period of unprecedented turbulence. In the industrial market economies, inflation has given way to stagnation with high unemployment and underutilized capacity. Third World countries have suffered a collapse of commodity prices, an intensification of debt service burdens, a recurrence of famine and an inability to meet basic needs for significant parts of the population. The centrally planned economies are faced with low growth and declining productivity.

In spite of determined efforts, by governments in developing countries and by international agencies, to reduce poverty and spread the effects of growth over larger sections of the community, the record of improvement remains patchy. It is believed that around one billion people in the Third World live below a modest subsistence line; half the world's population may not have access to safe drinking water; three-quarters of the population of the developing world have no adequate sanitary facilities; and about 200 million people lack basic shelter.[1] It has also been estimated that to meet minimum basic health needs the Third World may need an additional 4.5 million hospital beds, half a million physicians and 3 million other health workers; clearly the requirements are daunting.[2]

One of the few 'growth' areas of the global politico–economic system is military expenditure. Annual world-wide defence spending is approaching $1000 billion. Though most of it is spent in developed economies (both East and West), developing countries have also seen exceptional rises in defence spending. During the period 1975 to 1985, the poorest economies within the Third World experienced an increase of 71 per cent in their annual real military spending.[3]

Comparative data for industrial market economies and the Third World are shown in table 16.1. Centrally planned economies, as well as China, are excluded because of the lack of comparable data. The Third World has almost four times the population of the developed countries; but its aggregate output, consumption and investment are less than one-fifth of the total. On the other hand, when it comes to military expenditure the Third World share rises to 24 per cent—relatively high compared to the economic aggregates.

Table 16.2 is also revealing, clearly showing the disparity between rich and poor countries in terms of trade data. In terms of total imports, as well as of machinery alone, the Third World share is around 25 per cent. However, in the case of arms imports its share rises precipitously to about 67 per cent. Relatively poor economic status and high militarization tend to compound developmental problems.

It is tempting to believe that there is an *automatic* link between armaments and underdevelopment or between military expenditure and the global economic crisis; that is, that disarmament must produce development for the world economy. As is explained below, the linkages are much more complex and there may not always be obvious relationships between guns and butter. However, a substantial volume of research during the 1980s by analysts in the development studies community has shown that disarmament and development are conceptually interconnected and that one may lead to the other, but only with careful preparation, planning and political will.

The ICRDD was an important conference and merits detailed discussion. Section II gives some basic definitions, without which our understanding would be incomplete. Section III analyses the proceedings and the results. It is followed, in section IV, by an analytical evaluation; this includes a discussion of the conceptual framework within which the contents of the Conference are embedded. Conclusions are presented in the final section.

II. Basic definitions

To understand the essential linkages between disarmament and development we need to define the terms. Disarmament means a reduction in arms. This may be achieved through a lowering of military expenditure either in terms of its absolute level or in relation to other macroeconomic variables, such as the gross domestic product (GDP) or the total government budget. Military expenditure as a proportion of the national product is called the military (defence) burden and often its reduction signals at least a measure of disarmament, however weak. Other, more important allied concepts include force reduction, conversion of military industries to civilian purposes as well as

Table 16.1. Comparative economic and military data for industrial market economies and the Third World, 1985

	Third World (excl. China)	Industrial market economies
Population (m.)	2 659	737
Percentage share	*78.3*	*21.7*
GDP ($b.)	1 932	8 569
Percentage share	*18.4*	*81.6*
Consumption ($b.)	1 229	5 313
Percentage share	*18.8*	*81.2*
Investment ($b.)	422	1 799
Percentage share	*19*	*81*
Military expenditure (1980 $b.)	114	360
Percentage share	*24.1*	*75.9*

Source: Calculated from World Bank, *World Development Report 1987* (Oxford University Press: New York, 1987) and SIPRI data.

Table 16.2. A comparison of import shares for industrial market economies and the Third World, 1985

Figures are percentages.

	All imports	Machinery imports	Arms imports
Third World (excl. China)	*26*	*28*	*67*
Industrial market economies	*74*	*72*	*33*

Source: Calculated from World Bank, *World Development Report 1987* (Oxford University Press: New York, 1987) and SIPRI data.

the dismantling or destruction of weapon systems either in use or in inventories. Clearly, these measures must be brought about under international or bilateral control, and verification is crucial for their effectiveness.

Development and growth imply a process of social and economic change that increases per capita income and improves the quality of life of the maximum possible number of people in society. In addition to growth, development should bring about the right to full employment, the egalitarian distribution of income, the eradication of poverty, the provision of basic needs and entitlement to a higher physical quality of life as measured by, say, literacy, infant mortality, life expectancy, health care, nutritional availability, and so forth.

It should be noted that this notion of development is essentially open-ended and should not be associated only with underdevelopment, *per se*. The definition, clearly, is most relevant to Third World countries. But even in rich societies, certain deprived sections of the population could enjoy a better quality of life under greater prosperity and, *inter alia*, more development. The UN Secretary-General, Javier Perez de Cuellar, emphasized this aspect clearly in his opening address to the ICRDD: 'Problems of urban decay . . . industrial pollution, economic stagnation, changes in employment patterns . . . need for better provisions of services in health and education—these and other issues create demands for social and economic improvements in even the most developed societies. Thus the need for development is worldwide which governments can ignore only at the grave risk of social tensions, internal unrest and instability.'[4]

Governments and nation states have generally considered these two concepts—development and (dis)armament—as analytically separate. The primary objective of the state has been to provide national security in the traditional sense that its citizens needed to be protected from external threats while regime survival required protection from internal threats.[5] The level of armaments (or conversely disarmament) has generally been dictated by the needs of strategic security rather than by a concern for development or growth. Despite acceptance of the Keynesian paradigm, which seeks to guarantee the entitlement to full employment and the responsibility of the government to provide it, the primary function of developed nations' governments is usually still the provision of adequate military security. In similar fashion, Third World governments have attached great importance to economic growth and development through planning and state intervention; yet, once again, the needs of strategy and military security have been paramount—and the theme is one of eternal vigilance.

The optimum way to interrelate disarmament and development is to introduce the wider notion of security and to consider the linkages between this triad of concepts. The UN study on the relationship between disarmament and development (1981), produced by a group of governmental experts and chaired by the then Under Secretary of State for Sweden, Ambassador Inga Thorsson,[6] was the first analytical work to emphasize this triangularization. The report categorically states: 'the Group has placed the disarmament–development relationship in the context of a triangular interaction between disarmament, development and security'.[7]

The canonical concept of security, emphasizing defence spending, armed forces, external enemies, and so forth, is exclusively concerned with the military–political dimensions of the subject. There can be little doubt that military security is crucial. Nation states and their representative governments do indeed have legitimate security interests, particularly the right of self-defence. However, this narrow concept must be extended by considering the broader socio-economic dimension of security.[8] The latter is particularly relevant to the disarmament and development debate. If nations do not have economic prosperity and hence lack the wider elements of socio-economic security then they may be 'insecure' despite high levels of military preparedness. This seems to be the case for many Third World countries which have an adequate military machinery for local arms races and wars but are continuously subject to socio-economic problems which affect national welfare and regime survival. The centrally planned economies, with supply constraints and rationing, may also face similar problems since defence absorbs limited output which could be used for investment and consumption. Even industralized countries could find defence an economic burden in spite of short-term multipliers. Among OECD (Organization for Economic Co-operation and

Development) countries, low levels of defence burden in relation to perceived threats and military security needs (say for Japan, FR Germany and the Nordic countries) have generally provided high levels of growth, investment and productivity. Within this scenario, mutually verifiable and multilateral disarmament would reduce the economic costs, release resources domestically for more productive expenditures, increase growth rates and hence employment and consumption opportunities, and possibly allow a greater transfer of resources from developed to developing countries as well as foster economic co-operation and interdependence.

Disarmament, development and security must therefore be examined together. Effective disarmament at the national and global levels could lead to resources being released for growth and development. In addition, there are various beneficial trickledown effects and indirect spin-offs. Further, in the long term, disarmament can also contribute to lower threat perceptions since armaments can be seen as likely to trigger off an arms race; an excess of arms could lead to lower strategic security. This idea is not new. The Final Document of the UN Special Session on Disarmament in 1978 claimed: 'the accumulation of weapons, particularly nuclear weapons, constitutes much more a threat than a protection. . . . The time has therefore come . . . to seek security in disarmament'.[9] Thus, mutual disarmament can lead to greater military security. At the same time, the resource transfer, and concomitant benefits, can enhance economic security. This wider notion of security provides the context within which the ICRDD effectively examined the interrelationships between disarmament and development.

III. The Conference

Background

The United Nations has a long and distinguished history of formulating *principles* that relate disarmament to development. This is not surprising since the organization was initially set up to oversee the interests of world peace. As more Third World countries acquired membership, interest focused on economic development. It is natural that the linkages between the two have become increasingly emphasized.

Since the 1950s the UN General Assembly has repeatedly passed resolutions calling for reductions in defence expenditure and possible re-allocation of funds to developmental needs. Various studies written under the auspices of the UN have stressed, with increasing emphasis, the interrelationships and concepts behind disarmament and development. The expert report, *Economic and Social Consequences of the Arms Race and of Military Expenditures*,[10] explicitly recognized the linkages. A UN resolution of December 1970[11] called for a close link between the Second United Nations Development Decade and the First Disarmament Decade.

Specific proposals and action programmes which would institutionalize the links were also put forward. In 1955 the Prime Minister of France, Edgar Faure, proposed at the Disarmament Commission in Geneva that an

International Fund for Development and Mutual Assistance be set up to facilitate the transfer of funds available from possible disarmament measures.[12] The next few years saw a number of proposals from the Soviet Union calling for a reduction in the defence budgets of the major military powers (the USA, the USSR, France and the UK) and use of the monies saved to create a fund for development assistance.[13]

A major watershed in the history of these initiatives was the 1978 UN Special Session on Disarmament. It was an important, and possibly historic, meeting attended by numerous dignitaries from all over the world. Philip Noel-Baker, the elder statesman from Britain, called the final document of this special session 'the greatest state paper of all time'.[14] But most important was the strong emphasis that was placed on disarmament and development, linked together, during the deliberations. The final document claimed: 'There is also a close relationship between disarmament and development. Progress in the former would help greatly to the realization of the latter'.[15]

One important outcome of the Special Session was the setting up of the group of governmental experts which, three year later, produced the Thorsson Report. Such a study of disarmament and development was originally proposed by the Nordic countries[16] and the General Assembly had strongly endorsed the idea.

The Thorsson Report is a major study on the triangular relationship between disarmament, development and 'security', defining security in terms of both military-related factors and socio-economic determinants. It found 'non-military threats to security' to emanate from low growth, high unemployment, stagflation, retarded development, decline of non-renewable resources, and the fall in relative supply of food as population increases as well as inequitable distribution of wealth and income. Coupled with this wider notion of security, the effects of disarmament on development become more meaningful and clearer. The Thorsson Report also examines the socio-economic effects of armaments and the possibilities for conversion and redeployment of military resources towards the civilian economy.

The origins of the 1987 Conference can be traced to a speech by French President François Mitterrand in September 1983, in which he asked for such a meeting; he also called for the creation of an International Disarmament Fund for Development.[17] In 1985, France agreed to host the Conference, sponsored by the UN, in Paris during July–August 1986.[18] Unfortunately, a few months later, the invitation was withdrawn for various reasons: a change in the domestic political climate; the refusal of the USA to attend the meeting; and the feeling that such a forum should more appropriately meet at the Headquarters of the UN. After an initial postponement, the Conference was finally held in New York.[19]

In terms of participation the Conference must be considered a success. In addition to the 150 countries that took part there was observer representation from the Vatican, the Palestine Liberation Organization (PLO) and others. A large number of specialized organizations active in the field of economic development, such as the International Labour Organization (ILO), the United Nations Educational, Scientific, and Cultural Organization (Unesco), the International Monetary Fund (IMF) and the World Bank also participated in the deliberations. Intergovernmental organizations such as the Organization of American States (OAS), the Organization of African Unity (OAU), the European Community (EC) and the Council for Mutual Economic Assistance (CMEA) were also present. But, probably most significant, 183 non-governmental organizations were present in full force to represent grassroots public opinion. The UN also commissioned a number of expert reports which provided a comprehensive background of analytical information for the deliberations. A Panel of Eminent Personalities was also set up which submitted a comprehensive report.

The US absence

One question mark hung over the Conference. The United States, as a major force in world armaments and a crucial influence on the international economy, was conspicuous by its absence.[20] Both at the First Committee as well as the General Assembly (on 4 December 1986) its intentions were clearly stated: 'The United States delegation wishes the record of today's proceedings to show that the United States did not participate in the Assembly's action on the decision regarding the International Conference on the Relationship between Disarmament and Development . . . the United States will not participate in the Conference or in preparatory activities for it'.[21]

The reasons for the absence of the United States are not clear-cut, except that it sees no interrelationship between disarmament and development. But we have to try to understand the analytical causes since, as mentioned earlier, the USA is a major actor in the fields both of disarmament and development. The analysis must be partly speculative, but will be based on reasonable assumptions. Historically, the USA has always believed in concepts of national security as well as in relating economic and military policies. The formation of NATO and the implementation of the Marshall Plan are classic examples of such policy co-ordination, the former to ensure strategic security and the latter to provide economic security. It was always considered self-evident that unless post-war Western Europe was strong from an economic point of view it would not be able to defend itself from a military point of view.

The natural link through the broad notion of security, however, was not between disarmament and development but between armament and development. A strong military sector would protect NATO and Europe from potential WTO aggression. But rapid prosperity was also a *sine qua non* of overall security. Further, a rich economy would be able to afford, in the longer term, a higher level of military expenditure. The US contribution to European defence, as well as foreign aid for post-war recovery, was a means by which to facilitate the transformation to more developed *and* secure states.

Though the position is less conclusive, similar considerations have probably been applied to the case of Third World allies. Defence aid would be useful for strategic and military security while economic aid would facilitate development. In addition, the recipient economy concerned would have to spend less on the military (specifically, imported hardware) which, if there are major adverse economic effects, would help to remove a potential obstacle to higher growth. To give an example: in recent years, Egypt and Israel have received substantial amounts of economic as well as military assistance; and for both countries the grant element of foreign aid (economic and military) has been overwhelmingly large relative to loans. In 1986, for example, Egypt received $1293.3 million in economic assistance—$217.5 million as loans and $1075.8 million as grants—and $1245.8 million in military assistance, all as grants. Israel received $1898.4 million in economic assistance and $1722.6 million in military assistance, all as outright grants.[22] This indicates an implicit recognition that development contributes to the broad-based notion of security.

One of the economic hypotheses put forward in support of defence spending in Third World countries may also be useful in understanding the US perspective. The hypothesis claims that the *composition* of military expenditure is crucial in determining whether defence has a positive or negative impact on economic growth. In particular, expenditures on personnel, labour, food, housing, and so on, will usually have spin-offs which help the economy. On the other hand, procurement and capital expenditure, particularly on imported armaments, usually have unacceptably high economic costs and are detrimental to growth and development. If this is so, the US preference for linking military and economic aid, rather than fostering a linkage between disarmament and development, can be understood. As a global superpower, the USA chooses its allies from a strategic point of view. By giving them military help, specifically with capital-intensive arms imports, it can reduce the negative impact that defence spending would otherwise have on the economy. In effect there would be guns *and* butter, albeit with the help of an international power. The same analysis could be potentially applied to the Soviet Union too. The net effect is that there is little appreciation of disarmament and development.

The British view at the ICRDD (which was shared by some other participants, such as the Netherlands, though not necessarily by all of its European Community partners[23]) is instructive since it reflects implicitly what the US attitude could have been. The statement by the UK representative to the Conference makes very clear that only the narrow military-related definition of security is considered relevant. To quote: 'To provide security for the citizen . . . is the raison d'etre of government. Prosperity, welfare, all the rest, follow'.[24] Without such security, there would be no disarmament. Resource transfer is considered to be a separate issue which should not be linked with the usual procedures of arms control. A stronger indictment was that by Tim Eggar, the Under Secretary of State for Foreign and Commonwealth Affairs, to the First Committee at the 42nd Session of the UN General Assembly: 'We have recently witnessed a multilateral conference which in our view lost its way, which failed to live up to the important role which we believe the United Nations should be playing in this field'.[25]

The problem with such arguments is that they can also be used by other participants in international relations. If Third World countries accept that military security has primacy they may wish to act on this belief. In addition, if they also borrow the concept of nuclear deterrence (from the superpowers and the countries of the East and West), they may believe that peace is best kept through the acquisition of nuclear weapons. It will then be difficult to logically blame nuclear threshold countries, in the Third World, if they cite these arguments and acquire such arsenals. The logic of disarmament and development, if universally accepted, could even contribute to stopping nuclear proliferation.

The Final Document

The Conference proceedings were conducted relatively harmoniously under the Presidentship of Mr Natwar Singh of India. Three working groups were set up to examine: (*a*) the relationships between disarmament and development; (*b*) the effects of global defence expenditure, particularly of the major military spenders, on the international economy; and (*c*) recommendations for policies, particularly the means of releasing additional resources from disarmament towards developmental needs. The recommendations of the groups were processed by a 'Committee of the Whole'. The Final Document reflected many of the general principles enumerated by these specialist groups, but a few major elements were left out. For example, working group III proposed 'the utilisation of existing regional and international institutions *and the initial establishment of a special facility within such institutions* for the reallocation of resources'[26] (emphasis added). The words emphasized here were omitted, thus destroying any hopes of a special funding institution. This is discussed below.

The Final Document of the ICRDD has four principal parts.[27] The first, on the relationship between disarmament and development in all its aspects and dimensions, is clear on principles and lays down the philosophical basis for the analysis. It believes that disarmament and development are distinct processes but that they also have a 'close and multidimensional relationship'. It gives an important role to security but duly emphasizes the broader framework within which such security must be defined. It also prescribes multilateralism and expresses the belief that, in an interdependent world economy, no country can insulate itself from the adverse consequences of arms races and underdevelopment. The second part, on the implications of the level and magnitude of continuing military expenditures, is probably the most clearly argued section of all, dealing with 10 specific issues: information; defence-related research and development (R&D); energy consumption; arms trade; the downturn of the world economy; the contrast between civilian and military sectors; the opportunity cost of militarization; international debt problems; the inefficiency of the military–industrial complex; and economic interdependence. The third part, on ways and means of releasing additional resources, is probably the weakest section since it rarely enters into specifics and generally gives a vague notion of the possibilities.

The major interest lies in the fourth and final section, on the action programme. Here, the feelings expressed are somewhat mixed. The fact that Conference decisions were taken by consensus meant that suggested policy actions could not be very forceful.[28] Many of the participating nations were happy that the action programme stipulated multilateralism, called for strengthening the role of the UN, emphasized conversion studies and planning, recognized the need for more comprehensive defence expenditure data and stressed the need to explore disarmament measures which could be translated into developmental programmes. It was made clear that the United Nations will carry on working vigorously in the area and that future meetings will devote much more time and interest to the issues raised here. Various NGO forums, held during and after the Conference, were generally optimistic. Some critical observations were made, however, and the view of the dissenters was that the document was strong on principles but less effective in terms of actions suggested. Mexico's Ambassador is reported to have said that the document 'does not adequately reflect the minimum positions of the developing countries . . . it fails to include many of the positions with respect to disarmament and development which have been endorsed by the General Assembly'.[29]

One positive aspect of the action programme is the emphasis it places on improving the data base of national military expenditures.[30] Knowledge about mutual defence spending could be useful for disarmament and confidence-building measures. If more information is provided by member states to the UN mechanism, for monitoring trends and suggesting means of cutting down arms expenditures, then a preliminary positive step will have been taken. It is interesting to note that the Soviet Union promised to provide more comprehensive data on military spending—this must be considered a major breakthrough.

Military threats to security are emphasized strongly in the document. Paragraph 17 states: 'The use or threat of use of force in international relations, external intervention, armed aggression, foreign occupation, colonial domination, policies of *apartheid* and all forms of racial discrimination, violation of territorial integrity, of national sovereignty, of the right to self-determination . . . constitute threats to international peace and security'.

In so far as it relates to Third World countries, the major problem is that bilateral and regional political relations tend largely to be militarized. Part of the reason is once again the lack of economic development. For the élites in poor countries, regime survival requires the creation of external 'threats'; external vigilance is maintained at the cost of basic needs for the population. There are, of course, numerous other socio-cultural and historical reasons for regional conflicts, but prosperity would certainly help in minimizing these security problems.

It is interesting to note that the action programme has almost nothing to say about the arms trade. Yet, an earlier part of the Final Document mentions the destabilizing effects of such trade and remarks that the adverse developmental implications are greater than the military gains to the importers. It is extremely difficult to make concrete proposals for the reduction of arms transfers since even Third World countries may not wish to have effective measures. They believe that such measures as sanctions or embargoes would be half-hearted from the point of view of the suppliers and would therefore have different and disproportionate effects on the recipients. Military security would therefore be threatened particularly for small or neutral or non-arms-producing countries.

The most obvious, and major, disappointment from the Third World's point of view was that no mention was made of the much discussed 'special facilities' or 'international fund' linking disarmament measures to development. There is little doubt that if such an institution could be even agreed to in principle then the meeting would have been considered an outstanding success from the perspective of the developing countries. Unfortunately, geopolitical and economic realities dictate otherwise. The major Western aid donors were adamant in their refusal to even consider moves to transfer to the Third World part of any money saved by reducing military expenditures.

Major analytical and practical problems would face the establishment of a fund linking disarmament and development at the present time; however, it is a serious issue and one worthy of consideration. The fact that it did not even come near to inclusion in the political agenda is unfortunate. Although Third World countries were vociferous in asking for such a fund they did not co-ordinate their policies well. The non-aligned movement, which addresses disarmament issues, and the Group of 77, which concentrates on developmental issues, could have presented a more homogeneous front. The Soviet Union supported the idea strongly, but Soviet demands were dismissed since potential transfers would be based on reported military expenditures and it is widely believed that the Soviet Union understates its defence spending. The principal aid givers (including, by proxy, the United States) were easily able to override these pleas.

Even if a fund could not be set up at the present moment, it would be interesting to have some *concrete* proposals for resource transfer. Within the present institutional framework of the UN it is possible to earmark funds as a sort of 'disarmament dividend'.[31] This would have been a token gesture of policy co-ordination between the North (West), South and East. But clearly, on this point, unanimity is still far away. It is not surprising that some headlines focused on this issue, for example: 'West rejects Third World aid drive'.[32]

Nevertheless it would be unfortunate if overemphasis on the fund issue were to detract from the many positive achievements of the Conference. The creation of a fund could have been a step forward but it should not be seen as fundamental to the basic principles and the philosophy behind the ICRDD. The benefits of disarmament are multifarious and specific financial transfers are a minor aspect of the whole matter. The Final Document points out clearly the numerous ways in which the rewards of disarmament can be reaped: 'these could include trade expansion, technological transfers, the more efficient utilization of global resources, the more effective and dynamic international division of labour, the reduction of public debt and budgetary deficits, and increased flows of resources through development assistance . . .'. The concepts encompass a wide domain.

It must also be emphasized once more that the conclusions were adopted by *consensus*. Some give and take was inevitable and it is unwise to expect too much for the practical process which has just begun. The fact that, despite fundamental divergences among nations about security, disarmament, development and armaments, so much was actually agreed by the large number of participants is to be applauded.

IV. The analytical framework

The linkages for the Third World

Disarmament and development, as the ICRDD acknowledged, are distinct but strongly interconnected processes. The former is a political process with implications for military security. The latter is a socio-economic process which has important effects on economic security. As mentioned above, the interrelationships between disarmament and development can best be understood through the wider notion of security, which includes the traditional military dimension but also contains a socio-economic dimension.

For the Third World there are many channels and linkages; some, such as resource transfer, are obvious; others, such as co-operation among countries in both economic and military fields, are less evident. A summary of the linkages is given in table 16.3. The multi-dimensional facets of the subject can be seen through the threefold classification according to military–strategic, political and economic. The interconnections also unfold over the national economy, the regional blocs and the global system.

US defence spending and the international economy

Even though the emphasis above is on the Third World, potentially such a matrix can be constructed for the industrial economies too. A current and topical case illustrates some of the problems associated with rapid escalation of

Table 16.3. Disarmament and development in the Third World: the potential linkages

Sphere	National level	Regional level	Global level
Military/strategic	1. Reduction of military expenditure	1. Multilateral effort to end local arms races	1. Supplier control of arms transfer
	2. Use of defence personnel for civilian reconstruction	2. Strengthening of regional security	2. East/West arms reduction leads to allies in less-developed countries having lower commitments
	3. Conversion of military to civilian industries		3. UN peace-keeping strengthened
Political	1. Less control by the military	1. Less interference in political structure of neighbouring countries	1. Reduced importance of global power blocs
	2. Reduced internal threat to regime survival		
Economic	1. Release of domestic resources for additional consumption/investment	1. Economic and strategic co-operation among allies (like ASEAN)	1. Resource transfer from reduction of military expenditure in developed countries
	2. Reduction of taxation, government borrowing, inflation		2. Economic recovery in North acts as 'locomotive' to growth in the South

military expenditure in a major developed economy and the resulting economic crisis. Many explanations have been given for the Wall Street crash of October 1987 when stock prices fell to unprecedented low levels. Panic spread through the bourses around the world and there was speculation that we might even have been facing another Great Depression. Though some recovery has taken place and the international capitalist economy is not in fear of imminent collapse, the events of late 1987 clearly revealed the fragility of the system. We could be facing the downwards spiral of a major business cycle.

Equity (share) prices can fall rapidly either because a speculative 'bubble' has burst or because the 'fundamentals' of the economy cannot sustain high prices. Both these factors are important. The former is essentially short-term in nature and indicates *when* the decline takes place, whereas the latter is more deep-rooted and gives us a better picture of *why* the decline occurs. In terms of fundamentals, the crash can plausibly be attributed to US fiscal deficits engendered by rapidly rising defence spending throughout the 1980s.

The US budget deficit for fiscal year 1987 is anticipated to be about $150 billion. A more important source of worry is the national debt of some $2300 billion.[33] It is essential to consider the long-term implications of debt service and interest payments, which will be part of future deficits; currently, interest payment consumes 14 per cent of all federal spending.[34] The Pentagon budget is now around $300 billion.[35] It is interesting to note that if current US military expenditure was of the same order of magnitude as in 1980, its budget deficit would almost disappear.

In terms of economic theory, the use of defence spending to produce cyclical expansion is of course not new.[36] What is interesting is the rapidity with which this took place. More importantly, prior fears of inflation kept monetary policy very restrictive as the Federal Reserve Board strongly controlled the growth of money supply. Increased government spending, necessarily financed by bond issue and debt (since taxes were reduced), as well as contractionary monetary policy, raised the nominal (money) rate of interest. This in turn led to high levels of the real rate of interest since the rate of inflation was relatively low. An incidental feature of this was of course the international debt crisis, where Third World debtors had to pay very high real interest and debt service payments.

Increases in government spending usually raise the national product through what is termed the 'Keynesian multiplier'. In the USA the resulting rise in income in turn increased imports and created a huge trade deficit.[37] But high real-interest rates also caused an inflow of financial capital into the US economy. This produced a boom in the stock market which saw record increases in share prices. However, the short-term effect of capital flows into the economy, chasing interest-rate differentials from the rest of the world, causes a greater demand for domestic currency, which will appreciate. In the USA this led to overvaluation of the dollar, which made the US economy less competitive internationally.[38] In addition, increased emphasis on defence industries, and the potential diversion of resources, capital investment, skills and technology, makes civilian industries less efficient compared to international competitors.

The contributions of lower industrial competitiveness, a high interest rate, an over-valued exchange-rate, a large trade deficit and a massive budget deficit produce an unsustainable situation. Even though expansion of military expenditure creates a boom, the effects are temporary because most of the other economic indicators are misleading. The inevitable result was that the barometer of economic weather—Wall Street—turned adverse and the markets essentially gave a warning that the economy was not functioning well.

History reminds us that the Great Depression was begun by the Wall Street crash of 1929. In addition to world-wide economic stagnation it also led to the growth of protectionism and the beginning of extreme nationalism. It has even been suggested that the economic problems of the early 1930s contributed significantly to rearmament and laid the foundations for World War II. This is not to suggest that the same process will repeat itself; history is rarely that repetitive. In any case, policy makers have learnt their lessons from past experience. What we must note, however, is that economic insecurity can be closely linked with military insecurity and that international economic stagnation may have serious consequences for world peace.

It is often thought that disarmament and development are purely Third World phenomena. But, as our analysis for the USA shows, the economic implications of a rapid arms buildup could be adverse for rich industrial nations too. In the long run, the economy is sensitive to government budgetary imbalance and military expenditure contributes significantly to such disequilibrium. Thus, disarmament measures might even ease the economic constraints faced by industrial economies. One can even argue that arms control negotiations tend to succeed when economic constraints are binding. The massive arms buildups in both the USA and the USSR have produced major problems for their economies (though in radically different ways). Hence, the current interest in arms control might be a product of economic difficulties and a desire for higher growth.

A by-product of high interest rates and the overvaluation of the dollar, produced by expanding US military expenditure, has been the international debt crisis of the 1980s. Total Third World external debt now exceeds $1200 billion (see table 16.4). Annual debt service payments (interest plus amortization payments) are approaching $175 billion. For Latin American countries debt service accounts for more than half of their total annual exports; hence, export promotion brings little tangible benefit. Even for poor African countries, debt servicing alone can eat up one-third of their total export earnings. Large-scale default can hasten an international economic crisis and will also have grave implications for domestic regime survival and regional security. It is also important to note that if the dollar begins to fall (as is currently the case) a different problem arises. Imports become more expensive for the USA and therefore Third World countries will find it more difficult to sell their products in a major market. This may cause their export volume to fall, thus exacerbating the debt problem.

Recent economic problems may also produce a recession within industrial economies and particularly in the United States. This will mean a lower

Table 16.4. External debt of the Third World, 1987

Debt category	
External debt for all developing countries:	
Total (US $b.)	1 210.9
Percentage share of exports	*163.6*
External debt, by region, percentage share of exports:	
Africa	*233.1*
Asia	*90.2*
Western Hemisphere	*362.2*
Annual debt service for all developing countries:	
Total (US $b.)	171.5
Percentage share of exports	*23.2*
Debt service, by region, percentage share of exports:	
Africa	*33.2*
Asia	*12.1*
Western Hemisphere	*55.4*

Source: International Monetary Fund, *World Economic Outlook* (IMF: Washington, DC, Oct. 1987).

demand for Third World products and another collapse in international commodity prices. The final effect could be a decline in export revenues and an economic crisis in many poorer nations. Loss of income and basic needs provokes internal unrest. Ultimately, we may observe a rise in militarization as civilian governments fail to control the problems arising from the world economy, which are often beyond their control. Thus a complex web is established between economic and military factors. The nascent democratization of Latin America could be at particular risk in this situation.

The economic effects of military spending

To understand the numerous general relationships between defence and economic growth, we need to explore the issues further. We can use similar arguments to show the linkages between military expenditure and economic stagnation in both developed and developing countries. This could then lead to an analysis of disarmament on the one hand and growth and development on the other hand. There are obvious structural differences between advanced economies and Third World countries; hence the propagation mechanism and the transmission channels will have to be modified. For example, an industrial country can be viewed as a homogeneous economy; hence *aggregate* military expenditure will be the relevant variable whose impact effects need to be calculated. But poorer countries are usually 'dual' economies with fundamental structural heterogeneity between the advanced and backward sectors. The *form* of defence spending, whether it is on personnel or equipment, capital or labour, domestic spending or foreign imports, could be vital. Further, developed countries would be interested primarily in economic growth (of income and capital stock) while Third World economies would also be concerned with wider issues of socio-economic development.

In spite of these analytical divergencies, the fundamental theoretical paradigm is the same. At the macroeconomic level, the effect of defence spending on the economy can be explained in terms of multipliers and crowding out. If there is high unemployment and excess capacity (of capital stock) then defence, through the creation of aggregate demand, will raise output. This is the familiar Keynesian multiplier effect. In addition, since capital will be more fully utilized, the economy-wide rate of profit will also increase, thus contributing to more investment and growth.[39] All of this operates on the demand side and could be beneficial. The main problem, however, is that defence is a major, economically unproductive, consumption expenditure. Hence its impact on aggregate supply of the national product is bound to be minimal. Thus, in the longer term, when the economy faces supply constraints, defence spending has to be at the expense of something else. In so far as it crowds out other types of aggregate demand (private consumption, net exports, other government expenditure say on social welfare, and particularly investment) its long-term effects must be negative, either in terms of growth reduction or in terms of welfare losses.

Similar arguments can be made at the microeconomic or inter-industrial level. Defence industrialization produces employment and exports. Through its linkages with other sectors it can be the engine of growth. The use of sophisticated technology promotes learning by doing. Military R&D could, potentially, have civilian spin-offs. Yet, the resource argument against military expenditure remains strong, particularly over a longer period of time. R&D in the civilian sectors of industry has a much higher economic productivity as well as being a more profitable channel of technological progress. Sheltered from competition, using gold-plating technology, and utilizing non-economic methods to expand exports, defence industrialization is less efficient relative to civilian manufacturing sectors in advanced economies. For newly industrializing Third World countries, the potential benefits for other closely related sectors and inter-industrial spin-offs have been estimated to be rather low and insignificant.[40] The 'locomotive' theory of defence industrialization is not easy to justify for semi-industrialized economies.

The Declaration by the Panel of Eminent Personalities in the Field of Disarmament and Development in their submission to the ICRDD makes this very clear. 'When an economy has not utilised or underutilised resources, any kind of spending can have a stimulating effect. There is nothing unique about military expenditures in this regard. But in situations of resource constraints, military needs crowd out civilian needs in both industrial and developing countries. Scarce resources are better put to the formidable task of improving living standards rather than to military build-up.'[41]

Regarding the above analysis a cautionary remark should be made. One can ask: why do not other forms of state spending (such as on health or education) have the same adverse macroeconomic effects? It is not sufficient just to claim that military expenditure crowds out other forms of 'productive' expenditure. It must be analytically proved, and empirically demonstrated, that the alternatives (to defence) in government budgets have a less crowding-out effect, that by contributing to human capital and productivity, their long-term positive effects on the economy are stronger, and that social expenditures enhance welfare *and* provide opportunities for growth. In the absence of such economic logic it will be difficult to demolish the powerful strategic arguments that are given in favour of militarization.

Much theoretical and econometric research in recent years has shown that defence expenditures have a greater, and more pernicious, crowding-out effect than other related forms of national and governmental spending.[42] For developed countries, the military–industrial complex competes with the more competitive industrial sectors for the same stocks of capital, technology and skilled labour. Thus the trade-off with aggregate investment is crucial. It has been estimated that for OECD countries one dollar's worth of extra military expenditure reduces (private) investment by a dollar, both measured as a proportion of GDP.[43] This one-to-one inverse relationship between defence and investment has sizeable growth consequences. Thus, in the post-war period the high military spenders (USA, UK) tended to have lower investment shares and growth rates relative to the low military spenders (Japan, FR Germany). For the Third World, a different argument holds. Defence spending tends to reduce government socio-economic expenditures, such as on education, housing, health, social security, welfare, transport and economic services. This forces the people of these countries to spend more on health, education, and so on, thus increasing their consumption expenditure and reducing the saving rate.[44] In turn, lower saving leads to low investment and hence declining growth rates. In addition, government investment, as a major engine of growth in poor economies, falls with debilitating consequences on the economy. Finally, the state is a main provider of basic needs in such countries and a lowering of its commitments to social welfare reduces the entitlement of the masses to a better standard of living.

The North–South dimensions

The global aspects of development and disarmament are clearly crucial. One must also consider the North–South issues since, while the major part of arms exports are concentrated among developed countries, the majority of arms importers are Third World countries. During the 1970s the economic cost of arms imports increased as the grant and aid component declined, and it is now normal for bilateral arms trade to be financed in cash or credit terms. New institutional arrangements such as barter, though without a specific financial burden, are also expensive since they represent goods and services that are needed to compensate for arms purchase and hence are an opportunity cost. During the 1970s, availability of funds, either from oil revenues or relatively cheap credit, made it possible for the Third World to import massive amounts of armaments. But currently, with the decline of readily available petro-dollars and the rise in international debt, arms importers will find it increasingly burdensome to continue their purchases.

If global disarmament were to lead to a reduction in arms imports and a corresponding decrease in the cost of foreign exchange (and allied servicing) then the gains for development would be highly significant. More important, for typical Third World countries, intermediate imports such as machinery are exceedingly important in sustaining the level of growth. The output capital ratio of such foreign intermediates tends to be high precisely because there are no alternatives available domestically and substitution possibilities are non-existent. In so far as arms imports prevent imports of these 'essentials' they embody a far higher level of costs than conventional measurements would suggest.[45] Another factor that needs to be taken into account is the rapid cost escalation, due to technological improvements, that takes place in the modern armaments sector. For individual firms, or national arms-producing industries, higher prices mean lower international competitiveness. However, given the nature of mark-up pricing in the armaments industries, greater demand usually means a lower, rather than higher, equilibrium price. Thus, to mitigate the effect of lower international competitiveness industrial organizations tend to create export demand. There are incentives for arms suppliers (at the level of the firm or industry) to stimulate overseas demand for their products in an effort to keep inflation rates down.[46] In a sense, therefore, the burden of inflationary adjustments, in arms-producing economies, is passed on or transferred to the Third World.

Another North–South dimension to the problem arises in the field of the international debt crisis.[47] As the grant element has declined and credit sales have flourished, a significant part of Third World debt has arisen as a result of military imports. In 1979, for example, Argentina imported $480 million worth of arms. The change in *public* debt for that year was of the order of $1.6 billion. Thus, 30 per cent of that year's government debt (up to a maximum) could have been attributed to arms purchases.[48] Though the results should be treated with caution, there is little doubt that national debt and state purchase of military equipment can be closely linked, at least for some economies.

Summary

In summary, let us examine the specific links between disarmament and development. The most obvious and direct effect is that of resource transfer. At the national level, government expenditure on defence can be transferred to other categories of state spending such as economic services (agriculture, industry, infrastructure) as well as social services and welfare (education, health, social security, unemployment benefits).[49] At the international level similar effects could be obtained if the large military spenders could transfer some of the resources released by possible arms control measures towards the developmental needs of poorer nations. Here of course we need a more formal mechanism since there is no effective supra-national organization (a world government) which could channel these expenditures into socially desirable areas. The UN is the obvious candidate for such an institution.

Such transfers are essentially direct in nature. But there are numerous indirect effects which work through the 'structure' of the economy. Since arms control and disarmament will entail structural changes it will affect all other macroeconomic variables—investment, saving, net exports and so forth. Once again, estimates for both Third World and developed economies show that the *net* effects will be positive. A reduction in military spending will raise growth, investment and saving.[50]

At the microeconomic or industrial level we have the case of conversion. This implies a transformation of major components of the industrial base from defence production to more socially useful civilian output which is also more profitable and competitive. Though there are some crucial problems attached to industrial conversion, it is now well recognized[51] that such transformation is indeed possible provided it is well planned and that government, management and particularly the work-force are willing participants in the process. The technical, economic and social problems are surmountable. What is crucial is the political will.

It can be noted that market forces around the world are currently causing large-scale industrial re-structuring and even de-industrialization. Thus, the economy can and does adjust to major industrial transformation. Conversion requires similar changes and therefore it should be feasible. But a great deal of preparation and planning is needed, particularly to minimize the transition costs. Major studies and cost–benefit analyses, on the lines already conducted for Sweden, are therefore necessary for various countries with arms-producing capability.

Global disarmament must also tackle squarely the control and reduction of the trade in arms. For arms-importing countries in the Third World, more resources would be released for financing imports of essential intermediate investment goods (such as machinery), which must enhance the prospects for future growth. In so far as arms imports create debt, the burden of international debt will be eased and Third World nations can enjoy the fruits of export revenue. Though arms exporters, and specifically certain specialized industrial firms, will suffer, a dose of conversion will probably benefit everyone in the long run.

A more interesting side-effect may be discernible for Third World countries themselves. At the regional level, multilateral disarmament could enhance security and lead to more confidence-building measures among erstwhile belligerent neighbours. This could be the first step towards economic co-operation and policy co-ordination on developmental issues that benefit the regional community. If the antagonists of World War II can live harmoniously within the European Community, there is no reason why developing countries cannot follow suit. There are good current examples of regional coalitions (such as the Association of South East Asian Nations—ASEAN),[52] which demonstrate the practical feasibility of such ideas.

The central concept of *Common Security*, as envisaged by the Palme Commission[53] and appropriately adapted to our discussions, has three essential ingredients: strategic and economic policies should be in the interest of both opponents; policies should be undertaken jointly, that is by all interested parties together; activities which favour co-operation and reduce deceptions are preferable.[54] It is not difficult to see how the process of disarmament and development, if successful, satisfies the above-mentioned criteria.

IV. Conclusion

The International Conference on the Relationship between Disarmament and Development was a success since the basic underlying principles are now firmly on the political agenda. It is expected that the 1988 UN Special Session on Disarmament will devote a great deal of attention to the problem, that the issue will continue to be vigorously debated and that actions will be effectively implemented. The Conference failed only in its inability to produce more concrete policy proposals. However, given the fact that such a meeting was the first of its kind, and that major analytical problems must still be resolved, we should be hopeful about more positive action programmes in the future.

The fundamental principles must be repeatedly stressed. The links between disarmament and development are complex but crucial. They need to be understood within a re-defined notion of 'security'. For the Third World, there can be no true security, neither for the deprived majority nor the ruling élites, unless economic development occurs in the widest sense of the term. An elusive search for strategic security divorced from the wider concept of security from unemployment, hunger, disease and homelessness, can be self defeating. Unless this is realized by all there can be no release from the vicious circle.

Even the more developed economies (both market-oriented and centrally planned) need to consider the linkages between economic constraints, political expediency and military concerns. Armaments and crisis as well as disarmament and growth are interrelated. The public and the media are probably more aware of this than specialists or political leaders. To give a media example: 'The political, military and economic issues are intricately linked, though specialists who focus on details create the illusion that these are different worlds. But they must be seen as a whole . . .'. 'It is obvious to everybody . . .' except perhaps those 'who brush aside the stock market crash as unwarranted panic, that economic imbalance is threatening the West'. This 'creates social problems *and also affects military security*' (emphasis added).[55]

More research, greater awareness and firmer political will are required for the detailed implementation of specific projects for disarmament and development. The central point is clear: military expenditure is a major economic burden and disarmament presents a vital economic opportunity. It must be firmly grasped.

Notes and references

[1] See Deger, S., 'The social and welfare opportunity costs of military spending in developing countries,' *Homes Above All: Homelessness and the Misallocation of Global Resources* (The Building and Social Housing Foundation: Leicester, UK, 1987), pp. 31–46; and Deger, S. and West, R., 'Introduction: defence expenditure, national security and economic development in the Third World', *Defence, Security and Development*, eds S. Deger and R. West (Frances Pinter Publishers: London, 1987), pp. 1–16.

[2] This information comes from 'The health needs of developing countries', *Medicine and War*, vol. 4 (1988), pp. 49–52.

[3] These are those Third World countries (for which data are available) with 1985 per capita GNP of less than US $400, as reported by the World Bank. The change in defence spending was

calculated from the SIPRI military expenditure data—for 1975 from SIPRI, *World Armaments and Disarmament: SIPRI Yearbook 1983* (Taylor & Francis: London, 1983), and for 1985 from SIPRI, *SIPRI Yearbook 1987: World Armaments and Disarmament* (Oxford University Press: Oxford, 1987).

[4] The quotation is taken from the UN Secretary-General's address to the ICRDD, extracts of which are published in *New Perspectives*, vol. 18, no. 1 (1988), pp. 8–9.

[5] See the discussion on national security in Deger and West (note 1), introduction, pp. 5–8.

[6] *Study on the Relationship between Disarmament and Development*, UN document A/36/356, 5 Oct. 1981; henceforth referred to as the *Thorsson Report*.

[7] *Thorsson Report* (note 6), p. 163.

[8] See Stützle, W., 'Introduction: 1986—a year of peace?', SIPRI, *SIPRI Yearbook 1987: World Armaments and Disarmament* (Oxford University Press: Oxford, 1987), for a discussion of important examples of the social and economic elements of international security.

[9] Quoted from the article by Noel-Baker, P., 'The prospects for disarmament', in eds M. Graham, R. Jolly and C. Smith, *Disarmament and World Development*, 2nd edn (Pergamon Press: Oxford, 1986).

[10] *Economic and Social Consequences of the Arms Race and of Military Expenditures*, UN publication, Sales No. E.72.IX.16, 1972 (subsequently updated).

[11] UN Resolution 2685 (XXV), quoted in the *Thorsson Report* (note 6).

[12] *Official Records of the Disarmament Commission, Supplement for April to December 1955*, UN document DC/71.

[13] *Official Records of the General Assembly, Thirteenth Session*, UN document A/C. 1/L.204.

[14] See note 9.

[15] *Final Document of the Tenth Special Session of the General Assembly*, UN Resolution S-10/2, 30 June 1978.

[16] The background paper was prepared by Denmark, Finland, Norway and Sweden as mentioned in *Official Records of the General Assembly, Tenth Special Session, Supplement No. 1*. Detailed references are to be found in the *Thorsson Report* (note 6), p. 6, footnote 1.

[17] Fontanel, J. and Smith, R., 'The creation of an international disarmament fund for development' in Deger and West (note 1).

[18] Goldblat, J. and Ferm, R., 'UN General Assembly resolutions and decisions on arms control and disarmament, 1985–86', SIPRI, 1987.

[19] See organization details in *Report of the International Conference on the Relationship between Disarmament and Development*, UN document A/CONF. 130/39, 22 Sep. 1987.

[20] *The Christian Science Monitor*, 4 Aug. 1987, reports that the 'administration contends that disarmament and development should be dealt with as separate issues'.

[21] See *The United Nations General Assembly and Disarmament 1986* (United Nations: New York, 1987), pp. 201–2; also, the statement by the representative of the United States in UN document A/41/PV.96, 10 Dec. 1986.

[22] Data from *US Overseas Loans and Grants* (Office of Planning and Budgeting: Washington, DC, 1987), pp. 13, 18.

[23] See *Working Paper submitted by the Belgian Delegation on behalf of the Twelve States Members of the EC*, UN document A/CONF. 130/PC/5, 16 Apr. 1987.

[24] See the speech by Mr John Birch CMG, Deputy Permanent Representative of the UK Mission to the UN, in *Arms Control and Disarmament Quarterly Review*, no. 7 (Oct. 1987), pp. 23–30.

[25] For details see note 24, p. 21.

[26] Report of Working Group III, UN document A/CONF. 130/CW/WP.3, 4 Sep. 1987.

[27] International Conference on the Relationship between Disarmament and Development, New York, 24 Aug.–11 Sep. 1987, *Final Document* (United Nations: New York, 1987), Sales No. E.87.IX.8.

[28] 'Strong principles, weak actions in disarmament/development consensus report', *Disarmament Times*, 18 Sep. 1987, p. 1.

[29] See note 28, p. 1.

[30] The importance of data is discussed in Tullberg, R. and Hagmeyer-Gaverus, G., 'SIPRI military expenditure data', SIPRI, *SIPRI Yearbook 1988: World Armaments and Disarmament* (Oxford University Press: Oxford, 1988), chapter 6.

[31] An implicit suggestion of this sort is contained in the letter of 24 July 1987 from the Nordic countries to the Conference, UN document A/CONF./130/3.

[32] *International Herald Tribune*, 12–13 Sep. 1987 (article by Paul Lewis).

[33] *The Times*, 28 Jan. 1988. As early as 1983, Robert V. Roosa, Chairman of the Board of the prestigious Brookings Institution, said '. . . the biggest area of action, apart from new taxes, is to

find ways of cutting the projected growth in the defense budget'; see *The Brookings Review*, vol. 1, no. 4 (summer 1983), p. 31.

[34] *International Herald Tribune*, 20–21 Feb. 1988, p. 3.

[35] *The Independent*, 1 Feb. 1988, p. 8.

[36] Both the major schools of thought, neoclassical and Keynesian-radical, believe that defence is a major determinant of aggregate output in a capitalist economy. See, for example, Barro, R. J., 'Output effects of government policies', *Journal of Political Economy* (1981), pp. 1086–121 and Baran, P. A. and Sweezey, P. M., *Monopoly Capital* (Monthly Review Press: New York, 1966) for the two paradigms. Melman, S., *Profits Without Production* (Alfred Knopf: New York, 1983) is a good critique, using data from the USA, showing the inverse relationship between military expenditure and economic growth.

[37] The 1986 United States *trade* deficit was of the order of $156 billion. At the time of writing, January 1988, the trade deficit for 1987 is expected to be about $170 billion as reported in *International Herald Tribune*, 16–17 Jan. 1988, p. 1.

[38] See *Financial Times*, 28 Jan. 1988, p. 17, for a graph which implies that between 1980 and 1985 the value of the US dollar increased in real terms by more than 30 per cent in relation to the currencies of 15 other industrial countries.

[39] For a detailed discussion and formal modelling of the positive and negative impacts of military expenditure on economic development and growth see Deger, S., *Military Expenditure in Third World Countries: The Economic Effects* (Routledge and Kegan Paul: London, 1986). A broader point of view is taken by Kaldor, M., 'The military in Third World development', in *Disarmament and World Development* (note 9). Similar issues for the international economy are dealt with by Luckham, R., 'Militarism and international economic dependence', in the same volume.

[40] Deger, S. and Sen, S., 'Technology transfer and arms production in developing countries', *Industry and Development*, no. 15 (1985), pp.1–18.

[41] UN publication Sales No. E. 86 IX.5, 16–18 Apr. 1986.

[42] An overview is given in a paper prepared for the ICRDD: Deger, S., *Cross-Sectoral Analyses of Military Expenditure and Capital Formation, Productivity, Economic Growth and Competitiveness*, UN document, A/CONF. 130/PC/INF/16, 30 Apr. 1986. For developed countries see Smith, R. P., 'Military expenditure and capitalism', *Cambridge Journal of Economics* (Mar. 1977), pp. 61–76.

[43] Smith, R. P. 'Military expenditure and investment in OECD countries, 1954–1973', *Journal of Comparative Economics* (1980), pp. 19–32.

[44] Deger, S., 'Economic development and defence expenditure', *Economic Development and Cultural Change*, vol. 35, no. 1 (Oct. 1986), pp. 179–96.

[45] See note 40.

[46] Brzoska, M. and Ohlson, T., SIPRI, *Arms Transfers to the Third World, 1971–85* (Oxford University Press: Oxford, 1987).

[47] For the role of the debt crisis in security problems see Stützle (note 8). An empirical study, relating debt and defence, can be found in Tullberg, R., 'Military-related debt in non-oil developing countries 1972–82', SIPRI, *World Armaments and Disarmament: SIPRI Yearbook 1985* (Taylor & Francis: London, 1985), pp. 445–58.

[48] See Deger (note 39), and footnotes to that reference for the method of calculation.

[49] Some detailed cost-benefit exercises are reported in Deger, S., 'Resource transfer from defence to health care: problems and possibilities', *Journal of Tropical Pediatrics* (June 1987) and Deger (note 1).

[50] A macroeconometric model is estimated for 50 developing countries in the appendix to Deger (note 39).

[51] See the study in Thorsson, I., *In Pursuit of Disarmament: Conversion from Military to Civilian Production in Sweden*, vols 1 and 2 (Liber Allmänna Förlaget: Stockholm, 1984, 1985).

[52] The recent ASEAN meeting (Dec. 1987), though principally involved with accelerating trade co-operation, has also discussed strategic issues and security threats. See *Times of India*, 15 Dec. 1987, p. 1.

[53] *Common Security: A Programme for Disarmament*, The Report of the Independent Commission on Disarmament and Security Issues (Pan Books: London, 1982).

[54] See Rothschild, E., 'Common security and deterrence' in SIPRI, *Policies for Common Security* (Taylor & Francis: London, 1985).

[55] *International Herald Tribune*, 16–17 Jan. 1988, p. 4 (opinion column).

17. The SIPRI 1987 Olof Palme Memorial Lecture—'Security and disarmament: change and vision'

In October 1986, SIPRI's Governing Board decided to arrange an annual public lecture, named after the late Swedish Prime Minister Olof Palme. The lecture is to be delivered in Stockholm by a political leader of international stature or an eminent scholar in order to highlight the need for and problems of peace and security, in particular of arms control and disarmament. The lecture is also intended to draw attention to SIPRI's commitment to a future with fewer arms and more freedom. On 18 September 1987, Willy Brandt, former Chancellor of the Federal Republic of Germany, delivered the first annual Olof Palme Memorial Lecture.

WILLY BRANDT

I

I am well aware of the honour that my invitation to today's event means. I appreciate this very much, and I would like to wish the Institute the best of success for its work in the years to come, which—from what we know today—may turn out to be very interesting in terms of arms control and arms limitation.

It is not by lamenting that we will keep alive the memory of someone like Olof Palme, who struggled so hard for the security and welfare of so many people. Instead, we should try even harder in our endeavours; we should make an extra effort. The question then is: What can we do? What extra effort are we prepared to make in order to give humanity a better chance of survival—especially thinking about those who have been prevented so far, and repeatedly, from living a decent and, where possible, dignified life?

With your permission, I would like to start by stating a few facts. And in doing so, I can afford to do it without any tactical ulterior motives. I believe in the probability of progress in international negotiations on security policy. Nevertheless, it would be careless not to be prepared for new and further setbacks and aberrations.

1. When the date for today's event was agreed upon, none of us could possibly have known that, during the course of this week, the probability of a first real disarmament agreement between the two nuclear superpowers would be confirmed (as it in fact was on this very Friday, 18 September). Ill-tempered contemporaries, who tell us that this agreement will affect only a small portion of the nuclear destruction potential, fail to recognize the not only symbolic but almost fundamental importance of events to come, and they underestimate their potential as a basis for further, broader agreements. In any case, I want to congratulate the governments of the USA and of the Soviet Union on the agreement they have reached.

2. Follow-up negotiations on nuclear arms with a range of less than 500 kilometres are now within the realm of possibility. In addition, conventional stability—hopefully on a low scale—has generally been accepted as a topic by

the party which is superior in this field, although this party's relative advantage may have been exaggerated for obvious reasons. The Mutual and Balanced Force Reductions (MBFR) negotiations, which have been going on in Vienna for almost 15 years and which at an earlier time could have assumed a peace-setting function, have lost some of their importance. The corridor model—not necessarily limited to the two German states—which had been proposed in the report of the Palme Commission may turn out to be a useful vehicle on the path towards security in Europe with its certainly many trials and tribulations yet to overcome.

3. The dictate of reason described in the Palme Report—I am referring to the concept of Common Security—is gradually taken more seriously in both blocs and even in conservative government circles of both alliances. We should not, however, underestimate the power of the opposite approach based on conventional thinking. But how much has already changed was obvious last week, for instance, when a high-ranking official visitor from the GDR was expected in Bonn. When I first met with the leaders of the GDR in 1970, both sides already were in agreement at the time that never again should war be started from German soil. By now, these two countries discuss what they can do jointly—and individually in their own alliance and foreign policies—to make peace safer in Europe and in the world. And political parties which had fallen out mortally with each other have come to realize very calmly that the struggle between ideologies (or whatever it is that is given this name) can be civilized, that it should be a subsidiary issue when compared to the cause of peace. (This is the very essence of a paper that recently was published in Bonn and East Berlin and which I understand has provoked some misunderstandings.)

4. The Geneva negotiations—in this case, not those between the two nuclear superpowers but those of the larger committee which has been meeting since 1960 on behalf of the United Nations—have come very close to a result which would lead to a world-wide ban on chemical weapons. However, as long as major delays due to complications cannot be excluded, regional projects—such as the creation of a zone in Europe which would be free of any chemical weapons—in my opinion should not be shelved. Furthermore, the results and common recommendations worked out last year by the Stockholm Conference on Disarmament in Europe (CDE) on the issue of verification may turn out to be helpful in this particular context as well as in others.

5. Logic suggests that a reduction of tension in the relationship between the two superpowers may also ease tensions in several of the so-called regional conflicts. There seems to be some evidence of this at some trouble-spots, while there is none at others. I certainly do not want to nourish exaggerated expectations. But perhaps we should remember that nothing worthwhile has ever been achieved by displaying blasé negativism.

II

Political thinking has been slow in reflecting the new quality that the topic of 'War and Peace' has assumed. Often, the discussion on North–South problems is not very clear either, where international security issues are concerned.

It was this Institute (SIPRI) that drew our attention to the fact that at the end of last year (1986), the world was plagued by no fewer than 36 military conflicts, involving some five and a half million soldiers from 41 countries. The war between Iran and Iraq alone, in which also Olof Palme tried to act as a mediator, has been going on for over seven years now. More than 350 000 people have lost their lives in this war, and both sides have spent more money on it than Iran and Iraq have earned since the beginning of oil production. The fact that there has been no 'big' war so far is no consolation to those who have perished in the over 150 'limited' wars which have taken place all across the world since 1945. I am not even talking about all the victims of torture and hunger who have been silenced. Our world—which has been torn and for a long time dominated not only by the East–West confrontation, but also by the slowly aggravating North–South conflict as well as by serious regional crises on all continents—this world may dream of military security, but unfortunately one cannot count on it.

This becomes even clearer if we recall the current state of the world economy, and if we also bear in mind that leaders of the most powerful industrialized nations are unable to find solutions to pressing problems. In the light of repeated drops in commodity prices, an increasingly menacing ecological situation (described in vivid terms by the recent report of the Brundtland Commission) and, not least, the debt crisis affecting many Third World countries—and the life-threatening problems resulting from all this—it is hard to comprehend that the participants of the so-called economic summits behave as if it were appropriate for the congress to continue dancing. This is more than just annoying: it is a downright scandal.

There is a lot more at stake than what bankers and administrators of national debt would usually sort out amongst themselves. The debt crisis has reached proportions which have turned it into a political problem, and not just one of domestic policy for the countries involved. In some countries, especially in Latin America, this crisis touches upon the very substance of democratic institutions. It is hard to understand, therefore, why those who regard themselves as the guardians of democracy all across the world show so little readiness to help establish some of the fundamental economic and social preconditions for democratic progress. Unless there is a new sense of responsibility in the near future, I am afraid that this will lead not only to adverse effects on democracy but to chaotic conditions in more than one country. What this situation calls for is primacy of politics.

Any discussion on security and disarmament in my opinion must nowadays include North–South experiences and the substantial changes affecting the world economy. Global threats through weapons are paralleled by the global challenge of pressing problems in the South, where the slogan 'weapons instead of bread' has that topical relevance which it has lost in our part of the world.

At any rate, there can be no doubt that the major regional crises seem to be a greater threat to the world today than the East–West conflict. And those acting on behalf of the superpowers are no less preoccupied by those trouble-spots than they are by global security issues. It is in those hot-spots—which, after all, may spark off fires elsewhere—that their crisis-management skills must prove their value. There are many examples to quote from: Afghanistan's growing burden on the Soviet Union, which increasingly perceives it as such; the Gulf conflict, which in a way started out as a confrontation by proxy between the two superpowers; the United States' not very convincing handling of their 'backyard' or perhaps 'frontyard'—Central America—where the leaders of the countries involved no longer seem willing to grant the United States the controlling position that they used to hold during the past one and a half centuries, have now come nearer to a reconciliation amongst themselves; and last but not least, the aggravation of the situation in South Africa which may wind up in most severe bloodshed today or tomorrow. Anyone speaking here in Stockholm on an occasion like this, which is so closely related to Olof Palme, could not possibly leave this out.

All these problems—and, of course, many others—are in fact on the agenda, but where are they actually being tackled? If they were really top priorities for the superpowers, they would have discussed them with greater interest than they have so far; but, as I pointed out at the very beginning of these remarks, I assume—as a working hypothesis—that any real reduction of tensions in the relationship between the two superpowers may also help to defuse regional crises.

According to an old African saying which friends have told me, the grass will suffer when elephants fight, and it will not be much better off when they make love. I can easily sympathize with the profound scepticism expressed in this saying.

The concept of Common Security, however, does not imply at all that it is only of interest to Europe. I cannot think of any major conflict in other parts of the world where all-out victory is imminent for any one side.

By the way, serious negotiations on how to re-channel some of the funds currently spent on overarmament to finance development could very well produce positive global effects. Just last week, this was underlined by an interesting experience.

At the United Nations' Special Conference on 'Overarmament and Underdevelopment', one of the major parties was absent: the United States of America. Quite apart from this, I am afraid that the conference did not produce much more than general statements and tactical manoeuvres. And although I can very well understand that Western governments are not pleased if their past efforts are not duly recognized, I doubt that it has been a smart move for the most important power of the Western world to 'simply stay away'.

So one of the important tasks ahead of us is to convince political leaders in the West and in the East—and in particular, the superpowers—that the interrelationship between overarmament and underdevelopment will increasingly have a bearing on their own fields of interest. This 'underestimated interdependence', as I would like to call it, could be an area for constructive contributions from Europeans. And why wait for the superpowers once again? It would be worthy of Europe if its governments and its communities took an initiative in this important case.

III

For Europe, I can see at least one other opportunity to fulfil its responsibility in response to global needs. Against the background of last week's visit by Erich Honecker, the Chairman of the GDR's State Council, to the Federal Republic of Germany, I would like to make a few comments on the tasks that will arise after the conclusion of the first disarmament agreement on nuclear missiles. (If this agreement had not materialized, we would have been going through a very difficult period until a new US Administration would be fully functioning again. It might have come to a debacle.)

In this context, I shall say quite frankly that I do not particularly appreciate the type of language that often dominates the discussion on security policy. Too much of it is occupied by the military—in the dual sense of the term. The military occupation of the language of politics—in our case, of security policy—is an aberration that we should not accept, particularly against the background of our good European traditions. But this applies even more to all that empty talk about peace.

A prominent Prussian king is known to have once said that the military should not think, or else they would be poor soldiers. Whether that made sense at the time may be of no concern to us now. Politicians and political scientists, however, should certainly not allow themselves to become poor soldiers by condoning or actively encouraging any militarization of their language.

The issue of security is, of course, not only limited to military problems, inducing problems of arms limitation—important as these problems may be. The way things are today, however, one's own security depends to a large extent on the security of the other, or of others. This leads to the question as to what policy is most suitable and most likely to create the preconditions for technical military arrangements that secure peace. Such arrangements can only be achieved as a result of courageous foresighted policies—policies that are free of cheap opportunism.

It is both a political and a philosophical idea of considerable amplitude that, if the nations of this world are not to be doomed, they have to organize their life, their coexistence, by contractual arrangements. The problems that we will have to tackle are the challenge of hunger in the world, the threat to our environment and our biosphere, as well as the consequences of overpopulation. Against this background, disarmament seems to be reduced to a historical clearing-up operation, in which we attempt to remove the debris of a historical error, a remnant from the pre-nuclear age, which was to try and achieve security by building up growing arsenals of arms.

We need Common Security in order to be able to coexist. To me, this is the central message of the Palme Report (and also of the reports by the two commissions chaired by Gro Harlem Brundtland and myself). Common Security does not offer a recipe for solving concrete problems. Instead, it defines patterns of behaviour and of thinking, as well as methods that can help to solve many concrete problems. Agreements, for instance, should take the place of unilateral action; stability should be achieved by means of cooperation; and mutual strategic deterrence should be replaced by mutual strategic security. At a time when rapid changes take place all over the world, stability has become an indispensable factor to counterbalance our globe. It looks as if the opening of the Soviet Union could be a rather helpful element in this respect.

My own experience has taught me that usually no progress is achieved by ignoring the *status quo* but rather by taking note of it and by thinking about ways of how to change it so it gets improved. Often, substantial changes can be implemented under the political cloak of continuation. That is what we—my colleagues and I—tried to do years ago with what others called our 'Ostpolitik'. Since it helped to overcome the cold, the thick cloak was no longer needed.

The two alliances—NATO and the Warsaw Pact—will continue to be indispensable factors of stability. They will also remain indispensable for making peace so stable in Europe that it will become virtually unbreakable. The recognition of this reality can be expressed in many different ways. And this of course also concerns—I am sure—the neutral and nonaligned countries, because such an attitude is in keeping with their interests.

What we need is not a change on the European map but an inner recognition of borders so that these lose their dividing character and, instead, help to unite people from either side. This must not be confused with the fulfilment of dreams from times gone by. A change in awareness, however, may help to join what belongs together in a new way.

All this is actually not all that new any more. Our recognition of the GDR as a state in 1969 subsequently led not only to the signing of the so-called 'Grundlagenvertrag' by the two German states—it provided greater possibilities for human encounters, more security (maybe also a greater potential for development) for Berlin, and an easing of tension due to the renunciation of force in Europe and the development set off, despite all the obstacles, by the Helsinki Conference. The acceptance of the *status quo* paved the way for implementing changes without jeopardy for our 'European House'—an image that I find quite appealing although I would not recommend putting too much into it.

The fundamental principles laid down in the above-mentioned treaty in 1972 have just been sealed by the splendour of protocol, and, with its broadcast images, television has helped to make people aware of this, both in the East and in the West. The national anthems of the two countries provided the musical background, as it were, for an event which marked the end of a claim that had been an illusion for a long time, and maybe has also marked the beginning of hope for a new era.

How could this new era be characterized? If the two German states' independence and autonomy, as defined in the 'Grundlagenvertrag', are no longer challenged, and if—on the contrary—they are apparently supported by all relevant political forces in Germany, then unrealistic demands will no longer stop us from concentrating our efforts on co-operation. The Germans' prospects for the future now mainly rely on what they have in common. Anything else will be open to the course of history on which a lot of comments have been made recently, both in the West and in the East.

Simply by analysing what their common interests are and by translating their findings into proposals that they should submit to their respective alliances, the two German states may make important contributions, perhaps even indispensable ones. They will be all the more successful in doing so, the more their proposals reflect the European interest in *détente*, disarmament and security.

IV

This could be the beginning of a 'new German way of thinking' as part of a new approach towards Europe.

Gorbachev has introduced his notion of the House of Europe to describe his approach—an image which might provoke quite a few comments. For the time being, we are confronted with a situation where the two superpowers—who each hold different shares of this house—are arguing about who is to be in charge of it, with each of them trying to win the support of the owners and tenants for themselves and for their respective points of view.

It is time we remembered who the actual owners are, and hence, what their responsibilities are. Who else should have a say in this so-called European House if not those who live in it, who have grown up in it and who depend on it? It is time we thought not only in terms of the groupings that our countries belong to, but also in terms of the overall continental context. It is time we stopped waiting for the superpowers to come up with proposals, in keeping with their global responsibility, hoping that these proposals will be a pleasant surprise to us. It is time we developed our own European concepts in accordance with the criteria for our Common Security—criteria that would also be valid for the superpowers.

Whether a limitation of intercontinental machines of destruction—the so-called strategic weapons—can soon be achieved is a question which probably cannot be separated from the issue of future armament efforts in space. At this point, I do not want to start thinking aloud about the possibility of living in a world without nuclear arms. But if the main concern on the way towards this objective is maintaining a balance, this could also be achieved by keeping just a few weapons on either side.

If peace is to come to the so-called European House, we must make sure that no one in it is threatened or feels threatened. The task for us to tackle after the signing of the first intermediate-range nuclear forces (INF) agreement is to maintain—to negotiate about and organize—stability from the Atlantic Ocean to the Ural Mountains.

This will indeed be a gigantic task because we will have to deal with a large variety of armed forces and regions. The North, for instance, may opt for another approach than the South. In Central Europe, with its massive accumulation of weapons and troops, the problems seem to be most difficult and most pressing. If stability can be brought about there, it would make it much easier to bring about the same in neighbouring regions. (When I talk about Central Europe in this context, I am referring to the area extending from the western border of the Federal Republic of Germany to the eastern border of Poland, and from Denmark and the Benelux countries to Czechoslovakia and Hungary.)

As we all know, negotiations are currently under way in Vienna for a mandate within the Conference on Security and Co-operation in Europe (CSCE) framework. The first very important step to take, however, is to agree between East and West on the basic principles for stability, such as Common Security, the elimination of all superiority, taking into account geographical asymmetries, as well as eliminating attack potentials and military options that are considered to be particularly threatening by either of the two sides—and, of course, establishing verification procedures. Once these principles are accepted, one can then tackle the task of defining in detail how this will affect the structure and deployment of armed forces, and what impact this will have on strategies or doctrines (depending on whether Western or Eastern terminology is used) and on figures.

At any rate, I believe the squabble about figures must not be made the first item on the agenda. The experience of the MBFR negotiations should have taught us how time-consuming and unproductive it is to start by trying to agree on the size of each side's current inventory. I suggest that Europe has no time to repeat such a useless exercise. I am not all that interested in how many tanks the Warsaw Pact countries have today. What I would mainly like to know is how many tanks they will have as a result of negotiations, and where these tanks will be deployed. I am mentioning this only as an example of an area where superiority must be eliminated.

Attention should mainly be focused on the target and on the definition of the criteria for this target. I do not expect too much from the Soviet Union's proposals for percentage reductions. This would almost inevitably spark off a new discussion on data. Once the target is defined, the next step should be to determine what percentage share of a given arms category should remain in the Central European region: 40 or 50 per cent of the total envisaged for Europe? Or, to stick to my example, should 2000, 4000 or 5000 tanks be allowed to stay in Central Europe?

In this context, the proposal for creating a non-nuclear corridor is once again attractive, especially if it can be extended to comprise an area from which all heavy equipment that can be used for attacking should be removed. Such an arrangement would probably bring about an effective reduction in attack potential, because the lack of superiority would constitute an unacceptable risk for any aggressor.

This effect could be further enhanced if both sides had the right to deploy any number of highly modern, intelligent defence systems because this would provide a substantial advantage for the defending side. This is what may be called 'structural incapacity to attack'.

Recently there has been a rapprochement in the Federal Republic of Germany between large parts of the current coalition government and the opposition. Both are aware of the fact that the effect of weapons becomes more devastating for Germany, the shorter their range is. So there is an obvious interest—after the conclusion of an INF agreement—to press for negotiations on nuclear arms with a range of less than 500 kilometres. Disarmament must certainly not be excluded where weapons are concerned that, by their nature, would only be a threat for the battlefield represented by the two German states.

Any actions resulting from these considerations must, of course, be taken step by step, simply because of the interdependence between conventional stability and so-called tactical nuclear weapons. Their interdependence cannot be undone, neither by political nor by technical means. At the same time, however, this offers interesting opportunities for countries (like the two German states) which do not possess any nuclear arms.

The concentration on Central Europe is also indicative of the respect that France's independent nuclear arsenal will continue to command for an as yet unforeseeable period of time. To a large extent, the hopes—which I share—for closer co-operation among West European countries and for their combined responsibility in matters of defence, are based on the future role of France's conventional armed forces. These would be particularly important for the purposes that I have just outlined. But I do not want to conceal the fact that I think there are also some places in Western Europe where overcoming old patterns of thinking is as important a task as elsewhere.

V

Achieving Common Security for Europe by means of structural incapacity to attack—that is the opportunity that, providing we use some of our mental energy, history will be offering to us after the signing of the first nuclear disarmament agreement between the two superpowers.

This vision, which looked like a purely Utopian idea a couple of years ago, would all of a sudden move into the realm of possibility. One might also choose a different description: it would be tantamount to a partial demilitarization of the East–West conflict, replacing confrontation by peaceful competition and co-operation, and certainly not only in the economic field and that of cultural exchanges. This would truly be a breakthrough which might inaugurate a new chapter in European history.

Nevertheless, the 'ideological' differences, the incompatibilities of the systems, will remain: as much as the differences in preferences, aptitude and willingness on the part of the owners of the European House to furnish and decorate their own room. All this, however, would be subordinated to the law of survival: security—properly understood—comes first.

Achieving this goal would be the best contribution that Europe could make to the world. We would not only help ourselves but also set free energy to help cope with the major threats that jeopardize humanity. Whether the practical value of the concept of Common Security as a fundamental guideline for security policy can be put to a test will, to a large extent, depend on us, here in Europe.

Annexe A. Major multilateral arms control agreements

RAGNHILD FERM

For the full texts of the arms control agreements, see Goldblat, J., SIPRI, *Agreements for Arms Control: A Critical Survey* (Taylor & Francis: London, 1982).

I. Summaries of the agreements

Protocol for the prohibition of the use in war of asphyxiating, poisonous or other gases, and of bacteriological methods of warfare (Geneva Protocol)

Signed at Geneva on 17 June 1925; entered into force on 8 February 1928.

Declares that the parties agree to be bound by the above prohibition, which should be universally accepted as part of international law, binding alike the conscience and the practice of nations.

Antarctic Treaty

Signed at Washington on 1 December 1959; entered into force on 23 June 1961.

Declares the Antarctic an area to be used exclusively for peaceful purposes. Prohibits any measure of a military nature in the Antarctic, such as the establishment of military bases and fortifications, and the carrying out of military manoeuvres or the testing of any type of weapon. Bans any nuclear explosion as well as the disposal of radioactive waste material in Antarctica, subject to possible future international agreements on these subjects.

    At regular intervals consultative meetings are convened to exchange information and hold consultations on matters pertaining to Antarctica, as well as to recommend to the governments measures in furtherance of the principles and objectives of the Treaty.

Treaty banning nuclear weapon tests in the atmosphere, in outer space and under water (Partial Test Ban Treaty—PTBT)

Signed at Moscow on 5 August 1963; entered into force on 10 October 1963.

Prohibits the carrying out of any nuclear weapon test explosion or any other nuclear explosion: (*a*) in the atmosphere, beyond its limits, including outer space, or under water, including territorial waters or high seas; or (*b*) in any other environment if such explosion causes radioactive debris to be present outside the territorial limits of the state under whose jurisdiction or control the explosion is conducted.

Treaty on principles governing the activities of states in the exploration and use of outer space, including the moon and other celestial bodies (Outer Space Treaty)

Signed at London, Moscow and Washington on 27 January 1967; entered into force on 10 October 1967.

Prohibits the placing in orbit around the earth of any objects carrying nuclear weapons or any other kinds of weapons of mass destruction, the installation of such weapons on celestial bodies, or the stationing of them in outer space in any other manner. The establishment of military bases, installations and fortifications, the testing of any type of weapons and the conduct of military manoeuvres on celestial bodies are also forbidden.

Treaty for the prohibition of nuclear weapons in Latin America (Treaty of Tlatelolco)

Signed at Mexico City on 14 February 1967; entered into force on 22 April 1968.

Prohibits the testing, use, manufacture, production or acquisition by any means, as well as the receipt, storage, installation, deployment and any form of possession of any nuclear weapons by Latin American countries.

The parties should conclude agreements with the IAEA for the application of safeguards to their nuclear activities.

Under *Additional Protocol I* the extra-continental or continental states which, *de jure* or *de facto*, are internationally responsible for territories lying within the limits of the geographical zone established by the Treaty (France, the Netherlands, the UK and the USA), undertake to apply the statute of military denuclearization, as defined in the Treaty, to such territories.

Under *Additional Protocol II* the nuclear weapon states undertake to respect the statute of military denuclearization of Latin America, as defined and delimited in the Treaty, and not to contribute to acts involving a violation of the Treaty, nor to use or threaten to use nuclear weapons against the parties to the Treaty.

Treaty on the non-proliferation of nuclear weapons (NPT)

Signed at London, Moscow and Washington on 1 July 1968; entered into force on 5 March 1970.

Prohibits the transfer by nuclear weapon states, to any recipient whatsoever, of nuclear weapons or other nuclear explosive devices or of control over them, as well as the assistance, encouragement or inducement of any non-nuclear weapon state to manufacture or otherwise acquire such weapons or devices. Prohibits the receipt by non-nuclear weapon states from any transferor whatsoever, as well as the manufacture or other acquisition by those states of nuclear weapons or other nuclear explosive devices.

Non-nuclear weapon states undertake to conclude safeguard agreements with the International Atomic Energy Agency (IAEA) with a view to preventing diversion of nuclear energy from peaceful uses to nuclear weapons or other nuclear explosive devices.

The parties undertake to facilitate the exchange of equipment, materials and scientific and technological information for the peaceful uses of nuclear energy and to ensure that potential benefits from peaceful applications of nuclear explosions will be made available to non-nuclear weapon parties to the Treaty. They also undertake to pursue negotiations in good faith on effective measures relating to cessation of the nuclear arms race at an early date and to nuclear disarmament, and on a treaty on general and complete disarmament.

Treaty on the prohibition of the emplacement of nuclear weapons and other weapons of mass destruction on the sea-bed and the ocean floor and in the subsoil thereof (Sea-Bed Treaty)

Signed at London, Moscow and Washington on 11 February 1971; entered into force on 18 May 1972.

Prohibits emplanting or emplacing on the sea-bed and the ocean floor and in the subsoil thereof beyond the outer limit of a 12-mile sea-bed zone any nuclear weapons or any other types of weapons of mass destruction as well as structures, launching installations or any other facilities specifically designed for storing, testing or using such weapons.

Convention on the prohibition of the development, production and stockpiling of bacteriological (biological) and toxin weapons and on their destruction (BW Convention)

Signed at London, Moscow and Washington on 10 April 1972; entered into force on 26 March 1975.

Prohibits the development, production, stockpiling or acquisition by other means or retention of microbial or other biological agents, or toxins whatever their origin or method of production, of types and in quantities that have no justification of prophylactic, protective or other peaceful purposes, as well as weapons, equipment or means of delivery designed to use such agents or toxins for hostile purposes or in armed conflict. The destruction of the agents, toxins, weapons, equipment and means of delivery in the possession of the parties, or their diversion to peaceful purposes, should be effected not later than nine months after the entry into force of the Convention.

Convention on the prohibition of military or any other hostile use of environmental modification techniques (Enmod Convention)

Signed at Geneva on 18 May 1977; entered into force on 5 October 1978.

Prohibits military or any other hostile use of environmental modification techniques having widespread, long-lasting or severe effects as the means of destruction, damage or injury to states party to the Convention. The term 'environmental modification techniques' refers to any technique for changing—through the deliberate manipulation of natural processes—the dynamics, composition or structure of the Earth, including its biota, lithosphere, hydrosphere and atmosphere, or of outer space.
  The understandings reached during the negotiations, but not written into the Convention, define the terms 'widespread', 'long-lasting' and 'severe'.

Convention on the prohibitions or restrictions on the use of certain conventional weapons which may be deemed to be excessively injurious or to have indiscriminate effects ('Inhumane Weapons' Convention)

Signed at New York on 10 April 1981; entered into force on 2 December 1983.

The Convention is an 'umbrella treaty', under which specific agreements can be concluded in the form of protocols.

Protocol I prohibits the use of weapons intended to injure by fragments which are not detectable in the human body by X-rays.

Protocol II prohibits or restricts the use of mines, booby-traps and similar devices.

Protocol III prohibits or restricts the use of incendiary weapons.

South Pacific Nuclear Free Zone Treaty (Treaty of Rarotonga)

Signed at Rarotonga, Cook Islands, on 6 August 1985; entered into force on 11 December 1986.

Prohibits the manufacture or acquisition by other means of any nuclear explosive device, as well as possession or control over such device by the parties anywhere inside or outside the zone area described in an annex. The parties also undertake not to supply nuclear material or equipment unless subject to IAEA safeguards; and to prevent in their territories the stationing as well as the testing of any nuclear explosive device. Each party remains free to allow visits, as well as transit, by foreign ships and aircraft.

Under Protocol 1, France, the UK and the USA would undertake to apply the treaty prohibitions relating to the manufacture, stationing and testing of nuclear explosive devices in the territories situated within the zone, for which they are internationally responsible.

Under Protocol 2, China, France, the UK, the USA and the USSR would undertake not to use or threaten to use a nuclear explosive device against the parties to the treaty or against any territory within the zone for which a party to Protocol 1 is internationally responsible.

Under Protocol 3, China, France, the UK, the USA and the USSR would undertake not to test any nuclear explosive device anywhere within the zone.

II. Status of the implementation of the major multilateral arms control agreements, as of 1 January 1988

Number of parties

1925 Geneva Protocol	111
Antarctic Treaty	37
Partial Test Ban Treaty	116
Outer Space Treaty	89
Treaty of Tlatelolco	23
Additional Protocol I	3
Additional Protocol II	5
Non-Proliferation Treaty	137
NPT safeguards agreements	79
Sea-Bed Treaty	80

BW Convention	110
Enmod Convention	52
'Inhumane Weapons' Convention	28
Treaty of Rarotonga*	9

* On 21 April 1988 the USSR deposited the instruments of ratification of Protocols 2 and 3 to the Treaty of Rarotonga.

Notes

1. The table records year of ratification, accession and succession.

2. The Partial Test Ban Treaty, the Outer Space Treaty, the Non-Proliferation Treaty, the Sea-Bed Treaty and the Biological Weapons Convention provide for three depositaries—the governments of the UK, the USA and the USSR. The dates given for these agreements are the earliest dates on which countries deposited their instruments of ratification, accession or succession—whether in London, Washington or Moscow. The dates given for the other agreements, for which there is only one depositary, are the dates of the deposit of the instruments of ratification, accession or succession with the depositary in question.

3. The 1925 Geneva Protocol, the Partial Test Ban Treaty, the Outer Space Treaty, the Non-Proliferation Treaty, the Sea-Bed Treaty, the BW Convention, the Enmod Convention and the 'Inhumane Weapons' Convention are open to all states for signature.

The Antarctic Treaty is subject to ratification by the signatories and is open for accession by UN members or by other states invited to accede with the consent of all the contracting parties whose representatives are entitled to participate in the consultative meetings provided for in Article IX.

The Treaty of Tlatelolco is open for signature by all the Latin American republics; all other sovereign states situated in their entirety south of latitude 35° north in the western hemisphere; and (except for a political entity the territory of which is the subject of an international dispute) all such states which become sovereign, when they have been admitted by the General Conference; Additional Protocol I—by 'all extra-continental or continental states having *de jure* or *de facto* international responsibility for territories situated in the zone of application of the Treaty'; Additional Protocol II—by 'all powers possessing nuclear weapons'.

The Treaty of Rarotonga is open for signature by members of the South Pacific Forum; Protocol 1—by France, the UK and the USA; Protocol 2—by France, China, the USSR, the UK and the USA; Protocol 3—by France, China, the USSR, the UK and the USA.

4. Key to abbreviations used in the table:
S: Signature without further action
PI, PII: Additional Protocols to the Treaty of Tlatelolco
P1, P2, P3: Protocols to the Treaty of Rarotonga
CP: Party entitled to participate in the consultative meetings provided for in Article IX of the Antarctic Treaty
SA: Nuclear safeguards agreement in force with the International Atomic Energy Agency as required by the Non-Proliferation Treaty or the Treaty of Tlatelolco, or concluded by a nuclear weapon state on a voluntary basis.

5. The footnotes are listed at the end of the table and are grouped separately under the heading for each agreement. The texts of the statements contained in the footnotes have been abridged, but the wording is close to the original version.

6. A complete list of UN member states and year of membership appears in section III.

State	Geneva Protocol	Antarctic Treaty	Partial Test Ban Treaty	Outer Space Treaty	Treaty of Tlatelolco	Non-Proliferation Treaty	Sea-Bed Treaty	BW Convention	Enmod Convention	'Inhumane Weapons' Convention	Treaty of Rarotonga
Afghanistan	1986		1964	S		1970 SA	1971	1975	1985	S	
Algeria			S								
Antigua and Barbuda					1983[2]	1985[1]					
Argentina	1969	1961 CP	1986	1969	S[1]		1983[1]	1979	1987[1]	S	1986
Australia	1930[1]	1961 CP	1963	1967		1973 SA	1973	1977	1984	1983	
Austria	1928	1987	1964	1968		1969 SA	1972	1973[1]		1983	
Bahamas			1976[1]	1976[1]	1977[2]	1976[1]		1986	1979		
Bangladesh			1985	1986		1979 SA		1985			
Barbados	1976[2]			1968	1969[2]	1980		1973	1982		
Belgium	1928[1]	1960 CP	1966	1973		1975 SA	1972	1979		S	

MAJOR MULTILATERAL ARMS CONTROL AGREEMENTS 555

Belize							1985[1]	1986			
Benin	1986		1964	1986		1972	1986	1975	1986		
Bhutan	1978		1978			1985		1978			
Bolivia	1985		1965	S	1969[2]	1970	S	1975	S		
Botswana			1968[1]	S		1969	1972	S			
Brazil	1970	1975 CP	1964	1969[2]	1968[3]		S[2]	1973	1984		
Brunei Darussalam						1985 SA					
Bulgaria	1934[1]	1978	1963	1967		1969 SA	1971	1972	1978	1982	
Burkina Faso (formerly Upper Volta)	1971		S	1968		1970					
Burma			1963	1970			S	S			
Burundi			S	S		1971	S	S			
Byelorussia	1970[3]		1963[2]	1967[3]			1971	1975	1978	1982	

556 ANNEXES

State	Geneva Protocol	Antarctic Treaty	Partial Test Ban Treaty	Outer Space Treaty	Treaty of Tlatelolco	Non-Proliferation Treaty	Sea-Bed Treaty	BW Convention	Enmod Convention	'Inhumane Weapons' Convention	Treaty of Rarotonga
Cameroon			S	S		1969	S				
Canada	1930[1]		1964	1967		1969 SA	1972[3]	1972	1981	S	
Cape Verde	1970		1979			1979	1979	1977	1979		
Central African Republic	1970		1964	S		1970	1981	S			
Chad			1965			1971					
Chile	1935[1]	1961 CP	1965	1981	1974[4]			1980			
China	1929[4]	1983 CP		1983	PII: 1974[5]			1984[2]		1982[1]	P2: S[1] P3: S[1]
Colombia			1985	S	1972[2] SA	1986	S	1983			
Congo						1978	1978	1978			
Cook Islands											1985
Costa Rica			1967		1969[2] SA[16]	1970 SA	S	1973			

MAJOR MULTILATERAL ARMS CONTROL AGREEMENTS 557

Côte d'Ivoire	1970		1965		1973 SA	1972	S			
Cuba	1966	1984		1977[4]			1976	1978	1987	
Cyprus	1966[2]		1965	1972	1970 SA	1977[4]	1973	1978		
Czechoslovakia	1938[5]	1962	1963	1967	1969 SA	1971	1973	1978	1982	
Denmark	1930	1965	1964	1967	1969 SA	1972	1973	1978	1982	
Dominica					1984[1]	1971		1978		
Dominican Republic	1970		1964	1968	1971 SA	1972	1973			
Ecuador	1970	1987	1964	1969	1969 SA		1975		1982	
Egypt	1928		1964	1967	1981[2] SA		S	1982	S	
El Salvador	S		1964	1969	1972 SA		S			
Equatorial Guinea					1984	S				

State	Geneva Protocol	Antarctic Treaty	Partial Test Ban Treaty	Outer Space Treaty	Treaty of Tlatelolco	Non-Proliferation Treaty	Sea-Bed Treaty	BW Convention	Enmod Convention	'Inhumane Weapons' Convention	Treaty of Rarotonga
Ethiopia	1935		S	S		1970 SA	1977	1975	S		
Fiji	1973[1,2]		1972[1]	1972[1]		1972[1] SA		1973			1985
Finland	1929	1984	1964	1967		1969 SA	1971	1974	1978	1982	
France	1926[1]	1960 CP		1970	PI: S[6] PII: 1974[7]	SA[3]		1984		S[2]	
Gabon			1964			1974		S			
Gambia	1966[2]		1965[1]	S		1975 SA	S	S			
German Dem. Republic	1929	1974[1] CP	1963	1967		1969 SA	1971	1972	1978	1982	
FR Germany	1929	1979[2] CP	1964[4]	1971[5]		1975[4] SA	1975[5]	1983[3]	1983[2]	S	
Ghana	1967		1963	S		1970 SA	1972	1975	1978	S	
Greece	1931	1987	1963	1971		1970 SA	1985	1975	1983	S	

MAJOR MULTILATERAL ARMS CONTROL AGREEMENTS 559

Grenada									1986		
Guatemala	1983		1964[3]		1975[2]	1975[1]	1970 SA	S	1973		1983
Guinea						1985	S				
Guinea-Bissau			1976	1976		1976	1976	1976			
Guyana				S				S			
Haiti			S	S	1969[2]	1970		S			
Holy See (Vatican City)	1966			S	1968[2] SA[16]	1971[5] SA				S	
Honduras			1964	S		1973 SA	S	1979			
Hungary	1952	1984	1963	1967		1969 SA	1971	1972	1978		1982
Iceland	1967		1964	1968		1969 SA	1972	1973	S		S
India	1930[1]	1983 CP	1963	1982			1973[6]	1974[4]	1978		1984
Indonesia	1971[2]		1964	S		1979[6] SA		S			

560 ANNEXES

State	Geneva Protocol	Antarctic Treaty	Partial Test Ban Treaty	Outer Space Treaty	Treaty of Tlatelolco	Non-Proliferation Treaty	Sea-Bed Treaty	BW Convention	Enmod Convention	'Inhumane Weapons' Convention	Treaty of Rarotonga
Iran	1929		1964	S		1970 SA	1971	1973	S		
Iraq	1931[1]		1964	1968		1969 SA	1972[4]	S	S		
Ireland	1930[6]		1963	1968		1968 SA	1971	1972[5]	1982	S	
Israel	1969[7]		1964	1977							
Italy	1928	1981 CP	1964	1972	1969[2] SA[16]	1975[7] SA	1974[7]	1975	1981	S[3]	
Jamaica	1970[2]		S	1970		1970 SA	1986	1975			
Japan	1970	1960 CP	1964	1967		1976[8] SA	1971	1982	1982	1982	
Jordan	1977[8]		1964	S		1970 SA	1971	1975			
Kampuchea	1983[9]					1972	S	1983			
Kenya	1970		1965	1984		1970		1976			

MAJOR MULTILATERAL ARMS CONTROL AGREEMENTS 561

Kiribati										1986
Korea, Democratic People's Republic	1987				1985[1]		1987[7]	1984		
Korea, Republic of	1986	1964[3]	1967[4]		1985	1987	1987[6]	1986[3]		
Kuwait	1971[10]	1965[5]	1972[6]		1975,10 SA		1972[7]	1980[4]		
Lao People's Dem. Republic		1965	1972		S	1971	1973	1978	1983	
Lebanon	1969	1965	1969		1970		1975	S		
Lesotho	1972[2]		S		1970 SA	S	1977			
Liberia	1927	1964			1970 SA	S	S	S		
Libya	1971[11]	1968	1968		1970					
Liechtenstein					1975 SA		1982			
Luxembourg	1936	1965	S		1978[11] SA	1982	S	S	S	

State	Geneva Protocol	Antarctic Treaty	Partial Test Ban Treaty	Outer Space Treaty	Treaty of Tlatelolco	Non-Proliferation Treaty	Sea-Bed Treaty	BW Convention	Enmod Convention	'Inhumane Weapons' Convention	Treaty of Rarotonga
Madagascar	1967		1965	1968[7]		1970 SA	S	S			
Malawi	1970		1964[1]			1986		S			
Malaysia	1970		1964	S		1970 SA	1972	S	1978		
Maldives	1966[2]					1970 SA					
Mali			S	1968		1970	S	S			
Malta	1970[2]		1964[1]			1970	1971	1975			
Mauritania			1964								
Mauritius	1970[2]		1969[1]	1969[1]		1969 SA	1971	1972			
Mexico	1932		1963	1968	1967[,8] SA	1969[12] SA	1984[8]	1974[8]		1982	
Monaco	1967			1967							
Mongolia	1968[12]		1963	1967		1969 SA	1971	1972	1978	1982	

MAJOR MULTILATERAL ARMS CONTROL AGREEMENTS   563

Morocco	1970		1966	1967		1970 SA	1971	S	S	
Nauru						1982 SA				1987
Nepal	1969		1964	1967		1970 SA	1971	S		
Netherlands	1930[13]	1967	1964	1969	PI: 1971[9]	1975 SA	1976	1981	1963[5]	1987[4]
New Zealand	1930[1]	1960 CP	1963	1968		1969 SA	1972	1972	1984[6]	S	1986
Nicaragua	S		1965	S	1968[2,10] SA[16]	1973 SA	1973	1975	S	S
Niger	1967[2]		1964	1967			1971	1972		
Nigeria	1968[1]		1967	1967		1968	1973	1973		S
Niue										1986
Norway	1932	1960 CP	1963	1969		1969 SA	1971	1973	1979	1983
Pakistan	1960[2]		S	1968			1974	1974	1986	1985
Panama	1970		1966	S	1971[2] SA	1977	1974	1974		

State	Geneva Protocol	Antarctic Treaty	Partial Test Ban Treaty	Outer Space Treaty	Treaty of Tlatelolco	Non-Proliferation Treaty	Sea-Bed Treaty	BW Convention	Enmod Convention	'Inhumane Weapons' Convention	Treaty of Rarotonga
Papua New Guinea	1981[1]	1981	1980[1]	1980[1]		1982 SA		1980	1980		S
Paraguay	1933[14]		S		1969[2] SA[16]	1970 SA	S	1976			
Peru	1985	1981	1964	1979	1969[2] SA[16]	1970 SA		1985			
Philippines	1973		1965[3]	S		1972 SA	1971	1973		S	
Poland	1929	1961 CP	1963	1968		1969 SA	1975	1973	1978	1983	
Portugal	1930[1]		S			1977 SA	1974	1975	S	S	
Qatar	1976							1975			
Romania	1929[1]	1971[3]	1963	1968		1970 SA	1972	1979	1983	S[5]	
Rwanda	1964[2]		1963	S		1975	1975	1975			
Saint Lucia						1979[1]		1986[9]			

MAJOR MULTILATERAL ARMS CONTROL AGREEMENTS 565

Saint Vincent and the Grenadines										1986
Samoa, Western		1965	1968	1975 SA						
San Marino		1964		1970[9]		1975				
Sao Tome and Principe			1976	1983	1979	1979	1979			
Saudi Arabia	1971				1972	1972				
Senegal	1977	1964		1970 SA	S	1975				
Seychelles		1985	1978	1985	1985	1979				
Sierra Leone	1967	1964	1967	1975	S	1976	S			
Singapore		1968[1]	1976	1976 SA	1976	1975				
Solomon Islands				1981[1]	1981[13]	1981[9]	1981[7]		S[2]	
Somalia		S	S	1970		S				
South Africa	1930[1]	1960 CP	1963	1968		1973	1975			

566   ANNEXES

State	Geneva Protocol	Antarctic Treaty	Partial Test Ban Treaty	Outer Space Treaty	Treaty of Tlatelolco	Non-Proliferation Treaty	Sea-Bed Treaty	BW Convention	Enmod Convention	'Inhumane Weapons' Convention	Treaty of Rarotonga
Spain	1929[15]	1982	1964	1968		1987	1987	1979	1978	S	
Sri Lanka	1954		1964	1986		1979 SA		1986	1978		
Sudan	1980		1966			1973 SA	S			S	
Suriname					1977[2] SA[16]	1976[1] SA					
Swaziland			1969			1969 SA	1971				
Sweden	1930	1984	1963	1967		1970 SA	1972	1976	1984	1982	
Switzerland	1932		1964	1969		1977[11] SA	1976	1976[10]		1982	
Syria	1968[16]		1964	1968[8]		1969[9]		S	S		
Taiwan	[17]		1964	1970[9]		1970	1972[9]	1973[11]			
Tanzania	1963		1964				S	S			

MAJOR MULTILATERAL ARMS CONTROL AGREEMENTS 567

Thailand	1931		1963	1968		1972 SA		1975		
Togo	1971		1964	S		1970	1971	1976	S	
Tonga	1971		1971[1]	1971[1]		1971[1]		1976		
Trinidad and Tobago	1970[2]		1964	S	1970[2]	1986			1987	
Tunisia	1967		1965	1968		1970	1971	1973	1978	
Turkey	1929		1965	1968		1980[13] SA	1972	1974	S[8]	S
Tuvalu						1979[1]				1986
Uganda	1965		1964	1968		1982			S	
UK	1930[1]	1960 CP	1963[6]	1967	PI: 1969[11] PII: 1969[11]	1968[14] SA[15]	1972[10]	1975[12]	1978	
Ukraine			1963[2]	1967[3]					1978	
United Arab Emirates	1977							S		1982
Uruguay		1980[4] CP	1969	1970	1968[2] SA[16]	1970 SA	S	1981		

State	Geneva Protocol	Antarctic Treaty	Partial Test Ban Treaty	Outer Space Treaty	Treaty of Tlatelolco	Non-Proliferation Treaty	Sea-Bed Treaty	BW Convention	Enmod Convention	'Inhumane Weapons' Convention	Treaty of Rarotonga
USA	1975[18]	1960 CP	1963	1967	PI: 1981[12] PII: 1971[13]	1970 SA[16]	1972	1975	1980	S[6]	
USSR	1928[19]	1960 CP	1963	1967	PII: 1979[14]	1970 SA[17]	1972	1975	1978	1982	P2: S[2] P3: S[2]
Venezuela	1928		1965	1970	1970[2,15] SA[16]	1975 SA		1978			
Viet Nam	1980[1]			1980		1982	1980[11]	1980	1980	S	
Yemen Arab Republic	1971		S			1986	S	S	1977		
Yemen, People's Dem. Republic of	1986[20]		1979	1979		1979	1979	1979	1979		
Yugoslavia	1929[21]		1964	S		1970[18] SA	1973[12]	1973		1983	
Zaire			1965	S		1970 SA		1977	S		
Zambia			1965[1]	1973			1972				

MAJOR MULTILATERAL ARMS CONTROL AGREEMENTS 569

The 1925 Geneva Protocol

[1] The Protocol is binding on this state only as regards states which have signed and ratified or acceded to it. The Protocol will cease to be binding on this state in regard to any enemy state whose armed forces or whose allies fail to respect the prohibitions laid down in it.
Australia withdrew its reservation in 1986.

[2] Notification of succession. (In notifying its succession to the obligations contracted in 1930 by the UK, Barbados stated that as far as it was concerned the reservation made by the UK was to be considered as withdrawn.)

[3] In a note of 2 Mar. 1970, submitted at the UN, Byelorussia stated that 'it recognizes itself to be a party' to the Protocol.

[4] On 13 July 1952 the People's Republic of China issued a statement recognizing as binding upon it the 1929 accession to the Protocol in the name of China. China considers itself bound by the Protocol on condition of reciprocity on the part of all the other contracting and acceding powers.

[5] Czechoslovakia shall cease to be bound by this Protocol towards any state whose armed forces, or the armed forces of whose allies, fail to respect the prohibitions laid down in the Protocol.

[6] Ireland does not intend to assume, by this accession, any obligation except towards the states having signed and ratified this Protocol or which shall have finally acceded thereto, and should the armed forces or the allies of an enemy state fail to respect the Protocol, the government of Ireland would cease to be bound by the said Protocol in regard to such state. In Feb. 1972, Ireland declared that it had decided to withdraw the above reservations made at the time of accession to the Protocol.

[7] The Protocol is binding on Israel only as regards states which have signed and ratified or acceded to it. The Protocol shall cease to be binding on Israel as regards any enemy state whose armed forces, or the armed forces of whose allies, or the regular or irregular forces, or groups or individuals operating from its territory, fail to respect the prohibitions which are the object of the Protocol.

[8] The accession by Jordan to the Protocol does not in any way imply recognition of Israel. Jordan undertakes to respect the obligations contained in the Protocol with regard to states which have undertaken similar commitments. It is not bound by the Protocol as regards states whose armed forces, regular or irregular, do not respect the provisions of the Protocol.

[9] The accession was made on behalf of the coalition government of Democratic Kampuchea (the government in exile), with a statement that the Protocol will cease to be binding on it in regard to any enemy state whose armed forces or whose allies fail to respect the prohibitions laid down in the Protocol. France declared that as a party to the Geneva Protocol (but not as the depositary) it considers this accession to have no effect. A similar statement was made by Australia, Bulgaria, Cuba, Czechoslovakia, GDR, Hungary, Mauritius, Netherlands, Poland, Romania, USSR and Viet Nam, which do not recognize the coalition government of Kampuchea.

[10] The accession of Kuwait to the Protocol does not in any way imply recognition of Israel or the establishment of relations with the latter on the basis of the present Protocol. In case of breach of the prohibition laid down in this Protocol by any of the parties, Kuwait will not be bound, with regard to the party committing the breach, to apply the provisions of this Protocol.

[11] The accession to the Protocol does not imply recognition of Israel. The Protocol is binding on Libya only as regards states which are effectively bound by it and will cease to be binding on Libya as regards states whose armed forces, or the armed forces of whose allies, fail to respect the prohibitions which are the object of this Protocol.

[12] In the case of violation of this prohibition by any state in relation to Mongolia or its allies, Mongolia shall not consider itself bound by the obligations of the Protocol towards that state.

[13] As regards the use in war of asphyxiating, poisonous or other gases and of all analogous liquids, materials or devices, this Protocol shall cease to be binding on the Netherlands with regard to any enemy state whose armed forces or whose allies fail to respect the prohibitions laid down in the Protocol.

[14] This is the date of receipt of Paraguay's instrument of accession. The date of the notification by the depositary government 'for the purpose of regularization' is 1969.

[15] Spain declared the Protocol as binding *ipso facto*, without special agreement with respect to any other member or state accepting and observing the same obligation, that is, on condition of reciprocity.

[16] The accession by Syria to the Protocol does not in any case imply recognition of Israel or lead to the establishment of relations with the latter concerning the provisions laid down in the Protocol.

[17] The Protocol, signed in 1929 in the name of China, is taken to be valid for Taiwan which is part of China. However, unlike the People's Republic of China, Taiwan has not reconfirmed its accession to the Protocol.

[18] The Protocol shall cease to be binding on the USA with respect to the use in war of asphyxiating, poisonous or other gases, and of all analogous liquids, materials, or devices, in regard to an enemy state if such state or any of its allies fail to respect the prohibitions laid down in the Protocol.

[19] The Protocol only binds the USSR in relation to the states which have signed and ratified or which have definitely acceded to the Protocol. The Protocol shall cease to be binding on the USSR in regard to any enemy state whose armed forces or whose allies *de jure* or in fact do not respect the prohibitions which are the object of this Protocol.

[20] In case any party fails to observe the prohibition under the Protocol, the People's Democratic Republic of Yemen will consider itself free of its obligation.

[21] The Protocol shall cease to be binding on Yugoslavia in regard to any enemy state whose armed forces or whose allies fail to respect the prohibitions which are the object of the Protocol.

570 ANNEXES

The Antarctic Treaty

¹ The GDR stated that in its view Article XIII, paragraph 1 of the Treaty was inconsistent with the principle that all states whose policies are guided by the purposes and principles of the UN Charter have a right to become parties to treaties which affect the interests of all states.

² FR Germany stated that the Treaty applies also to Berlin (West).

³ Romania stated that the provisions of Article XIII, paragraph 1 of the Treaty were not in accordance with the principle according to which multilateral treaties whose object and purposes concern the international community, as a whole, should be open for universal participation.

⁴ In acceding to the Treaty, Uruguay proposed the establishment of a general and definitive statute on Antarctica in which the interests of all states involved and of the international community as a whole would be considered equitably. It also declared that it reserved its rights in Antarctica in accordance with international law.

The Partial Test Ban Treaty

¹ Notification of succession.

² The USA considers that Byelorussia and Ukraine are already covered by the signature and ratification by the USSR.

³ With a statement that this does not imply the recognition of any territory or regime not recognized by this state.

⁴ FR Germany stated that the Treaty applies also to Berlin (West).

⁵ Kuwait stated that its signature and ratification of the Treaty do not in any way imply its recognition of Israel nor oblige it to apply the provisions of the Treaty in respect of the said country.

⁶ The UK stated its view that if a regime is not recognized as the government of a state, neither signature nor the deposit of any instrument by it, nor notification of any of those acts, will bring about recognition of that regime by any other state.

The Outer Space Treaty

¹ Notification of succession.

² Brazil interprets Article X of the Treaty as a specific recognition that the granting of tracking facilities by the parties to the Treaty shall be subject to agreement between the states concerned.

³ The USA considers that Byelorussia and Ukraine are already covered by the signature and ratification by the USSR.

⁴ With a statement that this does not imply the recognition of any territory or regime not recognized by this state.

⁵ FR Germany stated that the Treaty applies also to Berlin (West).

⁶ Kuwait acceded to the Treaty with the understanding that this does not in any way imply its recognition of Israel and does not oblige it to apply the provisions of the Treaty in respect of the said country.

⁷ Madagascar acceded to the Treaty with the understanding that under Article X of the Treaty the state shall retain its freedom of decision with respect to the possible installation of foreign observation bases in its territory and shall continue to possess the right to fix, in each case, the conditions for such installation.

⁸ Syria acceded to the Treaty with the understanding that this should not mean in any way the recognition of Israel, nor should it lead to any relationship with Israel that could arise from the Treaty.

⁹ China declared as illegal and null and void the signature and ratification of the Outer Space Treaty by the Taiwan authorities.

The Treaty of Tlatelolco

¹ On signing the Treaty, Argentina stated that it understands Article 18 as recognizing the rights of parties to carry out, by their own means or in association with third parties, explosions of nuclear devices for peaceful purposes, including explosions which involve devices similar to those used in nuclear weapons.

² The Treaty is in force for this country due to a declaration, annexed to the instrument of ratification in accordance with Article 28, paragraph 2, which waived the requirements for the entry into force of the Treaty, specified in paragraph 1 of that Article: namely, that all states in the region deposit the instruments of ratification; that Protocol I and Protocol II be signed and ratified by those states to which they apply; and that agreements on safeguards be concluded with the IAEA. (Colombia made this declaration subsequent to the deposit of ratification, as did Nicaragua and Trinidad and Tobago.)

³ On signing the Treaty, Brazil stated that, according to its interpretation, Article 18 of the Treaty gives the signatories the right to carry out, by their own means or in association with third parties, nuclear explosions for peaceful purposes, including explosions which involve devices similar to those used in nuclear weapons. This statement was reiterated at the ratification. Brazil also stated that it did not waive the requirements for the entry into force of the Treaty laid down in Article 28. *The Treaty is therefore not yet in force for Brazil.*

⁴ Chile has not waived the requirements for the entry into force of the Treaty laid down in Article 28. *The Treaty is therefore not yet in force for Chile.*

⁵ On signing Protocol II, China stated, *inter alia*: China will never use or threaten to use nuclear weapons against non-nuclear Latin American countries and the Latin American nuclear weapon-free zone; nor will China test, manufacture, produce, stockpile, install or deploy nuclear weapons in these countries or in this zone, or send its means of transportation and delivery carrying nuclear weapons to cross the territory, territorial sea or airspace

of Latin American countries. The signing of the Protocol does not imply any change whatsoever in China's stand on the disarmament and nuclear weapons issue and, in particular, does not affect its stand against the Non-Proliferation Treaty and the Partial Test Ban Treaty.

China holds that, in order that Latin America may truly become a nuclear weapon-free zone, all nuclear countries, and particularly the superpowers, must undertake not to use or threaten to use nuclear weapons against the Latin American countries and the Latin American nuclear weapon-free zone, and implement the following undertakings: (1) dismantle all foreign military bases in Latin America and refrain from establishing new bases there, and (2) prohibit the passage of any means of transportation and delivery carrying nuclear weapons through Latin American territory, territorial sea or airspace.

[6] On signing Protocol I, France made the following reservations and interpretative statements: The Protocol, as well as the provisions of the Treaty to which it refers, will not affect the right of self-defence under Article 51 of the UN Charter; the application of the legislation referred to in Article 3 of the Treaty relates to legislation which is consistent with international law; the obligations under the Protocol shall not apply to transit across the territories of the French Republic situated in the zone of the Treaty, and destined to other territories of the French Republic; the Protocol shall not limit, in any way, the participation of the populations of the French territories in the activities mentioned in Article 1 of the Treaty, and in efforts connected with the national defence of France; the provisions of Articles 1 and 2 of the Protocol apply to the text of the Treaty as it stands at the time when the Protocol is signed by France, and consequently no amendment to the Treaty that might come into force under Article 29 thereof would be binding on the government of France without the latter's express consent.

[7] On signing Protocol II, France stated that it interprets the undertaking contained in Article 3 of the Protocol to mean that it presents no obstacle to the full exercise of the right of self-defence enshrined in Article 51 of the UN Charter; it takes note of the interpretation of the Treaty given by the Preparatory Commission for the Denuclearization of Latin America and reproduced in the Final Act, according to which the Treaty does not apply to transit, the granting or denying of which lies within the exclusive competence of each state party in accordance with the pertinent principles and rules of international law; it considers that the application of the legislation referred to in Article 3 of the Treaty relates to legislation which is consistent with international law. The provisions of Articles 1 and 2 of the Protocol apply to the text of the Treaty as it stands at the time when the Protocol is signed by France. Consequently, no amendment to the Treaty that might come into force under the provision of Article 29 would be binding on the government of France without the latter's express consent. If this declaration of interpretation is contested in part or in whole by one or more contracting parties to the Treaty or to Protocol II, these instruments would be null and void as far as relations between France and the contesting state or states are concerned. On depositing its instrument of ratification of Protocol II, France stated that it did so subject to the statement made on signing the Protocol. On 15 Apr. 1974, France made a supplementary statement to the effect that it was prepared to consider its obligations under Protocol II as applying not only to the signatories of the Treaty, but also to the territories for which the statute of denuclearization was in force in conformity with Article 1 of Protocol I.

[8] On signing the Treaty, Mexico said that if technological progress makes it possible to differentiate between nuclear weapons and nuclear devices for peaceful purposes, it will be necessary to amend the relevant provisions of the Treaty, according to the procedures established therein.

[9] The Netherlands stated that Protocol I shall not be interpreted as prejudicing the position of the Netherlands as regards its recognition or non-recognition of the rights or of claims to sovereignty of the parties to the Treaty, or of the grounds on which such claims are made.

[10] Nicaragua stated that it reserved the right to use nuclear energy for peaceful purposes such as the removal of earth for the construction of canals, irrigation works, power plants, and so on, as well as to allow the transit of atomic material through its territory.

[11] When signing and ratifying Protocol I and Protocol II, the UK made the following declarations of understanding:

In connection with Article 3 of the Treaty, defining the term 'territory' as including the territorial sea, airspace and any other space over which the state exercises sovereignty in accordance with 'its own legislation', the UK does not regard its signing or ratification of the Protocols as implying recognition of any legislation which does not, in its view, comply with the relevant rules of international law.

The Treaty does not permit the parties to carry out explosions of nuclear devices for peaceful purposes unless and until advances in technology have made possible the development of devices for such explosions which are not capable of being used for weapon purposes.

The signing and ratification by the UK could not be regarded as affecting in any way the legal status of any territory for the international relations of which the UK is responsible, lying within the limits of the geographical zone established by the Treaty.

Should a party to the Treaty carry out any act of aggression with the support of a nuclear weapon state, the UK would be free to reconsider the extent to which it could be regarded as committed by the provisions of Protocol II.

In addition, the UK declared that its undertaking under Article 3 of Protocol II not to use or threaten to use nuclear weapons against the parties to the Treaty extends also to territories in respect of which the undertaking under Article I of Protocol I becomes effective.

[12] The USA ratified Protocol I with the following understandings: The provisions of the Treaty made applicable by this Protocol do not affect the exclusive power and legal competence under international law of a state adhering to this Protocol to grant or deny transit and transport privileges to its own or any other vessels or aircraft irrespective of cargo or armaments; the provisions of the Treaty made applicable by this Protocol do not affect rights under international law of a state adhering to this Protocol regarding the exercise of the freedom of the seas, or regarding passage through or over waters subject to the sovereignty of a state, and the declarations attached by the United States to its ratification of Protocol II apply also to its ratification of Protocol I.

[13] The USA signed and ratified Protocol II with the following declarations and understandings:

In connection with Article 3 of the Treaty, defining the term 'territory' as including the territorial sea, airspace and any other space over which the state exercises sovereignty in accordance with 'its own legislation', the ratification of the Protocol could not be regarded as implying recognition of any legislation which does not, in the view of the USA, comply with the relevant rules of international law.

Each of the parties retains exclusive power and legal competence, unaffected by the terms of the Treaty, to grant or deny non-parties transit and transport privileges.

As regards the undertaking not to use or threaten to use nuclear weapons against the parties, the USA would consider that an armed attack by a party, in which it was assisted by a nuclear weapon state, would be incompatible with the party's obligations under Article 1 of the Treaty.

The definition contained in Article 5 of the Treaty is understood as encompassing all nuclear explosive devices; Articles 1 and 5 of the Treaty restrict accordingly the activities of the parties under paragraph 1 of Article 18.

Article 18, paragraph 4 permits, and US adherence to Protocol II will not prevent, collaboration by the USA with the parties to the Treaty for the purpose of carrying out explosions of nuclear devices for peaceful purposes in a manner consistent with a policy of not contributing to the proliferation of nuclear weapon capabilities.

The USA will act with respect to such territories of Protocol I adherents, as are within the geographical area defined in Article 4, paragraph 2 of the Treaty, in the same manner as Protocol II requires it to act with respect to the territories of the parties.

[14] The USSR signed and ratified Protocol II with the following statement:

The USSR proceeds from the assumption that the effect of Article 1 of the Treaty extends, as specified in Article 5 of the Treaty, to any nuclear explosive device and that, accordingly, the carrying out by any party to the Treaty of explosions of nuclear devices for peaceful purposes would be a violation of its obligations under Article 1 and would be incompatible with its non-nuclear status. For states parties to the Treaty, a solution to the problem of peaceful nuclear explosions can be found in accordance with the provisions of Article V of the Non-Proliferation Treaty and within the framework of the international procedures of the IAEA. The signing of the Protocol by the USSR does not in any way signify recognition of the possibility of the force of the Treaty being extended beyond the territories of the states parties to the Treaty, including airspace and territorial waters as defined in accordance with international law. With regard to the reference in Article 3 of the Treaty to 'its own legislation' in connection with the territorial waters, airspace and any other space over which the states parties to the Treaty exercise sovereignty, the signing of the Protocol by the USSR does not signify recognition of their claims to the exercise of sovereignty which are contrary to generally accepted standards of international law. The USSR takes note of the interpretation of the Treaty given in the Final Act of the Preparatory Commission for the Denuclearization of Latin America to the effect that the transport of nuclear weapons by the parties to the Treaty is covered by the prohibitions in Article 1 of the Treaty. The USSR reaffirms its position that authorizing the transit of nuclear weapons in any form would be contrary to the objectives of the Treaty, according to which, as specially mentioned in the preamble, Latin America must be completely free from nuclear weapons, and that it would be incompatible with the non-nuclear status of the states parties to the Treaty and with their obligations as laid down in Article 1 thereof.

Any actions undertaken by a state or states parties to the Treaty which are not compatible with their non-nuclear status, and also the commission by one or more states parties to the Treaty of an act of aggression with the support of a state which is in possession of nuclear weapons or together with such a state, will be regarded by the USSR as incompatible with the obligations of those countries under the Treaty. In such cases the USSR reserves the right to reconsider its obligations under Protocol II. It further reserves the right to reconsider its attitude to this Protocol in the event of any actions on the part of other states possessing nuclear weapons which are incompatible with their obligations under the said Protocol. The provisions of the articles of Protocol II are applicable to the text of the Treaty of Tlatelolco in the wording of the Treaty at the time of the signing of the Protocol by the Soviet Union, due account being taken of the position of the USSR as set out in the present statement. Any amendment to the Treaty entering into force in accordance with the provisions of Articles 29 and 6 of the Treaty without the clearly expressed approval of the USSR shall have no force as far as the USSR is concerned.

In addition, the USSR proceeds from the assumption that the obligations under Protocol II also apply to the territories for which the status of the denuclearized zone is in force in conformity with Protocol I of the Treaty.

[15] Venezuela stated that in view of the existing controversy between Venezuela on the one hand and the UK and Guyana on the other, Article 25, paragraph 2 of the Treaty should apply to Guyana. This paragraph provides that no political entity should be admitted, part or all of whose territory is the subject of a dispute or claim between an extra-continental country and one or more Latin American states, so long as the dispute has not been settled by peaceful means.

[16] Safeguards under the Non-Proliferation Treaty cover the Treaty of Tlatelolco.

The Non-Proliferation Treaty

[1] Notification of succession.

[2] On the occasion of the deposit of the instrument of ratification, Egypt stated that since it was embarking on the construction of nuclear power reactors, it expected assistance and support from industrialized nations with a developed nuclear industry. It called upon nuclear weapon states to promote research and development of peaceful applications of nuclear explosions in order to overcome all the difficulties at present involved therein. Egypt also appealed to these states to exert their efforts to conclude an agreement prohibiting the use or threat of use of nuclear weapons against any state, and expressed the view that the Middle East should remain completely free of nuclear weapons.

[3] France, not party to the Treaty, declared that it would behave like a state adhering to the Treaty and that it would follow a policy of strengthening appropriate safeguards relating to nuclear equipment, material and technology. On 12 Sep. 1981 an agreement between France, the European Atomic Energy Community (Euratom) and the IAEA for the application of safeguards in France entered into force. The agreement covers nuclear material and facilities notified to the IAEA by France.

[4] On depositing the instrument of ratification, FR Germany reiterated the declaration made at the time of signing: it reaffirmed its expectation that the nuclear weapon states would intensify their efforts in accordance with the undertakings under Article VI of the Treaty, as well as its understanding that the security of FR Germany continued to be ensured by NATO; it stated that no provision of the Treaty may be interpreted in such a way as to hamper further development of European unification; that research, development and use of nuclear energy for peaceful purposes, as well as international and multinational co-operation in this field, must not be prejudiced by the Treaty; that the application of the Treaty, including the implementation of safeguards, must not lead to discrimination of the nuclear industry of FR Germany in international competition; and that it attached vital importance to the undertaking given by the USA and the UK concerning the application of safeguards to their peaceful nuclear facilities, hoping that other nuclear weapon states would assume similar obligations.

In a separate note, FR Germany declared that the Treaty will also apply to Berlin (West) without affecting Allied rights and responsibilities, including those relating to demilitarization. In notes of 24 July, 19 Aug. and 25 Nov. 1975, respectively, addressed to the US Department of State, Czechoslovakia, the USSR and the GDR stated that this declaration by FR Germany had no legal effect.

[5] On acceding to the Treaty, the Holy See stated, *inter alia*, that the Treaty will attain in full the objectives of security and peace and justify the limitations to which the states party to the Treaty submit, only if it is fully executed in every clause and with all its implications. This concerns not only the obligations to be applied immediately but also those which envisage a process of ulterior commitments. Among the latter, the Holy See considers it suitable to point out the following:

(*a*) The adoption of appropriate measures to ensure, on a basis of equality, that all non-nuclear weapon states party to the Treaty will have available to them the benefits deriving from peaceful applications of nuclear technology.

(*b*) The pursuit of negotiations in good faith of effective measures relating to cessation of the nuclear arms race at an early date and to nuclear disarmament, and on a treaty on general and complete disarmament under strict and effective control.

[6] On signing the Treaty, Indonesia stated, *inter alia*, that it attaches great importance to the declarations of the USA, the UK and the USSR affirming their intention to provide immediate assistance to any non-nuclear weapon state party to the Treaty that is a victim of an act of aggression in which nuclear weapons are used. Of utmost importance, however, is not the action *after* a nuclear attack has been committed but the guarantees to prevent such an attack. Indonesia trusts that the nuclear weapon states will study further this question of effective measures to ensure the security of the non-nuclear weapon states. On depositing the instrument of ratification, Indonesia expressed the hope that the nuclear countries would be prepared to co-operate with non-nuclear countries in the use of nuclear energy for peaceful purposes and implement the provisions of Article IV of the Treaty without discrimination. It also expressed the view that the nuclear weapon states should observe the provisions of Article VI of the Treaty relating to the cessation of the nuclear arms race.

[7] Italy stated that in its belief nothing in the Treaty was an obstacle to the unification of the countries of Western Europe; it noted full compatibility of the Treaty with the existing security agreements; it noted further that when technological progress would allow the development of peaceful explosive devices different from nuclear weapons, the prohibition relating to their manufacture and use shall no longer apply; it interpreted the provisions of Article IX, paragraph 3 of the Treaty, concerning the definition of a nuclear weapon state, in the sense that it referred exclusively to the five countries which had manufactured and exploded a nuclear weapon or other nuclear explosive device prior to 1 Jan. 1967, and stressed that under no circumstance would a claim of pertaining to such category be recognized by Italy for any other state.

[8] On depositing the instrument of ratification, Japan expressed the hope that France and China would accede to the Treaty; it urged a reduction of nuclear armaments and a comprehensive ban on nuclear testing; appealed to all states to refrain from the threat or use of force involving either nuclear or non-nuclear weapons; expressed the view that peaceful nuclear activities in non-nuclear weapon states party to the Treaty should not be hampered and that Japan should not be discriminated against in favour of other parties in any aspect of such activities. It also urged all nuclear weapon states to accept IAEA safeguards on their peaceful nuclear activities.

[9] A statement was made containing a disclaimer regarding the recognition of states party to the Treaty.

[10] On depositing the instrument of ratification, the Republic of Korea took note of the fact that the depositary governments of the three nuclear weapon states had made declarations in June 1968 to take immediate and effective measures to safeguard any non-nuclear weapon state which is a victim of an act or an object of a threat of aggression in which nuclear weapons are used. It recalled that the UN Security Council adopted a resolution to the same effect on 19 June 1968.

[11] On depositing the instruments of accession and ratification, Liechtenstein and Switzerland stated that activities not prohibited under Articles I and II of the Treaty include, in particular, the whole field of energy production and related operations, research and technology concerning future generations of nuclear reactors based on fission or fusion, as well as production of isotopes. Liechtenstein and Switzerland define the term 'source or special fissionable material' in Article III of the Treaty as being in accordance with Article XX of the IAEA Statute, and a modification of this interpretation requires their formal consent; they will accept only such interpretations and definitions of the terms 'equipment or material especially designed or prepared for the processing, use or production of special fissionable material', as mentioned in Article III of the Treaty, that they will expressly approve; and they understand that the application of the Treaty, especially of the control measures, will not lead to discrimination of their industry in international competition.

¹² On signing the Treaty, Mexico stated, *inter alia*, that none of the provisions of the Treaty shall be interpreted as affecting in any way whatsoever the rights and obligations of Mexico as a state party to the Treaty of Tlatelolco.

It is the understanding of Mexico that at the present time any nuclear explosive device is capable of being used as a nuclear weapon and that there is no indication that in the near future it will be possible to manufacture nuclear explosive devices that are not potentially nuclear weapons. However, if technological advances modify this situation, it will be necessary to amend the relevant provisions of the Treaty in accordance with the procedure established therein.

¹³ The ratification was accompanied by a statement in which Turkey underlined the non-proliferation obligations of the nuclear weapon states, adding that measures must be taken to meet adequately the security requirements of non-nuclear weapon states. Turkey also stated that measures developed or to be developed at national and international levels to ensure the non-proliferation of nuclear weapons should in no case restrict the non-nuclear weapon states in their option for the application of nuclear energy for peaceful purposes.

¹⁴ The UK recalled its view that if a regime is not recognized as the government of a state, neither signature nor the deposit of any instrument by it, nor notification of any of those acts, will bring about recognition of that regime by any other state.

¹⁵ This agreement, signed by the UK, Euratom and the IAEA, provides for the submission of British non-military nuclear installations to safeguards under IAEA supervision.

¹⁶ This agreement provides for safeguards on fissionable material in all facilities within the USA, excluding those associated with activities of direct national security significance.

¹⁷ The agreement provides for the application of IAEA safeguards in Soviet peaceful nuclear facilities designated by the USSR.

¹⁸ In connection with the ratification of the Treaty, Yugoslavia stated, *inter alia*, that it considered a ban on the development, manufacture and use of nuclear weapons and the destruction of all stockpiles of these weapons to be indispensable for the maintenance of a stable peace and international security; it held the view that the chief responsibility for progress in this direction rested with the nuclear weapon powers, and expected these powers to undertake not to use nuclear weapons against the countries which have renounced them as well as against non-nuclear weapon states in general, and to refrain from the threat to use them. It also emphasized the significance it attached to the universality of the efforts relating to the realization of the Non-Proliferation Treaty.

The Sea-Bed Treaty

¹ On signing and ratifying the Treaty, Argentina stated that it interprets the references to the freedom of the high seas as in no way implying a pronouncement of judgement on the different positions relating to questions connected with international maritime law. It understands that the reference to the rights of exploration and exploitation by coastal states over their continental shelves was included solely because those could be the rights most frequently affected by verification procedures. Argentina precludes any possibility of strengthening, through this Treaty, certain positions concerning continental shelves to the detriment of others based on different criteria.

² On signing the Treaty, Brazil stated that nothing in the Treaty shall be interpreted as prejudicing in any way the sovereign rights of Brazil in the area of the sea, the sea-bed and the subsoil thereof adjacent to its coasts. It is the understanding of Brazil that the word 'observation', as it appears in paragraph 1 of Article III of the Treaty, refers only to observation that is incidental to the normal course of navigation in accordance with international law.

³ In depositing the instrument of ratification, Canada declared: Article I, paragraph 1, cannot be interpreted as indicating that any state has a right to implant or emplace any weapons not prohibited under Article I, paragraph 1, on the sea-bed and ocean floor, and in the subsoil thereof, beyond the limits of national jurisdiction, or as constituting any limitation on the principle that this area of the sea-bed and ocean floor and the subsoil thereof shall be reserved for exclusively peaceful purposes. Articles I, II and III cannot be interpreted as indicating that any state but the coastal state has any right to implant or emplace any weapon not prohibited under Article I, paragraph 1 on the continental shelf, or the subsoil thereof, appertaining to that coastal state, beyond the outer limit of the sea-bed zone referred to in Article I and defined in Article II. Article III cannot be interpreted as indicating any restrictions or limitation upon the rights of the coastal state, consistent with its exclusive sovereign rights with respect to the continental shelf, to verify, inspect or effect the removal of any weapon, structure, installation, facility or device implanted or emplaced on the continental shelf, or the subsoil thereof, appertaining to that coastal state, beyond the outer limit of the sea-bed zone referred to in Article I and defined in Article II. On 12 Apr. 1976, FR Germany stated that the declaration by Canada is not of a nature to confer on the government of this country more far-reaching rights than those to which it is entitled under current international law, and that all rights existing under current international law which are not covered by the prohibitions are left intact by the Treaty.

⁴ A statement was made containing a disclaimer regarding recognition of states party to the Treaty.

⁵ On ratifying the Treaty, FR Germany declared that the Treaty will apply to Berlin (West).

⁶ On the occasion of its accession to the Treaty, the government of India stated that as a coastal state, India has, and always has had, full and exclusive rights over the continental shelf adjoining its territory and beyond its territorial waters and the subsoil thereof. It is the considered view of India that other countries cannot use its continental shelf for military purposes. There cannot, therefore, be any restriction on, or limitation of, the sovereign right of India as a coastal state to verify, inspect, remove or destroy any weapon, device, structure, installation or facility, which might be implanted or emplaced on or beneath its continental shelf by any other country, or to take such other steps as may be considered necessary to safeguard its security. The accession by the

government of India to the Treaty is based on this position. In response to the Indian statement, the USA expressed the view that, under existing international law, the rights of coastal states over their continental shelves are exclusive only for the purposes of exploration and exploitation of natural resources, and are otherwise limited by the 1958 Convention on the Continental Shelf and other principles of international law. On 12 Apr. 1976, FR Germany stated that the declaration by India is not of a nature to confer on the government of this country more far-reaching rights than those to which it is entitled under current international law, and that all rights existing under current law which are not covered by the prohibitions are left intact by the Treaty.

[7] On signing the Treaty, Italy stated, *inter alia*, that in the case of agreements on further measures in the field of disarmament to prevent an arms race on the sea-bed and ocean floor and in their subsoil, the question of the delimitation of the area within which these measures would find application shall have to be examined and solved in each instance in accordance with the nature of the measures to be adopted. The statement was repeated at the time of ratification.

[8] Mexico declared that in its view no provision of the Treaty can be interpreted to mean that a state has the right to emplace nuclear weapons or other weapons of mass destruction, or arms or military equipment of any type, on the continental shelf of Mexico. It reserves the right to verify, inspect, remove or destroy any weapon, structure, installation, device or equipment placed on its continental shelf, including nuclear weapons or other weapons of mass destruction.

[9] Ratification of the Treaty by Taiwan is considered by Romania as null and void.

[10] The UK recalled its view that if a regime is not recognized as the government of a state neither signature nor the deposit of any instrument by it, nor notification of any of those acts, will bring about recognition of that regime by any other state.

[11] Viet Nam stated that no provision of the Treaty should be interpreted in a way that would contradict the rights of the coastal states with regard to their continental shelf, including the right to take measures to ensure their security.

[12] On 25 Feb. 1974, the Ambassador of Yugoslavia transmitted to the US Secretary of State a note stating that in the view of the Yugoslav Government, Article III, paragraph 1, of the Treaty should be interpreted in such a way that a state exercising its right under this Article shall be obliged to notify in advance the coastal state, in so far as its observations are to be carried out 'within the stretch of the sea extending above the continental shelf of the said state'. On 16 Jan. 1975 the US Secretary of State presented the view of the USA concerning the Yugoslav note, as follows: In so far as the note is intended to be interpretative of the Treaty, the USA cannot accept it as a valid interpretation. In addition, the USA does not consider that it can have any effect on the existing law of the sea. In so far as the note was intended to be a reservation to the Treaty, the USA placed on record its formal objection to it on the grounds that it was incompatible with the object and purpose of the Treaty. The USA also drew attention to the fact that the note was submitted too late to be legally effective as a reservation. A similar exchange of notes took place between Yugoslavia and the UK on 12 Apr. 1976. FR Germany stated that the declaration by Yugoslavia is not of a nature to confer on the government of this country more far-reaching rights than those to which it is entitled under current international law, and that all rights existing under current international law which are not covered by the prohibitions are left intact by the Treaty.

[13] Notification of succession.

The BW Convention

[1] Considering the obligations resulting from its status as a permanently neutral state, Austria declares a reservation to the effect that its co-operation within the framework of this Convention cannot exceed the limits determined by the status of permanent neutrality and membership of the UN.

[2] China stated that the BW Convention has the following defects: it fails explicitly to prohibit the use of biological weapons; it does not provide for 'concrete and effective' measures of supervision and verification; and it lacks measures of sanctions in case of violation of the Convention. China hopes that these defects will be corrected at an appropriate time, and also that a convention for complete prohibition of chemical weapons will soon be concluded. The signature and ratification of the Convention by the Taiwan authorities in the name of China are considered illegal and null and void.

[3] On depositing its instrument of ratification, FR Germany stated that a major shortcoming of the BW Convention is that it does not contain any provisions for verifying compliance with its essential obligations. The Federal Government considers the right to lodge a complaint with the UN Security Council to be an inadequate arrangement. It would welcome the establishment of an independent international committee of experts able to carry out impartial investigations when doubts arise as to whether the Convention is being complied with.

[4] In a statement made on the occasion of the signature of the Convention, India reiterated its understanding that the objective of the Convention is to eliminate biological and toxin weapons, thereby excluding completely the possibility of their use, and that the exemption with regard to biological agents or toxins, which would be permitted for prophylactic, protective or other peaceful purposes, would not in any way create a loophole in regard to the production or retention of biological and toxin weapons. Also any assistance which might be furnished under the terms of the Convention would be of a medical or humanitarian nature and in conformity with the UN Charter. The statement was repeated at the time of the deposit of the instrument of ratification.

[5] Ireland considers that the Convention could be undermined if the reservations made by the parties to the 1925 Geneva Protocol were allowed to stand, as the prohibition of possession is incompatible with the right to retaliate, and that there should be an absolute and universal prohibition of the use of the weapons in question. Ireland notified the depositary government for the Geneva Protocol of the withdrawal of its reservations to the Protocol, made at the time of accession in 1930. The withdrawal applies to chemical as well as to bacteriological (biological) and toxin agents of warfare.

⁶ The Republic of Korea stated that the signing and ratification of the Convention does not in any way mean or imply the recognition of any territory or regime which has not been recognized by the Republic of Korea as a state or government.

⁷ In the understanding of Kuwait, its ratification of the Convention does not in any way imply its recognition of Israel, nor does it oblige it to apply the provisions of the Conventions in respect of the said country.

⁸ Mexico considers that the Convention is only a first step towards an agreement prohibiting also the development, production and stockpiling of all chemical weapons, and notes the fact that the Convention contains an express commitment to continue negotiations in good faith with the aim of arriving at such an agreement.

⁹ Notification of succession.

¹⁰ The ratification by Switzerland contains the following reservations:

1. Owing to the fact that the Convention also applies to weapons, equipment or means of delivery designed to use biological agents or toxins, the delimitation of its scope of application can cause difficulties since there are scarcely any weapons, equipment or means of delivery peculiar to such use; therefore, Switzerland reserves the right to decide for itself what auxiliary means fall within that definition.

2. By reason of the obligations resulting from its status as a perpetually neutral state, Switzerland is bound to make the general reservation that its collaboration within the framework of this Convention cannot go beyond the terms prescribed by that status. This reservation refers especially to Article VII of the Convention as well as to any similar clause that could replace or supplement that provision of the Convention.

In a note of 18 Aug. 1976, addressed to the Swiss Ambassador, the US Secretary of State stated the following view of the USA with regard to the first reservation: The prohibition would apply only to (*a*) weapons, equipment and means of delivery, the design of which indicated that they could have no other use than that specified, and (*b*) weapons, equipment and means of delivery, the design of which indicated that they were specifically intended to be capable of the use specified. The USA shares the view of Switzerland that there are few weapons, equipment or means of delivery peculiar to the uses referred to. It does not, however, believe that it would be appropriate, on this ground alone, for states to reserve unilaterally the right to decide which weapons, equipment or means of delivery fell within the definition. Therefore, while acknowledging the entry into force of the Convention between itself and Switzerland, the USA enters its objection to this reservation.

¹¹ The deposit of the instrument of ratification by Taiwan is considered by the Soviet Union as an illegal act because the government of the People's Republic of China is regarded by the USSR as the sole representative of China.

¹² The UK recalled its view that if a regime is not recognized as the government of a state, neither signature nor the deposit of any instrument by it nor notification of any of those acts will bring about recognition of that regime by any other state.

The Enmod Convention

¹ Argentina interprets the terms 'widespread, long-lasting or severe effects' in Article I, paragraph 1, of the Convention in accordance with the definition agreed upon in the understanding on that article. It likewise interprets Articles II, III and VIII in accordance with the relevant understandings.

² The FRG declared that the Convention applies also to Berlin (West). The USSR and the GDR stated that the West German declaration was 'illegal', while France, the UK and the USA confirmed its validity.

³ It is the understanding of the Republic of Korea that any technique for deliberately changing the natural state of rivers falls within the meaning of the term 'environmental modification techniques' as defined in Article II of the Convention. It is further understood that military or any other hostile use of such techniques, which could cause flooding, inundation, reduction in the water-level, drying up, destruction of hydrotechnical installations or other harmful consequences, comes within the scope of the Convention, provided it meets the criteria set out in Article 1 thereof.

⁴ Kuwait made the following reservations and understanding: This Convention binds Kuwait only towards states parties thereto; its obligatory character shall *ipso facto* terminate with respect to any hostile state which does not abide by the prohibition contained therein. It is understood that accession to this Convention does not mean in any way recognition of Israel by Kuwait; furthermore, no treaty relation will arise between Kuwait and Israel.

On 23 June 1980, the UN Secretary-General, the depositary of the Convention, received from the government of Israel a communication stating that Israel would adopt towards Kuwait an attitude of complete reciprocity.

⁵ The Netherlands accepts the obligation laid down in Article I of the Enmod Convention as extending to states which are not party to the Convention and which act in conformity with Article I of this Convention.

⁶ New Zealand declared that, in its interpretation, nothing in the Convention detracts from or limits the obligations of states to refrain from military or any other hostile use of environmental modification techniques which are contrary to international law.

⁷ Notification of succession.

⁸ On signing the Convention, Turkey declared that the terms 'widespread', 'long-lasting' and 'severe effects' contained in the Convention need to be more clearly defined, and that so long as this clarification was not made, Turkey would be compelled to interpret for itself the terms in question and, consequently, reserved the right to do so as and when required. Turkey also stated its belief that the difference between 'military or any other hostile purposes' and 'peaceful purposes' should be more clearly defined so as to prevent subjective evaluations.

The 'Inhumane Weapons' Convention

[1] Upon signature, China stated that the Convention fails to provide for supervision or verification of any violation of its clauses, thus weakening its binding force. The Protocol on mines, booby traps and other devices fails to lay down strict restrictions on the use of such weapons by the aggressor on the territory of the victim and to provide adequately for the right of a state victim of an aggression to defend itself by all necessary means. The Protocol on incendiary weapons does not stipulate restrictions on the use of such weapons against combat personnel.

[2] France stated that it regretted that it had not been possible to reach agreement on the provisions concerning the verification of facts which might be alleged and which might constitute violations of the undertakings subscribed to. It therefore reserved the right to submit, possibly in association with other states, proposals aimed at filling that gap at the first conference to be held pursuant to Article 8 of the Convention and to utilize, as appropriate, procedures that would make it possible to bring before the international community facts and information which, if verified, could constitute violations of the provisions of the Convention and the Protocols annexed thereto.

Not being bound by the 1977 Additional Protocol I to the Geneva Conventions of 1949, France considers that the fourth paragraph of the preamble to the Convention on prohibitions or restrictions on the use of certain conventional weapons, which reproduces the provisions of Article 35, paragraph 3, of Additional Protocol I, applies only to states parties to that Protocol. France will apply the provisions of the Convention and its three Protocols to all the armed conflicts referred to in Articles 2 and 3 common to the Geneva Conventions of 1949.

[3] Italy stated its regret that no agreement had been reached on provisions that would ensure respect for the obligations under the Convention. Italy intends to undertake efforts to ensure that the problem of the establishment of a mechanism that would make it possible to fill this gap in the Convention is taken up again at the earliest opportunity in every competent forum.

[4] The Netherlands made the following statements of understanding: A specific area of land may also be a military objective if, because of its location or other reasons specified in Article 2, paragraph 4, of Protocol II and in Article 1, paragraph 3, of Protocol III, its total or partial destruction, capture, or neutralization in the prevailing circumstances offers a definitive military advantage; military advantage mentioned in Article 3, paragraph 3 under c, of Protocol II, refers to the advantage anticipated from the attack considered as a whole and not only from isolated or particular parts of the attack; in Article 8, paragraph 1, of Protocol II, the words 'as far as it is able' mean 'as far as it is technically able'.

[5] Romania stated that the provisions of the Convention and its Protocols have a restricted character and do not ensure adequate protection either to the civilian population or to the combatants as the fundamental principles of international humanitarian law require.

[6] The USA stated that it had strongly supported proposals by other countries to include special procedures for dealing with compliance matters, and reserved the right to propose at a later date additional procedures and remedies, should this prove necessary, to deal with such problems.

The Treaty of Rarotonga

[1] In signing Protocols 2 and 3 China declared that it respected the status of the South Pacific nuclear-free zone and would neither use nor threaten to use nuclear weapons against the zone nor test nuclear weapons in the region. However, China reserved its right to reconsider its obligations under the Protocols if other nuclear weapon states or the contracting parties to the Treaty took any action in 'gross' violation of the Treaty and the Protocols, thus changing the status of the zone and endangering the security interests of China.

[2] In signing Protocols 2 and 3 the USSR stated the view that admission of transit of nuclear weapons or other nuclear explosive devices by any means, as well as of visits by foreign military ships and aircraft with nuclear explosive devices on board, to the ports and airfields within the nuclear-free zone would contradict the aims of the Treaty of Rarotonga and would be inconsistent with the status of the zone. It also warned that in case of action taken by a party or parties violating their major commitments connected with the nuclear-free status of the zone, as well as in case of aggression committed by one or several parties to the Treaty, supported by a nuclear-weapon state, or together with it, with the use by such a state of the territory, airspace, territorial sea or archipelagic waters of the parties for visits by nuclear weapon-carrying ships and aircraft or for transit of nuclear weapons, the USSR will have the right to consider itself free of its non-use commitments assumed under Protocol 2.

III. UN member states and year of membership

In the following list of names of the 159 UN member states, the countries marked with an asterisk are also members of the Geneva-based Conference on Disarmament (CD).

Afghanistan, 1946
Albania, 1955
*Algeria, 1962
Angola, 1976
Antigua and Barbuda, 1981
*Argentina, 1945
*Australia, 1945
Austria, 1955
Bahamas, 1973
Bahrain, 1971
Bangladesh, 1974
Barbados, 1966
*Belgium, 1945
Belize, 1981
Benin, 1960
Bhutan, 1971
Bolivia, 1945
Botswana, 1966
*Brazil, 1945
Brunei Darussalam, 1984
*Bulgaria, 1955
Burkina Faso, 1960
*Burma, 1948
Burundi, 1962
Byelorussia, 1945
Cameroon, 1960
*Canada, 1945
Cape Verde, 1975
Central African Republic, 1960
Chad, 1960
Chile, 1945
*China, 1945
Colombia, 1945
Comoros, 1975
Congo, 1960
Costa Rica, 1945
Côte d'Ivoire, 1960
*Cuba, 1945
Cyprus, 1960
*Czechoslovakia, 1945
Denmark, 1945
Djibouti, 1977
Dominica, 1978
Dominican Republic, 1945
Ecuador, 1945
*Egypt, 1945
El Salvador, 1945
Equatorial Guinea, 1968
*Ethiopia, 1945
Fiji, 1970
Finland, 1955
*France, 1945
Gabon, 1960
Gambia, 1965
*German Democratic Republic, 1973

*FR Germany, 1973
Ghana, 1957
Greece, 1945
Grenada, 1974
Guatemala, 1945
Guinea, 1958
Guinea-Bissau, 1974
Guyana, 1966
Haiti, 1945
Honduras, 1945
*Hungary, 1955
Iceland, 1946
*India, 1945
*Indonesia, 1950
*Iran, 1945
Iraq, 1945
Ireland, 1955
Israel, 1949
*Italy, 1955
Ivory Coast (see Côte d'Ivoire)
Jamaica, 1962
*Japan, 1956
Jordan, 1955
Kampuchea, 1955
*Kenya, 1963
Kuwait, 1963
Lao People's Democratic Republic, 1955
Lebanon, 1945
Lesotho, 1966
Liberia, 1945
Libya, 1955
Luxembourg, 1945
Madagascar, 1960
Malawi, 1964
Malaysia, 1957
Maldives, 1965
Mali, 1960
Malta, 1964
Mauritania, 1961
Mauritius, 1968
*Mexico, 1945
*Mongolia, 1961
*Morocco, 1956
Mozambique, 1975
Nepal, 1955
*Netherlands, 1945
New Zealand, 1945
Nicaragua, 1945
Niger, 1960
*Nigeria, 1960
Norway, 1945
Oman, 1971
*Pakistan, 1947
Panama, 1945

Papua New Guinea, 1975
Paraguay, 1945
*Peru, 1945
Philippines, 1945
*Poland, 1945
Portugal, 1955
Qatar, 1971
*Romania, 1955
Rwanda, 1962
Saint Christopher and Nevis, 1983
Saint Lucia, 1979
Saint Vincent and the Grenadines, 1980
Samoa, Western, 1976
Sao Tome and Principe, 1975
Saudi Arabia, 1945
Senegal, 1960
Seychelles, 1976
Sierra Leone, 1961
Singapore, 1965
Solomon Islands, 1978
Somalia, 1960
South Africa, 1945
Spain, 1955
*Sri Lanka, 1955
Sudan, 1956
Suriname, 1975
Swaziland, 1968
*Sweden, 1946
Syria, 1945
Tanzania, 1961
Thailand, 1946
Togo, 1960
Trinidad and Tobago, 1962
Tunisia, 1956
Turkey, 1945
Uganda, 1962
*UK, 1945
Ukraine, 1945
United Arab Emirates, 1971
Uruguay, 1945
*USA, 1945
*USSR, 1945
Vanuatu, 1981
*Venezuela, 1945
Viet Nam, 1977
Yemen Arab Republic, 1947
Yemen, People's Democratic Republic of, 1967
*Yugoslavia, 1945
*Zaire, 1960
Zambia, 1964
Zimbabwe, 1980

Annexe B. Chronology

RAGNHILD FERM

Since the INF Treaty was negotiated and signed in 1987, many chronology entries concern these theatre nuclear weapons and their subcategories. The terminology of the original documents is adhered to as strictly as possible. It should be noted that in the INF Treaty land-based missiles with a range of 1000–5500 km are called 'intermediate-range'; in Soviet terminology these missiles are often called 'medium-range'. Land-based missiles with a range of 500–1000 km are called shorter-range and are also to be eliminated under the Treaty. Weapons with ranges of less than 500 km are not included in the Treaty but are variously referred to as short-range, battlefield or tactical nuclear weapons.

January–December 1987

1 January A six-month cease-fire in Afghanistan, starting on 15 January, is announced by the ruling People's Democratic Party of Afghanistan.

9 January The USA and Thailand sign an agreement for the construction of two US arms and ammunition stockpiles in Thailand.

13 January President Reagan asks the US Senate to give its advice and consent to ratification of the 1974 Threshold Test Ban Treaty (TTBT) and the 1976 Peaceful Nuclear Explosions Treaty (PNET), provided that the USSR will agree to improved verification procedures.

15 January The Soviet Defence Ministry announces that it will withdraw one division of troops from Mongolia between April and June. The withdrawal will include 10 000–12 000 of the 70 000 Soviet troops stationed in Mongolia.

16 January The Soviet news agency Novosti makes public comparisons between the number of Soviet and US nuclear weapons. This is the first time the USSR officially declares figures on the size of its nuclear arsenals.

17 January The seven Mujahideen groups of Afghanistan issue a joint statement in which they firmly reject the cease-fire proclaimed by the ruling People's Democratic Party of Afghanistan.

22 January At the beginning of the fourth session of the US–Soviet discussions on nuclear testing issues the USA states that it is prepared for immediate negotiations to limit nuclear testing. The negotiations should concern: first, effective verification provisions for the TTBT and the PNET; second, a step-by-step parallel programme to limit and ultimately end nuclear testing in association with a programme to reduce and ultimately eliminate all nuclear weapons.

26–29 January The fifth summit meeting of the Islamic Conference Organization is held in Kuwait, with Iran refusing to participate because of this choice of venue. On the main issue, the Iraq–Iran War, the summit calls for an end to hostilities but makes no specific proposals to this end. The President of Egypt proposes a non-aggression pact for the Muslim world and the convening of a preparatory committee for a Middle East peace conference.

5 February At the Conference on Disarmament (CD) the Soviet delegate declares that because of the US nuclear test on 3 February the USSR no longer considers itself bound by its unilateral moratorium on nuclear explosions. It will resume, at the appropriate time, its own programme of nuclear testing. However, the USSR is prepared to stop the implementation of its test programme if the USA halts its testing. Verification could be implemented both by national technical means and on the basis of international procedures, including on-site inspections.

5 February The USA announces that in view of its global security interests and responsibilities it is not, under current circumstances, in a position to sign the Protocols to the South Pacific Nuclear Free Zone Treaty (Treaty of Rarotonga).

8 February The IAEA Convention on the physical protection of nuclear material (opened for signature on 3 March 1980) enters into force.

9 February The Sino–Soviet border talks are resumed after a break of more than eight years.

10 February China signs Protocols 2 and 3 of the South Pacific Nuclear Free Zone Treaty (Treaty of Rarotonga), with reservations.

17 February At the CD the USSR announces that it will agree to describe the precise locations and to declare the detailed inventory of its chemical weapons upon entry into force of a CW convention.

17 February The 16 NATO states and the 7 WTO states (the so-called Group of 23), start talks in Vienna on the mandate for a Europe-wide conventional arms negotiation and the connection of such talks with the Conference on Security and Co-operation in Europe (CSCE).

19 February At the CD the French Foreign Minister states that France does not rule out the possibility of acquiring limited and purely deterrent capability in chemical arms.

23 February The member states of the European Community give their support to the Soviet proposal for an international peace conference to solve the Arab–Israeli conflict.

26 February The USSR resumes nuclear testing after a moratorium of almost 19 months.

26 February The IAEA Convention on assistance in the case of a nuclear accident or radiological emergency (opened for signature on 26 September 1986) enters into force.

28 February General Secretary Gorbachev announces that the USSR could agree to a separate accord on the complete elimination of medium-range missiles in Europe over a five-year period, delinking the INF issue from the US–Soviet Nuclear and Space Talks. Only 100 missiles in Soviet Asia and as many on US territory would remain. The USSR will remove from the GDR and Czechoslovakia the shorter-range missiles as soon as an agreement is signed on the elimination of Soviet and US medium-range nuclear missiles in Europe. As for the elimination of short-range land-based missiles, the USSR is prepared to start talks immediately. An agreement on substantial cuts in and subsequent elimination of strategic arms will become possible after a decision has been taken on the non-deployment of weapons in space.

2 March The Soviet proposal for an agreement on medium-range nuclear forces, announced by General Secretary Gorbachev on 28 February, is presented at the US–Soviet Nuclear and Space Talks.

4 March The US proposal for an agreement on intermediate-range nuclear forces (INF) is presented at the US–Soviet Nuclear and Space Talks. It provides for the reduction of these INF missiles on each side to 100 globally, with zero in Europe.

5–8 March At a meeting between the Soviet Foreign Minister and the President of Indonesia it is stated that both states call for an international conference on the Indian Ocean as a zone of peace. The work on such a conference is to be started not later than 1988.

10 March President Reagan sends his annual report to the Congress on Soviet non-compliance with arms control agreements. According to the report the USSR has failed to correct its non-compliant activities; neither have sufficient explanations been provided to alleviate US concerns on other compliance issues.

13 March After having studied the Anti-Ballistic Missile (ABM) Treaty negotiating record, US Senator Nunn, Chairman of the Senate Armed Services Committee, states that there is no evidence which contradicts the Senate's original understanding of the meaning of the Treaty and that, consequently, the traditional ('narrow') interpretation of the Treaty should be supported.

20 March The UK announces that it will not sign the Protocols of the Treaty of Rarotonga, because signing would not serve its national interests.

23 March–10 April The UN Conference for the Promotion of International Co-operation in the Peaceful Uses of Nuclear Energy (PUNE) is held in Geneva. The participating states fail to agree on principles for the nuclear supplies.

24–25 March The Committee of the Ministers of Foreign Affairs of the WTO, meeting in Moscow, calls on the USSR and the USA to sign without delay a separate agreement for the elimination of US and Soviet medium-range missiles in Europe. The participants also declare that they consider that nuclear- and chemical-free zones in the Balkans, Central Europe, North Europe and other parts of the continent would strengthen European security. The session makes a separate statement in favour of a chemical weapon ban.

27 March The NATO Special Consultative Group (SCG) declares its full support for the US draft INF Treaty, tabled on 4 March. However, in the absence of a treaty, the Group confirms NATO's determination to continue the deployment of intermediate-range nuclear missiles as scheduled.

31 March The British Prime Minister, visiting Moscow, declares that the UK is not prepared to accept the denuclearization of Europe; that the British nuclear forces are and will remain critical; and that any agreement on intermediate-range nuclear missiles should include restraints on shorter-range missiles to prevent circumvention. She also declares that the UK does not want the Strategic Defense Initiative (SDI) to undermine the ABM Treaty and proposes a timetable spelling out the planned research programmes of both parties supported by a commitment not to withdraw from the ABM Treaty for a fixed period.

31 March During the British Prime Minister's visit to Moscow, the Foreign Ministers of the two states sign an agreement on upgrading the 'hot-line' communications link between Moscow and London.

7 April Canada, France, the FRG, Italy, Japan, the UK and the USA reach agreement on adopting identical guidelines to control the transfer of equipment and technology which could make a contribution to missile systems capable of delivering a nuclear weapon. The agreement is announced in the respective capitals on 16 April.

9 April At the MBFR talks the WTO states issue an appeal to NATO states suggesting that the military budgets of the states of the two alliances not be increased for one to two years.

10 April General Secretary Gorbachev, speaking in Prague, announces the Soviet offer to begin talks on the elimination of missiles in Europe with a range of 500–1000 km and says that the USSR has stopped production of chemical weapons.

12–15 April During the US Secretary of State's visit to Moscow the two sides agree that the intermediate-range land-based nuclear missile reductions should be accomplished in approximately four to five years. General Secretary Gorbachev offers to dismantle the entire shorter-range missile armoury in Europe. He further proposes the elimination of tactical missiles. He also proposes that a summit meeting be held in Washington later in 1987. In addition the Soviet Foreign Minister suggests that a US nuclear device be exploded at a Soviet test site and a Soviet nuclear device be detonated at a US test site.

27 April A new Soviet draft for an INF treaty is presented at the US–Soviet Nuclear and Space Talks. It is proposed that the Pershing 1a missiles in FR Germany be removed and that 100 US warheads be permitted on US territory and 100 Soviet warheads in Soviet Asia, east of 80 degrees longitude. The missiles deployed should not be capable of reaching the other's territory.

8 May The Chairman of the Polish Council of State, General Jaruzelski, presents a plan for conventional and nuclear disarmament in Europe (he Jaruzelski Plan), which includes gradual withdrawal of nuclear arms from Europe, gradual withdrawal of offensive conventional weapons, a change to defensive military doctrines, and a wide range of new security- and confidence-building measures and machinery for strict verification.

8 May At the US–Soviet Nuclear and Space Talks the USA presents a draft treaty on the reduction of strategic weapons. Each side would limit its strategic nuclear delivery vehicles to 1600 and warheads to 6000 over seven years from entry into force of a treaty. During that period both sides would agree not to withdraw from the ABM Treaty. After 1994 either side could choose to deploy defensive systems. Only 1650 warheads would be permitted on heavy ICBMs or on ICBMs with more than six warheads. Mobile ICBMs would be banned.

14 May The members of the UN Security Council again strongly condemn the repeated use of chemical weapons against Iranian forces by Iraqi forces and again demand that the provisions of the Geneva Protocol be strictly respected and observed. The members of the Council also condemn the prolongation of the conflict and express grave concern over the danger of an extension of the conflict to other states in the region.

15 May The NATO Nuclear Planning Group, meeting in Stavanger, Norway, welcomes the improved prospects for a US–Soviet agreement on land-based intermediate-range nuclear missiles. It reaffirms that appropriate global constraints on shorter-range missiles are indispensable.

17 May An Iraqi Mirage F-1 attacks the *USS Stark* frigate in the Persian Gulf, killing 37 US sailors.

28–29 May The Political Consultative Committee of the WTO, meeting in East Berlin, agrees to: seek to reach agreement on the elimination of medium- and shorter-range nuclear missiles; hold talks on missiles in the eastern USSR and on the territory of the USA; seek agreement on the reduction of strategic offensive arms (50 per cent reduction in five years), coupled with a strengthening of the ABM Treaty; reduce conventional weapons in Europe by 25 per cent in the early 1990s; and establish a nuclear-free corridor in Europe (proposed by the GDR and Czechoslovakia).

1 June The Government of the Federal Republic of Germany decides to support the elimination of all intermediate- and shorter-range land-based nuclear missiles. The 72 West German Pershing 1a missiles with their US warheads cannot be included in the US–Soviet agreement.

5 June The Canadian Government announces its decision to acquire a fleet of 10–12 nuclear-powered submarines.

6 June The USSR announces the completion of limited withdrawal of Soviet troops from Mongolia. (See *15 January*.)

8 June At the CD the WTO member states present a document on the Basic Provisions of a Treaty on the Complete and General Prohibition of Nuclear Weapon Tests. The draft treaty includes rules for unconditional on-site inspection by international teams for verifying compliance.

8 June The New Zealand Nuclear-Free Zone, Disarmament, and Arms Control Act enters into force. The zone comprises all of the land, territory and inland waters within the territorial limits of New Zealand; the internal waters and the territorial sea of New Zealand; as well as the airspace above all these areas.

12 June In a reply to the Six-Nation Initiative statement of 22 May, General Secretary Gorbachev says that the USSR is prepared to reach agreement with the USA on holding calibration experiments at each other's test sites using both the national seismographic equipment of the two countries and the seismic monitoring facilities of the six nations. The USSR also wants to take steps to reach an interim agreement with the USA on limiting the yield of underground nuclear tests to within the one-kiloton threshold and their number to two to three per year.

12 June In a communiqué issued by the North Atlantic Council, meeting in Reykjavik, the ministers support the elimination of all US and Soviet land-based missiles with a range of 500 to 1000 km as an integral part of an INF agreement. In addition the communiqué recalls that negotiations on conventional stability should be accompanied by negotiations between the 35 CSCE states building upon and expanding the confidence- and security-building measures agreed on in the Helsinki Final Act and in the Stockholm Document. These two future negotiations should take place within the framework of the CSCE process.

16 June At the US–Soviet Nuclear and Space Talks the USA proposes the global elimination of US and Soviet shorter-range land-based missiles. It also emphasizes the global elimination of US and Soviet intermediate-range land-based missiles.

19 June The Chancellor of the Federal Republic of Germany suggests that French and German troops are combined in an experimental joint brigade.

22 June The WTO states present a working document on the mandate for talks between the two blocs (the so-called Group of 23) on the reduction of conventional weapons, calling for: overall reductions, including reductions in tactical nuclear weapons and strike aircraft; corrections of existing imbalances; zones of reduced concentration of forces along the East–West boundary; and elimination of the possibility of surprise attack.

10 July The NATO countries propose that future negotiations on conventional weapons be held in two separate groups, one concerned with questions on confidence- and security-building measures and the other dealing with conventional weapons stability. In the first group all 35 CSCE states would participate. The other group would include only member states of the two alliances (the so-called Group of 23), but the remaining CSCE countries (neutral and non-aligned—NNA) would be periodically informed.

16 July In a joint communiqué the Prime Minister of Greece and the President of Bulgaria urge the other Balkan states to join the initiative for a nuclear-free zone in the Balkans.

20 July The UN Security Council unanimously adopts a resolution demanding that as a first step towards a negotiated settlement, Iran and Iraq observe an immediate cease-fire, discontinue all military actions, and withdraw all forces to the internationally recognized boundaries without delay.

21 July In an interview with the Indonesian newspaper *Merdeka* General Secretary Gorbachev states that the USSR is prepared to renounce the 100 nuclear warheads on medium-range land-based missiles in Soviet Asia (see *28 February* and *27 April*), provided the USA does the same for its territory. Shorter-range missiles will also be eliminated world-wide. This initiative is not linked to US nuclear presence in Asia. The USSR is also prepared not to increase nuclear-capable aircraft in its Asian region, providing the USA does not deploy in this region nuclear systems capable of reaching Soviet territory. The USSR also suggests a limitation on US and Soviet naval activities in the Pacific (as stated before); restrictions on nuclear-armed vessels in certain areas; and a ban on anti-submarine warfare activities in special zones. Naval exercises and manoeuvres in the Pacific, the Indian Ocean and the adjoining seas should be limited to one to two annually, subject to notification of their conduct.

23 July North Korea proposes a troop reduction plan for the Korean peninsula calling on both sides to have less than 100 000 troops by 1992. The proposal would also require the removal of the 40 000 US troops in South Korea.

27 July The NATO states present a plan for new negotiations on the reduction of conventional forces in Europe within the framework of the CSCE process. Three objectives for the future talks are outlined: a stable, secure balance of lower levels of forces; the elimination of imbalances between NATO and the WTO, in particular as regards tanks, helicopters and artillery; and the elimination of the capability to launch a surprise attack. The new talks should take place within the framework of the CSCE.

27 July The Prime Minister of Greece and the President of Romania issue an appeal to the other Balkan leaders for a summit meeting to promote the transformation of the Balkans into a zone free of chemical and nuclear weapons.

29 July At the US–Soviet Nuclear and Space Talks the USSR presents a draft treaty on space weapons. It provides for a mutual non-withdrawal from the ABM Treaty for 10 years and a mutual commitment to confine work on space-based ABM systems to research in laboratories.

31 July At the CSCE Sweden proposes that two separate negotiation groups be established in accordance with the NATO proposal of 10 July. It is confirmed that the

NNA group should regularly receive information about the talks in the group dealing with conventional arms reductions.

31 July At the US–Soviet Nuclear and Space Talks the USSR presents a draft treaty for 50 per cent cuts in US and Soviet strategic weapons. Over a five-year period the USSR and the USA will reduce their strategic offensive weapons such that the overall number of ICBMs, SLBMs and heavy bombers will be brought down to 1600 for each side. The nuclear warheads on the remaining strategic delivery vehicles will be limited to 6000 for each side. The USSR offers to reduce its heavy ICBMs by half. It is stated, however, that radical cuts in strategic weapons can be achieved only if there is an accord on reinforcing the ABM Treaty regime.

7 August In Guatemala City a preliminary peace agreement, entitled 'Procedure for the establishment of a strong and lasting peace in Central America' (the 'Arias Plan'), is signed by the presidents of Costa Rica, El Salvador, Guatemala, Honduras and Nicaragua.

10 August The USSR and the USA announce that the two sides have agreed to exchange visits to chemical weapon facilities in both countries to enable each party to observe the other's procedures for destroying chemical weapons.

11 August At the CD the USSR presents a proposal on compulsory on-site inspection of chemical facilities within 48 hours.

21 August Japan signs an agreement with the USA on conditions for its participation in the SDI programme.

24 August–11 September The UN International Conference on the Relationship between Disarmament and Development is held in New York.

26 August The Chancellor of the Federal Republic of Germany announces that with the definitive elimination of US and Soviet land-based nuclear missiles with a range of 500–5500 km, the Pershing 1a missiles will be dismantled.

28–30 August The USA carries out its first on-site inspection of a Soviet military exercise in the USSR under the terms of the Stockholm Document. The inspection is carried out north-east of Minsk. (Inspections were also conducted by the UK in the GDR, on 10–12 September; by the USSR in Turkey on 5–7 October and in the FRG on 28–30 October; and by the GDR in the FRG on 11–13 November.)

2 September The President of Brazil reveals that work has begun on the construction of a large uranium enrichment plant which is to be run by the Brazilian Navy. The plant is not covered by international safeguards.

5–6 September A US congressional delegation visits the Soviet radar site near Krasnoyarsk at the invitation of the Soviet Government. (After the visit a US State Department spokesman says that the group saw no evidence which would alter the US conclusion that the radar under construction constitutes a violation of the ABM Treaty.)

15 September The USA and the USSR sign the Agreement on the establishment of nuclear risk reduction centers. The agreement provides for notifications of ballistic missile launches and transmission of other information. Under the agreement each side will establish a nuclear risk reduction centre in its capital. These centres would act as a second communications link, parallel to the 'hot line'.

17 September At the talks between the US Secretary of State and the Soviet Foreign

Minister agreement is reached on a mandate for nuclear testing negotiations. As a first step the two sides will agree upon verification measures towards ratification of the 1974 Threshold Test Ban Treaty and the 1976 Peaceful Nuclear Explosions Treaty and later proceed to the negotiation of further limitations on nuclear testing as part of an effective disarmament process.

17 September In an article published in *Pravda* and *Izvestia* General Secretary Gorbachev suggests a direct communication line between UN headquarters and permanent member states of the Security Council. He envisages that, within two to three years, the USSR will be able to compare figures which would symmetrically reflect the defence expenditures of the sides. He proposes that nuclear and offensive weapons be withdrawn from the borders and subsequent creation of demilitarized zones along borders. He also suggests that the International Court of Justice be recognized by all, on mutually agreed conditions.

17–25 September A joint French–West German military manoeuvre is held in FR Germany. 55 000 men from the 2nd Bundeswehr Army Corps and 22 000 men from the French Rapid Action Force (FAR) participate.

18 September At the end of the talks between the US Secretary of State and the Soviet Foreign Minister in Washington it is announced that the two sides have agreed in principle to conclude a treaty on the elimination of all US and Soviet intermediate-range and shorter-range land-based missiles. Similarly intensive effort should be made to achieve a treaty on a 50 per cent reduction in strategic offensive arms. A summit meeting is planned for the autumn of 1987.

21 September The South African President states that his government is prepared to commence negotiations with each of the nuclear weapon states on the possibility of signing the Non-Proliferation Treaty (NPT) and would consider including in these negotiations safeguards on its installations subject to the NPT conditions.

24 September In a speech at the UN General Assembly, Pakistan's Prime Minister proposes a UN Conference on non-proliferation in South Asia which would lead to a nuclear-free zone and a regional nuclear test ban.

24 September At a joint French–West German press conference the French President announces that the two governments will start negotiations on the establishment of a joint defence council.

1 October In a speech at Murmansk, USSR, General Secretary Gorbachev proposes that the Arctic area be made a zone of peace. He suggests WTO–NATO consultations on restrictions on naval activities in the Baltic, the North Sea and the Norwegian and Greenland seas. Scientific co-operation among states on a programme for natural resources and energy in the region is also suggested. He further offers to reduce the nuclear tests on Novaya Zemlya to the minimum in terms of number and yield.

3–5 October In accordance with the agreement of 10 August delegations from 45 nations are shown standard samples of chemical munitions at the Soviet Shikhany military installation. Soviet CW destruction technology is also demonstrated.

16 October President Reagan sends the certification to the US Congress which would permit the manufacture of binary chemical weapons.

19 October In a speech at the UN General Assembly the Director of the IAEA says that an agreement on nuclear safeguards has been reached in principle with China.

19 October At the Group of 23 talks the WTO states present a new formula to define the types of armament to be included in future negotiations on conventional forces as 'conventional land-based armaments'. It was made clear that this language does not exclude either nuclear- or dual-capable systems.

23 October The USSR invites the USA to carry out on-site inspection of two radars considered by the USA to violate the ABM Treaty.

27 October The member states of the Western European Union (WEU) issue a declaration, 'Platform on European Security Interests', which calls for a cohesive European defence identity. It is stated that the revitalization of the WEU is an important contribution to European unification. The security of the West European countries can only be ensured in close association with the North American allies, and the presence of US conventional and nuclear forces is essential for the defence of Europe. The UK and France will continue to maintain their independent nuclear forces.

28–29 October The WTO Foreign Ministers, meeting in Prague, reaffirm their proposal to hold a meeting of the Foreign Ministers of the CSCE countries. The meeting would take a decision to start large-scale talks with a view to substantially reducing the armed forces and tactical nuclear and conventional arms in Europe, and reducing military expenditures accordingly; adjusting the difference in levels through adequate limitations; and averting the danger of a surprise attack. The ministers declared the readiness of their states to promote the implementation of the plan for arms limitation and building confidence in central Europe (the Jaruzelski Plan) as put forward on 8 May.

2 November The Group of 23 member states agree that negotiations on the reduction of conventional forces will start in 1988 within the framework of the CSCE. The NNA states will not be directly involved.

3–4 November The NATO Nuclear Planning Group, meeting in Monterey, California, USA, welcomes and fully supports in principle the forthcoming INF agreement for the global elimination of 500- to 5500-km range land-based missiles. However, the NATO strategy of flexible response will continue to be vital.

5 November Spain accedes to the Non-Proliferation Treaty (NPT).

9 November Spain notifies its decision to open talks to renew the 1982 US–Spanish Agreement on friendship, defense and co-operation, governing the use of US bases in Spain, due to expire in May 1988.

9–20 November During the first round of the US–Soviet negotiations on nuclear testing (see *17 September*) it is agreed that the USSR and the USA will visit each other's test sites during January 1988 to familiarize themselves with the conditions and operations at the other's test site.

11 November The Chairman of the Polish Council of State, General Jaruzelski, says that the WTO would be willing to negotiate reductions in tanks in return for NATO reductions in combat bomber aircraft.

18 November In a joint majority report, issued by Special House and Senate committees investigating the Iran–Contra affair, it is stated that President Reagan bore 'ultimate responsibility', but there is no evidence that he had known of the diversion of funds from arms sales to Iran to assist the Contras in Nicaragua.

19–20 November In accordance with the agreement of 10 August Soviet military experts visit the Tooele Army Depot in Utah, USA, to inspect US chemical weapons.

24–26 November The Committee of the WTO Defence Ministers, meeting in Bucharest, approves a US–Soviet accord on medium- and shorter-range land-based nuclear missiles as a first step towards destroying nuclear arsenals. It favours the earliest conclusion of an agreement on a mutual 50 per cent reduction of strategic offensive arms, provided the ABM Treaty is preserved for at least 10 years.

30 November In a US televison interview General Secretary Gorbachev says that the USSR is engaged in research into space-based defensive weapon systems similar to the US Strategic Defense Initiative, but it will not build or deploy such systems.

1–2 December The NATO Defence Planning Committee, meeting in Brussels, fully supports the forthcoming INF agreement. The progress made in Vienna to convene conventional stability negotiations covering all of Europe from the Atlantic to the Urals is also welcomed.

4 December The US fiscal year 1988 DOD authorization bill is signed. No funds are appropriated for SDI tests except for those tests which are in conformity with the 'narrow' interpretation of the ABM Treaty.

8 December The Treaty between the USA and the USSR on the elimination of their intermediate-range and shorter-range missiles (the INF Treaty) is signed in Washington. The Treaty contains two protocols: the first specifies the way in which the missiles will be destroyed, and the second deals with the agreed procedures for verification. A Memorandum of Understanding lists the total numbers of missiles and launchers covered by the Treaty and the geographical location of each.

9 December In a joint statement issued in Washington, the USA and the USSR confirm that they are proceeding to design a joint verification experiment (JVE) at each other's nuclear test sites.

10 December In the joint US–Soviet statement issued at the end of the summit meeting in Washington, President Reagan and General Secretary Gorbachev confirm their intention to work towards the completion of a Treaty on the Reduction and Limitation of Strategic Offensive Arms. The negotiators should build upon the agreement on a 50 per cent reduction achieved at the 1986 Reykjavik meeting, including agreement on ceilings of no more than 1600 strategic offensive delivery systems, 6000 warheads (1540 warheads on 154 heavy missiles). The cuts would lead to a 50 per cent reduction of the throw-weight of Soviet ICBMs and SLBMs. The two leaders had also instructed their negotiators to work out an agreement that would commit the sides to observe the ABM Treaty as signed in 1972 while conducting their research, deployment and testing permitted by the Treaty and not to withdraw from the Treaty for a specified period of time. It is agreed that the next summit meeting will take place in the USSR in the first half of 1988.

10–11 December The North Atlantic Council, meeting in Brussels, welcomes the INF Treaty. It states that it is the commitment of the Alliance to respond in solidarity to the Soviet military threat and for the foreseeable future there is no alternative to the strategy of deterrence. The speedy conclusion of a START agreement is expected with the goal of achieving a 50 per cent reduction in Soviet and US strategic arsenals. The commitment to two future security negotiations in the framework of the CSCE is reaffirmed.

11 December An agreement among the USA, Belgium, the FRG, Italy, the Netherlands and the UK regarding inspections relating to the INF Treaty is signed in Brussels.

14 December NATO and the WTO agree that only conventional armaments should be included in the objectives of a new arms reduction forum. These new talks would take place within the CSCE framework.

14 December It is announced in London that the UK and France consider a joint development of an air-launched nuclear cruise missile to arm RAF Tornado and French Mirage aircraft around the turn of the century.

15 December It is announced in Pyongyang that North Korea has demobilized 100 000 soldiers.

16 December The USA takes up the production of binary chemical weapons.

20–22 December US officials visit two sites near Moscow and Gomel, USSR, to inspect two radars believed by the USA to violate the ABM Treaty (see *23 October*).

21 December The US Congress approves a compromise to give the Contras $8.1 billion in 'nonlethal' aid until 29 February on condition that the money not be used to buy arms.

22 December In a resolution the UN Security Council deplores the Israeli Army's 'killing and wounding of defenceless Palestinian civilians' in the occupied West Bank and Gaza Strip. The USA abstains.

23 December The negotiations between Spain and the USA (see *9 November*) break off, and the Spanish Prime Minister demands that all 72 US F-16 fighter bombers and 5 US KC jet tankers stationed in Spain be withdrawn by 1991.

26 December The USSR announces that its stocks of chemical weapons do not exceed 50 000 tons in terms of poisonous substances and that all its chemical weapons are located on Soviet territory.

27 December Iran discloses that it is manufacturing 'sophisticated offensive chemical weapons' but it will not use the weapons unless forced to do so. (According to press reports, the announcement was later disclaimed.)

Errata

SIPRI Yearbook 1987: World Armaments and Disarmament

Table 7A.2, pages 220–1: In the column for 1974, the top eight figures should read: '4 732, 5 076, 4 481, 6 200, 1 263, 1 247, 1 071, 1 121'; and the last two figures in the column should read: '12 982, 14 894'.

Page 493, Index: Entries under 'Somalia' may refer to South Africa. Owing to a printer's error, the entry for South Africa does not appear in the index.

INDEX

ABM (Anti-Ballistic Missile) Treaty (1972): cancellation clause 309, 502; future of 500–3; reinterpretation 492–6, 498; SDI and 6, 32, 492, 495; Standing Consultative Commission 491
Achille Lauro 277
Aérospatiale 50, 185
Afghanistan: arms imports 177, 178; chemical weapons 102; conflict in 286, 290; military expenditure 142; Mujahideen 182, 191, 287; *see also under* Union of Soviet Socialist Republics
Africa: conflicts in 140, 286, 293–6; economic problems 140, 141; military expenditure 140–2, 160–1, 165–6, 170–1
AIDS 112
Airborne Optical Adjunct 85
aircraft: *general references:* life of 196; maritime patrol 269, 270–3, 274; numbers 33, 37; *individual countries:* Argentina 270; Australia 270, 280; Brazil 270; Canada 270; Chile 270; China 54, 270; Egypt 271; France 49, 50, 51, 52, 196; India 271; Indonesia 271; Iran 271; Iraq 271; Israel 271; Japan 271; Korea, South 272; Kuwait 272; Libya 272; Malaysia 272; Mexico 272; Morocco 272; New Zealand 272, 280; Pakistan 272; Papua New Guinea 272; Philippines 272; Saudi Arabia 273; Seychelles 273; Singapore 273; South Africa 273; Taiwan 273; Thailand 273; UAE 273; UK 42, 46; USA: ASW 37; bombers: Advanced Technology 24, 26, 27; B-1 23, 24, 26, 27, 36; B-2 27; B-52 23, 28, 36; F-111 29; FB-111 36; fighters: A-6 31; A-7 31; ATA 31; F-15 29, 86; F-16 29; F/A-18 196; USSR: ASW 40; bombers: Backfire 35, 40, 45, 379; Badger 40, 45; Bear 23, 35, 39; Bison 23, 35; Blackjack 35; Blinder 40; fighters: Fencer 45; MiG-27 178; MiG-29 178, 179; refuelling 35
Air Defense Initiative 82
Akhromeyev, Marshal Sergei 5, 133, 328
Albania 138, 159, 164
Algeria 160, 165, 170
Algernon, Carl 193
Alpha experiment 86
America *see* United States of America
Andrew Jackson, USS 32
Andropov, Yuri 382, 383
Angola: arms imports 178, 179, 181; conflict in 182, 286, 287, 293; military expenditure 140, 141, 160, 165, 170
Antarctic Treaty (1959) 549, 552, 554–68
Aquino, President Cory 145
Argentina: arms exports 190–1; arms imports 534; economic problems 150; military expenditure 150–1, 162, 167, 172; National Commission for Atomic Energy 151; nuclear capability 58–9, 365

Ariane rocket 81
Arias, President Oscar 148 *see also following entry*
Arias Plan 2, 287
arms control: military doctrine 12, 13; on-site inspections 116, 120; political goals 9; *see also under particular aspects*
ARMSCOR 141
arms trade: black market 190–5; controversies over 194; depression of 195; diversification of 197; fraud 192; grey market 190–5; information about 180; SIPRI's sources and methods 176, 180, 256–63; small deals 188–90; trends 175–98; updating 196; values of 202–3, 244–5; world 176
artillery, nuclear 28, 37, 38, 40, 44
ASAT (anti-satellite activities): USA 75, 86, 89; USSR 35, 75, 86
ASLP missile 50
ASMP missile 46, 50, 52
ASROC missile 37
ASTARTE programme 51
ASW systems 37
AS-X-16 35
ATBM (anti-tactical ballistic missile) 82, 90
Athens meeting 324
Atlas rocket 76, 77
atomic demolition munitions 30, 37, 38, 40
attack craft 266, 276
Australia: arms control and 366; arms imports 179, 188; chemical weapons and 103, 104, 112; military expenditure 146–7, 160, 165, 170; nuclear issues 361, 362; nuclear tests and 67
Australian Group 103, 105
Austria: arms exports 177, 192, 194; military expenditure 138, 139, 159, 164, 169
Avions Marcel Dassault 185

Bahrain 159, 164, 169, 184
Bangladesh 142, 143, 160, 164, 169
Bani-Sadr, President 508
Belgium: arms exports 194; military expenditure 158, 163, 168; missiles in 8
Benin 160, 165, 170
Berne meeting 324
Bertram, Christoph 4
Bessmertnykh, Aleksander 376
Biden, Senator Joe 183
Bigeye 108
Biological Weapons Convention (1972) 106, 112–13, 352, 355, 356, 551, 553, 554–68; Review Conference 111, 113
Blackwill, Robert 332
BMD (ballistic missile defence): USSR 36, 39, 88–9, 499; *for USA see* SDI; *see also* ABM Treaty
Boeing Aerospace 27
Bofors 188, 193

592 INDEX

Bolivia 162, 167, 172
bombs: ANT-52 50, 52; B57 38; B61 26; B83 23, 26; WE-177 46
Bork, Robert 183
Botswana 160, 165, 170
Brazil: arms exports 176, 177, 182, 204–5; arms imports 178, 185; Germany and 58; military expenditure 151, 162, 167, 172; nuclear capability 58–9, 365
Brezhnev, President Leonid, 4, 378, 379, 381
Britannia, Royal Yacht 275
Brundtland Commission 541, 543
Brunei 146, 160, 165, 170
Brussels Club 103
Brussels Declaration 331
Brzezinski, Zbigniew 311
Budapest appeal 8, 329, 334
Bulgaria 115, 137, 159, 163, 168
Burkina Faso 160, 165, 170
Burma 102, 146, 160, 165, 170, 291
Burundi 160, 165, 170

Cambodia *see* Kampuchea
Cameroon 161, 165, 170
Camp David Accords 2, 182
Canada: arms control 355; arms exports 177, 194; arms imports 179; chemical weapons 103, 104, 112; military expenditure 131, 158, 163, 168
Caribbean 269
Carlucci, Frank 25, 303, 498
Carrington, Lord 13, 317
Carter, President Jimmy 2, 29, 376, 377, 378, 379, 380
CDE (Conference on Disarmament in Europe) (Stockholm) 9, 315, 390, 540
Central African Republic 161, 165, 170
Central America: arms imports 202–3; conflict in 147, 287; military expenditure 147–9, 161–2, 166–7, 171
Ceylon *see* Sri Lanka
Chad 106, 107, 161, 165, 182, 187, 189, 286, 294
chemical weapons: ban on 103, 115–20, 328, 347–58; bilateral talks on 103, 118; chemical weapon-free zones 115–16; definition 120; destruction sites 108, 109–12, 118, 347; possessor states 101 102, 103, 104; proliferation 101–8; trade and 101; treaty violations alleged 106, 113–15
Chervov, Colonel-General Nikolai 69
Chile 2–3, 151–2, 162, 167, 172
China: arms exports 176, 177, 186–7, 190, 191, 195, 196, 204–5; chemical weapons and 102, 103, 349, 353; military expenditure 144; nuclear weapon tests 65, 68, 73, 74; Rarotonga Treaty and 67; strategic nuclear forces 24, 44, 52–4; Viet Nam and 292
Chirac, Jacques 48, 107, 194
Colombia 151, 162, 167, 172, 296
commodity prices 143, 541
Common Market *see* European Community
communications, strategic 51–2, 54
Conference on Disarmament: chemical weapons and 101, 115, 117, 118, 119–20, 350; nuclear weapon tests and 68, 366, 367
confidence-building measures 12, 111, 112, 118, 325
conflicts: characteristics of 286–7; growing number of 285; international community and 287; United Nations and 287
Congo 161, 165, 170
Conventional Defense Initiative 87, 317
Cook Islands 280
CORRTEX 68, 69
Costa Rica 148, 161, 166, 171
Côte d'Ivoire 161, 165, 170
Council for Mutual Economic Assistance 103
'creeping jurisdiction' 265, 276, 281
CSCE (Conference on Security and Co-operation in Europe): Helsinki meeting 12, 315; Madrid meeting 9, 10, 324; Stockholm Document 4, 111, 323, 324–5, 326, 327, 338; Stockholm meeting 12, 324, 331; Vienna meeting 8, 315, 325, 326, 331
Cuba 148–9, 161, 166, 171
Cyprus 159, 164, 169
Czechoslovakia: arms control and 330, 349; arms exports 176, 177, 181; arms imports 179; chemical weapons and 103, 112; military expenditure 137, 159, 163, 168; missiles in 41, 321

Damavand project 192
Dassault 49, 185, 197
Dean, Jonathan 332, 333
debts, international 2–3, 140, 147, 148, 149, 533, 534
Defense Meteorological Satellite Program 77
Défense Nationale 52
Defense Support Program 78
defensive defence 328
Delta test 85
Denmark: arms trade and 194; chemical weapons and 112; military expenditure 158, 163, 168; nuclear weapons and 362
détente 491, 500
deterrence 13, 305–7, 491, 493, 494
development and disarmament 517–36
Dobrynin, Anatoly 334
Dominican Republic 148, 162, 166, 171

Ecuador 162, 167, 172, 268, 285
EEC *see* European Community
EEZs (exclusive economic zones) 267, 279
Eggar, Tim 524
Egypt: arms control and 354; arms exports 176, 177; arms imports 178, 179, 181, 195; chemical weapons 102, 103; debt 195; Israel, treaty with 2; military expenditure 140, 159, 164, 169
El Salvador 149, 162, 166, 171, 285, 296
Energiya rocket 78
Enmod Convention (1977) 551, 553, 554–68
Ethiopia 102, 161, 165, 170, 294
Euratom 363
Europe: military expenditure 138–9, 159, 164, 169

European Community 8, 359
European Political Co-operation 8
expendable launch vehicles 76, 78, 89
Extended Range Interceptor programme 85

famines 287
Fangataufa atoll 67
Far East: arms imports 202-3; conflict in 286, 291-3; military expenditure 143-6, 160, 165, 170
Faure, Edgar 521
Fiji 147, 160, 165, 170, 280, 281
Finland 104, 112, 138, 139, 159, 164, 169
Five Power Defence Arrangement 279
Flexible Lightweight Agile-Guided Experiment 84
force, non-use of 12
France: arms control and 7, 9, 316, 324, 327, 330, 331, 332, 366, 392; arms exports 176, 177, 180, 182, 185, 190, 204–5, 278; arms imports 182; chemical weapons and 101, 102, 103, 116, 117, 348, 350, 351, 352; Evreux Air Base 51; Germany and 49, 391; hostages 194; Iraq and 514; military expenditure 131, 158, 163, 168; NATO and 329; nuclear co-operation 24, 50; nuclear weapon tests 65, 67–8, 72, 73, 74; Rarotonga Treaty and 67; strategic nuclear forces 7, 14, 43, 48–52; UK, co-operation with 23–4

Gabon 161, 165, 170
Galosh missile 36, 39, 499
Gaulle, Charles de 14
Gazelle missile 36, 39
General Dynamics 27, 31
Geneva Protocol (1925) 348, 352, 355, 358, 510, 549, 552, 554–68
German Democratic Republic: arms control 330, 366; arms imports 179; Germany and 115; military expenditure 137, 138, 159, 163, 168; missiles in 41, 42, 321; USSR forces in 10, 11
Germany, Federal Republic of: arms control 14, 331; arms exports 176, 177, 182, 187, 194, 204–5, 275; arms imports 179; Brazil and 58; chemical weapons and 103, 112; France and 49; German Democratic Republic and 115; military expenditure 131, 158, 163, 168; missiles in 8, 28; NATO and 318; USSR and 118
Ghana 161, 165, 170
Giraud, André 46, 81, 194
Goa missile 41
Goblet missile 41
GOES-6 spacecraft 77
Goldemberg, José 58
Goldwater, Senator Barry 495
Gorbachev, Mikhail: ABM Treaty and 309; arms control and 5, 6, 12, 13, 320, 323, 327, 328, 334, 384, 390; arms exports and 180; changes made by 12; chemical weapons and 5, 108; economy and 6; INF Treaty and 6; leader, becomes 383–4; military, leadership over 5; military expenditure and 129; radar and 35; reform and 133; SDI and 81, 497
Gostev, Boris 133
Great Britain *see* United Kingdom
Greece 115, 158, 163, 168, 185
Gromyko, Andrei 4, 384
Group of 77, 527
Grumble missile 36, 41
Grumman 187, 196
Guadalupe 378
Guatemala: conflict in 285, 297; military expenditure 149, 162, 166, 171
Gulf War *see* Iraq–Iran War
Guyana 162, 167, 172

Hadès missile 48–9
Haig, Alexander 381
Haiti 162, 166, 171
Hawaii 34
Helms, Jesse 33
herbicides 352
Hernu, Charles 194
Hizbollah 277
Honduras 149, 162, 166, 171, 183
Honecker, Erich 543
Honest John missile 37, 38
Hong Kong 145, 160, 165, 170
Hungary 103, 112, 137, 159, 163, 168, 179
Huntington, Samuel 311
Hussein, President Saddam 509, 513
'hyper-velocity glide vehicle' 389

IAEA (International Atomic Energy Agency) 55, 56, 57
Iceland 131
Iklé, Fred 311
India: arms imports 178, 179, 180, 186, 188, 193; chemical weapons 103; conflict in 285, 287, 290–1; EEZ 276; military expenditure 143, 160, 164, 169; nuclear capability 56, 142, 363, 364; nuclear weapon tests 56, 74; Pakistan and 142, 285; Sri Lanka and 142, 278–9, 286
Indonesia: arms imports 275; chemical weapons 103; conflict in 292; EEZ 275, 276; military expenditure 145–6, 160, 165, 170
INF Treaty: Memorandum of Understanding 38, 407–9; missile numbers 3, 4; negotiations 375–93; nuclear force structures 28–9; origins 376–8; political value 4; shortcomings 7; shorter-range systems 7; significance of 389–93; terms of 385–7; text 395–489; time negotiating 7; verification 3, 4, 120, 319, 323, 380, 387
'Inhumane Weapons' Convention (1981) 552, 553, 554–68
International Institute for Strategic Studies 143
International Maritime Bureau 277
International Monetary Fund 139, 146, 150, 152, 153
IRA (Irish Republican Army) 190, 191
Iran: arms imports 178, 186, 189, 190, 191, 192, 193, 194, 195; chemical weapons 102, 104–5, 106, 114, 115, 348; conflict in 288–9; military

Iran – *cont.*
  expenditure 159, 164, 169; NPT and 59; Persian Gulf mined by 195; revolutionary guards 277; *see also* Iraq–Iran War
Iraq: arms imports 178, 179, 180, 181, 185, 194, 195; chemical weapons and 102, 103, 106, 107–8, 113, 114, 348; conflict in 289; debt 195; military expenditure 159, 164, 169; NPT and 59; *see also following entry*
Iraq–Iran War: arms embargo and 511, 512, 514–15; arms shipments and 287; black market and 190; chemical weapons and 104, 114, 509–10; China and 186, 187; civilians and 1, 510, 515; commentary on 289; internal components 285; missile war 1, 7, 184, 515; tanker war 1, 509, 510, 511, 512; UN and 1, 193, 195, 286, 507–16
Ireland 138, 159, 164, 169
Israel: arms exports 176, 177, 182, 187, 191, 194, 204–5; arms imports 178, 179, 181, 182; chemical weapons 102, 107; conflict in 289; Egypt, Treaty with 2; existence of 2; Gaza Strip 1, 2; maritime surveillance 277; military expenditure 140, 159, 164, 169; nuclear capability 2, 55; terrorists and 277
Italy: arms exports 176, 177, 187, 204–5; arms imports 179, 182; chemical weapons 103; military expenditure 158, 163, 168; missiles in 8
Izvestiya 13

Jackson, Senator Henry 32
Jamaica 148, 162, 167, 171
Janus experiments 86
Japan: arms imports 179; chemical weapons 103, 104; fishing 268; military expenditure 144, 160, 165, 170
Jaruzelski proposal 329
Jayewardene, President 279, 286
Jericho missile 55
Jordan 140, 159, 164, 169, 185
Junejo, Prime Minister 184

Kampuchea 106, 144, 287, 292
Kangaroo missile 35
Karber, Philip 332
Karpov, Victor 33
Kashlev, Yuri 328–9
Kennedy, President John F. 11
Kenya 103, 161, 166, 170
Khomeini, Ayatollah 512, 513
Kissinger, Henry 311
Kitchen missile 35
Kockums 188
Kohl, Chancellor 385
Korea, North: arms exports 189, 190, 191; arms imports 186, 190, 192, 194; chemical weapons and 102; military expenditure 146, 160, 165, 170
Korea, South: arms exports 177; arms imports 178, 179; military expenditure 143, 146, 160, 165, 170
Kuwait 159, 164, 169, 184

Kvitsinsky, Yuli 382

Laird, Melvin 495, 496
Lance missile 28, 37, 38, 84
Laos 144, 292
Large Advanced Mirror Programme 86
lasers 35, 83, 84, 86, 87–8
Latin America: conflicts in 286–7, 296–9
Laveikin, Aleksander 78
Law of the Sea, Convention on 265, 266–9, 276–8
Lebanon 140, 159, 164, 169, 277, 285, 289–90
Leonid Brezhnev 45
Levin, Senator Carl 329
Liberia 161, 166, 171, 189
Libya: arms exports 189, 191; arms imports 181, 190; Chad and 182, 187, 189; chemical weapons 102, 105–7; military expenditure 141, 161, 166, 171; NPT and 59
Lode experiment 86
Louzeau, Admiral 52
Luchaire 193
Luxembourg 158, 163, 168

M687 projectile 108
McDonnell Douglas 27, 29, 31
McHenry, Donald 507
McNamara, Robert 321
Madagascar 161, 166, 171
Maddanas 278
Malawi 161, 166, 171
Malaysia: conflict and 293; EEZ 276; fishing 268; military expenditure 146, 160, 165, 170
Mali 161, 166, 171
Mandela, Nelson 1
Marcos, President Ferdinand 145
Martin Marietta 188
Mauritania 161, 166, 171
Mauritius 161, 166, 171
Mexico: arms control and 350, 351; debts 2–3, 148; military expenditure 149, 162, 167, 171
Middle East: arms imports 202–3; conflicts in 286, 288–90; military expenditure 139–40, 159; nuclear-weapon-free zone 55
military activities, notifiable 338–46
military aid 196
military doctrine, talks on 329, 334
military expenditure: debt and 149–50; definition 130, 131; economic effects 129, 531–3; information on 129; limiting 129, 518; SIPRI methods and sources 129
mines 190, 193
Mir space station 78
MIRVs (multiple independently targetable re-entry vehicles): China 44, 52; France 51; UK 47; USSR 23, 33, 35
missiles, ballistic: *general references:* accuracy 34, 305; fuel 53, 78; numbers 33, 36, 37, 39, 40; silos 34; *individual countries:* China 7, 53; France 50, 51, 52; India 56; Israel 55; Saudi Arabia 7; UK 42, 46–8, 66; USA: ICBMs: Midgetman 303; Minuteman 23, 36; MX 23, 24–5, 36; small 24, 25; IRBMs: Pershing II 8,

28, 37, 38; SLBMs: Poseidon 36; Trident 24, 25, 26, 34, 36, 306; USSR: ICBMs: SS-11 23, 34, 39, 376, 378; SS-13 39; SS-17 23, 36, 39; SS-18 34, 39, 306; SS-19 23, 34, 39; SS-24 23, 33, 34, 39, 303, 306; SS-25 5, 23, 33, 34, 39, 303, 306; SS-X-26 34; IRBMs: SS-1 40; SS-4 28, 38, 40, 41, 376, 378; SS-5 38, 376, 378; SS-12 28, 38, 40, 41, 42; SS-20 4, 28, 38, 40, 41, 321, 376, 378, 379, 380, 383, 384, 388; SS-21 40, 44; SS-23 28, 38, 40, 41–2; SS-C-1 40; SLBMs: SS-N-5 40; SS-N-6 39; SS-N-17 39; SS-N-18 34, 35, 39; SS-N-20 34, 35, 39; SS-N-23 34, 35, 39; *see also* MIRVs
missiles, cruise: arms control and 304–5; USA: ACMs 24, 26, 27; ALCMs 23; GLCMs 8, 28, 37, 38; SLCMs 31, 37; USSR: ALCMs 23, 35; GLCMs 38; SLCMs 38, 40, 44–5
Mitterrand, President François 14, 49, 193, 522
Mongolia 146, 160, 165
Monte Ruby 278
Morocco 141, 161, 166, 171
Mozambique 140, 161, 166, 171, 286, 294–5
Mururoa Atoll 67
Mutual and Balanced Force Reduction Talks 8, 9, 315, 316, 319, 322–3, 540

Namibia 295
NATO: arms control and 8, 9, 14, 15, 321–2, 325, 326, 327, 330–3, 334; cohesion of 11; Defence Planning Committee 30, 317; first-use doctrine 30; flexible response strategy 14, 30, 131, 321, 329, 377, 379, 390, 391; Follow-on Forces Attack doctrine 328; General Political Guidelines 29, 30; Gleaneagles meeting 29; Gorbachev and 14; High Level Task Force 330; inconsistencies in 321; Long Term Defence Programme 133; military expenditure 130–3, 158, 163, 168; Montebello 14, 317, 382; Nuclear Planning Group 30; nuclear war planning 29; two-track decision 7, 375, 378–9; WTO, asymmetries with 317–19
naval arms trade 265–81
Navy Navigation Satellite System 77
Nepal 142–3, 160, 164, 169
Netherlands: arms control 354; arms exports 176, 180, 187, 278; arms imports 179; chemical weapons and 103, 112; military expenditure 158, 163, 168; missiles in 8
neutral and non-aligned states 325, 330, 331
neutron weapons 29, 48, 49, 378
New Zealand: chemical weapons 104, 112; military expenditure 147, 160, 165, 170; Nuclear Free Zone 361; nuclear weapon tests and 67
Nicaragua: arms imports 180–1; conflict in 285, 287, 297; Contras 148, 182, 189, 194, 287; military expenditure 162, 167, 171
Niger 161, 166, 171
Nigeria: arms exports 278; chemical weapons 103; military expenditure 141, 161, 166, 171; South Africa and 57
Nike Hercules missile 37, 38
Nitze, Paul 382

Noel-Baker, Philip 522
Non-Proliferation Treaty (1968) 7–8, 55, 57, 178, 358, 363, 364, 365, 550, 552, 554–68
non-provocative defence 13
North Atlantic Council 331
Northern Ireland 286, 288
Northrop 24, 27
Norway: arms control 355; arms exports 177; arms imports 179; chemical weapons and 104, 112; military expenditure 158, 163, 168; nuclear exports 55; nuclear weapons and 362
nuclear explosions, peaceful 66
Nuclear Material, Convention on the Physical Protection of 359
nuclear risk reduction centres 32–3, 386
nuclear threshold countries 358, 364
nuclear-weapon-free zones 115, 329
nuclear weapons, no-first-use 320, 321
nuclear weapon tests 65–73; ban on 365–9; unnoticed 65
Nunn, Senator Sam 6, 89, 329, 495

Obukhov, Ambassador 310
Oceania, 146–7, 160, 165, 170
OECD 103, 152, 533
Oerlikon–Bührle 188
Oman 140, 159, 164, 169, 184
Ottawa meeting 324
Outer Space Treaty (1967) 550, 552, 554–68

Pacific Patrol Boat programme 280
Pakistan: arms imports 178, 184, 186; chemical weapons and 104, 350; conflict in 290; India and 142, 184, 285, 291; military expenditure 143, 160, 164, 169; nuclear capability 56, 142
Palk Straits 278
Palme, Olof, 508, 509, 539, 541, 542 *see also following entry*
Palme Commission 535, 540
Panama 162, 167, 171
Papua New Guinea 280
Paraguay 162, 167, 172
Partial Test Ban Treaty (1963) 69, 367, 549, 552, 554–68
Patriot missile 85
patrol craft 274, 275–6, 277
PAXSAT programme 89
Peaceful Nuclear Explosions Treaty (1976) 68, 70, 367–8
Perez de Cuellar, Javier 519
Perle, Richard 5
Pershing 1 missile 4, 28, 37, 38, 376, 385
Persian Gulf 195, 281, 509 *see also* Iraq–Iran War
Peru: arms imports 178, 180; conflict in 297; military expenditure 162, 167, 172; nuclear weapon tests 67
Philippines: conflict in 285, 286, 293; EEZ 276; military expenditure 145, 160, 165, 170; Moro National Liberation Front 277
Pikalov, General 110
piracy 276, 277, 278
plutonium 56

Pluton missile 49
Poland: arms control 330; arms exports 181, 189, 194; chemical weapons 103, 112; military expenditure 137, 159, 163, 168
Polaris Sales Agreement 47, 48
political prisoners 1
POMCUS 318
Portugal: arms exports 190, 191; military expenditure 158, 163, 168
Powell, General Colin 310
Pravda 13
Proton launcher 78, 80
Pryor, Senator David 183
public opinion 11, 376, 377, 382, 383, 392
Pugwash conferences 329

Qadhafi, Colonel 107, 181
Queen Match programme 85

Rabuka, Colonel 280
radar 35
Rarotonga, Treaty of (1985) 67, 361, 552, 553, 554–68
Razuvanov, General 111
Reagan, President Ronald: ABM Treaty 32; arms control and 5, 6, 68, 301, 305, 311, 381, 382, 392; B-1 and 27; INF Treaty and 8; military expenditure and 130; MX missile and 245; nuclear risk reduction centres and 33; SDI and 492; strategic forces 24; USSR's alleged treaty violations 68
refugees 286, 288
Resolution 46
Rockwell 27, 51, 188
Romania 115, 137, 159, 163, 168, 189
Russia *see* Union of Soviet Socialist Republics
Rwanda 161, 166, 171

SALT (Strategic Arms Limitation Talks) 23, 24, 32, 33, 34, 304, 376, 377, 379, 491, 500 *see also* ABM Treaty
Satellite Data System 77
satellites: *general references:* arms control and 76; failures 75, 78, 79, 89; radar on 81; rocket fuel 78; use of 75; *individual countries:* Canada 80, 89; China 75, 78, 80, 94; France 75, 80, 81, 89; India 56; Japan 78; NATO 80; UK 75, 80; USA: communications 77, 97; early-warning 76, 78; meteorological 77, 97; navigation 77, 98; ocean-surveillance 76, 96; reconnaissance 76, 77, 93; search and rescue 77; USSR: communications 97; early-warning 96; geodetic 98; meteorological 75, 97; navigation 80, 98; ocean-surveillance 8, 79–80, 96; reconnaissance 79, 93–4, 95
Saudi Arabia: arms control and 177; arms imports 178, 179, 181, 182, 184, 187; Iraq–Iran War and 182; military expenditure 139, 140, 159, 164, 169
SA-X-12 missile 36
Scarab missile 107
Schmidt, Helmut 7, 379, 382

Schmitz, Karl-Erik 193
Scout booster 77
SDI (Strategic Defense Initiative): ABM Treaty and 6, 32, 87; aims lowered 89; ASAT and 82; change in 492–3; computers 82, 83, 85; funding 83, 131, 498, 499; interceptor technology 83–9; origins 309; sensors 82–3
sea: surveillance 269–80; *see also* Law of the Sea, Conference on
Sea-Bed Treaty (1971) 551, 552, 554–68
Sea Lance missile 31
seismic monitoring 67
Senegal 161, 166, 171
Sergeant missile 38
Shevardnadze, Eduard 32, 70, 286, 309, 327, 498
Shultz, George 32, 70, 384, 498
Sierra Leone 161, 166, 171
Singapore 103, 143, 160, 165, 170, 176
Singh, Natwar 525
Skylite experiment 87
Slater, Rear Admiral 47
smuggling 276, 280
Solomon Islands 268, 280
Somalia 161, 166, 294
South Africa: arms embargo 190, 192; arms imports 194, 202–3; chemical weapons 103; conflict in 285; guerrillas and 140; military expenditure 141, 161, 166, 171; nuclear capability 2, 56; political prisoners 1
South America: arms imports 202–3; military expenditure 149–52, 162, 167, 172
South Asia: arms imports 202–3; conflict in 286, 290–1, 295; military expenditure 142–3
South China Sea 279
Southerland, USS 268
South Pacific Nuclear-Free Zone *see* Rarotonga Treaty
spacecraft, manned 79, 86, 99
space shuttle 75, 76, 77, 78, 86, 89
Spain: arms exports 176, 177, 187, 190, 191, 194, 204–5; arms imports 179; chemical weapons and 112; military expenditure 131, 158, 163, 168; nuclear activities 358; USA and 29
SRAM missile 24, 26, 27
Sri Lanka: conflict in 142, 285, 286, 287, 291; India and 142, 278–9, 286; military expenditure 143, 160, 164, 169
stability talks 316, 317, 321, 323, 326–30, 330–3
Standard Missile-2 31
Stark, USS 184, 195
START (Strategic Arms Reduction Talks) 6, 25, 28, 34, 301–8, 383, 491, 501
Star Wars *see* SDI
Staunch, Operation 191
stealth techniques 52
strategic defence *see* BMD, SDI
Strypi-II rocket 85
submarines: Brazil 58; Canada 363; China 53; France 50–1; India 178, 364; UK 46, 47–8; USA 23; USSR 34, 45
SUBROC missile 31, 37
Sudan 161, 166, 171, 285, 295

summit meetings: Geneva 32; Reykjavik 6, 14, 15, 301, 309, 331, 384, 392; Washington 6, 7, 34, 286, 301, 303, 307, 375, 497, 499, 501
Surveillance, Acquisition, Tracking and Kill Assessment 83
Sweden: arms exports 176, 177, 188, 193; chemical weapons and 112; Hagfors Observatory 68; military expenditure 138, 139, 159, 164, 169; National Defence Research Institute 69; nuclear weapons and 362–3
Switzerland: arms exports 177, 188; chemical weapons 103, 104; military expenditure 138, 159, 164, 169
Syracuse programme 81
Syria: arms imports 178, 179, 181, 195; chemical weapons and 102, 107; conflict in 290; military expenditure 159, 164, 169

Taiwan: arms imports 178, 179, 187; chemical weapons 102; military expenditure 146, 160, 165, 170
Tamil Tigers 279, 286
Tanzania 161, 166, 171
TASM missile 28
Terrier missile 31, 37
terrorism 33, 183, 277
Thailand: arms imports 178; conflict in 293; fishing 268; maritime surveillance 277; military expenditure 146, 160, 165, 170
Thatcher, Margaret 47, 317
Third World: arms exports 204–5; arms imports 176, 178, 180, 181, 186, 266, 533; debts of 531; health needs 517; military expenditure 518, 524
Thompson, James A. 332
Thorsson, Inga 520
Threshold Test Ban Treaty (1974) 68, 70, 367, 368
Till, Geoffrey 265
Titan rocket 76, 77, 78
Tlatelolco Treaty (1967) 58, 354, 550, 552, 554–68
TN-70 warhead 51
TN-71 warhead 50, 51
TN-75 warhead 51, 52
Togo 161, 166, 171
Tonnant, Le 50
torpedoes 31, 40, 45
Trinidad and Tobago 162, 167, 171
Triomphant, Le 51, 52
Tunisia 141, 161, 166, 171
Turkey 158, 163, 168, 179, 186, 187, 327
Tuvalu 280

Uganda 161, 166, 171, 189, 295
Union of Soviet Socialist Republics: ABM Treaty and 497–500; Academy of Sciences 69; Afghanistan and 1, 113, 286, 287, 276, 379, 513, 541–2; aircraft flight across 36; arms control and 6, 8, 381, 390, 497 *see also under* Gorbachev, Mikhail; arms exports 176, 177, 178–81, 189, 194, 195, 204–5; arms imports 179; Chapayevsk 109; chemical weapons and 102, 103, 106, 108, 109–11, 112, 116, 118, 120, 347, 349, 350, 353, 354, 356; Chernobyl accident 69; Communist Party control of military 5; economy and 6, 497; Europe, forces in 10, 11, 319; foreign policy changes 4; Germany and 118; *glasnost* 180; Iraq and 513; Krasnoyarsk 35, 309, 499–500; MBFR and 322; military aid 196; military expenditure 133–6, 159, 163, 168, 527; Navy 44–5; Novaya Zemlya 69; nuclear weapon tests 65–6, 69, 72, 73, 74, 366; Rarotonga Treaty and 67; reform 320, 333; resources 10; SDI and 497–500; Semipalatinsk 69, 70; Shikhany facility 108, 109, 110, 111; strategic arms reduction 301, 303, 306, 307, 309, 310; strategic nuclear forces 33–45; theatre nuclear forces 38–44; treaty violations, alleged 68, 113, 119, 495, 499
United Arab Emirates 159, 164, 169
United Kingdom: arms control and 7, 66; arms exports 176, 177, 180, 182, 185–6, 191, 194, 196, 204–5, 278; arms imports 179, 182; Atomic Weapons Research Establishment 46; Audit Office 48; chemical weapons and 101, 103, 111–12, 113–14, 116, 119, 120, 354; France, co-operation with 23–4, 45; Hong Kong and 145; Iranian procurement office closed 194; military expenditure 132, 158, 163, 168; nuclear co-operation 23–4, 45, 46, 47; nuclear weapon tests 65, 66, 72, 73, 74; Rarotonga Treaty and 67; strategic nuclear forces 7, 42, 45–8; US missiles in 8
United Nations: Charter 1, 507, 514, 515; chemical weapons and 352; Disarmament and Development Conference 517–36; Israel and 55; military expenditure and 129, 153, 521; Overarmament and Underdevelopment, Conference on 542; peacekeeping troops 139, 147; Secretary-General 287, 508, 509, 510, 511, 512, 514, 515; South Africa and 56; Special Session on Disarmament 521; *see also* Law of the Sea, Convention on
United States of America: Agency for International Development 141; arms control 14, 176, 177, 181–4, 191, 192, 195, 204–5, 278; Arms Control and Disarmament Agency 69; Arms Export Control Act 183; arms imports 182, 186; Army War College 49; Cape Canaveral 25; chemical weapons and 101, 102, 103, 104, 106, 108–9, 112, 113, 117–18, 348, 352, 356; CIA 33, 134, 136; Congress 31–3, 65, 86, 108, 130, 181, 182, 183, 491, 498; Defense Authorization Act 108; Defense Intelligence Agency 33, 110, 134; Defense Science Board 113; Disarmament Development Conference and 517, 522, 523–5; Eastern Test Range 47; Ellsworth AFB 26; Europe, forces in 318; F. E. Warren AFB 23, 25; fish 'wars' 268; Forum Fishing Association 268; Freedom of Information Act 113; Grand Forks AFB 26, 499; House Armed Services Committee 24, 86; Iran and 513; Iran–Contra scandal 183, 191, 287; Iraq and 513; K. I. Sawyer AFB 27;

United States of America – *cont.*
  Lawrence Livermore Laboratory 27; Los Alamos Laboratory 27; military aid 196; military doctrines 29; military expenditure 25, 130–1, 132, 158, 163, 168, 528–31; Natural Resources Defense Council 69, 70; Navy 31, 196; Nevada Test Site 48, 66, 69, 70; nuclear exports 55; nuclear guarantee 321, 375; nuclear weapon tests 65–6, 72, 73, 74, 366; Rarotonga Treaty and 67; Senate Armed Services Committee 86; Seymour Johnson AFB 29; Single Integrated Operational Plan 26; strategic arms reduction 301, 305, 308, 310, 311; strategic nuclear forces 24–33, 36, 37, 38; theatre nuclear forces 28–9, 37; Tooele base 111; treaty violations, alleged 68, 69; Tuna Association 268; Vandenberg AFB 25
Urban, Jerzy 194
Uruguay 162, 167, 172

Valsella Meccanotecnica 193
Vanguard, HMS 47
Vanuatu 280
Venezuela 162, 167, 172
Venice meeting 324
very-low-threshold test ban 369
Vessey, John 311
Viet Nam 102, 106, 144, 279, 292
Vortex programme 76, 82
Votkinsk Machine Building Plant 5

Waldheim, Kurt 508, 513

Warner, John W. 32
Warsaw Pact *see* WTO
Weinberger, Caspar 5, 108, 303
West African Coastal Surveillance 278
Western Sahara 296
Western Samoa 280
Westinghouse 58
White Cloud programme 76
Wickham, General 101
Wohlstetter, Albert 311
World War II 10
WTO (Warsaw Treaty Organization): air defences 376; arms control and 8, 12, 120, 319–20, 321, 325, 326, 327–30, 332, 391; instability 320, 321; military expenditure 133–8, 159, 163, 168; NATO, asymmetries with 317–19; stability of 10
Wu Xueqian 195

Xinhua 54

Yazov, Dmitry 13
'yellow rain' 113
Yemen, People's Democratic Republic of (South) 159, 164, 169, 275
Yemen Arab Republic (North) 159, 164, 169
Younger, George 46
Yugoslavia 115, 138, 159, 164, 169

Zaïre 161, 166, 171
Zambia 161, 166, 171
Zimbabwe 140, 161, 166, 171, 186, 296